King John: New Interpretations

King John: New Interpretations

Edited by S. D. Church

THE BOYDELL PRESS

First published 1999
The Boydell Press, Woodbridge
Reprinted in paperback 2003

ISBN 0 85115 736 X hardback
ISBN 0 85115 947 8 paperback

The Boydell Press is an imprint of Boydell & Brewer Ltd
PO Box 9, Woodbridge, Suffolk IP12 3DF, UK
and of Boydell & Brewer Inc.
PO Box 41026, Rochester, NY 14604–4126, USA
website: www.boydell.co.uk

A catalogue record for this book is available
from the British Library

Library of Congress Catalog Card Number: 99–14590

This publication is printed on acid-free paper

Printed in Great Britain by
St Edmundsbury Press Ltd, Bury St Edmunds, Suffolk

Contents

List of Illustrations   vii–viii

Editor's Preface   ix

Abbreviations   xi–xviii

Introduction   xix–xxvi

Historians Without Hindsight: Coggeshall, Diceto and Howden on the Early Years of John's Reign   1–26
  John Gillingham

The English Economy in the Early Thirteenth Century   27–40
  J.L. Bolton

Early Thirteenth-Century Prices   41–73
  Paul Latimer

The Revenues of John and Philip Augustus Revisited   75–99
  Nick Barratt

The Norman Exchequer Rolls of King John   101–116
  V.D. Moss

King John and the Norman Aristocracy   117–136
  Daniel Power

Eleanor of Aquitaine: The Last Years   137–164
  Jane Martindale

Isabella of Angoulême: John's Jezebel   165–219
  Nicholas Vincent

John and Ireland: the Origins of England's Irish Problem   221–245
  Seán Duffy

John King of England and the Kings of Scots   247–271
  A.A.M. Duncan

King John and Wales   273–287
  Ifor W. Rowlands

John and the Church of Rome   289–315
  Christopher Harper-Bill

John and Justice   317–333
    Ralph V. Turner

King John and the Empire   335–346
    Natalie Fryde

Philip Augustus and King John: Personality and History   347–361
    Jim Bradbury

Illustrations

Early Thirteenth-Century Prices

Table 1	The Geographical Distribution of Wheat Price Data from the Exchequer Pipe Rolls 1165/6–1210/11	55
Table 2	The Geographical Distribution of Oxen Price Data from the Exchequer Pipe Rolls 1162/3–1210/11	56
Table 3	Wheat and Oxen Prices 1162/3–1210/11: Overall Average Price Levels for Selected Periods	57
Table 4	Exchequer Pipe Roll Wheat Prices 1165/6–1210/11: Selected Counties/Selected Periods	58
Table 5	Exchequer Pipe Roll Oxen Prices 1162/3–1210/11: Selected Counties/Selected Periods	59
Table 6	A Comparison of Prices per Summ and per Quarter in the Exchequer Pipe Rolls and the Winchester Pipe Rolls	60
Table 7	Wheat Prices: Printed Exchequer Pipe Rolls Compared with Winchester Pipe Rolls	61
Table 8	Oxen Prices: Printed Exchequer Pipe Rolls Compared with Winchester Pipe Rolls	61
Table 9	Wheat and Oxen Prices: Miscellaneous Accounts Compared with the Winchester Pipe Rolls	62
Table 10	Exchequer Cloth Prices 1180/1–1241/2 (cloth for table and for windows combined)	63
Table 11	Linen Purchases 1155/6–1254/5	64
Table 12	Wax Prices 1157/8–1257/8	65
Table 13	Lead Prices 1167/8–1258/9 (shillings per cartload)	66
Table 14	Wine Prices 1159/60–1253/4	67
Table 15	Palfrey Prices 1156/7–1259/60	68
Figure 1	Wheat Prices 1165/6–1250/1	69
Figure 2	Oxen Prices 1162/3–1250/1	69
Figure 3	Wheat and Oxen Prices 1165/6–1250/1	70
Figure 4	Sheep and Wool Prices 1162/3–1250/1	70
Figure 5	Exchequer Cloth 1180/1–1220/1	71
Figure 6	Wax Prices 1171/2–1250/1	71
Figure 7	Lead Prices 1167/8–1250/1	72
Figure 8	Wine Prices 1170/1–1250/1	72
Figure 9	Palfrey Prices 1156/7–1250/1	73

The Revenues of John and Philip Augustus Revisited

Tables 1–3	Comparison of Revenue 1202–3: Disposable War Revenue; Comparison of Revenue 1202–3: Ordinary Net Revenue; Comparison of Revenue 1202–3: Ordinary Disposable Revenue	93
Tables 4–6	Military Wages 1202–3; Expression of Revenue as Potential Military Capacity; Expression of Revenue as Potential Length of Service	94
Table 7	Analysis of Utilised Revenue in the War Zone	95
Table 8	Comparison of Revenue: John and Richard I	96
Table 9	Revenue for the 1214 Campaign (1)	97
Table 10	Estimated Military Wages 1214	98
Table 11	Expression of Revenue as Potential Length of Service	98
Table 12	Disposable Revenue 1214	99
Table 13	Comparison of Annual Revenue 1222	99

The Norman Exchequer Rolls of King John

Table 1	Debts of Bailliages 1198 and 1203	103
Table 2	Returns of Bailliages in 1203 compared with 1198	110–111
Table 3	Comparative Returns of Bailliages 1180 and 1195	111

King John and the Norman Aristocracy

Map	The Duchy of Normandy 1193–1204	118

Isabella of Angoulême: John's Jezebel

Map	Beneficiaries of Plantagenet Charters South of the Loire	166
Table 1	The Counts of Angoulême	171
Table 2	Pedigree of Isabella of Angoulême	180
Table 3	Pedigree of Isabella of Angoulême	181

Editor's Preface

The conference on King John, of which this volume constitutes the papers, was hosted by the School of History at the University of East Anglia during the Easter vacation of 1997. In running a conference such as the one which this volume records, many debts are incurred not all of which can be repaid by a mention in the preface. There are, however, some whose support and encouragement made sure that the conference did not remain a pipe dream. I owe a special debt of gratitude to Christopher Harper-Bill who, as my colleague and mentor in another place, suggested that I should do a conference on King John. Now that he is translated to East Anglia, the 'team' is restored in a happier location. I also owe a great deal to my wife, Maria Sophia Quine, who, during a difficult pregnancy and the first months of our son's life, made it possible for me to organise the conference and see its proceedings through to the press. From his base in the University's conference office, Simon Wray made events run much more smoothly than at one point had seemed likely: to him I owe any remaining credibility I might have as a conference organiser. I should also like to thank Louise Gregory, Amanda Ingham, Rob Liddiard, Claire Noble and Maria Reigger, all of whom rallied together to make the wheels of the conference run smoothly and did much to foster good relations between the conference delegates. The conference would not have happened but for the moral and financial support provided by the School of History at the University of East Anglia. The Royal Historical Society provided generous support for a number of postgraduate students to attend the conference. I would also like to record my thanks to the staff of Boydell and Brewer, and in particular Caroline Palmer, for their help and support in the production of this volume.

S. D. Church

Norwich
Ascension Day 1998

Abbreviations

Actes de Philippe Auguste	*Recueil des actes de Philippe Auguste, roi de France*, ed. H.-F. Delaborde *et al.*, 4 vols, Paris 1916–79
AD	Archives Départementales
AgHR	*Agricultural History Review*
AHP	*Archives Historique du Poitou*
AHR	*American Historical Review*
AN	Archives Nationales, Paris
Ann. angevines	*Recueil d'annales angevines et vendômoises*, ed. L. Halphen, Paris 1903
Ann. Mon.	*Annales Monastici*, ed. H.R. Luard, 5 vols, RS XXXVI, London 1864–69
ANS	*Anglo-Norman Studies*
Antiqs Journ.	*Antiquaries Journal*
Arch. Journ.	*Archaeological Journal*
Baldwin, *Government*	J.W. Baldwin, *The Government of Philip Augustus*, Berkeley 1986
Barratt, 'Revenue'	N. Barratt, 'The Revenue of King John', *EHR* 111, 1996, 835–55
Baumol and Blinder, *Economics*	W.J. Baumol and A.S. Blinder, *Economics: Principles and Policy* 5th edn, Orlando 1991
Bib Mun	Bibliothèque Municipale
BIHR	*Bulletin of the Institute of Historical Research*
BL	British Library
BN	Bibliothèque Nationale, Paris
Bolton, 'Inflation'	J.L. Bolton, 'Inflation, Economics, and Politics in Thirteenth-Century England', in *Thirteenth Century England IV: The Proceedings of the Newcastle upon Tyne Conference, 1991*, ed. P.R. Coss and S.D. Lloyd, Woodbridge 1992, 1–14

Book of Fees	*Liber Feodorum. The Book of Fees Commonly Called Testa de Neville*, 3 vols, London 1920–31
Bridbury, *English Economy*	A.R. Bridbury, *The English Economy from Bede to the Reformation*, Woodbridge 1992
Bridbury, 'Thirteenth-Century Prices'	
	A.R. Bridbury, 'Thirteenth-Century Prices and the Money Supply', *AgHR* 33, 1985, 1–21
Britnell, *Commercialisation*	R.H. Britnell, *The Commercialisation of English Society 1000–1500*, Cambridge 1993
Britnell and Campbell, *Commercialising*	
	R.H. Britnell amd B.M.S. Campbell, ed., *A Commercialising Economy: England 1086 to c.1300*, Manchester 1995
Britnell and Hatcher, *Progress and Problems*	
	R.H. Britnell and J. Hatcher, ed., *Progress and Problems in Medieval England*, Cambridge 1996
Cal. Docs France	*Calendar of Documents preserved in France*, ed. J.H. Round, HMSO London 1899
Cal. Docs Ireland	*Calendar of Documents Relating to Ireland*, ed. H.S. Sweetman, 4 vols, London 1875 etc.
Cal. Docs Scotland	*Calendar of Documents Relating to Scotland*, ed. J. Bain, 4 vols, Edinburgh 1881–88
C & S	*Councils and Synods and other Documents relating to the English Church*, ed. D. Whitelock *et al.*, 2 vols in 4, Oxford 1964–81
Cheney, *From Becket to Langton*	
	C.R. Cheney, *From Becket to Langton: English Church Government, 1170–1213*, Manchester 1956
Cheney, *Hubert Walter*	C.R. Cheney, *Hubert Walter*, London 1967
Cheney, *Innocent III and England*	
	C.R. Cheney, *Pope Innocent III and England*, Stuttgart 1976
Chron. Bower	*Scotichronicon by Walter Bower*, iv, General Editor D.E.R. Watt, Edinburgh 1994
Chron. Fordun	*Johannis de Fordun Chronica Gentis Scotorum*, 2 vols, ed. W.F. Skene, Historians of Scotland, Edinburgh 1871–72

Chronica Majora	*Matthaei Parisiensis, Monachi Sancti Albani, Chronica Majora*, ed. H.R. Luard, 7 vols, RS LVII, London 1872–83
Chron. Melrose	*The Chronicle of Melrose*, ed. A.O. Anderson *et al.*, London 1936
Close Rolls	*Close Rolls of the Reign of Henry III*, 14 vols, HMSO, London 1902–38
CLR	*Calendar of Liberate Rolls of the Reign of Henry III*, 6 vols, HMSO, London 1917–64
Coggeshall	*Radulphi de Coggeshall Chronicon Anglicanum*, ed. J. Stevenson, RS LXVI, London 1875
CRR	*Curia Regis Rolls of the Reigns of Richard I, John, and Henry III preserved in the Public Record Office*, 17 vols, HMSO, London 1922–
Devizes	*The Chronicle of Richard of Devizes of the Time of King Richard the First*, ed. J.T. Appleby, London 1963
Dialogus de Scaccario	*De Necessariis Observantiis Scaccarii Dialogus qui vulgo dictur Dialogus de Scaccario*, ed. C. Johnson, London 1950
Diceto	*The Historical Works of Master Ralph de Diceto, Dean of London*, ed. W. Stubbs, 2 vols, RS LXVIII, London 1876
Diplomatic Documents	*Diplomatic Documents preserved in the Public Record Office, 1101–1272*, ed. P. Chaplais, HMSO, London 1964
Docs of English History	*Documents Illustrative of English History in the Thirteenth and Fourteenth Centuries*, ed. H. Cole, Record Commission, London 1844
EcHR	*Economic History Review*
EEA	*English Episcopal Acta*
EHD	*English Historical Documents*
EHR	*The English Historical Review*
GEC	*Complete Peerage of England, Scotland, Ireland, Great Britain and the United Kingdom, Extant, Extinct or Dormant*, ed. G.E. Cokayne, new edn V. Gibbs *et al.*, 13 vols in 14, London 1910–59

Gervase	*The Historical Works of Gervase of Canterbury*, ed. W. Stubbs, 2 vols, RS LXXIII, London 1879–80
Gesta Regis Henrici	*Gesta Regis Henrici Secundi Benedicti Abbatis*, ed. W. Stubbs, 2 vols, RS XLIX, London 1867

Gillingham, *Richard Coeur de Lion*

J. Gillingham, *Richard Coeur de Lion: Kingship, Chivalry and War in the Twelfth Century*, London 1994

Gillingham, *Richard the Lionheart*

J. Gillingham, *Richard the Lionheart*, London 1978

Giraldi Cambrensis Opera	*Giraldi Cambrensis Opera*, ed. J.S. Brewer *et al.*, 8 vols, RS XXI, London 1861–1918
Glanville	*Tractatus de legibus et consuetudinibus regni Anglie qui Glanville vocatur*, ed. G.D.G. Hall, London 1965

Goldstone, 'Urbanization and Inflation'

J.A. Goldstone, 'Urbanization and Inflation: Lessons from the English Price Revolution of the Sixteenth and Seventeenth Centuries', *American Journal of Sociology* 89, 1984, 1,122–60

Guillaume le Breton	*Oeuvres de Rigord et de Guillaume le Breton*, ed. H.-F. Delaborde, 2 vols, Société de l'histoire de France, Paris 1882–85
Harvey, 'English Inflation'	P.D.A. Harvey, 'The English Inflation of 1180–1220, *Past and Present* 61, 1973, 2–30
Hist. ducs de Normandie	*Histoire des ducs de Normandie et des rois d'Angleterre*, ed. F. Michel, Société de l'histoire de France, Paris 1840
Hist. Guillaume le Maréchal	*Histoire de Guillaume le Maréchal*, ed. P. Meyer, 3 vols, Société de l'histoire de France, Paris 1891–1901
HMCR	*Historical MSS Commission Reports*
HMSO	Her Majesty's Stationary Office
Holt, *Magna Carta*	J.C. Holt, *Magna Carta*, 2nd edition, Oxford 1992

Holt, *Magna Carta and Medieval Government*

> J.C. Holt, *Magna Carta and Medieval Government*, London 1985

Holt, *Northerners*

> J.C. Holt, *The Northerners: a Study in the Reign of King John*, Oxford 1961

Howden

> *Chronica Magistri Rogeri de Hovedene*, ed. W. Stubbs, 4 vols, RS LI, London 1868–71

Interdict Documents

> *Interdict Documents*, ed. P.M. Barnes and W.R. Powell, PRS, n.s. 34, 1960

JBS

> *Journal of British Studies*

JEH

> *Journal of Ecclesiastical History*

JMH

> *Journal of Medieval History*

Jolliffe, *Angevin Kingship*

> J.E.A. Jolliffe, *Angevin Kingship*, 2nd edition, London 1963

Jolliffe, 'Chamber'

> J.E.A. Jolliffe, 'The Chamber and the Castle Treasuries under King John', in *Studies in Medieval History presented to F.M. Powicke*, ed. R.W. Hunt *et al.*, Oxford 1948, 117–42

Judgements

> *Recueil des judgements de l'Échiquier de Normandie au XIIIe siècle*, ed. L. Delisle, Paris 1864

Knowles, *Monastic Order*

> D. Knowles, *The Monastic Order in England: A History of its Development from the Times of St Dunstan to the Fourth Lateran Council, 943–1216*, Cambridge 1940

Landon, *Itinerary*

> L. Landon, *Itinerary of King Richard I*, PRS, n.s. 13, London 1935

Layettes

> *Layettes du Tréor des Chartes*, ed. A. Teulet *et al.*, 5 vols, Paris 1863–1909

Letters of Innocent III

> *The Letters of Pope Innocent III (1198–1216) concerning England and Wales: A Calendar with an Appendix of Texts*, ed. C.R. Cheney *et al.*, Oxford 1967

Life of St Hugh

> *Magna Vita Sancti Hugonis*, ed. D.C. Douie *et al.*, 2 vols, Oxford 1985

Lloyd, *English Wool Trade*

> T.H. Lloyd, *The English Wool Trade in the Middle Ages*, Cambridge 1977

Mayhew, 'Modelling'

> N.J. Mayhew, 'Modelling Medieval Monetisation', in Britnell and Campbell, *Commercialising*, 55–77

Mayhew, 'Money and Prices'	N.J. Mayhew, 'Money and Prices in England from Henry II to Edward III', *AgHR* 35, 1987, 121–32
Mayhew, 'Population'	N.J. Mayhew, 'Population, Money Supply, and the Velocity of Circulation in England, 1300–1700', *EcHR* 2nd series 48, 1995, 238–57
MGH	*Monumenta Germaniae Historica*
Miskimin, 'Population Growth'	H.A. Miskimin, 'Population Growth and the Price Revolution in England', *Journal of European Economic History* 4, 1975, 179–86
Monasticon	W. Dugdale, *Monasticon Anglicanum*, ed. J. Caley *et al.*, 6 vols, London 1846
MRSN	*Mangi Rotuli Scaccariae Normanniae*, ed. T. Stapleton, 2 vols, London 1840–44
Newburgh	William of Newburgh, *Historia Rerum Anglicarum*, in *Chronicles and Memorials of the Reigns of Stephen, Henry II, and Richard I*, ed. R. Howlett, 4 vols, RS, London 1884–90
ns	new series
Painter, *Reign of King John*	S. Painter, *The Reign of King John*, Baltimore 1949
Painter, *William Marshal*	S. Painter, *William Marshal: Knight Errant, Baron, and Regent of England,* Baltimore 1933
PBA	*Proceedings of the British Academy*
PR	*Pipe Roll*
Premier budget	F. Lot and R. Fawtier, *Le premier budget de la couronne française*, Paris 1932
PRO	Public Record Office
PRS	Pipe Roll Society
Powicke, *Loss of Normandy*	F.M. Powicke, *The Loss of Normandy, 1189–1204*, 2nd edition, Manchester 1961
Powicke, *Stephen Langton*	F.M. Powicke, *Stephen Langton*, London 1929
QN	'Querimoniae Normannorum', in *RHF* XXIV, i, 1904, 2–73

Red Book	*Red Book of the Exchequer*, ed. H. Hall, 3 vols, Record Commission, London 1896
Registres	*Les registres de Philippe Auguste*, ed. J.W. Baldwin, i (*texte*), Paris 1992
RHF	*Receuil des historiens de la Gaule et de la France*, ed. M. Bouguet *et al.*, 24 vols in 25, Paris 1738–1904
Richard, *Comtes*	A. Richard, *Histoire des comtes de Poitou, 778–1204*, 2 vols, Paris 1903
Rigord	*Oeuvres de Rigord et de Guillaume le Breton*, ed. H.F. Delaborde, 2 vols, Société de l'histoire de France, Paris 1882–85
RO	Record Office
Rot. Chart.	*Rotuli Chartarum in Turri Londinensi Asservati*, ed. T.D. Hardy, Record Commission, London 1837
Rot. de Lib.	*Rotuli de Liberate ac de Misis et Praestits*, ed. T.D. Hardy, Record Commission, London 1844
Rot. de Obl.	*Rotuli de Oblatis et Finibus in Turri Londinensi Asservati*, ed. T.D. Hardy, Record Commission, London 1835
Rot. Litt. Claus.	*Rotuli Litterarum Clausarum in Turri Londinensi Asservati*, ed. T.D. Hardy, 2 vols, Record Commission, London 1833–44
Rot. Litt. Pat.	*Rotuli Litterarum Patentium in Turri Londinensi Asservati*, ed. T.D. Hardy, Record Commission, London 1835
Rot. Norm.	*Rotuli Normanniae in Turri Londinensi Asservati*, ed. T.D. Hardy, Record Commission, London 1835
Rymer's *Fœdera*	*Fœdera, Conventiones, Litterae et cuiuscunque Generis Acta Publica*, ed. T. Rymer, new edn, ed. A. Clark *et al.*, Record Commission, London 1816
SATF	*Société des Anciens Textes Français*
SLI	*Selected Letters of Pope Innocent III concerning England (1198–1216)*, ed. C.R. Cheney *et al.*, London 1953
Torigny	*Chronique de Robert de Torigny*, ed. L. Delisle, 2 vols, 1971–72

TRHS *Transactions of the Royal Historical Society*

Turner, *King John* R.V. Turner, *King John*, London 1994

VCH *Victoria County History*

Walter of Coventry *Memoriale Fratris Walteri Coventria*, ed. W. Stubbs, 2 vols, RS LVIII, London 1872–3

Warren, *Henry II* W.L. Warren, *Henry II*, London 1973

Warren, *King John* W.L. Warren, *King John*, 2nd edn, London 1978

Wendover *Roger of Wendover, Flores Historiarum*, ed. H.R. Luard, 3 vols, RS XCV, London 1890

Wordie, 'Deflationary Factors' J.R. Wordie, 'Deflationary Factors in the Tudor Price Rise', *Past and Present* 154, 1997, 32–70

Introduction

The reign of King John (1199–1216) is undoubtedly one of the most important periods in English history. In 1199, when he succeeded to Richard I's lands, John could legitimately claim that he was king of England, lord of Ireland, duke of Normandy, duke of Aquitaine and count of Anjou. He was the inheritor of a form of governance based upon the exercise of the royal will. And John practised this form of kingship as effectively as any of his predecessors. But by the time of his death in October 1216, his dominion lay in tatters. He had lost control over most of his continental inheritance, and, had he lived, it is doubtful that he could have retained control of the land that remained to him. Moreover, John was confronted by a confederation of his barons who were determined to limit the impact of Angevin kingship on their lives. To this end they drew up a charter of liberties (Magna Carta) that made clear the terms under which they were prepared to accept John as their king. When this failed to limit John's power, these barons went into open civil war and invited the son of the king of France, Prince Louis, to take the kingship for himself. It is the purpose of the essays gathered together in this volume to explore some of the causes of these events of John's reign.

In the first essay, John Gillingham revisits some of the debates about King John's early reputation. He explores the views of three contemporary commentators, Abbot Ralph of Coggeshall, Ralph of Diceto and Roger of Howden, each of whom has been used by others to show that King John stood high in the estimate of his contemporaries before the disaster of the Loss of Normandy in 1204. Gillingham shows that, by a careful reading of the context of these writers' comments on John and his reign, all three had a far more circumspect attitude toward John than historians have traditionally allowed. Roger of Howden, for example, had a moment in November 1200 when he was positive about King John, praising him for the peace he had achieved with King William of Scotland and with the Cistercian order in England. But either side of the events of that good month for John, Howden was critical of the new king. Ralph of Diceto, too, was more censorious of King John than we have been taught to believe. He was certainly disapproving of John's marital antics, and he thought of the Treaty of Le Goulet as a defeat for the king. And Abbot Ralph of Coggeshall, thought by some to be quite positive about John in the years before 1204, was also, in fact, far from enthusiastic about the new king. Gillingham concludes that the beginnings of the decline in John's reputation are to be found in the first year of his reign, rather than in 1204. It was in the autumn of 1199 that Arthur of Brittany, John's rival for King Richard's lands, fled John to the safety of the court of Philip Augustus because he did not trust his uncle. It was also in the autumn of 1199 that the alliances that Richard had constructed against Philip Augustus began to fall apart, again because of the lack of trust engendered by King John. The opinions of Gillingham's historians are clear: John was a bad king from the very outset of his reign.

Four articles bring together the latest research and ideas on the economy in John's reign. The first in this collection is that by J.L. Bolton, who provides an important reinterpretive essay on the early thirteenth-century economy. Bolton argues that the established view on the economy in the period 1180–1220 – that it was characterised by steady inflation – is, in fact, far too simplistic. In reality there was a short period of inflation at the beginning of John's reign, but thereafter, because of the huge amounts of money being raised and stored by the king in preparation for the reconquest of his lost continental lands, there was a period of deflation. This new model for the early thirteenth-century economy further argues that it was only after 1220, when the minority government of King Henry III began to put the royal finances back onto a more secure footing, that England began to witness an upturn in its economic fortunes.

The contributions by Paul Latimer and Nick Barratt provide us with the sound economic data to begin the process of reappraising English royal finances during John's reign. Latimer, in his essay on early thirteenth-century prices, has provided in tabular form the results of his research on the prices of a range of essential goods. And it is from his work and the evidence presented in his essay that all future debates on the English economy in the twelfth and thirteenth centuries must begin. Likewise, Barratt, in his article on the revenues of John and Philip Augustus, has provided valuable new data on the incomes of kings John, Philip Augustus and Richard I. This work allows us to see at a glance the relative wealth of the protagonists in the wars for the Angevin continental lands. Importantly, Barratt shows that John does seem to have been at a financial disadvantage not only to Philip Augustus, but also compared with his brother Richard. It is a remarkable discovery, and one which will add yet more fuel to the debate about how Philip was able to take Normandy from John in 1204.

The general conclusions reached by Barratt concerning the wealth of John, Philip Augustus and Richard receive more specific support from the contribution of V.D. Moss to this volume. Moss shows that Richard I was able to extract far more money from the duchy of Normandy than King John was able to do in the years between 1199 and 1204. Indeed, Moss even goes so far as to place relative values on the amounts the brothers were able to raise. On the eve of the duchy's fall to Philip Augustus, Moss argues, 'King John could only extract approximately half the revenue that was raised by King Richard in 1198.' It is an extraordinary claim, and one which historians will have to consider carefully in their attempt to explain the Loss of Normandy by King John. Moss suggests that the reduction in revenue raised between 1198 and 1203 may reflect a kind of 'fiscal exhaustion' brought on by Richard's excessive demands for money to fight his campaigns. But it may also reflect an unwillingness by some of the Norman aristocracy to continue to support the Angevin cause. And this suggestion seems all the more likely in the light of the analysis of the duchy's fall given by Daniel Power in his contribution to this volume.

Power seeks to answer the question: 'did John forfeit the support of his subjects in Normandy?' The reason for needing to know the answer to this question is clear: if John did loose their support, then no amount of gold would have saved the duchy from the aggression of Philip Augustus. But this is not a simple question to answer. The Normans, Power argues, were not a homogenous group and their reactions to John and to the circumstances of the reign were not uniform. Power would like us to see three distinct regions in the duchy: the eastern marches, the southern marches and central Normandy. The first of his regions, the eastern marches, was very much subject to the influence of the Capetian kings of France. Long before John ascended the throne, Philip Augustus had been busy spreading his influence in this region. As well as actually taking control of certain strategic castles, Philip also consistently offered disgruntled Normans 'an alternative source of patronage' to the duke; and it is clear from Power's study, that many Normans did turn to the French king when they failed to achieve redress at the ducal court. According to this interpretation, then, ducal rule was already circumscribed by 1199 in the eastern marches. In southern Normandy, too, ducal authority was already limited by the actions of Richard in giving away important ducal castles. Moreover, in this region there was a political community that stretched from central Normandy to northern Poitou. And when in the wake of the victory at Mirebeau in 1202 John treated his Poitevin captives shabbily, he also alienated men in southern Normandy. Once these two important regions had turned against John, it was only a matter of time before central Normandy, too, turned its back on its duke. By using his 'hated *routiers*', and by abandoning the duchy in 1203, leaving it leaderless, John forfeited the support of even those nobles of central Normandy who might have fought with him to the bitter end.

In her contribution to this volume, Jane Martindale demonstrates that Queen Eleanor had just the sort of qualities of leadership that were so patently lacking in John, as evidenced by his defence of Normandy. In the period from Richard's death in 1199 and her own death in April 1204, she played a very active role in the rule and defence of Aquitaine. For example, it was Eleanor's idea, according to Martindale, for her to do homage in her own right (an unprecedented action) to the French king for Aquitaine. In performing this act, Eleanor hoped to thwart Arthur of Brittany's claim to the Angevin inheritance in that region and to mediate John and Philip Augustus, thus protecting her son and chosen heir from the demands of the French king. Moreover, when the need arose, Queen Eleanor was more than prepared to become involved in the harsher side of medieval government. Martindale points to at least one occasion when the queen can be seen to wage war on her grandson, Arthur of Brittany. Jane Martindale's Eleanor of Aquitaine is not a passive victim of events, neither is she the 'old dowager queen' nostalgic for the days of her youth; rather she is a powerful queen playing an active and extremely important role in the rule of the Angevin lands.

For too long, according to Nicholas Vincent, Isabella of Angoulême, King John's second wife, has languished in her husband's shadow, playing a bit part in the events that led to the loss of the Angevin continental lands. Admittedly Isabella was young when she married John in August 1200 (she was at least eighteen years younger than John, if not more), and this disparity in age meant that Isabella was kept very much in the background. Throughout her time as King John's consort, for example, she had little control over her dower lands; and it is Vincent's contention that the financial arrangements made for Eleanor were 'mean'. As a queen, Vincent concludes, at least in comparison with Eleanor of Aquitaine, Isabella was little more than a 'wife', even having no say over the membership of her own household.

Isabella's life as queen of England, however, formed only one part of her career. Within a few short months of John's death, Isabella abandoned her children by him and returned to Angoulême. In her home county, she emerged from the shadow of her late husband to become one of the most remarkable women rulers of the thirteenth century. She married Hugh X of Lusignan (son of her betrothed in 1200), bore him nine children and ruled the 'unified lordship' of Angoulême, Lusignan and La Marche jointly with her husband. Between them, Isabella and Hugh extended comital control of Poitou to a remarkable degree. Only at the end of her life did this rule begin to unravel. In 1242, she and Hugh unwisely rebelled against Louis IX of France. The resultant campaign waged by St Louis brought Isabella and Hugh to their knees and Poitou firmly into the domain of the French kings. The second half of Isabella's two-part career differed markedly from that of the first, and when she died in 1246 at the abbey of Fontevraud, it was 'with a prayer on her lips, not for King John or her children in England, but for the sons that she had born to . . . Hugh'. It was as if her life with King John had never existed.

As one of the contributors to this volume notices, it has been all to easy for English historians to think of Ireland, Scotland and Wales as forming a 'Celtic Fringe', somehow united in their views of the English and in their ways of dealing with their most powerful neighbour. But as the three essays by Seán Duffy, A.A.M. Duncan, and Ifor Rowlands demonstrate, the lordship, the kingdom and the principality each had its own characteristics and its own way of dealing with King John. John, too, approached each of these parts of the British Isles as separate units, not as a unified whole.

In his study of John and Ireland, Seán Duffy takes issue with what has become received wisdom about John's achievements in that island. Historians have traditionally looked to King John's Irish policies, and in particular the campaign of 1210, to show that John could at least be successful at something. But Duffy argues that even here it is possible to say that John replicated the mistakes he made elsewhere. Moreover, in the campaign of 1185, which W.L. Warren attempted to rescue from the more usual damning criticism levelled at it, John was also a failure. Furthermore, John's policy toward Ireland, which

Warren characterised as being a 'clever and well-thought-out plan for the expansion of the English colony', was, in Duffy's view, also a disaster which eventually led to the 'failure of the medieval conquest of Ireland'. And, Duffy argues, far from remaining loyal to John during the troubled years at the end of the reign, the native Irish took advantage of John's difficulties to 'stage a recovery' in their fortunes. In short, in his article on Ireland, Duffy offers a complete reinterpretation of the relationship that John had with his lordship.

In his article on Scotland, A.A.M. Duncan, too, provides an important re-interpretation of Anglo-Scottish relations. Duncan demonstrates, for example, that there is little evidence 'for a reception of French culture in Scotland', and that the real impact on the Scottish court and aristocratic society came from English clerics entering royal service in Scotland. These were the men who served in the royal household and instituted English practice in the Scottish exchequer and chancery. Some of these men also went on to join the upper reaches of the Scottish episcopate. The 'old alliance' between Scotland and France against England had an important part to play in Anglo–Scottish relations during John's reign. In 1199, for example, as Duncan demonstrates with a careful reading of the text of John's safe-conduct to William in 1205, Philip encouraged the king of Scots to prepare for war against John. Duncan's analysis does much to explain King William's reluctance to come to John in the immediate aftermath of the new king's coronation in May 1199. But once the terms of the treaty of Le Goulet had been agreed in May 1200, William, bereft of support from the king of France, was forced to come to terms with John. Duncan also throws new light on the causes of King John's campaign waged in Scotland in the summer months of 1209. He shows that this, too, had its root cause in a Franco–Scottish alliance against John. King John's anger at King William was, it seems, sparked by a proposal of marriage between Philip Augustus and Margaret, King William's daughter. Despite the fact that Philip was hardly in a position to make good his offer because of his own marital circumstances, William was still prepared to countenance the suggested union. John's response was to make threats to William and to launch an army of invasion. There was no battle, as is well known, but the outcome was yet another humiliation for the king of Scots as he was forced to hand over his daughters to John for safe-keeping.

In his essay on Wales, Ifor Rowlands reminds us of some of the fundamental features of Wales and Welsh society which dictated the way in which John approached that country. For instance, although the Welsh saw themselves as 'one people', there was no 'one Wales', no *dominium Wallie* with which John could deal. John had various lordships in Wales that he himself controlled, such as those lands he had in right of his first wife, Isabella of Gloucester. Then there were the marches of Wales, those bits that were under English domination. And finally there were the great Welsh princes who, in Rowlands' words, 'recog-nised the dominance of the king but did not conduct themselves as if subject to his domination'. And it was in his dealings with these great Welsh princes, most notably Gwenwynwyn of southern Powys and Llywelyn of Gwynedd, that John made his greatest mistake: allowing Llywelyn to gain the upper hand because he feared Gwenwynwyn too much. And in the end, his high-handed dealings with Wales, especially his attitude towards hostage-taking, meant that 'the mastery that John had achieved in 1211 . . . proved illusory and began to unravel within a year'. And in 1212, the hand of Philip Augustus can be seen to be manipulating the situation on John's borders once again. Rowlands shows that John's invasion of Wales in 1212 may well have been in response to news that Philip and Llywelyn of Gwynedd had entered into an alliance.

In an up-beat survey, Christopher Harper-Bill makes a strong case for judging that the English church was in a very healthy state. 'The overall picture', he concludes, 'is of a church that was efficiently administered and which provided the essential means of salvation . . . to the whole population of England.' In his administration of the Church, John seems to have been a typical English king: no better and no worse than his predecessors. What damned John in the eyes of his contemporaries was the attitude of Pope Innocent III to his activities and, of course, the conflict between John and Innocent III over the appointment of Stephen Langton to the see of Canterbury. The way that John handled the Canterbury election was a 'shambles'; he allowed himself to believe that Innocent III would see the election his way, despite evidence to the contrary. And once the two sides had got themselves into a cycle of dispute it became very difficult for either side to back down. The result was an interdict on England. But what were the results of this interdict on the day-to-day lives of most English men and women? The administration of the church seems to have continued uninterrupted, but the 'rhythm of life was disrupted': there was no church attendance and the bells were tied up (it must have been eerily silent in the countryside during the years of the interdict). And what, in the end, did the Roman Church get out of the long dispute with King John? Innocent got his man accepted at Canterbury, but Stephen Langton turned out to be a disappointment, unwisely allowing himself to be accused by the pope of supporting the rebel cause during the civil war. The Church got a penitent sinner, but John continued to appoint his own men to the episcopacy, as did his successors. There was, however, one area to which Harper-Bill points where the interdict does seem to mark a watershed, and that was in the area of election to the headships of royal or other monasteries. From this point onwards, kings of England allowed the members of these communities free election of their heads. The real benefactor of the interdict, or more especially the resolution of the dispute and the lifting of the interdict, was King John. He won in return for his submission to Innocent III the staunch and unwavering support of the papacy against his enemies.

In his paper, Ralph V. Turner provides us with an assessment of King John's administrative achievements. Perhaps John's greatest accomplishment, according to Turner, was the 'extension of royal justice to humble landholders'; a 'fragile and fleeting . . . expansion of royal jurisdiction', undone by the regime of Henry III which allowed the aristocracy to dominate justice in the localities. He created the court *coram rege* which provided an alternative source of justice to the Bench at Westminster, and, more importantly, it allowed 'his subjects an opportunity to conclude their cases more promptly' by providing regular sittings in the localities. Turner also gives us an insight into the attitudes that John displayed toward kingship and justice. For example, he explains that for King John, 'law of the land' meant the 'judgement of professional royal servants', not the judgement of peers. Turner also reminds us of the great hold John had over the inheritance claims of his magnates, refusing to allow those with even a perfect claim to enter into an inheritance without the payment of an 'exorbitant' fine. This influence over his barons' lives also extended to their marriages, even over those of full age. These provide us, says Turner, with 'striking evidence of his control over the lives of the English aristocracy'.

Throughout most of the twelfth century, English kings looked to the Hohenstaufen rulers of Germany as their natural allies; but the capture of Richard I by the emperor Henry VI changed that attitude. Henry extorted from Richard a large ransom and, even more humiliatingly, forced Richard to submit as an imperial vassal. In the wake of these events Richard, needless to say, turned away from the alliance between the English kings and the Hohenstaufens, and when Henry died in 1197, Richard threw his weight behind the candidature of the Welf, Otto of Brunswick. Natalie Fryde shows that John, too, followed his brother's lead; but whereas Richard had actively sought to support Otto, John, at least until Normandy was lost in 1204, and quite possibly until Otto's rival, Philip of Swabia, had died in 1208, kept a distance from his nephew. During this period, it seems that John's diplomatic interest lay in the Low Countries, from which he could raise troops for his campaigns. Until Otto had fully established himself as king of Germany, all he represented was a potential drain on John's resources as he looked for financial and military support in his bid to become undisputed king of Germany. After 1208, however, Otto, now firmly established in Germany, became an essential ally in John's plans to retake his lost continental lands. The alliance between John and Otto reached its full fruition in 1214 when, at the Battle of Bouvines, the forces of Otto, John and their allies met and were defeated by Philip Augustus.

In his essay, Jim Bradbury attempts to bring to the fore the attitudes of contemporary historians concerning Philip Augustus and King John. To the French observers of Philip, their king was a strong and powerful warrior; and to Bradbury, he was a military commander who was a 'match for both Henry II and Richard I . . . and he was more than a match for John', as he showed in his capture of Normandy. According to Bradbury, Philip was a pious man, as contemporary French chroniclers saw; it is only modern historians who suggest that 'Philip lacked devotion.'

The John who emerges from the pages of this volume is not a sympathetic character, but then no medieval king could, or indeed should, be seen in this light. In the eyes of John Gillingham's historians, he made errors of judgement early on in his reign and he was a difficult man to trust. These character-flaws led Arthur of Brittany into the arms of Philip Augustus and Hugh IX of Lusignan into rebellion. They also resulted in John's expulsion from his continental inheritance. Daniel Power, too, sees personal defects as the cause of the loss of Normandy. Inevitably, though, there is a tension in this volume between those who look to John's personality and those who look to the structures of early thirteenth-century society for their explanations of this king's failures. The works of Jim Bolton, Paul Latimer, Nick Barratt and V.D. Moss published here place to the fore the economic factors that led to John's problems. Moss, for example, has shown that in Normandy John could not match the revenue- raising feats achieved by his brother Richard. And Barratt's work demonstrates that despite being cash-rich, John was not as wealthy as Philip Augustus or, indeed, Richard I. The cost of the war with France obviously caused economic hardship throughout the Angevin realm. And once John was confined to England, the financial pressure on the kingdom increased. John did manage to raise large sums of money for his intended reconquest of the Angevin continental lands, but, as Bolton shows, this was at the cost of causing a recession in England.

On the wider stage, John's dealings with his near neighbours and with the universal church also do not reflect well on him. To Seán Duffy, John's failings in his governance of Ireland, from first contact in 1185 to the end of the reign, show him to have been incompetent. Indeed, Duffy would go so far as to lay the blame at John's feet for the eventual failure of the medieval conquest of Ireland. In Wales, too, John's careless handling of the Welsh princes led to failure. Only in his dealings with Scotland can John be said to have enjoyed any real success. But it was in his relationship with the universal church that John showed the best and the worst of his character traits. According to Christopher Harper-Bill, the Canterbury dispute which led to an interdict being placed on England was caused by John's failure to see that Innocent III was quite capable of choosing his own candidate for the see. It was, therefore, an avoidable confrontation which John, to his discredit, failed to avoid. But in his reconciliation with the papacy, John showed himself to be a masterful tactician. By appearing as a penitent sinner, John was able to remove all legitimate cause for Philip Augustus' intended invasion of England in 1213; and, although John could not have foreseen it, his actions gave him and his successor the unfailing support of the papacy throughout the civil war of 1215–17 and beyond.

If there is one criticism that can be levelled at historians of John's reign, it is that sometimes we are guilty of excusing the fact that the reign ended in the disaster of civil war. No group of subjects, no matter how numerous and powerful, lightly takes on the task of unseating a medieval king. The fact that his subjects undertook forcibly to remove him from office must, in the end, be the lasting judgement on King John.

Historians Without Hindsight: Coggeshall, Diceto and Howden on the Early Years of John's Reign

John Gillingham

In his 'Good and Bad Kings in Medieval English History', published in 1945, V.H. Galbraith suggested that 'a new approach to the problem of John's character' would probably result in the emergence of 'the notion of a king capable of a consistent policy of state-building, better in conception than in execution, but nevertheless still in the true line of Henry II'.[1] The 'new approach' was to be based on the systematic use of record evidence. As Sir James Holt put it in 1963, 'Stubbs and his contemporaries relied mainly on the chroniclers; modern writers rely mainly on records.'[2] According to Lewis Warren, 'the personality of John is writ large on the records that survive, and we can get closer to him there than through the pages of any chronicle'.[3] It is unlikely that anyone has ever known the historians of the late twelfth and early thirteenth centuries as well as Stubbs did, and while historians continued to rely on chronicle sources, it is not surprising that it was his fierce condemnation of John which held the field.[4] Thus, in 1902 Kate Norgate concluded her biography, in many ways still unsurpassed, with an allusion to John's 'almost superhuman wickedness'.[5] For Sir James Ramsay, John was 'a selfish cruel tyrant of the worst type'.[6]

Galbraith's observations were to be the harbinger of a new orthodoxy. This was established by Warren and, above all, by Holt, and it has lasted, as Ralph Turner's recent biography makes plain, to the present day.[7] Central features of the current orthodoxy are the following notions. John's early career was bad – in 1185 in Ireland, in 1189 when he rebelled against his father, and in 1193–4 when he rebelled against his brother. But he then became a reformed character.

---

[1] V.H. Galbraith, 'Good and Bad Kings in English History', *History* 30, 1945, 119–32, at pp. 128–30, reprinted in his *Kings and Chroniclers*, 1982.

[2] J.C. Holt, *King John*, Historical Association 1963, 4; reprinted in his *Magna Carta and Medieval Government*, 85–109.

[3] Warren, *King John*, 143.

[4] *Walter of Coventry*, ii. xi–lxxx. Reprinted in W. Stubbs, *Historical Introductions to the Rolls Series*, ed. A. Hassall, London 1902, 439–87.

[5] K. Norgate, *John Lackland*, London 1902, 286.

[6] Sir J.H. Ramsay, *The Angevin Empire*, London 1903, 502.

[7] This goes back to J.R. Green's view that he was 'the ablest and most ruthless of the Angevins', *A Short History of the English People*, London 1882, 122–3.

He served Richard well from 1195 on, and when he became king he showed that he possessed many admirable qualities.

> It is now recognised that John took a thoroughly intelligent and immensely energetic interest in the running of the country. . . . The total achievement was enormous, fit to stand alongside that of Henry II or Edward I. Together, these two and John represent a standard which was never again equalled in the medieval period.[8]

So far as I can see no one denies that in the end John was a failure, but they believe that he was a failure above all because he failed to recover Normandy and because the attempt to do so, in particular to raise money to fund the campaign of reconquest, led him into oppressive ways and so provoked barons and churchmen to rebel. Sidney Painter saw the loss of his continental possessions as 'the turning point in John's career, the event that warped his character beyond repair'.[9] Thus, in Holt's words, 'in the chronology of John's reign, 1204, not 1199, is the crucial date'. Moreover it is widely held that the loss of Normandy was not John's fault. 'King Philip's financial accounts for the year 1202–3 suggest that French resources along the Norman frontier were already far greater than anything John could bear.'[10] If it was war, John would be defeated. Hence he had no choice in 1199 but to make peace.

> A peace policy at the beginning of the new reign was closer to necessity even than to prudence . . . John's mustering of forces in 1199 was impressive . . . But behind them lay an economy at full stretch and a Normandy suddenly weary of war. The harsher truths of the military situation escaped contemporary chroniclers . . . The contrast with Richard . . . no doubt justified to small minds the epithet 'Softsword', but if John had tried a firm sword it would have shattered in his hand.[11]

Whether or not this view can be sustained is an argument which here I shall leave to others. I note only that it involves setting aside early thirteenth-century opinion. Just possibly Adam of Eynsham thought the king of France was richer than the king of England, but three well-informed and fairly detached contemporaries writing both before and after the loss of Normandy imply that he was not. According to an anonymous monk from the Cistercian house of Clairmarais near St Omer, 'John . . . abandoned Normandy, Aquitaine and all their appurtenances, thinking little of the shame of flight, struck down by cowardice rather than by lack of money.'[12] Since this was written c.1220, it could perhaps be argued that the author's opinion was influenced by his knowledge of

---

[8] Holt, *King John*, 13–14; cf. 'John was capable and dedicated to the work of kingship, in many ways a worthy successor to his father Henry II and great grandfather Henry I', Turner, *King John*, 263.

[9] Painter, *Reign of King John*, 227.

[10] Holt, *Northerners*, 144; cf. Turner, *King John*, 259.

[11] Warren, *King John*, 72, 79.

[12] 'Flandria Generosa', *MGH, Scriptores*, IX, 330.

subsequent events: John's retreat from Roche-au-Moine as well as the lavish scale of expenditure in 1213–14. But another author from north-eastern France, Lambert of Ardres, writing in about 1203 (at any rate before the loss of Normandy), thought that in the late 1190s Richard had been outbidding Philip with barrels full of gold and silver; and a third observer from the same region, the anonymous chronicler of Béthune, made the same point.[13] Modern English historians have sometimes pointed to the undoubted burdens which war placed on English and Norman taxpayers, without drawing attention to the evidence that the king of France's subjects suffered in the same way – as Coggeshall, for one, emphasised very strongly.[14] Rigord of St Denis complained that the kingdom of France in 1199 and 1200 was suffering from an intolerable burden of taxation.[15] Thus contemporaries did not excuse John's retreat from Normandy in 1203 in the way modern historians often have. In the view of the Melrose Chronicle, he returned to England 'having ignominiously lost his lands and castles across the sea'.[16] The damage to his reputation was noted by the Barnwell writer. 'Having been abandoned by his men, John left Normandy, pre-ferring to yield for the moment with some loss of reputation and material, rather than give himself and his followers over to destruction.'[17] Historians have cited this passage in support of their view that John was bowing to the inevitable. But for this author what was decisive was the fact that John's men abandoned him. Only after that did he have to choose between retreat and destruction. Why they abandoned him, whether it was because he lacked money or leadership, the Barnwell chronicler did not say. So this is the key question. Why was John abandoned? A question which is all the more puzzling if, as alleged, he had begun his reign rather well.

I shall attempt to answer this question by returning to the methods of Stubbs. Holt's own mastery of records did not prevent him, in his superb Historical Association pamphlet on King John, from setting out in ten lucid pages a crisp analysis of chronicle opinion.[18] He divided contemporary historians into three groups: firstly, those who completed their work before or just after John's accession; secondly, those who wrote by the time of John's death; thirdly, those who wrote after the king's death. In the first group he listed just four historians: Richard of Devizes, William of Newburgh, Roger of Howden and Ralph of Diceto. He used Devizes (whose work ended in 1192) and Newburgh (whose work ended in 1198) to demonstrate that John already enjoyed bad repute with some before he ascended the throne, culminating in William of Newburgh's famous judgement on John: 'nature's enemy'. However Holt felt that at times

---

[13] Lambert of Ardres, *Chronique de Guines et d'Ardre*, ed. M. de Godefroy Menilglaise, Paris 1855, 371. According to the anonymous of Béthune 'li rois Richars estoit trop riches et de terre et d'avoir, asés plus que li rois de France n'estoit', *RHF*, XXIV, pt 2, 758.

[14] *Coggeshall*, 76.

[15] *Rigord*, 148.

[16] *The Chronicle of Melrose*, ed. A.O and M.O. Anderson, London 1936, s.a. 1203.

[17] *Walter of Coventry*, ii.197.

[18] Holt, *King John*, 16–25.

Richard of Devizes' attitude to John was 'almost hysterical'. In contrast both Howden (whose work ended in 1201) and Diceto (whose work ended in 1202) 'took a calmer view'.[19] This assessment of Howden and Diceto was of crucial importance. It enabled Holt to conclude that 'the chroniclers' opinions of John roughly follow the pattern of his career. They were hostile to his behaviour while Richard was on crusade; they reacted reasonably towards him by the time he was king and during his early years; they turned hostile again, this time excessively so, from the middle years of his reign and especially after his death.[20] Turner has supported this line of argument, writing that Howden and Diceto took the positive view of the civil servant and

> combated the anti-government bias of most monastic writers . . . Unfortunately for John's reputation, the golden age of medieval English historiography ended in his first years. No chronicler after the deaths of Diceto and Howden early in his reign took a positive view of royal government.[21]

So the orthodoxy is that while the two best historians were still around, John's reputation stood reasonably high. But they were both dead by 1202. As Lady Stenton put it, 'no king of England was ever so unlucky as John'.[22] This was to return to Protestant orthodoxy as expressed by John Speed. Had John's story not fallen into 'the hands of exasperated writers, he had appeared a King of as great renown as misfortunes'.[23]

In this paper I shall concentrate on Coggeshall, Diceto and Howden – three historians who wrote before 1203. David Carpenter has recently subjected the pre-1203 section of Ralph of Coggeshall to close scrutiny, but Howden's and Diceto's narratives of John's reign have not been similarly studied – despite their importance for the argument that both modern historians and sensible contemporaries took a broadly similar view of John. Warren, for example, in his lively analysis of 'The Chroniclers and the Angevins', treated them not as historians of John, but of John's father and brother. This allowed him to assert that all 'the strictly contemporary' chroniclers were members of religious orders whose feelings about John were 'inevitably distorted' and that among them there 'was no one who knew him personally'.[24] Had he included Howden and Diceto in his analysis he would not have been able to make these claims.

---

[19] Holt, *King John*, 19.
[20] Holt, *King John*, 27. He acknowledged that both Howden and Diceto were 'at times critical', *Northerners*, 145.
[21] Turner, *King John*, 5, 8.
[22] D.M. Stenton, *English Society in the Early Middle Ages*, Harmondsworth 1951, 44. Cf. 'No such good fortune attended John. The era of great historical writing came to an end shortly after he ascended the throne', Warren, *King John*, 21.
[23] John Speed, *Historie of Great Britaine*, 3rd edn, London 1632, 572. Speed's assessment depended upon treating John's loss of his continental possessions as of little moment. Thus he proclaimed that John's work in Wales and Ireland was 'of greater import for England's peace than all the French titles ever yet have proved'.
[24] Warren, *King John*, 21.

There are, however, five other historians who wrote before 1203 and who should at least be mentioned: Gerald de Barri (better known as Gerald of Wales), Giselbert of Mons, Rigord of St Denis, Jocelin of Brakelond and Andreas of Marchiennes.[25] Gerald de Barri had many opportunities to observe John in action and indeed later claimed to have been amongst his *familiares*.[26] In the *Conquest of Ireland*, written in the late 1180s, Gerald regarded John's susceptibility to 'bad advice' as the main cause of the failure of the 1185 expedition to Ireland.[27] In the second edition of his *Topography of Ireland*, written at about the same time, he portrayed him as an idle pleasure-seeker, but expressed the hope that he would learn sense when he grew up.[28] In some ways the tone of Gerald's *Life of Geoffrey Archbishop of York*, probably written soon after June 1193, is even more striking. Although this contains warm words in praise of John's chancellor, Stephen Ridel, and was composed in order to justify the political campaign against Longchamp, a campaign in which John himself took a leading part, it none the less puts John himself in a highly ambiguous light, all too willing to be tempted by bribes.[29] But perhaps this is not surprising in a work being written as John's association with Philip Augustus was becoming clearer. The universal detestation in which this was held is well illustrated by the fact that Giselbert of Mons and Rigord of St Denis, both writing c.1196 and both hostile to Richard I, none the less criticised John's alliance with the king of France.[30] Jocelin of Brakelond almost certainly finished writing his chronicle in 1201 soon after the last event mentioned. According to him, Abbot Samson was thought *magnanimus* because he excommunicated the rebels of 1193 without any fear of Prince John. He described John's visit to Bury St Edmunds soon after his coronation in 1199, and portrayed a new king recompensing the abbey's hospitality in a distressingly ungenerous and tight-fisted fashion.[31]

Ralph of Coggeshall

Although Ralph of Coggeshall's account of the period after 1207 may not have been written until the 1220s, his narrative of the beginning of John's reign

---

25 Another possible author is the man responsible for the Winchester Annals for 1196 to 1202. J.T. Appleby plausibly suggested that these entries were written by Richard of Devizes, *Devizes*, xxiv–vi. They are very favourable to Richard, brief and neutral on John.

26 *Giraldi Cambrensis Opera*, i. 86–7 for Gerald's claim, in his autobiographical *De Rebus a Se Gestis*, to have been John's *familiaris*.

27 Gerald, *Expugnatio Hibernica*, ed. A.B. Scott and F.X. Martin, Dublin 1978, 236–42.

28 *Giraldi Cambrensis Opera*, v. 200.

29 *Giraldi Cambrensis Opera*, iv. 397, 404, 406, 417, 430. On this work see R. Bartlett, *Gerald of Wales 1146–1223*, Oxford 1982, 65. Howden and Devizes also noted John's weakness for bribes, *Gesta Henrici*, ii. 239; *Devizes*, 62–3.

30 Giselbert of Mons, *Chronicon Hanoniense*, ed. L. Vanderkindere, Brussels 1904, 284; *Rigord*, i. vi–xi, 122, 126.

31 *The Chronicle of Jocelin of Brakelond*, ed. H.E. Butler, London 1949, 55, 116–17. I shall consider Andreas of Marchiennes later.

belongs, as Powicke suggested, to an instalment of his history which covered the years from 1195 to 1201, and which was completed by 1202. Powicke also showed that in 1195, when Coggeshall completed an earlier instalment, he was hostile to John. Antonia Gransden, focusing on the early years of John's reign, took the view that Coggeshall began 'by being fairly favourable' to the king, before 'quick disillusionment' meant that his 'attitude soon changed'.[32] Recently Carpenter has greatly strengthened the argument for an instalment composed in 1201 and has added weight to the view that Coggeshall at first took a comparatively positive view of John as king.[33] On this interpretation, Coggeshall's changing attitude exemplifies the orthodox opinion that sensible contemporaries began by being critical, then became rather more sympathetic, before finally turning hostile again.

Unquestionably, Ralph was hostile by the time, probably c.1206, he wrote of John giving orders for the 'detestable' and 'execrable' blinding and castrating of Arthur.[34] But I am not convinced that in 1201 his tone was quite as positive as has been claimed. His commentary on the treaty of Le Goulet has often been regarded as favourable to John. 'John, mindful of the way in which repeated wars had caused inconveniences to his father and brothers and to the whole realm, was a lover of peace and was planning to lead a quiet life.'[35] But this sentence did not end there. It went on to record John's demand for the 30,000 marks due under the terms of the treaty. In the very next sentence Coggeshall complained of the level of taxation which resulted. Indeed his commentary on the treaty occurs in a section which he headed 'On the royal exactions'.[36] In this way John's *pacis concordia* with France led directly into that *discordia* between John and the Cistercian order which takes up the greater part of his account of John's first twenty months as king – in the printed edition nine out of thirteen pages.[37] Here Coggeshall dwelt on John's financial oppression, on his iniquities, his 'cruel edicts' and his fierce threats. He drew attention to one of John's least attractive qualities – his habit of sniggering, or of encouraging his courtiers to snigger, at the discomfiture of others.[38] In the end, however, the

---

[32] Holt, *King John*, 22; F.M. Powicke, 'Roger of Wendover and the Coggeshall Chronicle', *EHR* 21, 1906, 286–292; cf. J. Gillingham, 'The Unromantic Death of Richard I', *Speculum* 54, 1979, 26. Gransden, *Historical Writing*, 318, 326–7.

[33] D.A. Carpenter, 'Abbot Ralph of Coggeshall's Account of the Last Years of King Richard and the First Years of King John', *EHR* 113, 1998, 1210–30. I am very grateful to David Carpenter both for showing me a draft of his article and for sharing with me the pleasures of disagreeing with one another. The present essay is a considerably revised version of the paper originally given in March 1997; the revision owes much to him.

[34] *Coggeshall*, 139; Carpenter, 'Abbot Ralph', 1228.

[35] However Ramsay regarded *utpote pacis amator* as a sneer, *The Angevin Empire*, 384.

[36] *Coggeshall*, 101–2.

[37] *Coggeshall*, 102–110, out of pp. 99–111.

[38] *Coggeshall*, 105. Other writers to observe this trait were Gerald de Barri, *Expugnatio*, 236; Richard of *Devizes*, 62; and the authors of the *Hist. des ducs de Normandie*, 112, of the *Histoire de Guilluame le Maréchal*, ll. 13846–51, and of a fragmentary Canterbury Chronicle, *Gervase*, ii. lix, to which Henry Summerson kindly drew my attention.

brave and anxious resistance of the Cistercians paid off when, in late November 1200, the king took Hubert Walter's advice and backed down. In return for the Cistercians agreeing to forgo their claims for damages, John remitted their payment of the tax and promised to found a splendid new house of their order in which he hoped to be buried. At this point and on this issue Coggeshall was full of praise. Peace had been restored. John's heart was full of gentleness ('mansuetudo') and 'the spirit of counsel and pity' ('spiritus consilii et pietatis').[39]

What are the implications of this for his view of the peace between the kings of France and England? John deserved praise for giving way to the Cistercians because the Cistercians were in the right. But in the struggle between the king of England and the king of France, Coggeshall was in no doubt that Philip was in the wrong. In that section of his history which he completed in 1201 he condemned Philip's invasion of Normandy in the strongest possible terms.[40] Did he approve of John making a peace which allowed Philip to keep some of his unjust conquests?[41] At one point in his account of the Cistercians' resistance to John, Ralph described a council of abbots in which they debated whether or not buying off the king's anger in order to enjoy the benefits of peace would lead them too far down the road to subjection to secular power. Eventually a letter from the General Chapter of their order persuaded them that if they offered money for such a peace ('talem pacis concordiam'), it would endanger the whole order. Hence they resolved to fight on and in the end victory went to the virtuous.[42] But John had done precisely what they had decided not to do. In order to enjoy the undoubted benefits of peace, he had offered Philip a huge sum of money and, in consequence, had made his subjects suffer the financial burden of a carucage levied on top of an unprecedentedly high scutage.[43]

Did Coggeshall think the king of France could be trusted to keep the peace? It seems unlikely. When writing in 1201 about Philip's conflict with Count Baldwin of Flanders, he referred to Philip's *malignitas* and to the way he tricked his enemies by simulated goodwill.[44] In his commentary on the treaty of Le Goulet he made no mention of the fact that John's peace with France involved the breaking of his alliances with Otto IV, Baldwin of Flanders and Reynaud of Boulogne. Coggeshall may not have rated the alliance with Otto very highly, but writing in 1201 he had emphasised the importance of Richard's alliances with Flanders and Boulogne in bringing God's judgment upon Philip

---

[39] *Coggeshall*, 108–9. It is likely that Ralph himself was an eyewitness of this scene.
[40] *Coggeshall*, 76; and 112 for his opinion of Philip as an adulterer and oppressor of churchmen.
[41] *Coggeshall*, 100, where he named Vernon, Pacy, Ivry and Nonancourt as in Philip's possession on the day that Richard, 'validissimus rex', died, and which were therefore conceded to Philip, together with the county of Evreux, Auvergne and Berry.
[42] *Coggeshall*, 105–6.
[43] *Coggeshall*, 101–2.
[44] *Coggeshall*, 77–9. Given his view of Philip, what are we to make of his observation, p. 103, that John's marriage to Isabella of Angoulême was on Philip's advice?

for his disgraceful attack on Normandy. Later, when he came to narrate the events of 1202 and Philip's renewed advance into Normandy, he emphasised the military leadership of Reynaud of Boulogne who, he said, had gone over to Philip because John had made peace with the king of France without him, and once again he referred back to Richard's alliances with Boulogne and Flanders.[45] In other words it is certain that Coggeshall appreciated the strategic significance of these alliances. Yet when writing about the treaty, and doing so in some detail, he omitted all mention of one of its most salient features: the rupture of old alliances. Coggeshall was clearly happy when John submitted to the Cistercians; but it is less clear that he approved of the peace of Le Goulet. If his account was written in the months after November 1200, when the happy memory of John's peace with his own order was still fresh in his mind, then may he not – naturally desirous of peace – have made the best he could of Le Goulet, suppressing the doubts which he surely had?

Ralph of Diceto

Ralph of Diceto was probably in his seventies in 1199; he had connections with the royal court going back to the 1160s, and had been dean of St Paul's from 1180/1. Although the history as printed by Stubbs extends as far as March 1202, Diana Greenway drew attention to evidence that Ralph may have died in November 1199 or November 1200 and that the history after the coronation of John may have been written by an anonymous continuator.[46] If he survived until November 1200, he could have continued as far as the coronation of Isabella in October 1200, and it does look as though a text of 'Diceto' going up to that point was available to the author of the Dunstable Annals.[47] In any event, even if written by a continuator, then it was a continuator who finished writing soon after March 1202 and who shared Diceto's interests. I shall confine myself to the period up to October 1200 and for convenience shall continue to refer to the author as Diceto. Stubbs fairly characterised him as writing 'with a strong feeling of attachment to Henry II and the Angevin family; with considerable political insight, and acquaintance with both the details and the moving causes of public affairs; in a temperate and businesslike style'.[48] Naturally he criticised John's conduct in 1193. Then, after describing how he 'fell at his brother's feet and begged for mercy' in 1194, he ignored him altogether until he inherited the throne.[49]

---

[45] *Coggeshall*, 77, 135–6.

[46] D.E. Greenway, 'The Succession to Ralph de Diceto, Dean of St Paul's', *BIHR* 39, 1966, 86–95. See also *Diceto*, ii.166 n.3 for Stubbs' own recognition of this point.

[47] *Ann. Mon.* iii. 28. See C.R. Cheney, 'Notes on the Making of the Dunstable Annals, AD 33 to 1242', in T.A. Sandquist and M.R. Powicke, eds, *Essays in Medieval History presented to Bertie Wilkinson*, Toronto 1969, 91 (reprinted in his *Medieval Texts and Studies*, Oxford 1973, 222), pointing out that entries for 1200 and 1201 resemble passages in the D text under the year 1200.

[48] *Diceto*, ii. lviii.

[49] *Diceto*, ii. 106, 114.

In Stubbs' edition the period from the accession to October 1200 takes up nearly six pages. The first episode dealt with was John's divorce. This was done, Diceto wrote, 'on the advice of evil men'. In the very next sentence we are told that John acted 'less than prudently' ('minus caute') in his dealings with Arthur, and that consequently 'Arthur went over to the king of France who, coveting his goods, had him brought up with his son at Paris.'[50] It is important to note that Diceto always wrote of Philip Augustus in a hostile and mocking tone.[51] So far as his actions in 1199 are concerned, John has made a very bad start. Under the year 1200, Diceto reported two episodes: the peace with France and John's marriage. All he had to say about the peace was to highlight, in a manner reminiscent of Coggeshall, the size of the dowry which John gave to Blanche of Castile as the price of peace: 'all his land of Berry and Auvergne, also castles and many honours both in Normandy and in Gascony and in many other places'.[52] Then he turned to the subject of John's marriage. He noted that since Isabella of Angoulême, it was said, had earlier been given to Hugh le Brun, there afterwards erupted a massive quarrel between John and Hugh. This may be critical. What certainly are hostile are the immediately preceding words.

> Lord John, king of England, having in mind to marry a daughter of the king of the Portuguese, whose reputation had captivated his thoughts, sent from Rouen some great notables, the bishop of Lisieux, William of L'Étang, Ralph of Arden and Hubert de Burgh and many others from both England and Normandy, to bring her back to him. But he married Isabella only daughter and heir of the count of Angoulême, and he did this while they were on the journey, without having warned them, taking much less care for their safety than was worthy of the royal majesty.[53]

Here then is an author highly critical of John's beginnings, describing him as acting 'less than prudently', 'on the advice of evil men', 'in a manner unworthy of the royal majesty'.

Roger of Howden

Roger, parson of Howden – 'the best historian of the English crown in the twelfth century', according to Southern[54] – entered royal service in the 1170s, probably as early as 1170. He was sent on a number of missions to Scotland and the curia, becoming an expert on Anglo–Scottish relations and in particular on

[50] *Diceto*, ii. 167.
[51] *Diceto*, ii. 116, 118, 168.
[52] *Diceto*, ii. 168.
[53] *Diceto*, ii. 170.
[54] R.W. Southern, *Medieval Humanism and other Studies*, Oxford 1970, 150. It is worth noting, however, that at the end of his life, the 'reliable' Howden was addicted to the kind of Sunday observance miracle stories for which Warren pilloried the 'unreliable' Wendover, *King John*, 25–6.

the affairs of the Scottish church. He went on crusade with Richard I, and when Philip Augustus returned early from Acre, he was entrusted with the important and delicate task of keeping a watching brief on him. Elsewhere I have argued that Howden remained in the service of both the king and the bishop of Durham throughout the 1190s and that, as before, this included important missions to Scotland and to the curia.[55] In 1199 he was, in other words, not so much a retired administrator living quietly in a north-country parsonage as a highly experienced diplomat. By the time John came to the throne, Roger had known him for at least twenty-five years, and had been writing about him for nearly fifteen.

In his brief account of the 1185 expedition to Ireland in the *Gesta Henrici Secundi*, he made the earliest known observation on John's capacity as a leader. What struck him was John's reluctance to pay the substantial army with which he had been provided by his father. As a result his troops deserted to the Irish and the expedition ended disastrously. When composing his *Chronica* at some date after 1192, Howden revised the account of the Irish expedition which he had given in the strictly contemporaneous *Gesta*. But though he changed the words, he retained the same diagnosis of John's mistakes: not shortage of money but an unwillingness to spend it properly.[56] Evidently the meanness which Jocelin of Brakelond was to observe at Bury in 1199 was already apparent in Ireland in 1185. In the *Gesta*, Roger described John's conduct in 1189 as 'the occasion, or rather the immediate cause, of his father's death'. In the *Chronica*, he said that it was seeing John's name at the head of the list of traitors which set the old king cursing the day on which he was born.[57] After his return from crusade, Howden obtained his material on the John–Longchamp quarrel from Hugh de Puiset, bishop of Durham.[58] This made him emphatically hostile to Longchamp. Despite this, his account of the quarrel is not at all favourable to John. We have to remember that Howden wrote this section of his *Gesta* shortly after he had travelled back from Palestine with King Philip and that he had probably been at the French court at Christmas 1191 listening to the French king 'safe and sound and impudently announcing he was about to devastate the lands of the king of England'.[59] By January 1192 at the latest Roger had learned of John being tempted to do a deal with Philip.[60] Thus it was only

---

[55] J. Gillingham, 'The Travels of Roger of Howden and His Views of the Irish, Scots and Welsh', *ANS* 20, 1998, 151–69. My discussion of Howden owes much to Archie Duncan.

[56] *Gesta Regis Henrici*, i. 336; *Howden*, ii. 305.

[57] *Gesta Regis Henrici*, ii. 72; *Howden*, ii. 366. This does not strike me as 'a mild account of his desertion of his father'. Holt also believes that Howden 'associated John with Richard's popularity in 1189', *King John*, 19–20. This is certainly the impression given by the account of their arrival in England in *Howden*, iii. 5–6. Here, however, Howden was abbreviating his own contemporary account, *Gesta Regis*, ii. 75–6, where he had made it clear that Richard and John travelled separately and that it was Richard who was greeted with joy.

[58] D. Corner, 'The *Gesta Regis Henrici Secundi* and *Chronica* of Roger, Parson of Howden', *BIHR* 56, 1983, 126–44, here pp. 134–9.

[59] *Gesta Regis Henrici*, ii. 235. See Corner, 'The *Gesta Regis*', 141.

[60] *Gesta Regis Henrici*, ii. 236–7.

natural that he should treat his behaviour in 1193–4 with contempt, reporting Richard's various remarks on John's treachery and feebleness.[61] Despite this he was clearly pleased and relieved by John's submission in May 1194. Although he devoted only one sentence to the subject, he none the less gave it a subheading: 'concordia facta'.[62]

From then on we are dealing with the reformed John, and there is reason to think that Howden was prepared to set aside his old animosity against him. He gave John, together with Mercadier, a share of the credit for a great military success, the capture of two senior French commanders, the bishop of Beauvais and William of Merlou, followed on the same day (19 May 1197) by the capture of Milli. In Howden's words, John and Mercadier returned from their *chevauchée* into the Beauvaisis as 'gloriosi triumphatores'.[63] The capture of the bishop of Beauvais in arms was a great propaganda success for Richard I, exploited for all it was worth. Howden played his part by including in his history a forged letter by which the pope was made to condemn both the soldier–bishop and the king of France in the strongest terms.[64] It may be that a contribution by John to this triumph explains why William of Newburgh, quite likely writing in 1197, took such a positive view of his service to his brother after 1194, noting that he served him 'fideliter et fortiter' against the king of France – in stark contrast to his earlier view of John as 'nature's enemy'.[65] But although the capture of Philip of Beauvais was widely and gleefully reported by English historians, only Howden explicitly associated John with this coup.[66] According to Coggeshall, the bishop was captured by Richard's *familia*.[67] It could be that, like Mercadier, John was serving as one of the commanders of the *familia regis*. This would have enabled Richard to keep a very close eye on him, and might have had the effect of rendering him at times almost invisible – which might help to explain why Diceto never once mentioned John in his account of 1195–98. According to Howden, in 1199 John's loyalty to Richard was put in doubt by Philip, but was vindicated by the readiness of two of John's knights to prove his innocence of the charge in Philip's court.[68] This passage,

---

[61] *Howden*, iii. 198. Roger was probably an eyewitness when John was disseised by *commune consilium* at Nottingham in March 1194 and 'forfeited all claims to the kingdom', iii. 237–42.

[62] *Howden*, iii. 252.

[63] *Howden*, iv. 16. He mistakenly placed this episode at the end of his entry for 1196. *Howden*, iv. 60 shows John in September 1198 enjoying further success in the Norman war.

[64] *Howden*, iv. 21–4.

[65] *Newburgh*, ii. 424.

[66] Newburgh, Gervase of Canterbury and the Winchester Annals mention neither John nor Mercadier, *Newburgh*, ii. 493; *Gervase*, i. 544; *Ann. Mon.*, ii. 65. Diceto gives the credit to Mercadier, *Diceto*, ii. 152, as does *Hist. Guillaume le Maréchal*, ll. 11, 265–9.

[67] *Coggeshall*, 77.

[68] *Howden*, iv, 81. If John was attached to the *familia regis* this might throw light on Coggeshall's story of him leaving Richard's court 'propter expensarum penuriam' shortly before the king was killed, *Coggeshall*, 99. Cf. Turner, *King John*, 47. The whole of this paragraph owes much to discussion with David Carpenter.

written after John's reign had already begun, suggests that Roger was ready to treat the new king sympathetically.

How then did he treat King John? According to Holt, Howden

> did not let John's previous treachery affect his account of his early years as king. When he finished his work in 1201 he had presented no wayward tyrant, but a vigorous monarch, a ruler concerned to maintain his rights and realize his authority, a typical Angevin king in short, whose accession had made little difference to the routine conduct of government. Howden had been a royal justice and knew what he was talking about.[69]

Certainly Roger knew what he was talking about, and it is certainly arguable that he thought John's accession made little difference to the 'routine conduct of government'. But then very few kings would make much difference to the *routine* of government – though it should be said that Roger was singularly unimpressed by the *implementation* of assizes in John's reign. He reported in characteristic detail the content of the Assize of Wines and then added, 'but this the king's first statute had hardly been put into force when it was suddenly annulled'. His last reference to an assize relates to June 1201 and to the failure of corrupt officials to enforce Richard's Assize of Measures. The passage bears the rubric 'De relaxatione statuti regis Ricardi' and it is with this headline that this most administrative-minded of historians made his final comment on the routine of Angevin government.[70]

What did he think of John's political judgement? At first sight it seems that his view was a balanced one. He generally reported John's actions in neutral language. His coverage of John's first two years is much more detailed than any other contemporary historian's – about 100 pages in Stubbs' edition, about half of which relates to John's conduct of business – and only four episodes provoked him into a judgement. These fall 2–2, for and against. Twice he accused John of acting on bad advice; once he complimented him for acting on the advice of good men, and once for being inspired by divine grace. Four times may not sound much, but it must be remembered that Roger is famous for his 'passionless, colourless narrative'.[71] To put these four judgements into context it is necessary to look more closely at the composition of his history for the period in question. We are fortunate to possess, in Bodleian Library Laud MS misc. 582, a manuscript copy of the *Chronica* on which he was working from 1199 until his death. This suggests that the greater part of his account of John's reign was written up in three blocks: the first covering the period from the accession to March 1200 (fos 178r–183r; iv.86–113); the second from Easter 1200 to the end of that year (fos 183r–190v; iv.113–46); and the third from Christmas 1200 to autumn 1201 (fos 194r–199r; iv.156–76). Each of these blocks was probably put together at the end of the

---

[69] Holt, *King John*, 20.
[70] *Howden*, iv. 99–100, 172.
[71] *Howden*, i. lxix.

period covered.[72] From fo.180v onwards the greater part is written in the hand which has been identified as Roger's own.[73]

The earliest of these four judgements relates to an episode occurring in the summer of 1199 when John, having decided to restore his brother Geoffrey to the estates of the archbishopric of York – a subject on which Howden, thanks to his contacts with the York chapter, was exceptionally well-informed – then chose to keep back the rents from the manors until Geoffrey himself had returned from Rome. This was a very minor matter but since Howden asserted that John acted on bad advice ('pravo consilio') he presumably thought the king was being mean and petty.[74] By contrast he thought that the king was acting on divine inspiration when he humbly fell at the feet of the Cistercian abbots whom he had been persecuting. This happened at the great court at Lincoln in November 1200. At last, after threats of war and spurning many invitations, the king of Scots finally attended the English court and did homage. Here too John made a good impression by helping to carry the coffin of Bishop Hugh of Lincoln. November 1200 was undoubtedly a triumph for the king; for lovers of peace it was the highpoint of his reign. Howden, writing very soon afterwards, duly gave him credit.[75] It was while he was writing the same section of his history that he praised John for the second time. After noting that John and Isabella were crowned at Westminster on 8 October 1200, he wrote that 'meanwhile' Geoffrey of York was disseised on the king's orders, and then that 'after a while' ('procedente autem tempore'), John restored his archbishopric to him and invited him to court to explain his actions. This was done, said Howden, 'on the advice of good men'.[76] Although these events are only roughly dated, it seems likely that John and Geoffrey were reconciled towards the end of 1200, presumably as part of the general atmosphere of goodwill. Undoubtedly Roger liked what he saw of John at that time.

---

[72] Within these blocks changes in ink do not generally coincide with the entry of new items of information. On Roger's working method see Corner, 'The *Gesta Regis*', 132–44. At the end of his entry for any given year, and also after his entry for the end of Richard's reign, he left a leaf or two blank on which to add information which came in later, e.g. the account of the March 1201 council of Soissons wrongly placed in 1200 (*Howden*, iv. 146–8). However there is no space left blank at the end of the entry for 1199 on f. 181v – a fact which reinforces the impression that there is something curious (cf. p. 12) about Roger's treatment of late 1199 and early 1200.

[73] For the identification of the hand see D. Corner, 'The Earliest Surviving Manuscripts of Roger of Howden's "Chronica" ', *EHR* 98, 1983, 296–310.

[74] *Howden*, iv. 92. He included the text of the letter which Stephen of Turnham, who had been custodian of the York estates, sent to his agents. Given that this was so ephemeral a document, it is curious that he did so – perhaps it was a letter that he himself had composed.

[75] *Howden*, iv. 141–5. For reasons which will become apparent, I think it likely that the second block, including this section, was composed by the end of January 1201. The agreement which ended the long drawn-out Stuteville–Mowbray dispute could also have been reached at Lincoln, even if it was not formally recorded until 21 January 1201, *Howden*, iv. 117–18.

[76] *Howden*, iv. 139–40.

Yet by the time he next sat down to continue his working copy of the
Chronica, probably in the autumn of 1201, the goodwill had evaporated.[77] He
reported that late in March 1201 John ordered the earls and barons to muster at
Portsmouth at Whitsun (13 May) in order to deal with the revolt of the
Lusignans.[78] They held a meeting at Leicester and informed the king that they
would not go to Normandy unless the king restored their rights. John's reaction
was to demand their castles, beginning with William d'Albini's Belvoir, and in
the end he only allowed William to keep it after he had handed over his son as
hostage. In acting like this John was, in Howden's words, badly advised, 'malo
usus consilio'.[79] Here it seems Roger would have agreed with Ramsay's
comment that taking hostages in this way was an 'abominable practice'.[80] Presumably we should at least bear in the mind the attitude expressed in 1201 when
reading Howden's seemingly neutral report, under 1199, that John restored to
Roger de Lacy his castle of Pomfret and took his heir as hostage, as well as his
laconic reference to one hundred and fifty hostages being taken from Angers in
1200.[81] There are indications that the positive view which Howden took of John
at the end of 1200 may have been undermined as early as late January 1201,
when the king crossed the Humber and came to Beverley, very close to the parsonage at Howden. By then John had quarrelled, yet again, with his brother; and
had also quarrelled with the chapter of Lincoln.[82] In February, still in the north,
he was pressing his subjects hard with forest fines – always a sore point with
Howden.[83] Howden certainly praised King John, but only in two passages both
written in the glow of November 1200. Before and after that time he was either
neutral or critical.

Howden's narrative of John's dealings with Arthur in 1199 is particularly
striking, despite the studiously neutral tone in which it, unlike Diceto's account,
was written. He reported that when Philip and John met in August 1199, the
king of France demanded Poitou, Anjou, Maine and Touraine for Arthur, which
the king of England in no way wished to concede, nor – added Roger – ought he
to have done.[84] This, it must be remembered, is the author who had heard
Philip's boasts at Fontainebleau at Christmas 1191. In the autumn John scored a
great success when he came to terms with William des Roches. As Howden told
the story, William was irritated by Philip's methods, so in October 1199 he cun-
ningly removed Arthur from Philip's custody and brought him and the city of

[77] The last datable news item in this block, all written in Roger's own hand, occurred on
24 August 1201, *Howden*, 173.
[78] By autumn 1201 he knew, probably from Robert of Turnham, that this was serious trouble,
Howden, iv. 176 – the last entry written in his own hand.
[79] *Howden*, iv. 161.
[80] Ramsay, *Angevin Empire*, 503. For the vestigial evidence of John's immediate predecessors
taking hostages, other than from the Irish or Welsh, see Holt, *Magna Carta*, 82 n. 35.
[81] *Howden*, iv. 91–2, 125.
[82] Roger dean of Lincoln may well have been one of Howden's informants, see *Howden*, iv.
98, 145–6, 156.
[83] *Howden*, iv. 156–7. Cf. *Gesta Regis Henrici*, i. 105.
[84] *Howden*, iv. 95.

Le Mans over to John. But that same day Arthur was told that the king of England would put him in prison. Also on that day John forced the viscount of Thouars to hand over Chinon. Next night Arthur, his mother, the viscount of Thouars and many others slipped away and took refuge in Angers.[85] Given the central importance of Arthur in the succession dispute of 1199, it is difficult to imagine a more serious blow for John. But not since Powicke did so in 1913 has a twentieth-century historian re-told the story of how Arthur and friends fled.[86] Modern historians mention the agreement between John and William des Roches; they even say that this was why Philip agreed to make peace.[87] But as Norgate pointed out long ago, Howden got the date wrong. The agreement was in fact made on 18 September 1199 – as is proved by a record in the Charter Roll.[88] Perhaps worried by the thought of Roger's unreliability here, modern historians have preferred to disregard his tale of the precipitate flight of Arthur and friends, treating it as a matter of no great moment (indeed until now I have done the same myself). Yet the story is critically important. It tells of a king who – early in his reign – was not trusted and who in consequence suffered a severe setback. Both Howden and Diceto in their different ways ascribed great significance to this episode. That they were right to do so is suggested by what happened in 1202 when John next had Arthur in his possession, and by the analysis offered by the author of the *Histoire de Guillaume le Maréchal* to explain why John then made the disastrous mistake of refusing the requests made by William des Roches, his principal ally in the triumph at Mirebeau. According to the *Histoire*, John refused because he remembered how Arthur had acted in 1199.[89] Neither Howden nor Diceto could possibly have known what would happen after Mirebeau since by then they were dead, but, writing in 1199–1200, they both unerringly put their fingers on a decisive moment.

Why did Howden, who clearly liked to give precise dates whenever possible, date this episode only vaguely to 'in October', and even then get the month wrong? It should be noted that his account of the first two years of John's reign, though massively more detailed than any other, is far from being uniformly well informed about the king's activities over the whole period. He is fairly detailed on the five months from the accession in April 1199 to late August, but much vaguer on the following seven months; another patch of detail for April and May 1200 is followed by four months about which he had little to say; he was well-informed about the period from October 1200 to 4 March 1201, then again about a few days in mid-May 1201, but otherwise much less so. What can

---

[85] *Howden*, iv. 96–7. He added that Arthur's mother left her husband and married Gui de Thouars, the viscount's brother.

[86] Powicke, *Loss of Normandy*, 138–9. However even Powicke did not make at all clear the significance of this episode for the weakening of John's position in the run-up to the negotiations leading to the treaty of Le Goulet.

[87] Warren, *King John*, 69; J. Bradbury, *Philip Augustus King of France 1180–1223*, London 1998, 133.

[88] *Rot. Chart.*, 30; Norgate, *John Lackland*, 70–1.

[89] *Hist. Guillaume le Maréchal*, ll. 12,487–92, as elucidated by Paul Meyer, iii. 169.

explain these variations in a historian who gives the impression of being an assiduous collector of information? He may well have been at Lincoln to see John at his most impressive in November 1200 and almost certainly he was an eyewitness of much of what John did at Cottingham and Beverley in late January 1201.[90] But what were his sources of information on the king's activities when the court was not in his own neighbourhood?

David Corner has very plausibly suggested that for these years his main informants were Robert of Turnham and Philip of Poitou, bishop of Durham.[91] Possibly Roger was not at Lincoln in November 1200, but both Robert and Philip certainly were. Robert of Turnham was surely his source for the events of April 1199 since he was the castellan of Chinon who, in the critical days after Richard's death, handed that stronghold and treasury to John.[92] Moreover his attestations to John's enrolled charters show that he was at court in July and August 1199, so he could well have been the source for Howden's fairly detailed account of those months. He was at court again from January to June 1200, so he could have told Roger about the death of Mercadier at Bordeaux on 10 April and the Treaty of Le Goulet (22 May). Given his special knowledge of Chinon he could well have told Roger the story of Arthur, William des Roches and Gui de Thouars, castellan of Chinon, in the autumn of 1199, while his absence from court at the time may explain Howden's imprecise dating of that crucial episode. The last item of information in the *Chronica* in Roger's own hand is the news of the appointment of Robert of Turnham as seneschal of Poitou.[93]

Bishop Philip of Durham is certainly another very likely informant. Consider Roger's account of John's marriage to Isabella of Angoulême.

> The king of England, by the advice of his lord Philip king of France, married Isabel daughter of Ailmar count of Angoulême, whom the aforementioned count, on the advice and wish of Richard king of England, had earlier given to Hugh le Brun count of La Marche; whom the count had received *per verba de*

---

[90] *Howden*, iv. 156–7. Roger of Howden may have been the Roger the Chaplain who witnessed a number of royal charters in Henry II's reign (see Gillingham, 'The Travels of Roger of Howden', 163), so it is intriguing to find a charter for Grimsby dated 28 January 1201 witnessed by 'R. capellanus', and given at Immingham, *Rot. Chart.*, 85. Generally it would seem more likely that R. stands for Robert (a more active royal chaplain) – but at Immingham from where John could cross the Humber to Cottingham?

[91] Corner, 'The Earliest Surviving Manuscripts', 309–10. Other potential informants (in addition to members of the chapter of York and the dean of Lincoln, see n. 82) were: Roger Beaumont bishop of St Andrews, *Howden*, iv. 91; Richard Malebisse, iv. 91, 117,163; Hugh Bardulf, iv. 90–1, and William de Stuteville, iv. 117–18.

[92] *Howden*, iv. 86. This would make him the most probable source for Howden's version of the story of Richard's death at Chalus-Chabrol. In the light of this, my account of Howden's usefulness, or lack of it, for events south of the Loire in 'The Unromantic Death of Richard I', *Speculum* 54, 1979, 23–5, reprinted in Gillingham, *Richard Coeur de Lion*, 160–2, needs modifying.

[93] *Howden*, iv. 176. After this the *Chronica* consists of nothing but documents and brief introductions to them.

presenti and she had received him *per verba de presenti*; but because she had not yet reached nubile years, Hugh had not wished to marry her *in facie ecclesie*. So her father snatched her from the custody of Hugh le Brun, and she was immediately married to John by the archbishop of Bordeaux.[94]

If Isabella was under the age of consent then her arrangement with Hugh le Brun was, in canon law, voidable, whether or not she had given her consent to the marriage *per verba de presenti*.[95] I do not know how old she was, I merely find Roger's wording extremely intriguing. In his emphasis on the *verba de presenti*, it seems to me that he puts the case in terms sympathetic to Hugh le Brun.[96] But why should a Yorkshire parson see things from the point of view of a Poitevin magnate? Was it because his account derived from Philip of Poitou, Richard I's confidential clerk and a man who could well have been involved in Richard's policy of arranging the betrothal of Hugh and Isabella? Certainly an informant from Poitou would explain why, in the immediately preceding sentence, Roger named the archbishop of Bordeaux, the bishop of Poitiers and the bishop of Saintes as the bishops who gave John his divorce. Diceto, after all, in his account of the divorce, had listed a group of Norman bishops.[97] If Roger did indeed have a Poitevin source for this item of news, then the bishop of Durham is the obvious candidate. And if Roger's words reflected the bishop's view of John's new marriage, it was presumably a view on which John did not look kindly. So it is intriguing to find that early in 1201 Philip of Poitou left England on a pilgrimage to Compostella, the classic action of a man out of favour.[98]

Philip of Poitou could also have provided Roger with information on Anglo–Scottish relations since this was an area for which bishops of Durham had a special responsibility.[99] For example, Howden noted that John summoned the Scottish king to attend his court and then, after his coronation, sent Philip to meet him.[100] Yet it would be odd indeed if Roger himself, in his dual role as servant of the crown and of Durham, had not been involved in this business, given the expertise on Scottish affairs which he had accumulated over the last

---

[94] *Howden*, iv. 119–20.
[95] For the view that she looked about twelve when crowned in October 1200, *Coggeshall*, 103.
[96] Though without any explicit criticism of John – hardly to be expected in an instalment written up after the Lincoln court.
[97] *Diceto*, ii. 166–7.
[98] *Howden*, iv. 157. Cf. N. Vincent, *Peter des Roches. An Alien in English Politics 1205–1238*, Cambridge 1996, 198–9.
[99] *Howden*, iii. 244–5 for Durham's part in conducting a king of the Scots to the English court.
[100] *Howden*, iv. 91. If King William had been summoned to Nottingham, this might explain why Roger believed John spent Whitsun waiting for him there. It may be that John, once he was informed of William's reluctance to attend, and keen to get back to Normandy, went no further north than Northampton, spending Whitsun there, as Diceto rightly noted, *Diceto*, ii. 166.

twenty-five years. He had visited Scotland several times, and frequently escorted ecclesiastical and secular magnates to and from Scotland. Moreover he clearly continued to be deeply interested in Scottish affairs in John's reign. Take the following brief note: 'in this year [1201] on the eve of the Purification of the Blessed Mary [i.e. 1 February] William bishop of Glasgow arrived in England at Dover, returning from his consecration'.[101] This is a remarkably trivial piece of news except to someone intensely interested in the Scottish church, perhaps especially Glasgow – as indeed Howden continued to be. He noted, for example, not only the day Bishop Jocelin of Glasgow died, 17 March 1199, but also where he was buried, 'in the monks' choir at Melrose, on the north side of the church'.[102]

In all probability Howden was personally involved in the negotiations with William of Scotland which went on from April 1199 onwards. In 1199 William refused to obey John's summons and instead threatened war. If Roger had the job of escorting the bishop of St Andrews and Richard Malebisse as they chased after King John as he hurried back to Normandy in June 1199, it would have been no more than a continuation of the sort of thing he had been doing for the last twenty-five years.[103] It would, moreover, have taken him to Normandy in time to learn the precise details of events there from 24 June to 17 August which he then recorded in his *Chronica*.[104] In other words it may well be that Roger did not just sit back in his princely parsonage at Howden and wait for information to come to him, but that there is a sense in which his history of John's reign remained – as his history of the previous three decades had been – in large part a journal of his own travels.

In October 1200 John sent emissaries headed by Philip of Durham to escort William to Lincoln. They were provided, noted the royal clerk, 'with royal letters patent of safe conduct'.[105] After his diary of events at Lincoln on 21, 22, 23 and 24 November (including William's act of homage), Roger first reported the death of Roland of Galloway (one of those Scots who had attended the ceremony at Lincoln) on 19 December at Northampton and his burial there at the abbey of St Andrews, and then incidents which had occurred in Scotland while King William was away. Then he noted that William celebrated Christmas at Lanark.[106] All this is consistent with Howden having a role in conducting the king from and to Scotland. He was probably back in Yorkshire by 9 March 1201 (when, he reports, an earthquake was heard at York), but he may well

---

[101] *Howden*, iv. 157. He had earlier, iv. 139, noted William's consecration at Lyons by the archbishop of the city on papal orders on 14 September 1200.

[102] *Howden*, iv. 85. This was a later entry made in his own hand. It was probably added to his entry for the last year of Richard's reign after his return from a visit to Scotland. See Gillingham, 'The Travels of Roger of Howden', 157f., for his earlier contacts with Bishop Jocelin and with Melrose.

[103] *Howden*, iv. 88–9, 91.

[104] *Howden*, iv. 93–5.

[105] *Howden*, iv. 140.

[106] *Howden*, iv. 145, 156.

have returned to the Scottish court around Easter (25 March), since he noted that King William celebrated that festival at Crail – a very obscure place indeed, at any rate in English eyes.[107] Despite many references to the activities of the king of Scots from 1174 onwards, Roger had never until Christmas 1200 and Easter 1201 noted where he held his Christmas and Easter courts (though he did this routinely for the kings of England). His interest in the Scottish court was, if anything, growing. It looks as though he went there again either at or soon after Easter 1201 and then reported back to John at Portsmouth. That he was at Portsmouth in mid-May is suggested by his unusually detailed account of the arrangements and military appointments which John made while he was there and on the Isle of Wight waiting to get back to Normandy. The contents of the message taken to John at Portsmouth can be inferred from Howden's report that the king then sent Bishop Geoffrey of Chester, Richard Malebisse and Henry de Puiset on a mission to Scotland, asking William to accept yet another postponement of consideration of his demand for the return of Northumbria.[108]

The journey to Portsmouth may well have been Roger's last. He probably never again went further afield than York or Durham. He talked to Philip of Poitou when he returned from his pilgrimage and at York with Cardinal John of Salerno who gave him the inside story of how Innocent III had been elected pope. Towards the end of his life, he showed a growing interest in the preaching of Eustace de Flay and miracles.[109] If this reconstruction of Howden's movements in 1201 is roughly correct, it means that it would have been, at the latest, at Portsmouth in mid-May that he learned of John's demand that the English earls hand over their castles. Thus his critical comment, 'malo usus consilio', would reflect the judgement formed by a man still close to the centre of political life.

In 1200, however, there had been an episode in the story of Anglo–Scottish relations about which Howden had remarkably little to say.

> Meanwhile John king of England crossed from Normandy to England, and took an aid of three shillings from each carucate throughout England. And in Lent King John came to York, hoping that William king of Scots would come to him, as he had ordered; but the king of Scots did not come and the king of England returned to Normandy.[110]

By Howden's standards this is an astonishingly vague account of the entire trip to England. What makes it especially astonishing is the fact that both Philip of

---

[107] *Howden*, iv. 156, 161. For Crail in Fife, see the index to G.W.S. Barrow, *Regesta Regum Scottorum II. The Acts of William I*, Edinburgh 1971. It was probably on one of these visits that he learned of the plan for Alexander of Scotland to marry a daughter of Philip of France, *Howden*, iv. 138. 174. On this see A.A.M. Duncan's essay in this volume.

[108] *Howden*, iv. 163–4. Presumably the choice of the bishop of Chester to head this embassy reflects the fact that Durham was now well on his way to Compostella, and York was as unreliable as always.

[109] *Howden*, iv. 167–76.

[110] *Howden*, iv. 107.

Durham and Robert of Turnham were with the king at York.[111] Roger was evidently not in the north of England in March 1200. Nor, given the fact that he had very little precise information on what happened in the struggle between John and Philip Augustus between 17 August 1199 and 22 May 1200, does it seem likely that he was in France. So where was he?

The answer may be that he was at the curia. Both the end of his entry for 1199 and the beginning of his entry for 1200 are totally dominated by the figure of Innocent III – he dwelt on the pope's handling of the Tours–Dol dispute, of Gerald de Barri's pursuit of metropolitan status for St David's, of King Philip's treatment of Ingeborg, as well as providing a full text of Innocent's letter of 27 December 1199 taxing the clergy on behalf of the land of Jerusalem.[112] Howden could have left Normandy at the end of August 1199, spent six months or so in Rome and then returned home via Normandy probably in April or early May. He would then have heard Robert of Turnham's summary of recent episodes in the political and diplomatic struggle against Philip Augustus, before returning to the north of England and reporting local events, notably the floods that had washed away the bridge at Berwick, and yet another episode in the interminable dispute between Geoffrey and his chapter.[113] Elsewhere I have argued that he went to the curia on the king's business in 1171, 1179, 1183, 1192 and 1197–8. If this were even roughly right, then a mission to the curia in 1199–1200 would have been no more than a continuation of Roger's earlier activities.[114] If he was indeed at the curia, then on whose behalf, Durham's or the king's?

I have not so far managed to discover any evidence of Bishop Philip having Durham business at the curia in 1199–1200.[115] A possibility that should be considered is that Roger was part of an embassy sent by John to urge the pope to give more strenuous support to his nephew Otto IV. In his history, immediately after dealing with the events of late August in France, Howden reported that

---

[111] *Rot. Chart.* 39b, 40b, 41.

[112] *Howden*, iv. 100–113. In Roger's working copy, the account of the Tours-Dol dispute is in the hand of one of his scribes; the account of Gerald's struggle and of the first three months of 1200 is in his own hand. On his admiration for Innocent III see Gillingham, 'The Travels of Roger of Howden', 166.

[113] *Howden*, iv. 96–100. Corner, 'The Earliest Surviving Manuscripts', 309–10 for the suggestion that Howden received a packet of information from Robert of Turnham at about Easter 1200. Although he included a copy of Eugenius III's letter which Gerald had discovered in the papal archives, the fact that Roger did not have the texts of any of the letters written by Innocent III about St David's on 5 May 1200 (*Letters of Innocent III*, nos. 223–227) suggests that he left Rome before obtaining copies of them, though not before he knew (roughly) what they were going to say, *Howden*, iv. 106.

[114] Gillingham, 'The Travels of Roger of Howden', 165–6. David Corner had already suggested that Roger went to Rome in 1189, Corner, 'The *Gesta Regis*', 136.

[115] I am grateful to M.G. Snape for re-assuring me on this point. *Letters of Innocent III*, no. 216 and p. 216, concerns Durham cathedral priory rather than the bishop; in any event as confirmation of a decision made by papal judges delegate it might not have detained an envoy for long.

meanwhile Pope Innocent and the Romans chose Otto king of Germany as emperor . . . and that the cry '*Vivat* our emperor Otto' rang out on the Capitol and throughout the city. So having been chosen as emperor, Otto sent to his uncle King John, advising him not to make peace with King Philip of France for he would soon be able to bring him aid on an imperial scale.[116]

In fact, although Innocent had written about working for Otto's honour and advantage in a letter sent to the archbishop of Cologne in May 1199, it had been expressed only in very general terms, and there had certainly been no such imperial acclamation in Rome. Just another of Howden's occasional mistakes? Doubtless, but it is likely that Otto's envoys at John's court had talked up their lord's prospects when urging John to fight on. If Roger was there in August 1199, he would almost certainly have heard them do it.[117] Undoubtedly at this time John was actively concerned on Otto's behalf.[118] Did his concern stretch to the sending of an embassy to Rome? According to Innocent in a letter written in February 1203, John had sent him many letters and envoys urging him to support Otto and assuring the pope that he would devote his own resources to his nephew's cause.[119] Just when had John sent those many letters and envoys? He would not have done so once seriously engaged in making peace with King Philip. Had they all been sent since the breakdown of that peace and the renewal of John's alliance with Otto in September 1202? It is possible but unlikely. It is much more likely that some were sent in August–September 1199. In which case two very likely candidates for that embassy would have been Roger of Howden and Philip of Poitou. Philip had gone to Rome on Richard I's behalf in the dispute with the church of Rouen over the building of Château-Gaillard, and he had also gone to Germany to promote the election of Otto as emperor.[120] If Philip went he was back at court at Windsor by 4 March 1200.[121] Roger, however, to judge by the brevity of his account of John's visit to England in spring 1200, had still not returned. None of this can be proved, of course, but it seems to make sense both of what Howden wrote and of what he did not write about the events of September 1199 to April 1200.

If this reconstruction is roughly right, then we should read Howden's history as the work of an experienced diplomat who was still active – and this at a time when foreign affairs were amongst the most pressing items on John's political agenda. It is certain that Roger was well aware of the importance of

---

[116] *Howden*, iv. 95–6.

[117] T. Holzapfel, *Papst Innozenz III, Philipp II August, König von Frankreich and die englisch-welfische Verbindung 1198–1216*, Frankfurt am Main 1991, 45 n. 160.

[118] *Rot. Chart.*, 11–12, 31, dated 23 and 25 August. See Natalie Fryde's essay in this volume.

[119] *SLI*, no. 17. As noted there, John's letters on this matter do not survive. That Innocent received such assurances is suggested by the tone of his letters to John, especially no. 8, where he protested strongly against John's abandonment of Otto at Le Goulet.

[120] *Howden*, iv. 16–17, 37; ed. L. Landon, *The Itinerary of Richard I*, PRS 1935, 135.

[121] *Rot Chart.*, 37. Nothing is known of Philip's whereabouts between May 1199 and March 1200 (information from M.G. Snape).

alliances, as his treatment of Richard I's alliances with German and French princes shows.[122] An apparently trivial detail such as the information that a brother of the count of Flanders was knighted when John was installed as duke at Rouen – added as a marginal note in his own hand to his working copy – gains significance only in the light of his appreciation of the diplomatic context.[123] How then would he have regarded the Treaty of Le Goulet? As late as August 1199 he seems to have thought John's position a strong one. He noted that he had a large army in Normandy, that the count of Flanders and the other French counts and barons who had supported Richard had now done homage to him, and had sworn to support him against the king of France; both parties promised not to make peace without the consent of the other. Roger knew perfectly well that Philip's marital problems disturbed Innocent III, and that Otto IV had promised to help.[124] With all his diplomatic experience he surely sensed that, as Ramsay was to put it, 'John had an extraordinary opportunity for a coalition, with, for once in a way, both Pope and Emperor in accord, and on his side.'[125] By mid-September 1199 when William des Roches delivered Arthur to John, the king of England was in an even stronger position. But by January 1200 the coalition was in tatters.

Howden was well aware of the price John now had to pay for peace. According to his account of negotiations between Richard and Philip in January 1199, it had been proposed that Louis of France should marry Richard's niece, Blanche of Castile, that Gisors would be her dowry, and that King Philip would swear to help Richard's nephew Otto obtain the Empire.[126] According to his account of the terms arranged only a year later in January 1200, Louis was to marry Blanche, she was to receive a considerably larger dowry and John was to swear to give no help in any shape or form to his nephew Otto.[127] Roger must have been keenly aware of the difference that a year had made. When Otto's envoys – Henry duke of Saxony and William of Winchester – visited John, it was because of his oath to Philip, Howden wrote, that John refused to help.[128] If he had been sent to Rome in 1199 to assure the pope that John would support Otto, he must have felt that he had wasted his time. But whether or not he had been part of some such diplomatic initiative, given his known view of Philip Augustus, he can only have seen the terms agreed in January 1200 and finalised at Le Goulet in May as a defeat.

Commenting on the treaty, Gervase of Canterbury wrote that it led to John's enemies and detractors calling him Softsword. As Holt pointed out, Gervase

[122] *Howden*, iii. 234, iv. 19–20, 54–5, 61.

[123] *Howden*, iv. 87; Corner, 'The Earliest Surviving Manuscripts', 306.

[124] *Howden*, iv. 85–6, 93, 95–6, 112–13. Robert of Turnham witnessed John's treaty with Boulogne, *Rot. Chart.*, 30.

[125] Ramsay, *Angevin Empire*, 383. For a similar view see J. Ahlers, *Die Welfen und die englischen Könige 1165–1235*, Hildesheim 1987, 199–200.

[126] *Howden*, iv. 81.

[127] *Howden*, iv. 107.

[128] *Howden*, iv. 116.

was writing with later events in mind.[129] But that there were some critics who called him Softsword in 1200 is likely enough. Indeed it is certain that there was one contemporary who took that view of John's conduct in 1199–1200. This was Andreas of Marchiennes, a historian judged by K.F. Werner to have been an independent-minded man of firm opinions. As a monk of the Benedictine abbey of Marchiennes near Douai, Andreas – like Lambert of Ardres and the Béthune anonymous – was well placed to observe the Plantagenet–Capetian struggle, and since he died in January 1202, there is no question of his attitude to John being influenced by the hindsight of 1203–4. In his view, John pursued sluggishly ('segniter') the war which Richard had prosecuted 'viriliter et potenter'. His comment on the peace of Le Goulet was that in it John gave up those castles 'for which the whole war had been fought'.[130]

Howden might well have felt the same. Yet in his account of Le Goulet there is no word of blame or criticism. It may be worth noting, however, that he referred to the peace with France twice, once when summarising the terms provisionally agreed in January 1200, and then when summarising the treaty itself. His summary of the January agreement, which he dated no more precisely than 'after Christmas', consisted entirely of concessions made by John, including the promise not to help Otto in any way.[131] His summary of the treaty in May was couched in terms of Philip restoring territory to John, of John doing homage to Philip, and of Arthur doing homage to John for Brittany and his other lands.[132] In other words the second summary took a noticeably more positive view of the identical agreement. It went much further in indicating that Philip acknowledged John, not Arthur, as heir to Poitou, Anjou, Maine and Touraine and it made no mention of John's promise not to help Otto. The first of these passages was in the first main block of material, i.e. it was probably written up soon after Easter 1200, and in it Howden seems, discreetly, to have taken a fairly jaundiced view of the peace terms. But the second was in the second block of material, i.e. probably composed while Roger, like Ralph of Coggeshall, was still influenced by the impression made by the Lincoln court and while the English people were still enjoying the peace John had made. Moreover who could deny that in the short term at least, John in the summer of 1200 made effective use of the respite peace had given him? As Howden put it, 'immediately after the treaty with the king of France, John advanced into Aquitaine with a large army; but there he found no one who resisted him'.[133]

---

[129] *Gervase*, ii. 92–3; Holt, *King John*, 20–1.

[130] 'Sigeberti Continuatio Aquicincta', *MGH, Scriptores*, 6, 435–6. See K.F. Werner, 'Andreas von Marchiennes und die Geschichtsschreibung von Anchin und Marchiennes in der zweiten Hälfte des 12. Jahrhunderts', *Deutsches Archiv* 9, 1952, 402–63. Like everyone else, Andreas took a stern view of John's conduct in 1193.

[131] *Howden*, iv. 106–7. He also provided a text of the treaty itself, iv. 148–51, but this obviously reveals nothing of his own attitude to the peace terms.

[132] *Howden*, iv. 115.

[133] *Howden*, iv. 119; cf. *Coggeshall*, 103. This is how it seemed in retrospect to *Gervase*, ii. 92.

Conclusion

Modern English historians have mostly felt – as presumably John felt – that he had done well to get Philip to recognise him as Richard's sole heir, and hence to resolve the great problem of the disputed succession.[134] But had John been able to keep Arthur at his court he would not have had to pay so high a price. As it was he had to abandon the structure of alliances that Richard had built up. This meant that for peace John was now dependent upon the goodwill of the king of France. By April 1202 at the latest he came to realise that he had miscalculated badly and he tried to re-activate the old alliances.[135] But by then it was too late. His most important allies amongst the French aristocracy had taken the cross. According to William the Breton, presumably reflecting opinion at the Capetian court, they had done so because after Richard's death they found themselves deprived of both aid and counsel.[136] If it is thought that John failed because of the way he strained every nerve and sinew to build up the great coalition of 1212–14, then there is a sense in which the turning point came not in 1204, but in the first autumn of his reign, when the distrust he inspired precipitated Arthur's flight to the French court, and led to the collapse of the great coalition he had inherited from his brother.

If modern scholars have tended to underestimate the level of criticism voiced by Diceto and Howden between 1199 and 1201, it is partly a consequence of the new approach, the faith in record evidence on the grounds that the 'inner history of the reign' was 'writ large in the records, but barely perceived by the chroniclers'.[137] Many twentieth-century historians, especially those who specialise in record evidence, have tended to regard the historians of the time as mere chroniclers. They could sometimes – when they got their facts right – be useful sources of 'hard' information, but when they got their facts wrong, it was not worth wasting time on wondering why they were mistaken, or where they got their information from – they were, after all, mostly biased ecclesiastics, so, in a way, it was quite surprising that they got anything right. Even the better ones among them, such as Diceto and Howden, so often failed to see what really mattered – the 'harsher truths of the military situation' in 1199 for example – that their opinions were not really worth considering. In no less than four articles debating the subject of John's divorce and marriage to Isabella of

---

[134] See, for example, the view that the treaty 'has to be regarded as something of a triumph for John's diplomacy', Gillingham, *The Angevin Empire*, 67; reprinted in *Coeur de Lion*, 67. For a more realistic view see Bradbury, *Philip Augustus*, 134–5 and E.M. Hallam, *Capetian France 987–1328*, London 1980, 183. The modern French historian of the Plantagenet lands, Jacques Boussard, saw it as 'a great success for Philip', in R.H. Bautier, ed., *La France de Philippe Auguste*, Paris 1982, 279.

[135] Holzapfel, *Papst Innozenz III*, 94–5.

[136] *Guillaume le Breton*, i. 211. No contemporary English historian criticised Baldwin of Flanders for making his peace with Philip in January 1200 and taking the cross on Ash Wednesday.

[137] Warren, *King John*, 137.

Angoulême, not only did the protagonists, H.G. Richardson on the one hand, and Sidney Painter and Fred Cazel on the other, not notice how Howden presented the marriage, they did not even mention Diceto's outright condemnation of John for acting in a way unworthy of the royal majesty.[138] The dean's views were unimportant. Painter's only comment on the 1201 clash between John and the English earls was that 'none of Howden's statements can be confirmed from other sources'.[139] That Howden himself took a critical view of John's conduct went unmentioned. Jolliffe used the story of relations between Archbishop Geoffrey and the crown in his chapter entitled 'Kingship in Political Action' to argue that chroniclers with their preoccupation with spiritual factors managed to miss what was 'really' at stake and that in consequence none of them was either disturbed or shocked by the exercise of arbitrary royal power.[140] It is as though Howden had never used the words *pravo consilio* when writing about John's treatment of Geoffrey in 1199. Nor have modern historians bothered to look closely at John's 'less than prudent' dealings with Arthur in 1199. When modern historians disregard the views of past historians – whom condescendingly they like to call chroniclers – in this fashion, it is not surprising that they should take notice of contemporary opinion only when it was expressed with the vehemence of a Roger of Wendover.

Yet all contemporary historians, both English and non-English – the views of authors from non-Capetian France (St Omer, Ardres, Béthune and Marchiennes) are particularly worth noticing – took a critical view of John. This in itself is a highly significant political fact. Everyone disliked John. In the end, even though there was no rival member of John's family who could give would-be rebels a lead and a legitimate cause for which to fight, their dislike and discontent were so great that they invented a new kind of focus for revolt, a programme of reform: Magna Carta. If the three historians with whom I have been principally concerned here, all of them writing before the débâcle of 1203–4, did not evince what Holt called Wendover's 'uncomprehending hostility', they were none the less generally hostile.[141]

Undeniably there was, as modern orthodoxy proclaims, a more sympathetic view of John *during* his early years as king – but it did not last *throughout* his early years. The positive attitude expressed by Howden and Coggeshall, especially Coggeshall, was confined to what they wrote in the aftermath of the Lincoln court of November 1200. Ironically, although John is generally believed to have suffered at the hands of monks, in his early years the least critical voice was Coggeshall's, so great was a monk's longing for peace. But that moment of appreciation soon passed. In general Howden and Coggeshall criticised John, both before and after 1199. Diceto, of course, was always

---

[138] H.G. Richardson, 'The Marriage and Coronation of Isabelle of Angoulême', *EHR* 61, 1946 and 'King John and Isabelle of Angoulême', *EHR* 65, 1950; F.A. Cazel and S. Painter, 'The Marriage of Isabelle of Angoulême', *EHR* 63, 1948 and 67, 1952.

[139] Painter, *Reign of King John*, 48.

[140] Jolliffe, *Angevin Kingship*, 110–119.

[141] Holt, *Northerners*, 145.

scathing about him. The John who emerges from the pages of these three authors is an unreliable and unpredictable king; a suspicious ruler who took hostages from his own subjects; who arranged so crucial a matter as his own marriage in an unworthy fashion; who abandoned his allies; who was not trusted by people such as King William of Scotland and Arthur of Brittany; but who was himself prepared to trust Philip Augustus, a ruler whom all three disliked. If this is what John was like, it is not surprising that so many of his men chose to abandon him in 1203–4. Yet this is how he was seen by contemporaries who knew government circles well and whose perceptions are all the more telling since entirely free from the wisdom of hindsight that came after 1204.

The English Economy in the Early Thirteenth Century

J. L. Bolton

It is now some twenty-five years since P.D.A. Harvey published two of the most important articles on the economy of late-medieval England, 'The English Inflation of 1180–1220' and 'The Pipe Rolls and the Adoption of Demesne Farming in England'.[1] Their influence has been profound. They have helped mould a certain orthodoxy which sees these forty years at the turn of the twelfth and thirteenth centuries as a critical period of change. In the most general terms that orthodoxy may be stated thus: rising demand caused by a population perhaps just beginning to push against the limits of subsistence coupled with an influx, almost a tidal wave, of new silver brought to England, above all by the wool export trade, caused sudden and rapid price and wage inflation. That inflation, largely monetary in origin, stimulated or 'kick-started' significant economic changes. Great landlords, faced with rising costs and falling revenues from long leases at fixed rents, turned to the direct management of their estates in order to maximise their incomes by producing grain and wool for an expanding market. To secure the labour they needed they imposed or re-imposed labour services on a peasantry that became increasingly unfree. The increasing volume of coin in circulation combined with the need to market surpluses and the equal need for 'peasants' to participate in that market to raise the cash to pay their dues accelerated that commercialisation of society with which R.H. Britnell and B.M.S. Campbell have made us so familiar.[2] The silver that fuelled the inflation reached England mainly, though not exclusively, via the wool trade with Flanders. Without it the rapid expansion in the circulating medium, the silver penny, from perhaps less than £100,000 in 1180 to c.£250,000 in 1205 would not have been possible.[3]

Orthodoxy once established, and established so impressively, is hard to challenge without attracting charges of 'revisionism' with all that the term implies. Yet there must surely be some doubts about the supposed quickening of

---

[1] *Past and Present* 61, 1973, 3–30; *EcHR* 2nd series 27, 1974, 345–59.

[2] Britnell, *Commercialisation*, especially Part 2, 79–151; *Commercialising*, ed. Britnell and Campbell.

[3] Mayhew estimates mint output between 1158 and 1180 at around £125,000 so a figure of £100,000 or less of coin in circulation seems reasonable (Mayhew, 'Money and Prices', 121–32, at p. 125); Britnell has a figure of less than £125,000 but he seems to assume that nearly all mint output passed into circulation, which was not the case (*Commercialisation*, at p. 102). Mayhew, 'Money and Prices', also gives the figure of c.£250,000 for 1205.

economic expansion between 1180 and 1220 and the central role played by monetary inflation, especially in John's reign, in stimulating it. As long ago as 1971 Edward Miller warned us against drawing too strong a contrast between the economies of twelfth- and thirteenth-century England, pointing out that there could have been no expansion after 1180 unless the solid foundations had been laid for it earlier.[4] Recent work has only justified his arguments. Rosamond Faith has shown that on the manors of St Paul's Cathedral, leased out though they may have been, there was no dissolution of the demesnes and commutation of labour services in the twelfth century. Rather, there was growth, investment by the lessees in manorial buildings, increases in stock and more land brought into cultivation. The demesne arable was improved by double ploughing, marling and manuring and at the same time new service-bearing peasant holdings were created to provide the necessary labour. She argues that the evidence does not support Postan's assumption that the system of putting entire manors out to farm entailed economic stagnation and un-dynamic management. The depressed and unprofitable manorial economy of the twelfth century did not perhaps exist.[5] On a broader level, Edmund King largely agrees with her analysis. He sees the early twelfth century as a period of sustained economic development with a swift return to 'business as usual' after the temporary disruptions of the anarchy of Stephen's reign. In the same stimu-lating collection of essays honouring Edward Miller, Britnell has outlined the notable urban/market growth in northern England. 'New institutions, agricul-tural expansion and commercial growth', he argued, 'together created a powerful regional dynamism in the north, so that in this hitherto unurbanised region of England the marketing network of the thirteenth century was already substantially in place by 1216.'[6] So it was elsewhere, and for much the same reasons,[7] and probably the only dissenting voice here is that of A.R. Bridbury, who sees little but stagnation and decline in the twelfth and thirteenth centuries.[8] His views have not found wide acceptance, however. The consensus

---

[4] E. Miller, 'England in the Twelfth and Thirteenth Centuries: An Economic Contrast?', *EcHR* 2nd series 24, 1971, 1–14, at pp. 5–6.

[5] R. Faith, 'Demesne Resources and Labour Rent on the Manors of St Paul's Cathedral, 1066–1222', *EcHR* 2nd series 47, 1994, 657–78 and especially her conclusions at pp. 675–6. A.R. Bridbury has also attacked Postan's views on the actual leasing out of manors in a controversial article, 'The Farming Out of Manors', *EcHR* 2nd series 31, 1978, 503–20. He maintains his attack in his *English Economy*, Introduction, 1–42 at pp. 22–26, but does not see the twelfth century as a period of expansion: below, p. 29 and n. 10.

[6] E. King, 'Economic Development in the Early Twelfth Century', in *Progress and Problems*, ed. Britnell and Hatcher, 1–22; Britnell, 'Boroughs, Markets and Trade in Northern England 1000–1216', *ibid.*, 46–67, at p. 64.

[7] Britnell's earlier articles, on hundredal markets, 'English Markets and Royal Administra-tion before 1200', *EcHR* 2nd series 31, 1978, 183–96, and 'The Proliferation of Markets in England, 1200–1349', *EcHR* 2nd series 34, 1981, 209–221, at pp. 209–10 make this quite clear. See also Britnell, *Commercialisation*, Part 1, pp. 5–75 *passim*.

[8] 'The Domesday Valuation of Manorial Income', in Bridbury, *English Economy*, 111–25, at pp. 121–5.

seems to be that the twelfth century, the hiatus in Stephen's reign apart, was a period of steady expansion driven by the needs of a growing population.

1180, then, does not perhaps mark quite the clear break as once supposed. Nor would all historians accept that inflation of itself was necessarily the prime cause of economic change. The switch to direct management, demesne farming, on great estates has been attributed almost entirely to the sharp rise in prices and wages between 1180 and 1220.[9] Kathleen Biddick doubts that this was the case. She has drawn our attention to the problems faced by great landlords as a result of what she calls 'structural indebtedness'. From the mid-twelfth century, as English kings began to search for new sources of revenue to meet the ever-growing demands of war, lords were forced to scrabble to raise money where they could. Increasingly they contracted debts by taking advance payments from merchants for crops and animal products and especially for wool. They were drawn more and more into debt and had to increase sales of produce to compensate for the costs of borrowing. Money for agrarian loans was more costly than for commercial borrowing and 'structural indebtedness locked the English agrarian sector into cash cropping grain and wool for the expanding industrial sector'.[10] This is a persuasive argument, particularly in the light of the heavy demands for war and ransom made by the Angevins generally and John particularly. What it also offers is an alternative explanation, or at the least a partial alternative explanation, to inflation as the prime or only cause of economic change in this crucial period. Some of course do not think much at all of arguments for change. Bridbury points to the uncertain evidence of the pipe rolls for the movement towards demesne farming between 1180 and 1220. He argues that management decisions varied endlessly in accordance with the perceived needs of particular institutions and families. They switched from leasing to direct management and then back again as the situation required, to maximise the income from their estates.[11] M. Mate has shown that the monks of Canterbury Cathedral Priory saw no good reason at all for changing to direct management on their Kentish manors for most of the thirteenth century. Indeed, they soon abandoned their one brief experiment in that direction in the 1250s

---

[9] See above, p. 27.

[10] K. Biddick, *The Other Economy: Pastoral Husbandry on a Medieval Estate*, Berkeley and Los Angeles 1989, Chapter 3, 'From Consumption to Production: Peterborough Abbey in the Thirteenth Century', *passim* but especially pp. 50–3; *idem*, 'People and Things', *Comparative Studies in Society and History* 32, 1990, 3–23, at pp. 7–12. Here and in a later study of the Winchester estates in the thirteenth century the same arguments are used to explain management changes. Biddick argues, however, that the bishop of Winchester's household consumed much of the grain its estates produced and relied on the sale of animal products for much of its revenue: K. Biddick with C.C.J.H. Bijleveld, 'Agrarian Productivity on the Estates of the Bishopric of Winchester in the Early Thirteenth Century: a Managerial Perspective', in *Land, Labour and Livestock. Historical Studies in European Agricultural Productivity*, ed. B.M.S. Campbell and M. Overton, Manchester 1991, 95–123, at pp. 98–104, 119–20.

[11] 'Introduction', in Bridbury, *English Economy*, at p. 23; *idem*, 'Thirteenth-Century Prices and the Money Supply', *AgHR* 33, 1985, 1–21, at pp. 2–4.

because they found it brought them few cash benefits.[12] And, of course, if
we look at that supposed motor of the English economy, London, then P.
Nightingale argues that the late twelfth and much of the thirteenth century
brought nothing but setbacks for the city. The new direction for the chief export
trade in wool via the east-coast ports meant that London grew at a much slower
rate than the chief provincial towns.[13]

Nonetheless, structural indebtedness apart and Bridbury's opinions as always
honourably excepted,[14] these historians seem to agree that there was a period of
sustained inflation which accelerated or accentuated existing trends. In the
twelfth century the solid foundations for expansion were laid: in the early
thirteenth the walls of the edifice rose rapidly. Yet was there inflation between
1180 and 1220, and, if so, did it follow quite the inexorable path that Harvey
would have us believe? Doubts have been expressed both as to its severity and
about the dangers of relying too heavily on very limited price/wage information.[15] Paul Latimer's convincing reworking of the data has dispelled some of
those doubts but what he has shown is that inflation took a much more erratic
course than has previously been supposed. Two of his findings are of particular
interest. The first is that up to the late 1190s prices moved uncertainly. The
second is that the really sharp rise came in a very limited period indeed,
between 1199 and 1204. After that there was relative price stability at a higher
level, for reasons that will be discussed. At the same time Nick Barratt's outstanding analysis of John's revenues has revealed a king taking far more from
his kingdom than has hitherto been supposed.[16] In the remainder of this article
an attempt will be made to provide a synthesis of these two sets of data in order
to construct a new model for the early thirteenth-century economy. It will be
argued that, after the expansion of the twelfth century, John's reign and the
minority of Henry III, perhaps through the 1220s to the early 1230s, were difficult years for the English economy. The demands of the crown for war,
especially between 1204 and 1213–14, disrupted economic development,
causing some degree of hardship for most classes of society. Expansion could
not restart until coin again became abundant and then rose significantly in
amount per head in the 40 or so years of relative external and internal peace
after 1220. Much of the argument has to revolve around the questions of the
money supply and the demands of the crown and must therefore rely heavily on

---

[12] M. Mate, 'The Farming Out of Manors: a New Look at the Evidence for Canterbury
Cathedral Priory', *JMH* 9, 1983, 331–43.

[13] P. Nightingale, 'The Growth of London in the Medieval English Economy', in *Progress
and Problems*, ed. Britnell and Hatcher, 89–106, at pp. 90–91.

[14] See above, p. 29 and n. 10. A.R. Bridbury deserves our thanks for stimulating so much
fruitful debate about the performance of the medieval economy.

[15] Bolton, 'Inflation', 1–14, at pp. 3–7. My doubts about the severity of the inflation remain
but those on the 'recession' of the twelfth century should now be treated with some
caution.

[16] Barratt, 'Revenue', 835–55, *passim*.

the data supplied by Mayhew and Barratt.[17] There is an acceptance that some inflation occurred, particularly between 1199 and 1204, but also that it was held back after 1204 by major problems with the money supply. Some account will be taken of Biddick's arguments about structural indebtedness since a shortage of coin may have made it even more difficult than before for great landlords to meet the demands of the crown. Alternative explanations for relative price stability after 1204 will also be considered, and notably the Miskimin/Goldstone theory that increased velocity of circulation at a time of shortage of coin can have a marked effect upon prices.[18]

But the first question that has to be asked is, how much coin was actually in circulation, as opposed to having been minted? This question is fundamental to the whole debate. Without coin, or superfluity of coin perhaps, there would have been no price inflation. Without coin, commercialisation and a society relying increasingly on the market and market forces to regulate its affairs in town and countryside alike would not have been possible. Exchange, and the use of money as the principal medium of exchange, was as much a part of the commercialisation as organised markets and fairs governed by strict rules and regulations.[19] But, of course, we do not know precisely how much coin was in circulation. There are no figures for mint production in the late twelfth and thirteenth centuries, although that in itself is no sure guide to the size of the circulating medium. Estimates can only be made from the evidence of coin hoards and single coin finds, with all their attendant problems.[20] If we take Dolley's figure of £37,500 in 1086, however, there were about nine million silver pennies in circulation at the time of Domesday or, with a population of between 1.75 and 2 millions, somewhere around 5d or 4.5d per head. That would scarcely have allowed a high degree of commercialisation, as Britnell has shown.[21] By the 1170s and 1180s there was perhaps £100,000 in circulation (24 million silver pennies) rising to c.£250,000 in 1205 after the partial recoinage of that year. Given a population of around 3.5 to 4 million at the turn of the century, that meant about 17d or 16d a head, a trebling over a period of roughly one hundred years.[22] But whether we should accept the estimate of £250,000 is

[17] N.J. Mayhew's writings on the coinage and money supply are numerous but those chiefly used here are 'Money and Prices', 121–32 and 'Modelling', 55–77.

[18] The key articles here are Miskimin, 'Population Growth', 179–86 and Goldstone, 'Urbanization and Inflation', 1112–60.

[19] These are Britnell's arguments throughout his *Commercialisation*, a book of fundamental importance for any understanding of the medieval economy.

[20] Some coin drained abroad, or was sent to northern Europe to pay allies and for warfare in Normandy. Some was hoarded, some was lost or was kept out of circulation in stores of treasure. See below, pp. 32–4 and Mayhew, 'Population', 241–2. The present author hopes to discuss the problems of coin-hoard evidence in his *Money in the Medieval English Economy*, Manchester University Press, forthcoming.

[21] M. Dolley, *The Norman Conquest and the English Coinage*, London 1966, 14; Britnell, *Commercialisation*, 47–52.

[22] Estimates of the coinage are taken from Mayhew, 'Money and Prices', 124–5. In 'Modelling', 57, Mayhew also gives the various estimates for the population in the late

a moot point. There are no mint output figures for 1205 and it was, to say the least, a strange recoinage. Only worn and clipped light coins were to be replaced. All clipped money was to be exchanged between 2 November 1204 and 6 January 1205, winter months when there was little market activity. This explains the exemption given to country dwellers who were to have clipped money bored and returned to them until it could be exchanged. Old money that did not lack more than 2s 6d in the pound was to remain current.[23] How much of the 'old' money was surrendered, how much remained in circulation is simply not known. The reliability of coin-hoard and single-find evidence perhaps needs to be viewed more critically. Rigold's 'single-find' method shows an eleven-fold increase in the coinage between 1086 and 1300 whilst mint output evidence suggests at least a twenty-five-fold increase. £250,000 is, however, the currently accepted figure for the circulating medium, maintained at that level until the end of the reign as more silver supposedly flowed in from the profits of the wool trade.

   Here lies the first major question: how much of that silver was coined and actually in circulation as opposed to remaining in ingots, the silver marks some-times used to make payments abroad?[24] Had ingots been used in this way, then there would have been no drain of coin from England. But, as will be seen, that does not appear to have been the case. Coin was regularly sent abroad to pay troops and allies.[25] Up to 1199 there had already been large outward shipments to pay for wars in France, the Crusade and then Richard's ransom of 100,000 marks, or £66,666 13s 4d. This sum was paid, although not all of it was raised in England.[26] Simply for the sake of argument, let us say that it all was. That would have taken out of the country sixteen million silver pennies at a time when the total amount of coin in circulation was somewhere between twenty-four and sixty million pennies. This, of course, did not happen but suffi-cient silver seems to have flowed from England to cause a shortage of coin. In 1193 Queen Eleanor made a charter to Abbot Sampson and the monks of Bury St Edmunds redeeming the gold chalice they were proposing to give towards the king's ransom in lieu of their fine because they were suffering from a lack

eleventh century and c.1300. To these should be added the views of the 'Feeding London Project'. Its authors argue that England could not have sustained agriculturally a popula-tion of more than about 4.75 million in 1300: B.M.S. Campbell, J.A. Galloway, D. Keene and M. Murphy, *A Medieval Capital and its Grain Supply*, Historical Geography Research Series 30, Edinburgh 1993, 43–5. If that was the case, then there would have been fewer than 3.5 to 4 million people c.1200 and a greater amount of coinage per head. My feelings are that 3.5 to 4 million is still a valid 'guess' for 1200.

[23] The terms of the recoinage are given in *PR 7 John*, xxvii–xxviii.

[24] The use of silver ingots in international payments is discussed by P. Spufford in *Money and its Use in Medieval Europe*, Cambridge 1988, chapter nine, 'Ingots of Silver', 209–24 *passim*. The opening sentence of this chapter, at p. 209, is of particular interest.

[25] See below, p. 33.

[26] The ransom and its payment are discussed by Gillingham, *Richard the Lionheart*, 230–39; see also J.H. Ramsay, *The Angevin Empire or the Reigns of Henry II, Richard I and John (A.D. 1154–1216)*, iii, London 1903, 371–2.

of coin ('nummorum et pecuniae penuria laborantes').[27] Alongside this there were other shipments of the treasure of England and Ireland to pay for campaigns, for castle building and for subsidies for allies, all part and parcel of the costs of defending the Angevin territories. Roger of Howden tells us that Hubert Walter sent 1,100,000 marks, or £733,333 16s 8d or 175,999,920 silver pennies, abroad in 1196, which would have left England completely denuded of coin, silver ingots, plate or anything else containing bullion had it been true.[28] But the Norman Roll for 1195 shows at least £5,722 16s 10d remitted to the treasury at Caen from England, probably in the form of 1,373,280 silver pennies.[29] That at least gives us a realistic idea of the drain of money from the country in these years. The deflationary effects can only be imagined but they may in some way account for the uncertain course of inflation before 1199.

From 1199, however, and thanks to the work of Barratt, we have at least some clear idea of the king's revenues. In the first four years of his reign they ran at what can be called relatively modest levels, between £22,000 and £23,000 per annum. From 1203–4 there was a sudden rise in revenue to reach a new level of around £30,000 in 1205–6 and from then steadily upward to £52,000 in 1210, £83,000 in 1211 and £56,000 in 1212. Nor do these figures represent all John's income. Money extracted from the religious orders and particularly the Cistercians and from the Jews by way of tallages meant that John's revenue in 1211 was in fact somewhere in the region of £145,000. Moreover, perhaps up to 75 per cent of it was paid over in cash, and much of that cash, again perhaps 76 per cent of it, came not from the 'windfalls' produced by mulcting the church and the Jews, but from the ordinary revenues from the country at large. Between 1210 and 1212 those revenues contributed £118,115 out of a total of £157,051. The burden was falling on the population generally and most of the revenue was being raised through cash payments. Small wonder that Barratt concludes that 'John's attempts to maintain his financial position in this period represent the greatest level of exploitation seen in England since the Conquest.'[30]

Two points need to be made here. Firstly, it is worth noting the relatively low level of John's demands between 1199 and 1203, precisely the years in which there was a very sharp rise in inflation according to Latimer's calculations.[31] Perhaps, temporarily, not too much in the way of coin was being taken out of circulation by the new king, so fuelling price rises. But, secondly, although it is difficult even to estimate how much of the money raised after 1203–4 was sent abroad and how much remained in England, what we do know is that a great deal of it stayed in the kingdom and was not spent. Some fifty years ago J.E.A.

---

[27] L. Landon, *The Itinerary of King Richard I*, PRS n.s. 13, London 1935, 76; W. Dugdale, *Monasticon* iii, 154. I am very grateful to Dr Jane Martindale for these references.

[28] *Howden*, iv, 13.

[29] Ramsay, *Angevin Empire*, iii, 371–2. £4000 went towards paying the ransom, the rest to other expenses.

[30] Barratt, 'Revenue', 841–3, 855.

[31] See Paul Latimer's article in this volume.

Jolliffe published an article on the chamber and the castle treasuries under John.[32] Its findings have often been noted but perhaps never fully explored in relation to the amount of coin actually in circulation. Jolliffe showed that after 1207, and probably before, John was building up and retaining large sums of money 'on call' as it were, in these treasuries. He believed that most of it was in coin and that makes sense. As has already been seen, most of John's revenues came in cash from the country at large. Mercenaries, ship masters, merchants, victuallers and allies all needed to be paid in ready money if war was to be organised expeditiously. Moreover, the pipe rolls record payments for tonnels or small barrels in which the coin was packed and for the transport costs of the treasure, along with occasional reference to coin packed in sacks ready to be laid up in the treasuries.[33] Given this, the sums kept in the castle treasuries, when converted into silver pennies, are quite astonishing. In July 1207 20,000 marks were withdrawn from the central treasury at Winchester and dispatched to the castle treasuries at Devizes and Marlborough, with a further 11,000 to Nottingham. This decentralisation of the treasure continued throughout the autumn of 1207 and the spring of 1208 with 10,000 marks sent to Exeter in October, 6,500 to Salisbury, a further 2,000 to Exeter in March and 17,000 to Bristol in April. That amounts to £44,333 6s 8d or 10,640,000 silver pennies or 17.7 per cent of the coinage said to have been in circulation in 1205. Some of it must have been spent in England but clearly, by 1207, John already had a considerable store of treasure and was taking substantial amounts of coin out of general circulation. Then, between 1207 and 1213, he became intent on building up a huge war chest. In October 1213 there were apparently 120,000 marks on deposit at the castle treasury in Bristol – £80,000 or the equivalent of roughly one third of the circulating medium in 1205 – sent back there after the abortive Welsh campaign of that year and awaiting redistribution to other castle treasuries. Jolliffe suggests that over a period of years the provincial treasuries were capable of providing something like 200,000 marks on call. If that was all in coin, then it amounts to £133,333 or half the circulating medium.[34]

Unless there was considerably more money in circulation than has heretofore been supposed, then John's exactions must have had deflationary consequences. Even if the sums kept in the castle treasuries fluctuated as moneys were spent in England, a great deal was simply being hoarded. John was keeping substantial sums out of circulation on a long-term basis and in the last years of his reign sending equally substantial sums abroad.[35] Could the level of the circulating medium possibly have been maintained and replenished by the vast quantities of silver supposedly flowing into England as a result of

[32] Jolliffe, 'Chamber', 117–42.
[33] Jolliffe, 'Chamber', 133, 140–1; *PR 4 John*, xiii; *PR 5 John*, xi; *PR 10 John*, xxi; *PR 13 John*, xv.
[34] Jolliffe, 'Chamber', 130–5.
[35] Jolliffe, 'Chamber', 135.

favourable trade balances and above all from the wool trade? It was the export of wool to feed the cloth industry of Flanders and Brabant that provided the wealth of England in the eleventh century, or so P.H. Sawyer would have us believe.[36] He thought that the area for sheep grazing actually declined in the twelfth and thirteenth centuries. Perhaps, but there still seem to have been sufficient sheep for Harvey to see burgeoning wool exports to Flanders as the main reason why England was flooded with silver in the late twelfth and early thirteenth centuries.[37] Yet simply to maintain the coinage at a stable level of £250,000, quite heroic amounts of silver would have been needed. Would they have been forthcoming?

There is no firm evidence for the value of wool exports in these years nor indeed for the value of imports and exports generally, apart from those calculated from the returns of the Fifteenth of 1203–4. These suggest that imports and exports together were worth about £56,000 per annum, compared to the £200,000 for denizen exports alone in 1300.[38] Without detailed particulars of customs accounts, such as exist for the fourteenth and fifteenth centuries, separating imports from exports and attaching values to both is well nigh impossible. Nevertheless, England must have been dragging in substantial quantities of woad and other dyestuffs for the cloth industry as well as spices and other luxury goods, presumably paid for from the profits of the wool trade in one way or another. In the fifteenth century, admittedly in the very different circumstances of a growing shortage of bullion, the Italians paid for their exports of cloth and wool with the moneys earned from the sale of their imports. High levels of exports were also matched by even higher levels of imports in the sixteenth century, with adverse consequences for England's balance of trade and a flow of specie from the land. There is no evidence to suggest an imbalance in trade in the early thirteenth century. But surely there must have been some sort of relationship between imports and exports that might have limited the amount of silver flowing into the country.[39] Nor can we be certain how much English wool was flowing to Flemish and Brabantine looms. Both Sawyer and Harvey have supposed that it was absolutely vital for the high-quality product on which the Flemish export trade depended. Yet as long ago as 1950, E. Coornaert

---

[36] P.H. Sawyer, 'The Wealth of England in the Eleventh Century', *TRHS* 5th series 15, 1965, 145–164, at pp. 161–3.

[37] Harvey, 'English Inflation', 27.

[38] T.H. Lloyd, *The English Wool Trade in the Middle Ages*, Cambridge 1977, 9–11; *idem*, 'Overseas Trade and the English Money Supply in the Thirteenth Century', in *Edwardian Monetary Affairs (1279–1344)*, ed. N.J. Mayhew, British Archaeological Reports 36, Oxford 1977, 96–124, at pp. 100–3.

[39] For a discussion of the import trade in this period, much of it in Flemish hands, see P. Nightingale, *A Medieval Mercantile Community. The Grocers' Company and the Politics and Trade of London 1000–1485*, New Haven and London 1995, 52–63. Fifteenth-century trade is discussed by J.L. Bolton, *The Medieval English Economy 1150–1500*, London 1980, 305–14. The balance of trade in the sixteenth century in relation to the bullion supply is a central part of J.R. Wordie's argument in 'Deflationary Factors in the Tudor Price Rise', *Past and Present* 154, 32–70, at pp. 48–58.

questioned whether the Flemish towns did rely as heavily as Pirenne had suggested upon the production of luxury cloths made from English wool. He pointed to the quantities of cheaper cloth being produced, often using the inferior wools from the surrounding regions of northern France, from northern England, Scotland and Ireland. Taking up his argument, in 1972 A.E. Verhulst demonstrated the vital importance of local supplies of medium and low quality wools for the Flemish industry. More recently, Chorley and Munro have argued that the Flemish industry produced a great deal of cheap and medium-priced cloth, both for local consumption and for the export trade. Low-grade wool was employed in its manufacture and here what counted was not access to expensive wool but to cheap and middle-grade locally produced wools. English wool was employed only to a limited degree, less than Scottish and Irish wool and much less than *la laine nostree*, as it was called.[40]

This is not to say that fine English wool was not exported to Flanders in substantial quantities. It is to ask whether there was less of a flood and more of a moderately flowing stream. And, probably more importantly, that stream may well have been affected by a quite severe drought in the late twelfth and early thirteenth centuries. The constant interruptions in the wool export trade that were the product of war seem to have been completely ignored by those intent on the inexorability of silver flows. Between the late 1170s and 1193 Flemish merchants do seem to have traded freely with England. Thereafter there were constant interruptions. Lloyd argues that the consequences for the Flemish economy were so severe that Baldwin IX was forced to abandon France and form an alliance with Richard I in 1197. Freedom of trade did not long survive the outbreak of war between John and Philip Augustus, and between 1205 and 1213–14 the position of Flemish merchants in England remained precarious.[41] Given that this was a period of growing Flemish domination of the wool export trade, it seems doubtful that sufficient silver would have been flowing into England both to replace coins lost through hoarding or wear and tear and to make up for the substantial sums removed from circulation by John.

If that was so, then the economic consequences must have been quite considerable. Buying and selling would have been more difficult, simply because of a lack of coin, and the money left in circulation would have had to work harder, as will be seen. Putting together the cash to pay the king, be it for taxation in its various forms, reliefs, wardships and marriages must have posed

---

[40] E. Coornaert, 'Draperies rurales, draperies urbaines. L'évolution de l'industrie flamande au Moyen Age et au xvie siècle', *Revue Belge de Philologie et d'Histoire* 28, 1950, 59–96; A.E.Verhulst, 'La laine indigène dans les anciens Pays-Bas entre le XIIe et le XVIIe siècle', *Revue Historique* 248, 1972, 281–322; P. Chorley, 'The Cloth Exports of Flanders and Northern France during the Thirteenth Century: a Luxury Trade?', *EcHR* 2nd series 40, 1987, 349–79, at pp. 369, 373; J.H. Munro, 'Industrial Transformations in the North-West European Textile Trades', c.1290–c.1340: Economic Progress or Economic Crisis?', in *Before the Black Death*, ed. B.M.S. Campbell, Manchester 1991, 110–48, at pp. 110–11.

[41] Lloyd, *English Wool Trade*, 7–8, 11–14.

considerable problems. Here T.K. Keefe's analyses of proffers for heirs and heiresses recorded in the pipe rolls and the indebtedness they produced between 1180 and 1212 are of great interest. He has shown that the level of proffers soared first around 1194 and then in the opening years of the thirteenth century, precisely when Latimer has shown inflation to be at its sharpest. The level of debts owed to the crown by lay tenants-in-chief rose sharply in the first eight years of John's reign, by some 380 per cent, and although Keefe does not see repayment as a problem, it may well have been, given the scale of indebtedness and the shortage of coin.[42] Nor would credit have been readily available, since it is supposed to dry up when money is in short supply.[43] At a critical point in 1210 borrowing must have been very difficult, given John's savage mulcting of the Jews in that year. One chronicler states that they were charged with 66,000 marks and whilst such stories should not be believed, it is clear from the fragmentary evidence of the pipe rolls that the tallage was severe.[44] Even so, structural indebtedness must have increased sharply for both lay and ecclesiastical landlords and the response may not necessarily have been to switch to producing for the market, an uncertain lifeboat in stormy waters, but to scrambling to find the money to meet obligations by any means possible, even by asset stripping if necessary. The crown was already more than familiar with that practice. When it exercised its regalian right to administer the estates of the bishopric of Winchester during vacancies, livestock sales crippled the manorial economy, causing massive disinvestment.[45] The temptation for administrators of the estates of minors to do much the same must have been very great, especially if debt repayment became pressing. Selling the livestock on a depressed market may have been difficult and prices would have had to be adjusted accordingly. But continuing and sustained demand for basic cereal products and for essential livestock will bid up and help sustain price levels, as Wordie has recently shown for the sixteenth century.[46] As a short-term solution to immediate problems, asset stripping probably had much to recommend it, at least as much as creating elaborate and expensive management structures to produce for the market. Leasing may well also have been another attractive short-term option, but where demesne farming was practised, then labour services, imposed or re-imposed, were an attractive alternative to wage labour when coin was in

[42] T.K. Keefe, 'Proffers for Heirs and Heiresses in the Pipe Rolls: Some Observations on Indebtedness in the Years Before the Magna Carta (1180–1212)', *The Haskins Society Journal. Studies in Medieval History Volume 5*, Woodbridge 1993, 99–109, at pp. 103–7. My thanks are due to Professor Keefe for raising this issue with me.

[43] P. Nightingale, 'Money Contraction and Mercantile Credit in Later Medieval England', *EcHR* 2nd series 43, 1990, 560–75.

[44] S.K. Mitchell, *Studies in Taxation under John and Henry III*, New Haven 1914, 105–6; Painter, *Reign of King John*, 144.

[45] Biddick and Bijleveld, 'Agrarian Productivity on the Estates of the Bishop of Winchester', 101–4.

[46] Wordie, 'Deflationary Factors', 39–40.

short supply, for either landlord or demesne lessee.[47] As for commercialisation, it may well have slowed down, although how that could be measured remains, to say the least, problematic.

This was not long-term stagnation, but a recession when economic trends, never very clear in a society that looked from one harvest to the next, were both confused and confusing.[48] Real GDP does not in any case grow steadily, but oscillates. Since 1945 there has been a positive rate of growth in all advanced industrialised economies, but the actual rate of growth has varied considerably, with both the UK and USA experiencing falls of 2.5 per cent in 1982 and 1991.[49] Nevertheless, critics of this argument will rightly ask why, if the shortage of coin was so severe, prices did not fall after the substantial 'hike' of 1199–1204.[50] That would be fair comment, except that perhaps here we should look at two other inflationary tendencies counteracting monetary deflation. The first is simply population pressure. A sustained rise in demand at a time when the supply of foodstuffs, and particularly cereals, could not be rapidly increased will tend to push up grain prices and keep them high. This is certainly Wordie's argument in his analysis of the sixteenth-century price inflation, as has been seen, although we do not know enough about either wages rates or possible increases in manufacturing output to see whether they had the countervailing deflationary tendencies that he suggests.[51] The other and possibly quite serious inflationary factor involves the whole question of the velocity of circulation, the number of times each coin changed hands in monetary transactions. In two controversial articles Miskimin and Goldstone have argued that rising velocity of circulation and not an influx of American silver was largely responsible for the price revolution of the sixteenth and seventeenth centuries. Miskimin draws parallels between the levels of money and prices in the fourteenth and sixteenth centuries when expressed in constant terms of silver. Because there was a greater demand for money in the latter period, he thought that a greater velocity of circulation prevented prices falling. Goldstone sees rising population and increased urbanisation as the key to greater velocity of circulation. A much larger market network allowed more work to be done by the relatively small

---

[47] For the chronology of labour services see J. Hatcher, 'English Serfdom and Villeinage: Towards a Reassessment', *Past and Present* 90, 1981, 3–39, part vi at pp. 33–6.

[48] A.R. Bridbury's comments on the uncertainties of estate management in the thirteenth century are worth noting here: 'Thirteenth-Century Prices and the Money Supply', at pp. 2–4.

[49] M. Mackintosh et al., *Economics and Changing Economies*, Milton Keynes and London 1996, at p. 558. Gross Domestic Product (GDP) can be defined as the total money value of all goods and services produced in the economy over a one year period: Mayhew, 'Modelling medieval monetisation', at p. 56, n. 2; W.J. Baumol and A.S. Blinder, *Economics: Principles and Policy*, 5th edn Orlando, Fla, 1991, 355–6.

[50] For an explanation of the consequences for prices of alterations in the money supply, see below, n. 52.

[51] Wordie, 'Deflationary Factors', 44–5. Harvey, 'English Inflation', 16–17, discusses wage-rates but admits that the evidence is slender and that increases in the pay of mercenary soldiers may well be a special case.

amount of silver in circulation. Coin, in short supply, had to work a great deal harder, each unit changing hands much more frequently. Velocity of circulation thus rose faster than the total number of transactions and so, according to the simplified version of the Fisher equation or 'identity' used by most medieval historians, $P = \dfrac{MV}{T}$, prices would also rise.[52]

Miskimin and Goldstone's arguments have been much criticised by both early-modern historians and by medievalists.[53] Yet perhaps they deserve a more sympathetic hearing. In the twelfth and early thirteenth centuries there was the growth of both the population and of market networks, and presumably an increasing number of small transactions. That would have increased the velocity of circulation and so pushed up prices, *provided* there was no radical increase in the quantity of money in circulation. But, of course, it is widely accepted that there was. Mayhew argues that it was sufficient to allow for a fall in the velocity of circulation. More coin simply meant that each unit, each silver penny was used less frequently. In a cash-starved economy money moved from hand to hand rapidly and shortages of coin were such that queues of creditors waiting payment formed. High velocity of circulation of a very limited money supply went hand in hand with chronic illiquidity, inhibiting rather than facilitating trade. Successful urbanisation and monetisation demanded increased supplies of money which thereby permitted the velocity of circulation to fall, freeing one transaction from dependence on another.[54] Yet the Miskimin/ Goldstone and Mayhew models are not necessarily mutually incompatible, as long as one accepts the evidence offered here of a sharp reduction in the money supply between 1204 and 1214. The volume of transactions would not necessarily have fallen substantially. There had been a great expansion of market networks but, more importantly, the demands of the crown were such that all sectors of society needed to raise cash to meet them at a time when access to

52 This account of Miskimin and Goldstone's arguments owes much to N.J. Mayhew's elegant summation thereof in his 'Population', 239–40. Miskimin, 'Population Growth', *passim*; Goldstone, 'Urbanization and Inflation', *passim*. In the Fisher equation or 'identity', first developed by I. Fisher in his book *The Purchasing Power of Money*, New York 1911, P = prices, M = the quantity of money in circulation, V = the velocity of circulation and T = the total volume of transactions. As V and T are held to move together as constants, thus cancelling each other out, any change in M must force rises in P. Modern economists, however, hold that velocity is not a constant: Baumol and Blinder, *Economics: Principles and Policy*, 267–9. Fisher's original equation was $P = \dfrac{MV + M'V'}{T}$ where M' = the quantity of demand deposits and V' its velocity of circulation. Since these are largely unknown quantities in the middle ages, most medieval historians have chosen to ignore them.

53 Miskimin, 'Population Growth', *passim*; Goldstone, 'Urbanization and Inflation', *passim*. The most recent critiques of their theories are Wordie, 'Deflationary Factors', especially pp. 32–4; Mayhew, 'Modelling Medieval Monetisation', at 68–71; Mayhew, 'Population', especially pp. 239–40. As this current article demonstrates, I have been forced to rethink my doubts about these theories, put forward in 'Inflation, Economics and Politics', at p. 5 and n. 16.

54 Mayhew, 'Modelling', 68–71.

credit was very limited. Given that T remained fairly constant and V increased, this could have led to rising prices but it is more likely, and very much in line with Latimer's projections, that they were held at inflated but stable levels. As Wordie remarked of the sixteenth century, a severe shortage of specie could exercise a 'deflationary drag' on price levels.[55] That seems to have been the case in the early thirteenth century as well.

John's reign, then, was not a period of runaway inflation, except in its opening years. Thereafter, the sheer size of his exactions took so much money out of circulation that coin would have been hard to come by, credit scarce, indebtedness rapidly increasing. There must at best have been a slowing down of the economy, at worst a sharp recession. John's problems do not seem to have resulted from inflation as such but from the fiscal burdens he placed on all his subjects in his attempts to build up a war chest, and the economic difficulties that ensued. Hard times breed political discontent and this is as true of the early 1200s as it has been of the late 1980s and early 1990s. Political opposition grows as recession mounts. Yet we perhaps need to look beyond John's reign for a new model of the English economy in the late twelfth and early thirteenth centuries, a model tentatively advanced and in need of much more testing against the empirical evidence than has been possible here. The solid expansion of the twelfth century, more demographically led than is currently acknowledged, was first stimulated by new silver but then temporarily halted by a recession in John's reign and the civil wars and French invasion that followed. Expansion began again after 1220 but its full flowering may well have been in the forty or so years of internal peace and abundant coinage that then followed. It was precisely in these years that there probably was an influx of silver from the wool trade. Lloyd points to the severe disruptions to that trade caused by the war with France between 1216–17 and continuing difficulties with France and Flanders in the 1220s. He sees the years after 1236 as marking a new era in trade relations between England and Flanders, with a major expansion in trade. It is highly likely that there was an influx of silver in these years, such as to reduce the velocity of circulation quite dramatically and hold back price rises in spite of an increasing volume of transactions. After the recoinage of 1247–50 there was five times the amount of coin in circulation that there had been in the late twelfth century.[56] Henry III's military ineptitude, indeed his general ineptitude and the resistance to royal exactions in his reign, may have been just what an uncertainly expanding and commercialising economy needed.

---

[55] Wordie, 'Deflationary Factors', 69. This was also the case, of course, at other periods in the later Middle Ages, notably the early fourteenth century and, more controversially, the mid-fifteenth. For the literature on the earlier period see Bolton, 'Inflation, Economics and Politics', at p. 1 n. 2. For the second, see Mayhew, 'Population', 255–7. The most recent contribution to the debate on the depression of the mid-fifteenth century is J. Hatcher, 'The Great Slump of the Mid-Fifteenth Century', in *Progress and Problems*, ed. Britnell and Hatcher, 237–72. Not all will agree with him.

[56] Lloyd, *English Wool Trade*, 15–20, 22; Bolton, 'Inflation, Economics and Politics', at p. 6 for evidence of the increase in the money supply.

Early Thirteenth-Century Prices

Paul Latimer

When discussing anything in the reign of King John, even the economy, there is a temptation to try to relate it to the great, twin climaxes of that reign – the loss of Normandy in 1204 and the rebellion of 1215. Discussion of the price history of the reign has not been immune from the temptation to look for political consequences.[1] Nor is this illegitimate, except that it prompts us to look at the consequences of a price history the course of which has remained a matter for debate. The same problem of not being entirely sure what it is we are arguing about has also bedevilled the numerous attempts to discuss the causes of price changes in this period.[2] It seems necessary first to try to establish more securely what happened. The starting point is, and must be, the late D.L. Farmer's work on prices.[3] For the sake of brevity and simplicity, I will discuss in detail only two of the price series he constructed – for wheat and for oxen. All of the other

---

[1] Warren, *King John*, 163; P.D.A. Harvey, 'The English Inflation of 1180–1220', *Past and Present* 61, 1973, 3–30, at pp. 9–15; Turner, *King John*, 7, 89–91, 96–7.

[2] *The Cambridge Economic History of Europe, II: Trade and Industry in the Middle Ages*, 2nd edn, ed. M.M. Postan and E. Miller, Cambridge 1987, 217; M.M. Postan, *The Medieval Economy and Society*, London 1972, 235–41, 248–9; Harvey, 'The English Inflation of 1180–1220', 25–30; E. Miller and J. Hatcher, *Medieval England: Rural Society and Economic Change 1086–1348*, London 1978, 68–9; J.L. Bolton, *The Medieval English Economy 1150–1500*, London 1980, 72–8; A.R. Bridbury, 'Thirteenth-Century Prices and the Money Supply', *AgHR* 32, 1985, 1–21; N.J. Mayhew, 'Money and Prices in England from Henry II to Edward III', *AgHR* 35, 1987, 121–132; D.L. Farmer, 'Prices and Wages', in *The Agrarian History of England and Wales, II 1042–1348*, ed. H.E. Hallam, Cambridge 1988, 715–817, at pp. 718–25; J.L. Bolton, 'Inflation, Economics and Politics in Thirteenth-Century England', in *Thirteenth Century England IV, Proceedings of the Newcastle upon Tyne Conference 1991*, ed. P.R. Coss and S.D. Lloyd, Woodbridge 1992, 1–14, at pp. 1–6.

[3] Farmer, 'Prices and Wages', 715–817. This, however, only partially supersedes his earlier articles on prices: 'Some Price Fluctuations in Angevin England', *EcHR* 2nd ser. 9, 1956–57, 34–43; 'Some Grain Price Movements in Thirteenth-Century England', *EcHR* 2nd ser. 10, 1957–58, 207–20; 'Some Livestock Price Movements in Thirteenth-Century England', *EcHR* 2nd ser. 22, 1969, 1–16.

A note on dates: dates in the form 1180/1 will be used to indicate a period from Michaelmas (29 September) to Michaelmas. This convention agrees with that used by Farmer in 'Prices and Wages', but in his earlier articles he dated most prices by 'harvest year' whereby a price recorded in an account for 1180/1 would be dated as 1180: 'Some Price Fluctuations in Angevin England', 35–6.

series he produced fit broadly into the patterns generated by these two (see Figures 1 and 2).

Looking back from the mid-1190s, it is hard to detect any sort of clear trend in either wheat or oxen prices. There is a suggestion of a period of higher wheat prices from the mid-1170s to the mid-1180s, and a period of modestly higher oxen prices beginning in the mid-1180s. But both of these apparent upward movements seem to have been largely reversed in the 1190s. From 1200 to 1204, however, in the case of wheat, and from 1201 to 1205, in the case of oxen, there is a remarkable surge in prices. This surge in prices is especially evident in the case of wheat, but is still striking in the less volatile oxen series. Both sets of prices fall back to some extent in the following couple of years, wheat more so than oxen. But in neither case do prices return to the general level of prices before 1200. After 1207 the patterns of the two price series diverge somewhat for the rest of the first half of the thirteenth century. Wheat prices remain volatile, but fluctuate around a level somewhat more than twice the general level before 1200. Oxen prices, on the other hand, show a marked, if moderate, upward trend, so that by the 1230s and 1240s they often exceed the levels even of the early 1200s, something that does not happen in the case of wheat. Figure 3 plots indices of the seven-year moving averages of both wheat and oxen prices on a logarithmic scale. This makes the essential similarity between the price series for wheat and oxen much clearer. Although the upward trend in oxen prices between 1207 and 1251 is clear, it can be seen to have been very gradual in terms of the rate of change. Given the greater volatility of wheat prices, it is neither surprising nor particularly significant that no equally clear trend in wheat prices can be discerned. But the surge in prices in the early 1200s and the sustained nature of the consequent shift in prices appears as a striking feature of both series.

While Farmer's work is of great value and fundamental to this subject, it leaves some problems unsolved. The data collected by Farmer is dominated by prices either of food commodities or of livestock involved in the production of food. These are of obvious importance in a medieval economy, but we cannot automatically assume that these food-related prices, subject to particular supply constraints and demand pressures, behaved in the same way as other prices. I will try to make a start on looking at some of these other prices later in this article. A second, perhaps even more important problem concerns the reliability of the picture of food-related prices offered us by Farmer's various price series. Farmer himself was modestly cautious about their accuracy and others, such as A.R. Bridbury and, most recently, J.L. Bolton, have expressed some scepticism concerning the reality of a rapid rise in prices in the early thirteenth century. As the title of Harvey's 1973 article – 'The English Inflation of 1180–1220' – suggests, even historians who have accepted the fact of a significant rise in prices have sometimes been very cautious in trusting what Farmer's price series have to tell us about the timing and rate of price increases. It is this problem of the reliability of Farmer's food-related price series that I wish to discuss first.[4]

The catalogue of difficulties facing the student of medieval prices is a long and a familiar one, and does not need to be repeated here. What I do want to attempt is a categorisation of the kind of errors that these difficulties can introduce into our perception of prices, and then to assess the likely seriousness of these errors in dealing with Farmer's price series for the late twelfth and early thirteenth centuries. These errors may be divided into three categories, all of which potentially threaten the reliability of Farmer's price series. The first kind of error is that any particular price may be untypical. The restricted sample of prices that is available is likely to give a particular, abnormal price undue weight, and can thus distort any average in which it is used. Such distortions are not easy to identify in what we believe to be often genuinely volatile price series. This kind of error can, however, be mitigated to a considerable extent by comparing the price series of a number of commodities and by averaging prices over a number of years. The broadly consistent patterns generated by Farmer's different crop and livestock price series, and the stability of those patterns when subjected to various techniques and specifications of averaging, would seem to provide adequate reassurance against serious distortion from this kind of error.[5]

The second kind of error results from the fact that the samples of prices available to us as evidence are always biased towards particular localities and towards particular contexts within which the transactions have taken place.[6] 'Context' here should be taken to include any factors, aside from geographical location, which might affect the price of any particular item bought and sold. This could include, among other things, the measures used, the identities of the buyer and seller, or the purpose behind the transaction. It is usually impossible to correct either geographical or contextual bias and the limitations that these impose have to be accepted and assessed. If our data comes from a restricted range of contexts and, in some cases, a restricted geographical area, then we should certainly keep this in mind when framing our conclusions. The third kind of error is the most serious because it throws doubt on the whole idea of a continuous price series. Frequent, arbitrary changes in geographical bias or context can be countered in the same way as abnormal, particular prices, but where the geographical or the contextual bias in the sample of prices undergoes

---

[4] Farmer, 'Prices and Wages', 715, 779–80, 785; Bridbury, 'Thirteenth-Century Prices', 9; Bolton, 'Inflation', 4–5. Harvey writes of the 'chronology and scale of these price rises' as being 'defined with real precision', yet his arguments in the article do not rely on the precise chronology of the price rises: 'The English Inflation of 1180–1220', 3.

[5] Such techniques are not panaceas. Their results can be sensitive to their precise application. Conclusions in the present article have been reached after experimenting with several different specifications of such techniques and always with reference to the underlying data.

[6] For the geographical distribution of evidence in Farmer's work on grain and livestock prices in the thirteenth century, see 'Some Grain Price Movements in Thirteenth-Century England', 210–211; 'Some Livestock Price Movements in Thirteenth-Century England', 1, 11; 'Prices and Wages', 780–1.

a definite and sustained change, there is the risk that the price series before this change cannot be treated as at all comparable to the price series after this change.

From the 1160s to the middle of the thirteenth century all of Farmer's price data comes from two sets of source material – the Exchequer pipe rolls (in some cases up to 1210/11) and the Winchester pipe rolls (from 1208/9). In respect of the sections of price series that are derived from only one of these sets of source material, there is a considerable degree of contextual homogeneity.[7] Within the bounds of each set of source material, it seems unlikely that changes in the context of transactions contribute significantly to the major fluctuations of the price series. While the price data from the Winchester pipe rolls have a distinct geographical bias, it is fairly constant.[8] This is not the case, however, with regard to price data from the Exchequer pipe rolls. It is necessary to consider how far fluctuations in price series derived from these rolls may be explained by changes in geographical bias. That this is potentially a serious problem may be seen from Farmer's own work on regional variations in wheat and oxen prices in the thirteenth and fourteenth centuries.[9]

Tables 1 and 2 show the counties that contribute data from the Exchequer pipe rolls for certain periods of the price series for wheat and oxen. The periods were chosen to match the main fluctuations suggested by the seven-year moving averages of those price series. The results are reassuring, particularly in respect of oxen. Most of the periods draw data from a considerable number of counties, fairly widely distributed around the country. Tables 3–5 take the analysis further, taking the price levels of fixed groups of counties, averaged for each period, and comparing them with each other and with the overall average price levels for the same periods. All of the patterns suggested by the fixed groups of counties match in essence the patterns of the overall average price levels, though the decline of oxen prices in the 1190s, relative to the 1180s, appears less clear in the fixed groups of counties. With this slight exception, it

---

[7] The prices of grain purchases collected by Farmer from the Exchequer pipe rolls overwhelmingly concern royal purchases of military provisions, though there are a few purchases for seed, neither numerous enough nor anomalous enough to significantly affect the series. The prices of oxen purchases almost invariably represent the buying of working stock for estates in royal hands. For the Winchester pipe roll price data, Farmer was careful to distinguish between purchases of working stock and sales of stock which might be old or of poor quality. Concerning grain prices from the Winchester pipe rolls, he distinguishes sale prices from prices for the purchase of seed: 'Some Price Fluctuations in Angevin England', 34; 'Some Livestock Price Movements in Thirteenth-Century England', 6; 'Some Grain Price Movements in Thirteenth-Century England', 210; 'Prices and Wages', 745.

[8] The Winchester pipe rolls generally contain price data from Berkshire, Buckinghamshire, Hampshire, Oxfordshire, Somerset, Surrey and Wiltshire. See, for instance, the list of manors in *The Pipe Roll of the Bishopric of Winchester 1210–1211*, ed. N.R. Holt, Manchester 1964, 3–4.

[9] Farmer bases his analyses on 'marketing areas' which do not usually coincide with individual counties, but generally include manors from part of one county, or from neighbouring areas within two or three counties: 'Prices and Wages', 743–4, 751, 781.

would seem reasonable to conclude that changes in geographical bias do not significantly distort the price series derived from the Exchequer pipe rolls. Indeed, the patterns generated by the wheat and oxen price data demonstrate an encouraging and perhaps even surprising degree of robustness in this respect.

The risk that a definite and sustained change in geographical or contextual bias occurred is clearly present where reliance for price data on the Exchequer pipe rolls gives way, from 1208/9, to reliance on the Winchester pipe rolls. Although it is impossible to make precise comparisons with regard to the change in geographical bias between the two sets of sources, it is possible to consider separately the Exchequer pipe roll evidence that relates to southern counties, on the basis that the Winchester pipe roll evidence can be taken as broadly representative of southern conditions as a whole, as far as geographical factors are concerned. Tables 4(b) and 5(b) illustrate that the patterns of wheat and oxen prices from the Exchequer pipe roll data for southern counties were similar to the general patterns from those rolls. This in turn suggests that the change in geographical bias, between the data from the Exchequer pipe rolls and the data from the Winchester pipe rolls, does not produce significant distortion.

The most serious danger lies in the differences in context between price data from the Exchequer pipe rolls and the price data from the Winchester pipe rolls. Firstly, the predominant measure for grain changes, or at least its name does. Secondly, purchase prices for grain paid by royal officials to unspecified sellers on the Exchequer pipe rolls are not necessarily comparable with sale prices for grain on the Winchester pipe rolls obtained by the officials of the episcopal estates from unspecified purchasers. It is also true that most of the grain purchase prices on the Exchequer pipe rolls concern the purchase of military provisions, and this contextual factor could conceivably affect the price in a significant manner. Even with regard to the purchase of livestock, which on both sets of rolls has the similar purpose of stocking manors, the particular identities of the purchasers and sellers may have affected the level of the prices. These problems need to be considered.

The most common measure of grain in the Exchequer pipe rolls is the *summ*, though the *quarter* begins to become common by the 1190s and starts to overtake the *summ* in the first decade of the thirteenth century. In the Winchester pipe rolls the *quarter* is always used. Although these two measures are usually assumed to have been generally equivalent, early evidence for this is rare. A reference to the *summ* in the close roll for 1233 suggests that it comprised eight bushels – the same as the most common type of *quarter* – but it is not until the late thirteenth century that more direct evidence equating the two measures is found. The number of examples where it is possible to compare the prices of grain or salt, per *summ* and per *quarter*, in the same year, is small (see Table 6). Given the inherent volatility and variability of the prices, the most one can say is that these few examples do not show any consistent variation or a variation in any consistent direction between *summ* and *quarter*. They offer no reason to abandon the assumption, based on later evidence, that the *summ* and *quarter* were roughly equal in the twelfth and early thirteenth centuries, though it remains only an assumption.[10]

The overall effect of the other contextual factors on the price data in the Exchequer pipe rolls and Winchester pipe rolls is impossible to quantify directly. We have to accept that the two sets of sources provide us with two different lenses through which to view prices. Yet where the two sets of sources can be used in parallel, they point to generally similar price levels (see Tables 7 and 8). A thorough search of all the Exchequer pipe rolls for the first half of the thirteenth century would yield a fuller comparison, though while most of them remain unedited, it would be a tedious task. Other documents that have been edited offer some help. A Christchurch Canterbury roll of the issues of its lands in Kent in 1207/8 yields average wheat and oxen sale prices well within the range we would expect from the Exchequer pipe rolls and the Winchester pipe rolls.[11] Various edited accounts of lands in the king's hands, applicable to the years 1223/4, 1224/5 and 1232/3, provide a geographically diverse set of price examples. The average prices for wheat and oxen that these documents yield are on the whole close to their Winchester pipe roll counterparts (see Table 9). These examples, limited though they are, do not suggest that either the Exchequer pipe roll or the Winchester pipe roll price data are outrageously peculiar.[12]

The danger that our perception of food-related prices is distorted is real enough, particularly where one possibly idiosyncratic set of sources gives way to another. It seems over-pessimistic, however, to conjure up fears of huge distortions. The few indications that we have of the degree of distortion suggest that it is not large. It seems justifiable to accept provisionally that the price series collected by Farmer correctly delineate the main fluctuations in food-related prices in the late twelfth and early thirteenth centuries, at least for southern counties, and that the surge in these prices, of the years from 1199/1200 to 1204/5, is not just a mirage rising from poor and inconsistent data.

Turning to the problem of prices that are not related to food or food production, it must be admitted at the outset that it is impossible to obtain a fully representative set of price series for such items. What follows concerns very much a mixed bag of items for which I could find reasonable indications of price, paying no regard to the economic importance, or otherwise, of the items. Some of these series, considered individually, could not be said to tell us very much. Yet considered as a group, they represent a varied collection of price series and the results present a consistent enough picture to be used as at least indicative of

---

[10] *Close Rolls 1231–1234*, 190–1; R.D. Connor, *The Weights and Measures of England*, HMSO, London 1987, 149–51; R.E. Zupko, *A Dictionary of Weights and Measures for British Isles: The Middle Ages to the Twentieth Century*, Philadelphia 1985, 369; W.H. Prior, *Notes on the Weights and Measures of Medieval England*, Paris 1924, 18.

[11] *Interdict Documents*, 69–80. The oxen sale price is perhaps a little higher than one would expect from the sale of obsolete stock, but, given relations between King John and Canterbury at the time, it would not be surprising if many healthy oxen were being sold by the royal administrators.

[12] *Roll of Divers Accounts for the Early Years of the Reign of Henry III*, ed F.A. Cazel, PRS ns 44, 1982, 1–11, 28–30, 37–41, 49, 74–89.

prices unrelated to food. The items concerned are as follows: wool (with sheep prices being used as a surrogate in the twelfth and early thirteenth centuries); the cloth used for the table and curtains at the royal exchequer; linen; wax; lead; wine and palfreys. Except where I have made use of T.H. Lloyd's work on wool prices and Farmer's work on sheep prices, the price series are my own, using evidence taken mainly from the Exchequer pipe rolls, the close rolls and the liberate rolls. Each of these series has its own particular limitations, points of interest and difficulties.

It is unfortunate that we know so little about wool prices before the second decade of the thirteenth century, given the importance of wool in the English economy's external relations. Evidence for the period 1208/9 to 1250/1, taken from the Winchester pipe rolls, suggests a substantial increase in the level of wool prices from the early 1230s onwards. The average price from nine of the years between 1231/2 and 1248/9 is some 46 per cent higher than the average from thirteen of the years between 1208/9 and 1226/7.[13] In the case of sheep prices from the same period, which may be regarded as reflecting the value of wool, this increase in wool prices is substantially reflected in the purchase prices of wethers on the Winchester pipe rolls. The average price of wethers from eight of the years between 1231/2 and 1248/9 is some 36 per cent higher than the average from ten of the years between 1208/9 and 1226/7.[14] Before 1208/9 there is very little to go on as far as wool prices are concerned.[15] The fairly close correspondence between wool and sheep prices from 1208/9 onwards, however, may allow us to use sheep prices from the twelfth and the first years of the thirteenth century as some indication of wool prices before 1208/9 (see Figure 4).[16] The general pattern of sheep prices, both before and

---

[13] T.H. Lloyd, *The Movement of Wool Prices in Medieval England*, EcHR Suppl. 6, Cambridge 1973, 38–9.

[14] The purchase price of wethers seems the most appropriate basis for comparison. The sale prices of wethers, and the purchase and sale prices of ewes, all show increases (26 per cent, 15 per cent and 39 per cent respectively), but sale prices would be also likely to reflect the residual meat and hide value of old sheep and the price of ewes might be affected by the demand for and supply of breeding stock: Farmer, 'Some Livestock Price Movements in Thirteenth-Century England', 2–5, 7–8. Farmer indexes price data for wethers, ewes and wool in 'Prices and Wages', 799–810.

[15] There are two Exchequer pipe roll entries from 1197/8 and 1201/2 which give wool prices per sack. Making the dangerous assumptions that the sacks contained 26 or 28 stones of 14 lb, these entries would imply prices between 1s 10d and 2s 7d per 14 lb stone. Both of these prices are within the somewhat wide range of the early Winchester pipe roll prices: *PR 10 Richard I*, 182; *PR 4 John*, 129; Lloyd, *The Movement of Wool Prices*, 38–9.

[16] For the sheep prices in Figure 4, I have used, from 1208/9 onwards, wether or ewe purchase prices, which ever is available, or the average of wether and ewe purchase prices where both are available. The reason for this is that, in the Exchequer pipe rolls, sheep purchase price entries mostly record undifferentiated sheep, but it would make little difference if wether prices alone were used from 1208/9. All sheep prices are taken from Farmer, either 'Some Price Fluctuations in Angevin England', 41, or 'Some Livestock Price Movements in Thirteenth-Century England', 2–3. The wool prices are taken from Lloyd, *The Movement of Wool Prices*, 38–9.

after 1208/9, is similar to that of oxen prices. That this should be so is worth noting and is not at all self-evident, if one accepts the role of food prices in determining the price of oxen and of the role of wool prices in determining the price of sheep.

Cloth and clothing figure very frequently in the Exchequer pipe roll price information, but the many differences of type and quality generally make the patterns of prices difficult to discern. For one very particular set of cloth purchases, there is an exceptional series of prices which demonstrates a clear pattern. During each Easter term eight ells of woollen cloth, probably of the type known as *burell*, were purchased for the table of the upper exchequer, together with ten ells of linen cloth to cover the windows.[17] The cost of these purchases is recorded, at first separately but later in combination, for most years from 1180/1 onwards.[18] Figure 5 plots the prices of the combined purchases (table-cloth and curtains) from 1180/1 to 1220/1 (see also Table 10). Up to 1195/6 the level fluctuates gently between 11s 8d and 14s 1d. After that it begins to move up sharply, with a few lulls, more than doubling by 1201/2 and reaching a peak in 1211/12 at 42s 3d. After a few wild movements around the end of King John's reign it settles down again at 40s 1d from 1217/18 to 1220/1. In both 1229/30 and in 1241/2 the price was 40s 2d, barely changed from the beginning of Henry III's reign.[19] Though these purchases of cloth for the Exchequer present us with what is the most continuous of all available price series, it is obviously dangerous to draw broad conclusions from such a special group of transactions. Nevertheless, the stability before 1195/6 and, even more so, after 1217/18 is striking when set against the steep increases and erratic swings of the intervening period.

Nothing like such a clear picture can be obtained from the evidence for the prices of linen purchases, but it is possible to make some comments (see Table 11). It is obvious that the quality of linen could vary considerably even where there is no direct indication of quality in the records. Yet by giving regard to the size of purchases, to the recipients, to the purpose of the linen and, in conjunction with neighbouring prices, the price itself, it is possible to make a reasonable assessment as to which linen was of exceptional quality. Such purchases were necessarily individual and it is no surprise that there does not appear to be any pattern in their prices. For the rest, a pattern does emerge, albeit vaguely. Prices were mostly higher in the period from 1204/5 to 1254/5 than they had been earlier, but on the whole only modestly so. The peak in

---

[17] *Dialogus de Scaccario*, 6; *PR 27 Henry II*, 157; *PR 29 Henry II*, 161; *PR 33 Henry II*, 39.

[18] The form of the entries varies, and in particular appears to be abbreviated in later years, but nevertheless seems to represent a consistent series. See for example: *PR 1 Richard I*, 224; *PR 2 Richard I*, 156; *PR 10 Richard I*, 167; *PR 1 John*, 129; *PR 10 John*, 166; *PR 3 Henry III*, 74; *PR 5 Henry III*, 100.

[19] *PR 14 Henry III*, 98; *PR 26 Henry III*, 283. I have not checked the unedited Exchequer pipe rolls of the first half of the thirteenth century.

prices, such as it is, occurs not in the 1240s or 1250s but in the years 1204/5 and 1205/6.[20]

Wax was bought, often from abroad, in increasingly large quantities by representatives of the king for sealing documents and for candles and tapers.[21] Many of these purchases and the prices paid are recorded on the Exchequer pipe rolls and, in the thirteenth century, on the early close rolls and on the liberate rolls (see Table 12 and Figure 6).[22] That wax prices, after remaining fairly steady in the 1170s, had increased substantially by 1200/1, seems clear. Unfortunately, the gap in the evidence between 1179/80 and 1200/1 leaves us ignorant as to whether this change was gradual or abrupt. From 1200/1 to 1225/6 there is little sign of a clear trend, but from 1226/7 to 1250/1 there is more than a hint of a downward drift that continues and becomes more definite in the 1250s.

Gaps in the evidence also hamper the analysis of lead prices (see Table 13 and Figure 7).[23] Between 1187/8 and 1210/11 there is only one, possibly anomalous, example and none at all between 1229/30 and 1243/4.[24] The picture is further obscured by the probable variability of the principle measure for lead – the *caretata* or cartload.[25] In spite of these difficulties, it does seem clear that

[20] On Table 11 I have marked those purchases that can be tentatively placed in the category of 'exceptional quality' linen. The 200 ells bought at 9d per ell in 1205/6 'ad opus Regis' is something of a borderline case. Only the price marks it out as exceptional and it is possible that this is an exceptional price rather than exceptional linen. If so, it would accentuate the 'peak' in prices around 1204/5 and 1205/6.

[21] 1000 lb of wax were bought as early as 1157/8; 7000 in 1178/9; 10100 in 1204/5, and over 13000 in 1244/5: *PR 4 Henry II*, 112; *PR 25 Henry II*, 125; *PR 7 John*, 101, 113; *CLR*, ii, 285, 295, 298, 302, 309–10, 312, 320. See also M.T. Clanchy, *From Memory to Written Record*, 2nd edn, Oxford 1993, 78–80.

[22] It is often not clear exactly what number of pounds is represented by the various terms for hundred-weights and thousand-weights of wax. A hundred-weight could represent 100 lb, 108 lb, 112 lb or, conceivably, 120 lb and it is not even self-evident that a thousand-weight comprised always only ten hundred-weights: Connor, *The Weights and Measures of England*, 135–6; Zupko, *A Dictionary of Weights and Measures for the British Isles*, 190, 408; Prior, *Notes on the Weights and Measures of Medieval England*, 12. For simplicity I have treated all hundred-weights as 100 lb and all thousand-weights as 1000 lb, but it would be prudent to allow for the possibility that many of the prices given in Table 12 and Figure 6 may in truth be anything up to twenty per cent less than stated.

[23] The prices shown are taken from the printed Exchequer pipe rolls, from the early close rolls, from the liberate rolls, and from *Building Accounts of King Henry III*, ed. H.M. Colvin, Oxford 1971. Figure 7 shows all the different prices known for each year. In order to give greater weight to larger purchases, the seven year moving average is weighted over the seven years, rather than being a simple moving average of the weighted averages for individual years.

[24] In 1199/1200 10 *quadrigatas* of lead were purchased. The *quadriga* was a particular type of cart, but it is not clear whether the *quadrigata* was an unusual measure or just an unusual name for the normal *caretata* or cartload: *PR 2 John*, 89.

[25] At least three capacities of cartload are described with reference to Edward I's reign: the cartload of 2100 lb (30 fotmals, each of 70 lb); a cartload referred to as the great cartload of London of 1500 lb, and a cartload of the Peak that was much less. Evidence from Henry III's reign recognises the 2100 lb cartload, but also a *carrata minor* of 1680 lb

lead prices in the latter part of John's reign and the early years of Henry III's reign were significantly above those of the 1170s and 1180s, though exactly when and how abruptly this increase took place is hidden. The evidence also suggests that lead prices were tending to rise during the period from 1210/11 to 1250/1.

In certain contexts it might be appropriate to treat wine as a food, but not in the context of prices. Not only was it a luxury even to many among the upper ranks of society, but, owing to the potential for imports, its supply was increasingly unconstrained by limitations on domestic production. Thus, in terms both of demand and of supply, it differed quite radically from basic foodstuffs. In government records from the 1170s onwards there are a reasonable number of references to the prices paid for wine by the king.[26] There is, however, a problem peculiar to these purchases which arises from the prise of wine, the king's right to take a certain amount of wine from imported cargoes at a preferential price. In the late twelfth and early thirteenth century, the prise normally consisted of the right to take two tuns from each cargo and the price paid was in most cases twenty shillings per tun. Sometimes, for better wines, particularly wines of Auxerre, a price of two marks (26s 8d) per tun was paid, and on at least one occasion a price of 15s per tun was paid in respect of wines imported through the port of Bristol.[27] To use the prices of royal wine purchases as a surrogate for the prices of wine in general – a dangerous enough procedure in itself – it is desirable to try to exclude prices that were paid for wine taken under the

(24 fotmals of 70 lb). A cartload of 24 fotmals of unspecified size is also found in the accounts for building works in Henry III's reign: Connor, *The Weights and Measures of England*, 320; Zupko, *A Dictionary of Weights and Measures for the British Isles*, 87–8, 152, 154–5; Prior, *Notes on the Weights and Measures of Medieval England*, 11, 15; I.S.W. Blanchard, 'Derbyshire Lead Production 1195–1505', *Derbyshire Archaeological Journal* 91, 1971, 138–8; *Building Accounts of King Henry III*, 146–7, 148–9. A number of Derbyshire prices per cartload at 5s 0d and 6s 8d when other prices were between 9s 0d and 14s 7d per cartload in Henry II's reign suggests that the smaller 'Peak cartload' had a long history: *PR 14 Henry II*, 109; *PR 18 Henry II*, 7; *PR 23 Henry II*, 57; *PR 25 Henry II*, 30; *PR 26 Henry II*, 75, 137; *PR 28 Henry II*, 47, 102; *PR 29 Henry II*, 1; *PR 30 Henry II*, 2, 29; *PR 34 Henry II*, 199.

[26] There are only five references to the prices paid for wine before 1170 and three of these give the price in terms of the *modius*, the relationship of which to the later, more usual measure, the tun, is unclear: *PR 2–4 Henry II*, 112; *PR 6 Henry II*, 13; *PR 12 Henry II*, 100; *PR 13 Henry II*, 3. There are only a few later references to the *modius* as a measure for wine: *PR 21 Henry II*, 16; *PR 22 Henry II*, 12, 199; *PR 23 Henry II*, 177.

[27] The best account of the history of the wine prise is still N.S.B. Gras, *The Early English Customs System*, Harvard Economic Studies XVIII, Cambridge, Mass. 1918, 37–41. A.L. Simon, *History of the Wine Trade in England*, 3 vols, London 1906, is also useful, if unreliable. Neither Gras nor Simon notice the 26s 8d rate for the prise, though several instances make it clear: for example, *PR 12 John*, 193; *PR 14 John*, 98. The evidence for the 15s rate at Bristol in King John's reign rests on one Exchequer pipe roll entry: 'pro 4 tonellis de vino rubeo de prisa 60s scilicet 15s pro tonello' (*PR 12 John*, 111). It is doubtful, however, that this was a rate consistently used at Bristol. For example, two entries in 1199/1200 suggest wines bought at 20s per tun, although admittedly these are not explicitly *de prisa* (*PR 2 John*, 126).

prise. This task is complicated by the fact that not all such prices are identified explicitly and, particularly in the twelfth century, the level of the price itself does not always make it clear that the prise is involved. Where transport costs are or may be included, a definite identification of a price as a *de prisa* price is even more difficult.[28] Table 14 shows a series of weighted averages of wine prices.[29] It excludes all instances of prices that are identified explicitly as *de prisa*. It also excludes instances which, while not explicitly *de prisa*, seem likely to have been so, on the grounds that they match one of the prise prices or, where transport costs are or may be included, that they are very close to one of the prise prices. The overall effect of the exclusion of these doubtful cases is small. The series includes only purchase prices. For a number of reasons sale prices are generally much lower than purchase prices and as a group are clearly not comparable.[30] Figure 8 plots the series from Table 14. Two things are striking about the pattern of wine prices that it shows. Firstly, the general level of prices for the period from 1206/7 to 1250/1, while higher than that of the last thirty years of the twelfth century, is considerably less than double the level of prices in that earlier period. Secondly, something exceptional clearly happened to wine prices during the early years of King John's reign. Only rarely before the thirteenth century does the evidence providing these prices give an indication of the region of origin of the wines purchased. The relative importance of the different sources of wine probably changed in the late twelfth and early thirteenth centuries and, as wines of different regions were valued differently, this may affect the series.[31] A comprehensive history of the attempts by twelfth- and

[28] See, for example, two entries in 1176/7: 'pro 10 tonellis vini missis ad Windr' contra Natale £10 12s 4d' and 'pro 2 tonellis vini missis ad Gaitinton 46s 8d': *PR 23 Henry II*, 198.

[29] Prices are taken from the printed Exchequer pipe rolls, from the early close rolls, and from the early and later liberate rolls. Additionally a few prices are taken from the *Patent Rolls of the Reign of Henry III preserved in the Public Record Office*, ii, *1225–1232*, 1903, 415–17.

[30] Wine might be sold at a low price because it was old; medieval wines do not seem to have kept well: Simon, *History of the Wine Trade in England* i, 262–3. It is also possible that the king, on occasion, sold cheap English wine produced on lands he controlled, whereas most of his purchases were of imported wine. For example, this might be the explanation for the series of low-priced sales (from 16s 8d per tun to 26s 8d per tun) in 1209/10: *PR 12 John*, 3, 57–8, 82, 162, 192. The lower price of English wine is suggested by the isolated purchase at 10s per tun of wine specified as English in 1183/4: *PR 30 Henry II*, 113. The massive sale of wines by King John in 1201/2 is a special and interesting case, though again the average sale price is low: *PR 4 John*, 82–84.

[31] There must remain many uncertainties here. For instance, the predominance of Gascon wines is often linked to the capture of La Rochelle by the French in 1224, but they were already imported in large quantities earlier in the century. The largest single purchase of identified wines in King John's reign was of Gascon wines: *PR 13 John*, 110. It is also worth noting that the merchants buying grain in Kent in 1207/8 were from Bayonne: *Interdict Documents*, 71–2, 76. When, in the thirteenth century, it becomes practicable to produce separate series of prices for wine from Gascony and Anjou and, to a lesser extent for other particular wines, they do not deviate markedly from the pattern for wines as a whole.

thirteenth-century kings of England to regulate wine prices is still to be written and it is too complex a subject to be tackled fully here. While one would not want to discount automatically the effectiveness of these attempts, which were mostly aimed at the retail trade, there are signs that market pressures could overwhelm them.[32]

In the twelfth and thirteenth centuries, when a good war-horse might cost over one hundred times as much as a plough-horse, a horse was anything but just a horse. Plough-horses, as a substitute for oxen, fall within the class of food-related items and, as one would expect, the prices of plough-horses behaved in a manner similar to that of the prices of oxen. As for cart-horses, while they were not used exclusively in the production and distribution of food, the Winchester pipe roll evidence suggests that their prices maintained a level roughly double that of plough-horses for the period 1208/9 to 1250/1, thus fitting comfortably within the general pattern of agricultural livestock prices.[33] Outside of agriculture a broad range of types of horses occurs in the sources: pack- or sumpter-horses; rounceys; palfreys; hunters; chasers; destriers, and many beasts of widely differing value, described unhelpfully as 'horses'. The quality of these animals varies too much for the whole range to be treated as a single category, but for most individual types the number of examples is too small to produce meaningful price series. One of these types, palfreys, does, however, deserve some attention, not only because the palfrey is the most common type specified in the records, but also, as the staple riding-horse of lords, knights and officials, it constituted a normal and important expense for the upper ranks of society.

Two categories of palfrey prices in the sources will be considered here. Firstly there are prices that are, or at least approximate to, actual purchase prices. Secondly there are prices that represent expected prices or what were perceived to be reasonable prices. This kind of price is most evident when money is allocated for the purpose of purchasing palfreys. These categories are not strictly comparable, but it is often difficult to distinguish with certainty between them, nor does there seem to be any systematic difference between

---

[32] King John's wine assize of 1199 had to be revised immediately because the merchants would not tolerate it: *Howden*, iv, 99–100. Even after this the very numerous amercements for contravening the assize at this time may reflect the fact that the revised assize too was unrealistic, at least in its first few years of operation. In 1236 the assize in Oxford was suspended because of a shortage of wine, an event which roughly coincides with a period of high prices paid by the king in the mid-1230s: *Close Rolls*, iii, 333. Later levels of maximum prices under the wine assize in Henry III's reign, set either for individual boroughs or more widely promulgated, were sometimes, though not always, more generous than King John's revised assize: *ibid.*, i, 192, 230, 389, 576, 593; ii, 134, 142, 326–7; iii, 386, 407, 413, 512, 522–3.

[33] Farmer, 'Some Price Fluctuations in Angevin England', 41; 'Some Livestock Price Movements in Thirteenth-Century England', 2–3, 7; 'Prices and Wages', 799–806.

their prices.[34] Table 15 and Figure 9 include prices from both categories. It is likely that much of the volatility of the price series shown reflects a degree of variation in the quality of palfreys which the relatively small number of examples is insufficient to dampen.[35] It would be wrong to place too much weight on the lesser fluctuations in this series, but even if the timing and degree of the change in prices cannot be confidently asserted from this evidence, there seems little doubt that the prices of palfreys had risen significantly between the 1180s and the 1240s. An indication that the market in palfreys may at times have been distorted in John's reign is provided by an entry in 1209/10: 'Johannes filius Roberti debet 20m quia contra prohibitionem emit palefridum Regis.'[36] If this indicates that the king had reserved all purchases of palfreys to himself, it may help to explain the relatively low palfrey prices shown on Table 15 and Figure 9 for the latter part of John's reign, though there is no telling from the entry how long this prohibition lasted or how local it might have been.

The price series for wool and sheep, exchequer cloth and linen, wax, lead, wine and palfreys contain many weaknesses and uncertainties. The dangers of distortion are as great if not greater than for food-related prices, but the paucity of evidence and the limitations of the sources make these dangers harder to minimise. While further research and analysis is both possible and desirable, some provisional conclusions can be ventured. The general pattern of prices

---

[34] Prices that belong or may belong to the first category can be found on the Exchequer pipe rolls, the early close rolls and on the liberate rolls. An untypically clear and detailed example occurs in the Exchequer pipe roll for 1197/8 – 'Pro 20 palefridis emptis ad opus Regis ad feriam Sancti Yvonis £54 18s 4d. Et in custodia predictorum 20 palefridorum per 4 dies 19s 5d': *PR 10 Richard I*, 161. Most entries on the Exchequer pipe rolls that appear to refer to actual purchases provide much less detail, for example, 'In emptione 15 palefridorum ad opus Regis £17 16s' or, in the most common and least definite form, 'Pro palefrido ad opus Regine £2' (*PR 16 John*, 20; *PR 18 Henry II*, 79). Writs of Liberate on the liberate rolls also occasionally make it clear that they concern actual purchases, though often these include the cost of delivering the horse within the price: for example, *CLR*, iii, 82. Examples that probably belong to the second category of price are found on the Exchequer pipe rolls: for example, 'Normano de Camera eiunti in Alemanniam £4 ad unum palefridum emendum ad opus Regis Otonis' (*PR 5 John*, 9). They are, however, more commonly found in the form of writs of Liberate on the liberate rolls: for example, *CLR*, i, 37, 113, 118–119, 159. A third, interesting but distinct category concerns prices implied by the amounts for which debts to the king, expressed in terms of palfreys, could be commuted for cash. This practice, and especially its proliferation in King John's reign, contains many fascinating aspects, but will not be considered here, both for reasons of space and because the relationship between these 'prices' and market-prices was clearly indirect.

[35] In order to minimise the problem of varying quality as much as possible, the seven year moving average on Figure 9 is weighted over the seven years rather than being a simple moving average of the individual weighted annual averages. Also, so as not to extend unnecessarily the y-axis on Figure 9, the exceptional price of twenty marks for a single palfrey in 1249/50 is not shown, though it is included in the moving average (*CLR*, iii, 271).

[36] *PR 12 John*, 67. In September 1241 Henry III issued an order to seize all the suitable palfreys at Winchester fair and pay for them (*CLR*, ii, 73).

which emerges from the study of these commodities confirms rather than contradicts the more soundly based conclusions concerning food-related prices. As with food-related prices, there is little sign of a substantial, sustained rise in prices before John's reign. From 1198/9 to 1205/6, sheep prices, exchequer cloth prices and wine prices indicate a steep rise similar to that suggested by grain and food-related livestock prices. Linen prices, lead prices, wax prices and palfrey prices are all compatible with the notion of a general price surge during these years, even if they offer little positive evidence as to its timing. Thereafter, from 1206/7 to 1250/1, there is less consistency between the price patterns of different commodities. This should be no surprise. We should not expect the prices of very different commodities, subject to many special factors in their own particular markets, to move in concert in any but exceptional circumstances. Overall, it might be possible to say that, after a somewhat chaotic period in the latter part of John's reign, price trends were mostly either unclear or upwards – with only the price series for wax suggesting the gentlest of declines – and that the general level of these prices was substantially higher than before John's reign.

Caution is always advisable in dealing with medieval price series, but scepticism should be kept within reasonable bounds. There is a certain safety in numbers as far as price series are concerned. There is no indication that the shifting peculiarities of the sources create large distortions in terms of the very modest degree of accuracy that we might reasonably expect. Within the somewhat restricted range of contexts from which the data comes, the patterns of prices that were suggested by D.L. Farmer's figures would seem to deserve more trust than even he himself would have given them. The other price series introduced here not only offer some further evidence of the same patterns, but also suggest that these price patterns were not limited to food and food production. If we can conclude from this that an especially rapid, substantial and, as far as we can tell, fairly general, rise in prices did take place in the early years of King John's reign, and that this change in the price level was sustained thereafter, then we can move on to arguing from relatively firm ground about its causes and consequences, and also its relationship with the contemporary struggle to defend the lands of King John in France.

Table 1. The Geographical Distribution of Wheat Price Data from the
Exchequer Pipe Rolls 1165/6–1210/11

Counties	1165/6-1171/2	1172/3-1184/5	1189/90-1192/3	1199/1200-1210/11
Berkshire	X	X		X
Cambs. & Hunts.	X			
Cumberland				X
Dors. & Som.	X	X		X
Essex & Herts.	X	X	X	X
Gloucestershire	X	X		
Hampshire	X	X		X
Herefordshire	X			
Kent	X	X	X	X
Lancashire				X
Lincolnshire	X			
London & Middx.	X	X		
Norfolk & Suffolk		X		X
Northamptonshire	X		X	
Notts. & Derbys.	X	X		
Oxfordshire	X	X		X
Shropshire		X		
Staffordshire	X			
Surrey		X		
Sussex	X		X	
Warws. & Leics.	X	X		
Wiltshire	X	X	X	X
Worcestershire	X	X	X	
Yorkshire		X		X
Total Number of Counties:	18	16	6	11

Table 2. The Geographical Distribution of Oxen Price Data from the
Exchequer Pipe Rolls 1162/3–1210/11

Counties	1162/3-1181/2	1182/3-1188/9	1192/3-1198/9	1200/1-1210/11
Bedfordshire	X	X	X	
Berkshire	X		X	X
Buckinghamshire	X	X	X	
Cambridgeshire	X		X	
Cornwall		X	X	
Cumberland			X	
Derbyshire			X	X
Devon	X	X	X	X
Dorset		X	X	X
Durham				X
Essex	X	X	X	
Gloucestershire		X	X	X
Hampshire		X	X	X
Herefordshire			X	
Hertfordshire	X		X	
Huntingdonshire	X			X
Kent	X	X	X	
Lancashire				X
Leicestershire	X	X		X
Lincolnshire	X		X	X
Middlesex			X	
Norfolk			X	
Northamptonshire	X	X	X	X
Northumberland	X	X	X	
Nottinghamshire	X	X	X	X
Oxfordshire	X		X	X
Shropshire				X
Somerset	X	X	X	
Staffordshire	X		X	
Suffolk	X		X	
Surrey			X	
Sussex	X	X	X	X
Warwickshire		X	X	X
Wiltshire	X	X	X	
Worcestershire	X		X	
Yorkshire	X	X	X	X
Total Number of Counties:	22	18	31	18

Table 3. Wheat and Oxen Prices 1162/3–1210/11: Overall Average Price
Levels for Selected Periods

a) Wheat

Overall Average Prices for Each Period (pennies per summ/quarter)

1165/6- 1171/2	1172/3- 1184/5	1189/90- 1192/3	1199/1200- 1210/11
18.5	26.4	19.6	61.0

b) Oxen

Overall Average Prices for Each Period (pennies per ox)

1162/3- 1181/2	1182/3- 1188/9	1192/3- 1198/9	1200/1- 1210/11
36.5	51.4	40.8	78.2

Table 4. Exchequer Pipe Roll Wheat Prices 1165/6–1210/11:
Selected Counties/ Selected Periods

a) Counties with data for all periods

County	Weighted Average Prices for Each Period (pennies per summ/quarter)			
	1165/6- 1171/2	1172/3- 1184/5	1189/90- 1192/3	1199/1200- 1210/11
Essex & Hertfordshire	15.6	22.6	17.9	55.6
Kent	20.3	30.8	22.0	71.9
Wiltshire	23.4	40.3	25.8	96.0
Average (unweighted)	19.8	31.3	21.9	74.5

b) Counties with data for the first, second and fourth periods (These counties also
represent all the southern counties which have data for the fourth period.)

County	Weighted Average Prices for Each Period (pennies per summ/quarter)			
	1165/6- 1171/2	1172/3- 1184/5	1189/90- 1192/3	1199/1200- 1210/11
Berkshire	14.0	20.1	---	80.0
Dorset & Somerset	23.0	25.6	---	39.1
Essex & Hertfordshire	15.6	22.6	17.9	55.6
Hampshire	13.9	19.5	---	50.8
Kent	20.3	30.8	22.0	71.9
Oxfordshire	17.2	22.7	---	80.0
Wiltshire	23.4	40.3	25.8	96.0
Average (unweighted)	18.2	25.9	21.9	67.6

c) Counties with data for the first, second and third periods

County	Weighted Average Prices for Each Period (pennies per summ/quarter)			
	1165/6- 1171/2	1172/3- 1184/5	1189/90- 1192/3	1199/1200 1210/11
Essex & Hertfordshire	15.6	22.6	17.9	55.6
Kent	20.3	30.8	22.0	71.9
Wiltshire	23.4	40.3	25.8	96.0
Worcestershire	17.8	21.4	14.6	---
Average (unweighted)	19.3	28.8	20.1	74.5

Table 5. Exchequer Pipe Roll Oxen Prices 1162/3–1210/11:
Selected Counties/ Selected Periods

a) Counties with data for all periods

County	Average Prices for Each Period (pennies per ox)			
	1162/3- 1181/2	1182/3- 1188/9	1192/3- 1198/9	1200/1 1210/11
Devon	36.0	48.0	43.2	63.3
Northamptonshire	36.0	48.0	48.0	73.9
Nottinghamshire	48.0	60.0	48.0	87.7
Sussex	36.0	48.0	48.0	83.0
Yorkshire	39.0	60.0	48.0	77.1
Average	39.0	52.8	47.0	77.0

b) Southern counties with data for the third and fourth periods, and one or more other periods

County	Average Price for Each Period (pennies per ox)			
	1162/3- 1181/2	1182/3- 1188/9	1192/3- 1198/9	1200/1 1210/11
Berkshire	36.0	---	43.2	60.0
Devon	36.0	48.0	43.2	63.3
Dorset	---	48.0	36.0	72.1
Gloucestershire	---	48.0	48.0	74.1
Hampshire	---	36.0	40.0	68.9
Oxfordshire	36.0	---	47.5	66.8
Sussex	36.0	48.0	48.0	83.0
Average	36.0	45.6	43.7	69.7

Table 6. A Comparison of Prices per Summ and per Quarter in the Exchequer
Pipe Rolls and the Winchester Pipe Rolls

Year	Exch. Pipe Rolls Pennies Per Summ	Exch. Pipe Rolls Pennies Per Qtr	Win. Pipe Rolls Pennies Per Qtr
a) Wheat			
1170/1	18.0	17.8	----
1192/3	22.0	12.0	----
1206/7	47.3	52.0	----
1213/14	24.0	29.7	27.5
1214/15	24.0	32.0	----
1217/18	51.2	----	60.5
b) Barley			
1192/3	12.0	7.0	----
c) Oats			
1205/6	20.6	20.1	----
d) Beans			
1192/3	12.0	10.0	----
e) Salt			
1210/11	15.2	19.9	12.2

Table 7. Wheat Prices: Printed Exchequer Pipe Rolls Compared with
Winchester Pipe Rolls

Year	Exchequer Pipe Rolls: (pennies per summ/qtr.)			Winchester Pipe Rolls: (pennies per quarter)
	Purch.	Sales	Both	Sales
1208/9	----	----	----	31.5
1209/10	51.8	17.6	43.3	----
1210/11	48.0	----	48.0	41.8
1211/12	80.0	----	80.0	31.3
1212/13	----	----	----	----
1213/14	27.4	28.6	27.8	27.5
1214/15	29.3	----	29.3	----
1215/16	----	----	----	39.5
1216/17	----	----	----	----
1217/18	51.2	----	51.2	60.5
1218/19	----	----	----	63.8
1219/20	----	----	----	44.0
1220/1	----	----	----	62.5
1229/30	48.0	80.0	64.0	----
1241/2	47.0	----	47.0	----

Table 8. Oxen Prices: Printed Exchequer Pipe Rolls Compared with
Winchester Pipe Rolls

Year	Exchequer Pipe Rolls: (pennies per ox)		Winchester Pipe Rolls: (pennies per ox)	
	Purchases	Sales	Purchases	Sales
1207/8	73.8	----	----	----
1208/9	79.7	64.8	84.5	61.8
1209/10	81.7	----	----	----
1210/11	70.2	----	73.8	65.8
1211/12	73.8	----	79.5	59.3
1212/13	----	----	----	----
1213/14	88.1	104.0	92.3	68.5
1214/15	76.0	----	----	----
1215/16	----	----	75.8	55.5
1216/17	----	----	----	----
1217/18	----	----	88.3	60.3
1218/19	----	----	80.8	75.5
1219/20	----	----	91.8	78.5
1220/1	----	----	96.0	73.5
1229/30	94.5	70.5	----	----
1241/2	82.7	90.4	----	----

Table 9. Wheat and Oxen Prices: Miscellaneous Accounts Compared with the
Winchester Pipe Rolls

a) Wheat

Year

	Lands of Fawkes de Breaute (pennies per quarter)			Winchester Pipe Rolls (pennies per quarter)
	Purch.	Sales	Both	Sales
1223/4	----	33.0	33.0	31.3
1224/5	60.8	51.3	51.5	71.5

	Accounts of Escheats (pennies per quarter)			Winchester Pipe Rolls (pennies per quarter)
	Purch.	Sales	Both	Sales
1232/3	40.0	38.6	38.8	42.3

b) Oxen

Year

	Lands of Fawkes de Breaute (pennies per ox)		Winchester Pipe Rolls (pennies per ox)	
	Purchases	Sales	Purchases	Sales
1223/4	90.0	60.8	92.8	77.0
1224/5	67.0	----	90.3	77.3

	Accounts of Escheats (pennies per ox)		Winchester Pipe Rolls (pennies per ox)	
	Purchases	Sales	Purchases	Sales
1232/3	87.8	49.3	101.5	88.5

Table 10. Exchequer Cloth Prices 1180/1–1241/2
(cloth for table and for windows combined)

Year	Price	Year	Price
1180/1	14s 0d	1203/4	30s 10d
1181/2	12s 6d	1204/5	30s 1.5d
1182/3	11s 8d	1205/6	32s 1d
1183/4	----	1206/7	32s 1d
1184/5	12s 9d	1207/8	36s 11d
1185/6	11s 8d	1208/9	32s 1d
1186/7	14s 1d	1209/10	33s 6d
1187/8	12s 9d	1210/11	36s 3d
1188/9	14s 1d	1211/12	42s 3d
1189/90	12s 1d	1212/13	----
1190/1	12s 3d	1213/14	41s 3d
1191/2	12s 10d	1214/15	33s 2d
1192/3	14s 6d	1215/16	----
1193/4	----	1216/17	33s 2d
1194/5	----	1217/18	40s 1d
1195/6	13s 8d	1218/19	40s 1d
1196/7	16s 0d	1219/20	40s 1d
1197/8	19s 0d	1220/1	40s 1d
1198/9	20s 0d		
1199/1200	20s 0d	1229/30	40s 2d
1200/1	20s 0d		
1201/2	30s 0d	1241/2	40s 2d
1202/3	30s 9d		

Table 11. Linen Purchases 1155/6–1254/5

Year	Number of Ells	Pennies per Ell	Notes
1155/6	200	3.0	for napkins
1180/1	10	2.4	exchequer curtains
1181/2	10	3.0	exchequer curtains
1184/5	10	2.5	exchequer curtains
1185/6	10	2.0	exchequer curtains
1186/7	10	2.5	exchequer curtains
"	60	8.0	for the daughter of the duke of Saxony †
1187/8	10	2.5	exchequer curtains
1188/9	10	2.5	exchequer curtains
1195/6	10	3.6	exchequer curtains
1198/9	2000	2.5	for the coronation of King John
1203/4	100	2.4	
"	100	2.2	
1204/5	400	5.0	for the Christmas feast
"	200	5.1	for the Easter feast
"	60	12.6	'delicate' †
1205/6	200	9.0	for the king †
"	500	5.5	for Easter feast
"	60	8.0	for the countess of Gloucester †
"	500	4.2	for the king
1207/8	800	4.3	for the Christmas feast
1209/10	940	3.6	for the king for Christmas
1211/12	986	3.5	for the king's napkins for Christmas
1220/1	500	4.1	for the king's napkins for Christmas
1229/30	69	3.0	
1242/3 *	47	7.0	for sheets, etc for Prince Edward and Margaret his sister †
1243/4 *	48	6.0	to go round the king's bed †
1248/9 *	2000	4.3	
1253/4 *	600	3.3	for napkins
1254/5 *	566	3.5	

* Entries marked with an asterisk are from the liberate rolls. All the rest are from the Exchequer pipe rolls.

† 'Exceptional quality' purchases (?)

Table 12. Wax Prices 1157/8–1257/8

Year	Weighted Av. Price - pennies per lb	Year	Weighted Av. Price - pennies per lb
1157/8	(2.46)	1226/7	5.23
		1227/8	6.73
1171/2	(3.00)	1228/9	6.52
		1229/30	6.34
1174/5	(3.00)		
1175/6	(3.12)	1232/3	5.61
1176/7	(3.40)		
1177/8	(3.43)	1234/5	6.00
1178/9	3.26		
1179/80	(3.00)	1236/7	5.70
		1237/8	7.23
1200/1	(4.80)	1238/9	5.99
1201/2	(7.32)	1239/40	4.63
		1240/1	5.79
1203/4	(7.32)	1241/2	5.76
1204/5	4.81	1242/3	6.20
		1243/4	6.22
1206/7	(7.43)	1244/5	5.83
		1245/6	5.88
1208/9	(6.00)	1246/7	6.13
		1247/8	5.70
1210/11	4.03		
1211/12	3.76	1249/50	5.72
		1250/1	5.27
1213/14	8.92	1251/2	5.52
1214/15	5.70	1252/3	5.72
		1253/4	(5.00)
1219/20	4.86	1254/5	4.96
		1255/6	4.77
		1256/7	4.19
		1257/8	4.35

Figures enclosed in brackets are from a single entry.

Table 13. Lead Prices 1167/8–1258/9 (shillings per cartload)

Year	Price or Range of Prices	No of Cartloads	Weighted Average
1167/8	(9.0)	55	(9.0)
1171/2	(5.0)	40	(5.0)
1176/7	(6.7)	20	(6.7)
1178/9	(13.3)	100	(13.3)
1179/80	6.7 - 13.3	240	9.4
1181/2	12.5 - 22.0	44	13.4
1182/3	(7.0)	30	(7.0)
1183/4	12.5 - 14.6	75	13.7
1187/8	(6.7)	100	(6.7)
1199/1200	(20.0)	10	(20.0)
1210/11	23.8 - 27.7	80.5	24.2
1213/14	(40.0)	4	(40.0)
1219/20	(28.5)	4	(28.5)
1220/1	30.0 - 38.2	6.5	30.6
1221/2	28.0 - 36.0	25.1	29.8
1222/3	28.8 - 29.0	19.5	28.8
1223/4	(27.3)	20	(27.3)
1226/7	(48.0)	3	(48.0)
1228/9	(44.0)	3	(44.0)
1229/30	31.6 - 35.0	40	33.2
1243/4	(46.5)	14	(46.5)
1248/9	(40.8)	4	(40.8)
1252/3	43.5 - 45.3	63	44.5
1257/8	(46.0)	1	(46.0)
1258/9	(42.0)	4	(42.0)

Figures in brackets are taken from a single entry.

Table 14. Wine Prices 1159/60–1253/4

Year	Weighted Av. Price per Tun	Year	Weighted Av. Price per Tun
1159/60	(17s 0d)	1217/18	(39s 2d)
		1218/19	(40s 0d)
1166/7	(41s 0d)		
		1220/1	32s 9d
1172/3	(24s 0d)		
1173/4	(24s 0d)	1226/7	29s 6d
1174/5	36s 7d	1227/8	30s 10d
1175/6	(32s 2d)	1228/9	29s 5d
1176/7	(26s 5d)	1229/30	34s 0d
		1230/1	41s 9d
1180/1	(20s 10d)		
		1232/3	33s 2d
1183/4	25s 7d		
1184/5	24s 5d	1236/7	41s 10d
		1237/8	45s 11d
1186/7	(25s 0d)	1238/9	28s 7d
1187/8	(33s 4d)	1239/40	28s 5d
		1240/1	36s 3d
1189/90	24s 1d	1241/2	34s 4d
		1242/3	36s 1d
1193/4	30s 4d	1243/4	38s 3d
		1244/5	34s 4d
1199/1200	37s 9d	1245/6	37s 7d
1200/1	43s 6d	1246/7	40s 8d
1201/2	(50s 0d)	1247/8	33s 6d
1202/3	51s 11d	1248/9	30s 7d
1203/4	50s 3d	1249/50	34s 5d
1204/5	70s 9d	1250/1	31s 5d
1205/6	55s 1d	1251/2	32s 11d
1206/7	36s 10d	1252/3	36s 2d
1207/8	37s 3d	1253/4	37s 0d
1208/9	31s 8d		
1209/10	33s 0d		
1210/11	37s 3d		
1211/12	38s 1d		
1213/14	30s 0d		
1214/15	36s 7d		
1215/16	36s 4d		

For the prices included in the above weighted averages, see the text of the article.
Figures in brackets are taken from a single entry.

Table 15. Palfrey Prices 1156/7–1259/60

Year	Weighted Av. Price	No.	Year	Weighted Av. Price	No.
1156/7	(27s 0d)	1	1226/7	78s 4d	2
1157/8	20s 0d	2			
			1228/9	66s 8d	2
1162/3	(20s 0d)	1	1229/30	(66s 8d)	1
1165/6	(44s 5d)	3	1232/3	(66s 8d)	1
1171/2	(40s 0d)	1	1236/7	(66s 8d)	1
			1237/8	(66s 8d)	1
1173/4	(26s 8d)	1	1238/9	93s 4d	5
1174/5	(10s 0d)	1	1239/40	(40s 0d)	1
1175/6	(15s 7d)	3	1240/1	100s 0d	2
1176/7	28s 5d	3	1241/2	116s 8d	2
			1242/3	(100s 0d)	1
1188/9	(43s 4d)	1	1243/4	57s 9d	3
1189/90	32s 3d	6			
1190/1	(40s 0d)	1	1245/6	105s 4d	5
1195/6	(66s 9d)	1	1247/8	146s 8d	3
			1248/9	83s 4d	2
1197/8	(54s 11d)	20	1249/50	(266s 8d)	1
			1250/1	84s 0d	5
1201/2	(40s 0d)	1	1251/2	(133s 4d)	1
1202/3	(80s 0d)	1	1252/3	83s 4d	2
1204/5	(26s 8d)	1	1254/5	57s 9d	3
			1255/6	147s 5d	7
1210/11	(26s 8d)	1	1256/7	98s 4d	2
1211/12	32s 4d	12			
			1258/9	(173s 4d)	1
1213/14	(23s 9d)	15	1259/60	100s 0d	3

Bracketed figures are taken from a single entry.

Figure 1. Wheat Prices 1165/6–1250/1

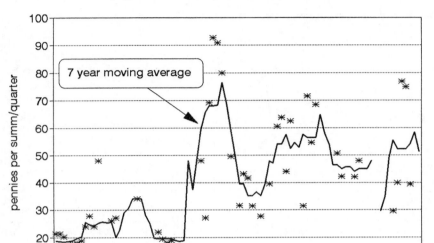

Figure 2. Oxen Prices 1162/3–1250/1

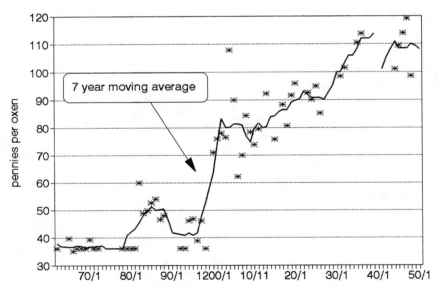

Figure 3. Wheat and Oxen Prices 1165/6–1250/1

7 year moving averages.
Indices: 1165/6 = 100

Figure 4. Sheep and Wool Prices 1162/3–1250/1

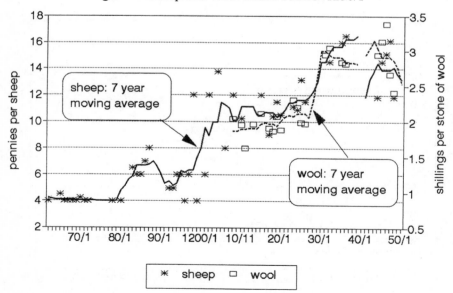

Figure 5. Exchequer Cloth 1180/1–1220/1

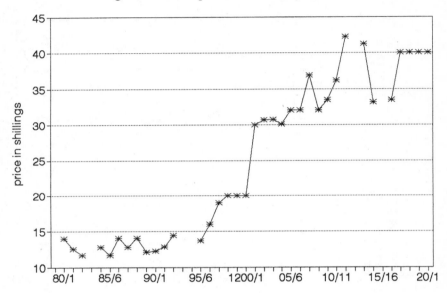

Figure 6. Wax Prices 1171/2–1250/1

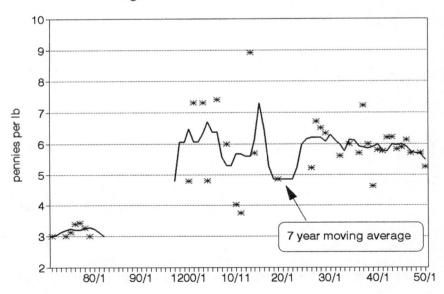

Figure 7. Lead Prices 1167/8–1250/1

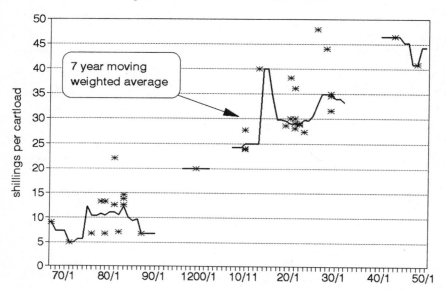

Figure 8. Wine Prices 1170/1–1250/1

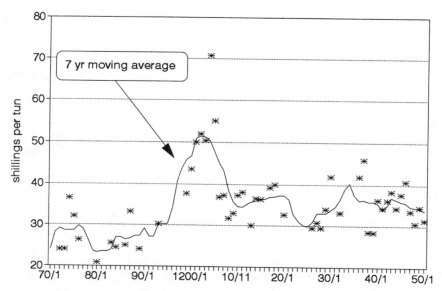

Figure 9. Palfrey Prices 1156/7–1250/1

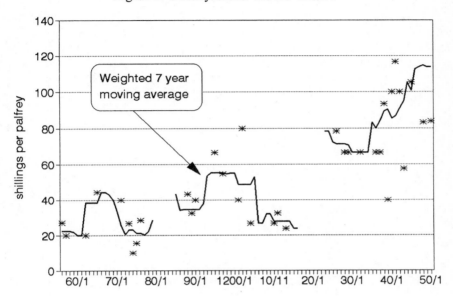

The Revenues of John and Philip Augustus Revisited

Nick Barratt

The loss of Normandy in 1204 has been a source of debate through the ages, with two main schools of thought emerging to explain John's sudden capitulation in the face of Capetian hostility. Current opinion can be summarised as follows: Sir James Holt has suggested that the conquests of Philip Augustus were largely inevitable, a result of the rapidly expanding resources of the French monarchy which had already outstripped the revenues of the Angevin monarchs of England by the end of the twelfth century. Based on the surviving records from France, Normandy and England for the 1202/3 financial year, Holt has calculated that on the eve of the war John was already struggling to compete with Philip's level of annual revenue, and that his attempts to retain Angevin possessions on the continent ultimately foundered on a lack of resources.[1] John Gillingham, on the other hand, has argued that the situation was not as clear-cut as Holt supposed, and that John's revenues were still a fair match for Philip's at this crucial time. Accordingly, the loss of Normandy should be primarily expressed in terms of diplomatic and military errors, attributable to John's personality and politics. Gillingham has supported this theory by demonstrating that Richard managed to hold his 'empire' together with resources similar to John's, despite long periods of absence from the heart of government.[2] Three more recent studies have added to this debate. The Capetian side of the equation has been closely analysed by John Baldwin, who regards Philip's finances as being 'adequate to his political designs against the Angevin lands on the continent',[3] a conclusion which is supported by Ralph V. Turner's recent assessment of John's reign.[4] Jim Bradbury has adopted a more cautious approach in his recent biography of Philip, stating that 'the records simply do not allow a conclusive view'. He does, however, suggest that 'Philip was improving his resources before this triumph', and that 'warfare from 1202, and the losses sustained from then onwards, must have seriously diminished [John's] continental income'[5].

[1] J.C. Holt, 'The Loss of Normandy and Royal Finance', in *War and Government in the Middle Ages*, ed. J.C. Holt and J. Gillingham, Woodbridge 1984, 92–105 at p. 98 in particular.

[2] Gillingham, *Richard Coeur de Lion*, 71–76.

[3] Baldwin, *Government*, 174.

[4] Turner, *King John*, 91–94.

[5] J. Bradbury, *Philip Augustus, King of France 1180–1223*, London 1998, 159–160.

It is therefore clear that crucial to the resolution of the debate is the precise level of revenue available to each side on the eve of the conflict. The first question to be addressed is why there is any ambiguity at all, given the survival of financial accounts from the three main territories for the same financial year. The French account for 1202/3 is the sole record of annual audit to survive in its entirety for the reign of Philip Augustus. Originally analysed by Brussel in 1727, it was subsequently re-examined by Lot and Fawtier in 1932.[6] Holt used Lot and Fawtier's calculations as the starting point for his comparison with the Angevins,[7] as did Baldwin, although he employed a slightly different analytical technique as part of a general study on Capetian finance. The second record source concerns the surviving Norman pipe rolls, edited by Thomas Stapleton in the mid-nineteenth century.[8] Those for 1195 and 1198 are virtually intact and provide a relatively clear picture of Norman revenue under Richard I, but the account for 1202/3 is incomplete. Finally, there is a virtually unbroken run of pipe rolls for England covering the reigns of both Richard I and John, with the exception of 1213, which have been published by the Pipe Roll Society.

Closer examination of the documents, however, reveals why historians have interpreted them in different ways. Firstly, all three sources are records of audit, not of receipt, and as such do not contain all revenue collected by the respective monarchs.[9] Key data is lacking in a number of areas; for example, moneys paid directly into the royal Chamber are largely lost,[10] and no figure survives for the total yield of English extraordinary taxation in 1203. Secondly, the French account survives in isolation, and so there is no way of telling whether it was a true reflection of Philip's revenue before 1203. This presents a problem when attempting to assess the standard level of Capetian finances before the war, as one of the key areas in the debate concerns the comparison of ordinary annual revenue for John and Philip, as opposed to the separate problem of calculating the funds that were utilised in the war zone. The incomplete Norman account of 1202/3 compounds this difficulty, as it becomes impossible to calculate accurately the revenue collected by John from the duchy on the eve of war, let alone assess the level of 'ordinary' revenue he received annually, without relying on the rolls for 1198 and 1195. Furthermore, no records survive to indicate the financial contribution of John's south-western territories to the campaign. Holt has argued that any drafts from these lands would have had a minimal effect on disposable revenue for the purpose of war,[11] but there is no concrete data to confirm or deny his suspicions.

---

[6] *Premier budget.*
[7] Holt, 'Loss of Normandy and Royal Finance', 94–95.
[8] *Rot. Norm.*
[9] For a fuller discussion of the relative merits and de-merits of using records of audit to provide revenue totals, see Barratt, 'Revenue', 835–855 at pp. 836–7, also n. 6.
[10] A fragment of a Norman chamber account for 1202/3 survives: *Miscellaneous Records of the Norman Exchequer*, ed. S.R. Packard in Smith College Studies in History xii, Northampton Mass. 1926–7, 67–69.
[11] Holt, 'Loss of Normandy and Royal Finance', 104–5.

Despite these apparent obstacles, enough material still remains to undertake a basic analysis of the accounts. The main aim of this paper is, therefore, to recalculate the overall resources of each side on the eve of hostilities in 1202/3, presenting figures for potential annual revenue and actual war revenue. This approach should determine whether normal Capetian resources had already outstripped those of the Angevins, whilst permitting a separate assessment of the level of revenue actually utilised in the war zone. A brief comparison of the relative position of John and Richard I will also be presented, based on the Norman and English pipe rolls for 1195 and 1198, to determine whether John was financially disadvantaged in comparison with his brother. Finally, an attempt will be made to analyse the funding for the 1214 campaign, and to consider the implications of its failure for Henry III.

A Definition of Revenue

When conducting a survey of this nature, the first task must be to provide a strict definition of all elements that constituted 'revenue' in the late twelfth and early thirteenth centuries. Holt has compiled a list of terms that he uses consistently throughout his calculations,[12] and the majority of these can be adopted for the purpose of this paper. 'Receipts' will be used to denote cash deposits into either the Treasury or Chamber, whilst 'expenditure' describes expenses made by local officials on behalf of the crown and authorised by royal writ. Holt, however, has defined regular allowances, such as fixed alms or *terrae datae* entries, as expenditure, and also includes pardons on the grounds that they were matched by some form of service or benefit to the crown. A decision has been taken to exclude these categories from all calculations of expenditure throughout this paper. Regular allowances, such as alms, were repeated annually in the rolls, and as such the king never expected to receive this income – it was essentially 'written off'. Similarly, a large number of *terrae datae* entries, that is land given away by the crown and subsequently deducted from the farms of the original accounts, answered for independent farms in the main body of the roll; this practice was particularly prevalent in the English pipe rolls. To include the initial *terrae datae* entries as 'expenditure' would be to count them twice, thereby artificially inflating the overall revenue total. Pardons have also been excluded, as there is no consistent way of analysing their impact on the overall revenue total. For example, during the later years of his reign, John was imposing heavy fines *pro benevolentia regis* as part of a punitive policy aimed at tying individuals to the crown. In many cases, however, these were never called for payment and were subsequently pardoned. His motives were as much political as they were financial, and the artificially high totals should not be regarded as an indication of the level of income that the crown expected to receive. Holt has also noted that 'withdrawals' from deposit are included in the accounts, along with 'transfers' between one

---

[12] *Ibid.* 93–94.

accountant and another. These are excluded to give 'net' revenue, a practice which has been followed in the current survey.[13]

The importance of providing disposable revenue totals is highlighted by Holt's arguments over the validity of including English 'expenditure' in the balance sheet.[14] If, as he suggests, expenditure recorded in the 1203 pipe roll is to be excluded, then it is important to maintain an element of consistency throughout the calculations. It is for this reason that the majority of French expenditure must also be removed from the final equation, as not all was devoted to military ends. As Normandy was the focal point of the war zone, however, it is reasonable to define all expenditure as being relevant to the defence of the duchy, especially in 1203 when the French threat was at its greatest. Similarly, it is important to exclude withdrawals from the initial equation. The main area of debate revolves around whether normal Capetian finances had outstripped those of the Angevins by the start of the thirteenth century. The inclusion of moneys withdrawn from deposit, generally for expenditure on specific projects, distorts the base level of new revenue produced during one financial year. Without any information on the size of reserves held by the Treasury, it is hard to speculate whether withdrawals were an indication of strength in depth, in the sense that large surpluses had been built up from ordinary revenue, or a sign that the royal coffers were being drained. Consequently, the purpose of this survey is to provide consistent totals for potential annual revenue that could have been devoted to the war, based largely around figures for net disposable income for France and England, and net total income for Normandy. The starting point for this exercise will be a re-examination of the Capetian position, based on the calculations of both Holt and Baldwin.

French Revenue 1202/1203

Holt states that his figures are derived from Lot and Fawtier's calculations of the 1202/3 account, and begins his survey by providing a total of 196,327 li.par. for gross revenue. If withdrawals totalling 59,375 li.par. are removed from this sum, net revenue can be put at 136,952 li.par. Holt also provides figures for gross expenditure (95,445 li.par.), generating a gross balance of 100,882 li.par. 'receipts', of which 27,370 li.par. was derived from the extraordinary levy for raising serjeants. Consequently, gross ordinary receipts can be put at 73,512 li.par. A net total would be preferable, but Holt does not state whether the withdrawals were fully expended on the various projects for which they were intended. It may be the case that unspent balances were returned to the Treasury or Chamber, thus inflating the level of recorded receipts. Furthermore, Holt gives no breakdown of the expenditure total, and so it is difficult to determine how much was devoted to the war effort on the Norman frontier. It is, therefore, difficult to provide an overall figure for Philip's disposable war revenue from

[13] *Ibid.* 93–94.
[14] *Ibid.* 97.

Holt's calculations, and a decision has been taken to use the gross total for receipts (100,882 li.par.) as the baseline for analytical purposes, as it best reflects Philip's disposable income. This equates to 147,288 li.ang.[15]

Baldwin has also analysed the French account presented in Lot and Fawtier's edition. His methodology is somewhat different to Holt's, as he immediately presents a total for net revenue (141,589 li.par.). This includes 26,453 li.par. receipts from the extraordinary levy, leaving a balance of 115,136 li.par. ordinary revenue.[16] On closer examination, this total comprised 76,965 li.par. receipts and 29,500 li.par. expenditure,[17] of which 17,100 li.par. related to military activities associated with the Norman campaign.[18] As a result, Philip's actual war revenue for 1202/3 can be put at 120,518 li.par. This total will be used as Baldwin's baseline figure, and equates to 175,956 li.ang. Given the marked difference compared with Holt's baseline total, both values will be put forward to represent the level of French war revenue on the eve of conflict.

Norman Revenue 1202/3

As outlined above, the 1202/3 Norman pipe roll is incomplete. The surviving accounts provide an overall revenue total of just over 9,000 li.ang., but it is clear that this does not fully reflect John's income from the duchy for the financial year. The breakdown in the audit process, and therefore in the compilation of the pipe roll itself, demonstrates that the conflict was imposing a great strain on the Norman administration, and it is highly likely that not all revenue collected was ever officially audited. Consequently, an alternative method of analysing John's Norman finances needs to be found. Holt suggests that the accounts of the bailiwicks that were audited in 1202/3 produced approximately 38% of their recorded yield in 1198, and if this 'yield ratio' is applied to all bailiwicks that accounted in the 1198 roll a more representative figure for 1203 can be produced.[19] Moss, however, has demonstrated that there are several flaws in Holt's methodology, and adopts a similar but more accurate approach based on the rolls for 1180, 1195 and 1198. A comparison between the bailiwicks accounting in 1180 and 1203 would give John an annual average revenue in the region of 26,000 li.ang.,[20] whereas 1195 would provide an average in the region of 45,000 li.ang. to 67,000 li.ang. It is his calculations for 1198, however, which are of particular relevance to this paper.

Moss suggests that total net revenue for 1198 was in the region of 99,000 li.ang., thereby excluding drafts from England, withdrawals from deposit and accounts of revenue from previous years. A total of 1,270 li.ang. received from

[15] Exchange rate used 1:1.46; for discussion see *ibid.* 95 n. 20.
[16] Baldwin, *Government*, 153–154; 502 n. 86.
[17] *Ibid.* 165; 507 n. 152.
[18] *Ibid.* 169.
[19] Holt, 'Loss of Normandy and Royal Finance', 96.
[20] See V.D. Moss's article in this volume.

Evreux, however, also needs to be removed from the 1198 roll before a figure for 1203 can be estimated, as the territory was surrendered to the Capetians in 1200 and revenue subsequently appears in the French account for 1202/3. For the purpose of this calculation, total revenue in 1198 amounted to approximately 97,730 li.ang. Using Moss' comparative approach on the bailiwicks that appear in the rolls for both 1198 and 1203, a yield ratio of 45% is reached as opposed to Holt's figure of 38%. If this is applied to the revised 1198 total, John's estimated average annual revenue from Normandy stood at approximately 44,000 li.ang. Overall, Moss suggests that a figure nearer 45,000 li.ang. should be used to represent John's potential revenue from Normandy if the data from the other rolls are taken into account, but he also notes that the decreasing fiscal performance of the Norman state since 1195 would tend to overstate the revenue yield by 1203.[21] It will be the lower figure of 44,000 li.ang., therefore, which will be used in this article to represent average annual net revenue.

But this total does not reflect the actual level of revenue John would have received on the eve of the war. Holt has identified 'extraordinary' revenue consisting of forced loans and tallages in the 1198 roll that amounted to 47,351 li.ang., which he argues should be removed before the yield ratio is applied to the 1198 total. Although forced loans and tallages had become a regular feature of Norman state finance by the late twelfth century,[22] there is no evidence from the accounts in the 1202/3 roll to suggest that John adopted similar measures before the conflict began. Consequently, the 1198 figure should also be amended to solely reflect the level of 'ordinary' revenue, and we arrive at a new total of approximately 50,400 li.ang. If the 45% ratio is applied, then John's estimated annual revenue is reduced to 22,680 li.ang., and will be used to represent his net disposable revenue for the 1202/3 campaign.

English Revenue 1202/3

The majority of John's revenue from England at this time can be found recorded in the 1202/3 pipe roll.[23] The net total is £23,391, consisting of £20,931 receipts and £2,461 expenditure. Holt discounts English expenditure from the equation on the grounds that it exclusively related to domestic affairs,[24] and a similar approach has been adopted here. Holt, however, also removes a large proportion of John's receipts, claiming that there is no documentary evidence that they were ever transferred to the war zone. If we are to build up a consistent picture of potential war revenue for both sides, any

---

[21] See V.D. Moss's article in this volume.

[22] V.D. Moss, 'Normandy and England in 1180: The Pipe Roll Evidence', in *England and Normandy in the Middle Ages*, ed. D. Bates and A. Curry, London 1994, 185–195; also V.D. Moss 'The Norman Fiscal Revolution 1191–1198', in *Crises, Revolutions and Self Sustained Growth: Essays in European Fiscal History 1130–1830*, ed. W.M. Ormrod, R. Bonney and M. Bonney, Stamford 1999, 41–61.

[23] *PR 5 John.*

[24] Holt, 'Loss of Normandy and Royal Finance', 97.

attempt to minimise John's disposable revenue from England cannot be justified unless a similar effort is made to analyse the way in which Philip utilised his resources in preparation for war. In 1203 John possessed cash receipts from England totalling £20,931, and it is therefore this figure that will be used to calculate potential revenue that was available for the campaign. The way in which this revenue was deployed will be discussed later, once the actual totals are calculated, and it is then that Holt's figures for moneys transported to Normandy from England will become relevant.

There are also two miscellaneous sources of revenue which need to be assessed. Firstly, a shipment of Irish treasure totalling £1,500 was received by the Norman Treasury at Caen on 18 October 1203, with an acknowledgement recorded in the English liberate roll.[25] Although there is no way of determining whether or not such payments from Ireland were made on a regular basis, the fact remains that this amount should be included in the calculations for 1202/3 as a source of extraordinary revenue. Secondly, an attempt must be made to estimate the contribution of the Seventh of 1203 to campaign funds. This is a difficult task, given the absence of any audit record for the collected receipts, or indeed the survival of a cumulative total for the tax. The lack of fines for evasion of payment in various records, in particular the pipe rolls, have led Holt to believe that the final yield was low. He estimates that approximately £7,000 from the proceeds of this tax were transported to Normandy,[26] and although the overall figure in England was probably higher, the lack of evidence for further receipts means that Holt's total will be used for the calculation. The inclusion of these extraordinary revenues gives John a war revenue from England and Ireland totalling £29,431, which equates to 117,723 li.ang.[27]

Balance Sheet 1202/3: Potential Revenue

Having determined the revenue totals, estimated and actual, for France, Normandy and England in 1202/3, it is now possible to compare the relative resources of the Angevins and Capetians on the eve of the war. Two analytical techniques will be employed for this purpose. The first approach is to present various revenue totals for both sides in Tables 1–3, all of which are expressed in li.ang. The relative disposable war revenues for each side are contained in Table 1, representing the realistic level of revenue that could be deployed in the war zone in 1202/3. If we take Holt's figure of 147,288 li.ang., John's revenue total of 140,403 li.ang. amounted to 95% of Philip's resources, whereas Baldwin's figure of 175,956 li.ang. reduces this ratio to only 80%. Alternatively, figures

---

[25] *Rot. de Lib.*, 70.

[26] Holt, 'Loss of Normandy and Royal Finance', 102–4.

[27] Exchange rate used 1:4, as is clear in the Norman pipe rolls; for example *Rot. Norm.*, 302, in the account of Geoffrey de Val-Richer 6859 marks 2 s. 3½ d. sterling is converted to 18,291 li. 2 s. 6 d. ang.

for ordinary net revenue in Table 2 represent the average level of annual income each monarch could reasonably expect to enjoy during the years that immediately preceded the conflict and excludes the estimated yield of the Seventh from England, the Irish treasures, and the receipts from the serjeants' levy from France. This method of analysis demonstrates that Angevin revenue would have stood at either 86% or 82% of the Capetian position, depending on whether Holt or Baldwin's figures are used. At face value it would therefore appear that the resources of the Capetians in the 1202/3 financial year were indeed superior to those of the Angevins. It would, however, also seem that the Capetian advantage was not as sizeable as some historians have previously claimed.[28]

Another approach swings the balance still further in John's direction. It is possible to analyse the level of 'ordinary' disposable revenue available to each side by excluding expenditure from England and France and focusing solely on ordinary net receipts as defined earlier. The figures in Table 3 show that John would have collected 106,464 li.ang.; this compares to Holt's revised total of 107,328 li.ang., which brings the ratio to 99%, and Baldwin's figure of 112,369 li.ang., which equates to 95%. No matter which set of data is used, it is difficult to describe Philip's revenue as having 'outstripped' John's on the eve of the war. This argument is further underlined by the fact that estimates for the Norman contribution in 1203 downplay the amount of revenue collected in the duchy, relying on the 45% yield ratio, and that the full yield of the Seventh from England is not known. Consequently the relative resources of the two monarchs are likely to have been even more closely matched.

Balance Sheet 1202/3: Potential Military Capacity

This method of comparison, however, fails to consider the varying military costs facing each side. A second analytical approach is required, and the survival of data for soldiers' pay in these financial records enables us to express revenue in terms of potential military capacity.[29] This is achieved by calculating the maximum number of troops each side could hire with their disposable war revenue, in effect incorporating an inflationary element into the equation. Care needs to be taken when adopting this approach, as only a proportion of disposable war revenue would actually be utilised for troop hire. Other uses of this revenue would have included 'bribes' to cement or undermine alliances with neighbouring dukes, counts or princes, which varied according to necessity or alignment. Similarly, further research is needed into the deployment of troops in castle garrisons throughout Normandy during this period, in particular the levels of mercenaries employed and the impact of feudal hosts in the

---

[28] Holt, 'Loss of Normandy and Royal Finance', 98.
[29] A similar technique was employed in W.M. Ormrod's 'State Finance in Thirteenth Century England', in *Thirteenth Century England V*, ed. P.R. Coss and S.D. Lloyd, Woodbridge 1995, 141–164, and has been adapted for the purpose of this paper.

compositions of the respective forces.[30] Consequently, the figures presented below are not intended to accurately reflect military expenditure during the campaign, but instead are used to highlight the fact that revenue totals alone are not sufficient to settle the debate one way or the other.

Only wages for soldiers hired in Normandy and France are considered for this exercise, as they provide a realistic reflection of where the bulk of troops were enlisted, and thus the reduced cost to John of importing English troops is largely overlooked. Nevertheless, it is still clear from the data in Table 4 that John would have enjoyed a financial advantage over Philip when raising an army. For example, at face value the daily cost of hiring one knight was identical, at 72 den.ang.[31] and 72 den.par.,[32] but when the exchange rate is taken into consideration the cost of a Norman knight in real terms was only two-thirds the price of a French knight. This ratio also holds true for foot serjeants at 8 den.ang.[33] and 8 den.par.,[34] but French mounted serjeants were more expensive at face value as well as in real terms, costing 36 den.par.[35] as opposed to 24 den.ang.[36] per day. Consequently, the conversion of revenue into military units tips the balance of power in John's favour.

Table 5 demonstrates that Holt's total for French disposable war revenue leaves Philip with the capacity to purchase less than three-quarters as many knights and foot serjeants as John, and under half as many mounted serjeants. If Baldwin's figures are used, the picture is more encouraging for Philip, but parity between the sides is still not attained – the Capetians could purchase 86% as many knights and foot serjeants as the Angevins, and 57% as many mounted serjeants. This line of argument can be taken further. Baldwin has estimated that the size of Philip's 'permanent' army on the Norman marches was based on a force that contained 257 knights, 1,608 foot serjeants and 245 mounted serjeants – a total of 2,110 troops altogether.[37] To keep an army of this size in the field would have cost Philip over 167 li.par. per day, or 244 li.ang., compared to 155 li.ang. for John (Table 6). Consequently, if he used the entire disposable war revenue for this purpose, Philip could afford to pay these troops for either 602 days (Holt) or 721 days (Baldwin). These figures compare unfavourably with John's potential length of service of 905 days, and equate to 67% and 80% of John's total respectively.

---

[30] I am grateful to the late T.K. Keefe for access to data on castle garrisons in the twelfth and thirteenth centuries, and on military wages. Further data can be found in 'Compte general des revenues du roy pendant l'anée 1202', in Edouard Audouin, *Essai sur l'armée royal au temps de Philippe Auguste*, Paris 1913, 42.

[31] *Rot. Norm.*, 513, 547, 548.

[32] Baldwin, *Government*, 169.

[33] *Rot. Norm.*, 547, 548.

[34] Baldwin, *Government*, 169.

[35] *Ibid.* 169.

[36] *Rot. Norm.*, 547, 548.

[37] Baldwin, *Government*, 168.

Actual Deployment of Revenue in the War Zone

This second method of analysis therefore confirms the suspicion that Capetian revenues had not outstripped those of the Angevins by 1202/3. The figures portrayed above demonstrate that although Philip may have enjoyed an advantage in the level of disposable revenue, he was faced with more expensive military costs. In real terms, it is likely that any financial superiority he might have enjoyed would have been negated. The causes for the loss of Normandy in 1204 must therefore be sought elsewhere, and the logical place to begin is by analysing the way in which potential disposable war revenue was actually utilised in the campaign. This is where Holt's figures for English funds sent abroad for the defence of Normandy become important. However, to maintain a fair comparison between Angevin and Capetian resources, French revenue must be subject to similar analysis. Accordingly, Baldwin has provided data for the level of revenue deployed in the war zone during the 1202/3 financial year, which is summarised in Table 7.[38]

It would appear that Philip devoted 83,031 li.par. (121,225 li.ang.) to the war effort in the marches during 1202/3, or 69% of his disposable war revenue. Of this, 17,100 li.par. (24,966 li.ang.) was legitimate military 'expenditure' for the campaign, whilst a further 8,671 li.par. (12,660 li.ang.) were 'receipts' collected by the march treasurers. The balance of 57,260 li.par. (83,600 li.ang.) consisted of Treasury drafts, or to use Holt's terminology, 'withdrawals'. Although these have been excluded from previous calculations of disposable war revenue on the basis that they did not constitute a 'new' resource derived in the 1202/3 financial year, the figure provides an indication of the reserves Philip was prepared to deploy in the campaign. If such a commitment had been made from the remaining new revenue collected in 1202/3, thus excluding the military expenditure and march receipts which we have just accounted for, Philip would have used 55% of the 103,418 li.par (150,990 li.ang.) collected from the *prevots, baillis* and the extraordinary *prisee*. However, Baldwin also notes that wages paid to soldiers in the marches during this period totalled 27,370 li.par. (39,960 li.ang.), which almost exactly matches the 26,453 li.par. (38,621 li.ang.) raised by the *prisee*.[39] In effect, these sums cancel each other out, as the proceeds were specifically earmarked for hiring troops, and can also be removed from the equation. The remaining withdrawals deployed by Philip would, therefore, have accounted for only 39% of the 'ordinary' receipts from the *prevots* and *baillis* collected in 1202/3.

In contrast, Holt calculates that John diverted £18,534 (74,136 li.ang.) from English revenue to the defence of Normandy in 1202/3.[40] If estimated funds derived from Normandy itself (22,680 li.ang.) are added to these drafts, John's actual resources in the war zone would have amounted to 96,816 li.ang., or 69%

---

[38] *Ibid.* 169.
[39] *Ibid.* 173.
[40] Holt, 'Loss of Normandy and Royal Finance', 97.

of his entire disposable war revenue. Nevertheless, despite utilising over two-thirds of total funds raised for the campaign, John's resources equated to only 80% of those deployed by Philip. Furthermore, the French total consisted mainly of cash drafted from funds held in reserve, and as we have seen Philip had sufficient new receipts to cover a campaign of this size. The Angevins, however, retained a slight advantage in the war zone if the revenue totals are expressed in military terms, although the gap between the sides is somewhat smaller. John could maintain an army of 2,110 troops, as defined earlier, for 624 days, whereas Philip could pay them for only 496. Holt's arguments concerning disposable income in the war zone would therefore seem to have some validity. Although Philip's superiority was not as decisive as had previously been thought, it would appear that a greater strain was indeed being placed on Angevin resources than on those of the Capetians. This is highlighted by the fact that Philip was able to use reserves built up in previous years which allowed current receipts to accumulate as surpluses, whereas John was struggling to raise sufficient new revenue to match Philip's resources in the combat zone. Baldwin, amongst others, has outlined the advances in Capetian state finance under Philip.[41] However, a further assessment based on the English and Norman records should be made before we can fully explain why the Angevins fought for their inheritance at a disadvantage.

Richard I and John: a Brief Comparison

A comparison of John and Richard's ordinary and extraordinary revenue, derived from the English and Norman pipe rolls for 1195, 1198 and 1203, is presented in Table 8. The criteria outlined earlier for totalling the rolls is applied here, and accordingly revenue earmarked for Richard's ransom or collected in previous financial years for a specific purpose has been discounted. English receipts in 1195 amounted to £23,029, or 92,117 li.ang.; to this can be added approximately 42,000 li.ang. from the Norman roll, making a grand net total of 134,117 li.ang. In 1198, English receipts were virtually identical to those in 1195, namely £23,024 or 92,097 li.ang., but as we have already seen the Norman total is complicated by the extraordinary revenue from the forced loans and tallages. The overall net total for the roll is 99,000 li.ang., but if Holt's figure of 47,350 li.ang. is removed, the revised total of 51,650 li.ang. can be combined with the revenue from England to give an overall net total of 143,747 li.ang. John's resources from Normandy are presented in the two ways as defined earlier, namely in terms of his potential annual revenue for the period 1199–1202, and also his estimated actual revenue for 1203.

Whichever way the data for these two sample years is viewed, it is clear that Richard enjoyed some form of financial superiority over his brother, although the scale is open to interpretation. The most relevant set of data is the comparison between Richard's position in 1198 and John's alternative figures. If

[41] Baldwin, *Government*, 141–152.

ordinary revenue is considered, then John was able to attain relative parity at 89% of Richard's total. However, it is clear that Richard was able to mobilise far larger sums of money than John if his 'extraordinary' funds are added, reducing the ratio to 67%. These ratios drop even further if John's actual revenue for 1203 is used in place of his potential average. The fact that John's revenue for 1199–1202 was based on a yield ratio of 45% of Richard's revenue for 1198 should not be overlooked, nor that extraordinary revenue from Ireland and the yield of the Seventh from England in 1203 are also excluded from the calculations. John's relatively poor fiscal performance needs to be examined in more detail, and an explanation can be found in the legacy bequeathed by his brother in 1199.

Richard had used Normandy to raise vast sums over a short period of time for purposes other than its defence, such as the crusade and his subsequent ransom; indeed, in 1195 16,000 li.ang. was paid to German envoys for this very reason.[42] Much of the revenue that was devoted to the defence of Normandy under Richard had been expended in improving existing fortifications and constructing new ones, such as Château-Gaillard. This policy had an impoverishing effect on the duchy,[43] leaving reserves low and making it harder to derive new revenue. Although this expenditure provided John with a series of strategically placed defences to repel potential French invasion, he was faced with the problem of providing the necessary finances to man them; for example, Powicke has calculated that the cost of maintaining a permanent garrison in all strongholds exceeded the fixed farms of the Norman bailiwicks.[44] These problems also faced Richard, but the use of English treasure and loans from Jewish financiers suggests that the duchy's resources were already insufficient for his needs. This picture of impending financial disaster is confirmed by a closer examination of John's revenue from England. It would appear that the traditional backbone of state finance, the county farm, had also been dramatically eroded in Richard's lifetime, in particular between 1190 and 1191, a policy that was in direct contrast to the achievements of Henry II in rebuilding revenue from this source after the civil wars of Stephen's reign. Although further research into this subject is required, it would appear that many of John's financial problems were indeed of Richard's making.

The Campaign of 1214

Having examined the comparative finances of John and Philip Augustus for 1202/3 in some detail, the next stage is to analyse the financial background to John's campaign of re-conquest, and to assess the impact of the extra revenue from the newly captured territories on Capetian finance. This task is complicated by the fact that there is even less surviving documentary evidence than for

---

[42] Powicke, *Loss of Normandy*, 233.
[43] *Ibid.* 232–234.
[44] *Ibid.* 234.

1202/3, making it extremely difficult to present accurate totals for the resources possessed by John and Philip in 1214. The calculations that follow are based on known data from England between 1210 and 1214, and estimated revenue totals for France and Normandy derived from the 1202/3 accounts. Although it is possible to identify expenditure related to the campaign from the surviving English records, no comparative data exists from the Capetian lands, and so the analysis will be restricted solely to disposable war revenue as defined earlier.

It is clear from Table 9 that John was generating an enormous amount of revenue from England between 1210 and 1214.[45] Audited Exchequer receipts, recorded in the surviving pipe rolls, amounted to £144,219 or 576,876 li.ang., as cash from the counties was swelled by the exploitation of Church resources. In addition, payments to other institutions, such as deposits in the castle treasuries or the king's Chamber, produced a further £31,116 (124,464 li.ang.), making a grand total of £175,335 (701,340 li.ang.). This is an enormous amount of money, and probably represents the greatest level of exploitation of English resources since the Conquest.[46] This does not even include sums from 1213, as the pipe roll is missing. One method of estimating the revenue from this year is to calculate the average annual level of 'ordinary' receipts between 1207 and 1212, the period that best reflects John's attempts to raise campaign funds. The yield of the 1207 Thirteenth has been excluded on the grounds that it represents an extraordinary levy, and only receipts from the counties have been considered in order to remove any distortions produced by Interdict revenues.[47] Accordingly, a total for 1213 of £30,173, or 120,692 li.ang., has been suggested, although this might be a little high due to the potential impact of concessions granted to the northern barons in this year.[48]

To this data can be added £46,526 (186,104 li.ang.) for the unaudited Church revenues paid directly into the chamber,[49] and it is important to include estimates for the yield of the Jewish tallage of 1210, and the contribution from miscellaneous religious sources in the same year. We know that the tallage was assessed at 66,000 marks (£44,000),[50] but no trace of the overall yield has been left in the records. Generally, Jewish tallages were well paid, and it will be assumed for the purpose of this survey that half of the sum demanded (£22,000, or 88,000 li.ang.) was paid between 1210 and 1214, either directly by the Jews or indirectly through unrecorded *debita Judeorum* that fell into the crown's hands.[51] Similarly, chronicle sources indicate that in 1210 John was demanding sums of money from various religious orders. The only cumulative total that can be found, £100,000, is, alas, probably an exaggeration; indeed, three separate figures for the Cistercian contribution are recorded – £18,000, £22,000

---

[45] Barratt, 'Revenue', 839–841.
[46] *Ibid.* 855.
[47] For the relevant pipe roll totals, see *ibid.* 841.
[48] *Ibid.* 851.
[49] S.K. Mitchell, *Studies in Taxation under John and Henry III*, New Haven 1914, 106–108.
[50] *Ibid.* 105.
[51] Holt, *Northerners*, 167–168.

and £40,000. Since there is no corroborating evidence for the overall amount, it is difficult to justify its inclusion in the calculations. Nevertheless, it is highly likely that funds were collected, and some provision must be made. Accordingly, the lowest recorded Cistercian total (£18,000, or 72,000 li.ang.) will therefore be used, thus erring on the side of caution.[52]

If these estimates for extraordinary revenue are added to the recorded sums, John's receipts from England for the period 1210–1214 were in the region of £292,034, or 1,168,137 li.ang., and can be used to represent potential disposable war revenue. This figure might seem unacceptably high, but material analysed by Jolliffe concerning the movement of treasure prior to the campaign would appear to support the argument that vast sums were being gathered in preparation for war.[53] For example, £80,000 was moved from Nottingham to Bristol in the autumn of 1213,[54] and Jolliffe has estimated that John's war chest for 1214 was in the region of 200,000 marks, or £133,333.[55] This total equates with 533,333 li.ang., or 46% of overall estimated receipts.

These two totals, 1,168,137 li.ang. and 533,333 li.ang., will be used as baseline figures for John's potential and actual disposable war revenue respectively. Similarly, Philip's resources for the same period need to be estimated. We have already provided rudimentary figures for annual French disposable revenue from the 1202/3 account, which vary according to whether Holt's or Baldwin's calculations are employed, and we have a similar estimate for potential Norman revenue between 1199 and 1202 based on the 45% yield ratio from 1198; the total used for 1214 has been raised to 44,550 li.ang. to take account of the revenue previously excluded from Evreux. Similarly, estimates for drafts from areas traditionally controlled by the Angevins, but had fallen into Philip's hands after 1204, can be produced from the surviving fragments of French accounts for 1221 and 1238. If these sources are combined, as in Table 9, it is possible to reach an amount that roughly equates to the level of ordinary annual war revenue, as defined earlier, which Philip might have received from his many possessions. Holt's figure for French revenue produces an annual figure of 162,098 li.ang., whereas Baldwin's calculations produce a total of 179,799 li.ang. If these sums are multiplied by five, we reach a figure for Philip's potential disposable war revenue accumulated between 1210 and 1214. Consequently, Holt's figures produce a grand total of 810,490 li.ang., which contrasts with Baldwin's total of 835,695 li.ang.

These are the baseline figures that will be used for comparison with those of King John. A further scenario is provided, however, which includes French receipts from the 1203 serjeants levy and extraordinary Norman revenue from 1198, such as the fixed loans and tallages. The intention is to replicate the impact of emergency measures previously imposed in these territories when

---

[52] Barratt, 'Revenue', 838.
[53] For discussion, see Jolliffe, 'Chamber', 117–142.
[54] Jolliffe, 'Castle Treasuries', 134.
[55] *Ibid.* 135.

invasion or war was imminent. Accordingly, as they were one-off measures, the yield for a single year has been added into the calculations, either 39,960 li.ang. (Holt) or 38,621 li.ang. (Baldwin) for France, and 47,350 li.ang. for Normandy. This produces alternative revenue totals for Philip of 897,800 li.ang. (Holt) or 921,666 li.ang. (Baldwin).

Given the uncertainty surrounding these calculations, it is difficult to draw concrete conclusions from the comparisons made at the foot of Table 9, which suggest that John collected more revenue than Philip between 1210 and 1214 in his attempts to mount a campaign of reconquest. What is apparent is that John was forced to rely exclusively on his English resources, which were quite clearly becoming strained by 1214,[56] whereas the estimates for Philip's annual revenue have been based on accounts that were at least ten years old; if the re-organisation of Capetian state finance prior to 1202/3 had continued after the capture of Normandy, it is likely that Philip's total disposable revenue between 1210 and 1214 would have been even higher. Furthermore, the estimates were based on ordinary revenue sources; the addition of potential extraordinary revenue from France and Normandy in the second scenario moves the two sides even closer together.

If the figures are analysed according to potential military capacity as defined earlier, the gap is reduced still further. A lack of raw data hinders this approach, as little information for soldiers' wages in 1214 survives. Consequently, a series of estimates is presented in Table 10; John's costs are derived from a variety of documentary sources,[57] but two alternatives are given for Philip depending on where he actually hired his men, France or Normandy, and both are based on the 1203 data, as no documentary evidence survives for either territory in this period. It is probable that Philip would have been able to hire troops at the rela-tively cheaper Norman price. If this assumption is correct then it is uncertain from the data presented in Table 10 which side enjoyed lower military costs. Baldwin has provided new estimates for the composition of Philip's army at Bouvines in 1214, suggesting that he was able to mobilise 1,300 knights and between 4,000 and 6,000 foot serjeants for the battle.[58] Using the wages por-trayed in Table 10, it is possible to calculate the daily cost of keeping a force of this size in the field. If potential disposable war revenue is divided by the figures for daily cost, we can express the maximum possible length of service for the army, and from the data in Table 11 it would appear that in terms of military purchasing power the two sides were approaching parity.

These estimates of the resources available to John and Philip Augustus do not, however, take into account the actual level of revenue used in the 1214 campaign. Yet again there is not enough surviving data to permit an analysis of

---

[56] Barratt, 'Revenue', 843.

[57] Again, I am grateful to the late T.K. Keefe for providing references for soldiers wages for John's reign, including *Rott. Litt. Claus.* i , 53a, 188b, 195b, 214b, 243b; *PR 14 John*, 47–48; *PR 16 John*, 109, 146; *Book of Fees*, 145, 452.

[58] Baldwin, *Government*, 218. For the purpose of this survey, an average figure of 5000 foot serjeants will be used.

the funds actually utilised in the war zone. Jolliffe's estimate for John's war chest of 533,333 li.ang. can, though, be used as a yardstick for assessing the financial strain imposed on each sides during the war (Table 12). For example, John's war chest would have absorbed 46% of potential disposable war revenue between 1210 and 1214. To commit a similar sum, Philip would have needed to devote a larger proportion of the estimated receipts collected between 1210 and 1214, although no allowance has been made for potential drafts of reserves held in the French Treasury.

Overall, it is difficult to draw any concrete conclusions from these hypothetical calculations, as there are just too many unknown factors that ought to be considered. The real worth of this survey is to demonstrate that John was fully committed to obtaining a decisive military victory. If successful, his own ordinary revenue would have reverted to its former level once the resources of Normandy and the other lost territories had been returned to his control, whilst Philip's new found advantage would have been simultaneously reversed. It also apparent that despite accumulating enormous reserves of cash, and transferring a sizeable proportion overseas for the campaign, John failed to open up a decisive financial advantage over his rival. Clearly, the loss of John's continental possessions in 1204 had tipped the financial scales firmly in favour of the Capetians, and he could not hope to maintain the level of English revenue seen between 1210 and 1214 for anything other than the short term. The defeat of John's allies at Bouvines was therefore a disaster in military, political and financial terms, and the implications can be examined in the years following his death in 1216.

The Legacy of Failure

The campaign of 1214, therefore, marked the second major turning-point of John's reign. Not only were the reverses of 1204 confirmed, but the Angevin–Capetian rivalry was also imported across the Channel when Philip's heir, Louis, launched an invasion of England when offered the crown by the rebellious barons. Although there were sufficient reserves left in the castle treasuries to mount a counter-offensive against the confederates,[59] John's sudden death in 1216 left his infant son, Henry III, with a precarious financial legacy. The English pipe rolls after 1218 depict a process of slow recovery from an initial position of extreme poverty, brought about by the exertions of winning the civil war, and paying Prince Louis's indemnity as part of the peace settlement.[60] Indeed, net total revenue only rose above £20,000 for the first time in 1224.[61] Furthermore, the surviving receipt rolls for the period 1220–1224 demonstrate

---

[59] For example, 10,000 marks were moved from Corfe in December 1215, and 20,000 marks were deposited at Winchester in the spring of 1216; see Jolliffe, 'Castle Treasuries', 137.

[60] A payment of £200 is recorded in the Exchequer receipt roll PRO E401/3B rot. 1d mem. 1.

[61] Figures for English royal revenue are provided in N. Barratt, 'English Royal Revenue in the Early Thirteenth Century and its Wider Context, 1130–1330', in *Crises, Revolutions and Self-Sustained Growth*, forthcoming.

that new funds brought in during each Exchequer term were barely sufficient to cover day-to-day administrative costs. For example, the Treasury realised surpluses of only £20, £688 and £200 during the terms for Easter 1220, 1222 and 1223 respectively,[62] whilst losses of £1,244 and £1,917 were recorded for Easter 1221 and Michaelmas 1224.[63] Although the rolls are incomplete in places, and there is no coverage of an entire financial year, it is nevertheless clear that in the aftermath of John's wars, English state finance was in no shape to fund an aggressive campaign of re-conquest.

This picture contrasts sharply with Capetian finances, as Table 13 demonstrates. The surviving fragment of the budget for 1221 (All Saints Term) suggests that Philip enjoyed an income of 73,657 li.par. per term, or an estimated net annual revenue of 194,898 li.par.[64] This equates with 284,551 li.ang. – nearly six times Henry III's net annual revenue for the same financial year (£13,184, or 52,736 li.ang.).[65] Royal disbursements from these receipts are also recorded in the account, and Baldwin uses them to calculate that Philip realised a surplus of 25,210 li.par. (36,807 li.ang.) per term, which roughly equated with 66,706 li.par. (97,391 li.ang.) for the year. Furthermore, the French Treasury already held reserves of 131,826 li.par. (192,556 li.ang.), a sum that was more than sufficient to maintain the territorial conquests of 1204.[66]

The capture of Normandy would therefore appear to be the decisive moment in the struggle between the Angevins and the Capetians. Before 1204, John's finances were already lagging behind Richard's, and he faced the added expense of manning the strategic defences constructed by his predecessor. Although, Capetian ordinary revenue had not yet outstripped that of the Angevins, military costs were subject to inflationary trends that worked in John's favour. The geographical spread of John's territories, however, meant that he could not draw on the combined total of his ordinary revenue for the defence of Normandy, whereas Philip was able to utilise his resources more effectively in the war zone. Once Normandy had been lost, it is clear that Angevin revenue was no match for the increased finances of the Capetians, which absorbed the new resources into the existing financial structure. The strain placed on England by the rapid accumulation of disposable income between 1210 and 1214 is clear in both the outburst of political protest after John's return from the continent, and the comparative poverty of the English crown during the minority of Henry III. English ambition after 1216 can be summed up by the 1225 campaign, which was a defensive expedition aimed at preserving the status quo in Gascony, rather than an attempt to re-conquer the possessions over which Henry III still claimed nominal lordship. Furthermore, as regular finance was insufficient to meet even this modest aim, extraordinary

---

[62] PRO, E401 (receipt rolls)/3B, 5 and 6 respectively. Balances produced by subtracting issues from recorded receipts.
[63] PRO, E401/4 and 7 respectively.
[64] Baldwin, *Government*, 352; 567 n.91.
[65] As recorded in *PR 6 Henry III*, and PRO, E401/5.
[66] Baldwin, *Government*, 352.

taxation in the shape of the Fifteenth had to be sought. Opposition to the levy was only overcome by the re-issue of the charters, demonstrating the revised priorities of the king and his baronage. The demise of the Anglo-Norman realm had thus been confirmed.

Table 1. Comparison of Revenue 1202–3: Disposable War Revenue
(all totals in livres angevin)

Capetian Revenue

	Holt	Baldwin
France	**147,288**	**175,956**

Angevin Revenue

England	117,723
Normandy	22,680
Total	**140,403**

Angevin Revenue Expressed as a Percentage of Capetian Revenue

	Holt	Baldwin
Ratio	**95%**	**80%**

Notes   France: Holt - gross receipts
France: Baldwin - net receipts, plus identifiable war expenditure
Normandy: estimated total, based on 45% of 1198 ordinary net total
England: net receipts, plus estimated yield of Seventh and recorded Irish treasure

Table 2. Comparison of Revenue 1202–3: Ordinary Net Revenue
(all totals in livres angevin)

Capetian Revenue

	Holt	Baldwin
France	**159,990**	**168,099**

Angevin Revenue

England	93,565
Normandy	44,000
Total	**137,565**

Angevin Revenue Expressed as a Percentage of Capetian Revenue

	Holt	Baldwin
Ratio	**86%**	**82%**

Notes   France: Holt - net total excluding serjeants' levy
France: Baldwin - net total excluding serjeants' levy
Normandy: estimated total, based on 45% of 1198 net total
England: net total excluding estimated yield of Seventh and recorded Irish treasure

Table 3. Comparison of Revenue 1202–3: Ordinary Disposable Revenue
(all totals in livres angevin)

Capetian Revenue

	Holt	Baldwin
France	**107,328**	**112,369**

Angevin Revenue

England	83,724
Normandy	22,680
Total	**106,404**

Angevin Revenue Expressed as a Percentage of Capetian Revenue

	Holt	Baldwin
Ratio	**99%**	**95%**

Notes   France: Holt - gross ordinary receipts
France: Baldwin - net ordinary receipts
Normandy: estimated total, based on 45% of 1198 net ordinary total
England: net ordinary receipts excluding estimated yield of Seventh and recorded Irish treasure

Table 4. Military Wages 1202–3
(all totals in respective currencies)

Daily rate of pay per individual

	Knight	Foot Serjeant	Horse Serjeant	
England	12	2	4	den. sterling
France	72	8	36	den. parisis
Normandy	72	8	24	den. angevin

Notes England: wages taken from 1202-3 pipe roll data
France: wages recorded by Baldwin from 1202-3 account
Normandy: wages taken from 1202-3 pipe roll data

Table 5. Expression of Revenue as Potential Military Capacity
(all revenue totals in livres angevin)

Disposable War Revenue

		Revenue	Total Number of Knights	Total Number of Foot Serjeants	Total Number of Horse Serjeants
Capetian	Holt	147,288	336,273	3,026,460	672,547
	Baldwin	175,956	401,726	3,615,534	803,452
Angevin		140,403	468,012	4,212,106	1,404,035

Capetian Military Capacity Expressed as a Percentage of Angevin Military Capacity

	Holt	72%	72%	48%
	Baldwin	86%	86%	57%

Notes All revenue totals based on disposable war revenue, as defined in Table 1
Total number of soldiers produced by multiplying revenue by daily wages
Capetian wages based on French prices, as defined in Table 4
Angevin wages based on Norman prices, as defined in Table 4, to reflect where soldiers were hired

Table 6. Expression of Revenue as Potential Length of Service
(all revenue totals in livres angevin)

Composition of Army
(number of units)
Cost Per Day

		Angevin	Capetian
257	knights	77	113
1608	foot serjeants	54	78
245	horse serjeants	25	54
2110	soldiers	**155**	**244**

Potential Length in Field

		Disposable War Revenue	Army Cost (per day)	Potential Length of Service (days)
Capetian	Holt	147,288	244	**602**
	Baldwin	175,956	244	**721**
Angevin		140,403	155	**905**

Capetian Length of Service Expressed as Percentage of Angevin Length of Service

	Holt	Baldwin
Ratio	**67%**	**80%**

Notes Cost per day produced by multiplying number of military units by daily cost
Potential length of service produced by dividing disposable war revenue by total cost per day

Table 7. Analysis of Utilised Revenue in the War Zone
(all totals in livres angevin)

Philip's Utilised Revenue in the War Zone

1. Total Revenue Deployed	**121,225**
Disposable War Revenue	175,956
2. Revenue deployed as percentage of disposable war revenue	**69%**
Expenditure (accounted for in Tables 1-3)	24,966
March receipts (accounted for in Tables 1-3)	12,660
Balance - drafts from Treasury	**83,600**
Non-march receipts (accounted for in Tables 1-3)	150,990
Drafts as percentage of non-march receipts	**55%**

Soldiers wages paid from drafts	39,960	
Balance of Treausry drafts		43,640
Extraordinary levy raised to pay soldiers	38,621	
Balance of non-march receipts		112,369
3. Drafts as percentage of non-march receipts		**39%**

John's Utilised Revenue in the War Zone

Transfers from England	74,136
Estimated revenue from Normandy	22,680
1. Total Revenue Deployed	**96,816**
Disposable war revenue	140,403
English disposable war revenue	117,723
2. Revenue deployed as percentage of disposable war revenue	**69%**
3. English transfers as percentage of disposable war revenue	**53%**
English transfers as percentage of English disposable war revenue	**63%**

Angevin Revenue as Percentage of Capetian Revenue

Capetian Revenue	121,225
Angevin Revenue	96,816
Ratio	**80%**

Expression of Revenue as Potential Length of Service

	Revenue	Daily Cost	Length of Service
Capetian	121,225	244	496
Angevin	96,816	155	624
Ratio (Capetian to Angevin)			**79%**

<u>Notes</u> French data provided by Baldwin
Transfers from England provided by Holt
Length of service produced by dividing revenue total by daily cost
Data entries labelled 1-3 are comparable

Table 8. Comparison of Revenue: John and Richard I
(all totals in livres angevin)

1. *(a) John 1199-1202 (potential annual revenue)*

English net total receipts	83,723
Norman estimated potential revenue	44,000
Total disposable revenue	**127,723**

(b) John 1203 (actual revenue)

English net total receipts	83,723
Norman estimated actual revenue	22,680
Total disposable revenue	**106,403**

2. *Richard 1195*

English net total receipts	92,117
Norman net total revenue	42,000
Total disposable revenue	**134,117**

3. *(a) Richard 1198 (ordinary net revenue)*

English net total receipts	92,097
Norman net ordinary revenue	51,650
Total disposable revenue	**143,747**

(b) Richard 1198 (total net revenue)

English net total receipts	92,097
Norman net total revenue	99,000
Total disposable revenue	**191,097**

John's Revenue Expressed as a Percentage of Richard's

		1195	(a) 1198	(b) 1198
Ratio	John (a)	**95%**	**89%**	**67%**
	John (b)	**79%**	**74%**	**56%**

Notes Norman net total revenue 1203 based on 45% yield of 1198 net total revenue
Norman net ordinary revenue 1198 excludes 47,350 extraordinary taxation

Table 9. Revenue for the 1214 Campaign (1)
(all totals in livres angevin)

Total English Disposable Revenue 1210-1214

Audited exchequer cash	576,876
Audited non-exchequer cash	124,464
Un-audited Interdict revenue (chamber)	186,104
Estimated Jewish tallage (50% yield)	88,000
Estimated religious contribution	72,000

Estimated revenue 1213		
Total audited receipts 1207-1212	724,156	
Annual average		120,693
Total Disposable Revenue 1210-1214		**1,168,137**

Total French Disposable Revenue 1210-1214

	Holt	Baldwin
Scenario 1		
French disposable revenue 1202-3	107,328	112,369
Estimated Norman annual revenue 1199-1202 (includes revenue previously excluded from Evreux)	44,550	44,550
Estimated contribution of other Angevin lands	10,220	10,220
Estimated Annual Disposable Revenue	162,098	167,139
Total Disposable Revenue 1210-1214	**810,490**	**835,695**
Scenario 2		
Addition of 1202-3 French extraordinary revenue	39,960	38,621
Addition of 1198 Norman extraordinary revenue	47,350	47,350
Total Disposable Revenue 1210-1214	**897,800**	**921,666**

Capetian Revenue Expressed as a Percentage of Angevin Revenue

Scenario 1	Holt	**69%**
	Baldwin	**72%**
Scenario 2	Holt	**77%**
	Baldwin	**79%**

Notes English audited receipts taken from pipe rolls only.
Estimated contribution from other Angevin lands based on figures from Anjou, Poitou and Touraine from the surviving French accounts form 1221 and 1238.
Reference: Holt, 'Loss of Normandy and Royal Finance', p. 105.

Table 10. Estimated Military Wages 1214
(all totals in den. angevin)

Daily Rate of Pay Per Individual

		Knight	Foot Serjeant	Horse Serjeant	
Angevin	**1214 recorded English wages**	**64**	**12**	**20**	
Capetian	1203 recorded French wages	105	12	53	(i)
	1203 recorded Norman wages	**72**	**8**	**24**	(ii)

Composition of Army (number of units)		*Cost Per Day* (all totals in livres angevin)			
Unit	Number				
		Ang.		Cap (i)	**Cap (ii)**
Knight	1300	**347**		570	**390**
Foot Serj.	5000	**250**		243	**167**
Total Cost		**597**		813	**557**

Notes English 1214 wages provided by Keefe
No data survives for 1214 from France or Normandy
Composition of army provided by Baldwin

Table 11. Expression of Revenue as Potential Length of Service
(all revenue totals in livres angevin)

Scenario 1

			Revenue	Daily Cost	Length of Service
Angevin			1,168,137	**597**	**1,957**
Capetian	(ii)	Holt	810,490	**557**	**1,455**
	(ii)	Baldwin	835,695	**557**	**1,500**

Capetian Length of Service Epxressed as a Percentage of Angevin Length of Service

		Holt	Baldwin
Ratio	John	**74%**	**77%**

Scenario 2

			Revenue	Daily Cost	Length of Service
Angevin			1,168,137	**597**	**1,957**
Capetian	(ii)	Holt	897,800	**557**	**1,612**
	(ii)	Baldwin	921,666	**557**	**1,655**

Capetian Length of Service Epxressed as a Percentage of Angevin Length of Service

		Holt	Baldwin
Ratio	John	**82%**	**85%**

Notes Daily cost calculated in Table 10
Length of service produced by dividing revenue total by daily cost

Table 12. Disposable Revenue 1214
(all totals in livres angevin)

John's War Chest as a Percentage of Disposable Revenue

		Revenue	Ratio of war chest to total revenue
Estimated war chest		**533,333**	
Estimated Revenue 1210-1214		1,168,037	**46%**

Philip's Relative War Chest

		Revenue	Ratio of war chest to total revenue
(John's estimated war chest)		**533,333**	
Scenario 1 Estimated Revenue 1210-1214	Holt	810,490	**66%**
	Baldwin	835,695	**64%**
Scenario 2 Estimated Revenue 1210-1214	Holt	897,800	**59%**
	Baldwin	921,666	**58%**

Notes Data for John's war chest provided by Jolliffe
There is no similar way of calculating Philip's relative war chest for this period

Table 13. Comparison of Annual Revenue 1222
(all totals in livres angevin)

Total Net Revenue

Capetian	**284,551**
Angevin	**52,736**

Angevin Revenue Expressed as a Percentage of Capetian Revenue

Ratio	**19%**

Termly Balances

Capetian All Saints 1221	**36,807**
Angevin Easter 1222	**2,752**

Angevin Balance Expressed as a Percentage of Capetian Balance

Ratio	**7%**

Treasury Reserves

Capetian	**192,556**	
Angevin		**no data**

Notes Capetian total net revenue calculated from account for All Saints term 1221 (Baldwin)
Angevin total net revenue calculated from 1222 pipe roll and 1222 Easter receipt roll
Capetian termly balance calculated from account for All Saints term 1221 (Baldwin)
Angevin termly balance calculated from 1222 Easter receipt roll
Capetian Treasury reserves calculated from account for All Saints term 1221 (Baldwin)

The Norman Exchequer Rolls of King John

V. D. Moss

The outstanding feature of the Norman Exchequer rolls of King Richard was a massive increase in revenue (by 1198 three-and-a-half-fold that of 1180) based on the systematic extraction of wealth by generalised tallages and forced loans made against the towns and bailliages of Normandy, especially those of the central region of the duchy.[1] This was achieved with only a minute drop in the rate of collection. In 1180, revenue paid into the Exchequer or expended amounted to 63% of money rendered.[2] In 1198 this yield ratio had only declined to 60%.[3] A further significant feature of this transformation was the contribution of urban Normandy which (once again led by central Normandy) accounted for over a fifth of the revenue.[4]

For once, therefore, we must begin with what is not present on the 1202/3 Norman Exchequer roll. Only three tallages (excluding those levied against the Jews) were present on the surviving records of 1203: 511 li.ang. was levied from Caen, 'ad mittendum servientes ad sedem de Alenchon'; 44 li.ang. in the 'vicomte between the Risle and the Seine' for military service on the march; and 80 li.ang. from Coutances there was a return for an old tallage 'ad mittendum servientes in Andegaviam'.[5] These totals were pitifully small compared to what was levied in 1195 and 1198.[6] There is no evidence whatsoever for any urban tallage, or forced loans against either town or bailliage in the Norman Exchequer roll of 1203. It is reasonable to argue that this evidence signals the end of the highly successful fiscal system of the 1190s.[7] The entry from Coutances may be a trace of a more generalised tallage from a previous year. Even if this were so, it was set at a very low level and was not made against the towns.[8]

---

[1] V.D. Moss, 'The Norman Fiscal Revolution 1191–1198', in W.M Ormrod, R. Bonney and M. Bonney, ed., *Crises, Revolutions and Self-Sustained Growth: Essays in European Fiscal History 1130–1830*, Stamford 1999, 41–61.

[2] Moss, 'The Norman Fiscal Revolution 1191–1198', 41–61.

[3] Moss, 'The Norman Fiscal Revolution 1191–1198', 41–61.

[4] Moss, 'The Norman Fiscal Revolution 1191–1198', 41–61.

[5] *MRSN*, ii, 524, 562, 570.

[6] V.D. Moss, 'Normandy and the Angevin Empire: a Study of the Norman Exchequer Rolls 1180–1204', unpublished University of Wales PhD thesis, 1996, 71, 78, 81.

[7] Moss, 'Normandy and the Angevin Empire', 60–89.

[8] Moss, 'Normandy and the Angevin Empire', 90–99.

The returns of the 1203 presented no new types of revenue which could even marginally compensate for the decline of the sources found on the Norman accounts of King Richard. There were, however, some new developments. The sum owed for the 'prepositura' farm of Vire was followed on this roll by a total of 70 li.ang. demanded 'de acrescenti de eodem anno'.[9] The first charge of this 'increment above the farm' can be dated to the roll of 1199.[10] The charge remained unpaid but it represented a unique attempt to import an 'increment above the farm' into Normandy.[11] The first mention of the Seine Valley as a distinct and separate bailliage is found on an 'extractus memorandum' dating from the reign of King John.[12]

Lucien Musset has argued that later Angevin Normandy saw Englishmen for the first time making administrative careers in the duchy.[13] In fact this practice was not new. One of the very examples that he takes, that of Geoffrey de Ripon, who (by 1200) was mayor of Caen, was already a Norman bailiff in 1186.[14] Richard of Cardiff was a Norman bailiff in 1180.[15] As is well known, Richard of Illchester became the seneschal of Normandy in 1176.[16] In addition non-Normans such as Robert the Angevin were also making an administrative career in the duchy in the 1180s.[17] A quantitative distinction might be made. In addition to the archbishop and two mayors whom Musset notes, Peter Stoke held the farm between the Vire and the Seine in 1201 and more importantly was the bailiff of Pont-Audemer in 1202.[18] In 1203 John Marshall held the bailliage of Falaise and later Exmes.[19] The qualitative transformation in terms of Englishmen making careers in Normandy, therefore, took place in the 1170–80s.

[9] *MRSN*, ii, 531.
[10] The sum of the 'prepositura' farm of Vire was 180 li.ang.; combined with the increment above the farm this rose to 250 li.ang. per annum. Fixed deductions from the farm were worth 25 li.ang. per year. The debt for three and four years earlier of 450 li.ang. from the 'prepositura' farm of Vire must include the increment above the farm since the total can only be based upon a sum of 250 li.ang. per year minus 50 li.ang. of fixed deductions over the two years.
[11] Moss, 'Normandy and the Angevin Empire', 162, 168–71.
[12] H. Legras, 'Un fragment de role Normand inedit de Jean sans terre', *Bulletin de la societe des antiquaires* 29, 1913, 27–28. For the 'extractus memorandorum' in general see 'Miscellaneous Records of the Norman Exchequer', ed. S.R. Packard, *Smith College Studies in History* 12, 1926–27, *passim* and Moss, 'Normandy and the Angevin Empire', 104–7.
[13] L. Musset, 'Quelques problèmes posés par l'annexion de la Normandie au domaine royal français', in R.-H. Bautier, ed., *La France de Philippe-Auguste: le temps des mutations*, Paris 1982, 291–307.
[14] Moss, 'Normandy and the Angevin Empire', 114–26.
[15] *MRSN*, i, 22–24.
[16] Moss, 'Normandy and the Angevin Empire', 91–99.
[17] Powicke, *Loss of Normandy*, 75.
[18] Moss, 'Normandy and the Angevin Empire', 252–3.
[19] *Rot. Litt. Pat.*, 24, 28. Whether the nephew of William Marshall is best described as English or Anglo-Norman is itself a difficult issue.

The Rise of Debt and the Deceleration of Revenue Collection

A pronounced feature of the 1203 Norman pipe roll was the rise of debt.[20] In order to analysis this we must compare the distinct debts recorded against the different bailliages on the 1202/3 Norman Exchequer roll with that of 1198.[21] Unlike their English counterparts each Norman bailliage account ends with a list of debts dating back from previous years. The great advantage of utilising these as a measure is that for the most part it avoids the problem of the returns of the current year and lessens the distortion created by new proffers with small down payments, since debts from the previous years will have smaller outstanding sums owed from previously rendered proffers. In addition, the debts referring to previous years can be traced back to entries on previous rolls. It is thus possible to take the debts recorded in the 1198 roll and find out how much there was still outstanding in 1203. Importantly, this gives us a glimpse (at least) as to what happened *vis à vis* Norman finances between 1197 and 1202.

There are a number of difficulties. Sometimes debts from the previous pipe-roll year appeared in the main body of the bailliage account.[22] The debts of the Cotentin do not survive for the records of 1203 and likewise the debts for Gavray were not found on the 1198 account. This means that between these years only five bailliages can be compared. Much more serious is the issue of large debts found in 1198 and not in 1203. It is quite possible that many of them may have been pardoned rather than paid. Whether this pardoning represented a form of patronage and therefore at least arguably revenue or, on the contrary, was simply the writing off of old uncollected debts cannot be resolved. The broad value of this approach can, however, scarcely be doubted.

Table 1. Debts in li. ang.

Bailliage	1198	1203	Outstanding
Coutances	250	1310	150
Vire	60	8900	50
Roumois	5890	3140	830
Pont Aud	950	3350	340
Inter	1750	560	150
Totals	*8900*	*17260*	*1520*

The results of the comparison show that debt had almost doubled between 1197 and 1202. Moreover, most of this increase is to be explained by the creation of new debts. Old debts accounted for less than 10% of the total. Two out of the five bailliages, however, performed better in 1202/3 than in 1197/8. But the comparative totals for the 'vicomte between the Risle and the Seine' of

---

[20] See Table 3.
[21] See Table 3.
[22] Moss, 'Normandy and the Angevin Empire', 166–68.

1,750 li.ang. compared with 560 li.ang. may well be distorted. One debt of
1,400 li.ang. concerning Robert de Harcourt was responsible for the over-
whelming bulk of the 1198 figure.[23] It is quite possible that this render was
pardoned rather than paid between 1197 and 1203. Indeed, given that such large
totals were generally paid off gradually, its complete disappearance leads one
strongly to suspect this was the case.

The same point cannot be made about the decrease in old debt in the
Roumois account.[24] Such a performance must be balanced against a very low
fiscal return rendered in the current year.[25] Nevertheless, between 1197 and
1202 there was a remarkable recovery of debt. Over 5,000 li.ang. had been
eliminated since 1198.[26] Some of this may have been pardoned and some even
transferred to the separate, non-surviving, account of Rouen. But it is difficult,
given the sheer number of debts, to believe that this was the entire explanation.
New debts totalled the rather small sum (given the size of the bailliage) of just
over 2,300 li.ang. This is a success story which bucked the general fiscal trend
of the times.

The other three bailliages represent fiscal disaster. The best was Pont-Audemer
with only a threefold debt increase.[27] The new debts were of a heterogeneous
nature including returns concerning justice, payments for military service and
revenues from the forests. Revealingly they cannot be explained by the creation
of large proffers and slow repayment. Next to the debt of Richard fitz Landri,
the highest total owed from one account was 250 marks for the 'goodwill of the
king' and the confirmation of a charter of King Richard.[28] William Ferrant
owed 300 li.ang. for a forest fine but all the other debts concerned 100 li.ang. or
less.[29] The returns revealed a generalised decline in the successful collection of
revenue from 1197 to 1202 at the most routine levels of administration.

Coutances tells a similar story to that of Pont-Audemer but written in even
more dramatic terms.[30] Total debt had increased six-fold. There was only one
large render made between 1197 and 1202, which was owed by William de
Pirou.[31] It was of a 'remansione finis sui' type and was made for having the land
of William de Tracaceio. It was worth just over 430 li.ang. All the other debts
were 100 li.ang. or less. Over two thirds of the value of the debt accumulated
since 1197 thus consisted of a large number of small payments of a heterogeneous type. In this instance, a simple count of the number of debts provides

---

[23] *MRSN*, ii, 492.
[24] *MRSN*, ii, 549–51.
[25] See the discussion later in this paper.
[26] *MRSN*, ii, 418–21.
[27] *MRSN*, ii, 555–560. Lack of space prevents me from examining all the technical problems
concerning the inclusion of the debts of William fitz Landri and the count of Meulan: for a
more detailed discussion see Moss, 'Normandy and the Angevin Empire', 166–8.
[28] *MRSN*, ii, 556.
[29] *MRSN*, ii, 559.
[30] *MRSN*, ii, 523–530, 298–300.
[31] *MRSN*, ii , 529.

the most graphic illustration of the decline in revenue collection. In 1198 there were just over 60. In 1203 there were more than 430.[32]

Vire and the Great Debt of the Earls of Chester

The returns from Vire illustrate an increase in debt of over 1000%. The major feature of this account was a vast, accumulated account owed by the earl of Chester.[33]

> Comes Cestrie (debit) £2598/6s/9d ang. de remanente compoti sui de baillis suis. Et 700 marcas quas Rex ei commodavit. Et 700 li.ang. de prestito Gasconie. Et 100 li.ang. pro habendo recto Petro de Sabrolio de honore de Croisilles. Et 185 li.ang pro relevio . . . milites de feodo Episcopi Baiocensis. Et 2250 li.ang. de firma Sancti Jacobi et de Vicomitatus Baiocensis et de prepositura Abrincensis et de baillis de Vira de iiii annis et dimidia. Et 240 quarterium avene de bernago Baillie de Vira de iiii annis.[34]

In addition, in the main body we see that the text the earl owed (again for four years) the revenue of the 'prepositura' and 'vicomte' farms of Vire as well as 'the increment above the farm'.[35] This was worth 940 li.ang. All of this totalled just under 8,530 li.ang., by far the greatest debt found against any individual on a Norman pipe roll.[36] In comparative terms it was worth roughly two-thirds of the entire annual farm revenue of Normandy.[37] The remaining item of his debt from Vire of just over 2,598 li.ang. was to be found in its entirety on the 1198 roll from the returns of Bayeux. Since 1197, not a single penny of it had been paid.[38] The next debt of 700 marks was also found in the 1198 returns from

---

[32] *MRSN*, ii, 523–530.

[33] *MRSN*, ii, 531, 536, 537. The secondary material, in terms of modern scholarship, for the consideration of the earls of Chester during this period is limited and tends to concentrate on English lands and practices. Despite all its sophistication J.C. Holt's *The Northerners* limits its comments on the earl to his English holdings and politics. J.W. Alexander's *Ranulf of Chester: A Relic of the Conquest*, Athens 1983, 12–13 has certainly more to say on Normandy. His judgement, however, might be considered somewhat problematic. Especially unfortunate, in the light of the forthcoming discussion, is his assertion that 'most of the Exchequer accounts for Ranulf's Norman lands before 1204 contribute nothing of interest to Ranulf's biography . . .' (121) The best of the modern discussions of the earl of Chester is that of B.E. Harris, 'Ranulph III, Earl of Chester', *Journal of the Chester Archaeological Society* 58, 1975, 99–114. This combines sound judgement and the recognition of the fundamental importance of the earl's Norman holdings. Its major fault is its brevity which allows little room for the consideration of the Norman Exchequer evidence.

[34] *MRSN*, ii, 536–37.

[35] *MRSN*, ii, 531.

[36] *MRSN*, ii, 531.

[37] Moss, 'Normandy and the Angevin Empire', 14.

[38] *MRSN*, ii, 383. The debt cannot be found on the returns from Bayeux on the 1195 Norman Exchequer roll. The only item in this context was the sum of just over 157 li.ang. owed by the count for the king's ransom (*MRSN*, i, 265). On the other hand the farm of the 'vicomte' of Bessin does not appear in these returns and the debt might be accumulated from that render.

Bayeux and once again there were no payments between 1197 and 1203.[39] The 'prestitum' for Gascony and the payment for 'having right' were fairly typical returns and have no great intrinsic interest.[40] The debts for the farms and the knights' fees were, on the other hand, extremely significant.[41] In order to understand them we must briefly consider the long term aims of the earls of Chester in Normandy.

The earls 'from their descent from Richard and Hugh de Avranchin' had claims to be hereditary holders of most of the farms of that area.[42] They had similar claims concerning the 'vicomte' of Bessin and the farms of Vire.[43] Much of this was recognised in a well-known charter of Henry II (then simply duke of Normandy and the count of Anjou) in 1153 at Devizes;

> ... sciatis me dedisse et concessisse Ranulfo comiti Cestrie omnem hereditatem suam Normannie et Anglie sicut unquam aliquis antecessorum suorum eam melius et liberius tenuit, et nominatim castellum Vira et Barbifluvium cum tali libertate ... et hoc unde erat vicecomes Abrincis, et in Sancto Jacobo de hoc feci eum comitem ... [44]

The general reading of this, mainly because of the extensive lands granted in England later in the text, has been that of a massive series of concessions to the earl. To some extent this was also true of Normandy. The grant of Barfleur was apparently new.[45] What is missing from the charter, however, is any mention of Bayeux. This is especially interesting since in a charter first mentioned by Le Patourel made by Robert of Gloucester in 1146 at Devizes, as the consul of the empress, he quitclaimed and granted to the bishop of Bayeux a series of rights, some of which referred to the earl of Chester:[46]

> Sciatis me clamasse quieta ... preter meum proprium feodum et molendinum de Crevequor quod comes Rannulfus apud Baiocas de episcopo tenebat ... Sciatis quoque quod idem Phillippus Baiocensis episcopus mihi concessit tenere terram quam Rannulfus comes Cestrie de eadem Baiocensi ecclesia

---

[39] *MRSN*, ii, 383, 536.

[40] *MRSN* ii, 536–37. The 'habendo recto' payment can, however, be dated to the second year of John's reign when it was rendered in the oblate roll, *Rot. Norm.*, 39.

[41] *MRSN*, ii, 531, 537.

[42] For Richard 'vicomte' of the Avranchin see D. Bates, *Normandy Before 1066*, London 1982, 115. For Hugh 'vicomte' of Avranchin see M. Chibnall, *Anglo-Norman England*, Oxford 1986, 19, 21, 22, 27, 34, 45, 109, 219. See also Powicke, *Loss of Normandy*, 76. The earls were hereditary farmers of the 'vicomte' farm of this area and the farm of St James-de-Beuvron. It seems unlikely that they had a claim to the 'prepositura' of Pontorson. The latter (perhaps significantly) was described as a bailliage in 1198: Moss, 'Normandy and the Angevin Empire', 134.

[43] Powicke, *Loss of Normandy*, 72, 73, 74.

[44] *Regesta Regum Anglo-Normannorum 1066–1154*, ed. H.A. Cronne and R.H.C Davis, Oxford 1968, iii, no. CLXXX, 65–66.

[45] Given the fact that most of the Norman section of this charter was the restoration of some of the previous rights of the earls it cannot be excluded that they once held Barfleur.

[46] J. Le Patourel, 'What did not happen in King Stephen's Reign', *History* 58, 1973, 14–15.

tenebat, salvo servitio ipsuis Baiocensis ecclesie, donec talis heres adveniat quem dux Normannorum justum heredem ipsius Ranulfi comitis Cestrie recognoscat et postea idem heres eadem terram de ecclesia Baiocensi et de episcopo in capite teneat . . . [47]

Now the logic of this text is to suggest that the land held from the bishop should be restored, if not to Ranulf then at least to his heir after the reconciliation of those that supported King Stephen in the reign of King Henry II.[48] But there is no evidence for this from any of the charters of King Henry II. Indeed the non-inclusion of the rights of the earl of Chester in Bayeux in the charter of 1153 as even the 'vicomte' of Bessin, suggests that Henry was unable to restore his rights. Moreover, the earl does not hold these lands on the list of knight service in Normandy for 1172.[49] In fact the first mention that we have to what were probably these lands is the debt on the 1203 Norman Exchequer roll.[50]

How far the actual terms of the 1153 charter were enacted can be gleaned from the Norman Exchequer rolls. By 1180 the earl's son had the farms of the Avranchin and, interestingly, the farm of the 'vicomte' of Bessin.[51] Barfleur was never held by the earl, however, on any of the surviving rolls, and Vire, as with the land held from the bishop of Bayeux, was only found in his hands on the 1203 account.[52] All of this suggests that the earls of Chester had extensive unrealised claims to lands and rights in Normandy prior to the reign of King John.

The circumstances of John's accession were the most unfavourable since the time of King Stephen. As well as facing a strong French monarchy, there existed an alternative claimant to the throne, namely Arthur, the count of Brittany.[53] This put landholders on the frontier between Normandy and Brittany in a rather strong bargaining position. It seems likely that the earl of Chester took full advantage of this situation since, according to Roger of Howden, Ranulf (with a number of other magnates) wavered in their support for King John.[54] In fact it was only when they were promised, by the justiciar and William Marshall, that the monarch would render all their rights, that they swore fealty to the king.

The debts on the 1203 Exchequer roll show us for the first time what concessions John had to make on his accession to win over just one of these magnates.

---

[47] *Regesta*, iii, no. LVIII, 22–3.

[48] It is possible that some of these lands held from the bishop may be referred to in the list of knight service from the church of Bayeux of 1133. 'Ricardus Comes Cestriae v milites', *Red Book*, ii, 645.

[49] *Red Book*, ii, 638.

[50] The payment of a relief suggests that these lands were recently passed into the hands of the earls of Chester.

[51] *MRSN*, i, 40.

[52] *MRSN*, ii, 536–7. It is just possible that the earl held the castle but did not administer the farm of Barfleur.

[53] Turner, *King John*, 49–54.

[54] Turner, *King John*, 51.

Vire was restored to the earls of Chester and no revenue was rendered to the Exchequer from its farms and the 'bernagium' for four-and-a-half years, that is, from the time of the coronation. No revenue was rendered from this time from the farms of Bessin and the earl's farms in the Avranchin. The lands that the earl held from the bishop of Bayeux were probably restored to him at the accession. Revenue was still owed to the Exchequer from these holdings in 1203. Finally the debts owed to King Richard from the earl were in effect frozen so that no revenue was collected from them.

This was an extremely high, if necessary, price to pay for the support of one magnate. It is true the debts could act as some kind of hold over the earl's loyalty. Indeed as we have seen they were increased from 1200 by increment above the farm in Vire. King John did not grant all of the Norman claims of the earl of Chester. Barfleur, for instance, was not placed in his hands. Nevertheless, what was conceded was highly significant. Great men such as Richard de Clare, William de Ferrers, Roger de Lacy and William de Mowbray were also promised their rights in return for swearing fealty to King John.[55] If concessions on the scale of those made to the earl of Chester were given to these individuals then the very process of accession would have severely weakened Angevin finance. Even on the basis of our existing knowledge the price of accession was considerable. If we add the accumulated debts of the earl of Chester to the relief of 20,000 marks King John paid to Philip Augustus on his accession, then we have a sum of over 60,000 li.ang.[56] This figure was comparable to the entire pipe-roll revenue for Normandy in 1195, and was considerably greater than the total for 1180.[57]

Total Revenue in 1202/3

The utilisation of the returns found on the 1202/3 Norman Exchequer roll as a source for the measurement of the revenue of Normandy is a matter of some controversy. John Gillingham has not used these records because of their extremely limited nature.[58] Holt, on the other hand, has estimated Norman revenue from these returns.

> Not surprisingly the pipe roll for 1203 is incomplete. By Michaelmas the Normandy defences were beset and Angevin control of Normandy was on the point of collapse. The account for the bailliage of Caux was rendered but it is not now included in the roll. Whether the other missing accounts were even rendered must be problematic. Quite apart from this the remaining accounts

[55] Turner, *King John*, 51. For some tentative discussion of the 'de Lacy' lands in Normandy during this time see W.E Wightman, *The Lacy Family in England and Normandy 1066–1194*, Oxford 1966, 215–26. It is interesting to note that these lands do not appear on any Norman record from 1199–1202. This might suggest that they had been restored to the family.

[56] Turner, *King John*, 53.

[57] Moss, 'Normandy and the Angevin Empire', 51–4.

[58] Gillingham, *Richard Coeur de Lion*, 72.

clearly reflect severely diminished resources. The revenues of the ten bailliages accounted is only 38% of the yield in 1198, 9654 l.ang. as against 25,366 l.ang.[59]

The approach adopted by Holt is in important respects both flawed and limited: the returns of 1203 can be used as a rough measurement of the revenue John could raise from Normandy during the period prior to its fall. This is not to say (given the effects of warfare, the areas of Normandy already conquered and the resulting problems of collection) that figures calculated from this account tell us precisely how much revenue was in fact collected in the year 1202/3.[60] We have detailed and complete returns from only eight of the nine (not ten) bailliages on the 1203 Norman Exchequer roll.[61] The account from Caen was incomplete.[62] The returns from the farm, judicial proceedings, land and water were not found on the records of 1203. The 1203 roll contained complete returns from the bailliages of Mortain and Vire.[63] On the 1197/98 Norman pipe roll these bailliages were not, in one sense, complete. The wealthy farms of Mortain were in the hands of the count and were therefore not rendered on the roll of that year.[64] Once, however, the count of Mortain, John, became duke of Normandy these returns were submitted, hence their presence in the bailliage of Mortain on the 1203 Roll.[65] The same point (although to a less financially significant extent) applied to the 'vicomte' and 'prepositura' farms of Vire which were not accounted for in 1198 but were rendered in 1203.[66] It may be that the distinct contents and the incomplete nature of the different bailliages illustrated by these three examples roughly balance each other out and that Holt's estimate is approximately correct. The point, however, is that very specific untypical factors affect no less than a third of the bailliages from which he drew his comparison.

[59] J.C. Holt, 'The Loss of Normandy and Royal Finance', in J.C. Holt and J. Gillingham, eds, *War and Government in the Middle Ages*, Woodbridge 1984, 92–105.

[60] A further complication is the 'fouage'. This was a three-yearly money tax that was due for collection in 1202/3. Unfortunately many of the bailliages present on the Norman Exchequer roll were exempt from this tax. Whether it was successfully collected in central Normandy we cannot say. For the latest discussion of the 'fouage' see D. Power in this volume, and Moss, 'Normandy and the Angevin Empire', 24–8.

[61] *MRSN*, ii, Cotentin 505–511, 572–74, Gavray 512–514, Coutances 515–530, Vire 531–537, Mortain 538–548, Roumois 549–553, Pont-Audemer 553–560, 'The vicomte between the Risle and the Seine' 560–568, and the partial returns from Caen 568–71. It is hard to know where Holt obtained his extra bailliage. It is possible that he has taken the very partial returns from the Avranchin (discussed later in this chapter) as another bailliage, or treated Cherbourg (*MRSN*, ii, 572–74) as a separate bailliage.

[62] *MRSN*, ii, 568–71.

[63] *MRSN*, ii, 531–48.

[64] The 'vicomte' and the 'prepositura' of Mortain, Le Tilleul, the 'vicomte' of Cerences, the 'prepositura' of Tenchebrai and the very wealthy farm of the fair of Mount Martin were all in the hands of the count of Mortain. See Moss, 'Normandy and the Angevin Empire', 248–62.

[65] *MRSN*, ii, 538–48.

[66] *MRSN*, ii, 531–37.

Moreover, Holt's calculation and conversion of this percentage into an actual revenue figure is problematic. Apart from the problems concerning his 1198 total, in his comparative calculations for Norman revenue in 1198, and thus resultingly for 1203, he has excluded an estimate of the revenue collected in 1196/97 in the construction of Château-Gaillard found on the 1198 roll.[67] This represents only about half of the revenue collected in the year 1196/7 but recorded on the 1198 roll.[68] Depending on whether one includes or excludes such revenue, Holt's estimate for 1203 would approximate to 46,000 li.ang. or 58,000 li.ang. A broadening and a refinement of Holt's approach is, fortunately, possible. This involves comparing the eight complete bailliages of the 1203 Roll with their counterparts found on not just the 1198 roll, but also those of 1180 and 1195. By utilising this method of calculation we arrive at three approximate estimates of Angevin revenue.

The Bailliages

The returns of the bailliages found on the 1203 compared to their counterparts in 1198 are displayed in Table Two. Mortain has been excluded, as has Caen, for reasons already mentioned. Vire, since its farms were only worth 200 li.ang., at least up to 1200, has been included.[69] The greater part of the debt of the earl of Chester has, however, been excluded, since it relates to bailliages which cannot be subject to comparison.[70]

Table 2 in li. ang.[71]

Bailliage	owed 1198	paid	owed 1203	paid
Mortain			3590	1450
Vire	980	740	3130	170
Inter	3000	870	1150	290
Pont Aud	2310	1260	3690	230
Cotentin	11510	4180	5190	2620

[67] Holt, 'Finance', 98 (n. 41). Holt's totals for the Norman Exchequer rolls of 1195 and1198 are substantially in error. See Moss, 'Normandy and the Angevin Empire', 36–59.

[68] Moss, 'Normandy and the Angevin Empire', 38.

[69] Moss, 'Normandy and the Angevin Empire', 168–70.

[70] See the discussion earlier in this paper.

[71] MRSN, ii, 1198, Gavray and Coutances 292–300 (for the forest sales from the former see 385), Vire 357–360, Roumois 416–420 (and 444), Pont-Audemer 450–9, Cotentin 471–481 and the 'vicomte between the Risle and the Seine' 459–60, 488–493, for 1203 see note 3. The calculation of the 1203 roll has none of the complexities in terms of income transfers found on the rolls of King Richard's reign. The only minor problem is making sure that the rolling account of Richard Fontenai which covers a number of bailliages (MRSN, ii, 511, 537, 546–548) is correctly treated, i.e. that the money spent or moved is considered in the bailliage from which it originates. In Vire a composite debt from that area and two other bailliages was made worth over 2200 li.ang., and 700 li.ang. has been included in our total as an estimate of Vire's proportion. All the figures in the Tables of this chapter have been rounded up to the nearest 10 li.ang.

Gavray	1510	1280	1770	1100
Coutances	2910	1120	3280	350
Roumois	7990	1690	3490	200
Totals	*30210*	*11140*	*25290*	*6410*

Table Three contains the comparative returns to 1203 from 1180 and 1195.[72] It should be noted that the records of Gavray were not present on the 1180 account and Roumois was absent from the returns of 1195.[73] In 1195 only the tallage from Vire appeared on the roll and this bailliage is thus excluded. It was worth just over 112 li.ang.[74] As the total found for the entire bailliage of Vire in 1203 was only 170 li.ang., it is very probable that this was in fact exceeded in 1195.[75] Only the escheats of Mortain were included in the surviving returns of 1195, which again is excluded from this table.[76]

Table 3 in li. ang.

Bailliage	owed 1180	paid	owed 1195	paid
Mortain	1720	1430		
Vire	260	250		
Inter	510	280	780	320
Pont Aud	1040	730	990	830
Cotentin	2100	1910	4300	2430
Gavray			670	660
Coutances	860	190	1010	940
Roumois			1780	720
Totals	*8270*	*5510*	*7750*	*5180*

Before calculating our estimates for the recorded revenue, a brief survey of the bailliages under consideration is necessary. A high proportion of the returns found on the 1203 roll came from the Norman south-west. The major feature of this area was its fiscal and administrative conservatism. The farms of the Coutances, Mortain and Vire were held in hereditary hands by the count of Mortain, the earl of Chester or William fitz John and his son throughout the period from 1180 to 1203.[77] The Avranchin (despite the debts of the earl of Chester) does not appear as a separate bailliage on the 1203 account but it

---

[72] References to all the bailliages found on the 1180 are to be found in Powicke, *The Loss of Normandy*, 68–78. For 1195 see *MRSN*, i, Coutances, 218–22, the 'vicomte between the Risle and the Seine' 146–153, Gavray 197–199, Pont-Audemer, 206–210, and Cotentin 143–45, 274–280, 285–288.

[73] The town of Rouen was present, but not the separately accounted for returns from Roumois.

[74] *MRSN*, i, 244.

[75] See Table 3.

[76] *MRSN*, i, 215.

[77] Powicke, *Loss of Normandy*, 66–78.

followed much the same pattern with its farms continuously held by the earl throughout the period.[78]

The returns from these bailliages still expressed many of the general features of Norman revenue in 1195 and 1198. Tallages and loans were made against them. They remained, however, far behind the fiscal performance of the north and never approached the stunning fiscal achievements of central Normandy in the time of King Richard.[79] Urban revenue from tallages and loans in 1198 from Vire, Mortain and Coutances reached the hardly dizzy heights of just under 240 li.ang.[80] Such returns from the bailliages were worth approximately 1,400 li.ang.[81] This was not a very impressive figure. It is hard not to suggest that administrative continuity and fiscal under-performance were linked.[82] It is possible that the proximity to the Breton frontier had a determinate affect on the history and administration of these farms.[83] It may well be that the predominantly low-level warfare of this area throughout most of the eleventh and twelfth centuries meant that the Norman dukes were satisfied with a situation of strong hereditary curia-like officials who kept the frontier safe but achieved little on the fiscal front.[84] One suspects this was so even when the dukes were perhaps powerful enough to have changed farm personnel and priorities if they had so wished.

The Cotentin, too, in a social sense may once (perhaps in the time of Count Giffard) have been part of this area. This, however, was slowly and unevenly changing. Returns from this area showed a significant improvement from 1180. Very unusually the figure for 1203 was greater than that of 1195 but not comparable with 1198.[85] In terms of revenue from tallages and loans in 1198 the performance of the bailliage was respectable compared to the rest of the south-west, coming just behind the great super-bailliages of central Normandy and Caux. On the other hand its figure for tallages and loans from the towns

---

[78] Powicke, *Loss of Normandy*, 66–78.

[79] Moss, 'Normandy and the Angevin Empire', 60–89.

[80] Moss, 'Normandy and the Angevin Empire', 81.

[81] Moss, 'Normandy and the Angevin Empire', 78.

[82] It is just possible that the amount of wealth found in these areas could also have been a factor. The whole issue needs far more research but it is interesting to note that Bates, *Normandy Before 1066*, 98, could describe Mortain before 1066 as 'poor'. For the English 'curial sheriff' see D.A. Carpenter, 'The Decline of the Curial Sheriff in England', *EHR* 91, 1976, 1–32.

[83] The whole issue of this frontier in this period and earlier, and its influence on Norman history, clearly needs more research. For the most recent general discussion of the frontier in the medieval period see R. Bartlett and A. Mackey, eds, *Medieval Frontier Societies*, Oxford 1992. Another contributing factor was the relative lack of ducal holdings in these areas before the conquest of England. See Bates, *Normandy before 1066*, 272. For the latest discussion see Power in this volume.

[84] One must not forget that Mortain was originally a Norman 'comté' with its own tradition of an area ruled by a member of the ducal family. See Bates, *Normandy Before 1066*, 99 and D.C. Douglas, 'The Earliest Norman Counts', *EHR* 61, 1946, 129–54.

[85] See Tables 2 and 3.

was extremely low, amounting to just 200 li.ang. paid in or expended.[86]

Gavray was the final bailliage from the south-west that appears on the 1203 account. Our interest in it lies in the fact that it broke all the rules. Revenue in 1203 was almost double the 1195 figure.[87] It failed to raise more revenue than the 1198 total, only because of the sale of forest land from that year and the collection of revenue from debts of tallages owed from 1193/4.[88] Moreover, its ratio of money owed to money paid in or expended in 1203 was astonishingly high: a 62% yield ratio compared to the pipe-roll average of a little over 25%.[89] The reasons for these achievements, which broke both temporal and geographical trends, remain to be discovered.

The returns from Roumois were accounted for separately from the city of Rouen on all the Norman Exchequer rolls. Rouen was never described as a separate bailliage, but de facto, if not de jure, they were treated as two distinct administrative units. In 1198 Roumois's fiscal performance was roughly comparable to the Cotentin – basically solid and substantial, but not as impressive as central Normandy. A sharp contrast exists between its excellent revenue performance in 1198 compared to 1180 and 1203. Much depends on how far this area can be seen as part of the economic hinterland of the city of Rouen. If this were so, then Richard's revenue achievements could well be part of the general picture of the 1190s, when, as argued elsewhere, there was much success in collecting urban revenue. On the other hand, as we have seen, Roumois made considerable progress in debt clearance between 1198 and 1203. This may help to explain the relatively bad performance concerning current revenue in the latter year. I have considered elsewhere the complex history of the bailliage of Pont-Audemer.[90] In fiscal terms the major contrast was between the highly impressive performance (given its size) in 1198 and the disaster of 1203.[91] Its revenue in 1180 and 1195, on the contrary, was roughly comparable.

The final bailliage found in the surviving records from 1203 was that of the 'vicomte between the Risle and the Seine'. This was one of the smallest and least-significant bailliages of Normandy. As an aside, it is probable that its most interesting feature was its title. This, very unusually, was not drawn from a diocese or a town but simply measured geographical space. Administratively it is one of the very few bailliages outside the south which was farmed by the same family from 1180 to 1204. So much so, that it was also called the 'bailliage de Londa' after the family that held the 'vicomte'.[92] The returns of 1198 were

---

[86] Moss, 'Normandy and the Angevin Empire', 78.

[87] See Tables 2 and 3.

[88] For forest sales and old tallages in this bailliage, see Moss, 'Normandy and the Angevin Empire', 66.

[89] See Tables 2 and 3. For a full discussion of the yield ratio see V. Moss, 'Normandy and England in 1180: the Pipe Roll Evidence', in D. Bates and A. Curry, ed., *England and Normandy in the Middle Ages*, London 1994, 185–95.

[90] Moss, 'Normandy and the Angevin Empire', 78, 80–2, 134, 166.

[91] See Tables 2 and 3.

[92] Powicke, *Loss of Normandy*, 70.

significantly higher than any other year. The returns from 1180, 1195 and 1203 in terms of revenue, if not their yield ratios, were very roughly comparable.[93]

The returns thus contain a number of major omissions and weaknesses. A disproportionate number of the bailliages were in the hands of hereditary officials. On the 1203 account there were no records found from central Normandy, the area of greatest fiscal achievement in the 1198 and of least continuity in governmental officials.[94] This is very unfortunate. It is highly unlikely, given the accounts that we have from elsewhere, that King John was able to repeat Richard's successes in this area. If he did not, an estimate of revenue based upon the records of 1198 for 1203 is likely to overstate the revenue of the latter. On the other hand, the non-inclusion of Gavray on the 1180 roll is likely to understate any estimate based on these records for 1203, given the continuous rise of revenue from this bailliage. A figure based on the rolls of 1195 and 1204 poses even greater difficulties. The figure for revenue in 1194/5 is actually that of a magnitude approximately between 51,000 li.ang. and 76,000 li.ang. This depends upon whether the massive sum for the king's ransom was collected in 1194/5 or in previous years, and whether this account can be linked up to other payments found on the Roll for the ransom, which could then be treated as income transfers and deducted from the total.[95] Moreover, the estimate can only be based on just the five bailliages that the two rolls had in common.[96] Besides suggesting that revenue in 1203 was less than that of 1195 and 1198 but more than 1180, the use of this comparison is thus limited.

Before calculating these estimates, it is worth briefly examining the results that can be drawn from the data in the tables against our existing knowledge from previously calculated rolls. The tables express a continuous decline in the yield ratio, 66% in 1180 and 1195, 36% in 1198, and 25% in 1203.[97] We know that these figures massively overstate the decline in yield from between 1180 and 1198, presumably because of the more fiscally effective returns from central Normandy in the latter year, which cannot be included in this comparison.[98] This again suggests that (unless we assume a similar increased fiscal performance in 1203 from records that we do not have) an estimate based on the 1198 figure is likely to overstate the revenue of 1203.

Revenue Estimates

Excluding the returns from Gavray the 1180 total works out at 5,510 li.ang. compared to 5,310 li.ang. for 1204, that is, a total less than that of 1180.[99] This

---

[93] See Tables 2 and 3.

[94] Moss, 'Normandy and the Angevin Empire', 60–89.

[95] Moss, 'Normandy and the Angevin Empire', 53.

[96] See Table 3.

[97] See Tables 2 and 3.

[98] The actual yield ratio for the 1194–5 Norman Exchequer roll was within a magnitude of between 50% and 70%. This is a not a great deal of use for checking our comparative totals.

[99] The forthcoming estimates are based upon Tables 2 and 3.

gives an estimate of revenue for 1203 of just under 26,000 li.ang. The totals for 1203 compared with 1195 work out at 4,590 li.ang. as against 5,180 li.ang. This would mean a total revenue estimate of between roughly 45,000 li.ang. and 67,000 li.ang. If we use the seven comparable bailliages from the 1198 roll we obtain totals of 4,960 li.ang. for 1203 compared with 11,140 li.ang.[100] As we have seen our own figure for 1198 of just over 99,000 li.ang. already excluded revenue collected in previous years.[101] It does, however, include the revenue of 1,270 li.ang. from Evreux.[102] As this was surrendered to Philip Augustus in 1200, our percentage of 45% most be taken from just under 98,000 li.ang.[103] This gives us an estimate of approximately 44,100 li.ang. for the revenue of 1203.

If nothing else, this shows the inexactitude of this method of estimation, but some useful information can be gleaned from these figures. All the totals show the revenue of Normandy in 1203 to be substantially below that of both 1195 and 1198. There are, as we have seen, good reasons to believe that the estimate from 1198 overstated the revenue of 1203 and that based which was based on 1180 understated this total. An estimate based on the 1195 figures is likely to overstate Norman revenue, since Vire (excluded from the comparison) was almost certainly worth considerably more in 1195 than in 1203, and Roumois, another area of poor fiscal performance on current account in 1203, is also excluded from this calculation.[104] If we suggested a prudent estimate of revenue somewhere between 44,000 li.ang. and 45,000 li.ang. (excluding the extreme variables) we would be wrong, but not, one suspects, enough to matter. If this is so, on the eve of the fall, King John could only extract approximately half the revenue that was raised by King Richard in 1198.

The Beginning of Fiscal Decline

The issue of when the revenue level began to decline is complex. As we have seen some debt accumulation dated back to the very accession of King John. Some problems may, therefore, simply have stemmed from the adverse circumstances of accession. One piece of evidence, however, suggests that things may not have been too bad during the first year of John's reign. The surviving returns of the Norman Exchequer roll for the year 1200/1 consist only of the account of Garin de Glapion, then seneschal of Normandy, dated from 6 June 1200 to 6 November 1201.[105] The record is about one fortieth of the size of the membrane from 1203. In terms of fiscal value it presented an account of no less than 7,365 li.ang. Its contents are far more important. In 1200 a tallage for the siege at Drincourt was levied in the bailliages of Arques and Blossville for

---

[100] See Tables 2 and 3.
[101] Moss, 'Normandy and the Angevin Empire', 51.
[102] Holt, 'Finance', 98.
[103] *Ibid.*
[104] See Tables 2 and 3.
[105] *MRSN*, ii, 501–2.

400 li.ang. and in the bailliage of Roumois for 300 li.ang. The 'comitatus' of Eu also rendered 400 li.ang.[106] Importantly the city of Rouen accounted (by tallage) for 300 li.ang. and the town of Eu contributed 200 li.ang.[107]

Some caution is needed. The membrane is minute. All the tallages came from the north of Normandy. They were relatively small in size. There were no examples of any forced loans levied against the towns or bailliages. Nevertheless, when one considers the smallness of the return, and the fact that it still recorded twice as many tallages as the entire surviving returns of 1203, it suggests, at the very least, that some elements of the fiscal system of the 1190s continued into the year 1201. This picture is to some extent reinforced by negative evidence. The extensive writs that we have recorded on the Rotuli Normannie show no significant movement of English money to the continent until September of 1201.[108] Moreover, the total amount of money sent (just under 24,000 li.ang.) is not greatly in excess of the revenue transferred from England as recorded on the 1198 Norman Exchequer roll.[109]

If all this is so, the crisis of Norman finance developed late in the day. Moreover, the crisis was relative in nature. King John was almost certainly extracting more revenue from Normandy than King Henry II did in 1180, despite the adverse conditions of accession and a declining rate of collection. It is only in comparison with King Richard that John's fiscal performance appears truly awful, and even up to 1201 something of Richard's fiscal system may have survived. Nevertheless, in terms of the maximum extraction of Norman revenue in a time of intense military competition, John was found wanting. Furthermore, the period of sharpest fiscal decline coincides with the time of Arthur's murder. It is difficult not to think that this act undermined confidence in the duke and may well have adversely affected revenue collection.[110] To what extent other factors such as fiscal exhaustion played a part in the fall of Normandy (and the shocking rapidity of this event may counsel against a monocasual explanation) awaits further research. In this respect the vast number of unexamined published and unpublished charters concerning the central areas of later Angevin Normandy may prove to be key sources. Nevertheless, whatever surprises new studies may reveal, John's failure to match Richard's fiscal performance as duke of Normandy must carry significant weight in any explanation of the duchy's fall.

---

[106] *MRSN*, ii, 501–2.

[107] *MRSN*, ii, 501–2.

[108] *Rot. Norm.*, 31, 36.

[109] *Rot. Norm.*, 31, 36.

[110] It must be noted, however, that Richard ordered Robert Brito to be starved to death and Roger of Wendover believed that Innocent III supported Arthur's execution. For the latest discussion see M. Strickland, *War and Chivalry*, Cambridge 1996, 256–57. His own assessment, however, that '. . . much of John's political failure was due to the delusion that fidelity could be maintained by fear and coercion' (p. 256) is all the more telling given his fine contextual study of Arthur's elimination.

King John and the Norman Aristocracy[1]

Daniel Power

In any assessment of King John his loss of Normandy and Anjou must loom large; and it does not reflect well upon his reputation. At the end of his days he had lost half the kingdom of England; but the early part of his reign was dominated by his acquisition and subsequent forfeiture of Normandy, Anjou and Maine, and part of Poitou. Yet John's failure in Normandy still leaves many questions unresolved; in particular, the actions and attitudes of the Normans themselves still elude satisfactory explanations. For the fall of Normandy was not simply a struggle between Capetian and Plantagenet. Caught between the warring kings were the local magnates: the wars eroded their incomes, they often had to fight their kith and kin, and many of the fortresses which the French besieged were not John's domain castles, but the treasured ancestral *capita* of Norman lords, the symbols of their lineages. A study of the Normans cannot wholly explain John's defeat in France in 1202–4, which was triggered to a large extent by factors elsewhere in the Plantagenet dominions, especially the Angoulême marriage and Lusignan rebellion, the claims of Arthur of Brittany, and the defection of William des Roches. Nevertheless, the form which the conquest of Normandy took is incomprehensible if the local aristocracy are left out of the equation. We cannot see the context in which castles changed hands or the king of France endowed the Norman church, for instance, without taking full account of the previous history of individual lordships.[2] Rather than seeking to revise the excellent narratives of Powicke and Warren for John's brief reign in Normandy, this article will concentrate upon the place of the Normans in those tumultuous events.[3]

The contemporary and near-contemporary accounts of the disasters of 1204 offered three main explanations for John's defeats. A common view, most

---

[1] I wish to thank the University of Sheffield for funding my attendance at the King John Conference, and the other participants for their comments upon this paper.
[2] See D.J. Power, 'What Did the Frontier of Angevin Normandy Comprise?', *ANS* 17, 1995, 181–201, at pp. 187–8 and n. 27, p. 196 and n. 68.
[3] Powicke, *Loss of Normandy*, 127–69, 251–64; Warren, *King John*, 48–99; K. Norgate, *England under the Angevin Kings*, 2 vols, London 1887, ii, 388–429, though not without errors, is also still valuable. N.C. Vincent, *Peter des Roches: an Alien in English Politics 1205–38*, Cambridge 1996, 42–7, offers a recent reassessment of the collapse of Plantagenet power in France. I use the term 'Plantagenet' rather than 'Angevin' for the dynasty, to distinguish it from the people of Anjou.

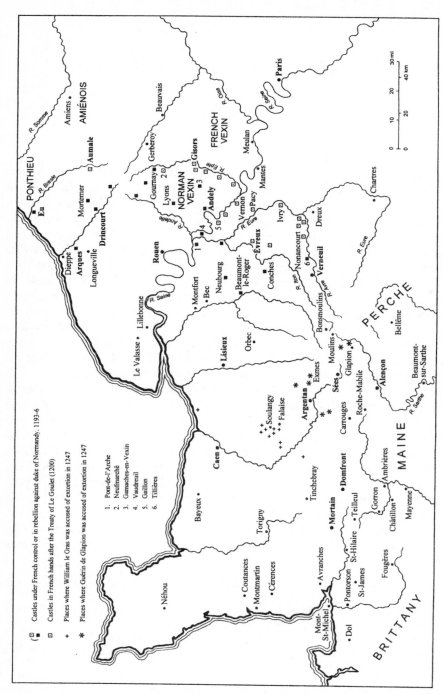

The Duchy of Normandy 1193–1204.

famously expressed by the author of *Histoire de Guillaume le Maréchal* and by Roger of Wendover, blamed these disasters on John's own failings.[4] A second explanation attributed the defeat to John's inferior resources in the face of superior Capetian resources.[5] Both these views have found their modern supporters,[6] and the most recent studies of the financial condition of Plantagenet government have not resolved this problem: they show that the Norman fiscal system was very robust,[7] but that John increased his income only after the disasters of 1204.[8] However, a third reason for John's defeat surfaces time and time again in the narrative sources: the Normans' reluctance to fight, or even their treachery.[9] Here we have a far more intangible problem than that of resources and account rolls, nothing less than the hearts and minds of the Normans themselves. For no amount of English silver or Norman tallages would enable John to defend his lands if he had forfeited the support of his subjects.

Yet most of these stories of betrayal have the same shortcoming: in contrast to narratives of King Stephen's reign or the Young King's rebellion, they generally treat the Normans as a single group. Only occasionally do the sources single out the actions of individual nobles: Count Robert of Sées and Hugh de Gournay are the most frequent,[10] and the Annals of Waverley stated that King Philip subjugated Normandy 'through the sedition of William du Hommet', the constable of Normandy, whose English lands were indeed confiscated before

---

[4] *Hist. Guillaume le Maréchal*, ii, lines 12,595–12,606 (iii, 171); *Wendover*, i, 316–17, ii, 8–9. Cf. *Ann. Mon.*, i, 26–7; ii, 256. *Giraldi Cambrensis Opera*, viii, 258–9, blamed the Normans' defeat on ducal tyranny generally.

[5] *Walter of Coventry*, ii, 197; cf. the comments attributed to Ranulf de Glanville (d. 1190), in *Giraldi Cambrensis Opera*, viii, 257–8.

[6] For the former, see especially Gillingham, *Richard the Lionheart*, 278–82; for the latter, *Premier budget*, 135–9; J.C. Holt, 'The End of the Anglo-Norman Realm', *PBA* 61, 1975, 223–65; *idem*, 'The Loss of Normandy and Royal Finances', in *War and Government in the Middle Ages*, ed. J. Gillingham and J.C. Holt, Woodbridge 1984, 92–105; J.W. Baldwin, 'La décennie décisive: les années 1190–1203 dans le règne de Philippe Auguste', *Revue Historique* 266, 1981, 311–37.

[7] V.D. Moss, 'Normandy and England in 1180: the Pipe Roll Evidence', in *England and Normandy in the Middle Ages*, ed. D. Bates and A. Curry, London 1994, 185–95, at 194–5. *Idem*, 'Normandy and the Angevin Empire: a study of the Norman Exchequer Rolls 1180–1204', unpublished University of Wales PhD thesis, 1996, 60–83, 224–40, portrays the developments in Norman finance in the 1190s as a 'fiscal revolution', but doubts if this was sufficient to counter the contemporaneous increase in Capetian resources.

[8] N. Barratt, 'The Revenue of King John', *EHR* 111, 1996, 835–55, especially pp. 844–5, 854; also his article in this volume.

[9] E.g. *Coggeshall*, 145; *Gervase*, i, 95; *Hist. Ducs de Normandie*, 97; *RHF*, XVIII, 351 (Savigny Chronicle); *Hist. Guillaume le Maréchal*, ii, e.g. lines 12,557–12,558 (iii, 170); *Ann. Mon.*, i, 57; iv, 392.

[10] For Hugh, see *Hist. Ducs de Normandie*, 92, and below, n. 14; for Count Robert, see below, pp. 128–32.

the surrender of Rouen.[11] Other sources tarred the Normans with a much broader brush. The *Histoire des Ducs de Normandie* stated that the English who garrisoned castles in Normandy believed that the Normans surrendered castles too easily.[12] The Annals of Saint-Aubin d'Angers alleged that John trusted his men guarding Normandy and was confident of returning from England in 1204, but panicked on hearing of his mother's death; Normandy then succumbed through treachery as even Rouen and Verneuil opened their gates.[13] Even one of the very few Norman sources for the period, the Annals of Jumièges, names only Hugh de Gournay and Peter de Meulan as traitors.[14] Besides, not all sources claimed that the Normans submitted tamely: one Picard chronicle thought that John's garrisons in Normandy were ready for a sturdy defence but were deserted by their lord.[15] It seems fair to conclude that contemporaries had only the vaguest impression of what most Norman lords were doing in this period; but many noted John's own fear of betrayal.[16]

The chroniclers' generalisations should be treated carefully, for it is doubtful whether the Normans really did react so uniformly. They had by no means always behaved as a single group in the past, and Normandy was in many respects highly regionalised. The duchy lacked natural and economic unity. The English Channel, the Seine and its tributaries, and the rivers flowing towards the Loire subjected different parts of the duchy to contradictory influences, from England, the Île-de-France, and Anjou, which were reflected, for instance, in styles of architecture.[17] The Normans' religious endowments show that the donors' interests were often quite localised, and the lordship based around its castle may have provided a more important focus for them than the Plantagenet or, indeed, the Capetian courts.[18] This in turn had political consequences: although the persistence of Norman identity in the late twelfth century can be seen in the provincial tournament teams described in the *Histoire de Guillaume le Maréchal*, for example,[19] the aristocracy along the duchy's borders often had

---

[11] *Ann. Mon.*, ii, 256; *Rot. Litt. Claus.*, i, 1. With his sons Jordan, bishop of Lisieux, Thomas, and Enguerrand, the constable had benefited when King John confiscated the property of defectors, including his son-in-law, Richard de Vernon, and Hugh de Gournay, in 1203: *Rot. Litt. Pat.*, 26, 33; *Rot. Norm.*, 81, 102, 107, 117; *Rot. de Lib.*, 67–8; Caen, AD Calvados, H 6597 (Gournay manor of Écouché); cf. *RHF*, XXIII, 619.

[12] *Hist. Ducs de Normandie*, 97. I wish to thank Dr Penelope Eley for her assistance with this source.

[13] *Annales angevines*, 21–2.

[14] *Les annales de l'Abbaye Saint-Pierre de Jumièges*, ed. J. Laporte, Rouen 1954, 85–7.

[15] *RHF*, XVIII, 713 (chronicle of Laon).

[16] *Coggeshall*, 143, 145–6; *Hist. Ducs de Normandie*, 97; *Hist. Guillaume le Maréchal*, ii, lines 12,569–12,584, 12,797–12,806 (iii, 171, 175); *RHF*, XVIII, 354, 358 (chronicles of Mortemer-en-Lyons and Rouen).

[17] L. Grant, 'The Architecture of the Early Savignacs and Cistercians in Normandy', *ANS* 10, 1987, 111–43.

[18] Cf. D. Crouch, 'Normans and Anglo-Normans: a Divided Aristocracy?', in *England and Normandy*, ed. Bates and Curry, 61–7.

[19] *Hist. Guillaume le Maréchal*, e.g. i, lines 2,780–2,787, 4,645–4,726 (iii, 39, 58–61).

far more in common with their immediate neighbours than with the inhabitants of central Normandy.[20]

Of course, there were a number of unifying elements in the duchy, most prominently the duke himself: his household and family, justice and courts, exchequer, patronage, the military services owed to him, and his place in the foundation myth and proud history of the Normans as a *gens*. Many Normans participated in the administration of their duchy, and Normandy had its own self-conscious body of customs long before these were set down in a custumal in about 1200.[21] The conquest of England had also given a great many Norman families an interest in English affairs which they shared with their duke. However, all of these unifying elements were flawed. The ducal family could divide, as well as unite, the Normans, and the history of the duchy is punctuated by periodic struggles within the ducal house, during which Norman fought Norman. In the rebellion of 1173–4, the faction of Henry the Young King had found its leadership in dissident Normans such as Hasculf de Saint-Hilaire, but other Normans rallied to Henry II were cajoled or forced into revolt, or remained indifferent to the uprising.[22] While it is debatable whether such factions were either rigid or long-lasting, these dynastic conflicts set a dangerous precedent of Norman nobles looking for other sources of patronage than their duke's largesse. In addition, by the reign of Henry I there was a strong contingent in the duchy with few or no interests in England, while many Norman nobles remained aloof from the ducal court.[23]

Perhaps there was some revival in harmony between the duke and his barons in the 1180s. The death of Henry II placed on the ducal throne one of his sons who had cultivated ties with dissident nobles, and the Third Crusade provided a common venture in which the aristocracy of the Plantagenet lands could sink their differences under the charismatic leadership of their new ruler. The repeated wars between the kings of England and France from 1187 also brought the magnates to the fore once more, for however much the dukes relied upon their household knights and mercenaries to wage war, they could not ignore the importance of the Norman aristocracy to the stability of the duchy, especially along the Norman frontiers. In the treaties of Messina (1191) and Le Goulet

[20] J.A. Green, 'Lords of the Norman Vexin', in *War and Government*, ed. Gillingham and Holt, 47–61; D.J. Power, 'The Norman Frontier in the Twelfth and Early Thirteenth Centuries', unpublished University of Cambridge PhD thesis, 1994. I discuss these cross-border connections in my forthcoming monograph on the Norman frontier.

[21] In general, see C.H. Haskins, *Norman Institutions*, Cambridge Mass. 1918, 156–95; D.J. Power, 'Angevin Normandy', in *A Companion to Anglo-Norman Studies*, ed. C. Harper-Bill and E.M.C. van Houts, forthcoming.

[22] Warren, *Henry II*, 117–36; for Hasculf's rôle see *Torigny*, ii, 35–6, 42–4. For the alignments of the chief Anglo-Norman magnates during the revolt see T.K. Keefe, *Feudal Assessments and the Political Community under Henry II and his Sons*, Univ. California 1983, 236–7.

[23] J.A. Green, 'King Henry I and the Aristocracy of Normandy', *111ᵉ Congrès National des Sociétés Savantes (Poitiers 1986), Histoire Médievale*, i (*La France Anglaise*), Paris 1988, 161–73; Crouch, 'Normans and Anglo-Normans', 51–67.

(1200) many of the sureties for the kings of England and France were magnates from either side of the eastern borders of Normandy.[24] So in 1199 the magnates were probably enjoying a political significance denied them since the early years of Henry II's reign; and their importance swelled still further at King Richard's sudden death. In Anjou and Maine, the success of the causes of both Arthur and John from 1199 to 1203 relied largely upon the lord of Sablé, William des Roches. In Normandy no single lord enjoyed such power, but elements within the Norman aristocracy could have seriously hindered John's success in 1199. On this particular occasion the Normans acted with one accord towards John by accepting him as their duke. The events of the next few years were to see them far less united.

The collapse of Plantagenet power in Normandy is most clearly understood if we treat the duchy as three main regions: the eastern marches; the southern marches; and central Normandy. It was in the eastern districts that the power of the king of France was most significant. By the late twelfth century the nobility all the way from Eu to Verneuil had to reckon with Capetian might and almost constant warfare.[25] In the southern frontier regions, along the borders of Perche, Maine and Brittany, French royal power was much less evident, but the magnates also had stronger traditions of independence and of conflict with the duke than elsewhere in Normandy. The central and north-western parts of the duchy from Rouen to the Cotentin constituted a third region, where ducal authority seems to have been at its most effective, the ducal peace most secure, and the aristocratic and economic connections with England strongest. Here the populace were totally unprepared for the appearance of mercenary armies in their midst in 1203, for there had been no major conflict in central Normandy since 1154.[26]

With this general political context in mind we can turn to John's relations with the Norman aristocracy between 1199 and 1204. Firstly, as count of Mortain, John himself had been a leading Norman magnate since 1189.[27] His county, a traditional apanage for cadets of the ruling dynasty, consisted of a compact marcher lordship, four castles (Mortain, Tinchebray, Le Teilleul and Cérences), estates scattered across much of Normandy, and revenues from the great fair of Montmartin.[28] John took an active interest in his Norman

---

[24] *Diplomatic Documents*, nos 5, 9.

[25] Power, 'Norman frontier', 150–3.

[26] *Torigny*, i, 282–3, 286–7 (sieges of Montfort and Torigny). An exception was King Richard's sack of Beaumont-le-Roger in 1194: Powicke, *Loss of Normandy*, 101–2.

[27] In 1189 Henry II had briefly considered making John heir to Normandy: Keefe, *Feudal Assessments*, 115, following *Giraldi Cambrensis Opera*, iv, 369.

[28] For the county's extent, see *Torigny*, i, 226; *MRSN*, i, 8–11, 14, 30, 215; ii, 538–48; Powicke, *Loss of Normandy*, 74–5; J. Boussard, 'Le comté de Mortain au IIe siècle', *Moyen Âge* 57, 1952, 253–79; M. Nortier, 'Le comté de Mortain au XIIIe siècle', *Melanges d'histoire normande: hommage à M. René Jouanne*, Flers 1970, 225–35. Little has been written about Mortain in the twelfth century, but see F.M. Powicke, 'The Honour of Mortain in the Norman *Infeudationes Militum* of 1172', *EHR* 26, 1911, 89–93. J. Pouëssel, 'Les structures militaires du unité de mortain (xie et xiie siècles)', *Revue de l'Avranchin et du Pays de Granville*, 58, 1981, 11–156.

county.[29] In addition he acquired part of the ducal forest of Lillebonne,[30] and Richard allowed him numerous other revenues in Normandy.[31] Indeed, the *Histoire de Guillaume le Maréchal* implies that John's familiarity with Normandy and England was a determining factor in his favour in 1199, for Arthur was deemed to be a hostile stranger by comparison.[32] Yet John had not always had cordial relations with the Norman aristocracy. His bid for the Plantagenet lands in 1193–4 had won support for him and Philip Augustus from several magnates in the eastern marches, notably the count of Meulan, Hugh de Gournay, and Richard de Vernon.[33] The Normans as a collective body, however, had rejected him in early 1193,[34] and we may suspect that the armed might and royal authority of Philip Augustus carried far more weight with his Norman partisans than did John. John's willingness to surrender most of Upper Normandy to the king of France in January 1194 cannot have endeared him to many in the duchy.[35] During the remainder of Richard's reign he played a modest part in Richard's victories, and may even have assisted Richard's captain, Mercadier, in capturing the bishop of Beauvais;[36] but his achievements were marred by the massacre of the French garrison of Évreux in 1194, apparently at his behest.[37] John's reputation with most Norman lords cannot have been particularly high when they accepted him as their duke in April 1199.

Nevertheless, John secured recognition in Normandy as Richard's heir, and within a year he had reunited virtually all the Plantagenet inheritance under him. Yet as duke his position was much weaker than Richard's had been ten years earlier. Since 1193 the king of France had seriously shaken the

---

[29] For John's acts as count (until their forthcoming publication) see *Rot. Chart.*, 18, 34, 57, 111; *Cal. Docs France*, nos 562, 565, 986; Caen, AD Calvados, H non classée, cartulary of Plessis-Grimoult, I, no. 31; AN, L 973, no. 828 (Savigny); L 979, no. 89 (Abbaye Blanche); Bib Mun Rouen, Y 51 (Fécamp Cartulary), fo. 10v; Rouen, AD Seine-Maritime, 18 HP 1 (Le Valasse). BN, ms. lat. 10065, fo. 91r–v, is a spurious or interpolated letter from John concerning the abbey of Blanchelande (*Cal. Docs France*, no. 869).

[30] Rouen, AD Seine-Maritime, 13 H 14 (act for Boscherville).

[31] Powicke, *Loss of Normandy*, 100; also *Cal. Docs France*, no. 873 (Jersey); Rouen, AD Seine-Maritime, 13 H 14 (property at Dieppe).

[32] *Hist. Guillaume le Maréchal*, ii, lines 11888–90 (iii, 160). For the uncertainty of John's legal claim to Normandy, see J.C. Holt, 'The *Casus Regis*: the Law and Politics of Succession in the Plantagenet Dominions 1185–1247', *Sewanee Medieval Colloquium 1987*, ed. E.B. King and S.J. Ridyard, Sewanee 1990, 21–42.

[33] *Howden*, iii, 218–9, 258–9 (Meulan, Gournay); *MRSN*, i, 148, 153 (lands of Richard de Vernon).

[34] *Howden*, iii, 204.

[35] *Layettes*, i, no. 412.

[36] *Howden*, iv, 16. He also took Gamaches-en-Vexin in 1196 and fired Le Neubourg to mislead the French into an ambush in 1198 (*ibid.*, iv, 5, 60). R.V. Turner, 'King John's Military Reputation Reconsidered', *JMH* 19, 1993, 171–200, at pp. 175–7, reassesses John's achievements in these combats, but treats Gamaches as Gamaches-sur-Bresle near Eu, which seems very unlikely.

[37] Powicke, *Loss of Normandy*, 101; cf. M. Strickland, *War and Chivalry: the Conduct and Perception of War in England and Normandy, 1066–1217*, Cambridge 1996, 53, 223.

Plantagenet hold on the duchy. In territorial terms, Philip Augustus had made headway chiefly in the eastern marches, where he could deploy his wealth and exert his guile directly.[38] In the Norman Vexin the barons had long been aware of Capetian claims to that *pagus* and were as likely to fight for the king of France as for the duke of Normandy;[39] but by 1199 the tentacles of Capetian power had spread along the Norman frontier both northwards and westwards from the Vexin. Northwards, the Capetian acquisition of the Amiénois in 1185 drastically altered the relationship between the local aristocracy and the king of France. Traditionally, power in the north-eastern marches of Normandy and adjacent areas of Picardy had been very devolved;[40] the authority of the duke of Normandy had apparently never been tightly defined in the region of Gournay and Aumale, where the aristocracy had lands and other interests running into Picardy. Other princes who jostled for control in western Picardy included the counts of Vermandois and Ponthieu and the bishop of Beauvais, but in practice the Picard castellans were very powerful, and perhaps only Philip d'Alsace, count of Flanders and, *jure uxoris*, of Vermandois, made good the claims of the counts of Vermandois in the region.[41] The significance of Flemish control of the Vermandois inheritance for north-eastern Normandy was clear. When Count Philip attacked Normandy in support of Louis VII in 1173, the invaders rapidly took Aumale and penetrated as far as Drincourt and Arques, whereas without Flemish help Louis VII could rarely campaign beyond the Vexin and Évrecin.[42]

However, when Philip Augustus acquired the county of Amiens from the count of Flanders in 1185 he overturned this order.[43] Henceforth, it was the king of France who sought to dictate events in this region: in 1192 he demanded the adjacent parts of Normandy, the counties of Eu and Aumale; in 1193 he secured Arques as a pledge for the truce with the Normans; and in 1195 he promised Eu and Arques, as his sister's dowry, to the count of Ponthieu, in a marriage alliance that strengthened Capetian influence in this region still further.[44] Although Richard I regained these fortresses, he soon lost Aumale again,

---

[38] Cf. Gillingham, *Richard the Lionheart*, 246 (map).

[39] Green, 'Norman Vexin', 47–61.

[40] Cf. Power, 'Frontier of Angevin Normandy', 190.

[41] Cf. Gilbert of Mons, *MGH Scriptores*, XXI, 531–2, 535–6. *Diceto*, ii, 32, and *Gesta Regis Henrici*, i, 321, state that William de Mandeville, then count of Aumale, gave military support to his lord the count of Flanders in 1184, although this could have been due to his Flemish upbringing; see Keefe, *Feudal Assessments*, 112.

[42] For the count of Flanders in this region in 1173, see especially *Newburgh*, i, 173 (cf. 190); also *Torigny*, ii, 39–41; *Gesta Regis Henrici*, i, 47, 49; *Diceto*, i, 373. The counts of Flanders and Ponthieu had also attacked Drincourt in 1167: J. Gillingham, 'War and Chivalry in the *History of William the Marshal'*, *Thirteenth Century England: Proceedings of the Newcastle upon Tyne Conference 1987*, ed. P.R. Coss and S.D. Lloyd, Woodbridge 1988, 1–13, at p. 2.

[43] Baldwin, *Government*, 24–6.

[44] *Howden*, iii, 287; *Actes de Philippe Auguste*, ii, no. 508.

probably for good.[45] In view of Capetian pressure in this district, it is no wonder that the lord of Gournay, even though his natural instincts may well have lain with his Plantagenet lords before any others, thereafter gained a name for unreliability and ultimately treachery, for his lands were now very exposed indeed. In his search for allies King Richard also conferred the county of Eu upon the Poitevin lord Ralph de Lusignan through marriage to its heiress, and then augmented this grant with the ducal fortress of Drincourt.[46] The ducal domain in this region was thereby diminished and Eu and Drincourt became embroiled in the tangled politics of Poitou.

An incident early in John's reign must have reinforced this view that the king of France now held sway within this part of Normandy. In the spring of 1201, the Lusignans revolted against John and set about besieging his castles, and in reply the seneschal of Normandy invested the count of Eu's fortress of Drincourt. Before John could cross from England, however, the king of France is said to have intervened and ended 'all the sieges', including, by implication, the siege of Drincourt.[47] If so, Philip Augustus was in effect already arbiter of the north-eastern Norman march. The inferior ducal resources in this region explain why Lyons-la-Forêt, Mortemer, the castles of Hugh de Gournay and several neighbouring fortresses fell so rapidly to the French once war recommenced in 1202,[48] and John's hope that the burgesses of Eu might resist their count for him were quickly dashed.[49] Soon Philip was able to raise revenues from this region for his own war effort through the cooperation of local knights.[50]

In the south-eastern marches, where Normandy bordered directly upon the French king's domains, Philip's acquisitions by the summer of 1199 were even more significant. During Richard I's imprisonment in Germany, King Philip had subdued the Norman Vexin, the Évrecin and the Eure and Avre valleys; and although Richard had reconquered most of this territory after his release in 1194, a number of important fortresses remained in French hands, including Gisors, Neaufles, Vernon, Pacy, Gaillon, Ivry and Nonancourt.[51] Since castles

---

[45] Powicke, *Loss of Normandy*, 110. *Diplomatic Documents*, no. 9, implies that the county of Aumale was under John's control in 1200, and *Coggeshall*, 136, states that Philip captured the castle and county of Aumale in 1202; however, in view of Richard's spectacular defeat there in 1196 and the failure of any author to record the Normans recapturing Aumale thereafter, the fortress itself had most probably remained in Capetian hands.

[46] S. Painter, 'The Houses of Lusignan and Châtellerault', in *Feudalism and Liberty*, ed. F.A. Cazel Jr, Baltimore 1961, 374–84, at p. 379; *Howden*, iv, 160–1.

[47] *Howden*, iv, 160–1; Powicke, *Loss of Normandy*, 144–5; for the siege, also *MRSN*, ii, 501; cf. *Rot. Chart.*, 102. *Guillaume le Breton*, ii, 155 (*Philippidos*, VI, lines 97–9) states that Drincourt actually fell to John's forces.

[48] Powicke, *Loss of Normandy*, 149–50.

[49] *Rot. Litt. Pat.*, 8, 13: Eu had fallen by 29 June 1202. *Coggeshall*, 136, alleges that King Philip met no resistance in this region.

[50] D.J. Power, 'John de Rouvray and the Knights of the Pays de Bray, c. 1180–1225', in *Family Trees and the Roots of Politics: the Prosopography of Britain and France from the Tenth to the Twelfth Century*, ed. K.S.B. Keats-Rohan, Woodbridge 1997, 361–84, at p. 379.

[51] Cf. Powicke, *Loss of Normandy*, 124.

had an offensive as well as a defensive capability, these fortresses gave Philip's soldiers easy access deep into the duchy: although Richard routed Philip Augustus outside Gisors in September 1198, the king of France was still able to attack Évreux immediately afterwards.[52] Richard's death revealed the significance of the French hold on these castles: not only was Norman pressure on Gisors instantly relaxed, but Philip rapidly seized Évreux and the surrounding district.[53] Indeed, if a charter for the abbey of La Noë near Évreux is dated correctly, Philip had taken the city and installed his own castellan less than a fortnight after Richard's death, so he may have renewed the war as soon as he heard that the king of England had been wounded.[54] In the first year of his reign John was in no position to regain these losses apart from Conches and he surrendered them at Le Goulet. When war broke out again, the king of France derived considerable advantage from control of the Évrecin. John Baldwin has shown that the French army planned to advance up the west bank of the Seine in 1202, and although this plan was abandoned because of the setback at Mirebeau, it was executed the following year.[55] Here, too, Philip's mastery won him local support. By May 1203 men from the Évrecin were serving in his army at Alençon with the former Plantagenet farmer of Évreux, Richard d'Argences.[56]

So by the time John had gained Normandy he held a considerably smaller territory than his brother had in 1189; his loss of control over the easternmost parts of Normandy was primarily a consequence of the superior might of the king of France, which neither he nor the Norman lords could withstand. Do we need to look further to account for most defections from John in this region in 1203? If other castles had been defended as resolutely as Château-Gaillard was in 1203–4, no doubt the French attack would have faltered; but this should not mask the political imbalance that existed in this region. Moreover, the French invasions in Richard's reign had done far more than merely deprive the duke of Normandy or his barons of various border castles; they had shaken the whole structure of Plantagenet authority in the duchy. King Philip had challenged the loyalty of the Norman aristocracy to their duke, offering an alternative source of patronage and redress; already some disgruntled Normans had sought to benefit from this before 1199.[57] In the treaty of Le Goulet John had to acknowledge another Capetian acquisition made during the Plantagenet succession

---

[52] *Howden*, iv, 60.

[53] *Rigord*, 145; *Howden*, iv, 85.

[54] BN, ms. lat. 5464, no. 20: act of Sibyl d'Émalleville for La Noë, witnessed by Hugh Branchart, 'castellan of Évreux'. It is dated '1198', which must be by the French system and can be no later than 17 April; King Richard had died on 6 April. Hugh had been King Philip's squire (*Actes de Philippe Auguste*, i, no. 402).

[55] Baldwin, *Government*, 167–8.

[56] See below, p. 131.

[57] E.g. Peter, brother of Hasculf de St-Hilaire (the rebel of 1173), who resented the division of Hasculf's lands made between him and Hasculf's daughter (Powicke, *Loss of Normandy*, 351–2). For his relationship to Hasculf, see AN, L 972, no. 647.

crisis: Philip was allowed to retain not only the city but also the bishopric of Évreux, with all its regalia. The unity of the Norman church had been one of the main foundations of ducal power and authority; its erosion had serious consequences for the stability and integrity of the duchy. Philip subsequently proclaimed that henceforth all episcopal elections in Évreux should be conducted freely, and it is this gratuitous propaganda *coup* which has attracted most attention from historians, but King John's cession was in many ways far more significant.[58]

The situation in the eastern marches suggests that the king of France had dealt several heavy blows to Plantagenet rule in Normandy, and perhaps it would have eventually collapsed simply because it was being progressively outstripped by Capetian resources and influence in these crucial border regions. Yet the war of 1202–4 that led to the demise of ducal power was by no means confined to eastern Normandy, and the rest of the duchy also requires consideration if we are to understand why it collapsed so rapidly. In the southern regions of Normandy, from Verneuil to the Breton border, we find a quite different political situation. Here the local aristocracy had a history of stubborn resistance to ducal authority, often centred around the control of particular fortresses, or even whole clusters of castles.[59] Many lordships were exempt from the ducal hearth-tax (*fouage*),[60] and fewer cases were brought to the Exchequer court at Caen.[61] In general the aristocracy here probably had fewest English connections,[62] but stronger links with Maine and Perche. Only in the far west, in the Avranchin and county of Mortain, did the aristocracy have somewhat closer ties to England or the ducal court; but the lords of Fougères in Brittany and of Mayenne in Maine wielded considerable influence as well.[63] Most significantly, the king of France was heavily dependent upon local cooperation in order to exert any political influence in the area. The French attacks upon Sées in 1151 and 1174 and the French invasions of northern Maine in 1189 and 1199 relied largely upon local help; when King Philip lost the support of William des Roches in 1199 he soon had to withdraw from Maine.[64] Yet even in the southern marches John inherited a political situation that was less favourable

---

[58] *Actes de Philippe Auguste*, ii, no. 637; cf. J. Baldwin, 'Philip Augustus and the Norman Church', *French Historical Studies* 6, 1969, 1–30, at pp. 4–6; Baldwin, *Government*, 179–81.

[59] Power, 'Frontier of Angevin Normandy', 186–9.

[60] T.N. Bisson, *The Conservation of Coinage*, Oxford 1979, 19–20, 204–5 (*Registres*, 556–7).

[61] Power, 'Norman Frontier', 198–9.

[62] L.C. Loyd, *Origins of Some Anglo-Norman Families*, ed. C.T. Clay and D.C. Douglas, Leeds 1951, Map (opposite 140), is very suggestive on this point.

[63] K.S.B. Keats-Rohan, 'The Bretons and Normans of England 1066–1154: the Family, the Fief and the Feudal Monarchy', *Nottingham Medieval Studies* 36, 1992, 42–78, at pp. 51–3, demonstrates various connections between the south-west Norman marches and north-east Brittany before 1150.

[64] For these attacks see *Torigny*, i, 254 (1151); *Diceto*, i, 379 (1174); ii, 63–4 (1189); *Gesta Regis Henrici*, ii, 67–9 (1189); *Howden*, iv, 96 (1199).

than in 1189. In his effort to win over allies King Richard appears to have conceded two important border castles, Moulins and Bonsmoulins, to the count of Perche.[65] In April 1199 Arthur of Brittany had given away three other ducal castles to Juhel de Mayenne: Gorron, Ambrières and Châtillon. These were the chief fortresses of the southern Passais and Juhel's family had ancient and persevering claims to them. Although John won back two of the castles after the failure of Arthur's cause in 1199, he had to hand them back to the lord of Mayenne in 1201 as the price of peace, a setback in an already unstable border region.[66] On both the southern and the eastern Norman frontiers, the material consequences of Arthur's challenge lasted beyond the Treaty of Le Goulet.

John's agreement with Juhel de Mayenne in 1201 gives us a vivid impression of where power really lay in this region. Juhel named as his sureties his half-brother Maurice de Craon, William des Roches, Count Robert of Sées, Guy de Laval, Stephen, brother of the count of Perche, and the viscounts of Beaumont and Châtellerault.[67] Together they represented the political community of the Loire provinces, lords closely related by blood or marriage whose power extended from central Normandy to Northern Poitou. In 1199 the Plantagenet succession dispute pitted several of them against one another; in 1202 the renewal of war between John and Arthur would have a similar effect, but their readiness to stand surety for Juhel de Mayenne demonstrated the level of trust that existed amongst them; and by January 1203 John had alienated them all.[68] Since this group included several lords with interests in or connections with Normandy, any serious challenge to John's control of Maine and Anjou threatened to engulf the southern regions of Normandy as well. Indeed, the revolt which William des Roches led in Anjou in 1202 must have contributed to the most significant and dramatic event in southern Normandy in John's reign: the rebellion of the count of Sées in January 1203.

This episode combined many of the factors described above: the ties between the southern Normans and neighbouring provinces, their grievances against the duke over the control of castles, and the lack of cohesion amongst the Normans overall. Count Robert was head of the Talvas family, southern frontier lords who were equally powerful in northern Maine.[69] They had long been isolated from the ducal court and had strong grounds to bear a grudge

---

[65] Power, 'Frontier of Angevin Normandy', 189n.; K.H. Thompson, 'The Counts of the Perche, c. 1066–1217', unpublished PhD thesis, Sheffield 1995, 135–6.

[66] Power, 'Frontier of Angevin Normandy', 187–8, which, however, fails to note that John had regained Gorron and Ambrières by 1201 (*Rot. Litt. Pat.*, 2).

[67] Rymer's *Fœdera*, I. i, 84–5.

[68] The fall of Anjou and Maine requires a separate study and will not be discussed in detail here. Stephen du Perche was absent on crusade.

[69] For the family in general, see Power, 'Norman Frontier', e.g. 124–7, 170–1, 317–19; K. Thompson, 'William Talvas, Count of Ponthieu, and the Politics of the Anglo-Norman Realm', in *England and Normandy*, ed. Bates and Curry, 169–84. For their comital title, see *ibid.*, 181–2; for simplicity's sake I refer to Count Robert by the title which the Plantagenet chancery accorded him.

against the dukes, for Henry II had taken their castles of Alençon and Roche-Mabile in 1166.[70] Count Robert may, however, have attempted to re-establish links with the dukes after he succeeded to the Talvas lands in 1191. It is probably not significant that he and his brother witnessed an act of Richard I in 1195, since it concerned a local priory;[71] but he seems to have profited from John's need for allies in 1199 by attaching himself to the Plantagenet court. He had joined John by 7 August, when he was with the new duke at Sées,[72] and he witnessed another seven of John's acts between 1199 and 1201.[73] Probably the count, aware of John's predicament at Richard's death, was seeking to regain his ancestral fortresses, even though he thereby had to oppose his neighbours and cousins from Maine who had quickly shown themselves to be Arthur's partisans. At first John did not restore the desired castles to him, and instead granted a commune to the burgesses of Alençon in September 1199.[74] Disappointed at this juncture, the count may have had more success when war began again in 1202, for he was certainly in control of the castle of Alençon when he deserted to King Philip.[75] Yet there is no evidence that he had been granted the castles as his inheritance rather than in custody, and rebellion may have been the only way he could secure his right to them.

Count Robert's close relations with the lords of the Loire provinces are, however, a more convincing reason for his desertion. As King John lost control of Anjou and Maine to William des Roches in the autumn and winter of 1202, the count would have been faced with a grave conflict of loyalties. His close kinsman, the Poitevin viscount of Châtellerault, had been captured at Mirebeau and was still John's prisoner;[76] his cousin Juhel de Mayenne was fervently upholding Arthur's cause again in Maine;[77] and Count Robert's powerful neighbour in Maine, the viscount of Beaumont, was clearly wavering by November 1202 when John appealed to him to ignore any rumours that John had spoken ill of him.[78] The story of Count Robert's dramatic defection to King Philip, immediately after John had stayed at Alençon, is well known;[79] yet, in the context of his family's history, Count Robert's actions are very understandable. Indeed,

---

[70] *Torigny*, i, 360.

[71] Bib Mun Rouen, Y 201, fo. 36: act for the priory of La Saute-Cochère (Exmes, 20 Dec. 1195).

[72] *The Cartæ Antiquæ Rolls 11–20*, ed. J. Conway Davies, PRS ns 1960, 116 ('Ricardo [*sic*] Comite Sagyen.').

[73] *Rot. Chart.*, 32, 64 (*bis*), 69, 71 (*bis*); Alençon, AD Orne, H 3349 (faulty copy of act of John at Caen, 6 Nov. 1201, also witnessed by Robert's brother William).

[74] *Rot. Chart.*, 17. Alençon had still been in the ducal domain in July 1199 (*ibid.*, 4).

[75] Cf. Powicke, *Loss of Normandy*, 182n.

[76] *Coggeshall*, 137–8; *Rot. Litt. Pat.*, 16, 22. The Châtellerault genealogy is extremely complex: this family was among the heirs to the Talvas lands in 1219–20, apparently through Count Robert's sister, but Painter, 'Houses of Lusignan', 380–4, does not explain the connection satisfactorily.

[77] Cf. *Rot. Norm.*, 61, 63, 65, 69.

[78] *Rot. Litt. Pat.*, 20.

[79] Powicke, *Loss of Normandy*, 157–8.

they were remarkably similar to those of his grandfather William Talvas, who had joined the Manceaux and Angevins in opposing the duke of Normandy, Stephen of Blois, in 1135.[80] When John left Alençon that midwinter day he evidently failed to give the count sufficient guarantees that he had more to gain by staying in John's camp than by leaving it. Others in the border region evidently felt the same way: the viscount of Beaumont followed Count Robert into revolt and John's position in Maine crumbled further.[81]

John's bitterness at this revolt is undoubted: his chancery even dated his fourth regnal year as 'the year in which Count Robert of Sées committed treason against us at Alençon', even though the charter thus dated had no connection with the count or his lands.[82] Twenty years later the *Histoire de Guillaume le Maréchal* was equally condemning. The count's action was shameful: 'Huntuz est qui de gré s'avile'.[83] Other accounts, however, do not denounce him: not only Rigord and William the Breton but also the Coggeshall chronicler and the *Histoire des Ducs de Normandie* record his defection without comment.[84] Perhaps most significant is the reaction of Philip Augustus. His disdain for *tournés* was proverbial; he treated Robert FitzWalter and Saher de Quincy harshly for their derisory defence of Vaudreuil against him and he exiled Hugh de Gournay rather than restoring him to his lost honours,[85] yet the count of Sées profited greatly at his hands. Perhaps Count Robert was too powerful to alienate; the flight of so many nobles to England in 1204 made him the greatest nobleman in Normandy. King Philip was not, however, afraid to chastise another count in Normandy, Renaud of Boulogne, when it suited him, and the marriage in 1205 between Count Robert's son and the daughter of King Philip's closest advisor, Bartholomew de Roye, suggests that the king of France held Robert in high regard.[86]

---

[80] Thompson, 'William Talvas', 174–7. Cf. D. Bates, 'The Rise and Fall of Normandy, c. 911–1204', in *England and Normandy*, ed. Bates and Curry, 19–35, at pp. 23–4.

[81] *Coggeshall*, 139. John's declining support in Anjou and Maine placed the viscount in a similarly difficult position: John was his cousin and had recently promoted his brother to the bishopric of Angers (*Rot. Litt. Pat.*, 14), and the viscount's sister, wife of Roger de Tosny, enjoyed John's favour (Powicke, *Loss of Normandy*, 134n.). His mother, lady of Le Lude, came to terms with John on 23 January, just after the Alençon revolt, but the viscount's adherents were suffering confiscation by 31 January (*Rot. Litt. Pat.*, 24; *Rot. Norm.*, 73). Another rebel in this district was the lord of Carrouges, Richard *de Vilers* (*Premier budget*, CCV; cf. *Rot. Norm.*, 75). Alençon, AD Orne, H 1986 (*vidimus* of act of Richard *de Vileris*, lord of Carrouges) establishes his identity.

[82] Rouen, AD Seine-Maritime, 3 H 16 (*Cal. Docs France*, no. 391), given at Bec-Hellouin, 20 April 1203: 'anno regni nostro quarto, quo comes Robertus Sagiensis fecit nobis proditionem apud Alenconem'. The charter confirms the rights of wardship of the abbey of Bec. Cf. Strickland, *War and Chivalry*, 225.

[83] *Hist. Guillaume le Maréchal*, ii, ll. 12.607–12,632 (iii, 171–2); the line quoted is 12,620.

[84] *Rigord*, 158; *Guillaume le Breton*, i, 211; *Coggeshall*, 139, linking the revolt to William des Roches; *Hist. Ducs de Normandie*, 96 (cf. the chronicle of Béthune, *RHF*, XXIV, ii, 762.).

[85] Strickland, *War and Chivalry*, 226–7; Powicke, *Loss of Normandy*, 285–6.

[86] *Actes de Philippe Auguste*, ii, no. 905. This was not a disparaging match for the Talvas, as the bride was a niece of Simon de Montfort.

The rebellion at Alençon also demonstrates that not all Normans shared the same interests, for few of the count's knights deeper into Normandy seem to have followed him into revolt.[87] The Talvas supposedly had some 112 Norman knights in their service and owed twenty more to the duke's army;[88] if all these had joined the insurrection, John would have confronted revolt even around Caen and Falaise. In the event, the revolt was very limited in its geographical scope, for John retained control even of Sées, just fifteen miles north of Alençon, as late as October 1203,[89] and freely gave away the count's central Norman lands.[90] More than a year after Count Robert's defection, one of his seneschals from central Normandy, Robert de Ri, attended the court of the Norman exchequer at Caen, where King John's seneschal of Normandy, William le Gras, was presiding.[91] Quite apart from the evidence which this provides that Norman government persisted until the king of France took Caen, it shows the lack of cohesion between the different parts of the Talvas inheritance. In June 1204 the garrison of Rouen included some of Count Robert's knights and squires who had preferred to stay loyal to their duke.[92] This was in keeping with the previous history of the Talvas lordships, for the counts had already fought against their own men in Stephen's reign and during the Young King's revolt.[93]

At about this time, perhaps because his central-Norman followers had failed to rise in revolt, Count Robert was alienating his woods near Alençon to secure more military support on the southern Norman border.[94] He also received Capetian aid, including from King Philip's newly acquired Norman territories: by May 1203 he had been joined at Alençon by the French king's marshal, Henry Clement, and Albert de Hangest, a leading Picard knight in King Philip's service, and by knights from the Évrecin with Richard d'Argences, the erstwhile Plantagenet custodian of Évreux.[95] These soldiers were supplemented by

---

[87] Powicke, *Loss of Normandy*, 175–7, lists the count's known adherents; *Jugements*, no. 366, appears to concern another one, at *Sifretot* (Chiffretot, Orne, cant. Vimoutiers, cne. Champosoult?).

[88] *Red Book*, ii, 626 (1172); for the number after 1204, see *RHF*, XXIII, 706, 707 (*Registres*, 283, 285), 715.

[89] *Rot. de Lib.*, 72, implies that John still controlled Sées Cathedral on 9 October.

[90] *Rot. Norm.*, 70–1.

[91] Caen, AD Calvados, H 6510, fo. 3v, no. 7 (dated 1204); the case concerned lands near Argentan. For Robert de Ri as the count's seneschal, see AD Calvados, H 6512, no. 7; for his lands at Ri as one of the count's fiefs, see AD Calvados, H 6511, no. 8.

[92] *Layettes*, i, no. 716.

[93] Thompson, 'William Talvas', 176; *Diceto*, i, 379.

[94] *Les Olim*, ed. le Comte de Beugnot, 3 vols, Paris 1839–48, i, 324–5: Count Robert 'of Alençon' grants the thicket of St-Aubin d'Appenai to Matthew le Véer in return for custody at the castle of Essay, dated '1202'. For Matthew, whose interests lay mainly in Perche, see Power, 'Norman Frontier', 124–5.

[95] Évreux, AD Eure, H 672: Robert de Bois-Gencelin enfeoffs Roger de Caugé with woodlands near Évreux, witnessed by Count Robert 'of Alençon', Albert de Hangest, Henry, marshal of the king of France, and Richard d'Argences, at Alençon. For Richard, see Powicke, *Loss of Normandy*, 172, 174–5, 331, 349; *Premier budget*, CXCVI, CCIX,

French subsidies,[96] and Juhel de Mayenne helped defend Alençon against John's counter-attack. Nevertheless, it is probable that King Philip could barely sustain the revolt. Certainly this was the view in Normandy twenty years later. In about 1227, a burgess of Caen called R. Gaudin wrote to Henry III to report the opinions of two Capetian officials in Normandy, including upon the events of 1203–4: they believed that if John had captured Alençon with Count Robert and Juhel de Mayenne inside, this would have ended the war. William the Breton curiously claimed that King Philip had to commandeer a tournament party near Paris in order to relieve Alençon; like Gaudin's letter, this strange tale implies that inadequate resources were preventing King Philip operating effectively so far from his domains.[97]

If King John's loss of southern Normandy was not due to superior Capetian strength, why did he fail to crush the disaffection there? The crucial setback was John's abortive siege of Alençon, with an army from central Normandy, in August 1203.[98] While William the Breton attributed the siege's failure to King Philip's hasty relief, Gaudin's letter ascribed it to the disaffection of the Norman barons: so outraged were the Normans at the depredations of John's mercenaries in central Normandy that they tricked him into believing that the king of France was close at hand, when the castle of Alençon was just about to fall.[99] Here, then, the chroniclers' stories of disaffection and treachery can be related to a specific, decisive incident. It brings us to those areas where ducal authority had remained largely unchallenged; and it leads us to ask whether John's misrule alienated his Norman supporters and led to the fall of Normandy at a speed the Capetian assaults in the east could not.

In general, it is true, there is little concrete evidence for the oppressions of John's regime. One illuminating, but late and fragmentary, source is the *Querimoniæ Normannorum*, the inquests into abuses that were executed for Louis IX in 1247.[100] A great many of the grievances which the commissioners recorded dated back to the 1200s, but mostly they concerned the confiscations which had followed John's expulsion from Normandy or injustices committed by Capetian *baillis* rather than under the Plantagenet regime. Against John there were only two specific complaints: he had built a mill at Verneuil and had

CCX. For Henry and Albert, see Baldwin, *Government*, 112–13, 168 (noting Henry's disappearance from Capetian fiscal accounts at this time).

[96] *Premier budget*, CCV: 500 li. paid to Count Robert, 300 li. to his brother William CCII (horses and harness for Juhel de Mayenne and the 'count of Alençon').

[97] *Diplomatic Documents*, no. 206; *Guillaume le Breton*, i, 211–12. For Gaudin's letter, see also Holt, 'Anglo-Norman Realm', 264–5.

[98] *MRSN*, ii, ccliii–cclxiv, 570; *Rot. Norm.*, 102, 115; Powicke, *Loss of Normandy*, 164.

[99] *Diplomatic Documents*, no. 206. The wording of Gaudin's letter is ambiguous: A. Cartellieri, *Philipp August, König von Frankreich*, 4 vols in 5, Leipzig 1899–1922, iv. I, 163–4, interprets it to mean that the seneschal of Normandy, William le Gras, was the special object of hatred, not John.

[100] For a discussion of this source, see C. Petit-Dutaillis, '*Querimoniæ Normannorum*', *Essays in Medieval History presented to T.F. Tout*, ed. A.G. Little and F.M. Powicke, Manchester 1925, 99–118. The text is in *RHF* XXIV, i, 1904, 2–73 [hereafter QN].

extended the fortifications of Falaise without compensating the burgesses whose property was harmed.[101] Now the recorded *querimoniæ* concern only about half the duchy, and some of John's 'oppressions' must have been redressed in the years after 1204; certainly King Philip attempted to right some wrongs after the fall of Normandy.[102] However, where John's rule was definitely found wanting was in the behaviour of his last seneschal of Normandy, William le Gras, about whom there were some twenty-two separate complaints in which he was accused of extorting lands or rights *per potenciam suam*. More than forty years after King John's flight from Normandy his seneschal's misdeeds were still notorious – or at least they furnished a credible excuse before St Louis's commissioners. Yet these do not amount to an indictment of Plantagenet government as a whole. All but one came from the district of Falaise,[103] mostly from parishes within a few miles of the seneschal's lands at Soulangy, where William was also enmeshed in a dispute with the abbey of Saint-Évroul.[104] So although he was apparently using his power as seneschal to acquire property, this was only in the vicinity of his estates. More importantly, he was not accused of acting oppressively on his royal master's behalf; that offence was restricted to the Capetian *baillis* after 1204. The recorded offences for an earlier Plantagenet seneschal of Normandy, Guérin de Glapion, were even more geographically restricted, to just three localities in southern Normandy, including around Glapion itself.[105]

Gaudin's letter shows, however, that William le Gras was remembered in the 1220s primarily for advising John to bring Louvrecaire and his *routiers* to garrison Falaise, from where they terrorised the very lands they were supposed to be defending, violating the wives and property of the Norman knights.[106] The

---

[101] QN, nos. 250, 403.

[102] *Jugements*, no. 366; QN, no. 412 (later reversed by the Capetian *bailli*).

[103] See Map. QN, nos. 379, 381, 382, 399, 406, 407, 412, 427, 430–2 concern Soulangy or the nearby parishes of St-Loup, Aubigny, St-Pierre-Canivet, Villers-Canivet, Aubigny, Tassilly, Martigny, Pierrepont, and (probably) Olendon, all north or west of Falaise; nos. 380, 440, and 441 are from Ste-Honorine-la-Guillaume, to the south-west. Nos. 448, 449, 454, 455, 459, and 462 concern Ifs-sur-Laizon, near St-Pierre-sur-Dives. Only no. 18 (Beuzeval in Auge) is not near Falaise. Nos. 384 and 400 mention William le Gras without making accusations, while no. 452 states that he took land in pledge. For William's origins and career, see N.C. Vincent, 'The Borough of Chipping Sodbury and the Fat Men of France', *Transactions of the Bristol and Gloucestershire Record Society*, 116, 1998, 42–59 at 44–6. I am grateful to Dr Vincent for allowing me to consult a draft of this paper.

[104] Alençon, AD Orne, H 770 (undated, c. 1200): act of William le Gras for St-Évroul, concerning Soulangy and promising to respect 'antiquas consuetudines' at 'Alnetum'.

[105] QN, nos 523, 527 (Ste-Scolasse, Le Plantis); 498, 516 (Exmes); perhaps 476 (Fontenay-sur-Orne near Argentan). Nos. 530 and 532 concern the claims of Guérin's heirs; nos. 542, 549 also mention him. For his property near Exmes and Fontenay, see QN, no. 530; Alençon, AD Orne, H 1977, H 3349. For Guérin, see Powicke, *Loss of Normandy*, 173–4, but the *Querimoniæ* hardly make him, in Powicke's words, 'a notorious robber of other men's property'.

[106] *Diplomatic Documents*, no. 206.

Histoire de Guillaume le Maréchal also regarded the marauding of Louvecaire's mercenaries as the chief cause of Norman desertions.[107] There certainly was a close connection between William le Gras and Louvrecaire in 1203–4, for the abbess of Caen fined to have the peace of the seneschal of Normandy and Louvrecaire and to have letters of protection against them and the *routiers*, as well as for restitution of her lands and men whom the mercenaries had seized.[108] The seneschal's unpopularity is also suggested by his exclusion from the general amnesty in June 1204.[109] It is, therefore, quite plausible that the growing hatred for his seneschal and mercenaries in central Normandy led in turn to John's military failures in the southern marches in 1203 and undermined his support in areas where he had hitherto been secure.

The setback at Alençon was followed by ineffective raids into the French marches and Brittany, and an equally fruitless attempt to relieve Château-Gaillard that starkly demonstrated the inferiority of John's resources in eastern Normandy. Confronting defeat in the marches and discontent in central Normandy, he abandoned the duchy altogether in December 1203. Normandy lost its duke and his household and faced the king of France leaderless, and, not surprisingly, those Normans still loyal to John failed to rally against the French and Breton armies that appeared in central Normandy in May 1204. Indeed, King Philip must have been aware of the disaffection in the previously loyal heart of Normandy, for after his stunning capture of Château-Gaillard in March, he profited from John's absence to march to Falaise and Caen before besieging Rouen. By then some Normans were pledging their English lands rather than risk their confiscation.[110] Soon there were other indications of Norman resignation or indifference. On 29 May, a small group of Normans gathered at Lanquetot, less than thirty miles north-west of Rouen in the Pays de Caux, to endow the nearby abbey of Le Valasse. Did it matter to them that the king of France was besieging the capital of Normandy that very day? The donor and his cronies clearly had their souls and their abbey to think about first.[111] Rather than resist, the Normans preferred to smooth the transition from Plantagenet to Capetian rule. When William Marshal yielded his castles to the king of France in May 1204, this was effected through a knight from the eastern marches, Osbert de Rouvray, whose brother, John, was prominent at the French court.[112] Yet Osbert was also in Rouen on 4 May with the archbishop of Rouen and two leading knights of the garrison, the brothers Geoffrey and Renaud de Bosco,

---

[107] *Hist. Guillaume le Maréchal*, ii, lines 12,595–12,606 (iii, 171). See Powicke, *Loss of Normandy*, 230.

[108] *PR 6 John*, 150.

[109] *Layettes*, i, no. 716.

[110] *Rot. Litt. Pat.*, 39 (Hugh le Portier of Lyons-la-Forêt, Robert de Gouvix).

[111] Rouen, AD Seine-Maritime, 18 HP 4 (act of Helias de Longueil). All the witnesses were very local.

[112] *Layettes*, i, no. 715; Power, 'John de Rouvray', esp. pp. 379–80.

which suggests that he himself was one of city's defenders.[113] Under the terms of the truce which heralded the capitulation of Rouen, the Normans were to surrender the castles according to the advice of John de Rouvray and John de Préaux – in other words, two knights from eastern Normandy who had joined the French king but with brothers within the garrison of Rouen.[114] After the surrender the king of France relied heavily upon Normans as he established his authority in the duchy, including several close associates of Count Robert of Sées.[115]

This readiness to accommodate the French king goes far to explain King John's relations with the aristocracy of Normandy after 1204. At the very least John should have attracted dissident Normans, for he represented an alternative source of patronage to Philip Augustus, yet he failed to destabilise Capetian rule in the duchy. In 1205 it is said that some of the Normans appealed to him against Philip's 'tyranny', and that the French knights defending Normandy were terrified that John would return, but there was only a brief uprising at Dieppe which was quickly suppressed.[116] In 1206 Philip Augustus reinforced his Norman castles because he expected, wrongly, that John would land there.[117] The king of France also felt obliged to go to Rouen and Verneuil in full force in 1207; and in 1214, he destroyed the walls of Verneuil and annulled the town's exemption from *fouage* because the citizens had offended him.[118] Such an incident, in the year of Bouvines, implies that Philip feared a Norman insurrection, but only one Norman lord, Fulk Paynel, actually joined John in Poitou.[119] By contrast, seventy Norman knights fought at Bouvines, and William the Breton vaunted the province's loyalty to the king of France.[120] Most striking of all is the passivity of the Normans when the count of Boulogne rebelled at Mortain in 1211. In view of the previous history of the Norman aristocracy, we can only conclude that this was a province which might resent its *baillis* but which tolerated its new Capetian ruler.

To find a single explanation for the fall of Normandy ignores the disunity of the Norman aristocracy. The lords of the eastern marches of Normandy had long been accustomed to having to deal with the king of France or his adherents, many of whom were also their lords. Here the experience of Richard's reign delivered a profound shock to Plantagenet rule, and John's control of

---

113 AN, S 5049: act of Walter archbishop of Rouen concerning money deposited with the Hospitallers; amongst the pledges for the sum were Geoffrey and Renaud de Bosco and Osbert de Rouvray.

114 *Layettes*, i, no. 716. The constable of Rouen was Peter de Préaux; for his brother John's desertion, see *Rot. Litt. Pat.*, i, 43.

115 E.g. Robert du Mesnil, one of the count's seneschals (*Rot. Norm.*, 70): *Jugements*, nos 79, 84, 205n., 729; *RHF*, XXIV. I, preuves de la préface, no. 30.

116 *Coggeshall*, 152, 154; Power, 'John de Rouvray', 364, 381.

117 *Annales angevines*, 22–3.

118 *Annales de Jumièges*, 89; QN, no. 253.

119 *Rot. Chart.*, 207.

120 *Guillaume le Breton*, ii, 302 (*Philippidos*, X, l. 499).

these regions was always uncertain; once war recommenced it was all he could do to prevent the French penetrating even more deeply into eastern Normandy. The fall of the remainder of the duchy, however, was a very different proposition. There the king of France had less influence, and the revolt in Maine, in rekindling old grievances amongst the magnates of southern Normandy, contributed far more substantially to John's difficulties. In the circumstances it is some testimony to John that he retained Count Robert's loyalty for several months after William des Roches had thrown the Loire provinces into turmoil. Yet neither Capetian penetration in the east nor rebellion in southern Normandy, serious as both undoubtedly were, made the duchy's collapse inevitable. King Philip's assaults were slow and might easily have ground to a halt; the southern rebellion diverted valuable resources but did not spread far into Normandy. John's decisive failures were in central Normandy. His experiences at the hands of marcher lords had evidently destroyed his trust in his Norman subjects, so that he relied too heavily upon his hated *routiers*, who so greatly undermined the loyalty of his remaining supporters that he fled the duchy altogether. John had therefore lost the active support of most Normans while they were still free of pressure from either the king of France or the lords of Maine and Brittany; and his own errors must account for their failure to defend Normandy for their duke.

Eleanor of Aquitaine: The Last Years[1]

Jane Martindale

> Mieus vaut lor ris et lor baisiers
> Que ne fait Londres ne Peitiers.
>
> (Their smiles and their kisses are worth more
> than are London or Poitiers. *Le roman de
> Thèbes*, ed. L. Constans, lines 971–2)[2]

A comparison of the attractions of the daughters of King Adrastus of Argos with two of the most important cities within the Angevin empire of the twelfth century would have been meaningless to the original audience of Statius's *Thebiad*. London and Poitiers would not have evoked any associations in first-century Rome; but for the *clerc* and *chivaler* to whom the vernacular *roman de Thèbes* was addressed around the mid-twelfth century, this matching of London and Poitiers would have been a topical allusion which they could understand. For them it could have been an amusing aside, as they heard (or read) the anonymous poet's romance transformation of the doom-laden Latin epic.[3]

---

[1] This paper owes much of its substance to the generosity of Sir James Holt in giving me access in Cambridge to the files of the Angevin *regesta*, and to Dr Nicholas Vincent in supplying me with his transcripts of Queen Eleanor's *acta*. I should like also to thank Professor John Gillingham (especially for his advice on the historian Howden), Dr Ruth Harvey, and the members of the King John conference for their helpful comments; and I hope that I have not misrepresented them. I owe a special debt, too, to the editor of the volume for his encouragement and patience.

[2] *Le roman de Thèbes publié d'après tous les manuscrits*, 2 vols, ed. L. Constans, *SATF*, 1890, 51; cf. also *Le roman de Thèbes*, ed, G. Raynaud de Lage, *Classiques Français du Moyen Age*, 2 vols, Paris 1966, 68; and *Le roman de Thèbes*, ed. F. Mora-Lebrun, *Lettres Gothiques*, Paris 1995, a single MS edn with modern French translation.

[3] The author appeals to a restricted audience to 'hear' him, 'Ainz me délet a aconter/ Chose digne de remembre./ Or s'en voisent de tot mestier,/ Se ne sont clerc o chevalier,/ Car aussi pueent escouter/ Come li asnes al harper' (. . . So it delights me to describe an affair worthy of being remembered. But if they are not clerks or knights, let all other professions recognise that they are no more qualified to listen, than an ass is to play the harp), *Thèbes*, lines 11–16, ed. Constans, 2. For the vernacular 'humanisation' of the Latin epic, J. Dufournet, 'La Thébaïde de Stace et le Roman de Thèbes (à propos du livre de G. Donovan)', *Revue des langues romanes* 82, 1976, 139–60 esp. pp. 147–59; cf. A. Petit, *L'anachronisme dans les roman antiques du XIIe siècle*, Lille 1985, 50–94.

This glancing reference in one of the earliest *romans antiques* to the attractions exercised by two Greek sisters over a pair of Theban refugees may seem an odd way to introduce a contribution to a volume discussing the tangled problems of King John's reign. I nevertheless deliberately and defiantly flaunt the opening quotation because – whatever might have been the reactions of Angevin contemporaries in the twelfth century – it seems unlikely that many members of this group of twentieth-century historians will think that Poitiers could ever have rivalled London in value or importance. At the time when John succeeded his brother Richard on the English throne, however, Poitiers had been the heart of Eleanor of Aquitaine's ancestral principality for centuries, and it kept that political importance until her death in 1204; but when the Capetian king Philip Augustus took Poitiers, and King John failed to recapture the city in the years after 1204 the especial relevance of a comparison between London and Poitiers would soon be destroyed. Since Queen Eleanor's activity was almost entirely confined to Poitou and her duchy of Aquitaine during her youngest son's reign, my opening quotation can stand as a declaration of intent for this paper, which will be especially (although not exclusively) concerned with Eleanor's ancestral principality. Furthermore, as *le roman de Thèbes* was almost certainly written for an Angevin court, it may also remind us how greatly the outlook and values of those twelfth-century 'clerks˙ and 'knights' differed from those of modern historians or readers of this.[4]

Before his succession to the English throne, John had never spent long in Aquitaine, nor (unlike Richard) had he ever been directly involved in the government of this region. Indeed, before his brother's death in 1199 John's last appearance here was during the fraternal struggles which marked the end of their father's reign: it occurred in a joint campaign of devastation with his brother Geoffrey during the summer of the year 1184.[5] All the same, the politics of the Angevin empire show that Poitiers and its surrounding county, together with the Loire valley and the concentration of Angevin territories between Angers and Tours, remained of vital importance to King John. Eleanor's background was, of course, utterly different. The Norman writer Wace describes Eleanor travelling southwards from the Capetian court to Poitiers, her 'natural

---

[4] *Le roman de Thèbes*, ed. de Lage i, xxvi–xxxi; ed. Mora-Lebrun, 8, suggesting that this romance was composed c.1150 'par un clerc poitevin des domaines d'Aliénor'. The twelfth-century topicality of the comparison between London and Poitiers was remarked on by R. Bezzola, *Les origines et la formation de la littérature courtoise en occident (500–1200)*, i, Paris 1967, 271–3. In general see the useful entry and bibliography in *Dictionnaire des lettres françaises: le moyen âge*, 2nd edn (various authors), Paris 1992, 1315–17.

[5] Gillingham, *Richard the Lionheart*, 100–103. At the time of Richard's death John was in Brittany with Arthur, and from there travelled to Chinon (where much of Richard's treasure was stored), Saumur and Fontevraud, *Life of St Hugh* ii, 137; cf. *Howden* iv, 86; Norgate, *John Lackland*, 59–61; Painter, *Reign of King John*, 8–9; Warren, *King John*, 64. John's favourable position in Poitou in 1199–1200 was due to the support of, and action taken by, some of the greatest magnates of the region, Gillingham, 'The Angevin Empire', in *Richard Coeur de Lion*, 66–9.

home' – 'A Peitiers s'en ala, sun naturel manage'.[6] During Richard's adolescence Eleanor personally presided over the government of the duchy during the years before the great revolt against her second husband's authority (i.e. between c.1168 and c.1173); many years later, following King Richard's release from imprisonment in Germany, she returned to northern Aquitaine – although not until after she had succeeded in reconciling John with the king. Eleanor then remained in 'her natural home'; but this time she almost certainly intended to give up the political responsibilities of the lay world and retire to the abbey of Fontevraud, since at about this time Richard appointed his nephew Otto of Saxony as count of Poitou (he was the son of Eleanor's daughter Mathilda who had married Duke Henry the Lion). In April 1199 news of Richard's mortal illness was brought to her at this abbey on the border of Poitou and Anjou.[7]

When Wace wrote of Eleanor's journey back to her 'natural home' he was describing her return to Aquitaine many years earlier in the year 1152, just after the divorce from her first husband, the Capetian King Louis VII. Her later activity suggests that Wace's statement was just as applicable to the last phase of her life, but in particular to the brief years of John's reign before her own death in 1204. It is confirmed by the details of her itinerary throughout these years, but notably during the course of the year immediately after Richard's death when there was considerable doubt throughout the continental territories of the Angevins as to whether John should indeed be regarded as his brother Richard's 'rightful heir'. After Richard's funeral, for instance, Eleanor came to Loudun in northern Poitou by late April 1199, then – moving steadily south – she passed through Poitiers, stopped at the important town and castle of Niort, then came to Saint-Jean d'Angély, La Rochelle, and the city of Saintes. In July she reached Bordeaux.[8] Queen Eleanor made an extended journey to Spain in early 1200, but otherwise – apart from a momentous visit to Tours where she did homage to King Philip in July 1199, and a brief visit to Normandy in the autumn of the same year – she never again left Aquitaine and the Loire region. Her final retirement to her chosen burial-place at the convent of Fontevraud signifies that in the few years before her death Eleanor's ancestral duchy had once more become her 'natural home'. The contents of the documents which allow historians to reconstruct the outlines of this itinerary also show that she

---

6 *Le roman de Rou de Wace*, ed. A.J. Holden, *SATF* 2 vols, 1970, i: *Chronique ascendante*, lines 32, 4.

7 Richard, *Comtes* ii, 299–315, 325, 331–2; Gillingham, *Richard the Lionheart*, 277; Norgate, *England under the Angevins*, ii, 385; J. Martindale, 'Eleanor of Aquitaine', in my *Status, Authority and Regional Power: Aquitaine and France, Ninth to Twelfth Centuries*, Variorum 1997, XI, 17–18 (paper first publ. 1992).

8 This part of her itinerary can be established from the places of enactment of documents drawn up in her name, Richard, *Comtes* ii, 335–45; below, n.49 for Eleanor's grant to the men of Bordeaux. For John's movements in 1199 and in 1200 when he travelled through Anjou, Touraine and Poitou before pushing further south to Gascony, *ibid.*, 357–64; Warren, *King John*, 68–70, 80–1; see N. Vincent's article in this volume.

remained much preoccupied with the affairs of the region throughout the few remaining years of her life. It therefore follows almost inevitably that she could not avoid becoming involved in the political and military problems with which the rulers of all the Angevin territories were confronted. They had to face Capetian pressure on their frontiers and constant doubts about the loyalties of their own men.[9]

Biographers of Queen Eleanor have often been reluctant to discuss her contribution to the government of either her own or her husbands' territories, or to consider seriously the political role which after her marriage to Henry of Anjou she played throughout the whole 'family assemblage' of Angevin lands – as the composite territories ruled by Henry II have been described by James Holt.[10] In the most recent biography of the queen, for instance, her involvement in two of the most politically significant episodes of the early years of King John's reign have been interpreted as though they provide little more than an opportunity for reflecting on Eleanor's dignified deportment, or on her nostalgia for lost youth. The comment on Queen Eleanor's homage to King Philip in the summer of 1199, for instance, is that 'we are left to imagine' the 'icy dignity' with which she confronted the Capetian king of the French in the city of Tours. Her journey to Spain in the early months of 1200 – and this must have been a winter journey – meant that 'once more she passed through the lands of her youth and no doubt heard the voices of the troubadours who were still charming the southern lords and ladies . . . What memories must have enlivened this journey, for her almost a pilgrimage . . .'[11] Imagination – perhaps also speculation – are not out of place in attempting to interpret two of the most interesting episodes of Eleanor's long life, but those comments certainly do not do the old queen justice, or enable anyone in the twentieth century to perceive the importance of the part that she played in Angevin politics and government at the end of her life. Eleanor's act of homage, for instance, which she performed at Tours in the first summer of John's reign, was unprecedented in the history of the relations between the

---

[9] Below, 155–64 for Eleanor's involvement with such problems after 1199.

[10] J.C. Holt following John LePatourel, 'The End of the Anglo-Norman Realm', in *Magna Carta and Medieval Government*, 27; cf. Gillingham, 'Angevin Empire', 21–37; R. Turner, 'The Problem of Survival for the Angevin "Empire": Henry II's and his Sons' Vision Versus late Twelfth-Century Realities', *AHR* 100, 1995, esp. 93–6.

[11] D.D.R. Owen, *Eleanor of Aquitaine, Queen and Legend*, Oxford 1993, 94, 97. Admittedly this is concerned with 'Eleanor the woman [rather] than Eleanor the politician', *ibid.*, 2; but since the intensely 'politicised' Angevin court and the world of Henry's Anglo-Norman ancestors was the setting for most of her existence after 1154, it is difficult to avoid discussion of how far she did play a political rôle in this world. A recent essay on 'Eleanor' is not concerned with political issues either, G. Duby, *Women of the Twelfth Century*, trans. J. Birrell, Oxford 1997, 5–20 (first publ. in French 1995); and neither is N. Cantor's 'The Glory of It All', in *Medieval Lives, Eight Charismatic Men and Women of the Middle Age*, New York 1994, 105–23 (where Eleanor's death is inexplicably given as occurring in the year 1194). This is not the place for a detailed discussion of the historiography of Eleanor's career, but for some assessment of studies appearing before 1992, see Martindale, 'Eleanor of Aquitaine', 17–18, 23, 36–44.

Capetians and Angevins. Its significance – incidentally this has repercussions also for discussions of the activity of women in positions of power – needs to be reconsidered in the light of the conduct of Angevin political affairs. The Spanish journey, also, raises a number of unanswered, and perhaps unanswerable, questions that were of more immediate importance in the year 1200 than the supposedly lingering romantic echoes of troubadour songs. Why, for instance, was a woman at least seventy-eight years old put in charge of the diplomatic mission to fetch a Castilian girl to marry the son of her own sons' most powerful political opponent? Did contemporaries really expect peace between Angevins and Capetians to be brought about by a Franco–Castilian marriage – even though, despite a series of treaties and truces, for fifty years every negotiated peace had always disintegrated into war?[12]

It will be assumed in this paper that Aquitaine was the centre of Queen Eleanor's activity during the reign of her youngest son, King John, but also that her contemporaries did regard this region south of the Loire as her 'natural home'. Her involvement in, and preoccupation with, political affairs in Aquitaine determine the nature of the detailed topics to be discussed in the last section of my contribution to this conference on King John. The first aim of what follows is, however, to investigate what Eleanor 'actually did' after King Richard's premature death. That is necessary because, as has already been implied, her modern biographers – and, indeed in general, most historians – do not examine in detail the range of her involvement in the government and politics of Angevin Aquitaine after 1199 – even though soon after his accession John acknowledged her as 'lady . . . of us and all our lands and affairs'.[13] The decisive part which Queen Eleanor played in the Anglo-Norman realm during the period of Richard I's absence on crusade and his captivity provides the background to her youngest son's later comprehensive recognition of her authority. Her involvement in the government of England and Normandy during the years between 1190 and 1194 must have contributed to her contemporaries' conviction that she could and should be trusted to deal with the defence of the realm, political revolt or negotiation with the formidable Emperor Henry VI. The first part of this study will therefore consider the scope of her contribution to the maintenance of Richard's power before 1199, as well as her later activity during John's reign. The second part will be more narrowly restricted to measures taken by the queen to avert threats to the security and integrity of her own 'inheritance' of Aquitaine during the years 1199–1204 – the crucial time when the first phase of King John's reign overlapped with the last years of his mother's life.

Immediately after Henry II's death, Queen Eleanor was entrusted with the widest possible powers by her son Richard. Ralph Diceto wrote that these

---

[12] For Henry II's troubled relations with Louis VII and the young Philip II, Warren, *Henry II*, 45–8, 64, 91, 101–2, 125–36, 145–7, 623–6; Gillingham, *Richard the Lionheart*, 245–75.
[13] Below, n. 43, and nn. 69–71.

powers were conveyed 'in mandates to the princes of the kingdom and laid down as if under a general edict' ('in mandatis regni principibus, et quasi sub edicto generali statutum') – in other words 'she received from her son the power of ordaining what she wished in the kingdom'.[14] Elsewhere her release from 'her husband's prison' is described as being secured by Richard's mandate *de ultra mare*; then 'she set out from city to city and from castle to castle just as it pleased her', 'leading around a queenly court' – although that literal translation scarcely does justice to the weight of the original phrase 'reginalem curiam circumducens'.[15] She is described as being personally responsible for sending clergy and laity throughout all the English counties to establish the peace, and to receive the oaths of 'every single freeman of the whole kingdom' who should swear to be faithful to King Richard 'as to his liege lord' ('sicut ligio domino suo') but also – perhaps rather unusually – to the queen herself.[16]

From these accounts Eleanor's role could perhaps be interpreted as being essentially ceremonial in character, of interest to contemporary writers and modern historians alike because of the dramatic changes in her fortunes after a decade of imprisonment and the cat-and-mouse treatment of the years 1183–9. During the first phase of Richard's reign she certainly did play a prominent ceremonial role in the affairs of the English kingdom: this can be glimpsed from references to her meeting with Richard outside Winchester on his entry into his new kingdom, or (at a rather more material level) from the considerable sums of money which her son authorised to be spent on her clothes for his coronation.[17] At a later date, too, after Richard's release from captivity, special attention was drawn to her presence at his second coronation. On that occasion she sat with her ladies in Winchester cathedral 'in the northern part of the church opposite the king' – perhaps that was thought particularly noteworthy because by that time Richard's queen, Berengaria, might have been expected to take part in the ritual.[18] Altogether it is understandable that Diceto should have interpreted Richard's accession after Henry II's death as a turning-point in the queen's life, commenting, in the words of one of Merlin's supposed 'prophecies', 'Aquila

---

[14] *Diceto* ii, 67; Gillingham, *Richard the Lionheart*, 128.

[15] *Gesta Ricardi* ii, 74–5; *Howden* iii, 4–5; Gillingham, *ibid*.

[16] *Gesta Ricardi* ii, 74 – includes the text of a precept ordering the release of prisoners; *Howden*, iii, 4–5. During the year c.1189–90, Howden was still close to the centre of English royal government and, indeed, was almost certainly the author of both these sources, even though the *Chronica*'s date of compilation is later: D. Corner, 'The *Gesta Regis Henrici Secundi* and *Chronica* of Roger, Parson of Howden', *BIHR* 66, 1983, 128–32; *idem*, 'The Earliest Surviving Manuscripts of Roger of Howden's "Chronica" ', *EHR* 98, 1983, 303–5; and below, n. 28.

[17] *Gervase* i, 453–4, 457; *Diceto* ii, 68–9; *PR 1 Richard I*, 223. Expenses for furs, *robbis*, horses and their trappings were allowed: it seems reasonable to suppose that these were for Richard's coronation since they are entered at the same time as repairs to Westminster Hall, the gates of the city and Westminster Bridge; cf. Martindale, 'Eleanor', 34 n. 36.

[18] 'Alienor vero regina mater eius cum puellis suis sedebat in boreali parte ecclesiae ex opposito regi', *Howden* iii, 248; Gillingham, 'Richard I and Berengaria of Navarre', in *Richard Coeur de Lion*, 133.

rupti foederis tertia nidificatione gaudebit' (The eagle of the broken agreement will have joy in [her] third nestling).[19]

Even in the preparations for Richard's first coronation, however, Eleanor apparently exercised considerable personal authority: after the archbishop of Canterbury had convoked his suffragans, she was consulted about the summoning of the laity – 'earls, barons and sheriffs' ('Mater comitis Alienor regina de vocatione comitum, baronum, vicecomitum fuit sollicita').[20] And, although her subsequent presence at councils in both England and Normandy might also be interpreted as having a ceremonial character, from what is otherwise known of her activity both before and during Richard's absence from Europe, there can be little doubt that such presence signifies continued active participation in the government of his kingdom. She attended councils at Canterbury in November 1189, for instance, and on both sides of the channel during the year 1190, at St Albans in June and Westminster in 1193; she was at Nottingham in March 1194 when King Richard required the court to make judgement on his brother Count John and Bishop Hugh of Coventry for their treachery during his captivity in Germany.[21] In any case, during the interval between Richard's succession to his father and his arrival in England, it was her direct administrative intervention which was used to curb the rapacity of forest officials, and to order the removal of royal horses from the stables of religious communities. She also ordered the liberation of all prisoners from their dungeons, and the 'in-lawing' of those who had been exiled.[22] Her specific involvement in administrative matters at this time is also shown by a writ in Eleanor's name dated in the first year of Richard's reign. It was addressed generally, and confirmed Maurice of Berkeley's barony for the service of five knights. She would have been able to draw

---

[19] *Diceto* ii, 67: his stated interpretation is that the 'broken agreement' refers to Eleanor's imprisonment between 1173–89, while Richard is identified as her third 'nestling'. (Richard was in fact Eleanor's fourth child by Henry, although her third son.) *Diceto* does not seem to have quoted literally from the 'prophecies' as found in the early MSS of Geoffrey of Monmouth's *Historia*, but this quotation might perhaps have been based on a short passage from one of those influential 'prophecies': 'Catuli leonis in equoreos pisces transformabuntur et aquila eius super montem Aravium nidificabit . . .', *The Historia regum Britannie of Geoffrey of Monmouth* i, ed. N. Wright, Cambridge 1984, 76. Elsewhere, however, the term 'aquila rupti foederis' is employed to refer to Eleanor's divorce from the Capetian King Louis VII, *Draco Normannicus*, ed. R. Howlett, *Chronicles of the Reigns of Henry II and Richard I*, ii RS 1885, I, lines 297, 603. For royal women's likely interest in the sibylline prophecies, E. van Houts, 'Queens and Would-Be Queens of England, 1000–1200', 11 (forthcoming). My thanks to Dr van Houts for sending me her paper before publication.

[20] *Diceto* ii, 68 and 69. Diceto was in a particularly good position to know of Eleanor's involvement since, as 'dean of the church of London' (i.e. St Paul's), he took a prominent part in the coronation because the bishopric was vacant; and see Gillingham, *Richard the Lionheart*, 129–30.

[21] Landon, *Itinerary*, 18, 26, 76, 87–8. For the political importance of the council held in March 1190 at Nonancourt, Holt, 'The *Casus Regis*: the Law and Politics of Succession in the Plantagenet Dominions, 1185–1247', in *Colonial England*, 314.

[22] According to the sources cited above, nn. 14–16.

on her experience many years previously, since she had been involved with the definition and performance of service by the knights and men of the abbeys of Malmesbury and Abingdon during the years 1158–59.[23]

Queen Eleanor played far more than a ceremonial rôle in the conduct of ecclesiastical affairs also, as can be seen from her involvement in the problems of the archbishops of Canterbury and their monastic chapter. Politically the most important episode of her involvement with this church relates to the delayed election of a successor to Archbishop Baldwin (he had died on crusade at Acre in 1190). In particular, although the Canterbury monks begged her to intercede with King Richard to allow them to hold a free election, she eventually made certain that one of her son's most trusted advisers, Hubert Walter, should be elected archbishop.[24] In spite of that, her achievement in securing 'concord' between the episcopal electors and the Canterbury monks was remarked on by Diceto.[25] Eleanor probably also played an important part at the Roman *curia* in two other matters of great importance to the church in England: her presence in Rome at the time of Pope Celestine III's consecration, for instance, has been associated with negotiations to secure the office of legate for William Longchamp, and also with the need to obtain papal approval for the appointment of Richard's bastard half-brother, Geoffrey, to the metropolitan see of York.[26] Those negotiations were successful, despite the queen's earlier decision in 1189 to forbid John of Anagni, the Pope's legate *a latere*, to move freely in the kingdom without royal permission.[27]

Eleanor's involvement in the 'high politics' of the Angevin world between

---

[23] '. . . Berchelay et totam Berchelayhurnesse . . . baronia de domino rege filio meo in feodo et hereditate . . .' This was merely calendared by I.H. Jeayes, *Descriptive Catalogue of the Charters and Muniments in the Possession of the Rt. Hon. Lord Fitzhardinge at Berkeley Castle*, Bristol 1892, no. 34, 18; I owe especial thanks to Nicholas Vincent for supplying me with the text of this writ (which survives in a damaged original). It was dated from Freemantle (Hants) 'xxx die Octobr regni regis Ricardi anno primo', where Richard was also at this date, Landon, *Itinerary*, 13. For the earlier writs, Holt, 'Feudalism Revisited', in *Colonial England*, 78–9 (the Abingdon writ referred to the services of both 'milit[es] and homin[es]').

[24] *Chronicles and Memorials of the Reign of Richard I*, ed. W. Stubbs, 2 vols, RS 1864–65, vol. 2; *Epist. Cant.* no. CCCLII, 332 (Prior Osbert to the queen); nos CCCXCIX, 362–3 (Richard requests his mother to speed up the election); CCCCIII, 364–5 (Richard to his mother ordering the election to take place: 'Mandamus vobis quod convocatis . . .'; cf. *Howden* iii, 226. For the confidence existing between Hubert and the king, Gillingham, *Richard the Lionheart*, 229, 243–4.

[25] He notes the rôle played by Archbishop Walter of Rouen too, *Diceto* ii, 108. Eleanor also intervened as early as 1189 in the long-running dispute between the monks of Canterbury and their archbishop over his plans to establish a chapter of canons at Hackington, *Gervase* i, 454. On this 'most celebrated lawsuit of the age', Cheney, *From Becket to Langton*, 4, 36–7, 73–5; I.S. Robinson, *The Papacy 1073–1198: Continuity and Innovation*, Cambridge 1990, 193.

[26] Landon, *Itinerary*, 47–8, 193–4; in general on legates, Robinson, *The Papacy*, 172–5.

[27] Interdictum est . . . per reginam Alienor ne procederet, quoniam citra conscientiam regis regnum suum intraverat', *Diceto* ii, 72; Robinson, *The Papacy*, 169.

her husband's death in the year 1189 and her own in 1204 is best perceived through the explicit and underlying aims of a number of the journeys which she made during these years to places outside the territories ruled by her sons. In early 1194, for instance, she travelled to Germany at Richard's express wish to become involved in the final negotiations for his release from captivity. There she was apparently responsible for advising her son to do homage to the Emperor Henry VI in order to bring to a close discussions which were being needlessly prolonged: 'Richard king of England, held in captivity by Henry [king] of the Romans, in order to escape from that captivity by the advice of his mother Eleanor, resigned the kingdom of England and transferred it to the emperor, as lord of all men . . .'[28] Her purpose in pursuing a long winter journey down the Italian peninsula to Sicily three years earlier seems less exclusively political in its aims, as she was then accompanying her son's new betrothed, Berengaria of Navarre, to meet her future husband. On the other hand, as John Gillingham has suggested, the old queen's meeting with the emperor-elect at Lodi during the winter of 1191, like her hurried return journey to Rome in April, almost certainly did have ulterior diplomatic and political motives. After the death of King William II the relations between the Staufen and the Sicilian kingdom were especially problematic, and the fate of Queen Joanna, Eleanor's widowed daughter, was uncertain.[29]

In John's reign, too, her voyage to Spain was (as has already been seen) connected with royal marriage plans and ambitions, and intended to find a bride of impeccable Angevin descent to marry the future Capetian king Louis VIII.[30] It was hoped – vainly as things turned out – to find a girl who would come to consolidate and symbolise the peace being negotiated between the Capetians and Angevins. Neither the Spanish nor the Sicilian journey was primarily a party of pleasure; indeed, on her Italian journey, after experiencing the dangers of the crossing of the Straits of Messina, Eleanor spent only three nights in Sicily before turning back to Rome just after the election of the new pope,

[28] 'Ricardus rex Anglie in captione Henrici Romanorum detentus, ut captionem illam evaderet consilio Alienor matris suae deposuit se de regno Angliae et tradidit illud imperatori sicut universorum domino . . .' *Howden* iii, 203. Howden's earlier career as royal clerk and crusader, his contacts with King Philip on the Capetian's return from the east, and his earlier association with Queen Eleanor, all surely help to account for his deep interest in the means by which the crusader Richard was eventually freed: see in particular D. Corner, 'The *Gesta Regis Henrici Secundi* and *Chronica*', 134–7. Eleanor moved to Mainz from Speyer, Landon, *Itinerary*, 82–3; see also a letter sent from Mainz by Archbishop Walter of Rouen to the author *Diceto* ii, 113; Gillingham, *Richard the Lionheart*, 235–6.

[29] Landon, *Itinerary*, 46; Gillingham, *Richard the Lionheart*, 159–61; D. Mathew, *The Norman Kingdom of Sicily*, Cambridge 1992, 285–91.

[30] As was guaranteed by the terms of the treaty of Le Goulet, but proposed even before Richard's death, Powicke, *Loss of Normandy*, 185–6, 203; Gillingham, 'The Art of Kingship', in *Richard Coeur de Lion*, 100; Warren, *King John*, 71; Baldwin, *Government*, 96–7; Bradbury, *Philip Augustus*, 125, 133–4.

Celestine, III.[31] But because the fate of dynasties and the peace of extensive territories could hang on the outcome of royal marriage plans, Eleanor did far more than play the role of royal chaperone in those two cases. And, since by the end of the twelfth century, it seems likely that plans for royal and aristocratic marriages could no longer wholly ignore such unpredictable variables as personal attraction or repugnance, the queen's voyages to Italy and Castile should be regarded as politically, as well as socially, momentous. Additionally, Queen Eleanor was undoubtedly playing a rôle for which royal women were later conventionally cast.[32]

Any suspicions that Eleanor was merely a royal figurehead, acting as a front for competent and highly trained Angevin officials and *familiares*, communicating with her sons at moments of crisis, are utterly dispelled by knowledge of the part which she played during King Richard's absence on Crusade – but more especially after John's ambitions erupted openly into rebellion. Eleanor's political influence during the years before Richard's early death, and the part which she played as mediator between Richard and John, surely explain her youngest son's acceptance of her position of authority in the years 1199–1204. Indeed, the powers attributed after 1199 to this woman in her late seventies, are only comprehensible if they are considered in the context of her activity during the successive crises of the period after Richard embarked for Jerusalem. According to Richard of Devizes, she made remarkable efforts both to sway the councils which teetered towards supporting John after his seizure of the castles of Wallingford and Windsor, and to prevent his embarkation from Southampton for Normandy to negotiate with the Capetian king.[33] The lengths to which John was prepared to go to achieve his premature political ambitions emerge starkly from the 'agreements' (*conventiones*) with King Philip which, as count of Mortain, he swore *in propria persona* to keep (January 1194). The agreements included the provision that John would not make peace with the king of England against the will of the King of France.[34] And, even though soon after his release Richard magnanimously pardoned John, that was the result of Eleanor's mediation ('mediante Alienor regina matre eorum'). She may well

---

[31] She and Berengaria crossed from Reggio (where King Richard came to meet them) to Messina on 30 March 1191: Eleanor left again to travel by sea to Salerno on 2 April, Landon, *Itinerary*, 47–8.

[32] Gillingham, 'Love, Marriage and Politics in the Twelfth Century', in *Richard Coeur de Lion*, 243–55; in particular, on the consequences of Philip Augustus's repugnance for his wife Ingeborg, 252–3. That example would surely have been in the minds of any royal matchmaker during Eleanor's journey to Castile; and Prince Louis had to marry Blanche of Castile in Angevin Normandy because of the interdict on Capetian territory resulting from King Philip's refusal to live with Ingeborg, Powicke, *Loss of Normandy*, 203. On royal women's part in promoting girls' marriages, J.C. Parsons, 'Mothers, Daughters, Marriage, Power: Some Plantagenet Evidence', in *Medieval Queenship*, ed. J.C. Parsons, Stroud Glos. 1994, 64–78.

[33] *Devizes*, 60–1; *Gesta Ricardi*, 236–7; Gillingham, *Richard the Lionheart*, 219–20.

[34] Teulet, *Layettes* i, nos 412, 175; for the dating, Powicke, *Loss of Normandy*, 146; Gillingham, *Richard the Lionheart*, 237–8; Bradbury, *Philip Augustus*, 111–13.

have been responsible, therefore, for the fact that John was spared the humiliation of a formal trial.[35] Like the queen mother Jocasta in *Le roman de Thèbes*, Eleanor sought ways to put an end to a potentially fratricidal war.[36]

As has already been seen, it was Eleanor whose presence in Germany was requested by King Richard when his release was finally negotiated with the emperor, and whose skill and authority were called on to secure the election of the 'right' candidate to Canterbury; but the range of measures taken by the queen during this time was far more extensive, and does not really seem to betray the 'near panic' which is supposed to have pervaded the Anglo-Norman realm after John allied with his brother's most dangerous enemy, King Philip.[37] Apart from being involved in measures which needed to be taken for the kingdom's defence – at that time Eleanor was occupied with affairs in both Normandy and England – the queen was also personally concerned with the business of raising Richard's ransom, which was eventually guarded 'under the seal of the lady queen, mother of the king and the seal of the lord archbishop of Rouen' – 'sub sigillo dominae reginae matris regis et sigillo domini Rothamagensis archiepiscopi'.[38] Eleanor's close attention to the procedures necessary to protect the kingdom and secure her son's release can be seen also from the responsibility attributed to her by contemporary writers – and also by the admiration which even a 'satirist' like Richard of Devizes lavished on her activities.[39] It is further confirmed by two interesting documents issued in the queen's name. In the first, on behalf of 'our dearest son King Richard . . .

---

[35] 'Interim Johannes frater regis, comes Moretonii, rediit ad regem fratrem suum; et mediante Alienor regina matre eorum, facti sunt amici rex et ille; sed rex nullum castellum neque terram aliquam ei reddere voluit', *Howden* iii, 252. Richard had been shown documents proving his brother's treacherous alliance with Philip (*ibid.*, 232, 236–8); and John was summoned by the Nottingham council of March 1194 to appear before May 5th; eventually – according to the itinerary compiled by Landon – the brothers met soon after Richard crossed to Normandy from Portsmouth, probably on May 12. Howden had merely noted that John met his brother in Normandy, but for the likelihood that this was at Lisieux see Landon, *Itinerary*, 93–4; Powicke, *Loss of Normandy*, 149–50; Warren, *King John*, 61–2. But for the fates of two of John's supporters, the bishop of Coventry and his brother, D. Desborough, 'Politics and Prelacy in the Late Twelfth Century: the Career of Hugh of Nonant, Bishop of Coventry, 1188–98', *Historical Research* 64, 1991, 6–7, 12.

[36] *Thèbes*, lines 4225–27, ed. Mora, 290: '. . . ceste dame qu'est lor miere;/ molt vodreient cercher et quere/ come ele fust fin de ceste guerre/'. At an earlier stage in the narrative Queen Jocasta is found exhorting one of her sons to accept his barons' counsel to make peace, and the poet calls on God to curse 'guerre de freres,/ et entre filz et entre pieres!' *ibid.*, lines 3923–4272.

[37] 'The government stiffened by the queen-mother, who knew how to cope with her sons . . .' Warren, *King John*, 60–1; Turner, *King John*, 46; although the crucial part which she played in this crisis is not always emphasised, Bradbury, *Philip Augustus*, 106–18.

[38] *Howden* iii, 210, 212; Landon, *Itinerary*, 76; Gillingham, *Richard the Lionheart*, 230; S.K. Mitchell, *Taxation in Medieval England*, ed. S. Painter, New Haven 1942, 14, 28, 285–7.

[39] *Devizes*, intro. xvi, 58–63 and at 59, 'matrona merito memoranda multotiens . . .'; Martindale, 'Eleanor of Aquitaine', 44–50.

detained by the Roman Emperor', she renounced works which had been exacted contrary to 'law and custom' from the men of the priory of Christ Church, Canterbury, 'on account of the disturbance of the land'.[40] According to the terms of the second, she personally remitted as alms in perpetuity a golden chalice worth thirteen gold marks to Abbot Samson and the monks of Bury St Edmunds 'pro salute karissimi filii nostri regis Ricardi'. This costly object had been offered by the monastic house to royal officials in lieu of the ready money which the community could not find, but which it owed to the Exchequer. The document was witnessed by the queen herself at Westminster and bears her personal authorisation, 'Teste me ipsa'. It seems plausible to attribute this, as Landon did, to the period when Richard's ransom was being collected.[41] Significantly, the two shrines that Richard visited immediately on his return to England after release from captivity in Germany were Bury St Edmunds and Canterbury.[42]

In a discussion of Richard as 'king of the English and duke of the Normans', Holt asserted that, rather than discussing 'the concept of monarchy', he would be concerned with 'what a king actually did in the late twelfth century'.[43] This paper, too, has been largely taken up with showing what Eleanor 'actually did' during the later years of her life, even though there is undoubtedly a need for further discussion on the 'concept of queenship' during the late twelfth century. Nevertheless, if, as Pauline Stafford has suggested, 'the ability to take part in events' and 'to have the means at . . . [one's] disposal' to achieve success, are two ways in which the actual exercise of power can be identified, then there can be no doubts about Eleanor's ability and capacity to exercise power.[44] This queen's intervention was frequently decisive during the last phases of her involvement in the politics and government of the Angevin empire. Moreover, documents issued in her name make it abundantly clear that her authority was regarded as legitimately ordained, whether – as in Aquitaine – based on powers derived from her own ancestors, or from those which she wielded on behalf of her sons in other territories which made up the 'family assemblage' of Angevin

---

[40] W. Somner, *The Antiquities of Canterbury or a Survey of that Ancient Citie with the Suburbs and Cathedrall*, London, 1640, 9–10.

[41] *Monasticon* iii, 154 (other witnesses included the Chancellor). The attribution of this undated document to the time when the ransom was being collected (to 1–5 June, 1193 precisely) was made by Landon, *Itinerary*, 76; that is surely confirmed by a different Bury account of a chalice being taken on behalf of the abbot and monks to London 'ad redempcionem regis Ricardi', and then being redeemed by the queen, *The Chronicle of Jocelin of Brakelond*, ed. H.E. Butler, *NMT* 1962, 46–7. Cf. n.44, below.

[42] Gillingham, *Richard the Lionheart*, 238.

[43] Holt, *'Ricardus rex Anglorum et dux Normannorum'*, in *Magna Carta and Medieval Government*, 67.

[44] Pauline Stafford, 'Emma: the Powers of the Queen', in *Queens and Queenship in Medieval Europe*, ed. A. Duggan, Woodbridge 1997, 11–12. Cf. also Stafford, 'The Portrayal of Royal Women in England, Mid-Tenth to Mid-Twelfth Centuries', in *Medieval Queenship*, 148, 161, 166; and also the remarks by the editors in *Women and Power in the Middle Ages*, ed. M. Erler and M. Kowaleski, Athens and London 1988, 1–2, 5, 10–12.

lands. This continued involvement is best conveyed, however, through a small group of documents which bear the signs of Eleanor's personal ratification – identifiable by the phrase *teste me ipsa* – and which show how closely she was concerned with the details of government and administration. The surviving eight documents, whose interest or significance does not seem to have been previously recognised, with two – possibly three – exceptions, date from John's reign. Apart from the Bury document just mentioned, all concern Aquitaine and the continental territories which were the setting for Eleanor's activity after 1199.

The odd one out of this group is the writ-charter for Bury St Edmunds which records the queen's return to the abbot and monks of St Edmund of the great golden chalice brought to Westminster to meet the Exchequer's demands for cash. Against the background of the urgent need to accumulate coin and bullion to pay Richard's ransom, the significance of the transaction seems obvious, and scarcely needs further comment.[45] Four of the rest of the group are mandates ordering regional officials to make redress for grievances brought to Eleanor's notice. For instance, she orders 'all prévôts from her land and her sergeants' ('prepositis omnibus de terra sua et suis servientibus') to preserve the immunity which her father had bestowed on the Poitevin abbey of Fontaine-le-Comte, and which had been confirmed 'by the judgment of the court of my son the king and of the burgesses and clerics of the city' [i.e. Poitiers] ('judicio curie filii mei regis et burgencium et clericorum civitatis'). That was *teste me ipsa* at Poitiers.[46] At Fontevraud on 6 October 1200, two charters were enacted in favour of the Poitevin abbey of Saint-Maixent, issued in Eleanor's name. One was authorised *teste me ipsa*, the other with the virtually identical phrase *teste me presente*. The first of this pair deplores the exactions made by her 'dearest son Richard, formerly king of the English' and prohibits further exactions on forest land held by the abbey (although she made the reservation 'salvo tantum et retento exercitu nostro et expeditione'). The second, however, contains concessions which were even more far-reaching, since all men who lived within the abbey's *bourg* were to be exempted from 'all tallages' '. . . et omni alia consuetudine, exercitu

---

[45] Above, n.41. The queen's attestation takes the form, 'Teste me ipsa apud Westmonasterium, et magistro W de Damartin, et magistro Radulpho Nigro, et Henrico de London charte presentis auctore, et Ricardo eleemosynario domine regine, et magistro Stephano de Sancto Edmundo, et abbate de Waltham, et episcopo Elyensi domini regis cancellario, et Galfrido, de Wauncy'. (The *Monasticon* reading of the last name is *Warren*: I have corrected this from Vincent's transcripts.) Cf. H. Prescott, 'The Early Use of *Teste me ipso*', *EHR* 35, 1920, 214–17, at 217 n.7.

[46] *Recueil des documents de l'abbaye de Fontaine-le-Comte (XIIᵉ–XIIIᵉ siècles)*, ed. G. Pon, *AHP* 62, 1982, no. 24. For the dating problems associated with this original charter – attributed by the editor only to the period of King Richard's reign, Pon, 36 n.1. The queen also issued her own confirmation of this abbey's immunity in response to injuries caused by her officials, *ibid.*, no. 26 (undated). Attribution to John's reign made at an earlier date now seems less plausible, Richard, *Comtes* ii, 338, 435–6.

et equitatione'.[47] A writ ordering her bailiffs to protect the possessions and animals of the religious house at Candeil was also authorised *teste me ipsa apud Chinon*'.[48] A more formal – but possibly partially corrupt – privilege enacted for the citizens of Bordeaux, on the other hand, emphatically renounces the evil customs that had been imposed on them, ('consuetudines pravas et inauditas et indebitas . . .'); but, despite the fact that this charter has an impressive witness-list, it still includes in its final protocol the affirmation that '*we* give it to the aforesaid people of Bordeaux with *my own hand*' (*teste me ipsa*). Although this privilege for Bordeaux is not laid out methodically or at great length like the texts modelled on *les Etablissments de Rouen*, it too ought to be included in discussion of the concessions made to cities and other urban communities by Eleanor and John in the years after 1199.[49]

Two further documents which are authorised *teste me ipsa* deserve especial attention for the light which they throw on the scope of Queen Eleanor's authority and on her determination to preserve Angevin power in her *hereditas*. The first is a mandate which in its present form has no other authorisation except the queen's attestation and, although it was enacted at Vaudreuil in Normandy, has an important bearing on the political situation in northern Aquitaine at a time when, after Richard's death, King Philip Augustus no longer needed to fear that speedy reprisals would *immediately* follow his attacks on Angevin territories. According to the terms of this undated writ, Queen Eleanor orders a man named Roger *Palestans* to do 'homage and liegeance' to Andrew of Chauvigny, who has been granted 'the whole fee of Ste-Sévère' ('feodum totum de Sancta Severa'). The document is undated, but by comparing it with other dated

---

[47] *Chartes et documents pour servir à l'histoire de l'abbaye de Saint-Maixent*, ed. A. Richard, *AHP* 18, 1886, no. 402: 'Teste me ipsa apud Fontem Ebraudi sexta die Octobris regni filii nostri Iohannis supradicti anno secundo'; cf. no. 403, later confirmed by John at Barbezieux with an impressive list of witnesses (on dating problems of that confirmation, *ibid.*, 18 n.1). For tallage in England, Mitchell, *Taxation*, 284–316; but tallage was a profitable exaction elsewhere, too, at this time.

[48] As it has survived, the text of this Candeil writ is corrupt – e.g. a grant made 'pro anima Raimundi filii nostri et nostra' ought presumably to be read as 'Ricardi'. If that emendation is made then it seems likely – on the basis of the wording – that his undated writ should be attributed to a period before Richard's death. Candeil is in the present département of the Tarn.

[49] The date is corrupt, since the year 1189 which appears in the transcript of the text – 'Actum est hoc anno Mo centesimo octuagesimo nono ab incarnatione domini prima die iulii . . . Datum apud Burdeguale per manum Rogerii capellanum nostrum . . . Teste me ipsa que cartam ipsam manu mea propria predicto populo Burdeguale tradimus' – is invalidated by the reference in the text of the charter to Richard's death – 'Noverit universitas vestra quod post mortem karissimi filii nostri Richardi regis Anglie . . .', *Livre des coutumes*, ed. H. Barckhausen, *Archives municipales de Bordeaux* 5, Bordeaux 1890, no. XLV, 437. What is known of Eleanor's itinerary indicates that this should be assigned to the months immediately after Richard's death in 1199, Richard, *Comtes* i, 345–6. This was presumably the document confirmed by John on 17 July – 'omnes libertates et liberas consuetudines quas A. regina mater nostra eis concessit et carta sua confirmavit', *Rot. Chart.*, 4b.

charters relating to the same transaction, and by considering it in the context of the queen's itinerary, this writ should almost certainly be attributed to the early months of John's reign (probably before 20 August 1199).[50] The queen's mandate is of major importance in establishing her determination that changes in King John's political and territorial policies should not alienate former supporters of King Richard in her own duchy. Andrew of Chauvigny had been one of her elder son's closest companions, prominent and trustworthy on crusade and earlier rewarded with marriage to the heiress to the important honour of Déols in Berry: it seems unlikely that King Richard would have been pleased with John's transfer of Déols to King Philip.[51]

The final document of this group is frequently cited both for the information that it supplies about the last years of Eleanor's life, but more particularly because it seems to foreshadow the imminent end of Angevin rule in much of Eleanor's duchy. It is a lengthy letter addressed by the queen to King John, and informs him that during her illness ('in infirmitate nostra') she has been visited at Fontevraud by Viscount Aimeri of Thouars: she reports that he and his friends are taking possession of John's castles in the region, and thus unjustly disinheriting 'you'. She goes on to assure her son that she has extracted a promise from the viscount that – as long as he can retain the possessions which he held on the day of Richard's death – he will remain faithful in John's service; but both she and John's constable exhort the king that he should either order the viscount to visit him, or on the other hand should himself come to Normandy – 'Teste me ipsa et eodem Guida de Diva const[abulario] de Dhinum apud Fontem Ebraud'.[52] Does it not seem likely that this letter was intended to convey a warning that the new king must employ a certain prudence in his dealings with the Poitevin aristocracy, if he does not wish to alienate them from the Angevin cause? In any case the importance of the political advice which

[50] Undated and only authorised *T[este] me ipsa apud Vallem Rodolii* [Vaudreuil]; Round, no. 1306 (where it is recorded as being witnessed *teste me ipso*). This will be printed from AN J440 (register of King Philip IV) in N. Vincent's catalogue of Eleanor's *acta*. It seems likely that it should be linked to another document by which the fee of Sainte-Sévère was transferred to Andrew de Chauvigny, 'Data apud Vallem Rodolii per manum Rogerii capellani nostri anno verbi incarnati MoCo XCo IXo . . .' *Layettes* i, 508; Round, no. 1307.

[51] On Andrew's relationship to Richard, Gillingham, *Richard the Lionheart*, 126–8, 155 and 221 (on crusade). Soon after Richard's succession to his father, Queen Eleanor was present at Salisbury at the wedding of Andrew of Chauvigny to the heiress of Déols in Berry, *Gesta Ricardi*, 76; on the regional importance of the position he thus acquired, G. Devailly, *Le Berry du Xe siècle au milieu du XIIIe*, Paris 1973, 411, 423, 438–41 (by 1201 Andrew had gone over to Philip Augustus); cf. for Sainte-Sévère (now dép. de l'Indre), L. Raynal, *Histoire du Berry depuis les temps les plus anciens jusqu'en 1789*, 4 vols, Bourges 1844–47, ii 101–2. (This is not therefore in Gascony, as was supposed by both A. Richard and J.H. Round.)

[52] *Rot. Chart.*, 102 (regnal year 2 John) – this roll preserves Queen Eleanor's letter, but also Viscount Aimeri's in which he protests his fidelity to John; cf. Richard, *Poitou* ii, 385–6, 401; Warren, *King John*, 88: 'a triumph of feminine diplomacy . . . not merely the worries of an old woman'.

was being communicated probably explains this letter's curiously irregular diplomatic form.

The phrase *teste me ipsa* may not be found so often in the documentary output of Queen Eleanor as is *teste me ipso* in King Richard's *acta*, but qualitatively the appearance of this formula in documents issued in her name also 'provides some kind of register of . . . personal interest and intervention', and serves as a sign of 'direct personal responsibility' for the matter being addressed in each of the documents discussed. Interestingly too, all Eleanor's documents attested in this fashion seem to conform to the categories of 'a formula . . . largely reserved for the important, the intimate or the confidential occasion'.[53] Elsewhere Pierre Chaplais argued that at this time the use of *teste me ipso* indicated that documents so attested were actually read in draft by (or to) the ruler: the missive sent by Eleanor to King John warning him about the seizure of Poitevin castles by Viscount Aimeri and his associates reads almost as though it had been personally dictated by her.[54] Today – for want of more personal and intimate letters and communications – it is impossible to tell whether Eleanor resented being disturbed by the pressure of secular affairs after her retreat to the convent of Fontevraud during the last years of Richard's reign; but it can scarcely be doubted that she regarded as supremely important matters which she attested 'my own self' at that abbey in 1199–1200, whether this attestation was appended to a document making reparation for her older son's exactions on the property of Saint-Maixent, or to a letter outlining the threats posed by Aimeri of Thouars and other members of the regional aristocracy to King John.

Even at the very end of her life it is surely a mistake to portray Eleanor as a passive victim – the 'old dowager queen' – waiting in July 1202 within the walls of the small fortified town of Mirebeau in northern Poitou to be rescued from the siege mounted against her by her grandson, Arthur of Brittany.[55] She may never have directed a prolonged military campaign, but even as a young woman, accompanying her first husband King Louis VII to Jerusalem and back, she seems likely to have been aware of what was at stake in the conduct of war; and, moreover, her *acta* show that the organisation of defence and military matters was included in the powers with which she was invested from the time of her marriage to Henry of Anjou. When she informed King John from Poitou that there was a danger that his castles in the region were being taken over 'without licence' by members of the regional aristocracy, she was surely

---

[53] Holt, '*Ricardus rex Anglorum et dux Normannorum*', 79 and 80; Prescott, above n.45.

[54] P. Chaplais, *English Royal Documents: King John–Henry VI*, Oxford 1971, 15–16.

[55] For the quotation, Baldwin, *Philip Augustus*, 191–2; Powicke, *Loss of Normandy*, 223–4; Warren, *King John*, 93–6; Painter, *Reign of King John*, 19 (identified as Mirebeau). For comments on the speed with which John moved and on the element of surprise in his relief of Mirebeau, Gillingham, 'The Fall of the Angevin Empire', in *Richard Coeur de Lion*, 193, 195; *idem*, 'The Angevin Empire', 69–70; Bradbury, *Philip Augustus*, 143–4; and in a more general context, M. Strickland, *War and Chivalry, The Conduct and Perception of War in England and Normandy 1066–1216*, Cambridge 1996, 10, 164, 184.

writing from an experience gained over many years – ironically in particular during John's own revolt against Richard; but it also seems likely that in her ancestors' principality she had a grasp of the strategic importance of the castles whose control was vital if members of her dynasty were to maintain their political power as rulers.[56] That inference seems to be borne out by the contents of the Canterbury document issued during Richard's imprisonment in Germany. It records that the priory's men, compelled by Eleanor herself because of 'urgent necessity' and by 'our intervention', had dug ditches, built walls, and engaged in other forms of unspecified castlework.[57] Examples like these lend support to the chroniclers' assertions that in the English kingdom it was the queen who set in motion the defensive measures taken to ensure that John would not be able to overthrow the government being exercised in the name of the absent King Richard. Howden, for instance, states that the royal 'castles of Windsor, and of Wallingford, and of the Peak were transferred into the hand of Queen Eleanor', although John was permitted to keep Nottingham and Tickhill.[58] The measures that the queen employed on Richard's behalf in opposition to John were later transferred to John's cause once he had become his brother's legal successor. But, whereas before 1199 she played a direct and crucial part in preserving Richard's position in the 'Anglo-Norman realm', after John's succession she exercised her authority almost entirely in the interests of securing Angevin power in Aquitaine and the Loire region.

Throughout the years 1189–1204, the queen had repeatedly shown that she recognised the need to make careful provision for defence in times of turmoil, and indeed that 'in urgent necessity' she would even be prepared to go over to the offensive. During the period of acute political crisis after Richard's death, Queen Eleanor even directed the *routier* Mercadier with his mercenary band ('cum ruta sua') against her grandson Arthur who was aiming to gain possession of the whole Angevin heartland. She led Mercadier's troops in an expedition of devastation, laying waste the country around the city of Angers, 'because they had accepted Arthur'.[59] Her involvement in this unwomanly – but essentially royal – activity implies that she had absorbed and understood the contemporary need for military action to 'conform' to a 'pattern of ravaging and besieging'. Political needs might in an emergency demand immediate

---

[56] Below, nn. 82–6.

[57] 'Cum autem ob terre turbationem Cantuarie civitas fossatis et muris et aliisque propugnaculis muniretur omnesque ad hoc compellerentur quidam homines prioris et conventus Cantuar' . . . quod operatio quam urgens necessitas et nostra interventio . . .', for the reference, see above, n. 40.

[58] *Howden* iii, 208; *Gesta regis Ricardi* ii, 232–4 – this records the Lacy constable of Chester's action against his men who gave up Tickhill to John in the year 1191 – two were hanged; *Devizes*, 62 – John had been residing in Wallingford. For an extended account of the problem of castle control in England during the years 1191–94, Norgate, *John Lackland*, 31–49.

[59] 'Interim regina Alienor, mater predicti ducis et Marchadeus cum ruta sua intraverunt in Andegaviam et devastaverunt eam, eo quod Arturum receperunt', *Howden* iv, 88; Norgate, *John Lackland*, 63; Warren, *King John*, 66.

military action; and in an emergency Eleanor (even at around the age of seventy-eight) was prepared to proceed to war.[60]

Queen Eleanor's involvement in a campaign of devastation around the city of Angers at the beginning of John's reign presents an extraordinary contrast to her retirement to the abbey of Fontevraud in the years following Richard's release in 1194. With her decisive return to the world of secular affairs she was drawn into the eye of the political storm which was gathering force after her elder son's death. For about five more years it is possible to trace some of Eleanor's attempts to hold together the Angevin 'assemblage of lands', but there are signs that she was determined in particular to preserve her own paternal inheritance as a political entity. Her activity during these years certainly suggests that for her Poitiers equalled London in worth, and that she wished to ensure that Poitou – indeed all Aquitaine – should be transmitted to John as her chosen successor, her *rectus heres*. Although her death in April 1204 meant that the 'loss of Normandy' was soon followed by the 'loss of Poitou', it still seems necessary to reconsider some of the well-known moves and events in this game of twelfth-century power politics. These may take on a rather different significance if viewed from a standpoint south of the Loire, rather than in terms of the interests of the Capetian or Angevin kings. The purpose and consequences of the arrangements Eleanor made with King John, for instance, are not easy to determine, while Eleanor's homage to King Philip, too, has provoked widely differing interpretations. Discussion of those events of the year 1199/1200 is still needed, and so is a brief survey of the means that the queen used in her attempts to retain the loyalty of the inhabitants of Aquitaine to the descendants of the Poitevin dynasty. These topics will be briefly considered in the rest of this paper.

Under the year 1199, the Capetian historian and apologist Rigord noted that during the course of this year at Tours 'Eleanor, the former queen of England, did homage [to King Philip Augustus] for the county of the Poitevins which belonged to her by hereditary right.'[61] Slightly surprisingly, Rigord's narrative appears to be the only contemporary source to make any reference to this momentous ceremony, for which no 'official' record survives; the 'English'

---

[60] 'Thus should war be begun: such is my advice./ First lay waste the land', Gillingham, 'Richard I and the Science of War', in *Richard Coeur de Lion*, 217 (citing Fantosme's metrical *Chronicle*), 218 (for the quotation in the text – applied to Richard's campaigns in Europe); cf. Strickland, *War and Chivalry*, 266–7, 285–7. Eleanor's part in initiating this campaign in Anjou is not remarked on by Powicke, *Loss of Normandy*, 196, nn. 2–3, nor by Richard, *Comtes* i, 337. Perhaps – either on grounds of Eleanor's age or sex – neither was prepared to credit Howden's assertion; cf. L. Huneycutt, 'Female Succession and the Language of Power in the Writings of Twelfth-Century Churchmen', in *Medieval Queenship*, 190, 194.

[61] *Rigord* i, 146: 'Alienordis, quondam Anglie regina apud Turonis Philippo regi fecit hominium pro comitatu Pictavensium, qui iure hereditario eam contingebat'; Richard, *Comtes* ii, 353; Powicke, *Loss of Normandy*, 195–7 – 'Eleanor did homage for the duchy of Aquitaine'; Warren, *King John*, 80.

narrative historians, for instance – even when they include detailed accounts of the events of these years – do not refer to it at all. It does not always seem to be realised just how exceptional this occurrence was: a woman did not normally perform homage in her own person. Almost as though to draw attention to the contrast, Rigord carefully notes that John's rival for the Angevin inheritance, his nephew Arthur, had earlier done homage to the Capetian king, whereas Arthur's mother Constance apparently merely renewed her fealty to Philip 'under oath'.[62] In practice too, ever since the time when, over sixty years previously, Eleanor had 'inherited' her father's principality, either her husband or a son had performed the ceremonial acts of homage on those occasions when Capetian rulers were in a position to exact them.[63] Eleanor's homage to King Philip Augustus had therefore the same legal and political consequences as if performed by a husband, son or one of her male kin, but also a symbolic importance in signifying that a woman could exercise an independent authority. It surely involves far more than a 'prudent confirmation of her position'.[64] Its unique character can be better understood if it is compared with 'Glanvill's' near-contemporary statement of practices in the English kingdom: his statement of what should happen if a daughter (or daughters) succeeded to an inheritance, is that homage should be performed by her husband – in the case of a divided inheritance, by the husband of the eldest sister, the *primogenita*. He certainly did not envisage homage being performed in person by an heiress.[65] In the context of Richard's unexpected death, however, Eleanor's act also had a

---

[62] *Rigord* i, 145: 'Arturius vero, adhuc puer, comes Brittanici littoris nepos regis Anglie . . . apud Cenomannis regi Francorum occurrens, hominium fecit et omnimodam fidelitatem cum matre sua sub iuramento firmavit'. This was elsewhere written up (in the present tense) to lay stress on the 'magnanimity' of the Capetian king, but without any reference to Eleanor's homage: 'Arturus puer, dux Britannie minoris, Andegavum civitatem nobilissimam et Cenomannum capit, et inde turpiter fugat Johannem Sine-Terra patruum suum . . . Arturus vero facit Philippo magnanimo hominium de comitatu Cenomannico, et Andegavico, et Turonensi et adducitur Parisius', *Guillaume le Breton*, 205. Only Philip's removal of the young prince to Paris in late July (*v kal. Aug*), not Arthur's earlier homage, is mentioned by Powicke, *Loss of Normandy, ibid.*; whereas Eleanor's homage is not mentioned by Bradbury, *Philip Augustus*, 130–9. On the issues of succession and inheritance involved, Holt, 'The *casus regis*', 305–13; *idem*, 'Aliénor d'Aquitaine, Jean sans Terre et la succession de 1199', *Cahiers de Civilization Médiévale* 29, 1986, 95–6.

[63] Or when, between the years 1156 and 1199, it had been in the political interest of Henry II or his various sons to perform these acts, Holt, 'The End of the Anglo-Norman Realm', 42, 44.

[64] Warren, *King John*, 80; but cf. H.G. Richardson, 'King John and Isabelle of Angoulême', *EHR* 65, 1950, 362: 'she exercised sovereignty in Poitou and in July 1199 went to Philip Augustus who accepted her homage . . .'.

[65] 'Maritus autem primogenite filie homagium faciet capitali domino de toto feodo', *Glanvill* VII, 3, 6 (i.e. even when the inheritance is divided). For the problems raised by these arrangements, Holt, 'Feudal Society and the Family, IV: The Heiress and the Alien', in *Colonial England 1066–1216*, esp. 251–4; J. Hudson, *Land, Law and Lordship in Anglo-Norman England*, Oxford 1994, 112; but for examples showing diversity of treatment and political exploitation of the position of heiresses during this period, J. Green, *The Aristocracy of Norman England*, Cambridge 1997, 377–83.

broader political significance because of a need to devise some method of coun-
tering the claims made on behalf of Arthur of Brittany to be Richard's heir, but
also so as to prevent the Capetian king taking advantage of the dispute. It is
generally agreed that between them Queen Eleanor and King John devised a
'diplomatic masterstroke' to achieve their political ends; but to appreciate that
'masterstroke' the queen's homage to King Philip in July 1199 has to be considered side-by-side with the famous written agreements made by the new king
and his mother.[66]

These arrangements are known only from the record preserved on the
charter roll for John's first regnal year.[67] The ingenuity of the moves made by
the old queen and her son can be glimpsed from the terms of these enrolled
charters. In the first place, Eleanor asserted that she had accepted John as her
'rightful heir' ('rectus heres') for all Poitou, and proclaimed that she had
accepted his homage; but she also transferred (attornavit) the fealty, homage
and services owed by all great clergy and laity to her son as 'to the king their
liege'.[68] John, too, in the charter drawn up in his name notes that he has performed homage to his mother; but on the other hand in many respects his
document allots a far wider authority to Queen Eleanor, who is to be lady
'. . . of us, and of all our lands and possessions'. It is also specifically laid
down that, 'except for the salvation of our souls' ('pro salute animarum
nostrarum'), neither of the parties to the agreements shall 'give away'
anything without the other's consent.[69] Both these documents must have been
intended to provide a basis in law for a transmission of power which, in
practice, had already occurred throughout those territories where John had
been accepted; they also proceed from the assumption that Eleanor was the
rightful holder of Poitou and could designate her chosen successor. In particular, of course, these documents would exclude the claims made on behalf of
Arthur that, as the son of John's elder brother Geoffrey, he ought to succeed to
the Angevin territories by representation. Underlying the dispute between uncle
and nephew was the thorny question of whether a grandson should 'succeed to
all that his father would have inherited had he survived, thereby representing

---

[66] Holt, 'Aliénor d'Aquitaine', 92: 'à la fois une manoeuvre légale très habile et un coup de
maître diplomatique'; Turner, *King John*, 52.

[67] *Rot. Chart.*, 30 (membr. 24 *in dorso*), for Eleanor's concession; for John's *ibid.*, 31
(membr. 10 *in dorso*) = Rymer's, *Foedera* I i, 113 (i, 36 of the edn of 1745) – i.e. the
document in Eleanor's name was not included by the *Foedera* editors. Although these
documents are normally treated by historians as a pair which were enacted reciprocally,
they were entered at different places on the roll – which suggests that possibly the
agreements were drawn up at different times and places (neither bears a precise date, nor a
place of enactment); although the king's was apparently witnessed, the names have been
omitted.

[68] *Rot. Chart. ibid.*: 'tanquam ad rectum heredem nostrum et dominum suum . . . regi suo
ligio . . .'

[69] '. . . volumus quod sit domina sed et de nobis et omnibus terris et rebus nostris', *Rot.
Chart.*, 31.

his father's title' – the dilemma that lawyers enigmatically alluded to as the *casus regis*, and which had been provoked because Geoffrey died before his younger brother John.[70]

These arrangements had many short- and long-term implications, but in the present context of Eleanor's last years they are especially interesting if they are related to late twelfth-century notions of lordship and to received opinion about the obligations and services owed by one individual who had performed homage to another. According to the terms of the agreements recorded on the charter roll it seems that, because Eleanor was 'lady' of John's lands and person, and because she had done homage to the Capetian ruler *in propria persona*, King Philip would not be justified in demanding services directly of John. At least, as far as his mother's Poitevin inheritance was concerned, John should rather respond to his mother's summons: in her turn she would be answerable for her son's actions to the lord to whom she had done homage: the implication of her act would be that she should appear in the royal court, if this were necessary. Although that eventuality is not directly alluded to, this is not merely a fanciful hypothesis, but should be compared to arguments which were advanced during the 1120s on behalf of the count of Auvergne by the duke of Aquitaine (Eleanor's grandfather) to Philip Augustus's grandfather (King Louis VI).[71] Moreover, it is sometimes overlooked that King Henry II advanced similar claims to King Louis VII: the counts of Auvergne, Henry asserted, were 'my men' ('homines meos'), and should therefore be subject to his, Henry's, jurisdiction.[72] In any case the *conventiones* concluded between King Philip and John when the latter was still merely count of Mortain also prove that the Capetian ruler regarded jurisdiction over his subordinates as an important issue: in order to gain King Philip's support in his revolt against Richard, John agreed in 1193–94 to perform the services and judicial requirements which were owed from each 'fee' for the French king *in his court* (my italics).[73] Furthermore, a number of contemporary references also suggest that different levels of lordship were invoked to evade the jurisdiction of a court which might be expected to be hostile. For instance, Gerard de Canvill, when accused of betraying the king

---

[70] Baldwin, *Government of Philip Augustus*, 94; Holt, 'The *Casus Regis*', 307 (for the quotation); Gillingham, 'The Angevin Empire', 35–6; Hudson, *Land, Law and Lordship*, 114, 118–19, 123.

[71] Martindale, 'Eleanor of Aquitaine', 29–30. Unfortunately Louis VI's biographer, Suger, never described the outcome of the dispute which had arisen when that Capetian king led an army to bring support to the bishop of Clermont against the count of Auvergne.

[72] E. Baluze, *Histoire généalogique de la maison d'Auvergne*, 2 vols, Paris 1708, ii, 68–9; and in general on the county of Auvergne, Warren, *Henry II*, 105–6, 143–6; J. Boussard, *Le gouvernement d'Henri II Plantagenêt*, Paris 1956, 524–6.

[73] 'De predictis vero terris, ego regi Francie et successoribus suis regibus Francie faciam servitia et iusticias in curia sua pro singulis feodis, sicut unusquisque feodum aportat, sicut antecessores mei antecessoribus suis fecerunt.' *Layettes* i, 175. These 'servicia' should not be interpreted as military ones, since in a later part of the agreement John was exempted from being compelled to go in *exercitum* or *equitationem*.

during Richard's captivity, claimed the right to be heard in John's court, not the king's, as he had become John's man.[74]

The methods designed to avert direct Capetian intervention in the Poitevin principality were ingenious, but within a few years – and certainly after Eleanor's death in early 1204 – it must have been apparent that, even though this 'diplomatic masterstroke' was logically coherent, it was not going to be effective for long in keeping back the tide of Capetian encroachments on the territories of the Angevin dynasty. All the same, a number of other aspects of this crucial phase of the Angevin-succession struggle need briefly to be reviewed. In the first place, the complexity of the political situation is obscured if it is supposed (as has been asserted by Baldwin) that Queen Eleanor 'did homage to' Philip 'in John's name'; indeed, as has just been argued, her personal performance of that ceremony was probably primarily intended to deprive the Capetian king of the legal basis for intervening in the affairs of Poitou and Aquitaine. Another aspect of these arrangements is far more specu- lative. The charters exchanged between Eleanor and her son during the first year of his reign firmly lay down that he should perform liege homage to her, and then that is surrounded with qualifications. Unfortunately no document specifies the terms on which Eleanor undertook to do homage to the Capetian king, and (as has already been mentioned) no account of this is provided by any narrative writer apart from the Capetian apologist, Rigord. Nevertheless, it seems to me a distinct possibility that in its outlines this 'diplomatic master- stroke' could well have been devised by Queen Eleanor herself, since it bears a close resemblance to the plan evolved at an earlier date by which Richard would perform homage to the Emperor Henry VI in order to hasten his release from prison – a scheme attributed by Howden to the 'counsel' given by Eleanor to her son.[75] Even if the agreements between John and his mother were rendered unworkable by changed political circumstances – for instance John's marriage to Isabella, Arthur's 'disappearance' and Eleanor's own death – that does not

---

[74] *Howden* iii, 242–3; Norgate, *England under the Angevin Kings* ii, 299. In the case of another man, Peter Bovencourt, the argument was reversed, since he was not permitted to 'purge' himself of the charge of betrayal in the *curia regis*, but was dismissed by the chancellor with the words: 'Vade ad dominum tuum constabularium, et in curia eius purga innocentiam tuam a crimine quod ipse tibi imponit . . .' The constable hanged him in chains, *Gesta regis Ricardi* ii, 233.

[75] Above, n. 28. Eleanor's role was not mentioned in a paper that drew attention to the diplomatic importance of these arrangements, A.L. Poole, 'England and Burgundy in the Last Decade of the Twelfth Century', in *Essays in History Presented to R.L. Poole*, ed. H.W.C. Davis, Oxford 1927, 261–73. But Howden, the chronicler who gave the most detailed account of the negotiations from the Angevin point of view, was in a special position to have good information about this plan and on the 'kingdom of Arles' which Henry VI apparently hoped to entrust to Richard, Gillingham, 'The Travels of Roger of Howden and his Views of the Irish, Scots and Welsh', *ANS* 20, 1997, 169 and in general 152–4.

detract from the intrinsic interest of this legally ingenious scheme with its underlying political aims.

Within the confines of the present discussion, it has finally to be recognised that the different facets of the plan devised by Eleanor, John and their advisers in the first year after his succession to his brother will be misunderstood unless these are also related to the Capetian king's own shifting attitudes and behaviour after Richard's death in April 1199. In the following years Philip's actions show some remarkable changes of policy. They certainly do not seem to reveal that he wished to establish a 'régime of fiefs' throughout his kingdom, organised according to a 'concept of hierarchy' and subordinated in an orderly manner to the jurisdiction of the royal court. That can be seen from his treatment of his most important Angevin opponents. According to Rigord, Arthur did homage at Le Mans before Eleanor came to Tours in July 1199 so that, if Arthur remained with the Capetian king during the intervening period, he could have been present when Philip acknowledged that Poitou was his grandmother's *hereditas*.[76] The separate homages performed at Le Mans and Tours show that King Philip was prepared to accept (probably to encourage) the division of the territories which the Angevins had ruled since the 1150s; but those homages also show that the Capetian king did not envisage the different parts of that inheritance being subject to uniform *ius* or practice. If inheritance practices had been uniform, the Capetian king would have been obliged to accept that Brittany was Constance's *hereditas* in the same way that Poitou was Eleanor's, and there could have been no justification for recognising Arthur as duke of Brittany in 1199.[77] By contrast, sometime before the summer of 1200, Philip's attitudes had changed drastically since, according to the terms of the Treaty of Le Goulet, John was now acknowledged by Philip as *rectus heres* to the Angevin territories (perhaps thereby bypassing the problems created by Eleanor's homage), while Arthur was subordinated to his uncle.

Soon, however, despite the hopes for peace attached to Prince Louis's marriage to Blanche of Castile – a marriage in which Queen Eleanor had been deeply implicated – Philip swung back to lend his support to Arthur's claims. In at least one of the documents that were issued in King Philip's name to advance Arthur's political position, the language of right and legality is almost entirely abandoned. Early in the year 1202, for instance, Arthur was promised a marriage to Maria (one of the king's legitimised daughters), then in July of the

---

[76] After the ceremony in Tours King Philip returned to Paris (which he reached by 28 July), and he was then certainly accompanied by Arthur, above n. 62.

[77] Arthur's own position changed on his mother Constance's death in August 1201. After a second marriage to Earl Ranulf of Chester she had remarried Guy, brother of Viscount Aimeri of Thouars, Gillingham, 'The Angevin Empire', 67; Painter, *Reign of King John*, 3–4, 8, 13, 201; Warren, *King John*, 89.

same year Philip took Arthur as his liegeman 'against all who live or die'.[78]
That second document only makes provision for Arthur's liegeance to be
applied to Poitou 'if God grants that either we or he shall acquire it by any
means whatsoever' – so Poitou is here being treated as a special case and seemingly recognised as subject to separate rules of succession.[79] It could be argued
that a clause like this could serve as a pretext for the young Breton duke's attack
on his grandmother in northern Poitou – indeed might it not be seen as a licence
to undertake that expedition? That hypothesis is lent greater weight by another
document in Arthur's own name which records that he has done homage to
Philip, and in which he is styled 'Arturus dux Brittanie et Aquitanie et comes
Andegavie et Cenomannie': so he was in fact being treated as 'duke of
Aquitaine' *de iure*, if not *de facto*.[80] Ever since King Richard's death in 1199,
King Philip's treatment of his Angevin opponents – including Queen Eleanor –
had been remarkable for the way in which the Capetian's actions were adapted
to his immediate territorial and personal ends: they may show a consistency of
political purpose, but scarcely suggest that the Capetian ruler paid much
attention to 'right' or legality as those would have been understood at the turn
of the twelfth century. 'Legal doctrines and arguments' were in fact 'concocted
to give . . . conflicting claims respectability'; but, it may surely be concluded, if
legal doctrines could not be accommodated to the required ends, they were
treated as superfluous and action without justification would do.[81]

The argument advanced in this article is that, in the immediate aftermath of
King Richard's death, Queen Eleanor was responsible for devising an ingenious
method for keeping political control over the destiny of her own *hereditas*.
Because of her age, however, it seems unlikely that she expected that situation
to be long lasting. Neither her homage to King Philip, nor the elaborate agreements between the queen and King John, necessarily secured the support of the
inhabitants of that *hereditas* for her or her youngest son. Surviving documents

---

[78] *Actes de Philippe Auguste* ii, nos 709 (Paris, April 1202), 723 (Le Goulet, July 1202);
Powicke, *Loss of Normandy*, 223. That followed the complicated episode of John's
deprivation of his continental lands on 28 April in an assembly which 'a pu . . . être
présentée, selon la tournure d'esprit plus ou moins juridique des chroniqueurs, tantôt
comme un conseil politique, tantôt comme une cour chargée de prononcer une sentence',
Ch. Petit-Dutaillis, 'Le déshéritement de Jean Sans Terre et le meurtre d'Arthur de
Bretagne: étude critique sur la formation d'une légende', part II, *RH* 148, 1925, 59–62
(quotation at 62).

[79] *Recueil* ii, no. 723: 'Insuper autem de dominio Pictavie recipimus eundem Arturum in
hominem ligium si Deus dederit quod nos vel ipse eam quocumque modo acquisieri-
mus . . .' The king also envisages that the Poitevins should do homage to Arthur, 'salva
fide nostra'.

[80] 'Insuper autem de dominio Pictavie feci eidem domino meo regi hominagium ligium si. . .'
The passage in this distinct document drawn up in Arthur's name is then followed by the
clause already cited in the previous note – surely proving the interdependence of the two
documents, *Layettes* i, no. 647, 236 (printed from the original); for the view that Arthur
violated his faith to John, Strickland, *War and Chivalry*, 257.

[81] Holt, 'The *Casus Regis*', 309.

indicate that Eleanor herself paid especial attention to the demands of the regional aristocracy, but also deliberately made efforts to retain the loyalty of towns and other communities through the grant of communal privileges. The last section of this examination of the queen's activity between 1199–1204 will deal very briefly with these two differing topics.

Eleanor's letter to John informing him of the disaffection of the aristocracy of northern Poitou shows her awareness of the need to placate men like the viscount of Thouars: a number of her charters from these years reveal the concessions she was prepared to make – and those which she was not. Among the most interesting of these was a grant made to Ralph of Mauléon within a few weeks of Richard's funeral – it was enacted at Loudun on 29 April 1199. In this lengthy writ-charter Queen Eleanor notifies all her *fideles* throughout Aquitaine of decisions which she has taken following requests made personally to her by Ralph. He had come to her and demanded ('requisivit') the 'return' of Talmond and La Rochelle which, he asserted, ought to belong to him 'by hereditary right' ('iure hereditario').[82] In the queen's charter Ralph's claim to a 'hereditary right' is not specifically accepted or denied but, since his claims were only in part conceded by the queen, there can be little doubt that his original demands must have been understood as a serious threat to the power of the Poitevin ruler. The queen did grant Ralph the castle of Talmond, and also added another castle at Benon which (as can be established from earlier ducal documents) had been built by Eleanor's grandfather, the 'troubadour' Duke William IX.[83] Nevertheless, the 1199 charter conveys the impression that these were grants made out of political necessity. Indeed, it is openly stated that the concessions were made to Ralph 'because we wish to have his service': the qualification that he got Talmond 'because he is a neighbour to us' is presumably a less direct allusion to Ralph's capacity to cause trouble for the ruler of Poitou. In return the queen did get Ralph's *homagium ligium*, and his gospel-oath 'to defend us, our land and honour against everyone living and dead . . .'. On the other hand, an implied threat seems to be concealed beneath his offer to prove his right ('paratus fuit probare') 'in our presence by his own oath and [the oaths] of one hundred knights' for, even though that was an appeal to a traditional method of legal proof, it could also be interpreted as a piece of political blackmail, designed to draw attention publicly to the amount of local support on which the lord of Mauléon could rely.[84] In the present context, however, the most interesting aspect of this lengthy document is that the queen utterly repudiated Ralph's

---

[82] Le Père Arcère, *Histoire de la ville de la Rochelle et du pays d'Aulnis*, 2 vols, La Rochelle 1756, ii (preuves), no. x; *Cal. Docs France*, no. 1099, 389–90 (English summary, witness-list in Latin); Richard, *Comtes* ii, 335.

[83] Martindale, 'Cavalaria et Orgueill', in *Status, Authority and Regional Power*, X 97 – this region was one of the most favoured hunting-centres of the Poitevin dynasty of dukes; cf. Richard, *Comtes, ibid.*

[84] Eleanor's grant was substantially confirmed by King John, *Rot. Chart.*, 24; Richard, *Comtes* ii, 359–60, comments that no earlier count of Poitou would have made such concessions.

demand to hold La Rochelle 'by hereditary right', and obliged him to renounce his claims to that important port and new town. Ralph obviously could apply a considerable amount of pressure in these months of crisis and, since he got possession of two castles in the traditional hunting-reserves of the Poitevin dukes, it might be thought that a high price was paid for his liege homage. But Eleanor's sticking-point is even more instructive: Ralph was obliged to declare that he and his successors would renounce La Rochelle in perpetuity ('quidquid iuris habebat in Rupella nobis et heredibus nostris in perpetuum quitavit et dimisit'). She would not alienate that urban settlement whose economic and strategic importance as a port had been greatly increased in the previous forty years.[85] Altogether, if both text and context of this charter are carefully examined, it yields a considerable amount of interesting information about the queen's topographical knowledge of her own province, and provides an interesting testimony to her political acumen. She was prepared to sacrifice what, by the turn of the twelfth century, had become the less important resources represented by two ancestral hunting-castles, in favour of the more substantial economic advantages attached to the possession of La Rochelle, and to the considerable political support which could be obtained from its citizens.[86]

La Rochelle provides a way back to the oblique reference to the city of Poitiers at the beginning of this article. Queen Eleanor made grants of liberties to both those urban communities: her grants suggest that she, like other members of her dynasty, realised the importance of the towns and cities of Aquitaine to its rulers. That importance is highlighted by the early issue (in 1199) of two charters of 'liberties' for 'our beloved and faithful men of the town of Poitiers', while (probably during the course of the same year) the queen granted a 'sworn commune' to 'all the men of La Rochelle and their heirs' – only reserving the fealty which they owed to her and her heirs.[87] Niort was also granted privileges by Eleanor, although that fact is known only from the confirmation made by John in the year following her death. That important fortified site and urban settlement on the River Sèvre had apparently also obtained, from the king during the course of 1199, the right to organise a commune: it seems to have been the first of the Poitevin towns to have its privileges confirmed by Philip Augustus in 1204 after the 'loss of Poitou'.[88] Other communities which

---

[85] Arcère, *ibid.* Ralph did obtain a substantial annual revenue from the resources of the town, however; Gillingham, 'The Angevin Empire', 46–7.

[86] Henry II had made a grant of liberties 'omnibus burgensibus meis de Rupella pro fideli servicio suo . . .', *Recueil des actes de Henri II roi d'Angleterre concernant les provinces françaises*, ed. L. Delisle and E. Berger, 4 vols, Paris 1909–24, ii no. DXIX. Eleanor, her husbands and her descendants were also extremely generous to the establishment of the Temple in La Rochelle, *Chartes de la commanderie magistrale du Temple de la Rochelle*, ed. Meschinet de Richemond, *Archives Historiques de la Saintonge et de l'Aunis*, I, 1874, nos I–IV, VI–VII.

[87] A. Giry, *Les Etablissements de Rouen*, 2 vols, Paris 1883–85 (reprint in 1 vol., Paris 1975), 357, ii, 143–5; for Poitiers; 68–9; La Rochelle, Richard, *Comtes* ii, 339–41.

[88] Giry, 238–40; Delaborde, ii, 828 (August, Actum Pictaris).

also secured grants from Eleanor – not all the texts survive in their entirety – were the city of Saintes,[89] and Oléron (which, as an island on which there were important monastic establishments and a fortified site, could scarcely qualify as an urban community).[90] The privileges of some of these places were based on the texts which were studied many years ago by Alfred Giry and called by him *Les Etablissments de Rouen*. The concessions – by no means identical – included the regulation of justice and jurisdiction, as well as important commercial concessions; burgesses or citizens were personally freed from fiscal impositions associated with marriage and wardship, and attributed the right to make their testaments. The grant of a commune also entailed the right to a considerable degree of self-government, including arrangements for self-defence.[91] South of the Gironde the picture is less clear, and concessions to urban communities appear to have been made either by King Richard or by John (e.g. at Bayonne).[92] However, the charter for the citizens of Bordeaux authorised by the queen *teste me ipsa* was drawn up in Eleanor's name to abolish 'iniquitous customs' imposed on the men of the city and, in particular, the practice of taxing wine for three successive weeks after the vintage to the benefit of Eleanor and her officials.[93]

The last years of Queen Eleanor's life are remarkable for the position of influence which she occupied during the reigns of her sons Richard and John; and the main aim of this article has been to convey some idea of how that influence was exercised. Few of the topics considered here could be followed up in enough detail to bring out the depth of Eleanor's involvement in the affairs of her 'natural home'; but it nevertheless seemed necessary to volume on some relatively narrow features of the last years of her active life. If those are neglected a distorted impression will inevitably emerge, not only of her contribution to the politics and government of the Angevin dynasty, but also of her life and 'career' as *regina Anglorum . . .* and *ducissa Aquitanorum*. And even though King John has been the central focus of this volume, it also seemed necessary to treat the years between the death of King Henry in 1189 and Eleanor's own death in 1204 as a continuum. For only after examining the evidence for Eleanor's activity during the crises of both Richard's and John's reigns does it become possible to argue that throughout these years she displayed a consistent attitude towards the exercise of power. Furthermore, her activity seems to display an underlying respect for principles of legitimacy as they were comprehended in the late twelfth century. It seems that she was also concerned to clothe political action in the prevailing legal forms and fashions.

---

[89] Teulet, *Layettes* i, 208; Giry, 1, 11, 67.

[90] Giry, *ibid.*, 9, 89–90.

[91] In addition to the documents already noted, see the trilingual text edited by Giry, *ibid.*, ii, 3–55.

[92] The 'provençal' text of the *établissements* represents *lo privilegi de le comunie que en Johan d'Angleterre de aus ciptadans de Baione*, Giry, *ibid.*, ii, 55; cf. i, 105 for two earlier grants by Richard (the earlier dated 1174).

[93] For the reference, above, n. 49.

Although that is more speculative, it is implied through her willingness to do homage to King Philip to preserve her ancestral lands from his encroachments or those of Arthur, and it is strengthened by the impression that she was responsible for advising Richard to do homage to the emperor in order to secure a speedy release from his German captivity. Like Queen Jocasta in the 'Romance of Thebes' she did not fear the 'perils' of political confrontation and, like that queen, she too was surely heard respectfully when she gave counsel:

> Li reis lor prie que se taisent
> et la reïne parler laissent;
> tout ce die que li plerra . . .

(The king requested them to be silent, and to let the queen speak, to say anything she pleased . . .).[94]

---

[94] *Roman de Thèbes*, ed. Mora, lines 4460–63, 304. The queen then says that she has given the 'best counsel that she knows' ('le meillor cunseil que j'en sai'), line 4465 *ibid*. But her advice to compromise and make peace is not accepted by the king.

Isabella of Angoulême: John's Jezebel*

Nicholas Vincent

A man's choice of his wife tells us more about him than most other things in his life. Not surprisingly, historians have made much of Eleanor of Aquitaine, the wife of the first Plantagenet king of England, Henry II. Far less has been written of Isabella of Angoulême, the wife of King John.[1] Apart from a heated debate conducted fifty years ago between H.G. Richardson and Sidney Painter, over the precise details and legal consequences of her marriage, Isabella is known to us chiefly by proxy, as the mother of the Lusignans, Henry III's plague of half-brothers, the blight of the Plantagenet court from the 1240s onwards.[2] She herself is remembered, if at all, for the mere fact of her marriage to King John, seen by many as a leading cause of the collapse of the Plantagenet dominion in France. For those who know their chronicles, she may also be marked out as a foreign harlot: 'More Jezebel than Isabel', as Matthew Paris says of her.[3] Yet, as I hope to show, there was far more to Isabella than just marriage, motherhood and a fierce temper. In particular, I wish to draw attention to the exalted nature of Isabella's birth, and, with this in mind, to draw some rather intriguing

* For assistance in the writing of this paper I am indebted to Stephen Church, Alain-Charles Dionnet, Michael Staunton, Rowan Watson and to the extremely valuable contributions made by those attending the Norwich conference. Work in France was facilitated by the Leverhulme Trust, the Newton Trust of Trinity College Cambridge, and the British Academy, which since 1994 has funded my work as Director of the Academy's Angevin Acta Project.

[1] The only extended biographies of Isabella are those by F. Marvaud, 'Isabella d'Angoulême ou la Comtesse-Reine', *Bulletin de la Société Archéologique et Historique de la Charente* 2nd series i, 1856, 116–252 (a hopelessly over-romanticized account), and H.S. Snellgrove, *The Lusignans in England 1247–1258*, Albuquerque 1950, ch. 1 (devoted largely to the years after 1217). Marvaud employs a legendary account of the marriage feast between John and Isabella, which first appears in the sixteenth century, and for which see A. Richard, *Histoire des Comtes de Poitou (778–1204)*, 2 vols, Paris 1903, ii, 379; M. Lecointre-Dupont in *Mémoires de la Société des Antiquaires de l'Ouest* xii, 1845, 125–7.

[2] H.G. Richardson, 'The Marriage and Coronation of Isabelle of Angoulême', *EHR* 61, 1946, 289–314, with ensuing debate between Richardson, S. Painter and F.A. Cazel in *EHR* 63, 1948, 83–9; *EHR* 65, 1950, 360–71; *EHR* 67, 1952, 233–5. Painter's contributions are reprinted in his collected essays, *Feudalism and Liberty*, ed. F.A. Cazel, Baltimore 1961, 165–77.

[3] *Chronica Majora*, iv, 253: 'Multi enim Francorum necnon et Pictavensium eam inexorabili odio persequebantur, asserentes eam potius impiissimam Zezabel quam Ysabel debere nominari'.

conclusions about her treatment at the hands of King John, about Isabella's financial and landed resources, and about her later relations with her eldest son, King Henry III. Marriage and the Plantagenet temper did not go well together. Richard I lived in almost total separation from his wife. The relations between his parents, Henry II and Eleanor, were so notorious as to have sparked a whole series of popular fictions. John himself may have fared little better than his father and elder brother in terms of conjugal harmony. But his consort, Isabella, was in her way just as interesting a woman as either of her two predecessors. The wives of the Plantagenet kings may have been quick tempered and hell to live with. Dull they never were.

John was already married at the time of his accession to the throne in 1199. He had been betrothed to his first wife, Isabella of Gloucester, since 1176, and had married her in 1189, shortly after the death of Henry II. Thereafter, she proved incapable of producing an heir. Since she was related to John within the prohibited degree of kinship, through their common descent from Henry I, John sought an annulment. The negotiations for this were put in train, perhaps as early as 1196, and were finalized shortly after John's accession to the throne in 1199.[4] John was free to marry for a second time. It was in these circumstances, in August 1200, that he married Isabella of Angoulême. At the time, Isabella can have been no more than fifteen years of age, perhaps considerably younger. She was the daughter and sole heiress of Adomar, count of Angoulême, himself the one surviving son of William IV Taillefer, count of the wealthy city and province of Angoulême in south-western France, straddling the valley of the Charente between Poitou and Gascony.[5] In theory the counts of Angoulême

---

[4] Richardson, *EHR* 1946, 289–95. Since Richardson wrote, the charters of Isabella of Gloucester have been published by R.B. Patterson, *Earldom of Gloucester Charters; the Charters and Scribes of the Earls and Countesses of Gloucester to A.D. 1217*, Oxford 1973. Various others, unnoticed by Patterson, can be found as Exeter, Devon RO ms. 1392M/Unsorted deeds, Kingsteignton no.1 (to Le Val Notre-Dame near Falaise, 1189 X 1199); Bristol RO ms. 36074(32) (to Maurice of Berkeley, 1189 X 1191); London, Lincoln's Inn Library ms. Hale 100 fo. 4r (to the earl of Winchester, 1216/17, during the rebel occupation of London); Canterbury Cathedral Library ms. Register B fo. 404r (to the monks of Canterbury, after 1217). The most interesting for present purposes is a charter issued as countess of Mortain at Bec on 1 August 1196, confirming a grant from the Gloucester estate made by John as count of Mortain at Lion-la-Fôret on the previous day: Worcester, Worcestershire RO ms. BA3814 ref.821 (Worcester Liber Ruber) fos 127v–128r, 144r–v, also in *ibid.* ms. BA2636 ref. 009:1 parcel 9 (Worcester cartulary) fo. 109r–v. This award suggests that John and Isabella may still have been cohabiting as late as the summer of 1196.

[5] For Isabella's age, see below. For the wider history of Angoulême during the twelfth and thirteenth centuries, the standard account by P. Boissonnade, *Quomodo Comites Engolismenses erga Reges Angliae et Franciae se gesserint*, Angoulême 1893, reissued in an expanded French translation as 'L'Ascension, le déclin et la chute d'un grand état féodal du Centre-Ouest: les Taillefer et les Lusignans comtes de la Marche et d'Angoulême et leurs relations avec les Capétians et les Plantagenets (1137–1314)', *Bulletin et Mémoires de la Société Archéologique et Historique de la Charente*, 1935, 1–258, has recently been supplemented and to a large extent superseded by A. Debord, *La*

were vassals of the dukes of Aquitaine, brought within the Plantagenet sphere of influence following the marriage of Henry II to Eleanor of Aquitaine in 1152. In practice they were semi-autonomous rulers, only loosely tied into the feudal hierarchy.[6]

When we think of the Plantagenet 'empire' in France, we are accustomed to picture the sort of map that appears in countless textbooks, in which a broad swathe of Plantagenet lands stretches unbroken from the English Channel to the Pyrenees. In the better sort of textbook, this 'empire' would most appropriately be coloured red. In reality, however, the Plantagenet dominion was no such seamless robe. The further south one goes, and certainly south of Poitiers, the 'empire' very soon breaks down into a series of isolated Plantagenet outposts surrounded by territories controlled not by the kings of England but by the local feudal aristocracy. This, I would suggest, was true of the whole of Gascony south of the Garonne. It also applied to the region between Poitiers and Bordeaux. Here, to judge from the surviving charter evidence, Henry II and his family issued only a handful of privileges and controlled very little in the way of ducal demesne. At most, they commanded a loose and often grudging allegiance from local magnates, by virtue of the position of Henry and Eleanor as successors to the once powerful dukes of Aquitaine. Despite regular campaigns, the levelling of rebel castles and the attempted suppression of their over-mighty subjects, Henry II and Richard established no effective administrative machinery to replace local aristocratic power in much of Poitou, let alone in the regions further south.[7] From Poitiers and the Talmond southwards, Plantagenet influence was restricted to a coastal strip along the Atlantic: the regions of the Aunis and the Saintonge, stretching from La Rochelle via Oléron to Saintes, and thence to Bordeaux. Inland, the Plantagenets held no castles and appear to have exercised little in the way of administrative authority.[8] We have only a few charters issued by Henry II, Eleanor or Richard to beneficiaries east of Saintes, for the most part simple letters of protection to the religious,

---

Société laïque dans les pays de la Charente X^e–XIIe siècles, Angoulême 1984, and the important but unpublished work of Rowan C. Watson, 'The Counts of Angoulême from the 9th to the 13th Century', unpublished University of East Anglia PhD thesis, 1979, which includes an invaluable register of more than 270 charters issued by the counts.

6 For the position of Angoulême within the Plantagenet dominion, see Debord, *Société laïque*, 390–6; Watson, 'Counts of Angoulême', 65–9, 111–14, suggesting that the homage rendered to the dukes of Aquitaine by the counts of Angoulême until 1127 did little to compromise their independence.

7 For the failure of the Plantagenets to stamp their authority upon Poitou, and for the rise of the great, local families of Lusignan, Mauléon, Thouars and L'Archévêque, see R. Hajdu, 'Castles, Castellans and the Structure of Politics in Poitou, 1152–1271', *JMH* 4, 1978, 27–54, esp. 27–41. For the regions further south, see Debord, *Société laïque*, 375–402.

8 See the map provided by Debord, *Société laïque*, p. 387 figure 66, showing the disposition of ducal castles and the seats of the ducal *prévôts*.

granting or confirming nothing in the way of land.[9] In particular, the two
semi-independent counties of Angoulême and Limoges, commanding the upper
reaches of the Charente and the Vienne, lay entirely outside Plantagenet control
for much of Henry II's reign, retaining a considerable degree of autonomy even
despite the campaigns of 1167–9, 1173–4, 1176, 1178–9, 1183, 1188 and 1194
in which Henry and Richard went to war against the local, inter-related feudal
aristocracy.[10] The counts of Angoulême meanwhile grew wealthy on the profits
of the trade routes criss-crossing their lands from La Rochelle to Bordeaux and
from the Atlantic to the Mediterranean. Much of this wealth was invested in
castle-building and the payment of mercenaries used in their wars against the
Plantagenets.[11] Any drift by Angoulême or Limoges towards allegiance to the
Capetians posed a serious threat to Plantagenet lines of communication between
Poitou and Bordeaux. Hence the speed, in 1183, 1188, 1194 and again in 1199,
with which Richard reacted to the threat of rebellion. As John Gillingham has
pointed out, it was far more than mere treasure-seeking that led Richard to his
death at the siege of Chalus in the Limousin in April 1199.[12]

It is possible that Count Adomar of Angoulême and his half-brother, the
viscount of Limoges, were already in alliance with Philip Augustus of France
by April 1198.[13] Certainly it was their rebellion against Richard that forced the
campaign in which Richard met his death. In April 1199, immediately after
Richard's demise, the two counts entered into a more formal treaty with the
French. Citing the injuries done to them by the late King Richard, count and

---

[9] East of Saintes, see the charters of Richard to Solignac, to St Martial Limoges (concerning
affairs in La Marche), and the various charters issued by Henry II, Richard and Eleanor in
favour of Grandmont: C. de Lesteyne, 'Deux chartes Limousines concernant l'abbaye de
S. Martial', *Bulletin de la Société Archéologique et Historique du Limousin* 55, 1905,
310–13; *Chartes, chroniques et memoriaux pour servir à l'histoire de la Marche et du
Limousin*, ed. A. Leroux and A. Bosvieux, Tulle/Limoges 1886, 59–60 no. 63; A. Lecler,
'Histoire de l'abbaye de Grandmont', *Bulletin de la Société Archéologique et Historique
du Limousin* 57, 1907, 71–2; Delisle and Berger, *Recueil des actes de Henri II*, nos 575,
627, 685, 729. Between Poitiers and the Lot, only the archives of the abbeys of
Dalon, Sarlat and Cadouin preserve charters of Henry, Richard and Eleanor: BN mss.
Périgord/Lespine 36 fo. 80r; Périgord/Lespine 37 fos 50r–51v, 56r–v, 91r–v, 203r; A.W.
Lewis, 'Six Charters of Henry II and his Family for the Monastery of Dalon', *EHR* 110,
1995, 652–65. To the north, even after his acquisition of La Marche in 1177, only a
handful of Henry II's charters are preserved amongst the archives of Charroux, Dorat and
Montazai: Delisle and Berger, *Recueil des Actes de Henri II*, nos 566, 733; Poitiers,
Bibliothèque Municipale ms. Fonteneau 30 part 2 p. 647; G. Thomas, *Les Comtes de la
Marche de la Maison de Charroux (Xᵉ siècle–1177)*, Paris 1928, 127 no. 110.

[10] See the remarks of Gillingham, *Richard Coeur de Lion*, 177, 190–1, and for the rebellions,
see Debord, *Société laïque*, 388–96; Watson, 'Counts of Angoulême', 118–123

[11] Debord, *Société laïque*, 394–6.

[12] Gillingham, *Richard Coeur de Lion*, ch. 6, esp. 174–80, and for a narrative of Richard's
campaigns against Angoulême and Limoges before 1199, see Gillingham, *Richard the
Lionheart*, 71–100, 113–14, 231, 234, 253, 259.

[13] *Actes de Philippe Auguste*, ii, no. 598, with suggested redating of Philip's letters to April
1198, by Gillingham, *Richard Coeur de Lion*, 176.

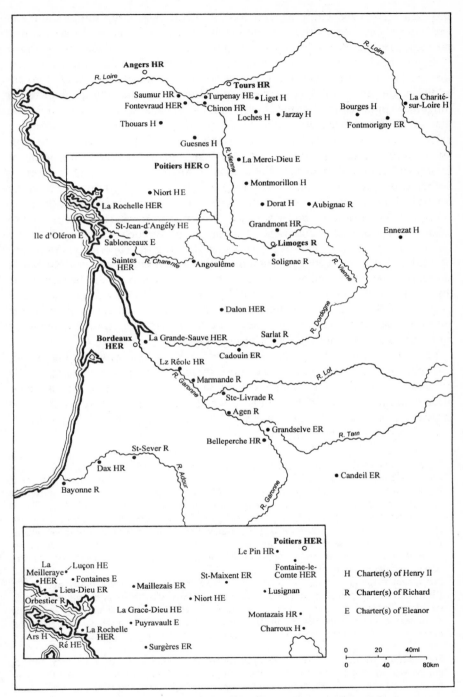

Beneficiaries of Plantagenet Charters South of the Loire.

viscount recognized Philip as their lord, allowing that Philip might commend (*adiungere*) them to another lord on condition that any such lord issue written guarantees to restore all the lands and rights that the count and viscount claimed to hold. Should this lord refuse their rights or fall foul of the king of France, then Philip, the count and the viscount would act in concert against him. In addition, the count of Angoulême obtained a pledge that Philip would give judgement in his court over the county of La Marche, a region of eastern Poitou that in 1177 had been purchased by Henry II in the light of the impending extinction of its comital family, but which thereafter had threatened to drift away from Plantagenet control into the hands of the neighbouring lords of Lusignan.[14] Through marriage, the counts of Angoulême possessed a claim to La Marche, vigorously contested by the Lusignans.[15] The lord referred to in the treaties of 1199 was presumably the successor to Richard, in the event King John, to whom the count and viscount fully expected to render homage, and to whom they were duly commended in the Anglo-French treaty made at Le Goulet in May 1200.[16] However, by acknowledging the superior overlordship of Philip Augustus, and by obtaining Philip's guarantees against Richard's successor, the count and viscount launched an appeal over the head of their immediate Plantagenet overlord, leapfrogging the customary feudal hierarchy to play off the Capetians against the Plantagenets – a threat to Plantagenet authority that had always been inherent in the homage for Aquitaine rendered by Henry II and his family to the kings of France.

From the moment of his accession, therefore, King John was confronted with Capetian intrusion into one of the most strategically significant parts of his dominion. In his first nine months as king, to counter this threat and to shore up his crumbling position in the south, he was forced to grant away much of his inheritance in Poitou to the greatest of the local magnates, the families of

---

[14] *Layettes*, i, nos 492–4, and for La Marche, see Warren, *Henry II*, 585; Gillingham, *Richard the Lionheart*, 78–9; Thomas, *Les Comtes de la Marche*, 49–51; *Rot. Norm.*, 56. That Richard did not entirely lose possession of La Marche, as has sometimes been supposed, is proved by his charter of March 1196 to St Martial Limoges, addressed to his seneschal of La Marche (above, n. 9), and by charters at Guéret, Archives départementales de la Creuse mss. H233 (Aubignac cartulary) fo. 140r (issued before the seneschal of Poitou); H256, Peter Bertin as seneschal of Poitou and La Marche addressed to the seneschal of *Briderio*, temp. Richard I, concerning the rights of the abbot of Aubignac. In general, see Watson, 'Counts of Angoulême', 125n.

[15] For Count Adomar's claim to La Marche, where at some time, most likely in 1199 or 1200, he is to be found issuing a charter to the monks of Aubignac, claiming to act as successor to 'predecessores mei comites Marchie', see A. Thomas, 'Une charte méconue d'Adémar conte d'Angoulême', in *Mélanges d'Histoire offerts à M. Charles Bémont*, Paris 1913, 201–9, esp. 205 n.3, and the genealogical tables in Debord, *Société laïque*, 390.

[16] For the terms of the treaty, see *Diplomatic Documents*, no. 9; *Layettes*, i, no. 578, and for the possibility that the treaty led to the restoration to Count Adomar of Angoulême of various lordships in the Saintonge and Oléron, previously seized by Richard, see Watson, 'Counts of Angoulême', 135–6.

Table 1. The Counts of Angoulême

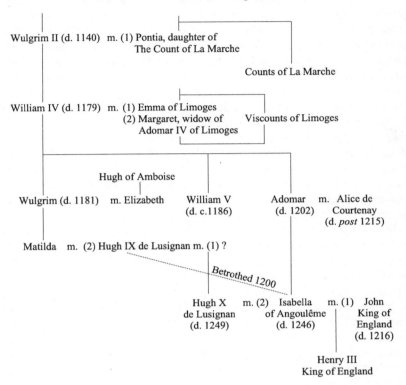

Mauléon, Thouars and Lusignan.[17] In particular, perhaps acting under duress following the kidnapping of his mother, Eleanor of Aquitaine, in January 1200, John recognized Hugh de Lusignan's claim to the county of La Marche, thereby backing the Lusignans against the appeal over La Marche brought by the count of Angoulême before the court of France.[18] Hugh de Lusignan could now look forwards to a vast expansion in his territorial lordship, as ruler of both Lusignan and La Marche. In fact, Hugh's ambitions soared even higher than this. The chronology here is far from certain, but within a few months of being granted La Marche, we know that Hugh was betrothed to Isabella, sole heiress to Count Adomar and to the entire county of Angoulême. Possibly he was already betrothed to Isabella by January 1200, as part of a pooling of the rival claims to

---

[17] *Rot. Chart.*, 24b, 25, 31–31b; Painter, *Feudalism and Liberty*, 27, 35, 66; Debord, *Société laïque*, 397.

[18] For John's treaty with the Lusignans, cemented at Caen on 28 January 1200, see *Rot. Chart.*, 58b–59, and for the supposed kidnapping of Eleanor, reported by Bernard Itier and Aubry de Trois-Fontaines, see Painter, *Feudalism and Liberty*, 66.

La Marche advanced by the houses of Lusignan and Angoulême. Possibly their betrothal did not take place until after the January settlement, as a means by which the count of Angoulême could maintain a stake in the succession to La Marche. Whatever the order of events – and, as we shall see, the precise chronology here is significant – the unification of the three lordships of Angoulême, Lusignan and La Marche under Hugh de Lusignan threatened to establish an entirely new balance of power in Poitou. On the whole, the probability is that Hugh's betrothal did not occur, or at least that it was not made known to King John, until after January 1200.[19] If, in January 1200, Hugh had already been set to inherit Angoulême, it is very hard to believe that John could have been persuaded to recognize him as count of La Marche. The unification of Lusignan and La Marche, sought by Hugh's ancestors since the eleventh century, was one thing. The unification of Lusignan, La Marche and Angoulême was quite another: a potential disaster for King John, in which Hugh de Lusignan would become master of most of Poitou, a rival and virtual equal to the hereditary Plantagenet dukes of Aquitaine.

It was against this background that in August 1200 John carried off Isabella of Angoulême and married her himself. Much as his father, Henry II, had laid the foundations of later Plantagenet dominion through his marriage to Eleanor of Aquitaine (in 1152, when she was only recently divorced from King Louis VII of France), so John may have hoped to bring off a similar coup in 1200. By marrying Isabella, John sought to acquire the rich but rebellious county of Angoulême, henceforth to form an integral part of the Plantagenet dominion. At the same time he hoped to dispose of the threat posed by a united lordship of Lusignan, La Marche and Angoulême. Had the scheme succeeded, John would have matched the success of his father, and would once and for all have stamped Plantagenet authority upon much of Aquitaine. In fact, his scheme backfired disastrously. Hugh de Lusignan rebelled, together with his brother Ralph, recently granted the important county of Eu in Normandy. Like the count of Angoulême before him, he carried his grievances to the court of France, where they provided the excuse for Philip Augustus to declare the forfeiture of King John's continental possessions. An initial set-back, in which Hugh and his allies were taken prisoner by John, was followed by the disappearance of Arthur of Brittany, presumed murdered at John's command, and by a general rising on behalf of John's barons in France. By the summer of 1204, the whole of Normandy, Maine, Anjou, the Touraine and much of northern Poitou had effectively been occupied by Philip Augustus and the allies of France.

In 1946, H.G. Richardson attempted to challenge the accepted chronology of John's marriage to Isabella, arguing that the marriage was arranged several months earlier than had previously been supposed, and in collaboration with the Lusignans, rather than as a hostile action against them. In January 1200,

---

[19] This is to discount the claim of *Howden*, iv, 119, that Isabella had been betrothed to Hugh de Lusignan with the assent of Richard I, for which see below.

Richardson argued, in return for John's agreement to recognize Hugh as count of La Marche, Hugh freely agreed to relinquish his fiancée. John then exchanged marriage vows with Isabella in a formal ceremony of betrothal, although not yet marriage. According to Richardson, this betrothal was referred to in May 1200, in the peace treaty with Philip Augustus made at Le Goulet, although John deliberately left the identity of his betrothed a secret, and may even have kept up a fiction that he was seeking a bride from the court of Portugal. He then married Isabella in August 1200. Shortly afterwards, the Lusignans rose in revolt, setting in train the events that were to lead to Capetian invasion and the loss of much of John's dominion in France. However, the cause of their revolt, Richardson argued, was not John's theft of Hugh de Lusignan's bride, but his treatment of Hugh's kinsman Ralph de Lusignan.[20] Richardson's interpretation was flawed in several respects. Although the status of Angoulême and Limoges was referred to in the Anglo-French truce of May 1200, there is no sign that formal negotiations between John and the count of Angoulême were opened until the following month.[21] As Sidney Painter has pointed out, John appears to have been entirely sincere in his negotiations for a wife from Portugal, as late as July 1200. The reference to a betrothal in the peace treaty of May 1200 implies merely that John intended to remarry, not that he was already betrothed. Thereafter, during the negotiations with the count of Angoulême, John was either suddenly captivated by the beauty of Isabella, as various of the chroniclers allege, or, more likely, for hard-headed reasons, made off with Hugh de Lusignan's intended bride, to prevent the creation of a united county of Lusignan, La Marche and Angoulême, and to claim the succession to Angoulême for himself.[22] The subsequent rebellion, Capetian invasion and defeat of King John can therefore be traced directly to the events of August 1200 and John's marriage to Isabella. John's marriage was a disastrous misjudgement which was to cost him Normandy and much of the Plantagenet dominion in France.

Richardson's interpretation may have been discredited, but various questions remain unanswered. To begin with, why was Hugh de Lusignan so outraged by the marriage of Isabella and John? The traditional answer here has been that Hugh was angered by the theft of his bride and the consequent collapse of his proposed annexation of the county of Angoulême. However, this may not have been all. Here we need to bear in mind the account of Hugh's betrothal supplied by Roger of Howden. According to Howden, Isabella was given in marriage to Hugh de Lusignan by her father, Count Adomar of Angoulême, 'on the advice and at the wish of King Richard'. Hugh received her by marriage vows by *verba de presenti*, and Isabella gave similar vows by *verba de presenti*, 'but because she had not yet attained the age of nubility, Hugh did not wish to

---

[20] Richardson, *EHR* 61, 1946, 298–307.
[21] For the negotiations of June, in which the count and viscount were summoned to a meeting with John at Lusignan for 5 July, see *Rot. Chart.*, 97.
[22] Painter and Cazel, above, n. 2.

espouse her ('copulare') in the face of the Church'.[23] In other words, Hugh was
married to Isabella in the full legal sense, save for his failure to consummate the
union because Isabella was as yet sexually immature.[24] In these circumstances,
two questions arise. Firstly, if Isabella and Hugh were effectively married by
verba de presenti, did Isabella obtain an official divorce before her betrothal to
John, most obviously on the grounds of the non-consummation of her marriage
to Hugh? The abrupt nature of John's decision to marry her makes this highly
unlikely, so that it seems that, as with his first marriage, contracted in spite of
the known consanguinity of husband and wife, John's betrothal to Isabella of
Angoulême was highly irregular.[25] Secondly, if Isabella was under age in 1200
so far as Hugh was concerned, then surely the same objection should have
applied to her suitability as a marriage partner for King John? Did John in fact
marry an under-age bride? Reporting Isabella's arrival in England in the
autumn of 1200, Coggeshall tells us that at the time Isabella appeared to be
about twelve years of age, 'que quasi duodenis videbatur'.[26] Twelve was the
accepted age of puberty for a girl, but in Coggeshall's uncertainty there may lie
a significant indication that Isabella appeared decidedly young for a bride, and
that her officially declared age of twelve was regarded with a certain degree of
scepticism.[27] Isabella's parents cannot have been married before 1184, when
her mother was still betrothed to a previous husband, and they are not in fact
recorded as husband and wife until 1191.[28] On this calculation, Isabella could
not have been more than fifteen, and was quite possibly as young as nine at the
time of her marriage in 1200. She did not give birth to her first child by King
John until October 1207, seven years after their marriage, an interval that once

---

[23] *Howden*, iv, 119, who also claims, much more implausibly, that John's marriage to
Isabella was arranged with the approval of Philip Augustus. Howden's version of events
was later copied by Wendover and Paris, *Chronica Majora*, ii, 462. It is worth noting the
specific, legalistic terminology employed here by Howden. For remarks on the unreliability of Howden for events in France after the mid 1190s, see Gillingham, *Richard
Coeur de Lion*, 161–2.

[24] For the law of marriage on this point, see C.N.L. Brooke, *The Medieval Idea of Marriage*,
Oxford 1989, 138–9.

[25] For the irregularity of John's marriage to Isabella of Gloucester, and for the haste of his
marriage to Isabella of Angoulême, see *Diceto*, ii, 72–3, 170, where John is said to have
married in 1200 without warning the ambassadors whom he had previously sent to arrange
a marriage in Portugal, thereby placing his envoys in a potentially dangerous position.

[26] *Coggeshall*, 103.

[27] For canon law forbidding betrothal before the age of seven and fixing the age of consent
for girls at twelve and fourteen for boys, see Brooke, *Marriage*, 138n., 140. John's sister
Eleanor, daughter of Henry II, had been married to the king of Castile in 1170 at the age of
only eight, although it is possible that their marriage was not consummated until she was
fifteen. However, Margaret, the fifteen-year-old daughter of Henry III, provoked scandal
in the 1250s when she sought to consummate her marriage to the fourteen-year-old King
Alexander III of Scotland: J.C. Parsons, 'Mothers, Daughters, Marriage, Power: Some
Plantagenet Evidence, 1150–1500', in *Medieval Queenship*, ed. J.C. Parsons, Stroud 1986,
67.

[28] See below, n. 41.

again suggests that she may have been as young as eight or nine in 1200.[29] Although in 1200 King John appears to have gone out of his way to obtain letters from the bishops of Bordeaux, Saintes, Périgueux, Limoges, Angoulême and Waterford, testifying to the legitimate nature of his marriage to Isabella, the suspicion remains that his bride was a pre-pubescent child in 1200, and that the king stepped in where Hugh de Lusignan, Isabella's betrothed husband, had believed it indecent to tread.[30] How happy it would have made Bishop Stubbs, indeed how happy it must make all the latter-day critics of King John, to know that the king may have been guilty not only of cruelty and murder but even, possibly, of child-molesting.

Thus far, and give or take a few details of interpretation, Isabella's paternal ancestry and her position as heiress to the count of Angoulême have long been recognized. But, like any heiress, Isabella had a mother as well as a father. Isabella's maternal ancestry, overlooked by both Painter and Richardson, was in many ways just as significant as her paternal inheritance. Her mother Alice was a daughter of Peter de Courtenay I (1125–1187), lord of Montargis and Châteaurenard south of Paris, himself the son of Louis VI of France and the brother of Louis VII.[31] In this way, via her maternal Courtenay kin, Isabella was not only a cousin of kings Philip Augustus, Louis VIII and Louis IX of France, but closely related to most of the royal houses of Europe. Her uncle, Peter de Courtenay II, was count of Nevers and Latin Emperor of Constantinople (1216–1218), and was succeeded as emperor by his sons Robert (1221–1228) and Baldwin (1239–1247). By marriage, the Courtenays were allied after 1200 to the kings of Hungary, Aragon and Castile, to the counts of Hainault, Namur, Nevers and Forez, and via Isabella herself to the kings of England.[32] In addition, Isabella could claim an even closer connection to

---

[29] For the children born to John and Isabella, see below, n. 100.

[30] For the episcopal letters, testifying *quod omnia in matrimonio canonice contrahendo processerunt*, later released to the archbishop of Canterbury, see *Rot. Norm.*, 36.

[31] Isabella's maternal descent is fully set out in a papal bull of 20 May 1254, retrospectively allowing for the annulment of a betrothal arranged between Isabella's son, King Henry III, and a daughter of the count of Ponthieu, later queen of Castile, on the grounds of their common descent from King Louis VI of France: BL ms. Cotton Cleopatra E i fo. 194, whence the eighteenth-century copies in Paris, Bibliothèque Mazarine ms. 1896 fos 3r–19r; Carpentras, Bibliothèque Municipale ms. 1772 fos 123r–130r. An edition of this letter is in preparation by Professor David d'Avray. Isabella's Courtenay descent is also cited as the cause for the annulment of a marriage arranged between Margaret, one of Isabella's daughters by Hugh de Lusignan, and Raymond count of Toulouse: *Layettes*, ii, 574–6 no. 3367.

[32] For the Courtenays, the standard authority is Jean Du Bouchet, *Histoire Généalogique de la maison royale de Courtenay*, Paris 1661, with further, but by no means entirely accurate, material on the English branch of the family supplied by E. Cleaveland, *A Genealogical History of the Noble and Illustrious Family of Courtenay*, Exeter 1735. H. Stein, 'Chartes inédites relatives à la famille de Courtenay et à l'abbaye des Echarlis', *Annnales de la Société Historique et Archéologique du Gatinais* 36, 1922, 141–65, prints various important evidences, mostly from the large collection of materials assembled in BN ms. Pièces Originales 891 *et seq.*

various of the lords of north-eastern France, since her mother, Alice de
Courtenay, had been married at least two times before she was betrothed to
Adomar of Angoulême.

Alice's first husband was Andrew lord of La Ferté-Gaucher in Champagne,
to whom she was married at some time after 1169.[33] By a previous marriage,
Andrew had fathered a son and heir, John de Montmirail, a knight in the service
of King Philip Augustus, who is said on one occasion to have saved the king's
life, and who later underwent a religious conversion, entering the Cistercian
abbey of Longpont in Picardy, where he died as a monk in 1217, and where by
the 1230s he was being venerated as a miracle-working saint.[34] It was this son
John who inherited his father's senior lordship of Montmirail, at the time of
Andrew de La Ferté's death, shortly after 1177. The lordship of La Ferté-
Gaucher itself was retained as dower for Alice de Courtenay, Andrew's
widow.[35] In this way, through her first marriage, Alice acquired not only a rich
lordship in Champagne, where she continued to exercise her rights as dowager
for the next thirty years, but close kinship, as step-mother, to one of the more
extraordinary warrior saints of thirteenth-century France.

As her second husband, at some time after 1177, Alice married William
count of Joigny near Auxerre.[36] By William she had a son, Peter, later count of

---

[33] For Alice's marriage to Andrew of La Ferté-Gaucher, see *Obituaires de la province de
Sens I: diocèses de Sens et de Paris*, ed. A. Molinier, Paris 1902, ii, 967, recording the obit
celebrated at the Hôtel-Dieu in Provins for Andrew and Adomar count of Angoulême,
'mariti quondam Aales comitisse Angolismensis que nobis multa bona contulit'. For the
date of the marriage, see H. Arbois de Jubainville, *Histoire des ducs et des comtes de
Champagne*, 8 vols, Paris 1859–69, vii (Livre des Vassaux), 16 no. 275, 251–2.

[34] For John de Montmirail, beatified in 1891, see *Acta Sanctorum*, September vol. viii,
Antwerp 1762, 186–235; J.-B. Machaut, *Histoire du B. Jean, seigneur de Montmirel et
d'Oysi*, Paris 1641; A.-C. Boitel, *Histoire du bienheureux Jean surnommé l'Humble*, Paris
1859; G. Larigaldie, *Chevalier et moine, ou Jean de Montmirail, connétable de France
1165–1217*, Paris 1909; A.-C. Dionnet, 'La Cassette reliquaire du bienheureux Jean de
Montmirail', *Revue française d'héraldique et de sigillographie* 65, 1995, 89–107. I am
extremely grateful to Monsieur Dionnet for bringing his important article to my attention.

[35] Arbois de Jubainville, *Histoire des ducs de Champagne*, vii, 16 no. 275, 251–2. For two
charters issued by Alice (de Courtenay) as countess of Angoulême in 1209 and July 1215,
the first with title as lady of La Ferté-Gaucher, confirming awards to the Hôtel-Dieu at
Provins, including a grant of corn from the mills of La Ferté made by John de Montmirail
before 1209, see Melun, Archives départementales de Seine-et-Marne ms. 11H depot B2
(with seal), with further copies in *ibid*. 11H depot A12 (Grand cartulaire) fo. 29v; A13
(Petit cartulaire) fo. 73r; B162 No. 1. For further charters, of 1197 and 1202, to the monks
of Jouy-en-Brie, with a drawing of Alice's seal displaying the Courtenay arms, see BN ms.
Latin 5467 pp. 129–30, 196.

[36] The genealogy of the counts of Joigny supplied by *L'Art de vérifier les dates*, ed. M.F.
Dantine and others, 3rd ed. vol. 2, Paris 1784, 593–7, needs to be corrected in the light of
W. Mendel Newman, *Les Seigneurs de Nesle en Picardie (XIIe–XIIIe siècles)*, 2 vols,
Paris 1971, ii, 332–42, and E. de Saint-Phalle, 'La première dynastie des comtes de Joigny
(1055–1338)', in *Autour du comte de Joigny XIe–XVIIIe siècles: Actes du colloque de
Joigny 9–10 Juin 1990*, Société généalogique de l'Yonne, Cahiers généalogiques vii,
organisé par G. Poissonier avec preface de J.-P. Rocher, 1991, 59–77.

Joigny (d.1222), a half-brother of Isabella of Angoulême.[37] We shall return to Isabella's relations with this half-brother in due course. In the meantime, we should note that William de Joigny, Alice's husband, was himself a son of Adela, daughter of the count of Nevers, and hence related to Alice's Courtenay ancestors within the prohibited degree of consanguinity, a fact which provided the grounds for his divorce from Alice c.1184.[38] The counts of Joigny could claim at least some association with the English royal family, even before the marriage of Isabella to King John. Count William of Joigny had encountered Richard I on the Third Crusade, and his wife, Isabella's mother Alice, finds a mention in the *Histoire de Guillaume le Maréchal*, where her beauty is said to have caught the eye of William Marshal and the Young King Henry during a tournament waged at Joigny c.1180.[39] Even before Isabella's betrothal to King John, there was a distant kinship established between the Plantagenets and Isabella's maternal, Courtenay kin, through their mutual ties to the Holy Land. The grandfather of Henry II of England, count Fulk of Anjou (d.1143), had married Melisand, heiress to King Baldwin II, through whom he had ruled as king of Jerusalem. The younger son of Fulk and Melisand, King Amalric I of Jerusalem (1163–1174), married a daughter of Jocelin II de Courtenay, titular count of Edessa and a direct descendant of the Courtenay lords of the Île-de-France. In turn, Amalric's eldest daughter, Sibyl, herself heiress to Jerusalem, had married as her second husband Guy de Lusignan, uncle of the Hugh de Lusignan IX who in 1200 was cheated of his marriage to Isabella of Angoulême. In this way, the families of Lusignan, Courtenay and Anjou/England were already closely intermarried, even before the rivalry between King John and Hugh de Lusignan over the hand of Isabella.

By virtue of her Courtenay ancestry Isabella would have been a desirable match, even without the added attraction of her inheritance in Angoulême. As a Courtenay, she was directly descended from the kings of France, from the very noblest of blood, close kinswoman to the kings of Jerusalem. Furthermore, by the first two marriages of her mother, contracted before 1184, Isabella enjoyed connections to some of the leading families of Champagne and Burgundy, which must greatly have enhanced her standing. Her behaviour in later life was to be consistent with this proud lineage. By marrying her, King John allied himself to the Courtenays, one of the greatest crusading families in medieval Europe, counts of Edessa from the early twelfth century, and participants in most of the crusades thereafter. Although in 1200 many of the most prestigious of the Courtenay marriages were still in the future, by 1216, through Isabella

---

[37] Aubry de Trois-Fontaines, ed. P. Scheffer-Boichorst, *MGH Scriptores* xxiii, Hanover 1874, 874 : *Alaydis comiti Guilelmo Ioviniaci peperit comitem Petrum et post Engolismensi comiti peperit Isabellam modernam Anglie regina*, and see P. Delon, 'Une Chronique inédite des comtes de Joigny', *Bulletin de la Société des Sciences Historiques et Naturelles de l'Yonne* 34, 1880, 213–14. See also my forthcoming article, 'Quelques précisions sur les comtes de Joigny 1166–1222', intended for *Annales de Bourgogne*.

[38] *Autour du comte de Joigny*, 66 and table 7.

[39] *Howden*, iii, 93; *Hist. Guillaume le Maréchal*, i, 125–6 lines 3425–3463, ii, 44–5.

and her mother Alice, John could claim kinship to the ruling house of Jerusalem, to the crusader king of Hungary, Andrew II, and to various of the leading families in the Latin empire of Constantinople, including the Latin emperor Peter de Courtenay, Isabella's uncle. Isabella was also close kinswoman to the kings of France. As a result, after 1200, she occupied a somewhat ambiguous position in Capetian–Plantagenet relations. She was, for example, the niece of Robert de Courtenay, butler of France, and a kinswoman of the count of Nevers. Both Robert de Courtenay and the count were to take leading roles in the French invasion of England after 1215.[40] The various marriages of Isabella's mother Alice may well have been arranged as a prop to Capetian interests. For example, Alice's marriage to the count of Joigny, although within the prohibited degree of kinship, may have been sponsored as a means of strengthening Courtenay–Capetian interest in the succession to the county of Auxerre–Nevers. Her divorce c.1184 coincided with the marriage of her brother, Peter de Courtenay, to the Nevers heiress, which had rendered her own Joigny connection not only redundant but a positive encumbrance.[41] Her subsequent alliance with Adomar of Angoulême can be seen as an early attempt on Adomar's part to establish links with the Capetian court. At the time of his marriage to Alice, Adomar had only recently succeeded to the county of Angoulême, following the deaths of his elder brothers Wulgrim (d.1181) and William V (d. c.1186), and in the aftermath of the Plantagenet campaign against Angoulême and Limoges mounted in 1183.[42] This war itself may well have been sparked off by an attempt made by Count William V to render homage for Angoulême, traditionally held from the dukes of Aquitaine, to the Capetian Philip Augustus. Adomar's marriage to Alice de Courtenay can be seen as a further subversive intrusion of Capetian influence into the Angoumois, just as earlier, presumably under Plantagenet sponsorship, the marriage of Adomar's elder brother Count Wulgrim (d.1181) to a daughter of the lord of Amboise, a subject of Henry II,

[40] Her kinship to Philip Augustus and to Robert de Courtenay the butler is remarked by William the Breton, in Bouquet, *Recueil*, xvii, 185, and the *Hist. Ducs de Normandie*, 202, and see below, pp. 201–2.

[41] *Autour du comte de Joigny*, 66, where the dating of Alice's divorce to 1186 follows Newman, *Seigneurs de Nesle*, ii, 333. This results from the misdating to 1186 of a charter actually dated 1184, recording Alice's last appearance as countess of Joigny: BN ms. Baluze 38 fo. 306v, and see also *ibid.* ms. Latin 17097 (Gaignières' transcripts for Les Escharlis), pp. 247–8. She is first recorded as the bride of Adomar of Angoulême in 1191; *Gallia Christiana*, ii, 1049, and see BN ms. 12898 fo. 122r, where as *Alaidis de Courtenai* she appears as Adomar's wife in an award to St-Amand-de-Boixe, datable to the time of Abbot Jocelin, 1186 X 1197.

[42] Adomar's first appearance as count of Angoulême occurs in a charter of Richard Plantagenet dated 1186: *Gallia Christiana*, ii, preuves cols. 285–6, which corrects the dating supplied by P. Boissonnade, 'Les Comtes d'Angoulême: les ligues féodales contre Richard coeur de Lion et les poésies de Bertran de Born (1176–1194)', *Annales de Midi* 7, 1895, 282–3. Watson, 'Counts of Angoulême', 127, makes the entirely plausible suggestion that this appearance at Richard's court in 1186 marks Adomar's recognition as count by Richard, his overlord.

suggests Plantagenet intrusion into the dynastic politics of Angoulême.[43] If rumour is to be believed, in 1181–2, long before John's marriage to Isabella of Angoulême, John's elder brother Richard had himself considered marrying Matilda of Angoulême, Isabella's cousin, the daughter of count Wulgrim, born to Wulgrim's marriage with Elizabeth of Amboise.[44] Instead, Matilda remained unmarried. In 1200, in the aftermath of John's betrothal to Isabella, Isabella's jilted fiancé, Hugh de Lusignan, carried off Matilda and married her himself, presumably as a means of maintaining his interest in the succession to Angoulême. As the daughter of an elder brother, Matilda arguably possessed a better, or at least as good a claim to Angoulême as her uncle Adomar or as Isabella her cousin. It was not until 1233 that Matilda, by then Hugh's widow, finally ceded any rights that she might have in the county to Isabella.[45] The claims of the daughter of an elder brother, Matilda, as opposed to those of a younger female cousin, Isabella, provide us with an intriguing point of comparison to King John's own claims to the Plantagenet succession, set against those of his nephew, Arthur of Brittany. They serve to remind us that the *casus regis* was only one amongst many such inheritance disputes, and that even in seeking the succession to Angoulême through his marriage to Isabella, John advanced a claim that was far from clear cut. Seigneurial inheritance in the year 1200 was still a potential battleground, in which might could on occasion triumph over any abstract theory of right.

The inter-relationships and inter-marriages described thus far may appear to supply nothing more than a confusing list of place-names and minor dynasties in France. They are indeed extremely complicated, as the accompanying family trees should make apparent. However, at root, they reveal the true splendour of Isabella's inheritance, not only on her father's, but on her mother's side also. Isabella was very much more than an innocent provincial heiress. The descendant of kings, she was close kinswoman to most of the ruling houses of Christendom. Moreover, the complex jigsaw of inter-marriages, into which her own betrothal to King John fits as only one small part, should serve to indicate both the significance that was attached to Angoulême by the Plantagenets and the Capetians, and the extent to which the

---

[43] A suggestion first made by Watson, 'Counts of Angoulême', 129–30, 133, whence Gillingham, *Richard the Lionheart*, 85. For Elizabeth *alias* Isabella, daughter of Hugh of Amboise and Matilda of Vendôme, dead by April 1213, buried at Fontaines-les-Blanches (dép. Indre-et-Loire), see C. Desages Olphe Galliard, 'Essai sur la chronologie et généalogie des comtes d'Angoulême', *Bulletins et Mémoires de la Société Archéologique et Historique de la Charente* 8th series 6, 1905–6, 235–6, citing evidences now Blois, Archives départementales de Loir-et-Cher ms. 17H19; Tours, Archives départementales de l'Indre-et-Loire ms. H710.

[44] Galliard, 'Essai', 235–6; Boissonnade, *Annales de Midi*, 1895, 291–2, citing the chronicle of Geoffrey de Vigeois as printed by Bouquet, *Recueil*, xii, 448. It is unclear from the chronicler's words ('qui cum puella terram obtinere tentavit') whether Richard hoped to marry Matilda or merely to obtain custody of her lands.

[45] S. Painter, *Feudalism and Liberty*, 80–1; *Cartulaire des comtes de la Marche et d'Angoulême*, ed. G. Thomas, Angoulême 1934, 40–43 nos 18–19.

Table 2. Pedigree of Isabella of Angoulême
showing her kinship to the kings of France, Jerusalem and England

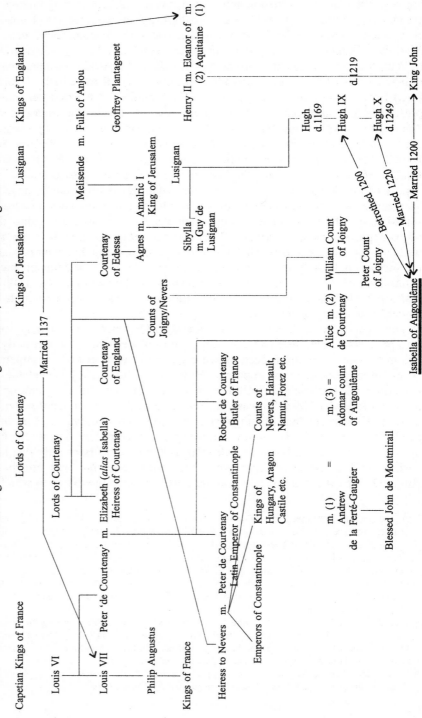

Table 3.

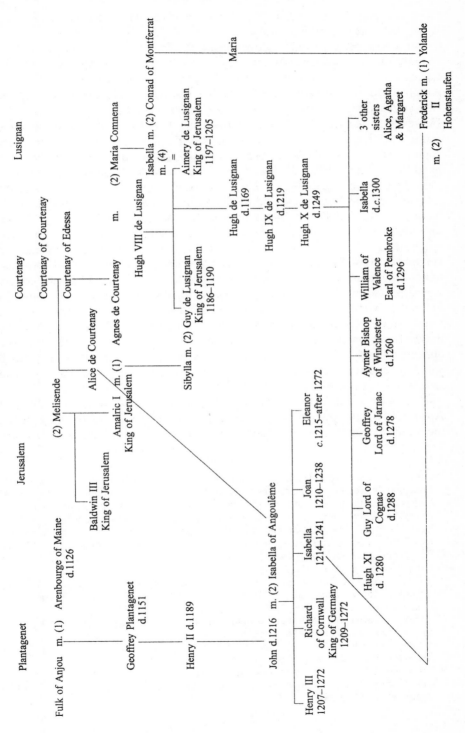

Capetians had already intruded upon Plantagenet lordship in Angoulême, long before the accession of King John.

For a brief period, and as a direct result of John's marriage, Angoulême was brought under Plantagenet control. Quite what degree of control can only be guessed at, since we are ignorant of the precise terms made between Count Adomar and John in 1200, save for the fact that they were embodied in at least two conventions, a public and a private treaty later delivered to England.[46] However, as Maurice Powicke has pointed out, there was at least some compensation to John for his marriage to Isabella. By marrying, John forfeited the support of the Lusignans who had never been trustworthy allies. On the other hand, for a time at least, the king's marriage established a much surer alliance with the count of Angoulême.[47] Count Adomar supported John throughout the rebellion by the Lusignans, and seems to have taken local command of the county of La Marche on behalf of the Plantagenets.[48] In February 1202 he led John on a tour of the newly consecrated abbey of La Couronne near Angoulême, during the negotiation there of a treaty between England and Navarre.[49] He died in June 1202, whereafter his widow, Alice de Courtenay, may have assumed the government of the city of Angoulême, whilst the county was expected to answer to John's seneschal for Poitou.[50] Alice was summoned to court in March 1203, and that autumn was awarded a monthly pension of 50 livres Anjou, payable at the Norman exchequer, presumably in return for any dower rights or claim that she might have over the county.[51] Thereafter, she appears to have retired to her estate at La Ferté-Gaucher in Champagne, which she had acquired some thirty years earlier by virtue of her first marriage, and where she was still living in July 1215.[52]

Having assumed the place of the late Count Adomar, between May 1204 and April 1205, John granted wide-ranging privileges to the city of Angoulême, including the right to have a mayor and commune, and quittance of customs

---

[46] For reference to the public and private conventions, see *Rot. Chart.*, 98b; *Rot. Norm.*, 36. Immediately after his marriage, John made an expectative award payable from his rents at La Rochelle pending the assignment of land in Angoulême, 'cum comitatus ille in manum nostram devenerit': *Rot. Chart.*, 74b, an award that was subsequently cancelled in 1201–2 in favour of an assignment of land elsewhere, apparently recorded in the lost charter roll for the third year of John's reign. In general, see Watson, 'Counts of Angoulême', 132–8.

[47] Powicke, *Loss of Normandy*, 142.

[48] For his authority over La Marche, see *Rot. Chart.*, 102; *Rot. Litt. Pat.*, 13; Thomas, 'Charte Méconue', 205–8. For his co-operation in the attack against the Lusignans, and for subsidies sent to Angoulême, see Rymer's *Foedera*, I i, 84; *Rot. Chart.*, 103; *Rot. Litt. Pat.*, 1, 3, 5b, 11; *Rot. de Lib.*, 2, 16.

[49] *Chronique Latine de l'abbaye de La Couronne*, ed. J.-F.E. Castaigne, Paris 1864, 69–70, and for the treaty, see Rymer's *Foedera*, I i, 85–6.

[50] For the seneschal, see *Rot. Litt. Pat.*, 13, 15.

[51] *Rot. Litt. Pat.*, 28, 36b; *Rot. Norm.*, 104.

[52] For a charter issued by Alice as countess of Angoulême in July 1215 at Provins, near her dower lands of La Ferté-Gaucher, see Melun, Archives départementales de Seine-et-Marne ms. 11H depot B2.

elsewhere in his lands.[53] However, with the collapse of John's dominion in France, both Alice's pension and John's day to day control over Angoulême probably lapsed. Alice was forced to issue an undertaking to Philip Augustus, supported by pledges of 2,000 marks of silver supplied by her Courtenay kinsmen, that she would enter into no arrangement with John without Philip's approval.[54] Philip himself, in a charter issued in May 1204, clearly anticipated a time when he would have jurisdiction over Angoulême, but in the event, the Capetian invasion penetrated only so far as the northern marches of Poitou.[55] Thereafter, for the next ten years, until Isabella returned in 1217 to take up her inheritance, Angoulême was placed under the command of an official appointed by John, Bartholomew de Le Puy (*de Podio*), styled variously *prepositus*, seneschal and mayor of Angoulême.[56] Isabella herself was sent to Angoulême in 1206, during John's first expedition to Poitou after the Capetian invasion, and again in 1214.[57] However, although she received the county's homage in 1206, and in 1214 may have been allowed various seigneurial privileges, she appears to have exercised no direct authority there until after the death of John.[58] In 1212, for example, it was to John and to Isabella's son, the infant Henry III, that the men of the county were expected to render homage,

---

[53] *Rot. Chart.*, 132b, 148, 149; *Rot. Litt. Pat.*, 48.

[54] *Gervase*, ii, 94–5; *Layettes*, i, nos 741–2, with suggested dating by L. Delisle, *Catalogue des actes de Philipe-Auguste*, Paris 1856, nos 811–12, taken from a abstract of various documents now missing from the Trésor des Chartes. There is a fuller abstract of these documents, including various details missing from the printed version, in BN ms. Pièces Originales 907 (formerly ms. français 27391) nos 3297, 3306, 3355.

[55] *Actes de Philipe Auguste*, ii, no.788, and see nos 799, 800, 847, 856, 859; Watson, 'Counts of Angoulême', 137, for the homage rendered to Philip by the count of Périgord and the bishop of Limoges, and for Philip's confirmation of the liberties of St-Jean-d'Angély. At much the same time, the monks of La Couronne near Angoulême sought letters of protection from Philip during a visit to Paris *en route* for the Cistercian general chapter: *Chronique de La Couronne*, ed. Castaigne, 73–4. The monks had earlier sought similar letters from John, in July 1200, even before John's marriage to Isabella; *Rot. Chart.*, 97b.

[56] *Rot. Litt. Pat.*, 92, 93b, 111 (as mayor); *Rot. Litt. Claus.*, i, 73b; *Rot.Litt. Pat.*, 116b, 152b, 175 (as *prévôt* 1206 and seneschal 1214–17). The implication is that Bartholomew was addressed as *prévôt* or seneschal during John's expeditions to Poitou in 1206 and 1214, but served as mayor in the meantime. He is to be found with some position of authority within the county as early as 14 June 1202, two days before the death of Count Adomar: *Rot. Norm.*, 54, and for the date of Adomar's death, at Limoges, see *Chroniques de Saint-Martial de Limoges*, ed. H. Duplès-Agier, Société de l'Histoire de France, Paris 1874, 68, 106–7. Watson, 'Counts of Angoulême', 204 is perhaps over-hasty in rejecting any connection between Bartholomew and the various men named *de Podio*, active in comital service at Angoulême in the late twelfth century.

[57] *Rot. Litt. Pat.*, 67b; *Chronica Majora*, ii, 572; *Rot. Litt. Pat.*, 117, where Isabella was to be sent to the king in Poitou together with her children Richard and Joan, although not, apparently, until a fairly late stage of the king's campaign.

[58] For the reservation to Isabella of the tongues and chines of venison taken by the king's huntsmen in 1214, which looks very much like a seigneurial perquisite (the haunches and rumps being retained for the king), and for the expectation that she would seal an award of land, see *Rot. Litt. Claus.*, i, 169b; *Rot. Chart.*, 196.

and in September 1214 we find John rather than Isabella receiving the surrender of a rent in the city of Angoulême with which he then invested Bartholomew de Le Puy, his local commander.[59]

Alice de Courtenay, Isabella's mother, lived on until at least 1215, and during John's expedition of 1214 was promised that her annual pension would continue to be paid.[60] As a link to the Courtenays, she was not without significance. As early as August 1201, we find John rewarding a kinsman of Alice, described as Reginald *prévôt* of Chartres, and it may be no coincidence that in 1214, shortly after the marriage of Alice's niece Yolande to the king of Hungary, we find Hungarian envoys active in England, perhaps to coordinate the crusading plans of King John and Andrew II.[61] Alice's nephew, Philip count of Namur, fought together with the Anglo-imperial forces against the French at Bouvines, whilst in 1217 the news of the imprisonment of Alice's brother, Peter de Courtenay, emperor of Constantinople, was swiftly communicated to England.[62] Isabella herself may have been allowed no direct authority over Angoulême during her husband's lifetime, but the exalted nature of her birth helps to explain the fact that in 1200, immediately on her arrival in England, she was crowned queen in a ceremony that appeared deliberately to invest her with a share in sovereignty. As Richardson pointed out, Isabella was not only crowned but anointed, whilst the solemnity of her position is deliberately referred to in letters of King John, where Isabella is described as 'by God's grace . . . crowned queen of England with the common assent and agreement of the archbishops, bishops, counts, barons, clergy and people of the whole of the realm': much the same terms that were used by the king in referring to his own coronation.[63] At least to begin with, it may be that John considered allowing Isabella the same vice-regal powers that had been exercised before 1173 by his mother, Eleanor of Aquitaine. In the event, as we shall see, Isabella achieved no such status. However, the coronation of 1200, and the solemn crown-wearings that followed it, should serve to remind us that Isabella was a descendant of the kings of France, herself crowned queen of England.

In these circumstances, was Isabella treated in a suitably royal fashion by her husband, King John? The answer must be a resounding 'No'. What evidence we have suggests that the financial and other practical provisions made for her during John's lifetime were modest, even downright mean. Here we need to bear in mind that there was a great distinction to be drawn between a wife's expectations, in terms of the dower that she might hope to receive after the death of her husband, and the actual resources that she could command during

---

[59] *Rot. Litt. Pat.*, 92; *Cartulaire des Comtes de la Marche*, ed. Thomas, 58–60 no. 27.

[60] *Rot. Litt. Pat.*, 119, 121b, 177; Melun, Archives départementales ms.11H depot B2, and see *Rot. de Lib.*, 118, for her dispatch of a messenger to King John in 1209.

[61] *Rot. de Lib.*, 19; Vincent, *Peter des Roches*, 68.

[62] *Hist. Ducs de Normandie*, 205, and see *The Letters and Charters of Cardinal Guala Bicchieri, Papal Legate in England 1216–1218*, ed. N. Vincent, Canterbury and York Society lxxxiii, 1996, 47–8 no. 59n.

[63] Richardson, *EHR* 61, 1946, 307–10, citing *Rot. Chart.*, 128; *Rot. de Lib.*, 1; *Rot. Norm.*, 34.

her husband's lifetime. In theory, Isabella would have been entitled to a dower comprising one third of John's estate. Even in practice, it is clear that John assigned various estates to serve as Isabella's dower, which, had she ever taken possession of them, would have made her rich. At Chinon, on 30 August 1200, six days after their marriage, John promised Isabella a dower comprising Saintes and Niort in Poitou, and a rich collection of estates in Anjou, including the towns of Saumur, La Flèche, Beaufort-en-Vallée, Baugé and Château-du-Loir.[64] The assignment is an intriguing one. By granting Isabella Saintes and Niort, John can only have fanned the flames of Lusignan resentment. Not only had he made off with Hugh de Lusignan's affianced bride, the heiress upon whom the Lusignans had pinned a large part of their hopes for territorial expansion, but, as John's bride, Isabella was promised two of the richest lordships in Poitou. Had she gained possession of these, she would have far eclipsed the wealth and power of the Lusignans and her former fiancé Hugh. This in itself should alert us to the fact that John's marriage was conceived from the start as a deliberate and hostile gesture against the Lusignans, indeed that it was tantamount to inviting a trial of strength, in which the Lusignans were quite deliberately goaded into rebellion.

The remainder of the dower settled upon Isabella in 1200 lay in Anjou and the Touraine, and made up a considerable portion of the demesne of the counts of Anjou. Why was Isabella promised these Angevin lands? The answer lies in the peculiar position in which Isabella was placed at the time of her marriage. In 1200 Isabella became merely one of three queens of England, the others being the widows Eleanor of Aquitaine and Berengaria of Navarre, both of whom were still alive. Eleanor's dower, which had been officially assigned in 1189, shortly after the death of her husband, had swallowed all of the English and Norman estates which traditionally comprised the dowers of the Anglo-Norman queens. Already, by 1189, there seems to have been an understanding that certain royal manors were, as a matter of course, to be included in any queen's dower. Roger of Howden makes this point, when he writes that in 1189 Richard granted Eleanor the entire dower which had previously been held by the wives of Henry I and Stephen.[65] Some of these estates, such as Exeter, enjoyed an even longer association with the queens of England, stretching back beyond the Norman Conquest to the Anglo-Saxon past.[66] Be that as it may, the endowment of the widowed Eleanor had left Richard with a problem when it came to assigning dower to his own queen, Berengaria of Navarre, solved in 1191 when Berengaria was promised all of Gascony south of the Garonne and various lordships in Anjou, pending the reversion of the estate that was currently held

[64] *Rot. Chart.*, 74b–75.
[65] *Howden*, iii, 27.
[66] M.A. Meyer, 'The Queen's "Demesne" in Later Anglo-Saxon England', in *The Culture of Christendom: Essays in Medieval History in Commemoration of Denis L.T. Bethell*, ed. M.A. Meyer, London 1993, 75–113.

by Eleanor.[67] These promises to Berengaria were never honoured. For example, in 1191 Berengaria had been promised the lordship of Château-du-Loir, which was nonetheless bestowed upon Isabella in 1200.[68] More importantly, when Eleanor did eventually die, in 1204, it was to Isabella rather than Berengaria that her dower was reassigned. In the meantime, no attempt seems to have been made to allow Berengaria possession of any of her dower in Gascony. The outcome was an acrimonious dispute between Berengaria and her brother-in-law, in which John was threatened with papal censure, and from which he was eventually forced to extricate himself, at the height of the political crisis in 1215, by promising Berengaria a cash alternative of several thousand pounds.[69] The interlocking interests of Berengaria and Isabella, Navarre and Angoulême, in these arrangements, may well explain the involvement of Count Adomar of Angoulême in the peace negotiated between England and Navarre at Angoulême in 1202.[70] Whatever the rights and wrongs here – and there can be little doubt that John's treatment of Berengaria was shoddy in the extreme – the dowers already held by Eleanor, or promised to Berengaria, ensured that in 1200 John had to find an alternative assignment for his own bride, Isabella.

Niort and Saintes, the two Poitevin lordships promised to Isabella in 1200, if added to her own, personal inheritance of Angoulême, would have ensured her a pre-eminent place amongst the Poitevin nobility. As to the assignment of estates in Anjou, perhaps Isabella or her advisors were unwilling to accept a dower in England or Normandy, far removed from her own homeland in the south. Alternatively, the king may have been reluctant to deplete the Anglo-Norman royal demesne. In any event, it seems that the assignment of 1200 was always intended to be a provisional one, pending the death of Eleanor of Aquitaine. Certainly, within a few weeks of Eleanor's death in 1204, the king made a second settlement upon Isabella. Whether this was intended to replace rather than to supplement the settlement made in 1200 is uncertain, although later Isabella herself was in no doubt that she was entitled to all the lands assigned both in 1200 and 1204. Since 1200, Isabella's dower in Anjou had been overrun by the Capetians, so that such a supplement would have had to be found sooner or later, regardless of the death or survival of Eleanor. As it was, in 1204 Isabella was promised possession of Eleanor's dower in England and Normandy, comprising the city of Exeter and various manors in Devon; Ilchester in Somerset; Wilton, Malmesbury and a further two manors in

---

[67] *Registres*, 469–72 nos 28, 30, noticed by Gillingham, *Richard Coeur de Lion*, 124n. from an earlier printing by E. Martène and U. Durand, *Veterum scriptorum et monumentorum amplissima collectio*, 9 vols, Paris 1724–33, i, cols. 995–97 For dissension from Gillingham's opinion on the significance of the offer of Gascony made to Berengaria, see Vincent, *Peter des Roches*, 44 n.6.

[68] *Registres*, 469–70 no. 28.

[69] *Howden*, iv, 164, 172–3; *Letters of Innocent III*, nos 210, 217–19, 355, 531–2, 580, 765–6, 789, 836, 868, 1050–2; Cheney, *Innocent III and England*, 101; Vincent, *Peter des Roches*, 67, 95, 124, and references there cited.

[70] Above, n. 49.

Wiltshire; the city of Chichester; Queenhithe in London; Waltham in Essex; the honour of Berkhamsted; the town of Rockingham; the county of Rutland; and in Normandy, Falaise, Domfront and Bonneville-sur-Toque.[71] In the light of the military collapse of 1204, Isabella was further promised that if anything should be lost from her dower lands, through war or for any other reason, the king would make good such losses with a supplementary award of lands in England.

The settlement of 1204, like that made in 1200, was a generous one, guaranteed by solemn oaths from a dozen bishops, earls and other magnates. However, far more significant than the theoretical generosity of these settlements is the fact that Isabella exercised absolutely no control over her dower during the lifetime of her husband. That this was to be so had been made plain as early as August 1200, when, on the day after assigning Niort as part of Isabella's dower, John immediately farmed the town to a local man, William Cocus, for an annual rent of 200 livres of Poitou. The money was to be paid to John, not to his queen.[72] Meanwhile, both Niort and Saintes remained under the overall authority of John's mother Eleanor, in her capacity as duchess of Aquitaine. In 1199, Eleanor had confirmed a commune to the men of Saintes, followed in 1203 by a similar award to the men of Niort.[73] In neither town were Isabella's interests so much as mentioned, let alone consulted. Throughout John's lifetime, Isabella derived no direct revenue from any of her dower lands in England or France. During the four years in which she was dowered with estates in Anjou and Poitou, she exercised no authority there. Likewise, the Norman lands awarded in 1204 were a dead letter from the very start. They had already been overrun by the French by the time that they were theoretically assigned to Isabella. In addition, Isabella faced a threat from within the Plantagenet royal family, since the dower of Eleanor, transferred to Isabella in 1204, had already been promised, as long ago as 1191, to the bride of Richard I, Berengaria of Navarre. In theory, according to this earlier settlement, Eleanor's dower should have passed to Berengaria in 1204, rather than to Isabella. Already, at the time of the first assignment of dower made to Isabella in 1200, there had been indications of a potential rift with Berengaria, in the award to Isabella of the lordship of

---

[71] *Rot. Chart.*, 128. It is worth pointing out that Eleanor's dower as listed in 1191 differs in several important respects from the estate settled upon Isabella in 1204. In particular, Isabella's settlement did not include the manors of Lambourne in Berkshire, Martock in Somerset, Stanton in Oxfordshire, the town of Northampton, Grantham and Stamford in Lincolnshire, and the honours of Berkeley and Arundel, referred to as parts of the queen's dower in 1191; *Registres*, 471–2 no. 30. Various of these manors were held by Eleanor merely as wardships and escheats.

[72] *Rot. Chart.*, 75.

[73] *Layettes*, i, 208–9 no. 507; M. Dillay, *Les Chartes de franchises du Poitou*, Catalogue des Chartes de Franchises de la France I, Paris 1927, 21–2 no. 28. Eleanor's grant of liberties to the men of Niort is referred to by King John, *Rot. Chart.*, 161. For further confirmations to the religious of Notre-Dame and St-Eutrope at Saintes made by Eleanor, one of them certainly after the accession of King John, see BN ms. Latin 12754 pp. 266–7, also in *ibid.* ms. Latin 13817 fo. 244v; Paris, Archives Nationales ms. JJ114 fo. 124v no. 239, also in *ibid.* ms. JJ123 fo. 118r no. 234.

Château-du-Loir, theoretically promised to Berengaria since 1191.[74] In 1204, this rift widened into outright rivalry, with Berengaria intervening, shortly after the death of Eleanor, to lay claim to the entire dower that had been promised her a decade earlier. Her claim could be ignored in England, but in France it was eagerly exploited by Philip Augustus. In 1204, Philip granted the newly captured city of Le Mans to Berengaria, in return for a charter, issued at Paris, by which she abandoned the dower rights that she claimed to hold in the Norman lordships of Falaise, Domfront and Bonneville-sur-Toque.[75] At the same time, in August 1204, Berengaria's brother, King Sancho VII of Navarre, issued a charter of protection for the men of Bayonne, the most important outpost of Plantagenet influence in southern Gascony, in theory saving Bayonne's fidelity to King John, in practice as part of Navarre's wider ambitions to extend its power north of the Pyrenees into Plantagenet controlled Gascony.[76] Sancho's actions here coincided with a full-scale invasion of Gascony mounted by King Alfonso VIII of Castile, himself seeking to lay claim to dower lands promised since 1170, from the time of his marriage to Eleanor, the sister of King John.[77]

It was not only Berengaria who threatened the integrity of Isabella's dower. A considerable part of Isabella's potential revenue from England and Normandy had already been granted away by Eleanor of Aquitaine to various of her own familiars and favourites. Only one of these awards was made in free alms: a grant by Eleanor of half of the manor of Winterslow in Wiltshire to the nuns of Fontevraud.[78] Most of Eleanor's awards were conditional upon the payment of rents and services. But the rents which she and her successors were to receive henceforth were negligible and well below their true market value.[79] In effect,

---

[74] *Rot. Chart.*, 74b–75; *Registres*, 469–70 no. 28.

[75] *Registres*, 493–4 no. 47, tentatively dated to August/September 1204. There are signs that Berengaria had been in attendance upon the French court since shortly after the death of King Richard. In April 1199 she had witnessed a charter of Eleanor of Aquitaine, bestowing alms for the soul of the late king, but by July of the same year she was at Chartres, together with Queen Adela of France, witnessing the marriage settlement between her sister Blanche and Theobald count of Champagne: *Layettes*, i, nos 489, 497. By January 1204, denied her income from King John, she is said to have sought refuge in Champagne: *Letters of Innocent III*, no. 531.

[76] J.-A. Brutails, *Documents des archives de la Chambre des Comptes de Navarre (1196–1384)*, Paris 1890, no. 3, also in *Catologo de los Cartularios Reales del Archivo General de Navarra años 1007–1384*, ed. F. Idoate, Pamplona 1974, 78–9 no. 137.

[77] Gillingham, *Richard Coeur de Lion*, 125.

[78] *Cal. Docs France*, no.1090, and see also *EEA* ii, *Canterbury 1193–1205*, no. 469.

[79] See, for example, Hertford, Hertfordshire RO ms. 17465 (Flamstead cartulary) fo. 28r, for a grant to Agatha de Gatesden of part of the wood of Hemel Hempstead and various rents, in return for an annual quit-rent of 1 lb of pepper, with a further award of the manor of Lifton Devon in hereditary fee, in return for an annual quitrent of 1 lb of incense, referred to in *Rot. Chart.*, 7b–8, 10b. For further awards to Eleanor's familiars in England, see *Rot. Chart.*, 8, 25. In Normandy, the awards made by Eleanor to the abbeys of St-Etienne Caen and Fontenay, may have involved lands that she held in dower; BN ms. Latin 12758 p. 574; *Rot. Chart.*, 6b. Within the forest of Domfront she undoubtedly granted extensive

between 1189 and 1204 Eleanor had greatly depleted the value of the dower subsequently assigned to Isabella, by bestowing large parts of it upon her faithful servants and their heirs, in return for quit-rents of pepper or incense. More significantly still, it is apparent that throughout John's reign, the king continued to dispose of Isabella's dower lands, regardless of any interest that the queen might have had in such awards. In this way, Rutland was assigned at fee farm by the king to Ralph de Normanville and his heirs in May 1205.[80] The remainder of Winterslow, Queenhithe and the honour of Berkhamsted were all granted between 1204 and 1208 in fee farm to the king's justiciar Geoffrey fitz Peter and his heirs. They were recovered by the Crown in 1213, as part of the wider attack made by John against Geoffrey's heir, Geoffrey de Mandeville. However, Geoffrey continued to press for their return, and they were not finally wrested from Mandeville family control until a few months before the king's death, in June 1216.[81] The city of Chichester and the site of the former castle at Malmesbury, again supposedly part of Isabella's dower, were both assigned by John, for life, or in fee farm, to the local religious.[82] Shortly after the assignment of Chichester, in May 1204, the king had issued a further confirmation to the bishop and chapter of Chichester, for the sake of his own soul and that of Isabella.[83] After John's death, Isabella herself confirmed his award of the town and site of the castle at Malmesbury to Malmesbury Abbey in return for a fee farm of £20 and prayers for the sake of herself and her late husband.[84] In this way, she at least extracted some indirect, spiritual services in return for the alienation of parts of her dower. However, a money farm and meagre spiritual services could in no way up make up for Isabella's complete lack of control over her own future estate. Between 1200 and 1216 the lands assigned to her in dower were entirely managed, and in large measure subject to alienation, by her husband, King John.

We have an interesting point of contrast here in the resources controlled by

privileges to Robert le Saucier, in return for a quit-rent of 1 lb. of pepper: Flers, Bibliothèque Municipale ms. 224 (G9) fo. 12r, also in *ibid.* ms. 181 (F50) pp. 27–8. A lost charter to St Albans Abbey confirming rights in Hemel Hempstead is referred to in Chatsworth House, Duke of Devonshire ms. St Albans cartulary endpapers, s.xiv, listing the titles to charters from the lost Redbourn section of the St Albans cartulary.

80 *Rot. Chart.*, 149, of which the original is now Lincoln, Lincolnshire RO ms. 3Anc1/34/1/1. The circumstances in which Ralph abandoned his custody of the county in 1209/10 (*PR 12 John*, 213–14) are unclear.

81 *Rot. Chart.*, 134b, 151b, 182b, 223; *Rot. Litt. Claus.*, i, 217; Holt, *Magna Carta*, 208; Vincent, *Peter des Roches*, 106–7. After 1216, and in compensation for her dower lands which had been lost in Normandy, Isabella was granted the farm of the manor of Aylesbury, held since 1204 by Geoffrey fitz Peter and his heirs, possibly as a detached portion of the honour of Berkhamsted: *Rot. Chart.*, 127b–128, 223; *Patent Rolls 1216–25*, 302, 431–2

82 *Rot. Chart.*, 127b, 222. The monks of Malmesbury had offered John 100 marks and a palfrey for the king's award, made in June 1216; *Rot. de Obl.*, 599.

83 *Rot. Chart.*,129.

84 Below, Appendix no. 3.

Isabella's predecessor as queen, Eleanor of Aquitaine. Not only was Eleanor duchess of Aquitaine in her own right, with a rich store of patronage at her disposal both before and after her marriage to Henry II, but even during Henry's lifetime she appears to have exercised at least some control over the estates that were later confirmed to her as dower. In this way, even before 1189, she had issued a writ commanding the knights of Malmesbury to render the services that they owed to the abbey there.[85] Beyond this we know that Eleanor enjoyed at least one other source of income during the lifetime of her husband that may well have been denied to Isabella: the proceeds of Queen's Gold. Queen's Gold was a supplementary levy of one mark of gold for every 100 marks of silver, taken on voluntary fines and on many of the king's transactions with moneyers and the Jews – an obligation that may well explain the widespread transfer of Jewish debts to Isabella's successors as queens of England, Eleanor of Provence and Eleanor of Castile. According to the *Dialogus de Scaccario* (1177), it was still a matter of dispute with Queen Eleanor whether the levy could only be applied to fines of 100 marks or more, or whether it could be taken on fines as small as 10 marks. Nonetheless, the *Dialogus* leaves us in no doubt that Eleanor had a clerk at the royal Exchequer, whose duty it was to claim her gold. This queen's clerk was responsible for rendering accounts to Eleanor, and for ensuring that a supplementary claim was written in to every relevant summons for debt sent out into the counties. Whilst the king might subsequently relax or remit a fine, the gold levy owed to the queen could in no way be reduced by the king, without the queen's express approval.[86] H.G. Richardson demonstrated that Eleanor continued to receive Queen's Gold, even after the death of Henry II, suggesting that it was assigned to her as part of her dower. A writ entered on the pipe roll for 1208 makes it plain that she was still issuing quittances for gold owed from the reign of Henry II, several years after Henry's death.[87] At Bury St Edmunds, she was granted a gold cup in place of the 10 marks of gold that were owing from a fine of 1000 marks that the abbot made with King Richard in 1189, and until at least Christmas 1192 her clerks at the royal Exchequer were assisted by a clerk of the abbot of Waltham in collecting and accounting for Queen's Gold.[88] All of this makes it extremely doubtful

---

[85] *Registrum Malmesburiense*, ed. J.S. Brewer and C. Trice Martin, 2 vols, RS LXXII, 1879–80, i, 335.

[86] *Dialogus de Scaccario*, 122–3.

[87] H.G. Richardson, 'The Letters and Charters of Eleanor of Aquitaine', *EHR* 74, 1959, 209–11; *PR 10 John*, 15. Richardson further suggested that Eleanor was deprived of Queen's Gold at the time of her disgrace in 1173, only recovering it towards the end of Henry's reign. However this would necessitate a revision to the accepted dating of the *Dialogus*, and finds no support from any other authority.

[88] BL ms. Additional 14847 (Bury Registrum Album) fo. 40r–v (44r–v), also in Cambridge University Library ms. Ff.2.33 (Bury sacrist's register) fo. 29v, whence *Monasticon*, iii, 154; *The Early Charters of the Augustinian Canons of Waltham Abbey, Essex, 1066–1230*, ed. R. Ransford, Woodbridge 1989, no. 36; Richardson, 'Eleanor', 211. The Bury charter, supported by the account in *The Chronicle of Jocelin of Brakelond Concerning the Acts of Samson Abbot of the Monastery of St Edmund*, ed. H.E. Butler, NMT 1949, 46–7, makes it

whether Richard's queen, Berengaria of Navarre, ever replaced Eleanor as the beneficiary of Queen's Gold. Just as Berengaria was denied any control over her promised dower lands, so from 1191 onwards she may have been denied her rights at the English Exchequer.

The evidence for the payment of Queen's Gold to Isabella is less than satisfactory, and allows for no certain conclusion. However, it remains a strong possibility that it was John, rather than his wife, Isabella, who benefited from a levy that should by custom have passed to the queen. To begin with, it is apparent that at some time, probably in the early months of 1201, a clerk went through the fine rolls for the first two years of John's reign, marking those fines which were liable to Queen's Gold, and then entering running totals on the dorse of various membranes of the roll. These jottings demonstrate that, whatever the custom before the 1170s, by 1200 Queen's Gold was being levied on fines as small as 4 marks, not merely upon those of 100 marks or more, suggesting that Eleanor's claim of the 1170s had been settled in her favour.[89] Nothing, however, is said of the destination of whatever sums were eventually collected. In theory, they could have been intended for John's mother, Eleanor of Aquitaine, or for his new bride, Isabella. Most likely, they were pocketed by John himself. Thereafter, from 1201 onwards, it has been assumed that any money collected passed to Isabella. However, in November 1207 John issued explicit instructions that the royal Exchequer was to hear accounts for Queen's Gold as for any others of the king's debts. A king's clerk named Alexander de Refham was to keep the appropriate rolls and to intervene when Queen's Gold was in question, replacing Alexander de Lucy who had previously exercised this office, and whose accounts were to be audited by the Exchequer.[90] From 1207 onwards, the Exchequer pipe rolls begin to record Queen's Gold, owed or received, as part of the ordinary sheriffs' accounts, from time to time listing it under individual subheadings, county by county, highlighted *aurum regine*.[91] Various aspects of these accounts are worth remarking. To begin with, they can record only a tiny number of the occasions upon which gold was either owed or paid, and they tend to be carried forwards from year to year in a way that suggests that old entries were being copied out on to the rolls, without any real attempt at collection. What we have here appears to be only the tip of what must have been a far more substantial administrative iceberg. Secondly, and contrary to the claim of the *Dialogus* that only the queen could licence any remission of her gold, the earliest such accounts on the pipe roll, for 1208, show that on at

---

plain that Richardson was correct in supposing that Eleanor continued to collect Queen's Gold on fines made after the death of Henry II, a point that has been questioned by M. Howell, 'The Resources of Eleanor of Provence as Queen Consort', *EHR* 102, 1987, 373 n.3.

[89] *Rot. de Obl.*, 1–31, 76–99, 141; Richardson, intro. to *Memoranda Roll 1 John*, xcvi.

[90] *Rot. Litt. Claus.*, i, 98.

[91] *PR 10 John*, 19, 21, 37, 59, 73, 91, 112, 126, 164, 188, 192. In the previous two years, a sum of 22 marks of Queen's Gold owed on Jewish debt by Elias Martin had been separately listed on the pipe rolls: *PR 7 John*, 213; *PR 8 John*, 97.

least two occasions sums owed in Queen's Gold were being written off by the
Exchequer against various debts to the king. Thus Henry de Bohun was
pardoned his gold by the Exchequer, the debt being written off against the
superplus or various other credits that he had built up elsewhere in his account
through sums spent on the king's behalf.[92] In the same year, the memoranda roll
records a fine of three marks offered to the king by Roger de Somerville, to be
quit of six marks that he had previously owed in Queen's Gold.[93] In other
words, John and his Exchequer officials were exercising a degree of control
over the collection and remission of Queen's Gold that suggests that the queen
herself was allowed little or no interest in what was, in theory, her own
resource. Of the two clerks mentioned in November 1207 as being responsible
for the auditing of gold at the royal exchequer, both appear to have been the
king's, rather than the queen's men.[94] Neither man is found on any other
occasion in the service of Isabella.

After John's death, although no new accounts were rendered, sums owing in
gold from before 1216 continued to be entered on the early pipe rolls of
Henry III. One or two were cleared by payments into the Exchequer.[95] Others
were subsumed within larger debts to the king whose payment was then
rescheduled at fixed annual rates.[96] This too suggests that it was the king's
administration, rather than the queen, which was taking the admittedly small
sums referred to in the pipe rolls. One other piece of evidence may be relevant
here. In the 1190s, when Eleanor of Aquitaine levied Queen's Gold on a fine
between the abbot of Bury and the king, she received a gold cup in lieu of cash.
Such renders in gold may well have been a customary way of discharging debts
to the queen. By contrast, the pipe roll for 1203–4 records expenses of 37 marks
on gold and £1 spent on its fashioning into a golden cup for Isabella, and again
in April 1206, we find King John issuing special instructions to release 3 marks
of gold collected from the Jews and to have it made into a cup for the use of the
queen.[97] In other words, on the two occasions where we read of Isabella receiving gold, it came as a gracious gift from the king, rather than as hers by right.

In this way, Isabella enjoyed no revenue from her dower lands. She may have
received little or nothing from the collection of Queen's Gold, whilst her own
personal inheritance in Angoulême remained in practice beyond her personal

---

[92] *PR 10 John*, 21, 188.

[93] *Memoranda Roll 10 John*, 30.

[94] Both Alexander de Refham (or *Roffam*, Rochester) and Alexander de Lucy appear earlier
in the reign, charged with administering the receipts from the vacant bishoprics of
Canterbury and Carlisle: *Rot. Litt. Pat.*, 30b, 35b, 65; *Rot. Litt. Claus.*, i, 42, 44, 46b, 50,
57b, 65b, 112b.

[95] See the debt of Ralph of Pembridge, repaid by 1220: *PR 16 John*, 136; *PR 3 Henry III*,
166; *PR 4 Henry III*, 195.

[96] See the debts, including gold, rescheduled to William Paynel, Joceus de Plugenet, Oliver
de Punchardon and the heirs of James of Newmarket: *PR 4 Henry III*, 83; *PR 5 Henry III*,
3, 18–19, 84.

[97] *PR 6 John*, 175; *Rot. Litt. Claus.*, i, 68b.

control. Instead, Isabella appears to have depended entirely upon the grace and favour of the king. Here, at last, we are forced to enter the murky waters of the king's private life. Our evidence for judging the more personal side of the relations between king and queen is far from ideal. Are we to accept or to reject the scandal put about by contemporary chroniclers? The chroniclers are almost universally hostile to John, accusing him of cruelty and debauchery, often in the most extravagant terms. Victorian scholars, most notably Bishop Stubbs, had a natural inclination to credit such accounts, presenting a 'Bad King John', a true model of evil, stained with every form of moral pollution, so unlike the home life of their own Dear Queen. Sidney Painter and his successors, writing in an atmosphere of greater moral relaxation, accepted that the king was cruel, suspicious and an unfaithful husband, but turned a blind eye to some of the grosser crimes with which the king was charged, rejecting them as the exaggerations of hostile chroniclers, composed after the events of 1215–16, at a time when John was being transformed into the bogey man of later legend. What judgement are we to pass upon the king, looking back from the late twentieth century, from an age of such moral laxity that even 'Bad King John', let alone Bishop Stubbs, might have regarded us as moral degenerates?

John undoubtedly fathered several bastards. At least two of these children, Oliver and Richard fitz Roy, were born to noblewomen whose liaisons with the king might well be regarded as scandalous.[98] A king who dallied with the wives and daughters of his leading barons was likely to excite far more bitter resentment than a king who confined his extra-marital entertainments to low-born courtesans. However, what evidence we have suggests that all of John's bastards were born before he ascended the throne, before his marriage to Isabella of Angoulême. Thereafter, references to the king's lady friends, such as the *amica domini regis* who was sent a chaplet of roses in June 1212, or the Susan, 'maidservant of the king's friend [*amice*]', perhaps the same *amica* as before, who received a dress in the spring of 1213, have long given rise to suspicion. However, there is no outright proof that such 'friends' were John's mistresses.[99] The fact that the king fathered at least five legitimate children by Isabella – the eldest son, the future King Henry III, born in 1207, the youngest daughter, Eleanor, perhaps as late as 1215 – suggests, at the very least, that John and his wife maintained normal conjugal relations for most of their

---

[98] For Oliver, see S. Painter, 'Who was the Mother of Oliver fitz Roy', *Medievalia et Humanistica* 8, 1954, 17–19, reprinted in Painter, *Feudalism and Liberty*, 240–43, and in general, see Painter, *Reign of King John*, 231–5, which is merely summarized by C. Given-Wilson and A. Curtis, *The Royal Bastards of Medieval England*, London 1984, 127–31.

[99] 'Misae Roll 14 John', in *Docs of English History*, 234, 267, cited, although slightly warped by Painter, *Reign of King John*, 234. Painter's reference (p. 234 n.30) to a mistress of the king paid £30 by Peter des Roches is the outcome of mistakenly substituting the feminine *amica* for *amicus* in the account printed as *PR 11 John*, 10.

marriage.[100] It was this evidence, above all, that led H.G. Richardson to conclude that, although 'there are dark stories of Isabella's licentiousness and of her imprisonment by John, . . . we can dismiss any suggestion of the one and be extremely sceptical of the other. The pair must have lived together in tolerable amity.'[101]

In support of this picture of relative marital harmony, the Chancery and Exchequer records supply several examples of the king's courtesy to the queen. From the 'strong wine of Poitou' and the 'best cloth' purchased for her wardrobe in Normandy in 1203, through to the 'roaches and little pike' which the king asked be caught for her table at Marlborough in 1215, there are occasional references throughout the reign to gifts from husband to wife.[102] Perhaps even more tellingly, it was not only the king who extended such courtesies. Peter des Roches, always the most astute of courtiers, provided a cheese and a bacon pig for the queen at Downton in 1210–11, and in the same year spent thirty-two pence in buying birds, possibly song birds, for her at Witney.[103] Bishop Peter, it might be argued, was unlikely to have bothered with such attentions had the queen been entirely out of royal favour. In the same way, the records suggest that for much of the reign Isabella enjoyed relative freedom of movement, and that she was accompanied on her travels by a conventional, if by no means lavish, household of valets and maid-servants.[104] A regular stream of messages passed between husband and wife, and perhaps most instructively, the name chosen for the king's daughter Isabella, later married to the Emperor Frederick II, was presumably intended to honour the queen: unlike the names chosen for the remainder of John's legitimate children, it enjoyed no previous

---

[100] The children of John and Isabella are listed by the *Handbook of British Chronology*, 3rd ed., ed. E.B. Fryde, D.E. Greenway and others, London 1986, 37. However, although the *Handbook* suggests that John's daughters were all born after 1210, already in 1208–9 the bishop of Winchester had spent twelve pence at Witney in carrying birds to the king's daughter (*filie regis*) at Winchester: *The Pipe Roll of the Bishopric of Winchester 1208–9*, ed. H. Hall, London 1903, 17, lines 48–9. It is conceivable that the daughter in question was illegitimate. Despite a highly confused attempt to redate the birth of the legitimate Joan to 1203 by G.R. Stephens, 'The Early Life of Joan Makepeace', *Speculum* 20, 1945, 301–2, the daughter of the king whose expenses in Normandy were accounted in 1203, was most likely the illegitimate Joan, later married to Llywelyn ap Iorweth; *MRSN*, ii, 569. It would be unwise to place much confidence in the statement of a papal letter of 1238 that at the time of her betrothal in 1214 the legitimate Joan was at least seven years old. Seven was the age at which canon law permitted betrothal, but in practice, children were frequently betrothed even younger than this: *Les Registres de Grégoire IX (1227–41)*, ed. L. Auvray, 4 vols, Bibliothèque des Écoles françaises d'Athènes et de Rome 1896–1955, ii, no. 2580. It seems to have gone unremarked that in 1214 the king referred to a son named John, either the same as a bastard namesake referred to in 1200, or possibly a legitimate son who may conceivably have died in infancy: *Rot. Litt. Pat.*, 117.

[101] Richardson, *EHR* 61, 1946, 310–11.

[102] *Rot. de Lib.*, 7; *Rot. Norm.*, 107–8, 110, 115; *Rot. Litt. Claus.*, i, 213b.

[103] *The Pipe Roll of the Bishopric of Winchester 1210–1211*, ed. N.R. Holt, Manchester 1964, 37, 65.

[104] For her household, horses and men, see for example, *Rot. Litt. Claus.*, i, 26, 62b, 184b.

currency within the Plantagenet royal family. In England, the queen is to be found at Marlborough in 1200, December 1203 and 1207; at Tickhill and Nottingham in 1201; Woodstock in 1203; Tewkesbury, Ludgershall and Dorchester in 1205; Gloucester in 1207; Ludgershall again in 1210; Northampton, Corfe and Sturminster in 1212; at Winchester for the birth of the future Henry III in 1207, and at Devizes for the birth of Richard of Cornwall in 1209.[105] In 1203 she was in Normandy, and in 1206 and 1214 she was with the king in Poitou.[106] Only from the time of John's return to England, from October 1214, do the Chancery rolls suggest that she was kept under guard, and then, we may assume, more for her own safety than for any sinister reason. During the civil war, she appears to have travelled in the company of various of the king's hostages and prisoners, including a brother of the constable of Chester, who to some extent appear to have been placed under her personal custody.[107]

The first signs of concern for the queen's safety come on 3 November 1214, when Terric the Teuton was ordered to ensure Isabella's passage under armed escort, from the coast at Freemantle, via Reading to Berkhamsted.[108] In December she was moved to Gloucester, in May 1215 to Winchester, and later to Marlborough and eventually Bristol where she is to be found in the summer of 1216.[109] In this context, the close roll records a remarkable letter from the king to Terric the Teuton, Isabella's chief guardian. Dated 30 October 1214, to the time when Terric first took up his charge, it seems to have escaped any previous notice by historians. 'Know', the king writes,

> that by God's grace we are safe and well, and we order you to return the horse that you borrowed from Richard the Fleming. We shall shortly be coming to the place where you are, and we shall think of you like a hawk ('cogitabimus de vobis de austurco'), and although we may have been absent from you for ten years, when we come to you, it will be to us as if we had been absent no more than three days. Keep your charges carefully. Let us know frequently about the state of your charge.[110]

Was this letter intended more for Isabella than her guardian: a promise (or perhaps a threat) that the king would soon rejoin her? Certainly, the veiled tone in which it is written, its failure to name the queen as the charge in Terric's keeping, or the place where she was being kept, suggest fear that any more open

---

[105] *Rot. de Lib.*, 7–9, 75, 155; *Rot. Litt. Claus.*, i, 96b; *Docs of English History*, 252, 256–7; *PR 3 John*, 89, 100, 174; *PR 6 John*, 187; *PR 7 John*, 103, 133; *PR 9 John*, 125, 139; *PR 14 John*, 129–30; *Rot. Litt. Claus.*, i, 40b; *Gervase*, ii, 107.

[106] *Rot. Litt. Pat.*, 117; *MRSN*, ii 569.

[107] *Rot. Litt. Pat.*, i, 143b, 192b.

[108] *Rot. Litt. Claus.*, i, 177. Isabella appears to have returned from Poitou with the king, with whom she stayed briefly at Exeter on her return: *Rot. Litt. Claus.*, i, 433.

[109] *Rot. Litt. Claus.*, i, 180b, 189b, 242, 275, 285; *Rot. Litt. Pat.*, 124b; 'Prestitae Roll 17 John', in *Docs of English History*, 271, 274; 'Close Roll 16 John', in *Memoranda Roll 10 John*, 137.

[110] *Rot. Litt. Claus.*, i, 175b.

message might result in harm to the queen. All of this might argue genuine, affectionate concern. We should bear in mind here that only two years earlier, in 1212, wild rumours are said to have circulated throughout England that the queen had been raped at Marlborough, and that her younger son, the future Richard of Cornwall, had been murdered.[111] John himself was no stranger to the mistreatment of women and children, at least if we are to believe the chroniclers and their accounts of the cruel death by starvation that he inflicted upon Matilda de Braose and her offspring after 1210.[112] Three or four years later, Isabella's cousin Yolande de Courtenay was married to King Andrew II of Hungary following the death of Andrew's first wife, brutally murdered as part of a more general conspiracy amongst the barons and even the bishops of Hungary.[113] The chivalric code of honour was never much more than a light veneer, a superficial application of courtesy and civilization to what was underneath, a far grimmer and more violent reality. At the court of King John, the veneer appears to have worn perilously thin.

Here, if we probe a little deeper, we begin to unearth various indications that the marriage of John and Isabella was by no means so amicable or so tolerant as Richardson and others have supposed. We have already seen that the king may have maintained one, perhaps several mistresses, even after his marriage. Isabella of Angoulême was his second wife. There is rarely much love lost between a man's first and second wives, and yet throughout his reign, John continued to maintain his first wife, Isabella of Gloucester, with her own household of knights and maid-servants, supplying her with gifts and pensions on a scale not far short of the expenses recorded for the household of Isabella of Angoulême.[114] Until at least March 1207, Isabella of Gloucester appears to have stayed at Winchester castle. She was removed thereafter to Sherborne, and later still to Bristol, perhaps so as to avoid the embarrassment of having both of the king's wives staying in Winchester at the time of Isabella of Angoulême's

---

[111] *Memorials of St Edmund's Abbey*, ed. T. Arnold, 3 vols, RS XCVI, 1890–96, ii, 23.

[112] Painter, *King John*, 242–50. Beyond the annals of Margam, Roger of Wendover and the *Histoire des ducs de Normandie*, the cruel death of Matilda de Braose is included amongst John's crimes, together with his murder of Arthur and his imprisonment of Eleanor of Brittany, in the so-called 'Invective against King John', a tract in circulation at some time after 1250, but drawing upon much earlier sources of information: BL ms. Cotton Vespasian E iii fo. 175v: 'matrem cum filio sine causa iusta crudeliter fame et siti interemit'. I am currently preparing an edition.

[113] Aubry de Trois-Fontaines, in *MGH Scriptores* xxiii, 898, a story known to Matthew Paris, *Chronica Majora*, iii, 51. For a modern account, see J.M. Bak, 'Queens as Scapegoats in Medieval Hungary', in *Queens and Queenship in Medieval Europe*, ed. A.J. Duggan, Woodbridge 1997, 226–7.

[114] *PR 3 John*, 55, 101; *PR 4 John*, 280; *PR 5 John*, 139, 154–5; *PR 6 John*, 125, 131, 213; *PR 7 John*, 113, 121; *PR 8 John*, 47, 149, 150, 181; *PR 9 John*, 54, 139, 144; *PR 10 John*, 97, 103; *PR 11 John*, 97; *PR 13 John*, 221; *PR 14 John*, 43, 113. After her removal to Sherborne in 1207, and, perhaps more significantly, after the birth of the king's son Henry, Isabella of Gloucester's expenses were gradually scaled down, from more than £80 a year to just over £50.

confinement for the birth of her first child, the future Henry III, in the autumn of 1207.[115] Earlier on in the reign, however, in 1205 and 1206, the two Isabellas were being supplied with wine and expenses in such a way as to imply that they may have been lodged together in the same place.[116] There is no certain proof that this was the case, but it is possible that an even worse indignity was inflicted on the queen. Painter and others have suggested that a peculiar fine entered in the fine roll at Christmas 1204, by which the wife of Hugh de Neville offered 200 chickens to lie one night with her husband, may imply that Neville's wife was a royal mistress, anxious to escape for a time into her husband's bed.[117] More innocent explanations might be advanced: for example, that Neville's wife was simply protesting, light-heartedly, against the constant absence of her husband in royal service.[118] Nonetheless, Hugh de Neville himself was later to join the rebel barons, surrendering Marlborough castle to them in a way that suggests that he had grievances aplenty against King John. If he had indeed been cuckolded by the king, then it is worth pointing out that for extended periods Isabella of Angoulême was maintained at Neville's castle of Marlborough.[119] Neville, the cuckold, and Isabella, the bride abandoned for Neville's wife, lodged together in one and the same place: it seems hardly the most happy of *ménages*. Richardson sought to dispel any sinister interpretation of the claim made by a Canterbury chronicle that in 1209 Isabella was shut up ('includitur') at Devizes, pointing out that her 'enclosure' was probably nothing more than her confinement that year for the birth of her son Richard.[120] Less easy to explain is the claim made in the same chronicle that in 1208 John had placed the queen at Corfe under close custody ('sub arta custodia').[121] We might note here that Isabella's supposed removal to Corfe in 1208, and the royal order issued in November 1207, that Queen's Gold henceforth be accounted for at the king's Exchequer, both came shortly after the birth to Isabella of John's eldest legitimate son, the future Henry III. Could it be that having discharged his responsibilities by fathering an heir by Isabella, the king felt no further need to maintain either the queen's income or her day-to-day comfort?

---

[115] *Rot. Litt. Claus.*, i, 44b, 92; *Rot. Litt. Pat.*, 77; *PR 10 John*, 97, 103. In 1214, at the time of her marriage to Geoffrey de Mandeville, Isabella was in the custody of Peter de Chanceaux, then constable of Bristol: *Rot. Litt. Claus.*, 161b; *Rot. Litt. Pat.*, 108b.

[116] *PR 7 John*, 12, 121; *PR 9 John*, 144; *Rot. Litt. Claus.*, i, 64.

[117] Painter, *Reign of King John*, 231–2, and see N. Vincent, 'Hugh de Neville and his Prisoners', *Archives* 20, 1992, 190–7.

[118] As suggested to me, several years ago, by Sir James Holt.

[119] For Isabella's expenses at Marlborough, see, for example, *Rot. de Lib.*, 7; *PR 6 John*, 187; *PR 9 John*, 125; *Docs of English History*, 271, 274; *Rot. Litt. Claus.*, i, 213b. For building work undertaken at Marlborough castle by King John, see *The History of the King's Works I: The Middle Ages*, ed. R.A. Brown, H.M. Colvin and A.J. Taylor, 2 vols, London 1963, ii, 734–5.

[120] *Gervase*, ii, 107; Richardson, *EHR* 61, 1946, 310–11n.

[121] *Gervase*, ii, 102: 'reginam, sponsam suam, sub arta posuit custodia in castello de Corf'. This particular story forms part of a more wide-ranging diatribe against the king's cruelty, and, we must assume, was deliberately intended to elicit a hostile reaction to John.

Whereas for John's father, and John and Isabella's son Henry III, it was entirely customary for the king to mention the welfare of his queen in confirming or granting land to the religious, from time to time requesting prayers for her soul as well as for his own, under John we find no such indication of even conventual, pious solicitude. The one exception is an award to the cathedral church of Chichester, made by John at the time that Isabella was promised her dower in 1204: an award that directly affected Isabella's rights in the city of Chichester.[122] Thereafter, for the rest of their married life, Isabella goes entirely unmentioned in any of John's charters, or even in his will: a stark contrast to John's father, mother and elder brother, who are frequently referred to in John's charters as the spiritual beneficiaries of his acts of charity.[123] After John's death, Isabella herself made three awards to the religious for the soul of her late husband. Two of these merely confirmed earlier awards made by the king or by Geoffrey fitz Peter, who for a time had enjoyed custody of Isabella's lands at Berkhamsted.[124] The third involved a grant of the fair of Exeter to the local monastery of St Nicholas. All three were made in England, in the few months before Isabella's departure for France.[125] Thereafter, not a single charter issued by her during the remaining thirty years of her life, so much as mentions her late husband.

Isabella's decision to leave England in 1217 serves to remind us that after the king's death she took the earliest possible opportunity to abandon four of the five children that she had born to John. Already, as early as 1212, aged only four, the future King Henry seems to have been taken out of her custody and placed in the household of John's close confidant, the bishop of Winchester. After the king's death, the bishop was also entrusted with the care of John's youngest daughter Eleanor, whilst John's other two children still in England were given into the hands of the alien constables Peter de Maulay and Philip Mark.[126] We shall return to Isabella's relationship with her children in due course. For the moment, whatever Isabella's abandonment of them may tell us about her previous feelings for their father, there can be little doubt that in 1217 the queen was anxious to return to her homeland. In part this may reflect her exclusion from the inner circles of the minority council, convened to govern on behalf of her son. In 1217, for example, the council had issued instructions that a separate room be prepared for Isabella at Exeter castle, since it was 'unfitting' that the queen continue to occupy her present lodgings, which were judged

---

[122] *Rot. Chart.*, 129.

[123] Perhaps most notably here, see John's foundation charter for Beaulieu, 25 January 1205, made out of love of God, for the souls of Henry II, Henry the Young King, Richard I, Eleanor, and all John's ancestors and heirs, but without any mention of his wife: *The Beaulieu Cartulary*, ed. S.F. Hockey, Southampton Record Series vii, 1974, 3–5 no. 1.

[124] That Geoffrey had originally granted the tithes of mills at Berkhamsted to the order of St Thomas Acon is proved by *Calendar of Patent Rolls 1324–7*, 128; *Rot. Litt. Claus.*, i, 198b.

[125] Below, Appendix nos 1–3.

[126] Vincent, *Peter des Roches*, 71, 153 and notes.

entirely inadequate.[127] However, this exclusion in turn only goes to prove the extent to which Isabella had failed to become the central figure in any sort of queen's party, a stark contrast to the political power wielded by her mother-in-law Eleanor of Aquitaine, or her future daughter-in-law Eleanor of Provence. Both Eleanors were accompanied to England by large numbers of servants and supporters from their own particular homelands in Poitou and Savoy. So generously were the Savoyard uncles of Eleanor of Provence rewarded in England, that in the 1250s they became a leading incentive to baronial rebellion against the crown. Eleanor of Aquitaine, to judge from the witness lists to her charters, maintained a mixed Anglo-French household, including a large number of knights and clerks from her native Poitou. Isabella by contrast was allowed no such body of kinsmen or servants from Angoulême to serve her in England. After 1200, although the king kept open channels of communication with Angoulême, and at the height of the civil war introduced a few knights from Angoulême into English custodies, Isabella herself was served by a household that seems entirely to have been made up of knights and servants chosen for her by the king.[128] Her closest guardian, Terric the Teuton, we can assume was not even a native French speaker, but a German, first employed in England as a go-between with the court of the Welf emperor Otto IV and later responsible for missions on behalf of Henry duke of Saxony.[129] In 1213 Terric had been appointed constable of Berkhamsted, and it may be that the connection between Berkhamsted, the queen's dower, and Isabella herself explains his *entrée* the following year into Isabella's household.[130] Thereafter, he was entrusted with Isabella's safe-keeping throughout the civil war.[131] In 1217 he joined her expedition to Angoulême, whereafter he vowed to go on

---

[127] *Patent Rolls 1216–25*, 53.

[128] For embassies from Angoulême, including the abbot of St Eparch (1207) and the mayor of Angoulême (1213), see *Rot. Litt. Claus.*, 90b, 92, 95, 143b. For the knights Oliver and Geoffrey de Boutteville, introduced to custodies in England, including custody of Belvoir castle and the gate of Devizes castle during the civil war, see *Rot. Litt. Claus.*, i, 73, 260, 275b, 278, 287; *Rot. Litt. Pat.*, 165, 168; *Chronica Majora*, ii, 622, 639. William of Bath, who occurs as the queen's clerk in 1205–6, may be the same William *Bathion* restored to property within the city of Angoulême in 1214; *Docs of English History*, 271, 274–5; *Rot. Litt. Claus.*, i, 172.

[129] Terric appears from 1199 with land held from the royal demesne in Hampshire, and from 1202 as a royal valet (*vadletus*) with custodies in Normandy, after the loss of Normandy granted the manor of Ringwood in Hampshire as an escheat previously held by Juhel de Mayenne: *PR 1 John*, 2; *Rot. Norm.*, 51, 70, 112; *Rot. de Lib.*, 30; *Rot. Litt. Claus.*, i, 13, 32, 62b, 96, 169b; *Rot. Litt. Pat.*, 30, 46; *The Cartularies of Southwick Priory*, ed. K.A. Hanna, 2 vols, Hampshire Record Series 9–10, 1988–9, i, 98 no. 162, ii, 341–2 no. 840. For his contacts with Otto and Henry of Saxony, see *Rot. Litt. Claus.*, i, 82b, 108, 121b; *Rot. de Lib.*, 77, 238.

[130] *Rot. Litt. Pat.*, 105b; *Rot. Litt. Claus.*, i, 154b, 162b. During the ensuing war, Berkhamsted castle was held on Terric's behalf by his brother Walerand the Teuton; *Rot. Litt. Pat.*, 155, 169b, 174b; *Rot. Litt. Claus.*, i, 195, 198b, 217b, 258b, 293; *Patent Rolls 1216–25*, 254.

[131] *Rot. Litt. Claus.*, i, 177, 180b, 189b, 242, 275; *Rot. Litt. Pat.*, 124b, 143b.

crusade, dying at some time in 1223.[132] Terric's appearance in Isabella's house-hold, even after the death of King John, suggests that he had won the queen's trust. Nonetheless, so far as we can judge, he and his brother Walerand were the only men who had served Isabella in England whom she later chose to accompany her to her homeland. As with Eleanor of Aquitaine's lordship over Poitou, Isabella was theoretically ruler of Angoulême from the time of the death of her father in 1202, throughout the reign of John. In practice, and in contrast to Eleanor, this seems to have made no difference to Isabella's day-to-day subjection to King John, to her material well-being, or to her freedom to select her own household from amongst her fellow natives of Angoulême.

According to the *Histoire des ducs de Normandie*, a chronicle with close access to sources at court, King John blamed his marriage and Isabella for the loss of his French dominions in 1204: a charge which is said to have resulted in angry exchanges between husband and wife.[133] Even more remarkable is the account of John and Isabella's marriage inserted in the *Chronica Majora* of Matthew Paris, some twenty years after John's death. This has been dismissed, by Painter and Richardson amongst others, as a malicious fiction. Certainly it conflicts directly with a claim made in the chronicle of Roger of Wendover, later copied by Paris, that it was his excessive lust and devotion for Isabella that kept John in his bed-chamber in 1203, when he would have done better to make war against the king of France.[134] Paris' account comes as part of an extended report on the activities of master Robert of London, who, Paris claims, was sent by King John to the court of the Moslem emir of Morocco in 1211, and who had supposedly supplied the chronicler with a first-hand account of his embassy. According to this, Master Robert informed the emir that John was married to a shrew of a wife: 'Hateful to him, and who hates him too. She has often been found guilty of incest, sorcery ('maleficam'), and adultery, so that the king, her husband, has ordered those of her lovers who have been apprehended to be strangled with a rope in her own bed'.[135] So fanciful is the entire account in which this story appears, that it has never found acceptance with historians, and probably never will. There are, nonetheless, various aspects to it which cannot so readily be dismissed. The suggestion that John may have offered to surrender his realm to Islam is clearly preposterous, intended as a gross parody of John's later surrender of his realm to the pope. Likewise, most of the details of the

---

[132] He witnesses charters issued by Isabella, after John's death, at Taunton and Angoulême: below, Appendix no.1; G. Babinot de Rencogne, 'Nouvelle chronologie historique des Maires de la ville d'Angoulême', *Bulletin de la Société Archéologique et Historique de la Charente*, 1868–9, and separately, Angoulême 1870, 98–9 no. 5, whence Watson, 'Counts of Angoulême', 390 no. 209. For his proposed pilgrimage to the Holy Land and his death between March 1222 and February 1223, see *Rot. Litt. Claus.*, i, 457b, 534, 541b; *Patent Rolls 1216–25*, 274, 301, 377. For Walerand the Teuton and Geoffrey de Boutteville in Isabella's service after 1217, see *Diplomatic Documents*, no. 39.

[133] *Hist. ducs de Normandie*, 64–5.

[134] *Chronica Majora*, ii, 481–2, 489.

[135] *Chronica Majora*, ii, 563.

embassy which Paris supplies can be shown to be apocryphal. However, the basic idea that in 1211 or 1212 John attempted to initiate diplomatic relations with Moslem Spain or North Africa has much to commend it, given that at precisely this time the king was engaged in forging alliances with Toulouse and Aragon against the French.[136] Moreover, the remarks that Paris inserts about Isabella, whether or not they were spoken as he claims, at least give some idea of the sort of rumours that were in circulation during Isabella's lifetime.

Faced with the charge that Isabella was guilty of incest, Sidney Painter remarked, with withering irony, that 'it is hard to conceive how Isabella could find anyone in England to commit incest with'.[137] Would that we could be so sure. Whilst Isabella had no paternal kinsmen in England; on her mother's Courtenay side, she had a whole host of relatives who, at least in theory, might have been her lovers. To begin with there were the Courtenays of Oakhampton and Oxfordshire, descended from the Reginald de Courtenay who first appears in the service of Henry II at some time after 1160. Later, family myth would present this Reginald as the rightful lord of Courtenay in the Gatinais south of Paris, dispossessed and forced into exile by Louis VII for his role in arranging the marriage between Louis's wife, Eleanor of Aquitaine, and Henry II.[138] There is absolutely nothing, save wishful thinking, to support such a suggestion. The last of the original line of Courtenays, Renaud or Reginald, simply disappears at the time of the Second Crusade, in all probability deceased.[139] His daughter, or possibly his sister, Elizabeth, was married to Peter, a younger son

---

[136] N. Barbour, 'The Embassy Sent by King John of England to Miramolin, King of Morocco', *Al-Andalus* 25, 1960, pp. 373–81. In an unpublished paper, 'Two Christian Embassies to the Almohad Emir Muhammad Al-Nasir at Seville in 1211', Barbour revises his dating of the mission from 1212 to June–July 1211. For my knowledge of both of these papers I am indebted to Sir James Holt. For further remarks on the murky diplomatic negotiations of these years, and the fears to which they gave rise, see N. Vincent, 'Simon of Atherfield (d.1211): A Martyr to his Wife', *Analecta Bollandiana* 113, 1995, 349–61, esp. 355–6.

[137] Painter, *Reign of King John*, 236.

[138] The first appearance of this mythical account of the Courtenay pedigree that I have been able to trace, occurs in BL ms. Additional 49359 (Courtenay register, s.xiv/xv) fo. 54v, where Henry II is said to have granted the heiress of Oakhampton to Reginald de Courtenay, 'qui adduxerat ei reginam Alyanor'. It appears again in Philémon Holland's edition of William Camden's *Britain or a Chorographicall Description of the most flourishing Kingdomes*, London 1610, 207–8, but not in Camden's original Latin edition, *Britannia*, London 1586, 88, which merely notes that the Courtenay earls of Devon were of the blood royal of France. The copy of the 1610 edition of Camden in BN livres imprimées N-10, contains extensive manuscript corrections to the Courtenay pedigree by an English antiquary. I hope to deal with Reginald de Courtenay and his heirs at greater length in a forthcoming article.

[139] He is probably to be identified as the Renaud de Montargis (Montargis being a subsidiary lordship of Courtenay), who is said to have taken the cross in 1146: Bouquet, *Recueil* xii, 126, 199. In c.1149 Abbot Suger received complaints of Renaud's attacks upon merchants of the count of Champagne between Orléans and Sens, suggesting either that he had returned before the king from crusade, or that he had never fulfilled his crusading vows: Bouquet, *Recueil*, xv, 511 nos 73–4 . Thereafter he simply vanishes.

of Louis VI of France, who thereafter assumed the name Peter de Courtenay.[140] The Courtenays to whom Henry II awarded lands in England, although related to the original Courtenay line, appear to have been only distant cousins. Nonetheless, cousins they were, so that in 1217, when Robert de Courtenay of Oakhampton was asked to surrender Exeter to Isabella, he is described in King Henry III's letter as 'our kinsman'.[141] Perhaps because of his kinship to one of the leading families of France, Robert de Courtenay of Oakhampton appears to have been singled out for particularly harsh treatment by Louis and the French during the civil war of 1216–17, being deprived of his lands in one of Louis' few surviving English charters. The fact that the original of this charter survives amongst the Courtenay family archives in France provides further proof, if such were needed, of the kinship between the English and French Courtenays.[142] Robert appears as witness to Isabella's charter in favour of the monks of St Nicholas Exeter, issued at Exeter in May 1217.[143]

Even closer in kinship than the Courtenays of Devon, Isabella enjoyed regular contact, from at least 1207, with her French half-brother, Peter de Joigny, the only child born to the marriage of Isabella's mother, Alice, with William count of Joigny, before 1184. Peter himself was in some senses a child of incest, since his parents were related within the third or fourth degree of kinship via their joint descent from a Courtenay daughter married to the count of Nevers: a fact that provided the grounds for their subsequent divorce.[144] In May 1207, during Isabella's first pregnancy, King John had written to Peter,

---

[140] All of the standard accounts here depend upon the so-called continuator of Aimo of Fleury, a twelfth-century source, now BN ms. Latin 5925a fo. 188r, partially printed by Bouquet, *Recueil*, xi, 276, and cf. *ibid.*, xii, 219, which states that Peter son of Louis VI was married to Elizabeth the daughter of Renaud de Courtenay. Nowhere else have I found any evidence for Renaud being married, let alone to him fathering a daughter named Elizabeth. However, there is at least one proof, previously overlooked, that Renaud de Courtenay had a sister named Elizabeth: BN ms. Pièces Originales 891 (formerly ms. français 27375) no. 3, where William (Renaud's brother) and Elizabeth de Courtenay his sister appear in a charter issued by Miles their father and Elizabeth his wife to the monks of St-Pierre-de-Néronville near Sens. It is also worth noting that both Miles de Courtenay (d. after 1145) and Wiliam his son (d. before 1152) were married to women named Elizabeth *alias* Isabella: as above, and see A. Luchaire, *Etudes sur les actes de Louis VII*, Paris 1885, 183–4 no. 261.

[141] *Patent Rolls 1216–25*, 53.

[142] BN ms. Pièces Originales 892 (formerly ms. français 27376) no. 90, as printed by Stein, 'Chartes Inédites', *Annales de la Société Historique et Archéologique du Gatinais* 36, 1922, 154–5 no. 15; C. Petit-Dutaillis, *Etude sur la vie et le règne de Louis VIII (1187–1226)*, Paris 1894, 120 . This Robert, of Oakhampton, is to be distinguished from a French namesake, a son of Peter de Courtenay, who commanded part of the invading army in 1216–17, being captured at the battle of Sandwich in 1217, and whose kinship to Queen Isabella is noted by *Hist. ducs de Normandie*, 202, cf. Petit-Dutaillis, *Louis VIII*, 98, 165, 169–70, 295. It may be mere coincidence, but it worth remarking that the English Courtenays feature prominently amongst the handful of barons recorded in the pipe rolls of John's reign as owing Queen's Gold: *PR 11 John*, 148; *PR 16 John*, 51, 142.

[143] Below, Appendix no. 2.

[144] Above, nn. 38, 41.

begging him to come to England, 'since the queen, your sister, greatly desires to see you'.[145] Whether or not Peter obeyed this summons, in 1209 his messengers were twice entertained at the English court, and he went on to play an intriguing and previously unrecognized role in Anglo-French relations during the civil war.[146] Although a subject of Philip Augustus, and heir to one of the principal lordships of northern Burgundy, in 1214 he joined King John's expedition to Poitou, where he witnesses various royal charters.[147] In the following year, backed by pledges from his Courtenay kinsmen, he obtained licence from Philip to cross to England at the invitation of King John. For this he had to promise the French king to attempt no hostile action against him.[148] Nonetheless, during the ensuing French invasion, he was granted an annual pension of £200 by King John, and he did not return to France until the end of the civil war, in March 1217.[149] All the indications are that he fought in England on the Plantagenet side, the side of his half-sister Isabella, against Louis and the rebel barons.

Military service, even the remarkable appearance of a Burgundian baron fighting with John against the French, is a long way from incest. Peter died as count of Joigny in 1222, leaving a widow and a bitter dispute over his inheritance. It seems almost inconceivable that he could have enjoyed any sexual liaison with his half-sister, Isabella, not least because for most of the time that Peter de Joigny was in England, Isabella was pregnant with children by King John. Nonetheless, there is one piece of circumstantial and geographically remote evidence which might suggest otherwise. An Irish chronicler recording the events of 1233, reports the death that year of a man named Piers the Fair, killed fighting in county Cavan with the army of Walter de Lacy. Piers is styled in this account 'the son of the English queen'.[150] He can hardly have been the son of Berengaria, nor of Eleanor of Aquitaine. Could he, just possibly, have been, or be rumoured to have been, an illegitimate son of Isabella of Angoulême? In this case, his name – Piers or Peter – would be highly significant. Peter was the name both of Isabella's grandfather, Peter de Courtenay, and of her half-brother Peter de Joigny. Might it have been chosen in their honour? Certainly it was a name that had much to commend itself to Isabella.

Nothing more of this peculiar story is ever likely to come to light. In all probability, the Irish Peter was no queen's bastard. Isabella's reputation remains intact. However, both the report set down by Matthew Paris, and the

---

[145] *Rot. Litt. Pat.*, 71b, as noticed by Painter, *Reign of King John*, 236.

[146] *Rot. de Lib.*, 118, 132.

[147] *Rot. Chart.*, 200b, 201; *Rot. Litt. Pat.*, 113, 115.

[148] *Rot. Litt. Pat.*, 134b; *Rot. Litt. Claus.*, i, 203b; *Registres*, 412–3 nos 47–8.

[149] *Patent Rolls 1216–25*, 46; *Rot. Litt. Claus.*, i, 345b.

[150] *Annals of the Kingdom of Ireland by the Four Masters*, ed. J. O'Donovan, iii, Dublin 1851, 268–9, for 'Feorus' *alias* Piers. I am indebted to Richard Sharpe for his advice on the translation of this passage. O'Donovan's reference to *The Works of Spencer, Campion, Hanmer and Marleburrough*, 2 vols, Dublin 1809, ii, 353, supplies no new information.

later Irish source suggest that rumours of Isabella's adultery may well have circulated, whatever the actual reality. Isabella would not have been the first queen to have been accused of adultery or even of incest. Eleanor of Aquitaine, for one, had been suspected of conducting an affair with her uncle.[151] At the very least, Isabella must join the long line of Plantagenet kings and queens whose personal lives were put in the balance by English chroniclers, and found distinctly wanting. Henry II, so it was said, had not only proved repeatedly unfaithful to his wife, Eleanor of Aquitaine, but had been so sunk in lechery as to deflower Alice of France, the intended bride of his son Richard.[152] Eleanor's own rumoured sexual misconduct is well known. Richard, Henry's successor, was accused by some contemporaries of debauching the wives and daughters of his barons. By others, although most decidedly not by John Gillingham, he may even have been accused of sodomy.[153] John and Isabella, lecher and incestuous adulterer merely add to this list. Even their own son, the blameless Henry III, who fathered no bastards, and who lived a life of utter marital rectitude with Eleanor of Provence, was accused, perhaps precisely because of his avoidance of pre-marital sex, of impotence, feebleness and of being 'more a woman than a man'.[154] We are dealing here with the world of rumour, and especially with the malicious rumours that the ruled put out about their rulers. Like devotees of the modern tabloid newspapers, there was nothing that so titillated an observer of the Plantagenet court as sexual misdemeanour. The modern analogy might remind us that titillation is often less innocent than its purveyors would have us suppose. With the Plantagenets, as with more recent royal families, rumour and malicious report play no small part in the waxing and waning of a house's popularity. In certain circumstances, as perhaps with King John and Isabella, they can significantly undermine the standing of an otherwise powerful dynasty.

At least in material terms, John treated Isabella in much the same shoddy fashion that his brother Richard had treated Berengaria of Navarre. Isabella was crowned but never permitted to rule. Whatever the true state of her more personal relations with John, the very fact that these were subject to rumour tells us much about popular perceptions of the Plantagenet court. Isabella was kept in relative comfort, but without lands or assured resources. John, like Richard, had been very much a mother's boy, brought up as the favourite of Eleanor of Aquitaine. It may be that like many another son with an overpowerful mother, he found his own marriage difficult to reconcile with the ideal of mother–son relationship that had been imparted to him in childhood. Such speculations are best left to the devotees of D.H. Lawrence. We can, however,

---

[151] William of Tyre, *Chronicon*, 16.27, in *Willelmi Tyrensis archiepiscopi Chronicon*, ed. R.B.C. Huygens, H.E. Mayer and G. Rösch, 2 vols, Corpus Christianorum Continuatio Medievalis 63, Turnholt 1986, ii, 754–5.

[152] Gillingham, *Richard Coeur de Lion*, 129–30.

[153] Gillingham, *Richard Coeur de Lion*, 133–6, 184–90.

[154] *Chronica Majora*, iii, 618–19, and for the background to these rumours, said to have been circulated by Hubert de Burgh, see Vincent, *Peter des Roches*, 276.

state with some confidence that Isabella, like Berengaria before her, was allowed none of the autonomy or vice-regal power that had been wielded by her mother-in-law, Eleanor of Aquitaine. Whereas several of Eleanor's writs survive from before 1189, drafted by clerks of the royal chancery attached to her household, we have no single letter or charter issued by Isabella during John's lifetime, and for Berengaria only one issued during the lifetime of Richard I: a notification, in the name of Berengaria and her sister-in-law Joan dowager queen of Sicily, of the pledges issued by various of Richard's courtiers returning from crusade for a loan of 150 marks raised from the merchants of Rome.[155]

In this and many other respects Isabella and Berengaria provide an interesting contrast both to Eleanor of Aquitaine and to the first English queen for whom we have detailed household accounts: Eleanor of Provence, the wife of Henry III. As Margaret Howell has shown, Eleanor of Provence, like Berengaria and Isabella before her, enjoyed no control over her dower lands during her husband's lifetime. Nonetheless, Henry III's bride was granted some degree of financial independence. She was allowed full control over the collection of Queen's Gold, and from the time of her marriage had her own independent treasurer and financial office. Moreover, from 1250 or so, Eleanor of Provence received, if not land in fee, then the administration of a rich series of escheats and wardships from the crown. A skilful speculator in the feudal property market, she went on, during the period of baronial rebellion in the 1260s, to serve as one of Henry III's most successful fund-raisers and supporters.[156] Compared to Berengaria and Isabella, Eleanor of Provence might well be envied her freedom of action. Even more striking is the contrast between Isabella of Angoulême and Eleanor of Castile, the wife of Isabella's grandson, King Edward I. Whereas Isabella appears to have travelled with a retinue of twelve horses, by 1290 Eleanor of Castile had at least 200 servants in full time employment, ranging from stewards to dog handlers, a hairdresser and a large group of ladies-in-waiting, many of them Eleanor's own kinswomen, although of English rather than Spanish birth.[157] Eleanor of Castile was a patron of the arts on a lavish scale, a speculator in land, and the dedicatee of various literary romances.[158] Unlike Isabella, who seems to have been separated from her children when they were very young, Eleanor kept her children by her on her ceaseless and costly travels around the realm.[159] In part the contrast between the lifestyles of these queens may be merely an accident of record keeping – a result of the survival of the household accounts of Eleanor of Provence and Eleanor of Castile, when we have nothing comparable for Isabella. At root,

---

[155] *EEA*, iii, *Canterbury 1193–1205*, no. 578.
[156] Howell, 'The Resources of Eleanor of Provence', *EHR* 102, 1987, 372–93.
[157] For the cost of stabling Isabella's twelve horses, see *Rot. Litt. Claus.*, i, 62b. For Eleanor of Castile, see J.C. Parsons, *The Court and Household of Eleanor of Castile in 1290*, Toronto 1977, 1–55, 153–160.
[158] Parsons, *Eleanor*, esp. 11–14, 17–22 and references.
[159] Parsons, *Eleanor*, 9.

however, it suggests that Isabella of Angoulême was treated with less than royal courtesy by her husband King John.

John died in October 1216. Isabella outlived him by thirty years. The story of her later life can only be briefly touched upon here. Nonetheless, there are various aspects to it which demand comment. To begin with, from the time of her return to Angoulême in 1217, until her death, Isabella maintained only the most strained of relations with her children by King John. The alacrity with which she abandoned her children in England, and the speed with which she established her lordship over Angoulême argue considerable steeliness of will. For the remainder of her life she continued to use the title 'Queen of England'. Her letters, written in the first person plural, continue to employ the reginal style *Dei gratia* and were sealed with the seal that had been made for her as queen, displaying her titles as queen of England, lady of Ireland, duchess of Normandy and Aquitaine, and countess of Anjou, showing her robed and crowned.[160] Her tomb effigy likewise shows her crowned as queen.[161] The silver coins of Angoulême, minted after 1224, display Isabella's name alongside the titles of Louis of France and Hugh de Lusignan.[162] It is possible that having been denied much in the way of personal authority during the lifetime of her late husband, after John's death, Isabella was all the more keen to stand on her own dignity. Certainly, it seems that in 1241 she was to take mortal offence at the failure of the French royal family to accord her the respect that she believed to be her due.[163]

At least to begin with, on her return to her homeland in 1217 she had the support of the English minority council, which clearly expected her to govern Angoulême as part of the wider Plantagenet dominion. Isabella reasserted her control over Cognac, denied to the lords of Angoulême since the 1180s, and

[160] L.C. Douët d'Arcq, *Collection des Sceaux*, 3 vols, Archives de l'Empire Inventaires et Documents, Paris 1863–8, iii, 264 no. 10010, from Paris, Archives Nationales ms. J628 no. 10. The seal is presumably the same as that referred to in 1214: *Rot. Chart.*, 196. Watson, 'Counts of Angoulême', 225n. and catalogue no. 268, records a small seal used by Isabella in the absence of her seal as queen. Watson's catalogue provides a fairly comprehensive listing of the charters and letters issued by Isabella after 1217, to which can be added the various letters to King Henry III printed in *Diplomatic Documents*, ed. Chaplais, nos 39, 58, 84, and a privilege to the men of La Rochelle, confirming their customs in transporting wine through her lands, said to have been issued in response to a mandate from King Louis IX addressed to Hugh de Lusignan count of La Marche and Tibaut de Blazon seneschal of Poitou, July 1229; BN ms. nouv acq. français 7285 fo. 43r–v (French translation from a lost original).

[161] A. Erlande-Brandenburg, *Les Rois à Fontevrault*, Exhibition catalogue, Fontevrault, Centre Culturel de l'Ouest 1979, 15–16, 21, and for the introduction of the regalia to the tomb effigies of Eleanor of Aquitaine, Berengaria and Isabella, previously absent from the tombs of the Anglo-Norman queens, see the same author's *Le Roi est Mort: Etude sur les funérailles, les sepultures et les tombeaux des rois de France jusqu'à la fin du XIIIe siècle*, Paris 1975, 122–3.

[162] J.-F.E. Castaigne, *Notice historique sur Isabella d'Angoulême comtesse-reine*, Angoulême 1836, 26–7, and for the mint, see Watson, 'Counts of Angoulême', 175–6, 216.

[163] See below, p. 211.

entered into prolonged and violent disputes with Reginald de Pons over the castle of Merpins, and with Bartholomew de Le Puy, King John's former governor of Angoulême, in which Bartholomew was at one stage forced to surrender two of his sons as hostages.[164] Isabella also appears to have fallen foul of the bishop of Saintes who issued a sentence of excommunication against her.[165] Here we receive the first indication that, whatever the councillors of Henry III may have hoped, Isabella herself had no intention of acting as a Plantagenet viceroy within what she clearly regarded as her own personal inheritance. Beyond this, the imprisonment of Bartholomew de Le Puy and his sons might remind us of the hostage-taking practised by King John, one of the policies that did most to earn John his reputation for barbarity. Clearly John was not alone in adopting such methods. His widow, Isabella, a mother herself, was prepared to resort to hostage-taking, even the ransoming of children, when it suited her policy, just as a few years earlier she appears to have exercised some sort of custody over a series of John's hostages, including the brother of Roger de Lacy.[166]

Rivalry with Bartholomew de Le Puy aside, Isabella also harboured various other grudges against the minority council in England: that they were failing to send her the military aid that she requested, and that she was being denied a sum of money, 3500 marks, that she claimed had been willed to her by King John, or at least, as she put it, that John 'ought' to have willed to her.[167] In particular, it seems that she was dissatisfied with the dower that had been settled upon her in 1216, in accordance with the assignment promised by King John. As we have seen, in 1200, Isabella had been promised various lordships in France, including the Poitevin strongholds of Saintes and Niort, followed in 1204 by a grant of dower lands in England and Normandy. It is unclear whether this second settlement was intended to replace or merely to supplement the award that had included Saintes and Niort. Nonetheless, Isabella herself clearly believed that she was entitled to both awards of land, in Poitou and Anjou, and in England and Normandy. In 1216 she had been compensated for the loss of various of her dower lands in France with a grant of the Devon stannaries, and the manor of Aylesbury.[168] However, she continued to demand the Poitevin lordships of Saintes and Niort promised to her in 1200.[169] Here there was a

---

[164] For Cognac, see *Comptes d'Alfonse de Poitiers (1243–1247)*, ed. A. Bardonnet, Archives Historiques du Poitou, Poitiers 1875, 21–2. For Reginald, Bartholomew and his hostages, see *Diplomatic Documents*, nos 58, 108; *Regesta Honorii Papae III*, ed. P. Pressutti, 2 vols, Rome 1888–95, no. 2725; *Patent Rolls 1216–25*, 85.

[165] *Regesta Honorii III*, ed. Pressutti, no. 1939 (17 March 1219), perhaps related to an earlier papal privilege, exempting her private chapel in time of interdict, *ibid.* no. 1538 (21 July 1218).

[166] *Rot. Litt. Pat.*, 143b.

[167] *Diplomatic Documents*, nos 39, 84; *Patent Rolls 1225–32*, 103.

[168] *Patent Rolls 1216–25*, 34, 431–2; *Rot. Litt. Claus.*, i, 349b.

[169] For letters from the king's council to the men of Niort, requesting their assistance to Isabella on her returning to France, 24 July 1217, and for her subsequent claims to Niort and Saintes, see *Patent Rolls 1216–25*, 113, 431; *Patent Rolls 1225–32*, 98–9.

complication, since the city of Saintes had been reassigned by John in 1214, to form part of the marriage portion of John and Isabella's daughter Joan, betrothed to Hugh de Lusignan X, the son of Isabella's former fiancé Hugh IX.[170] Isabella's claim to Saintes may well lie behind the sentence of excommunication issued against her by the bishop of Saintes in 1219. It may also have played no small part in her decision, made in 1220, to ignore the earlier marriage settlement between Joan and Hugh X and to marry Hugh de Lusignan herself. In so doing – through one of the most extraordinary marriages in history – Isabella effectively recreated precisely the circumstances which had prevailed twenty years earlier, uniting the three lordships of Angoulême, Lusignan and La Marche, through marriage to the Lusignan lord. In 1200, it had been the threat of this united lordship that had persuaded King John to make off with Isabella, setting in train the events which were to lead to the loss of much of the Plantagenet dominion in France. In 1220, the councillors of Henry III were in no position to emulate King John. Faced with the establishment of a vast new territorial lordship in Poitou, the minority council could only request, as politely as possible, the return of Joan and her marriage portion. Since this, in turn, involved Hugh and Isabella in abandoning their claim to Saintes and the Isle of Oléron, the request was refused.[171] An attempt by the English court to force compliance, with the seizure of Isabella's dower lands in England in September 1221, only raised the nightmarish prospect of an alliance between Hugh and Isabella and the Capetian kings of France.[172] The council backed down, and in April 1222, Isabella's dower was restored.[173] However, Isabella and Hugh continued to play off the Capetians against Isabella's own son, Henry III, seeking the most favourable terms from both parties. In particular, Isabella continued to press for the lordship of Niort, promised to her in 1200 as part of her dower.[174] In short, she asked not only that the Plantagenet court accept precisely the conditions that had first led John into warfare in Poitou – a unified lordship of Angoulême, Lusignan and La Marche – but also that she and her Lusignan husband be allowed to retain the lordships of Niort and Saintes which would never have granted to her in dower had it been known that they were likely to fall into the hands of the Lusignans. In these circumstances, Isabella's protests to Henry III – that she had married Hugh de Lusignan only to prevent Hugh from marrying an ally of France, and that she was motivated solely by concern for Henry's best interests – ring entirely hollow.[175]

---

[170] *Rot. Chart.*, 197b. The *Hist. ducs de Normandie*, 206, implies that Isabella had encouraged the marriage between Hugh de Lusignan and Joan as a means of furthering her own interests at Angoulême.

[171] D. Carpenter, *The Minority of Henry III*, London 1990, 193–4, 200, 221; *Diplomatic Documents*, no. 85.

[172] For the seizure of the dower, see *Patent Rolls 1216–25*, 302, 318.

[173] *Patent Rolls 1216–25*, 329–30.

[174] *Patent Rolls 1216–25*, 431; *Patent Rolls 1225–32*, 102.

[175] *Diplomatic Documents*, no. 84.

In 1220 Isabella 'went native'. It was the failure of her son, Henry III, and his councillors, to come to terms with this harsh reality which ensured, over the next twenty years, that Isabella and Hugh proved the blight of all Plantagenet initiatives in France. In 1224, having first sworn fealty to Henry III, Hugh de Lusignan defected to Louis VIII during the Capetian invasion of Poitou, with Louis promising Isabella 2000 livres Parisis each year in return for her dower lands forfeit in England, and the annual revenues of Langeais near Tours in exchange for the rights that she claimed as dower at Saumur in Anjou.[176] Two years later, Isabella issued a formal acknowledgement that she had received sufficient compensation for her dower lands, and in 1230 Hugh and Isabella once again entered into alliance with Louis IX, who granted Isabella an annual pension of 5000 livres Tours in return for her resignation of the dower rights that she claimed in England, Normandy and Anjou and the revenues that she had previously been granted at Langeais.[177] The English court, however, continued to hope that Isabella's claims could be satisfied and that she, if not her husband, could be prised away from the Capetians. In 1224, and again in 1226, offers were made from England, including the recognition of Isabella's claims to Niort, to the 3500 marks supposedly willed to her by King John, and to compensation for the dower lands which she had lost in Normandy and Anjou.[178] Both of these offers were rejected, having been trumped by the Capetians. In 1230, having at last launched a campaign of reconquest in France, Henry III still hoped that a personal interview with his mother, planned to take place at Dinan, would lead to a reconciliation.[179] Whether or not the proposed interview took place, in May 1230 Hugh de Lusignan simply renewed his treaty with the French.[180] Henry's expedition was rendered a costly disaster, with wide ramifications for the history of government in England.[181] Meanwhile, as early as 1228, it seems that English proctors at Rome were pressing the pope to annul Isabella's marriage to Hugh de Lusignan.[182] The marriage itself was certainly an extraordinary one, in which Isabella stood to Hugh de Lusignan not only as wife to husband, but as mother to Hugh's former fiancée, and as one-time fiancée to Hugh's father. However, whatever the scandal this might excite, and despite a further attempt to involve the pope a decade later, there was no

---

[176] *Patent Rolls 1216–25*, 431, 444–5; Martène and Durand, *Amplissima Collectio*, i, 1162–3, 1184–6.

[177] *Layettes*, nos 1924, 2052, 2065, 2068; Martène and Durand, *Amplissima Collectio*, i, 1238–9.

[178] *Patent Rolls 1216–25*, 431–2; *Patent Rolls 1225–32*, 98–9, 102–3.

[179] *Diplomatic Documents*, no. 219.

[180] Martène and Durand, *Amplissima Collectio*, i, 1236–8; *Layettes*, ii, no. 2052.

[181] For the longer term consequences of the failure of the 1230 expedition, see Vincent, *Peter des Roches*, 268ff.

[182] *Patent Roll 1225–32*, 217, a letter requesting that the process be halted, which in turn suggests strongly that it was Henry III and his councillors who had first persuaded the pope to initiate the enquiry into Isabella's marriage.

inherent impediment, of consanguinity or legal form, to justify an annulment.[183] So far as we can judge, from her own point of view, Isabella's marriage to Hugh de Lusignan was a far more satisfactory affair than her earlier marriage to King John. Whereas John had allowed her little or no freedom of action, after 1220 Isabella appears together with Hugh, acting on almost equal terms. As countess of Angoulême in her own right, her name appears together with Hugh's in a large number of charters issued to the local religious.[184] It is hard to imagine King John extending a similar courtesy. Isabella gave birth to at least nine children by Hugh. The future wellbeing of this Lusignan brood appears to have excited far greater concern in her than she was ever to show for her children by King John.[185] Together, as Rowan Watson has shown, Hugh and Isabella imposed a remarkable degree of seigneurial control over their joint inheritance, for the first time bringing the castellans and minor lords of Angoulême under firm comital rule, greatly extending their power along the frontiers of the ancient county of Angoulême. Until 1224 they were assisted here by the money sent to them from England, and thereafter by the pensions paid to them by the kings of France. Between 1226 and 1229 Hugh defended his lands against an expeditionary force from England led by Richard, Isabella's second son, hastily created count of Poitiers, and went to war against the neighbouring viscount of Limoges. Elsewhere, he and Isabella imposed their authority over the lords of Barbezieux, Montendre, Aubeterre, Chabanais and Confolens. Indeed, it was the very extent of this increase in comital power, and the imposition of feudal customs on the previously independent lords of the Angoumois that may have driven various of Hugh and Isabella's vassals into their short-lived alliance with Henry III, during the king's disastrous continental expedition of 1230.[186]

So far as we can judge, after 1217, Isabella spared only a passing thought for her children in England. She may possibly have met her eldest son, Henry III, during Henry's expedition to Brittany and Poitou in 1230. Thereafter, for the next twelve years, even the impersonal contacts, via nuncios and messengers, that had persisted between mother and son throughout the 1220s, dwindled to a mere formality. Henceforth, Isabella's maternal feelings may well have been reserved for her children by Hugh de Lusignan, and just possibly for Richard of Cornwall, her younger son by King John. In 1227 it was to Richard of Cornwall that the English court granted custody of the dower lands confiscated from Isabella.[187] In the long term, this was to lay the foundations of Richard's

---

[183] For the later enquiry, referred to in royal and papal letters of 1235 and 1238, see *Treaty Rolls 1234–1325*, ed. P. Chaplais, London 1955, no. 88; *Registres de Grégoire IX*, ed. Auvray, no. 2580.

[184] Watson, 'Counts of Angoulême', 390–443 nos 209–272 *passim*.

[185] For a genealogical chart, see Snellgrove, *The Lusignans in England*, 24.

[186] Watson, 'Counts of Angoulême', 142–8.

[187] *Rot. Litt. Claus.*, ii, 197b, 198; *Patent Rolls 1225–32*, 140. The lands were not fully granted to Richard until 1231: *Calendar of Charter Rolls 1226–57*, 129, 139; Vincent, *Peter des Roches*, 271–3.

financial security, bringing him an additional 1,000 marks or more a year, part of the great fortune that was to enable Richard to prop up the tottering finances of King Henry III during the 1250s, and in his own right make a bid for the crown of Germany.[188] In the immediate term, however, Richard's acquisition of the dower was overshadowed by controversy. In particular, Richard objected to the fact that Isabella's honour of Berkhamsted was withheld on behalf of a nephew of the justiciar, Hubert de Burgh. This dispute brought Richard close to rebellion: one of our first indications of the longer-term consequences of the tangled history of Isabella's dower lands.[189]

Isabella made her last, and in some ways her most dramatic, appearance on the public stage in 1241–2, by which time she was nearing 50 years of age. In 1241, Louis IX demanded that oaths of fealty be sworn to his brother Alfonse, newly created count of Poitiers. Hugh de Lusignan, Isabella's husband, complied, but faced a furious backlash from Isabella. According to Matthew Paris, Isabella was anxious to protect the rights of her English son, Richard of Cornwall, who had held the title count of Poitiers by grant of his brother, Henry III, since 1225. Richard was highly favoured, according to Paris, because of the renown he had won as a crusader, and the special courtesy he had shown in freeing various of Hugh de Lusignan's knights from captivity in the Holy Land.[190] By contrast, and perhaps more plausibly, a local informant, writing to Blanche the queen-mother of France, reports that Isabella was prompted to rebel by what she regarded as the indignities inflicted upon her by the French royal family. At Poitiers she had attended the French court to render the homage that had been demanded from her, but was made to stand together with what she regarded as *hoi poloi* whilst Louis IX, the queen of France, the countess of Chartres and the countess's sister, the abbess of Fontevraud, remained seated, according Isabella none of the respect she believed to be her due. Enraged, she made first for Lusignan, where she stripped the castle and its chapel of their furnishings before fleeing to her castle at Angoulême. When Hugh, her husband, attempted to console her, she poured out a stream of abuse against him, threatening to deny him access to her bed and to see him no more. Hugh – presented in this account very much as a hen-pecked husband – then gathered together the barons of Poitou in a league against the French.[191] Whatever the truth of this account, it confirms the version supplied by Matthew

---

[188] N. Denholm-Young, *Richard of Cornwall*, Oxford 1947, 167–8, and see the valuation placed upon the English dower by Louis IX in 1230 of 2500 livres Tournois p.a.: Martène and Durand, *Amplissima Collectio*, 1236.

[189] Denholm-Young, *Richard of Cornwall*, 9–14; Vincent, *Peter des Roches*, 265–6. Besides the dispute over Berkhamsted, Richard was also denied possession of various manors from his honour of Cornwall, retained by Walerand the Teuton, brother of Terric, and a one-time servant of Isabella.

[190] *Chronica Majora*, iv, 178.

[191] L. Delisle, 'Mémoire sur une lettre inédite adressé à la Reine Blanche par un habitant de La Rochelle', *Bibliothèque de l'Ecole des Chartes* 17, 1856, 513–55, esp. 525–9.

Paris, that it was Isabella who took the leading role in persuading Hugh de Lusignan to rebel against the French and to seek assistance from England.

The resulting campaign proved a disaster for Isabella, for Hugh and for Henry III.[192] Louis IX was allowed to take the offensive, and spent more than a month, before the arrival of the English army, suppressing rebellion in Poitou. The English army, when it did arrive, was greatly out-numbered by the French. Hugh de Lusignan failed to provide the allies and men from Poitou that he had promised, leading to bitter recriminations. At Taillebourg, in July 1242, the English only narrowly escaped a disastrous encounter with the army of Louis IX. Henry III fled via Saintes and Pons to Bordeaux, abandoned at every turn by his erstwhile French allies. Meanwhile, within a week of the débâcle at Taillebourg, Hugh and Isabella sued for peace. In return for a pardon from Louis IX, they were forced to relinquish the rich pensions that had been paid to them since 1224, to meet the cost of installing French garrisons in three of their principal castles, and to abandon their claim to Saintes.[193] In effect, having established a hegemony over much of Poitou during the past twenty years, Hugh and Isabella were forced in 1242 to hand over their hard-won gains to the Capetians Louis IX and Count Alfonse. The virtual principality of Lusignan, La Marche and Angoulême, established after 1217, merely served as a stepping stone on the path to Capetian conquest.[194]

On a more personal level, the rebellion of 1242 was also to have momentous consequences for Isabella. Blamed by the French for stirring up revolt, and by the English and the Poitevins for the failure of that revolt when it came about, Isabella found herself condemned on all sides. Her reaction, according to the French chronicler William de Nangis, was tantamount to a nervous breakdown. When it became clear that the rebellion had failed, Nangis claims that Isabella sent assassins to poison Louis IX and his brother. The plot was unmasked, and according to later testimony Isabella tried to kill herself with a dagger.[195] This is a splendid story, with plenty of classical resonances. It may or may not be true. By a fortunate accident, our evidence for the settlement made between Hugh, Isabella and the king of France in 1242 extends beyond the treaties themselves to include a remarkable work of art: an enamelled, Limoges-work coffer, measuring some two feet in length and six inches in depth, in which the bones of the blessed John de Montmirail are stored at the abbey of Longpont north of Paris. A recent and plausible account of this reliquary has suggested that the fifty or more heraldic devices with which it is emblazoned, including those of Louis IX, Alfonse of Poitiers, Hugh de Lusignan and many of the participants,

---

[192] The best narrative of the campaign remains that by C. Bémont, 'La Campagne de Poitou 1242–1243', *Annales de Midi* 5, 1893, 289–314, and see also R.C. Stacey, *Politics, Policy and Finance under Henry III 1216–1245*, Oxford 1987, 183–200.

[193] *Layettes*, ii, no. 2980.

[194] Crucial here is the analysis by Hajdu, 'Castles, Castellans and the Structure of Politics in Poitou', *JMH* 4, 1978, 27–44.

[195] Nangis in Bouquet, *Recueil*, xx, 334–5, whence the chronicle of St-Denis in *ibid.*, xxi, 113.

both from the Capetian and the Lusignan armies in the rebellion of 1242, demonstrate that it was made shortly after the Lusignan surrender to King Louis, as a token of the peace and of Hugh de Lusignan's submission to Capetian power.[196] What has not been appreciated is that the body of John de Montmirail, the warrior saint and one-time servant of Philip Augustus, would have been a particularly appropriate relic over which to swear a peace between Louis and the Lusignans. The blessed John was, as we have seen, a close kinsman of Isabella of Angoulême, being the step-son of Isabella's mother, Alice de Courtenay by her first husband Andrew of La Ferté-Gaucher. Linked to the Capetians by military service, and to the Lusignans and Isabella by marriage, John de Montmirail and his heraldic reliquary serve to remind us of the extraordinary wealth of contacts enjoyed by Isabella of Angoulême, both with the Capetian and the Plantagenet courts. If his relics did indeed play a role in the peace settlement of 1242, then this would suggest that Isabella was a more active participant in the peace than we might otherwise suppose.

Whatever the precise truth here, it is certain that Isabella was humiliated by the events of 1242, and that she found herself increasingly estranged from her husband Hugh de Lusignan. In March 1243 she and Hugh drew up a division of their estates, between their various Lusignan sons.[197] Shortly afterwards, Isabella retired to the abbey of Fontevraud, where she asked to be veiled as a nun and where she died on 4 June 1246. Only two days before her death, she had written to Louis IX, reminding him of her earlier pleas that he allow her Lusignan sons to take possession of her estates.[198] By her will, she bequeathed 1000 livres to the nuns of Fontevraud, of which 100 livres were to pay for a chantry priest, and the remainder for the repair of the nuns' clothing.[199] At the last, then, the various strands of Isabella's life were drawn together. She chose to die at Fontevraud, the great necropolis of the Plantagenet kings of England, with a prayer on her lips, not for King John or her children in England, but for the sons that she had born to her Poitevin husband Hugh de Lusignan.

In England, the news of her demise was greeted with a brief display of mourning. Over the next few weeks, Henry III set aside small sums of money to pay for obit celebrations at Westminster and Malmesbury, and for a feast for the

---

[196] A.-C. Dionnet, 'La Cassette reliquaire du bienheureux Jean de Montmirail', *Revue française d'héraldique et de sigillographie* 65, 1995, 89–107. Besides identifying the various heraldic shields on the reliquary, which show beyond a doubt that it was commissioned at some time in the early to mid 1240s, Monsieur Dionnet, who was unaware of the relationship between Isabella and John de Montmirail, suggests that it may originally have been given by Hugh de Lusignan to Alfonse of Poitiers as a receptacle in which to store the documentary proofs of Hugh's submission, and that only much later was it granted to Longpont for use at the tomb of the blessed John, perhaps at the time of one or other of the translations of John's relics, previously assumed, on no very firm evidence, to have taken place c.1253 and again at some time after 1272.

[197] *Layettes*, ii, no. 3049.

[198] *Layettes*, ii, no. 3523.

[199] See the obituary notice from Fontevraud, printed below, Appendix no.5.

friars and poor scholars of Oxford and Cambridge.[200] However, it is perhaps more indicative of the king's true feelings that in October 1246, less than six months after Isabella's burial at Fontevraud, Henry ordained that his own body was to be buried, not at Fontevraud with the bodies of his mother and ancestors, but at Westminster Abbey.[201] Eight years later, in 1254, Henry did eventually make a pilgrimage to Fontevraud, where with his own hands he helped to transfer Isabella's corpse from the humble resting place she had selected in the chapter-house, to a position beside the tombs of Eleanor of Aquitaine, Henry II and Richard I. It was probably on this visit of 1254 that Henry paid for the surviving wooden effigy of Isabella, showing her robed and crowned as queen of England.[202] Much later, he willed his own heart to Fontevraud, where it was buried with due ceremony in 1291.[203] In the meantime, in October 1249, he had referred to Isabella by name, together with King John, as the spiritual beneficiary of an award to the hospital of St Anthony Vienne, and Isabella occurs once again, together with John, Eleanor of Provence and Henry III's children, as the named spiritual beneficiary of an award to the lepers of Windsor in April 1251.[204] It remains questionable, however, whether Henry felt any true remorse for his mother, who had abandoned him in infancy, and who, for the next forty years had effectively blighted all attempts at a Plantagenet reconquest in Poitou. The mourning and the obits carried out in 1246 were perfunctory in the extreme. On the other hand, within a year of Isabella's death, Henry went on to provide a haven and rich rewards for Isabella's Lusignan offspring, sowing the seeds of the resentment against these Lusignan half-brothers that in the 1250s was to boil over into open rebellion amongst the English baronage. In this, he may have been prompted more by dynastic than by personal motives. Through Isabella, Henry continued to possess a claim to the county of Angoulême. It was a claim that Henry himself formally renounced under the terms of the Anglo-French treaty of Paris after 1258, but which his brother, Richard of Cornwall, and his sister, Eleanor the wife of Simon de Montfort, insisted upon reserving, even after the Anglo-French treaty, maintaining a theoretical but nonetheless contentious link between the Plantagenets and Isabella's

---

[200] *Calendar of Patent Rolls 1232–47*, 485; *Calendar of Liberate Rolls 1245–51*, 71, 78, 288; *Close Rolls 1242–7*, 448–9; B. Harvey, *Westminster Abbey and its Estates in the Middle Ages*, Oxford 1977, 391, citing *Calendar of Charter Rolls 1226–57*, 304.

[201] Westminster Abbey Muniments 6318A, enrolled in *Calendar of Charter Rolls 1226–57*, 306. The chancery enrolment survives only a mutilated form.

[202] For the effigy, see above, n. 161.

[203] *Calendar of Patent Rolls 1281–92*, 463, and see A. Pommier, 'Observations sur une relique', *Bulletin de la Société Archéologique et Historique de l'Orléanais* 17, 1918, 275–85; Carpenter, *Reign of Henry III*, 428.

[204] *Calendar of Charter Rolls 1226–57*, 345, 357, 361, and for the grant to St Anthony Vienne of the church of All Saints at Hereford, see also *The Manuscripts of St George's Chapel, Windsor Castle*, ed. J.N. Dalton, Windsor 1957, 275; *Charters and Records of Hereford Cathedral*, ed. W.W. Capes, Hereford 1908, 114–16.

continental lordship in the Angoumois for at least thirty years after her death.[205] Eleanor de Montfort was still laying claim to an annual pension from the Lusignan lords of Angoulême as late as 1269.[206]

Isabella left a bitter legacy to her Plantagenet kin. But for her marriage to King John in 1200, there might have been no Poitevin rebellion against John, and no Capetian invasion of John's lands. Arthur of Brittany might have grown up to be a disappointment to his friends, and French would now be the principal language of the British Isles. Thereafter, had the relations between John and Isabella been more equitable, in particular had John allowed Isabella a greater role in the administration of her dower lands, then she might never have abandoned England after John's death. Angoulême would have been united to the English crown, with Henry III as its first Plantagenet count. Isabella would never have married Hugh de Lusignan, so that the foreign policy of Henry III would have taken a very different course. Richard of Cornwall might never have succeeded to Isabella's dower, which would have passed instead to Henry's queen, Eleanor of Provence. Hence, there might have been no Richard king of Germany and no diversion of Richard's financial resources to his German ambitions, away from the needs of Henry III and the English Crown. Above all, there would have been no Lusignan half-brothers at the court of Henry III, poisoning relations with the native English baronage.

There is one final legacy that Isabella may have bequeathed to her eldest son: a legacy with which this study can fittingly conclude – the abiding devotion of Henry III to the cult of Edward the Confessor. Much has been written of Henry's piety, and of his devotion to Edward the Confessor, as the very model of an English royal saint ruling in peace and harmony with his barons.[207] It seems to have escaped attention that Henry III shared more in common with the Confessor than just his piety and his pacific approach to government. Both Henry and the Confessor were the sons of queens of England who effectively abandoned their children. Emma, the Confessor's Norman mother, abandoned her children by Æthelred in order to marry the Danish usurper Cnut. Thereafter it is doubtful whether Edward saw her again for the best part of twenty years.[208] Isabella of Angoulême abandoned her children by King John to marry one of the greatest barons of Poitou, and with him to forge a virtual principality for herself and her new husband, very much at the expense of Henry III. Apart from brief meetings in 1242, and possibly in 1230, she had no personal contact with Henry III, her eldest son, for the last thirty years of her life. Might this

---

[205] Denholm-Young, *Richard of Cornwall*, 97; M.W. Labarge, *Simon de Montfort*, London 1962, 191–2, 201; J.R. Maddicott, *Simon de Montfort*, Cambridge 1994, 204–5, 221.

[206] Labarge, *Simon de Montfort*, 264.

[207] In particular, see P. Binski, 'Reflections on "La estoire de Seint Aedward le rei": Hagiography and Kingship in Thirteenth-Century England', *JMH* 16, 1990, 333–50, and the same author's *Westminster Abbey and the Plantagenets: Kingship and the Representation of Royal Power 1200–1400*, New Haven and London 1995.

[208] For Emma's relations with her son, see F. Barlow, *Edward the Confessor*, London 1970, 34–5, 38, 45–7, 57–9, 76–8, 117.

similarity, between Emma and Isabella, and Edward and Henry III, provide at least one key to Henry's later devotion to the cult of the Confessor? It is certainly remarkable than in all of Henry's devotions to St Edward, the figure of Edward's mother should be so conspicuous by her absence.[209]

To this extent, it is arguable that without Isabella, and without the treatment that she met at the hands of King John, there would have been no Plantagenet collapse in 1204, no civil war, no Magna Carta, no humiliating setbacks for Henry III in Poitou, no Lusignans at Henry's court, and, perhaps most intriguingly, no sense of affinity between Henry III and the Confessor: in other words, no Westminster Abbey. From language to architecture, from Aachen to Angoulême, and from Burgundy to the court of France, Isabella cast a remarkable shadow over the course of European politics. Historians of the reign of King John and of his son, Henry III, would do well to remember this, and to accord Isabella, John's Jezebel, the respect that is properly her due.

Appendix

I have attempted to assemble here all of the charters issued by Isabella before her return to Angoulême in 1217. Thereafter, for a catalogue of her charters issued as countess of Angoulême and La Marche, for the most part in association with Hugh de Lusignan, see above n. 160; Watson, 'Counts of Angoulême', 390–443 nos. 209–72, with remarks on her comital chancery and seals at pp. 209, 224–5.

1. St Thomas' Acon

Grant to St Thomas' Acon, for the soul of King John, of the hospital of St John the Baptist Berkhamsted together with the tithes of all her mills in Berkhamsted and Hemel Hempstead.   Taunton, 1 March 1217

B = PRO C53/105 (Charter Roll 12 Edward II) m.10, in an inspeximus 9 Dec. 1318.

Pd (calendar from B) *Calendar of Charter Rolls 1300–26*, 399–400.

Omnibus Cristi fidelibus ad quos presens scriptum pervenerit Isabella Dei gratia regina Angl(ie) domina Hibern(ie) ducissa Norm(annie) et Aquit(anie) comitissa Andeg(avie) salutem et dilectionem. Noveritis nos divine pietatis intuitu et pro salute anime domini nostri I(ohannis) regis Angl(ie) illustris et

---

[209] Emma makes only a perfunctory appearance in the 'Estoire de Seint Aeward', which Binski argues was very much a product of the court circle of Henry III. Nor, so far as we can judge, was any attempt made to revise or copy the eleventh-century *Encomium Emmæ*, which presumably went unnoticed at the court of King Henry.

animarum omnium antecessorum nostrorum et heredum nostrorum et omnium Dei fidelium defunctorum dedisse et concessisse et hac presenti carta nostra confirmasse Deo et beate Marie et ecclesie sancti Thome martiris site in civitate Acon' et canonicis regularibus ibidem Deo servientibus et imperpetuum servituris hospitale sancti Iohannis Baptiste in Berkamsted' cum omnibus pertinentiis, cui scilicet assignavimus et dedimus et presenti carta confirmavimus totam decimam molendinorum nostrorum omnium tam molendinorum ad bladum quam fulloratorum in soca de Berkamested' et in soca de Hammelhamsted' tam de profectu bladi quam denar(iorum) et aliorum profectuum inde provenientium. Concessimus etiam eis et hac presenti carta confirmavimus quindecim acras terre in Selidone et totum fossatum cum herbagio inter vivarium et ipsum hospitalem quantum vivarium durat in longitudine, scilicet a via que vocatur Waterlane usque ad ecclesiam sancti Iacobi in Berkhamested', et similiter totam terram que fuit Rogeri Corduanar' cum pertinentiis et omni servicio quod ipsa terra reddere consueverat, et quandam placiam quam Ricardus le Caretur aliquo tempore tenuit iuxta hospitalem qui de dicta placia annuatim reddere solet dicto hospitali servicium decem et octo denar(iorum). Preterea dedimus eis quindecim carectatas busch(i) in haya de Berkamested' per annum, et viginti quinque carectatas busch(i) in bosco de Bunnendon' per annum, et viginti porcos in haya de Berkamstede et in bosco de Bunendon' singulis annis cum porcis nostris quietos de pannagio, et pasturam ad averos suos et ad vaccas et animalia sua in communi pastura de Berkhamsted' infra boscum et extra. Confirmavimus etiam eis omnes terras et ten(ementa) que rationabiliter adepti sunt in feudo nostro de Berkamsted' et in Hammelhamste(de) et rationabiliter adipisci poterunt. Quare volumus et firmiter precipimus quod predictum hospitale et fratres ibidem Deo servientes habeant et teneant omnes elemosinas, decimas, terras, ten(ementa) et omnia alia supradicta de nobis et heredibus nostris imperpetuum in puram et perpetuam elemosinam, libere et quiete ab omni seculari servicio et exactione, et ut hec nostra donatio, concessio et confirmatio firma et illesa in perpetuum permaneat, huic presenti carte sigillum nostrum apposuimus. Hiis testibus: Teodoro Teutonico, Willelmo de Sorewill', Walerando Teutonico, Hug(one) et Nich(olao) et Thom(a) de Meriet, Thom(a) de Fluri, Olivero Auenel, Wakelino de Bremfeld', Roberto capellano, Thoma de Cirestr', Waltero persona de Ciselbergh' et multis aliis. Dat' per manum nostram kal' Marcii apud Tanton', anno regni domini Henr(ici) regis Angl(ie) filii nostri primogeniti primo.

2. Exeter, St Nicholas' Priory

Grant of the fair of the city of Exeter   Exeter, 29 May 1217

B = BL ms. Cotton Vitellius D ix (Cartulary of St Nicholas' Exeter) fo. 65r–v (62r–v), s.xiii.

Universis Cristi fidelibus ad quos presens scriptum pervenerit Isabel Dei gratia regina Angl(ie), domina Hib(ernie), ducissa Norm(annie), Aquit(anie) et comitissa Andeg(avie) salutem. Noverit universitas vestra nos divine karitatis intuitu et pro salute anime nostre et anima domini I(ohannis) bone memorie quondam regis Angl(ie) et mariti nostri et omnium liberorum nostrorum et omnium antecessorum et successorum nostrorum dedisse et concessisse et hac presenti carta nostra confirmasse Deo et ecclesie sancti Nicholai Exon' et monachis ibidem Deo servientibus in puram et perpetuam elemosinam feriam civitatis Exon' cum omnibus profectionibus et consuetudinibus eidem ferie pertinentibus, habendam et tenendam libere et quiete, plenarie et integre, bene et pacifice sicut umquam dominus I(ohannes) quondam rex Angl(ie) et maritus noster eam liberius et quietius tenuit et nobis in dotem assignavit. Ut autem hec nostra donatio, concessio et confirmatio in perpetuum rata permaneat et inconcussa eam presenti scripto et sigilli nostri appositione corroboravimus. T(estibus) domino Simon(e) episcopo Exon' et capitulo sancti Petri Exon', dominis Henrico et Rob(erto) capellanis nostris, domino Rob(erto) de Curtenay vic(ecomite) Devon', Rogero de Langefort, Willelmo Hastem't tunc maiore Exon', Waltero Probo et Waltero la Thawe tunc prepositis Exon', Willelmo Derling, Waltero Turb', Iohanne filio eius, Baldwino Hoel, Willelmo Lud, Ylar(io) Blundo, Laur(encio) le Taillur civibus Exon', Waltero clerico nostro et aliis. Dat' per manum nostram apud Exon' iiii° kal' Iun' anno regni regis H(enrici) primogeniti nostri primo.

3. Malmesbury Abbey

Confirmation of the vill and site of the castle of Malmesbury in fee farm
[1216 x 1217]

B = PRO. E164/24 (Malmesbury cartulary) fos. 169v–170r, s.xiii/xiv.
C = BL ms. Lansdowne 417 (Malmesbury cartulary) fo. 69r–v, s.xiv/xv.

Pd (from B) *Registrum Malmesburiense*, 430 no. 93.

Isabella Dei gratia regina Angl(ie) etc. uniuersis Cristi fidelibus hanc cartam inspecturis salutem in domino. Sciatis quod nos intuitu Dei et pro salute anime nostre et domini nostri felicissime recordationis Iohannis quondam regis Anglie illustris concessimus et hac carta nostra confirmauimus Deo et ecclesie sancti Aldhelmi de Malmesbr' et abbati et monachis ibidem Deo seruientibus villam de Malmesbr' cum omnibus pertinentiis suis que est de dote nostra habendam et tenendam ita libere et quiete, integre et pacifice cum hundredis et omnibus pertinentiis et libertatibus et liberis consuetudinibus et omnibus aliis ad villam illam pertinentibus sicut idem dominus rex bone memorie eandem villam cum suis pertinentiis eis dedit et carta sua confirmauit, ad feodi firmam per xx. libras sterlingorum ei et heredibus suis inde ad duos terminos anni soluendos, quas ipsi abbas et monachi nobis reddent tota vita nostra ad duos terminos, videlicet ad festum sancti Michaelis x. libras et ad Pascha x. libras pro omni seruicio et exactione. Concessimus etiam predictis abbati et monachis imperpetuum locum illum in quo situm fuit castrum in ipsa curia ecclesie de Malm' quem in usus suos ad edificia sua dilatanda conuerterunt ut locum illum sine omni difficultate pacifice possideant sicut ius ecclesie sue nec inde aliquo tempore per nos vel nostros in aliquo vexabuntur. Ut autem hec rata sint et inconcussa, hanc cartam nostram eis fecimus et sigilli nostri impressione roborauimus. Hiis testibus: domino H. Dublin' archiepiscopo, P. Wynton' et I. Bath' episcopis et multis aliis.

4. Winchester, David of

Charters of Isabella granting David of Winchester land in *Alrichestun'*, *Wik'* and Hemel Hempstead are referred to in a mandate of Henry III, 6 December 1221, ordering the restoration of these lands to David: *Rot. Litt. Claus.*, i, 483.

5. Isabella's Obituary Notice from Fontevraud

B = BN ms. Latin 5480 part 1 (Gaignières transcripts for Fontevraud) p. 1, copy from the lost necrology of Fontevraud, s.xvii.
C = Angers, Archives départementales ms. 10H225bis, copy from B, s.xvii.

Pridie Nonas Iunii migr(auit) domina Helisabeth venerabilis regina Anglie comitissa Angolisme et Marchie mater illustris domini Henrici regis Anglie, que dum in mundo viueret multas aduersitates passa fuit, manens nobiscum paruo tempore, nobis mille libras in helemosinam contulit, centum pro capellano, residuum ad camisias comparandas, in nostro capitulo sepulturam suam elegit, nostro velamineque petierat monacabiliter velata. Postea euoluto octo annorum spacio, ab illustrissimo filio suo Anglorum rege Henrico de capitulo nostro in ecclesiam nostram propria manu ipsius deportata est, ab archiepiscopis Burdegal' et Biturice', baronibusque et militibus iuxta sepulturam regiam regum sicut ipse elegerat tumulata

John and Ireland: the Origins of England's Irish Problem

Seán Duffy

Henry II's son John was lord of Ireland for just some months short of forty years, in other words, nearly two and half times longer than he was king of England or held the county of Mortain, his most valuable Continental asset prior to his accession to the throne, and eight times longer than he could credibly claim to be duke of Normandy. Ireland and John, therefore, go back a long way. He was its lord nearly twice as long as he knew his own father, longer than he knew his mother or any of his brothers, and a lot longer than he had the pleasure of knowing his wives or in-laws. And yet it can reasonably be said that Ireland has featured only peripherally in the historiography of John. None of his biographers since Kate Norgate has dealt with the matter in any depth (and even she confined comment largely to his two Irish expeditions),[1] while Lewis Warren's several important contributions to the subject were made after the appearance of his biography, the first a full thirty years ago,[2] but they have not been incorporated into its reissues.

There is, of course, an easy explanation for this neglect, apart altogether from the excessive fear to tread which Ireland seems to provoke in scholars deeming themselves non-specialist intruders. It is the task of the historian to assemble the pieces of the past in order to describe how things came to be the way they are, rather than what might have been. Consequently, that which would have been important if things had worked out differently, and one needed to tell a different story, appears with the benefit of hindsight to be a matter of little consequence. John is a classic case of this kind. For the first half of his life, a period of a quarter of a century, few people, except perhaps the wily John himself, thought that he would ascend the throne of England. When contemporaries did think of him, which was not often – as Warren rather unkindly put it, 'fourth sons, even of a king, are among the more insignificant of God's creatures'[3] –

---

[1] Kate Norgate, *John Lackland*, London 1902, 17–19, 150–56.

[2] See 'The Interpretation of Twelfth Century Irish History', *Historical Studies*, vii, ed. J.C. Beckett, London 1969, 1–19; 'The Historian as "Private Eye" ', *ibid.*, ix, ed. J.G. Barry, Belfast 1974, 1–18; 'John in Ireland, 1185', in *Essays presented to Michael Roberts*, ed. J. Bosy and P. Jupp, Belfast 1976, 11–23; 'King John and Ireland', in *England and Ireland in the Later Middle Ages: Essays in Honour of Jocelyn Otway-Ruthven*, ed. J.F. Lydon, Dublin 1981, 26–42; 'Painter's *King John*: Forty Years On', *Haskins Society Journal* I, 1989, 1–9.

[3] Warren, *King John*, 26.

they thought initially not in terms of the English throne, but of the niche in life which had been carved out for John by his father and his father's advisers. Ireland, for the most part, was that niche.

Ireland and John are therefore inseparable. No Irish historian who contemplates the rendering or reduction of Ireland into an English colony places John far from the top of his list of dramatis personae. But, because of the intimacy of John's association with Ireland, both before and, possibly even to a greater extent, after his accession to the throne, the reverse should surely also apply: that, rather than read history backwards with the aid of hindsight, no student of John should place Ireland too far from centre-stage. Instead, though, the subject tends only to appear when fine words are needed with which to praise him or bury him. The public-relations disaster that surrounded his expedition to Ireland in 1185 is therefore frequently cited as evidence of John's youthful folly. On the other hand, and more importantly, historians grasping for something good to say about his subsequent reign have latched onto the apparently more slick operation executed in Ireland in the summer of 1210. When, for instance, Sidney Painter was summing up John's reign after his early humiliations, he said:

> History has not, I believe, fully recognised, either the full scope of John's plans to recover his prestige or how near they came to fruition . . . He humbled the great Anglo-Irish barons and the native chieftains and vastly increased his authority in that lordship.[4]

The entry on King John in the *Dictionary of the Middle Ages* puts it even more bluntly: 'Since 1200 John's only success had been the Irish expedition of 1210.'[5] Such statements abound, all to similar effect: by and large, it seems, students of John, while not devoting much of their efforts to coming to grips with his relationship with Ireland, are content to cite its example as one of the pitiably few success-stories of his notorious reign.

It is, of course, quite unfair to blame non-Irish historians for this. Those who are not specialists in Irish history are entitled to expect that up-to-date reputable secondary literature is available on the subject, capable of providing them with a reasonably sound assessment. They may feel that it would be unwise, or even impertinent, to butt in, as it were, and offer a contrary opinion of their own. When Ralph Turner, for example, was writing on the Irish question in his recent biography of John, he consulted the *New History of Ireland. Volume II*, a generally very reliable read.[6] The section for John's reign in this multi-authored tome is written by F.X. Martin, and this is what Professor Turner makes of his discussion:

---

[4] Painter, *Reign of King John*, 227.
[5] B. Lyon, 'John, King of England', in *Dictionary of the Middle Ages*, ed. J.R. Strayer *et al.*, New York 1986, vii, 130.
[6] *A New History of Ireland. Volume II. Medieval Ireland*, ed. A. Cosgrove, Oxford 1987.

A modern authority on medieval Ireland finds it a great irony that in Ireland of all John's possessions, he should have demonstrated 'qualities of foresight and constructive leadership'. The author [Martin] continues, 'John, so often described as the worst of the kings of England, was, paradoxically, the best for Ireland.'

Professor Turner then adds: 'Whether or not one accepts this judgement, John made a strong impact, perhaps stronger than any other medieval English monarch.'[7] The latter is a cautious and balanced assessment, which, with respect, cannot be said for that upon which it was based.[8] The former, however, has now joined the lexicon of historical aphorisms so beloved of the under-graduate essayist, though admittedly coming a poor second to Warren's sub-limely over-the-top 'King John was the most successful high-king Ireland had ever seen.'[9] That such conclusions have obtained currency, and been allowed to retain that currency, is all the more unfortunate in view of the fact that one does not have to scratch too far beneath the surface to detect signs that John was far from an unqualified success in his dealings with Ireland and the Irish, and that his mistakes and failures elsewhere were replicated in this instance also. This is what I propose to examine in this paper.

One should perhaps begin any assessment of John and the Irish question by briefly summarising the standard interpretation. There are two stages of this: the pre-Lewis Warren view, and then the re-assessment which Warren provided in his series of articles on this subject. The pre-Warren view was a bit of a curate's egg. John campaigned in Ireland twice, the first time disastrously in 1185, the second time triumphantly in 1210; in the interval and subsequently he was quite successful, certainly in terms of introducing to Ireland the rudiments of the English governmental system, so that he was, in Edmund Curtis' phrase, 'the founder of Anglo-Ireland',[10] although earlier, Goddard Orpen had been consistently critical of the king, and more inclined to credit royal ministers, par-ticularly John de Gray, bishop of Norwich, with many of the later administra-tive improvements.[11]

Lewis Warren offered a highly revisionist account of John's lordship. Not only was the 1210 campaign an unqualified success, but the failures of the earlier expedition had, he believed, been exaggerated.[12] Whatever his initial wobbles, in and after 1185 John and his advisers masterminded a clever and

---

7   Turner, *King John*, 145.
8   Such views, of course, are not new, and bear the imprint of Curtis' view that 'John dealt with the baronage of Ireland as he dare not deal with those of England, and as the founder here of a central government, and as the repressor of an overgrown feudalism, must be counted one of the best of the foreign Kings': E. Curtis, *A History of Mediaeval Ireland from 1110 to 1513*, 1st edn, Dublin 1927, 108.
9   Warren, 'King John and Ireland', 39.
10 Curtis, *Mediaeval Ireland*, chap. V.
11 G.H. Orpen, *Ireland under the Normans*, 4 vols, Oxford 1911–20, ii, chap. 21.
12 Warren, 'John in Ireland, 1185'.

well-thought-out plan for the expansion of the English colony in Ireland, and its gradual extension to cover the whole island. This involved the construction of a strategic arc of both royal and baronial castles and interlocking lordships, which would provide for the security of the colony's heartland and main administrative and economic centres, and be a bridgehead for later expansion.[13] Furthermore, although John had fallen out with many of the Anglo-Irish barons and came to Ireland in 1210 to bring them to heel, Warren notes as one of John's major achievements the fact that these same barons remained loyal to him through the Magna Carta crisis and the civil war, indeed right to the bitter end. He suggests that the explanation for the Anglo-Irish barons' peculiar steadfastness is that they extracted a deal from John: in return for their loyalty he reversed an earlier royal policy of conciliation towards the native Irish province-kings, and gave the barons free rein in Ireland, which would conceivably involve the wholesale expropriation of the Irish kings and the erection of legal obstacles in the way of their progress.[14]

Overall, this is a very attractive picture and, if some of the more technical detail has not percolated through from the academic journal or *festschrift* to the textbook and undergraduate lecture-course, its main tenets have, and have won general acceptance.[15] But nagging doubts remain, partly in reaction to the very neatness of the Warren thesis,[16] partly, as I hope to demonstrate, because the evidence demands it. The first concerns the 1185 expedition, an unmitigated disaster, not merely in terms of John's losses in the field against his Irish subjects, but more especially from a long-term policy standpoint. Warren would contend that a major change in policy towards the native Irish only occurred after the year 1212, over a quarter of a century later, and was one wrested from John by the Anglo-Irish barons at a time of weakness at the beginning of the king's crisis years. It would appear, however, that that change of policy, if things were ever otherwise, began with the 1185 expedition, and that the undoubted irreparable damage it caused, and which led ultimately to the failure of the medieval conquest of Ireland, began to manifest itself before the young Lord John had even left the country. A further point concerns the 1210 expedition, which I have discussed elsewhere, arguing that in its own way, contrary to the accepted view, it was as disastrous, militarily and politically, as the first campaign.[17] Finally, there is the matter of the barons' war and the French invasion. There is an implicit acceptance on the part of many historians, and

---

[13] Warren, 'King John and Ireland'.

[14] Warren, 'The Historian as "Private Eye" '.

[15] For the most recent regurgitation of Warrenesque theory, see S. Duffy, *Ireland in the Middle Ages*, London and Dublin 1997, chap. 4.

[16] Robin Frame has hinted at his own doubts about the existence of 'elaborate royal policies towards the Lordship' in his 'England and Ireland, 1171–1399', in *Ireland and Britain 1170–1450*, London 1998, 17 (reprinted from *England and her Neighbours, 1066–1453: Essays in Honour of Pierre Chaplais*, ed. M. Jones and M. Vale, London 1989 (at p. 141)).

[17] S. Duffy, 'King John's Expedition to Ireland, 1210: the Evidence Reconsidered', *Irish Historical Studies* 30, 1996–7, 1–24.

explicitly in the case of Lewis Warren, that Ireland remained at peace through-out this troubled period, the Anglo-Irish remaining firmly loyal to John and the native Irish not taking advantage of his adversity. I propose to look again at this troubled period and to see if such an analysis stands up to scrutiny.

There is something almost prophetic about the fact that John's birth in 1167 coincided with the most significant development in the story of Ireland's relationship with England: in that very year, a certain dispossessed Irish province-king, the famous Diarmait Mac Murchada, having come to the court of Henry II in search of aid to recover his ancestral patrimony of Leinster, and having sworn fealty to him, landed on the shores of Ireland with his first band of Cambro-Norman allies. What followed, the full-scale Anglo-Norman invasion of Ireland and King Henry's assertion of lordship over it, is a story too familiar and too complex to retell here.[18] It was the single most formative development in Irish secular affairs, and John, whose first breath all but coincided with its formal initiation, was in on the act from the start.

The question of Henry II's interest in Ireland, whether it was an item of marginal concern to him or of prolonged preoccupation, has been subjected to extensive study and need not detain us unduly.[19] He did certainly think that he had found some sort of solution to the matter of how best to govern the country, even if only *pro tempore*, when he made the formal agreement in 1175 with the reigning high-king of Ireland, Ruaidrí Ua Conchobair of Connacht, usually known as the Treaty of Windsor. That settlement, however, did not last, not least because the most powerful of the new resident barons, Richard 'Strongbow' de Clare, earl of Strigoil, who had acted as Henry's justiciar for Ireland, died within a year, leaving behind something of a power-vacuum. Gerald of Wales states that envoys were then sent to the king in England, 'informing him of the changed situation arising out of the earl's death', and that Henry immediately sent William fitz Audelin to Ireland as his *procurator*.[20] Roger of Howden reports both events, placing them correctly in 1176, but, curiously, precedes them by this statement: 'Eodem anno dominus rex Angliae pater dedit Johanni filio suo Hyberniam'. There is no other record of Henry giving Ireland to John at this point, and, since other accounts record that this did not occur until the Council of Oxford in 1177, there is no reason to accept Howden's statement, were it not for the fact that he too records the Oxford grant, this time again stating that Henry created John king of Ireland, but adding, 'having a grant and confirmation thereof from Alexander the

---

18 The most recent detailed investigation of the subject is M.T. Flanagan, *Irish Society, Anglo-Norman Settlers, Angevin Kingship*, Oxford 1989.

19 See Flanagan, *Irish Society*; eadem, 'Strongbow, Henry II and the Anglo-Norman Intervention in Ireland', in *War and Government in the Middle Ages: Essays in Honour of J.O. Prestwich*, ed. J. Gillingham and J.C. Holt, Woodbridge 1984, 74–77; Warren, *Henry II*, 187–206.

20 Giraldus Cambrensis, *Expugnatio Hibernica: The Conquest of Ireland*, ed. A.B. Scott and F.X. Martin, Dublin 1978, 169.

Supreme Pontiff'.[21] If the latter is true, and we know that Alexander III had consistently supported Henry's Irish intervention,[22] then preparations for the transference of Ireland to John may indeed have been underway, as Howden has it, since 1176.

The point is of no great significance other than to alert us to the fact that Henry may have been concerned about the state of Ireland for quite some time before the deliberations at Oxford. During the rebellion of the young King Henry, in 1173–4, Ireland had been in a very disturbed state,[23] but 1176 was also a bad year. When the Dublin garrison marched north to what is now Co. Armagh, they were overtaken by the local forces of Airgialla, and 500 of them were slain in the flight back to Dublin.[24] The Airgialla later joined with the more significant army of Cenél nEógain in mid-Ulster and invaded Meath, destroying Slane Castle, and killing another 500 'foreigners', including its commander Richard Fleming, causing the Anglo-Normans to raze three more of their own castles in Meath 'for fear of Cenél nEógain'.[25] These figures may appear exaggerated, though the same annals report a figure of forty of the foreigners being killed in the same year by the Midlands lord Ua Ciarda, suggesting that the numerical exaggerations involved are not of enormous proportions. The essential point seems to be that the colonists were coming under pressure, enough perhaps to cause Henry to focus his attention on the problem.

More than one contemporary commentator thought that the men left in charge by Henry on his hurried departure from Ireland in 1172 had abused their positions. William of Newburgh, who is always worth heeding, states that 'the military commanders left there by him [Henry] for the government of this subjugated province, desirous either of booty or fame, by degrees extended the boundaries allotted them'.[26] Roger of Howden has a lengthy story, apparently about the king of Thomond, Domnall Ua Briain, whom he calls Monoculus, king of Limerick, claiming erroneously that he was slain, in or before 1177, and that 'one of his issue, a powerful and active man, invaded the kingdom of Limerick, gained possession of it, and ruled it with a strong hand, acknowledging no subjection to the king of England and refusing to obey his officers'. The facts are confused but the explanation offered by Howden is interesting; he claims that the rebel king opposed Henry's officers 'because of their faithless conduct and the evils they had inflicted on the people of Ireland, without them

---

[21] Howden, ii, 100, 133; only the 1177 grant is recorded in *Gesta Regis Henrici*, i, 161–5, though the latter *precedes* its account of Oxford with a reference to John's future coronation in Ireland (at p. 161), again implying that the matter had previously been aired.

[22] J. Watt, *The Church in Medieval Ireland*, Dublin 1972, chap. 2.

[23] See S. Duffy, '1169 as a Turning-Point in Irish–Welsh Relations', in *Britain and Ireland, 900–1300*, ed. B. Smith, Cambridge, forthcoming.

[24] *The Annals of Tigernach*, ed. W. Stokes, 2 vols, Felinfach 1993 (reprinted from *Revue Celtique* 16–18, 1895–7) ii, 440.

[25] *Annals of Tigernach*, ii, 442; *The Annals of Ulster*, ed. W.M. Hennessy and B. MacCarthy, 4 vols, Dublin 1887–1901, ii, 185.

[26] *Newburgh*, i, 238–40.

deserving them'. He adds that as a result 'the king of Cork [Mac Carthaig] and many other wealthy persons rose in rebellion against the king of England and his officers'.[27]

These statements, from reputable English sources, highlighting the early failures of Anglo-Norman government in Ireland and the abuses of the barons and royal officials, have been rather ignored, but if they are indicative of a widespread contemporary awareness of the situation in Ireland, it may help to explain the background to its transference to John. 1177 was meant to mark a new departure. The Irish annals seem to capture the sense of this when they laconically report for this year: 'Three fleets of Saxons arrived in Ireland, that of Hugh de Lacy to Dublin, William fitz Audelin to Wexford, and Philip de Briouze to Waterford.'[28] At the same council at which John had obtained a grant of Ireland, de Lacy, in addition to receiving the custody of Dublin, had been confirmed as lord of all Meath, fitz Audelin was given custody of Wexford, and the lordships of Cork and Limerick were likewise disposed of, the latter eventually (at the later Council of Marlborough) to de Briouze. Howden makes a point of concluding his account of these developments by stating that 'after the king, at Oxford, had divided the lands of Ireland and their services, he made all the persons to whom he had entrusted the custody thereof do homage to himself *and* to his son John, and take oaths of allegiance and fealty to *them* for their lands in Ireland'.[29] John, a nine-year-old child, had come into his inheritance.

Not surprisingly, the evidence for John's personal involvement with his new lordship in these early years is slight to the point of non-existence. When 200 seams of wheat were sent by Henry II into Ireland in 1178–9, it was for the sustenance of *familia sua*; a year later, a similar gift arrived, 'by the king's writ'.[30] Sources emanating from within Ireland as yet make no allusion to John's new status: Hugh de Lacy was described in an annal for 1178 as 'the constable of the king of England in Dublin and in east Meath', while the castle constructed at Leighlin, Co. Carlow in 1180 was said to be the work of 'muintir Rí Saxan' ('the people of the king of England').[31] It was at this point that worries started to mount about de Lacy's ambitions. Gerald of Wales states that he 'was strongly suspected of wanting to throw off his allegiance and usurp the government of the kingdom [of Ireland], and with it the crown and sceptre', as a result of which he was recalled, his place being taken by his namesake John de Lacy, constable of Chester, and Richard de Pec, who were 'sent by the king of the English' to take joint control of the government.[32] Howden states that the two were sent 'to take charge of the city of Dublin, of which Hugh de Lacy had had

[27] *Howden*, ii, 135–6; *Gesta Regis Henrici*, i, 173.

[28] *Annals of Tigernach*, ii, 444.

[29] *Howden*, ii, 134–5; *Gesta Regis Henrici*, i, 162–5 (my italics).

[30] *Cal. Docs Ireland*, i, nos. 53, 58.

[31] *Annals of the Kingdom of Ireland by the Four Masters*, ed. J. O'Donovan, 7 vols, Dublin 1851, iii, 43; *Miscellaneous Irish Annals*, ed. S. Ó hInnse, Dublin 1947, 71.

[32] *Expugnatio Hibernica*, 191, 193–5.

the keeping', adding the often-cited detail that 'our lord *king* was unwilling that he should have charge of it any longer, because he had, without his permission, married the daughter of the king of Connacht, according to the usage of that country'.[33] When Hugh was subsequently restored, Robert of Shrewsbury was sent to Ireland, 'to act on the *king's* behalf in assisting and advising him, and to keep a watch on all his activities'.[34] Clearly, young John might be Ireland's titular lord, but old Henry was still master.

Nevertheless, the worry of de Lacy acquiring de facto lordship in Ireland was very real. An Irish annal for 1184 describes Hugh as 'tigerna Gall Éirenn' ('lord of the foreigners of Ireland').[35] William of Newburgh states that de Lacy 'was esteemed the chief and most powerful' of the English barons in Ireland, who had been conferred with extensive possessions and responsibilities there after the death of Strongbow in 1176, adding:

> But, in a short time this Hugh so extended his boundaries, and prospered, and increased so much in ingratitude of wealth and power, that he now became formidable, not only to his enemies but even to his associates . . . He appeared to seek the kingdom of Ireland for himself rather than the king of England, so much so, indeed, that rumour states that he procured himself a royal diadem.[36]

Removing de Lacy permanently from the scene made little sense as he was by far the most effective bulwark against Irish rebellion, but it was becoming urgent to inject a new focus for the colonists' loyalties, such as John's presence in person would provide. In 1184, therefore, Henry took steps to transfer to John what Gerald calls 'totum Hibernie dominium', adding that it was something which he 'had long had in mind', and that John had 'already received all the homage due from Ireland with his father's full consent'.[37] John Cumin, archbishop of Dublin, was sent to Ireland to prepare the way for John's arrival, Hugh de Lacy was recalled, and, Gerald says, Philip of Worcester was sent to the island as *procurator*. The impression here is of Henry still calling the tune, but the *Annales Cestrienses* are a useful source for Irish affairs in this period, and they say that when Henry gave John what they term 'dominium de Hibernia', it was the latter who 'sent Philip of Worcester with a great multitude into Ireland for the purpose of undertaking its defence'.[38]

Either way, preparations were set in train to pack John off to see for the first time, and to take personal charge of, the lordship over which he had been

---

[33] *Howden*, i, 270 (my italics); for the significance of the marriage, see S. Duffy, 'The Problem of Degeneracy', in *Law and Disorder in Thirteenth Century Ireland*, ed. J.F. Lydon, Dublin 1997, 90.

[34] *Expugnatio Hibernica*, 195 (my italics).

[35] *Miscellaneous Irish Annals*, 73.

[36] *Newburgh*, i, 239–40.

[37] *Expugnatio Hibernica*, 198–9.

[38] *Annales Cestrienses; or the Chronicle of the Abbey of S. Werburg, at Chester*, ed. R.C. Christie, Lancashire and Cheshire Record Society, xiv, 1886, 24–5.

nominal ruler for the previous seven years. He would, in fact, become king of Ireland. This was the view within Ireland itself, where native annalists record for 1185 that 'the son of the king of England came to Ireland with sixty ships to assume its kingship'.[39] It was also the view in England, where Roger of Howden wrote that, at Windsor on the fourth Sunday of Lent, King Henry 'dubbed his son John a knight, and immediately afterwards sent him to Ireland, appointing him king thereof';[40] while the Chester annals likewise record that, from Pembroke in Wales, John 'started for Ireland, in order to be crowned king there'.[41] He did not, however, as yet possess a crown. Howden has the background to this story, which is to the effect that the pope, Lucius III, had 'stoutly refused' various requests from Henry, 'one of which was that such one of his sons as he thought fit should be crowned king of Ireland'; only when Lucius died, late in 1185, to be replaced by Urban III, was Henry's request acceded to by the pope, 'who confirmed it by his bull, and as proof of his assent and confirmation thereof, sent him a crown made of peacocks' feathers, embroidered with gold'.[42] By this point, however, John had returned from Ireland, in ignominy, and the peacock-feathered crown, if it existed, was never worn.

The reasons most probably lie in the events that took place in Ireland in 1185, and its immediate aftermath. Gerald of Wales accompanied John to Ireland, travelling in the same ship, having been, as he puts it, 'specially sent with John by his father'.[43] Henry's insistence on sending Gerald suggests his interest in preserving a record of the proceedings and perhaps, as duly emerged, of the history of the colony to date, and that he expected it to mark a new beginning. Things, of course, did not turn out as planned, but Henry's arrangements cannot be faulted. Gerald says that the expedition was 'one that he had prepared for with such care', but which 'came to nothing and was totally unsuccessful, so that all his careful preparation and expenditure of money was wasted'.[44] Evidently John made a lot of mistakes in Ireland, and, according to Gerald's testimony, though one should stress that on this point we have his word alone for it, the first was made almost the moment John and his entourage disembarked at Waterford:

> As soon as the king's son arrived in Ireland, there came to meet him at Waterford the Irish of those parts, men of some note, who had hitherto been loyal to the English and peacefully disposed. They greeted him as their lord and received him with the kiss of peace.

[39] *Annals of the Four Masters*, iii, 67; *The Annals of Loch Cé*, ed. W.M. Hennessy, 2 vols, RS, 1871, i, 171.
[40] *Gesta Regis Henrici*, i, 336.
[41] *Annales Cestrienses*, 32–3.
[42] *Howden*, ii, 306–7; *Gesta Regis Henrici*, i, 339.
[43] *Expugnatio Hibernica*, 229.
[44] *Expugnatio Hibernica*, 205.

Gerald then describes the famous beard-pulling incident in which members of John's entourage showed discourtesy towards, and made fun of, their Irish guests, and he continues:

> As soon as they regained their freedom, they . . . made for the court of the king of Limerick [Ua Briain]. They gave him, and also the prince of Cork [Mac Carthaig], and Ruaidrí [Ua Conchobair] of Connacht, a full account of all their experiences at the king's son's court. They reported that the son himself was a mere youth, with an entourage composed only of youths, a stripling who listened only to youthful advice. They held out no hope of mature counsels or stable government in that quarter, and no hope of any security for the Irish.
>
> The three main buttresses of Ireland at that time, the princes of Limerick, Connacht, and Cork, had been prepared to come to the king's son and, by declaring their submission to him, to bind themselves to him with the bonds of that obedience which was his due. But when they heard all this, they deduced that these small injustices would be followed by greater ones, and debated among themselves how the English must intend to act against the overweening and rebellious, when men of goodwill, who had kept the peace, received this treatment. So with one accord they plotted to resist, and to guard the privileges of their ancient freedom even at the risk of their own lives. In order that they might be more effective in fulfilling this aim, they made pacts with each other throughout the country, and those who had previously been enemies now became friends for the first time.[45]

This may or may not be true, but it sounds at least plausible. There were certainly many Irish who had previously been loyal to the English, who had accepted Henry II's overlordship and sworn fealty to him, and presumably they intended to do likewise when John arrived. Perhaps John's mistreatment of them pushed them into rejecting him and rebelling against him, though there is likely to have been more to it than that alone.

We have a considerable number of charters from John's visit, drawn up at various stages of his itinerary. Several were issued at Waterford, in the immediate aftermath of his arrival, one of which is a joint grant to Theobald Walter, brother of the archbishop of Canterbury and ancestor of the Irish Butlers, and to Ranulf de Glanville, John's former guardian, the famous justiciar of England, bestowing on them a very substantial grant in what is now north Co. Tipperary and adjacent areas, forming the core of what later became the earldom of Ormond.[46] At Wexford, meanwhile, John granted half a cantred at Kilsheelin, Co. Tipperary, to William de Burgh, brother of Hubert, another subsequent English justiciar, and, to his chamberlain Alard fitz William he made a further grant of land near Waterford, but including, in addition to other estates elsewhere, 'terram que fuit Vecranethan et que fuit

---

[45] *Expugnatio Hibernica*, 237–9.
[46] *Calendar of Ormond Deeds*, ed. E. Curtis, 6 vols, Dublin 1932–43, ii, no. 426.

Ubrenan', near Wexford.[47] This latter component, in other words, is specifi-
cally stated to be made up of the patrimonies of two local Irish lords, whose
dispossession presumably followed. In addition to these grants, we know that
John built several castles in the area: one at Lismore, Co. Waterford, one at
Ardfinnan, in the barony of Iffa and Offa in Co. Tipperary, and one at
Tibberaghny, in the barony of Iverk, Co. Kilkenny.[48] From what we can tell,
the Irish or some of the Irish in these areas had previously acquiesced in the
Anglo-Norman settlement. But evidently, now, there was going to be no place
for them. Perhaps this lies behind another of the criticisms that Gerald makes
of John's expedition:

> Another additional reason [for its failure] is that we went back on our
> promises and bestowed on our new arrivals lands belonging to our supporters
> among the Irish, who had stood by us right from the arrival of [Robert] fitz
> Stephen and the earl [Strongbow] in Ireland. They immediately went over to
> our enemies, and, changing their role, spied against us and guided the enemy
> to us, being in a much better position to harm us because they had previously
> been on much closer terms with us.[49]

Gerald's account needs to be taken with a large pinch of salt because he clearly
did not hold John in high regard, or, at least, disapproved of the company he
kept. Gerald was a brother of Robert de Barri, the first of that family to settle in
Ireland, and he was a nephew of Robert fitz Stephen, again another of the early
leaders of the invasion. He was also closely related to the Geraldines. These
people, having paved the way for the establishment of the colony, evidently
resented John's intrusion of newcomers in 1185. Yet Gerald's account cannot
be dismissed entirely, and surely some credence can be given to his statement
near the end of the *Expugnatio Hibernica* to the effect that

> I have thought it useful to explain briefly how and why this first enterprise by
> the king's son did not come up to his expectations, and why an undertaking
> on such a large scale did not meet with the success it might reasonably have
> expected, [so that it] may serve as a warning for the future, although it cannot
> put right what has happened in the past.[50]

What Gerald is suggesting is that the Lord John made some serious errors of
judgement in the early days after his arrival in Ireland, and provoked opposition
even from unlikely quarters. For instance, Domnall Mór Ua Briain, the king of
Thomond, had been among the first to submit to Henry II when he arrived at
Waterford in 1171. Yet in 1185, almost certainly because of these speculative

---

[47] For the latter, see *Calendar of Ormond Deeds*, i, no. 7. I am very grateful to Dr Nicholas
Vincent, Director of the Angevin Acta Project, for his generosity in making available to
me the text of the former and of John's other early charters.
[48] *Expugnatio Hibernica*, 235.
[49] *Expugnatio Hibernica*, 239.
[50] *Expugnatio Hibernica*, 235.

grants which John proceeded to make of lands on the borders of his kingdom, Ua Briain refused to cooperate. The annals and Gerald report that twice he defeated the garrison in the new castle at Ardfinnan (killing a total of 23 knights), and that he attacked Tibberaghny Castle, this time without victory though. As for Mac Carthaig of Desmond, King Diarmait was treacherously killed during the 1185 campaign while parleying with the men of Theobald Walter at Cork.[51] Meanwhile, in spite of John's presence in the country, there was extensive warfare in Meath, which had been invaded, if unsuccessfully so, by the northern army of Cenél nEógain.[52] 1185, therefore, saw difficult days, and his campaign was anything but trouble-free for John. Far from being a triumphal procession through his new lordship, it became in the end a real embarrassment. And we do not have to rely on the begrudging Gerald of Wales or the bias of Irish annals for this. Roger of Howden observes that John behaved selfishly while he was in Ireland, and would not pay his troops their wages, leading to large-scale desertion on their part. More importantly, he adds that John 'lost most of his army in numerous conflicts with the Irish'. In the end, he says, after a stay of less than eight months, John was compelled to return to England penniless.[53]

If, as few would dispute, John's 1185 expedition was a military failure, it was disastrous too in a political sense. Lewis Warren says of the alliance he suspected was forged between John and the Anglo-Irish barons after 1212 that 'John's volte face over the royal policy towards Ireland and the settlers there marked the demise of any hope of the creation of a kingdom of Ireland in which Irish and Normans were equal partners.'[54] Yet, if there ever was a volte face, if there ever was a moment when the prospect of the native Irish and the settlers being 'equal partners' was abandoned, it came at least twenty-seven years earlier: the policy which we see in action in Ireland in 1185, involving territorial expansion, dispossession of Irish lords, new castle-construction, and a further wave of colonisation, left no room for an equal partnership with the Irish. John, in this, his first direct intervention in Irish affairs, showed no desire to act as an impartial lord of both native and newcomer; he was clearly an advocate of the latter's interests. On the other hand, if it is the case that he did somehow clumsily seek the loyalty and coop-eration of the Irish, evidently he had no comprehension of how that could best be obtained. He could not or would not envisage a form of government for Ireland which did not involve the alienation of the native lords. For the rest of the Middle Ages, the bulk of the Irish remained beyond the law, denied access to justice or participation in government, and this policy began with John's lordship, in 1185, if not indeed as early as the fateful decisions made at the Council of Oxford in 1177.

[51] *Expugnatio Hibernica*, 235; *Annals of Loch Cé*, i, 171.
[52] *Expugnatio Hibernica*, 235.
[53] *Gesta Regis Henrici*, i, 339.
[54] Warren, 'The Historian as "Private Eye" ', 18.

How did John get it so wrong? Apart from being ill-behaved and ill-advised, John's honeymoon was undoubtedly spoiled by Hugh de Lacy. As constable of Dublin, de Lacy controlled the colony's capital,[55] and, since Strongbow's death, in the absence of a resident lord of Leinster, Hugh's own lordship of Meath was fuelling most of the colonial expansion. At his death in 1186 an Irish annalist described him as 'king of Meath and Bréifne and Airgialla', an area that would have stretched from north Co. Dublin to south Armagh, and from the east coast to the river Shannon; indeed the same writer adds that, at Hugh's death, 'Meath from the Shannon to the sea was full of castles and foreigners.' He also notes that 'it was to him that the tribute of Connacht was paid, and it was he who won all Ireland for the foreigners'.[56] An Anglo-Irish annal, in recording his death, simply states: 'ibi cessavit conquestus'.[57] Whatever threat de Lacy posed to royal prestige abroad was, therefore, more than compensated for by his capacity to ensure continued English rule in Ireland. One suspects John came to realise this during his expedition. John was perhaps at Dublin when trophies in the form of one hundred severed heads arrived, including that of the king of Cenél nEógain and many of his invading army, having been defeated in Meath by one of de Lacy's lieutenants, William le Petit.[58] There was no 'showdown' between both men. Indeed, de Lacy accompanied John on at least part of his itinerary, witnessing several charters, including one issued at the newly constructed castle at Ardfinnan, Co. Tipperary, another at Kildare, and a third at Dublin, usually topping the list of witnesses, and usually bearing the title *constabularius*.[59] It may or may not be significant, however, that Hugh only appears in the testing clause of grants and confirmations to the church and a confirmation of Henry II's first Dublin charter; that he did not act as witness to any of John's major new Irish land-grants is possibly a sign of his opposition to the development.

De Lacy certainly seemed to make little effort to hide his position of power. The Irish annals record that after John had taken control of Leinster and Dublin, and attacked Munster (without success, they say) from his new castles, he 'returned to his father complaining of Hugh de Lacy, who controlled Ireland for the king of England before his arrival, and did not allow the Irish kings to send him tribute or hostages'.[60] There is presumably some truth to this, because, according to William of Newburgh, the announcement of de Lacy's death at the hands of an Irish axe-man some months later was 'very agreeable news' to Henry.[61] De Lacy's removal either cleared any obstacles in the way of John's

---

[55] For its importance, see S. Duffy, 'Ireland's Hastings: the Anglo-Norman Conquest of Dublin, *Anglo-Norman Studies* 20, 1998, 69–85.

[56] *Annals of Loch Cé*, i, 173.

[57] *Chartularies of St Mary's Abbey, Dublin*, ed. J.T. Gilbert, 2 vols, RS, 1885–86, ii, 305.

[58] *Expugnatio Hibernica*, 235.

[59] See, for instance, *Historic and Municipal Documents of Ireland*, ed. J.T. Gilbert, RS, 1870, 49; *Crede Mihi: the Most Ancient Register Book of the Archbishops of Dublin*, ed. *idem*, Dublin 1897, 31–2.

[60] *Annals of the Four Masters*, iii, 68–9; *Annals of Loch Cé*, i, 171.

[61] *Newburgh*, i, 237.

return to Ireland, and his coronation, or, most probably, the instability it was likely to generate necessitated it. 'When King Henry heard of it', say the Chester annals, 'he prepared to send his son John once more into Ireland.'[62] He also seems to have been in contact again with the papacy on the subject of John's coronation, and Howden tells us that after Christmas 1186, Cardinal Octavian arrived at Henry's court, in the company of Hugh de Nunant, whom Pope Urban had appointed legate to Ireland, 'for the purpose of there crowning John, the king's son'.[63] In the meantime, however, Henry's plans had changed. The Chester annals assert that John came all the way to Chester and was awaiting a favourable wind for the voyage to Ireland, when news arrived of the death of his brother Geoffrey, count of Brittany, whereupon Henry 'caused his son John to be recalled, and sent Philip of Worcester with some others into Ireland'. By the time, therefore, that the papal legate arrived to crown young John in Ireland, it was too late; instead, as Howden puts it, 'the king put off that coronation' and brought the legates to the continent with him to deal with the more pressing matters now needing his attention there.

Ireland was now therefore a kingdom (as contemporary accounts, official and otherwise, continued to call it) without a king, while its would-be king held lordship over it, apparently confirmed by the papacy, but, as long as his father lived, used the style *filius Domini Regis*, even in charters specifically to do with Irish affairs, before that of *Dominus Hibernie*, which is by no means always employed. In fact the limitations on John's authority, after his return from Ireland and prior to his father's death, are apparent from his grant to Theobald Walter of the strategic castle and vill of Arklow, Co. Wicklow, the charter for which states that the grant was made 'by assent of my father'.[64] This undated charter was issued at Winchester, with an impressive list of witnesses that included Ranulf de Glanville and Hubert Walter, and it may just be relevant that at least two other charters drawn up at the same location, and probably at the same time, but dealing with minor ecclesiastical rights and possessions in Ireland, have rather inferior witness-lists and, significantly perhaps, do not contain the 'by assent of my father' formula.[65] One is tempted to conclude that after 1185 John's actions were subjected to serious scrutiny by King Henry, and his freedom of action with regard to Ireland rather heavily circumscribed.

That situation changed with his father's death. At Chinon in Touraine, where Henry died in July 1189, John granted Hubert Walter what he calls 'all *my* vill of Lusk', in north Co. Dublin.[66] Among the witnesses to this grant were Bertram de Verdon and Gilbert Pipard, and in 1189 or 1190, shortly after the

---

[62] *Annales Cestrienses*, 34–5; see also, *Gesta Regis Henrici*, i, 350.

[63] *Howden*, i, 317; *Gesta Regis Henrici*, ii, 3–4.

[64] *Calendar of Ormond Deeds*, i, no. 17.

[65] *The Irish Cartularies of Llanthony Prima & Secunda*, ed. E. St J. Brooks, Dublin 1953, nos. 60, 61.

[66] *Calendar of Ormond Deeds*, i, no. 863 (my italics).

new king, his brother Richard, had given John the county of Mortain, both were the recipients of very substantial estates carved out of the kingdoms of Airgialla and Airthir, covering much of Co. Louth (though John kept part of this for himself), and, more speculatively, south-east Co. Monaghan and south Co. Armagh.[67] In 1192 he granted Henry Tyrel a carucate of land in Meath and the sergeancy of Co. Dublin.[68] By this time he had appointed as co-justiciars William le Petit and Peter Pipard, and in January 1193 the latter received a large grant, consisting of three cantreds of land in the south Ulster marches.[69] That same August, Theobald Walter, now butler of Ireland, was given the manor of Tullow in Ossory, and the Steine, an area in the eastern suburb of Dublin where the priory of All Hallows was located.[70] And at some point in the following year he made his most sweeping grant yet when he gave away all of Connacht to William de Burgh.[71] Though *ex silencio* speculations are dangerous, these land-grants do appear to point to a more interventionist approach by John in Irish affairs following the death of Henry II.

It is noteworthy that two of the three Irish castles built by John in 1185, Lismore and Tibberaghny, were attacked and razed by the Irish in 1189,[72] and, while one hesitates to suggest that this may indicate an Irish revolt following news of Henry's death in July, one can well understand how that event would necessitate a reassertion of English lordship. There is a record preserved by Matthew Paris to the effect that when William Longchamp, bishop of Ely, was appointed papal legate in 1190, his area of jurisdiction included England, Wales, and 'those parts of Ireland in which the noble man John, count of Mortain, brother of that king [Richard], has power and lordship'.[73] There may, of course, be no grounds to the statement but it does show the contemporary or near-contemporary doubts that hung over John's claim to be *Dominus Hibernie*, a title he employed consistently from 1189, though, interestingly, almost always, even in Irish charters, preceded by what was obviously considered the more prestigious *Comes Moretain*.

With this new assertion of lordship went the land-grants just mentioned, and what seems to have been, to judge from the amount of comment on the subject in contemporary accounts, a major new phase of castle-construction. The Annals of Inisfallen report for 1192 that 'many castles were built this year against the men of Munster'.[74] Another set of annals specifies two castles – Kilfeacle and Knockgraffon, Co. Tipperary – as having been built by the English of Leinster in this year during a campaign against Domnall Ua Briain of

[67] A.J. Otway-Ruthven, 'The Partition of the de Verdon Lands in Ireland in 1332', *Proceedings of the Royal Irish Academy* 66, C, 1968, 401–55.

[68] *Calendar of Patent Rolls, 1334–8*, 415.

[69] *Calendar of Ormond Deeds*, i, nos. 12, 863.

[70] *The Red Book of Ormond*, ed. N.B. White, Dublin 1932, no. 2.

[71] *Cal. Documents Ireland*, i, no. 653.

[72] *The Annals of Inisfallen*, ed. S. Mac Airt, Dublin 1951, 315.

[73] *Chronica Majora*, ii, 358.

[74] *Annals of Inisfallen*, 317.

Thomond.[75] In the same year, but as part of a different westward push, castles were built at Ardnurcher and Kilbixy, Co. Westmeath,[76] while a year later, in 1193, we hear of the construction of castles at Bruis, Co. Tipperary, and at Donaghmoyne, Co. Monaghan.[77] The Irish, needless to say, were conscious of the threat that this new expansionary wave represented, and knew that the key to its containment lay with the castles. Hence the compliment paid to the king of Cenél nEógain, Muirchertach Mac Lochlainn, at his death in 1196: he was described pithily as 'destroyer of the foreigners and of castles'.[78] This opposition to the castle-building programme had led to an inter-provincial alliance in the previous year which the Annals of Inisfallen describe in these remarkable terms: 'Cathal Crobderg Ua Conchobair, king of Connacht, came to Munster and demolished many castles, but they were rebuilt; everyone expected that he would destroy all the foreigners on that expedition, and he arranged to come back, but he did not come.'[79]

Another account of this campaign casts it in an entirely different light: according to this source, Cathal Crobderg's army marched into Munster as far as Emly and Cashel, Co. Tipperary, and burned 'four large castles and some small ones', but, curiously, he had in his company one of the leading de Lacy tenants in Ireland, Gilbert de Angulo, 'with some of the English and Irish of Meath'.[80] In other words, the Irish were facilitated in their opposition to this new expansionary phase by elements within the colony itself, or, more likely perhaps, the latter were manipulating the Irish for their own purposes, using them to gain advances at the expense of their rivals for power within the lordship. Though the course of these internal conflicts in the 1190s and later is confused, and the alliances themselves sometimes of a transient nature, they do herald the emergence within Ireland, under John's stewardship, of unchecked – indeed, one suspects on occasions, deliberately promoted – baronial rivalries, the worst excesses of which could verge on civil war.

These dissensions were partly the product of John's rebellion against Richard in 1193–4, mirroring, therefore, divisions further afield, but they were partly also power-blocs and factions peculiar to the Irish situation where the *casus belli* was nothing more noble than lust for land. Old enmities die hard and it is no great surprise to find that one of the two leaders of another army that marched in 1195 'to conquer the English of Leinster and Munster' was a son of the late Hugh de Lacy, probably Walter.[81] The other leader was the conqueror of Ulster, John de Courcy, whom the Lord John had removed as justiciar in the early 1190s, and was perhaps therefore a Richard loyalist. John interpreted the actions of de Lacy and de Courcy at this point as being hostile to him – one of

---

[75] *Annals of the Four Masters*, iii, 95.
[76] *Annals of Loch Cé*, i, 187.
[77] *Annals of Inisfallen*, 319; *Annals of Loch Cé*, i, 187.
[78] *Annals of Ulster*, ii, 223.
[79] *Annals of Inisfallen*, 321.
[80] *Annals of the Four Masters*, iii, 101.
[81] *Annals of the Four Masters*, iii, 101; *Annals of Ulster*, ii, 223.

his first instructions to the Irish justiciar, Meiler fitz Henry, upon ascending the throne in 1199, was to enquire whether Henry Tyrel had 'sided with John de Courcy and W. de Lacy and aided them in destroying the king's [John's] land of Ireland'[82] – but the targets of their assaults were really henchmen of John whose successes at land-grabbing in the south-west of Ireland were beginning to challenge the older ascendancy. Their 'loyalty' to the king may therefore have simply been opposition to John's favourites. Nevertheless, although we have barely any evidence of intrusion by Richard I into Irish affairs, one of the few instances, after his return to England and John's restoration to favour, is his intervention on behalf of Walter de Lacy. When, in June 1195, John gave to Walter and his heirs all the land of Meath as it had been held by his father Hugh at his death, his charter was effectively a confirmation of a similar charter issued by King Richard at the same time.[83] Likewise, whereas John had earlier tried to prevent Strongbow's son-in-law, William Marshal, from gaining possession of his lordship of Leinster, it seems to have been at about this point that Richard intervened to secure it for him.[84]

It may thus be the case that, just as in the aftermath of his 1185 expedition, John's freedom of action in regard to his lordship of Ireland was apparently restricted by Henry II, so in the mid-1190s a similar threat loomed. After his surrender to Richard, John ceases to make new grants of land in Ireland to lay tenants (other than displays of favour to the de Lacys forced on him by the king), and confines himself to confirmatory grants to the church. We may have one other example of Richard's circumscription of John's authority in this period. During his rebellion John introduced a newcomer to the Irish scene, Hamo de Valognes, who was granted, in the summer of 1193, custody of Waterford, 'to sustain him in my service',[85] then somewhat later obtained a grant of the territory of Uí Chonaill Gabra, now the baronies of Upper and Lower Connello, Co. Limerick,[86] and who acted as justiciar from 1196 to 1198/9. Roger of Howden preserves for 1197 a story to the effect that de Valognes 'and other guardians of Ireland, liegemen of Count John, brother of Richard, king of England, did great injustices to John Cumin, the archbishop of Dublin', who, 'preferring to go into exile than have these enormities against him and his church go unpunished any longer', excommunicated de Valognes and others, we are told, and pronounced a sentence of interdict upon his archdicese; but 'the rest of the bishops of Ireland ignored the losses and injuries that the above servants of Count John had done to their brother bishop'. Archbishop Cumin then 'went into England to Richard and John', says Howden, 'but found no redress'.[87] If Howden is to believed, the archbishop here appealed over

---

[82] *Cal. Docs Ireland*, i, no. 90.
[83] *Calendar of the Gormanston Register*, ed. J. Mills and M.J. McEnery, Dublin 1916, 177–8.
[84] *Hist. Guillaume le Maréchal*, lines 9,581–9,618.
[85] *Facsimiles of Royal and other Charters*, i, no. 74 (plate 48).
[86] *Cal. Docs Ireland*, i, no. 92.
[87] *Howden*, iv, 29–30.

John's head to the king, and, as ever, Howden is not far off the mark, though his concluding statement is in fact inaccurate. Shortly afterwards, Hamo de Valognes granted Archbishop Cumin twenty carucates of land in Uí Máil (Imaal, Co. Wicklow), 'for the injuries and wrongs done to the church of Dublin by him and his when he was the justiciar of Ireland'.[88] One of the witnesses to this grant was Hugh, bishop of Lincoln, who died in November 1200, and as John himself issued several undated charters to the archbishop while count of Mortain, which may have been part of the same conciliatory exercise, it may reasonably be inferred that Richard did seek to address the archbishop's concerns.

If there was a new restraining influence on John's actions, it was removed when Richard I died in April 1199 and the lord of Ireland had himself crowned king of England. It is difficult to resist the conclusion that the freedom of manoeuvre which John now possessed resulted in a similar splurge of land-grants, castle-construction, and colonisation to that which followed the death of his father a decade earlier. On a single day, 6 September 1199, Hamo de Valognes was confirmed in his lands in Connello, William de Burgh received Ardpatrick, Co. Limerick; Thomas fitz Maurice, ancestor of the earls of Desmond, was granted lands in Uí hAinmire, north of Limerick city, and 'Eleur' in the cantred of Fontymkill, apparently near Kilfinnane, Co. Limerick; Thomas's brother William, baron of Naas, received the manor of Carrickittle in the cantred of Grean, Co. Limerick; and other grants in the same area went to Lambkin fitz William and Robert Sergeant.[89] A week later, the vill of Athlongford on the river Suir was given to Elias fitz Norman, Humphrey de Tickhill received Kildruma, and Milo le Bret got lands in the same area.[90] In mid-October further estates in Co. Limerick came the way of Geoffrey fitz Robert and John's long-standing servant, John de Gray.[91] Meanwhile, two sets of Irish annals report in the same year the construction of castles at Askeaton, Co. Limerick, and Granard, Co. Longford,[92] while, in the following summer, Tipperaghny Castle was given over to the ambitious William de Burgh, and, as regards the exploitation of these new estates, Hamo de Valognes was given licence 'to lead his men to colonise his land ['ad terram suam hospitandam']'.[93]

John, as king, was therefore authorising a vigorous programme of westward expansion in Ireland that, it goes virtually without saying, had little or no regard for the sensitivities of the indigenous rulers. For instance, when he next turned his attention to his lordship, at the end of October 1200, John granted to Meiler fitz Henry three cantreds in Co. Kerry, one of which, the land of Eóganacht Locha Léin in the Killarney area, is specifically stated to have belonged to the

---

[88] *Calendar of Archbishop Alen's Register, c. 1172–1534*, ed. C. McNeill, Dublin 1950, 27.

[89] *Rot. Chart.*, 19b; see also C.A. Empey, 'The Settlement of the Kingdom of Limerick', in *England and Ireland in the Later Middle Ages*, ed. Lydon, 1–25.

[90] *Rot. Chart.*, 20b.

[91] *Rot. Chart.*, 28.

[92] *Annals of Inisfallen*, 325; *Annals of Loch Cé*, i, 207.

[93] *Cal. Docs Ireland*, i, nos. 120, 122.

Irish lord Ua Muirchertaig.[94] No mention is made of what was to become of the latter: John's need to reward his justiciar for services rendered patently out-weighed any responsibility he felt to attend to the welfare of his Irish subjects. On this matter there are two assumptions which it seems reasonable to make. One is that King John cared little for the concerns of the Irish, which need hardly surprise us. The other is that, even had he given thought to the matter, his primary concern had to be the retention of control over Irish affairs. His problem in this respect was that serious internal frictions now existed within the colonial community there, and, for a king whose vantage-point was inevitably going to be somewhat distant, staying in command of the situation would be no mean feat. He would need good deputies, he would need to reward loyalty, and he would need to be on his guard against individuals or coalitions whose ambitions posed a challenge to his authority. These considerations seem to have dictated John's relations with Ireland for the rest of his life. Combined with the fact that suspicion was second nature to him, and that he delighted in applying the principle of 'divide and rule', they help to explain some of the many apparent contradictions in his actions in the years that followed.

John inherited in Ireland, if he did not create, an unruly frontier society, and for the early years of his reign evidence of the lengths to which he may have gone to ameliorate the situation is slight. In October 1200 he instructed that no recognisance be made or no outlawry proclaimed, 'save in or by the king's court', and on the same day ordered all those holding lands 'in the marches of Ireland' to fortify their castles by a given date, 'otherwise the king will seize their lands'; at about this same time, when a former tenant of the late Hugh de Lacy requested an inquisition to determine whether the latter had unlawfully disseised him of his lands in Meath, John ordered the justiciar to summon twelve men to the next county court of Dublin to pronounce on the matter, 'if the state of the land of Ireland permit this to be done without damage'.[95] These appear to be the actions of a man anxious for the security of his lordship, but one wonders whether the concerns at work in these instances were to protect the colony from Irish rebellion or from internal lawlessness and dissension.

The early aftermath of his accession saw a period of intense and, it must be said, confusing, jostling for power among the resident barons, when some-thing of the fever of a gold-rush took hold at the prospect of territorial expan-sion across the Shannon into Connacht.[96] This led to warfare between rival groups of barons, each sponsoring rival Ua Conchobair claimants to its kingship, or what was left of it. While William de Burgh sought to implement his earlier grant of the province by lending aid to one side, John de Courcy of Ulster joined forces with the de Lacy brothers, Walter and the younger Hugh,

---

[94] *Cal. Docs Ireland*, i, no. 124.

[95] *Cal. Docs Ireland*, i, nos. 125, 126, 164.

[96] The subject is expertly examined in Helen Perros [Walton], 'Crossing the Shannon Frontier: Connacht and the Anglo-Normans, 1170–1224', in *Colony and Frontier in Medieval Ireland*, ed. T.B. Barry, R. Frame, K. Simms, London 1995, 117–38.

in supporting the claims of another. The justiciar, Meiler fitz Henry, was inclined to take the latters' side in the affair and led the English of Leinster to war in Connacht in 1200.[97] But King John's response was to inject a further complicating element into the equation by the revival, in the early weeks of 1201, of the de Briouze interest in the lordship of Limerick, in the form of William, nephew of Philip de Briouze.[98] The latter was presumably expected to be the strong man who could intervene to keep de Burgh's ambitions in check, but it led only to another bout of hostility, as Philip of Worcester had an interest in these lands: the Irish annals report a war between de Worcester and de Briouze in 1201,[99] while Roger of Howden reports how Philip, 'escaping with difficulty from the hands of the king, returned to Ireland by passing through the territories of the king of Scots, and recovered part of his lands by waging war'.[100]

The civil wars of 1200–1 persisted throughout the first decade of John's reign, when the Irish headlines, as it were, were dominated by these men – Meiler fitz Henry, William de Briouze, William de Burgh, Philip of Worcester, Theobald Walter, Geoffrey de Marisco, John de Courcy, Walter and Hugh de Lacy. Not all of them survived the period, and the most prominent of all, William Marshal, only finally arrived to take charge of his lordship of Leinster early in 1207. But throughout it all each was engaged in a potentially deadly game of snakes-and-ladders with the king, the rules of which may have been known to them, though to us they remain largely a mystery. There seems little doubt that against some of them at least the dice were heavily loaded, and the stakes were raised by John's insistence on obtaining as hostages, and holding onto, some of their closest relatives and leading tenants. This atmosphere of distrust and insecurity must surely account, to some extent at least, for the tension between these barons, which is writ large on the pages of the historical record for these years, and also for the complex see-saw relationships between them, which resulted, for instance, in young Hugh de Lacy committing treachery on an erstwhile ally, John de Courcy, and saw each rise and fall in royal favour, for reasons of which our only clue lies in the rumours of contemporary chroniclers.

Although, in the early weeks of 1208 John was sufficiently worried about the situation in Ireland, primarily the feuding between the barons and their suspected disloyalty, to make preparations for an Irish expedition, he was in fact eleven years on the throne before he made it to Ireland in person. Once more, however, John's actions during his 1210 campaign suggest a perpetuation of the same contemptuous attitude towards the native kings. The aspect of the expedition which many modern accounts emphasise is that King John, anxious to bring his troublesome barons to book, embarked on an elaborate display of

---

[97] *Annals of the Four Masters*, iii, 125.
[98] *Cal. Docs Ireland*, i, nos. 145–8.
[99] *Annals of Inisfallen*, 329.
[100] *Howden*, iv, 152–3.

generosity to the native Irish kings, and in return found that they were more than willing to accept him as their lord, so that close relations developed between both sides.[101] The essential assumption here is that John's negotiations with the Irish kings in the summer of 1210 were concluded successfully in his favour, and that he left Ireland on good terms with them, but, as I have attempted to prove elsewhere, this is an assumption which cannot be sustained by the evidence.[102]

For instance, the *Histoire des ducs de Normandie* describes, in very colourful detail, how the king of Connacht, Cathal Crobderg Ua Conchobair, submitted to John, joined his host, and marched northwards to Ulster with him to capture Carrickfergus Castle from John's principal baronial opponents in Ireland, the de Lacy and de Briouze factions. It then describes how, while there, John was approached by the most powerful of the northern kings, Áed Méith Ua Néill, and has elaborate discussion of how negotiations proceeded between both sides, as John sought that Ua Néill become his vassal, and pay him an annual tribute for his lands.[103] But the Irish annals are very clear about Ua Néill's reaction when asked to go one step further and hand over hostages:

> Messengers came to him [Ua Néill], to his house, to seek hostages, and he said: 'Depart, O foreigners, I will give you no hostages at all.' The foreigners departed and he gave no hostages to the king.[104]

As regards Cathal Crobderg, the annals report that he withdrew from John's forces at Carrickfergus and returned to Connacht, but promised to rejoin the king in a fortnight, bringing with him his son Áed, his intended heir, whom King John meant to hold as a hostage to ensure Cathal's future good behaviour. However, Cathal was cautioned by his wife and followers not to hand Áed over to the king, and thus when he went to meet King John, two weeks later as arranged, he came without the son. John was angered by this and apprehended four of Cathal's sub-kings and royal officers, whom he brought back to England with him.[105]

At this point, therefore, relations were soured between both sides, and, after John's departure, there was a clear government backlash. The king left instructions that John de Gray of Norwich, the 'foreign bishop', as the annals put it, should erect three castles in Connacht, a major new and threatening enterprise that included the building of a castle at the important ecclesiastical site of Clonmacnoise on the Shannon,[106] and the very strategically placed bridge and

---

101 Painter, *Reign of King John*, 227; Warren, *King John*, 196; A.J. Otway-Ruthven, *A History of Medieval Ireland*, London 1968, 81; Warren, 'The Historian as "Private Eye" ', 17; J. Lydon, *The Lordship of Ireland in the Middle Ages*, Dublin 1972, 65.

102 S. Duffy, 'King John's Expedition to Ireland, 1210'.

103 *Hist. ducs de Normandie*, 112–14.

104 *Annals of Inisfallen*, 339.

105 *Annals of Loch Cé*, i, 243.

106 'The Annals of Multifernan', ed. A. Smith, in *Tracts relating to Ireland*, ii, Irish Archaeological Society, Dublin 1843, 11.

royal fortress, again overlooking the Shannon, at Athlone.[107] Furthermore, the government organised an invasion of Connacht by the colonists of Meath and Leinster, and another invasion from the south, by the forces of Munster and rival members of the Ua Conchobair dynasty. This, therefore, is the price that Cathal Crobderg paid for refusing to hand over his intended heir to King John. He was wise. Later that year, as the pressure mounted, he gave John instead another of his sons, but the latter was never released and died in England some years later.[108] Ua Néill too suffered for his stance. Within a year, an English army came northwards to try to force him into submission, but it was routed by a widespread alliance of northern kings assembled behind Áed Méith's banner. John de Gray himself came north in 1212 and castles were built at Cáel Uisce, near Belleek on the Erne, and at Clones in Co. Monaghan, from which raids were launched into the heart of Ua Néill's territory of Tír nEógain, while at the same time a fleet led by Thomas, brother of Alan of Galloway, evidently hired by King John for the purpose, was attacking Derry to Ua Néill's rear. Yet Áed Méith withstood these challenges, John de Gray was humiliatingly defeated, and little progress was made in undermining northern resistance.[109]

In other words, King John left Ireland at war with perhaps the two most powerful Irish kings, Ua Conchobair and Ua Néill. The view, therefore, that the 1210 expedition was an out-and-out triumph needs to be considerably modified. Some of the principal Anglo-Norman barons who had been causing problems for the king on both sides of the Irish Sea were dealt with effectively, John displaying his customary but unpredictable mixture of lenience and cruelty. Yet the campaigns of the summer of 1210 were intended to do more than call the bluff of William de Briouze or the de Lacys. They were intended to produce a settlement between the king of England and his subject-kings of Ireland. But the negotiations collapsed, and John's elaborate Irish expedition failed to produce such a settlement. It is hardly surprising that it was nearly two hundred years before another royal expedition to Ireland took place – and that, perhaps not coincidentally, was led by another man of whom it is sometimes said that he was one of the worst kings of England but paradoxically the best for Ireland, the unfortunate Richard II.

John might well have come to grips with his Irish problem – he made reference to a future visit to Ireland in a grant to the archbishop of Dublin made in July 1213[110] – if crisis had not struck quite so soon afterwards. Warren was right, I believe, when he said that the barons of Ireland, or at least the great majority of them, remained loyal to John during the emergency, rather as the barons of the Welsh March did. Indeed, there is a strong interconnection between events in Ireland and Wales in these years. It seems likely that it was

---

[107] *Annals of Loch Cé*, i, 245.
[108] Duffy, 'King John's Expedition to Ireland, 1210', 17.
[109] See K. Simms, 'The O'Hanlons, the O'Neills, and the Anglo-Normans in Thirteenth-Century Armagh, '*Seanchas Ardmhacha* 9, 1978–9, 70–94 (at p. 77).
[110] *Cal. Docs Ireland*, i, no. 475.

John's absence in Ireland in the summer of 1210 that triggered a Welsh rising, instigated in part by the very people he went to Ireland to dislodge, de Briouze and de Lacy, though Llywelyn ab Iorwerth of Gwynedd seems to have responded to their urgings.[111] When John returned from Ireland at the end of the summer, Llywelyn's rivals took heart: Rhys Gryg of Deheubarth, for instance, used royal troops to undermine Llywelyn that September.[112] In the following summer, 1211, John undertook two major campaigns to deal with the Welsh problem, and the leading Anglo-Irish barons left Ireland to come to his aid.[113] He planned a similar campaign for 1212, again calling for massive assistance from Ireland,[114] though it had to be cancelled when he heard rumours of the baronial conspiracy. In these new circumstances, all thoughts of subduing Llywelyn were shelved, and, indeed, by the winter of 1214–15 John was busy offering inducements to the Welsh princes in hopes of obtaining their assistance.[115] Likewise with the kings of Ireland: instead of harassing Cathal Crobderg, in August 1214 and again in February 1215, John took him under his protection and ordered that no force of horse or foot was to proceed against him so long as he remained in the king's service, and, at about the same time, the archbishop of Dublin was ordered to buy scarlet cloth to make robes for the Irish kings.[116]

But by this stage the battle-lines had been drawn. By and large the Marcher barons in Wales proved loyal to John, and almost inevitably, therefore, the native Welsh under Llywelyn lined up with the reform party. In Ireland too, the barons remained loyal, and experience would suggest that the native Irish would take advantage of their preoccupation with English affairs to try to stage a recovery.[117] However, the standard works on this period of Irish history make little or no reference to attempts by the Irish to profit from the king's flagging cause. This is partly because one has to look rather carefully to find evidence for it: the Irish annals are meagre at this point and lack detailed accounts of events. But there was certainly something afoot. In May 1214 King John wrote to Henry of London, archbishop of Dublin, requesting a report on the state of Ireland.[118] Had the archbishop's reply survived, it might have made allusion to Áed Ua Néill's defeat of the English in Ulster that year, his destruction of Clones Castle, and his burning of the port of Carlingford, Co. Louth, to the death of Gilbert de Angulo when the Irish attacked Cáel Uisce Castle, and to

[111] *Walter of Coventry*, ii, 202.
[112] J.E. Lloyd, *A History of Wales from the Earliest Times to the Edwardian Conquest*, 2 vols, London 1939, ii, 633.
[113] *Annals of the Four Masters*, iii, 167.
[114] *Rot. Litt. Claus*, i, 131b.
[115] Lloyd, *History of Wales*, ii, 642.
[116] *Cal. Docs Ireland*, i, nos. 509, 530, 531.
[117] See, for example, S. Duffy, '1169 as a Turning-Point in Irish–Welsh Relations'.
[118] *Cal. Docs Ireland*, i, no. 503.

Cormac Ua Maíl Sechnaill's assault on the castle of Kinclare, Co. Westmeath.[119] Cormac attacked castles at Athboy, Co. Meath, and at Birr, Co. Offaly, in the following year, 1215,[120] which may have prompted the instruction, issued by King John to the justiciar in July, to ensure that the barons of Ireland fortified their lands in the marches by Michaelmas.[121] Then, in January 1216, the constable of Carrickfergus Castle was ordered to allow the justiciar to enter it with any force he might wish to place there in order to defend the castle and neighbouring parts; while in June the justiciar was instructed to fortify the castle and take the outer bailey into the king's hand.[122]

These orders indicate considerable anxiety about the state of Ireland, and perhaps it is worth pointing out that, circa February 1216, Innocent III wrote to his legate in Ireland, the archbishop of Dublin, directing him 'to put down conspiracies against the king throughout the kingdom of Ireland'; unfortunately, the full text of the letter does not survive, and neither does that sent by the pope at the same time ordering the punishment of clerics 'who communicate with those excommunicated for insurrection against the king'.[123] John, of course, died in October, but the archbishop received two interesting mandates from the pope soon afterwards. The first, dated 17 January 1217, ordered him 'to take measures to preserve to King Henry the fealty of his subjects in Ireland, and to recall those who have opposed him', adding that the pope has heard that a conflagration of the kind that had gripped England 'has taken hold as far as Ireland'.[124] We gain, perhaps, a clue as to what this may have concerned from the command issued in January 1217 to William Gorm de Lacy, half-brother of Walter and Hugh, ordering him to restore to the justiciar, Geoffrey de Marisco, the castles of Carlingford, Co. Louth, and Dundrum, Co. Down, and 'to satisfy the justiciar for the damage done to the king and the country by his taking of those castles'; clearly William Gorm, if not actually an enemy of the king, was prospering from the civil war across the Irish Sea.[125] More direct evidence concerning the rebellion of a prominent member of the Anglo-Irish baronage comes in June, when the justiciar was ordered to restore to Nicholas de Verdon his castle of Dundalk, Co. Louth, 'whereof he was disseised because he went against King John in the war'.[126]

The second papal mandate, dated 29 April 1217, is of greater interest still. It too is addressed to the archbishop of Dublin and orders him 'to fulfil his office faithfully and prudently in bringing about a peace between the Irish and the

---

[119] *Annals of the Four Masters*, iii, 179, 181; *Annals of Ulster*, ii, 257; *Annals of Loch Cé*, i, 249.

[120] *Annals of Loch Cé*, i, 251.

[121] *Cal. Docs Ireland*, i, no. 574.

[122] *Cal. Docs Ireland*, i, nos. 674, 697.

[123] P.J. Dunning, 'The Letters of Innocent III to Ireland', *Traditio* 18, 1962, 246–7.

[124] *Vetera Monumenta Hibernorum et Scotorum Historiam Illustrantia*, ed. A. Theiner, Rome 1864, 4.

[125] *Cal. Docs Ireland*, i, no. 755.

[126] *Cal. Docs Ireland*, i, no. 790.

king'.[127] As far as the pope was concerned, therefore, the Irish and the new king were at war. Whether this refers to a temporary state of unrest during which the Irish had sought to exploit King John's plight, or to a perception abroad that the two nations in Ireland were condemned to a state of perpetual war, is impossible to determine, and perhaps irrelevant. One this is certain: King Henry III, the new lord of Ireland, had inherited a dubious legacy from his father.

---

[127] *Calendar of Entries in the Papal Registers relating to Great Britain and Ireland: Papal Letters*, ed. W.H. Bliss *et al.*, London 1893–, i, 47.

John King of England and the Kings of Scots

A. A. M. Duncan

In a beguiling piece of social analysis, the Barnwell chronicler contrasted the rebel Guthred of the ancient line of Scottish kings, with 'the more recent kings of Scots [who] profess themselves to be rather Frenchmen both in race and manners, language and culture; and after reducing the Scots to utter servitude, they admit only Frenchmen to their friendship and service'.[1] There is no doubting the migration of Anglo-French families to Scotland from about 1120 and their ousting of all save the native earls from the royal court. G.W.S. Barrow has traced both their roots in France and the origins in England from which they came to Scotland.[2] Frenchmen in race, yes, but not in birth or place of upbringing. And by the last quarter of the twelfth century Anglo-Norman migration was largely internal to Scotland;[3] the younger son in England – and he should surely be called English – who now looked for a fief in new lands was liable to cast his eye westward to Ireland.

By proximity to Cumbria, the descendants of Fergus lord of Galloway preserved a unique closeness to the kings of England. Duncan of Carrick was brought up as a hostage in England under Henry II, and his cousin, Lachlan, who significantly adopted the Roland form of his name, managed to put an acceptable veneer over the reputation of their province for uncivilised behaviour. By marriage Roland inherited the lands of the Scottish de Morevilles and seized the opportunity of King William's homage at Lincoln to John in 1200 to offer 500 marks for succession to various fees lost by the de Morevilles in the young Henry's rebellion.[4] Roland died the following month, leaving two sons. By January 1205 Thomas of Galloway, the younger son, had entered the service of John from whom he borrowed armour, and to whom he sent galleys for the planned French expedition. He certainly accompanied John to Poitou and was rewarded with various lands; by 1207 he was speculating in lands in royal wardship, and went on to serve John and Henry III in Ireland, as both a Scottish

---

[1] *Walter of Coventry*, ii, 206.

[2] G.W.S. Barrow, *The Anglo-Norman Era in Scottish History*, Oxford 1980.

[3] The exception of men coming to the Garioch in the service of Earl David is to be explained by his unique position as earl in England and brother of the king in Scotland. K. Stringer, *Earl David of Huntingdon, 1152–1219*, Edinburgh 1985, chapters 4, 8.

[4] *PR 3 John*, 182; *Cal. Docs Scot.* i, no. 294.

earl (Atholl) and a mercenary captain.[5] His older brother Alan played a small part in events in 1212, but the Alan fitz Roland who was with John at Dublin in 1210 was a Berkshire and Oxfordshire tenant, not the lord of Galloway.[6] Alan of Galloway, despite the approaches of John for mercenaries, remained faithful to the Scottish king throughout his life.

The argument for a reception of French culture in Scotland is slight. The cult of knighthood certainly pervaded aristocratic society, but the castles which symbolised knightly (or even kingly) standing were rarely if ever in stone; there is no Dover or Norwich, Gisors, Les Andelys or Falaise in Scotland. Our sole Scottish–French romance, the *roman de Fergus*, has a hero who swears by St Mungo, and the author, William the clerk, was well familiar with Scotland's geography. But the text is in Picard French, and its two manuscripts are of French provenance.[7] This is slender evidence for Scottish readers of French *romans* or for the speaking of Anglo-Norman in cloister or castle north of the Tweed.

'They admit only Frenchmen to their friendship and service.' The English example was particularly influential in royal service in late twelfth-century Scotland. An exchequer audit was instituted, perhaps in the 1180s, when a survey of royal rents was made.[8] Chancery, which in the 1170s had added *Dei gratia* to the royal style, in 1195 adopted a recent English royal practice of giving the month date in royal charters; the oath for the keeping of the peace introduced by Hubert Walter in 1195 was adapted and extended for Scotland in 1197.[9] The conduit here was a steady trickle of foreign, especially English, clerics into King William's service, including two who were for a time royal chancellor.[10] Between 1178 and 1186 King William had anticipated at St Andrews what King John was to do at Canterbury, had been excommunicated and threatened with interdict for intruding a royal clerk and exiling the canonically elect bishop – a fierce dispute which weakened his hold on the Scottish church not a whit. In exercising that control he favoured his own clerks without regard to their land of origin.

The two wealthiest Scottish sees show how that produced a cosmopolitan

---

5 *Cal. Docs Scot.* i, nos 357–62. On Thomas, see *The Scots Peerage*, i, Edinburgh 1904, 419–22.
6 *PR 13 John*, 11, 62, 201. He died in 1210 or 1211.
7 Guillaume le Clerc, *The Romance of Fergus*, ed. W. Frescoln, Philadelphia 1983. At pp. 12, 28, he reports a study of the language by Alois Stefan in 1893: 'the dialect of the author is predominantly Picard, although it contains some traits of the dialect of the Île-de-France and characteristics of the Champenois and Burgundian dialects'. For the MSS *ibid.* 2–6, and at p. 7 an account of the Dutch translation known in a single MS. For the authorship see Guillaume le Clerc, *Fergus of Galloway: Knight of King Arthur*, translated by D.D.R. Owen, London 1991, xiii, 162–9.
8 *Acts of the Parliaments of Scotland*, i, 118.
9 Duncan, *Scotland, Making of Kingdom*, 211, 201–2, 207; and see my paper on 'Roger Howden and Scotland, 1187–1201', in *Church, Chronicle and Learning . . .* ed. B. Crawford, Edinburgh forthcoming.
10 *RRS*, ii, 29–31.

episcopate. Roger, son of the earl of Leicester, who took service with William in the 1180s, was briefly chancellor about 1188, promoted to the see of St Andrews in 1189, but waited nine years before his consecration in 1198.[11] Roger had brought after him John of Leicester, presumably a relative, who climbed the ecclesiastical ladder at St Andrews to win the see of Dunkeld in 1212.[12] With Roger probably came William Malveisin who also took service with the king and in 1199 was appointed first as chancellor then as bishop of Glasgow. His origins are uncertain, but perhaps French rather than English,[13] for he has been suggested as the most likely William the clerk to have written the *roman de Fergus*. He was translated from Glasgow to St Andrews in 1202, and Glasgow was given to the king's nephew, Florence of Holland, nominally chancellor for a time, who resigned, still unconsecrated, in 1207 and was succeeded by Walter of St Albans, a chancery clerk with a Glasgow prebend, who was said to have paid the queen and the chamberlain for his nomination.[14] Bishops Roger and William Malveisin will appear again as royal envoys.

The family of Roland of Galloway apart, King John had little contact with earls and barons of Scotland, and this paper is perforce largely about the elderly king of Scots, who, as William de Warenne, had become earl of Northumberland forty-seven years before John became king, and who held that earldom for five years before being stripped of it so that his brother, King Malcolm, might enjoy the earldom of Huntingdon. Their claims, the first theme in the counterpoint of Anglo-Scottish relations, were derived from Matilda daughter of Earl Waltheof who had at different times held Northumbria and the midland earldom. Matilda had married Simon de Senlis and if earldoms had descended by male primogeniture her heir was a de Senlis, even while her second husband David I extorted Northumberland from King Stephen for their son Earl Henry, and after his death for Earl Henry's son, William. A title derived from Stephen had no validity in the court of Henry II, and the return of the northern counties in 1157 was part of the general settlement after the anarchy, a return to the heritage of Henry I's reign without the conquests of Stephen's; Malcolm IV was treated according to a consistent principle. To William, however, his inheritance and seisin of the earldom gave him an indefeasible claim, and however compensated by Huntingdon, to which he succeeded with the Scottish kingdom in 1165, he could not let that claim rest.

---

[11] For an account of Bishop Roger, *Series Episcoporum Ecclesiae Catholicae Occidentalis, Series VI (Britannia)*, tom. i, Ecclesia Scoticana, curavit D.E.R. Watt, Stuttgart 1991, 89–91; J. Dowden, *The Bishops of Scotland*, Glasgow 1912, 10–12; *Charters of the Abbey of Coupar Angus*, ed. D.E. Easson, Edinburgh 1947, i, no. XI. Roger was the uncle, not the brother, of Robert earl of Leicester, and his non-clerical status may have been preserved lest the earldom should fall to him.

[12] D.E.R. Watt, *Biographical Dictionary of Scottish Graduates to AD 1410*, Oxford 1977, 336–7.

[13] Watt, *Biog. Dict. of Sc. Graduates*, 374–9.

[14] A. Theiner, *Vetera Monumenta Hibernorum et Scotorum Historiam Illustrantia*, Rome 1864, 13.

Although David I would doubtless have annexed the three northern shires to Scotland if he could have got away with it, his successors, who are persistently presented as seeking this end, never articulated any such claim. In the year before John's birth William drove Henry II into a fury by his importuning for the earldom,[15] and in 1173, despite a party of magnates who argued against, William listened to the young men and engaged with the young Henry against the old king because he promised it.[16] The disastrous outcome, whereby he lost Huntingdon and became a liegeman-king with English garrisons in four, three and eventually two of his Scottish castles, warned William against engaging again in such a trial of strength and initiated a period of remarkable collaboration with English kings and receptivity to English clerks. But it may have been an even stronger lesson to those Scottish magnates, young and old, who had to swear fealty to Henry II at York in 1175. For England, overlordship arose in defence against an unjust war for the earldom, and as a means of ensuring that the Scottish king and kingdom did not adhere to an enemy of Henry II; it did not arise from English pursuit of ancient precedents.

There was no interference in Scotland by Henry II who gradually settled issues in William's favour. His wish to marry a daughter of Henry the Lion was stymied by Rome,[17] but Henry II found him another wife, Ermengarde de Beaumont; the earldom of Huntingdon was restored to be held of William by his brother David;[18] one by one the castles were returned and at Canterbury in 1189 the submission of 1174 was cancelled, restoring the position of William to that of Malcolm IV,[19] a phrase of deliberate ambiguity since William had held Northumberland in the early part of Malcolm's reign, but had lost it in the later part. Because of Richard's absence it took another four years before the touchy claims of the Scottish king to conduct (sustenance and escort) on his visits to the English court were satisfied, but the settlement could not be called ungenerous.[20] A new relationship of compliance replaced homage, and a policy of financial inducement replaced insistence on William's right to Northumbria. We do not know how William raised the 10,000 marks which he had to pay for the Quit-Claim of Canterbury, though some at least was probably borrowed from English Jews[21] against the security of something quite new in Scotland, a tax, probably a carucage.[22] By 1191, when Longchamps was told of Richard's nomination of Arthur as his heir, the chancellor immediately sought the support

---

[15] *Materials for the History of Thomas Becket*, ed. J.C. Robertson, 7 vols., RS LXVII, 1875–85, vi, 72.

[16] *Jordan Fantosme's Chronicle*, ed. R.C. Johnston, Oxford 1981, 20–35.

[17] *Benedict*, i, 313–14, 322. It is sometimes suggested that Henry II stimulated the pope to reject the application for a dispensation. No source suggests this.

[18] *Howden*, ii, 285.

[19] *Anglo-Scottish Relations, 1174–1328, Some Selected Documents*, ed. E.L.G. Stones, Oxford 1970, 12–17.

[20] *Anglo-Scottish Relations*, 18–23.

[21] *Cal. Docs Scot.*, i, no. 433 shows William owing Aaron of Lincoln £2,776 in 1209.

[22] Duncan, *Scotland, Making of Kingdom*, 213, 238n.

of King William in carrying out that succession should Richard die.[23]

Whatever the response, in 1193 not only did William reject John's request for men to help him seize power on news of Richard's captivity, but he sent 2,000 marks as a contribution to the king's ransom.[24] The aim was probably to secure Richard's favour and the Northumbrian earldom, for William went south in 1194 to the second coronation, petitioning for it. After refusal, he offered 15,000 marks, could have had it without the castles, but refused, and had to be satisfied with a promise from Richard to look at his claim on his return from France.[25] It was an answer such as William was to hear at intervals for the remaining twenty years of his life. Even his plea 'sell me justice!' could not achieve the resolution he desired.

When Richard died William had to choose at a distance whom he should support for the English throne and what price he could extract for that support. He offered fealty to Duke John in Normandy in return for the northern earldom, but his messengers were detained in England by John's supporters who sent Earl David to William to ask for patience, while John sent Eustace de Vescy renewing Richard's promise of an early decision if he would keep peace.[26] Immediately after John's coronation on 27 May 1199, attended by the earl of Leicester and his uncle Roger, bishop of St Andrews, William's ambassadors put forward their master's demands and offer, but, of course, without the clout which John's pre-royal status had given them. The answer, sent by Philip bishop of Durham, was to require William's presence at John's court, which moved to Northampton to meet him; Bishop Roger was sent to bring him south.[27]

What John intended we do not know, but it is possible that if William had come with humble mien and a large cheque, John would have accommodated him for a time. Instead William sent Roger back with a threat that if the earldom were not handed over, William would seize it, and giving a forty-day time-limit during which he mustered an army – the complementarity of these two acts is noteworthy. John was forced into concessions to other reluctant magnates but did not budge; William lost courage and cancelled his host despite John's absence in France for the second half of 1199.[28] Then, during his brief return to England from February to April 1200, John went to York in March to meet William, whom he had summoned but who did not come, and matters were again dropped until after John's return and second coronation in early October 1200. Immediately thereafter, Howden tells us he sent a powerful seven-man embassy, including Earl David, with letters patent of safe-conduct, to bring

---

23 *Chron. Melrose*, 48; *Newburgh*, i, 335–6.
24 *Gervase*, i, 515; *Chron. Melrose*, 48.
25 *Howden*, ii, 243–4, 249–50.
26 *Howden*, iv, 88–9.
27 *Howden*, iv, 90–2, ascribing the proposed meeting to Nottingham; *Diceto*, ii, 166 says Northampton, which the itinerary of John shows to be correct.
28 *Howden*, iv, 92, 100.

William to him at Lincoln on 21 November.[29] Yet, on 30 October John wrote again; an embassy from William had explained that he did not know that John had sent a conduct (presumably men and letters) so he now sent four men, including Bishop Roger, giving conduct by them for William's visit to court. The embassies had evidently crossed, but the second one confirms what John's moves to Northampton in 1199 and York in 1200 suggest – that he was extremely anxious to bring William to him, to obtain William's homage.

This detail, I believe, gives a context for a remarkable safe-conduct issued in November 1205, for William to meet John at York in February 1206. The seven-man escort sent included only two of the escort of 1200, but the list ended 'and more of the ancient conduct whom he sought from us', a reference to the 1194 settlement, which suggests that seven in 1205 replicates seven in 1200. Then the letter continues: 'we grant him also, if perchance, God forbid, we leave through ill ['recesserimus per malum'], a truce of forty days after he has returned to his land, so that in the meantime there shall be no forfeiture of him or his land or his men by us or ours'. Finally, as William asked, Earl David was sent to Scotland to remain there until William's return.[30] It is difficult, if not impossible, to find a context for what were clearly William's fears, in 1205–6. There can be no doubt that the forty-day truce was to allow the assembly of an army, yet nothing in 1205 suggests that the kings were then close to war. They met in 1206 and again in 1207 without quarrel or achievement, and the 1207 safe-conducts are entirely straightforward. That of 1205, I suggest, must have been a recycling and adaptation of an earlier safe-conduct from a period when we know William thought of using a forty-day truce to call out his host, but with the 1205 addition of a sentence about Earl David.

If the seven-man safe-conduct of early October 1200 (of which no text survives) was that reused in 1205, its reassurances for William must have been sought by him before John left England in April 1200. This helps to explain the abortive meeting demanded by John for York in March 1200 – the safe-conduct sent for that occasion did not sufficiently assure William, who asked for the forty-day truce; by the time his request reached England, John had departed for France. So William's fears and hopes belong to early 1200. They were the result, I suggest, of his willingness to think of war against the English king as early as the summer of 1199, a striking departure from his complaisance towards Richard. The explanation for that is surely to be found at the court of Philip II of France. At Richard's death either William approached not only John, but also Arthur at the French court, offering fealty in return for Northumbria; or Philip, recalling William's alliance of 1173–74, approached him with an offer that Arthur would accept his fealty. The existence of some

---

[29] *Howden*, iv, 107, 140; *CRR*, i, 135; Howden lists the mission sent (on 8 or 9 October 1200) with a safe-conduct.

[30] *Rot. Litt. Pat.* i, 56a. *Concessimus . . . si forsan quod absit per malum tunc recesserimus, treugam XL dierum postquam in terram suam reversus fuerit it quod interim ei aut terre sue aut hominibus suis a nobis aut nostris non forisfiet.*

proposal of alliance appears in Howden who, discussing Agnès de Méran, twice (in 1200–1) tells us that Philip had promised his older child by Agnès, Marie, born about 1196–97, as spouse to Alexander of Scotland.[31]

The date of that offer can only be surmised, but it would surely be before both the peace of Le Goulet in May 1200 and the truce and understanding reached in the preceding January – in other words it belongs to 1199. Such a proposal, if made soon after Richard I's death, and the offer of alliance which would certainly accompany it, would explain as nothing else does why William found the courage to threaten John in the summer of that year, and why some eight months later in March 1200, he would not come to meet John, for fear of the latter's anger. Philip would have no further interest in a Franco–Scottish alliance once John had made his peace and done homage for his French possessions.

William's obduracy crumbled in November 1200. If he wished to retain his modest English possession, Tynedale, he had no choice but to do homage to John, though evidently on the understanding that he could raise his other claims. Bishop Roger, again at John's court, went north and brought William to the impressive homage-ceremony at Lincoln in November 1200, after which William made his petition and John promised a reply by Whitsun 1201, extended later to Michaelmas and doubtless postponed again and again thereafter;[32] John had time to visit the northern shires but not to sit in judgement on the northern earldom. These embassies suggest that Earl David was not alone in being a compliant agent of John, and that Bishop Roger, too, firmly disapproved of William's stand and was in effect exiled from Scotland for many months, having followed John to France, remaining there till the end of 1199, but returning to Scotland by the summer of 1200.[33] In return John gave him the vacant abbacy of Peterborough and also sought to secure his election as bishop of Lincoln.[34] He remained at John's court from November 1200 until February 1201[35] and must be connected with the tantalising letters issued by John on 6 January 1201, safe-conducts for Harald earl of Orkney and his chaplain Adam, announcing that John had sent for the earl to come to speak with him;[36] we may presume that Adam was then at court. The aged Earl Harald Maddadson had been deprived of his northern revenues from Shetland by Sverre king of Norway and sought to replace the loss by obtaining the most

[31] *Howden*, iv, 138, 174. Howden says she was five in September 1200, but Cartellieri, *Philipp II*, iv, 83 n.3 argues that she cannot have been born before early 1197.

[32] *Howden*, iv, 141, 163–4.

[33] *Rot. Chart.*, 9b, 32a.

[34] *Howden*, iv, 156; *Life of St Hugh*, ii, 84–85; *Historiae Anglicanae Scriptores*, ed. J. Sparke, London 1723, iii, 106. Roger stripped the abbacy of its goods. The pressure for the bishopric may have come early in 1200 on Hugh's death, but more probably in November when John, William, Roger and Bishop Hugh's corpse were all at Lincoln cathedral.

[35] See the index to *Rot. Chart.*, under *Sancti Andree, episcopus*, for the many occasions when Roger witnessed charters of John. For February 1201, *Rot. Chart.*, 85.

[36] *Rot. Chart.*, 100.

northerly earldom in Scotland. From 1196 William had been involved marginally in the feud of Earl Harald with his rival for the earldom, resolved by
Harald's victory. In 1198 or early 1199 he was brought to William's court by
Bishop Roger, where he offered the king money for the earldom of Caithness.
William set further conditions which Harald refused, returning home without
the earldom.[37] Probably in the autumn of 1200 he invaded and seized it, his men
mutilating the bishop's tongue in the process; William emasculated Harald's
son whom he held hostage and sent an army north late in 1201 which achieved
little.[38] At court in January 1201 Adam may have been seeking John's help for
Harald, but it is equally possible that he was on his way to Rome to seek absolution for the men who cut the bishop's tongue,[39] having been diverted to court by
Bishop Roger, who could interpret the situation for John. For it is surely curious
that John had a sudden desire to meet the earl in the kingdom of Norway who
had offered to buy the most northerly earldom in Scotland from King William,
then had taken it by force. His ambitions were exactly parallel to William's in
England, but since he did not come, and Adam and his companions sailed home
from Northumberland in John's third exchequer year, 1201–2,[40] we can only
guess at John's motives. Whatever they were, they encouraged William to settle
on £2,000 as the price which gave Harald Caithness in the spring of 1202 when
Bishop Roger brought Harald to him at Perth[41] – just when John was about to
lose *his* northern possessions in France.

William's importuning and John's stonewalling continued by letter and
embassy for five years without a meeting. In July 1205, in a letter written while
Scottish messengers were at John's court and English ones at William's, John
claimed that he wished to hear from the latter before hastening to meet William.
'And know that we are well pleased by the exception which you made in your
letters about retaining for yourself the land of Tynedale, of which mention had
not been made in the agreement discussed between us, and of which you were

[37] *Howden*, iv, 10–12.
[38] *Chron. Fordun*, i, 276; *Orkneyinga Saga*, ed. H. Pálsson and P. Edwards, London 1978,
221–4. Fordun says William sent the army *infra ipsum Natale Domini*, the saga that he led
the army immediately after Christmas. I feel sure that William did not lead the army, but
the saga's chronology is rather more persuasive. These events are dealt with in chapters
added at the end of the saga, on which see the edition by A.B. Taylor, *The Orkneyinga
Saga*, Edinburgh 1938, 91–4, 342–9, 408–10. See in general, Patrick Topping, 'Harald
Maddadson, Earl of Orkney and Caithness, 1139–1206', *Scottish Historical Review* 62,
1983, 105–20. In this paper I have attributed the *Gesta Annalia* to Fordun as an inherited
convenience; their authorship is, however, under review.
[39] The letter of Innocent III fixing the penance on *Lomberd laicus* responsible for cutting the
bishop's tongue is printed by A.C. Lawrie, *Annals of the Reigns of Malcolm and William,
Kings of Scotland, 1153–1214*, Glasgow 1910, 339. The bull is dated at Subiaco, where
Innocent was in August–September, 1202. It seems unlikely to me that the sacrilege
occurred less than a year earlier, and I place it in 1200, which fits with Fordun's rather
vague chronology.
[40] *PR 3 John*, 244.
[41] *Chron. Fordun*, i, 276.

seized before.'[42] The implication is clearly that the two kings had agreed tentatively on attributing William's English lands to someone acceptable to him – William's son Alexander or Earl David. It is in the context of this outline 'agreement' that the safe-conduct of November 1205, which I have already discussed, makes so little sense. There is a lingering distrust in William's insistence that Earl David be sent to stay in Scotland while the king was in England. Yet when they met in February 1206 John was surely looking only for a quiet border and men to accompany him to Poitou; we know only that William is said to have cured a sick boy by his touch and blessing. Of the meeting at York in late May 1207 we know nothing, but the notice John gave for another meeting on 11 November was too short, and there was no further movement in the relations of the kings till 1209.[43] That was their crisis year.

Contemporary evidence for it is slight: William's promise to pay 15,000 marks, copied into Liber A, and a valuable narrative in the Melrose chronicle, which says that John ordered William to meet him in late April.[44] But John's invitation of 10 April is in the most friendly terms, rejoicing at William's recovery from illness, sending an escort which included William's two sons-in-law, Eustace de Vescy and Robert de Ros, and expressing a desire to complete the negotiations which had been going on for a long time.[45] The place of meeting was Newcastle not York, perhaps a friendly gesture to William's fragile health, perhaps because it was chief place of Northumberland. The two kings met briefly at Bolton near Alnwick, William bound for Newcastle, John going to Norham which was in his hands after the death of Philip bishop of Durham. Having inspected it, he returned to Newcastle where the two kings had some discussion for two days, parting on 26 April.[46] The fifteenth-century chronicler, Walter Bower, using an early-thirteenth-century St Andrews chronicle, now lost, adds the valuable information that Earl David came with John, that William fell ill at Newcastle, and that John left, having urged William to go home to recover; the households of the two had the impression that they had made peace, though they had not.[47] The settlement here postponed by William's collapse would have been of his claims in England, but if a compromise was to be discussed, we do not know what it was.

But John must have had opportunity to put his proposed deal to William, for on his return, as Bower recounts, William held a council at Stirling on 24 May to agree a reply to the English king, a reply sent by a powerful embassy including William Malveisin, bishop of St Andrews[48] who was

[42] *Rot. Litt. Claus.* i, 43.
[43] *Rot. Litt. Pat.*, 69b, 76; *Rot. Litt. Claus.* i, 86, 90. *Chron. Fordun*, i, 279.
[44] *Chron. Melrose*, 54. The verb used is *mandavit.*
[45] *Rot. Litt. Pat.*, 91.
[46] *Chron. Melrose*, 54.
[47] *Chron. Bower*, iv, 449.
[48] The others were Walter bishop of Glasgow, William Comyn and Philip de Valognes. All these witness *RRS*, ii, no. 491, dated at Stirling on 20 May, and therefore of 1209. No. 492, at Edinburgh on 23 May would probably not be of 1209.

clearly responsible for the chronicle used by Bower. They found John in a very hostile frame of mind, offended by the response and thundering threats against kings of Scotland and their land – threats which they retailed to William at Forfar.[49] Gervase of Canterbury is chronologically imprecise but tells of John demanding that three castles on the border, perhaps Berwick, Roxburgh and Jedburgh, be restored, or that Alexander be sent as hostage,[50] a demand which would fit this juncture well, for fear of an English invasion now threw the king and kingdom into a panic. The army was called out, castles reinforced, and the king moved to Lothian while sending another embassy, including Malveisin again, to mollify John with a friendlier message urging peace between them.

That embassy crossed Saer de Quincy and Robert de Ros, both men with Scottish interests, coming from John to William at Edinburgh. Without waiting for Malveisin's return, William replied with an even more ingratiating message, but Malveisin came back to William, now at Traquair – and we must now be in July 1209 – with news that John was coming to the border with an army, expecting to fight a Scottish army. Malveisin was sent south again to delay John with negotiations until William could collect again ('recolligeret ad plenum') his full host. Evidently the first muster had been dropped, but the summons was now renewed. When John was at Bamburgh William was near Melrose while his men streamed in.[51] From John's itinerary, the date must have been about 31 July.

The fourteenth-century Scottish chronicler, John of Fordun, becomes increasingly well informed from the mid-twelfth century, and used contemporary sources for these events; the origin is unfortunately obscured by his addiction to rhetorical embellishment. In his version William lay ill at Traquair as John marched to Norham intent on punishing the Scots, then moved to Roxburgh, assembling his army.[52] The overlap with Bower is obvious, for Roxburgh is no great distance from Melrose. What is new here is the claim that William had again been ill, at Traquair, explaining why he so desperately needed to buy time and why, eventually, notwithstanding the presence of his army, William negotiated by messenger, submitting to humiliation in the treaty of Norham in early August.

It would seem that long years of desultory but amicable negotiation came to an abrupt end after the Newcastle conference of April 1209, about June of that year, and that the cause is unlikely to have been only the message brought from Stirling to John. After all, John had the earldom William wanted, and if William refused to pay a price for it, John had only to shrug his shoulders; he had no need or incentive to invade Scotland just for that. Various explanations have

[49] *Chron. Bower,* iv, 449–51. To this occasion in 1209 might be dated *RRS*, ii, no. 498, dated at Forfar, 11 June, though none of the ambassadors witness it.
[50] *Gervase,* ii, 102–3.
[51] *Chron. Bower,* iv, 451.
[52] *Chron. Fordun,* i, 276–7.

been offered for John's sudden determination to launch on William the war for which he took a scutage of a mark on the knight's fee. Thus Wendover attributes the tension to William having received fugitives and enemies of John from England – a clear reading back of the two bishops and Eustace de Vescy who fled to Scotland later.[53] Fordun also has an explanation, widely accepted in modern literature, for the sudden deterioration: John had begun to strengthen a castle at Tweedmouth, to destroy Berwick; William found this intolerable and twice had it demolished, driving away or killing the on-site workmen.[54] This version of events, too, is entirely wrong. Berwick bridge had been destroyed by floods in 1199, and its reconstruction had been delayed by the refusal of Philip bishop of Durham to allow work at Tweedmouth, his land, until an agreement between William and Bishop Hugh Puiset, presumably about sharing tolls, had been confirmed.[55] Once that was done, work on the bridge proceeded, until, as the Lanercost chronicle states, Bishop Philip built the castle which he cheekily called 'Malveisin' and which in the agreement of 1209 was called 'the castle above the port'.[56] The silence of English sources about any Scottish attack on this castle discredits Fordun when Lanercost offers a far more probable version exonerating both William and John. The former paid money 'for the liberty of the port of Berwick and got leave to demolish the castle which Bishop Philip built opposite Berwick'. Here Lanercost has added 'the port of Berwick' to his source, the contemporary Melrose chronicle.[57] Bower's version first adapts Fordun, saying erroneously that John had tried to build the castle, but then, using the St Andrews chronicle, makes it clear that in 1209 the two kings agreed that this castle should never be built in future, and that as compensation for the *inhonoratio* done to John by its throwing down, *dirupcio*, by the Scottish king, the latter should pay £4,000 – a figure which Bower alone preserves. The destruction of the castle clearly followed the treaty, and was the result of a financial agreement made in the interests of the burgesses of Berwick at the expense of those of the see of Durham, fortuitously vacant and sold out by John at this time. I have little doubt that most of the £4,000 was promised to William by the guildsmen of Berwick.[58]

Then there is a later Yorkshire explanation for the 'war', found in the 1291 Bridlington chronicle, in Langtoft and Trivet, and added by Bower to his chronicle, claiming that John made war on William because the latter had married his daughter to the count of Boulogne; this appears also in Guisborough, but as the

[53] *Wendover*, ii, 50.

[54] *Chron. Fordun*, i, 277.

[55] *Howden*, iv, 97–8.

[56] Appendix, I no. 1; and next note.

[57] *Chronicon de Lanercost*, ed. J. Stevenson, Edinburgh 1839, 4, 7; *Chron. Melrose*, 54.

[58] To this payment I would ascribe an entry in the inventory of Scottish records, 1282: Appendix, I no. 16. *Chron Bower*, iv, 452–3. The translation of *inhonoracio* is difficult, but it seems to mean 'lack of prestige' rather than 'dishonour'.

count of Flanders, who, in 1209, did not exist.[59] Even if this were only a proposal of marriage, it should refer to Renaud de Dammartin in 1208–9, when he was still a vassal of Philip II. But he held the county in right of his wife who was alive in 1213.[60] My suggestion of twenty years ago, of a proposed marriage to Philippe Hurepel, younger son of Philip II, who acquired the county much later, having married Renaud's daughter in 1210, is equally impossible,[61] but the story may be the result of confusion between this marriage and reports of the proposal in 1200, when Philippe was born, that his sister Maria should marry Alexander of Scotland. None of the reports of this supposed Boulogne marriage knows the name of William's daughter or of the count, suggesting a common source.

F.X. Martin and Lewis Warren made a northern English conspiracy the reason for John's warlike advance to Norham.[62] The sole evidence for this, as J.C. Holt pointed out, is a letter of Philip II, dated 1209, to John de Lacy, indicating that a Norman intermediary, Roger des Essarts, had told Philip that Lacy planned a rising 'by friends and by attacks ['imprisios'] in England, and by friends and defence of castles in Ireland'. He has also pointed out that the letter is an insertion in Philip's register, that John de Lacy was then probably seventeen years old, his father, Roger constable of Chester, loyal to King John, and that there is no evidence to connect anyone else to this plan. The letter promises that once Philip is sure of the rebellion he will take such advice about the lands held by Lacy's ancestors in England as is irrefutable on the matter. If this meant a restoration of lost fiefs, as it seems to do, Painter was unable to find any such of John de Lacy in England.[63]

There is no other evidence of John de Lacy's treason, and no evidence that

---

[59] *Documents and Records illustrating the History of Scotland*, ed. F. Palgrave, London 1837, i, 66–7; *Chronicle of Pierre de Langtoft*, ed. T. Wright, RS XLVII, London, ii, 130; *Nicholai Triveti Annales*, ed. T. Hog, London 1845, 281; *Chron. Bower*, iv, 472–3; *The Chronicle of Walter of Guisborough*, ed. H. Rothwell, London 1957, 149.

[60] Baldwin, *Government*, 200–202; A. Cartellieri, *Philipp II August, König von Frankreich*, 4 vols., Leipzig 1899–1922, iv, 312–13. Dr Nicholas Vincent kindly showed me evidence that Renaud's father, who was count of Dammartin, received lands in the earldom of Northampton (=Huntingdon) when it was held by Simon de Senlis in the decade after 1174. But that does not explain the story.

[61] Duncan, *Scotland, Making of Kingdom*, 244. In November 1209 Renaud gave an undertaking to Philip II to respect the agreement they had made for the marriage of Renaud's daughter to Philippe Hurepel, promising to hand over his daughter when they asked for her. *Registres*, 392–3.

[62] *A New History of Ireland, ii, Medieval Ireland 1169–1534*, ed. A. Cosgrove, Oxford 1987, 139; Warren, *King John*, 193.

[63] *Actes de Philippe Auguste*, iii, 161–2, no. 1079; Painter, *Reign of King John*, 253–4; Holt, *Northerners*, 207–8. The letter is given in full in Register A without the abbreviation of formulae usual in that register, which covers the years 1204–11, and is cancelled. In 1211 a new register, C, was begun with many letters copied from A but in a rearrangement; letters in A which were not to be copied were cancelled. Thus no. 1079 had been registered by 1211, and its cancellation does not signify that it was invalid. M. Nortier, 'Les actes de Philippe Auguste: notes critiques', in *La France de Philippe Auguste, le temps des mutations*, ed. R.-H. Bautier, Paris 1982, 429–51, esp. p. 436.

King William or northerners were involved. Moreover the letter is addressed not to John but to I. or J. de Laciaco. John, or his father, is not known to have held castles, or, as far as I can tell, lands, in Ireland. But the Lacys who certainly did were the Herefordshire family which had been given the lordship of Meath by Henry II; Walter de Lacy succeeded in 1189, but his estates were sequestrated at least once by the crown thereafter; he was heir to the lands of his predecessors which the letter envisages restoring[64] so the initial I could be an error for U[altero]. His younger brother, Hugh, was made earl of Ulster by John in 1205, the lack of which title in the letter argues against the addressee J being an error for H[ugoni]; on the other hand Hugh was the bolder opponent of John, received de Briouse when outlawed, and fled by way of Scotland in 1210 to France in 1211, where he stayed for a decade, suggesting that he was already an ally of King Philip. Marginally Hugh seems the more likely of the two. The date of the letter, '1209', as Cartellieri pointed out,[65] could be as late as 17 April 1210, not long before Walter de Lacy gave refuge to William de Briouse in Meath, though his brother, not he, was ready to offer 'defence of castles'.[66] An Irish conspiracy was real, and was, I believe, the context of the letter, which had nothing to do with the Northerners or the king of Scots. Walter de Lacy agreed an enormous fine for his heritage in 1198 and it may be doubted that further English lands waited to be recovered with the help of Philip II. I suspect that des Essarts left a false impression and that de Lacy was really seeking a promise of restoration of his extensive lands in Normandy, as the Norman intermediary would suggest.[67] But even if that be wrong, the letter is noteworthy evidence of Philip II's readiness to embarrass John. A letter like this promising to help William's claims to land in England would explain the latter's fears in 1200. Another move along the same lines certainly explains the brink of war between John and Scotland in 1209.

The collapse of Anglo-Scottish relations in the summer of 1209, after the Newcastle meeting, as a result of which John demanded either key Scottish castles or custody of William's heir, must be explained from the substance of the agreement reached later between the two kings. Details were not publicised and the actual documents (save one) were surrendered to the Scots in 1237 and doubtless destroyed.[68] But the terms are preserved by Bower, drawing on the St Andrews chronicle: William's daughters, Margaret and Isabella, were given to John, Margaret to be married to John's son Henry, Isabella to an English noble of rank; if the older child of either king were to die before marriage, the younger would step into his or her shoes. Scottish merchants could freely trade in England; King William would retain intact his ancient honours, that is the

---

[64] W.E. Wightman, *The Lacy Family in England and Normandy, 1066–1194*, 192–4, 201–5, 223–6. Add to his references, *Registres*, 295.

[65] Cartellieri, *Philipp II*, iv, 282–3.

[66] *New History of Ireland*, ii, chapter v.

[67] Roger des Essarts, discussed by Painter, *Reign of King John*, 253–4. I have not found him in *Registres de Philippe Auguste*.

[68] *Anglo-Scottish Relations*, 49.

honourable conduct promised in 1194; in return for the marriages and observing all the articles, John was to be paid 15,000 marks within two years. William voluntarily gave John thirteen hostages for this peace.[69] The wording of these terms, humiliating to William, and which the Melrose chronicle says were made against the will of the Scots,[70] must have been English for they are presented as John's concession. William's promise to pay the 15,000 marks states that the money was for having John's goodwill and that the hostages were for prompt payment; the daughters, it says, were not 'hostages'.[71] Nonetheless the whole point of the peace, as it was called, was not to end a war, for war had been avoided, but to put William's daughters in John's hands, to deprive their father of the choice of their husbands; in fact they were handed over at Carlisle within two weeks – a detail again known only from Bower.[72]

The annals of Margam and Waverley give the only convincing explanation for John's anger: that William was said to have entered into an alliance with John's enemies. For in the Scottish archives in 1291 was 'a charter of King John sent to King William about negotiation of a marriage between the king of France and the daughter of King William'.[73] The word used is *maritagium*, but other entries in the list show that this was just *matrimonium*; the entry does not mean more than that a negotiation had been proposed. Now Philip Augustus notoriously already had a wife, but in 1208 a process before the legate Guala had offered the prospect of annulment until Philip sent Guala packing in January 1209,[74] and it is entirely possible that, to find another ally against John, with whom his two-year truce had just ended, Philip offered himself as husband to Margaret of Scotland during that process, just as in 1210 he offered himself to the daughter of the margrave of Thuringia if her father could procure a papal annulment for Philip.[75] On this view, John learned of the proposed negotiation between Philip and William between April and June 1209; we can, I believe, be more specific, pin-pointing arrival of the news at the payment of half a mark made at Arundel on 28 May 1209 through Robert de Vieuxpont to 'Fulcher, a secret messenger who came from overseas parts'.[76] John reacted forcefully with demands, threats and ultimately an army of invasion and a scutage. Bower's narrative of William's responses suggests that he desperately sought to assure John that there had been no negotiation with Philip, and that these assurances had some effect, for John did not invade, and as part of the peace at Norham,

[69] *Chron. Bower*, iv, 452–3.
[70] *Chron. Melrose,* 54.
[71] *RRS*, ii, no. 488; Lawrie, *Annals*, 369–70; Rymer's *Foedera*, I, i, 103.
[72] *Chron. Bower,* iv, 454–5.
[73] Appendix, II no. 8; *Annales Monastici*, i, 29; ii, 262.
[74] Baldwin, *Government*, 207; Cartellieri, *Philipp II*, iv, 277–81.
[75] Cartellieri, *Philipp II*, 296–7.
[76] 'Fulchero secreto nuncio qui venit de partibus transmarinis, dimidiam marcam, per R[ogerum de Vete]ri Ponte.' *Rot. de Lib.* 113. But *R[ogerum]* is surely an editorial error for *R[obertum]*. On Robert de Vieuxpont see Holt, *Northerners*, 220–1; I have found nothing further on Fulcher.

gave William a charter either recording his acceptance of William's denial, or perhaps remitting rancour for the very proposal – the 'goodwill' for which William paid so heavily. Thus was the crisis resolved and the foundations laid for another phase of Anglo-Scottish frictions.

If this peace was concerned with a ghost marriage to the king of France, it did nothing to heal the long-festering sore of Northumbria. In Scottish sources Fordun has an account of the treaty which, though less full than Bower, is accurate in most respects – far more so than any thirteenth-century account – and which adds to Bower a further agreement that William would resign all the lands he held of John who would give them back to Alexander to hold of him, and that in future the heir to the Scottish throne, not the king, would do homage and fealty for these lands, honours and possessions.[77] This was carried further when Alexander did homage to John at Alnwick in the same year. The homage is mentioned in a charter,[78] and the most likely occasion for it would be August 1209, after William had crossed the Tweed into Scotland, sending Alexander to John as he travelled south. The lack of comment upon this arrangement is perhaps surprising, but it explains much about the previous decade, and specifically why in 1205 Tynedale would be kept by William as an exception to an agreement already outlined. The ease with which it was carried out in 1209 suggests that it had been worked out long before but held up for lack of some final piece in the jigsaw. William resigned the empty lordship of the earldom of Huntingdon, gaining nothing, not even an end to his allegiance to John, for he kept Tynedale. But surely what lay behind this sleight of hand had been a much more serious hope – that the claim to Northumbria would be recognised at the cost of it being held by the king's son, as Earl Henry had held it sixty years before. This John had refused to concede during earlier meetings with William, though he was anxious to complete a deal which would eliminate William as claimant. In 1209 he had his way. I was quite wrong to suggest twenty years ago that in 1209 John promised Northumbria to Alexander. But not wrong to deny that William renewed homage to John on this occasion.[79]

For two years after the peace at Norham, the Scots did nothing to rock the boat for John, who got his money reasonably on time. It is unclear whether the two English bishops who came in 1209 did so by agreement between the kings or as true refugees, but William gave the heiress of the earldom of Atholl to John's mercenary, Thomas of Galloway. In 1210 Matilda de Briouse and her children were handed over to John by Duncan of Carrick, and while Hugh de Lacy, the deprived earl of Ulster, found refuge with King William, he soon departed for France. But in January 1211 a ghost emerged from William's past. Guthred mac William, son of a rebel of the 1180s, landed from Ireland with the

[77] *Chron. Fordun*, i, 277.
[78] See the discussion with references in Duncan, *Scotland, Making of Kingdom*, 255.
[79] *Ibid.* 244.

collusion of the magnates of Ross.[80] The king made great efforts in the summer to subdue by terror the territories which Guthred overran, and withdrew at Michaelmas, leaving the earl of Fife in charge of Moray, showing how far the trouble had spread; even so Guthred was able to besiege and take a castle built by William.[81] Guthred left no manifesto of his aims and claims, but he was descended from William son of Duncan II, certainly represented a Gaelic reaction to the spread of William's Anglo-Scottish lieges and sheriffs, and seriously threatened the inheritance of William's line.

In 1195 William had fallen ill, and, still lacking a son, proposed that his daughter should marry Otto of Brunswick who would succeed to the throne. Despite strong domestic opposition on behalf of Earl David, who had campaigned for Richard, both in England against Count John, and with Count John in Normandy against Philip II, and was now more closely associated with Huntingdon than with Scotland,[82] he procured the agreement of Richard that the couple would be endowed with Lothian and the northern English counties, with the two kings acting as guardians in possession of the castles in the kingdom of the other. It was a bizarre suggestion which fell through only because William recovered and pulled out when Ermengarde again became pregnant,[83] but it was taken very seriously by the two kings, for the disappointed Otto was compensated with the county of Poitou and title of duke of Aquitaine in September 1196.[84] Its significance is the length to which King William was prepared to go in pursuit of his right, his willingness to oust his brother's inheritance, and his indifference to domestic opposition.

The birth of a son, Alexander, to William and Ermengarde on 24 August 1198 certainly changed the situation, though only so long as the child lived. Almost a year after William's homage at Lincoln, at a ceremony at Musselburgh on 12 October 1201, the Scottish magnates swore fealty to the king's son Alexander, now three years old.[85] There was a precedent in the recognition of the ten- or eleven-year-old Malcolm as heir in 1152 when Earl Henry died, but in 1201 there was no such precipitant, and the fealty to this small child remains inexplicable in purely domestic terms. The explanation is surely to be found in William's great age – he was about sixty – and the demonstrable vulnerability of children inheriting a right to the throne while a mature adult male of close family survived to thwart that right – the wicked uncle syndrome. The death of

---

[80] *Chron. Fordun,* i, 278–79. Fordun calls them the thanes of Ross, but Fordun liked to people Gaelic Scotland with thanes.

[81] *Chron. Bower,* iv, 464–7.

[82] Stringer, *Earl David,* 40–1, 283.

[83] *Howden,* iii, 298–9, 308 (June–Dec. 1195). This pregnancy could have led to a birth in 1196; Ermengarde presumably became pregnant in November 1197, and it seems unlikely that the proposed marriage to Otto simmered on until so late a date.

[84] Bernd Ulrich Hucker, *Kaiser Otto IV,* MGH, Schriften 34, Hannover 1990, 12–16.

[85] *Chron. Melrose,* 51. See the discussion of measures taken by Louis VII, in his later years, to secure recognition of his son Philip [II] as his heir by fealty from the young king, Henry, in A.W. Lewis, *Royal Succession in Capetian France,* London 1981, 69–77.

William's niece, Constance of Brittany, in August 1201, must have seemed to confirm finally the exclusion of Arthur from the English throne, and probably determined William to insure against a like fate befalling Alexander in Scotland. He would have vivid memories of the defence of his brother David's claim mounted by some magnates in 1195, and would now have a new fear that David might be cajoled into playing the John to Alexander's Arthur – recognising John himself as the possible mastermind. But the other fear of William which must underlie this oath is that there would be those among the magnates prepared to exclude Alexander in favour of David. Relations between the two brothers became distant, for David, busy at William's court in the 1190s, disappears from it thereafter. He was in France with John in 1199, 1200 and 1202–3, and intended to go to Poitou in 1205. True, he was in Scotland in 1202 and 1204, but he joined the Scottish magnates in homage to the boy Alexander only in 1205, and when in February 1206 the two kings at last met at York, William asked that David should stay in Scotland while he was in England,[86] presumably in order that David should be out of John's hands while the Scottish king was in them. David in Scotland was less of a threat to Alexander's succession than if he were at large in John's service. After 1209 David remained in England, where his age did not protect him from John's distrust. But in 1211 Guthred replaced him in William's fear that Alexander might be excluded from the throne.

These were the circumstances in which the king went to John yet again, dragging himself all the way to Durham for a meeting on 2 February 1212 and staying there for a week. There, by the mediation of Queen Ermengarde, they renewed the peace and love between them and reached a further agreement whose content is preserved by Bower: within six years Alexander was to be provided with a wife by John (whose daughter Joanna had been born in 1210); each king swore to protect the other in his just quarrels, and that the survivor would help, protect and cause to be invested in the kingdom the heir of the other.[87] Our evidence is patchy and reticent on what were evidently very confidential negotiations, but William felt in need, even desperate need, of John's assistance, went to Durham to seek it, and brought in Ermengarde to press the case.[88] For the provision for Alexander's marriage reported by Bower there is confirmation in a text of William's letter of 8 February which grants to John the marriage of Alexander within six years. But the letter continues with a promise by William and Alexander that whatever happens to John, they will maintain fealty to his son Henry as their liege lord, helping him to maintain himself in his realm, saving their faith to King John.[89] Despite John's position as an

---

[86] Stringer, *Earl David*, 46–7.

[87] *Chron. Fordun*, i, 278; *Chron. Bower*, iv, 466–9.

[88] I do wonder if Ermengarde's role may not have been rather more mundane – interpreting between French and Early Scots. Fordun claims that they returned to Norham, but John's itinerary rules this out.

[89] 'Concessimus eidem domino nostro Iohanni regi Anglie quod quicquid de ipso contingat, nos et Alexander filius noster Henrico filio eius tanquam ligio domino nostro contra

excommunicate, he was far from a papal threat to disinherit him and his heir, and this undertaking makes no sense on its own. I can only make sense of it as a sentence written when Henry III was king, to replace an original wherein William promised to help and support the succession of John's heir. But if Bower is right John gave a parallel undertaking to William, to support his heir, which fits completely with all that happened in 1212.[90]

When William returned to Scotland he sent Alexander to London to be knighted by John, while Saer de Quincy remained in Scotland. The knighting may have been to mark Alexander's fourteen years, but it also allowed him to command the army sent in the summer to subdue Guthred, which included a force of Brabançons supplied by King John,[91] while in May Reginald king of the Isles was brought to Lambeth to swear fealty to John, conveniently ignoring his overlord, the king of Norway.[92] Although Reginald in Man had lost control of the southern Hebrides, he remained lord of Lewis, Harris and Skye, and might offer or deny help or transit of Irishmen to Guthred, a route which John could now close for William. The Melrose chronicle is almost silent on Guthred, and this has led us to underestimate not only the threat but also William's perception of it. The Barnwell chronicler commented that William, 'now of advanced age, was not able to pacify the interior districts of his kingdom, [and] disturbed by revolts he fled to the king of the English and entrusted to his care himself, his kingdom and his only son. And [John] presented the boy with the belt of knighthood and he (that is, surely, Alexander, not John) set out with an army to those parts; sending his men through the interior of the kingdom, he seized the leader of the revolt, Guthred.'[93] Even if the chronicler exaggerates, William does seem to have turned to John almost in desperation, after his failure in 1211, to secure the professional service which

omnes mortales fidem et fidelitatem tenebimus, et iuvabimus eum pro viribus nostris ad tenendum ipsum in regno suo salva fide qua predicto domino nostro regi Iohanni tenemur.' *Anglo-Scottish Relations*, 24–7; *RRS*, ii, 456–7, where there is an important comment.

[90] In 1236 (according to Matthew Paris) Alexander was to argue that John had promised him Joanna as his wife and the earldom of Northumberland, presumably in 1212; if there was such a statement, Alexander was foolish to take it as a promise. *Chronica Majora*, iii, 372.

[91] The Bury chronicle says that the Brabançons were led by 'a certain noble', a leader usually identified as Saer de Quincy earl of Winchester, because John gave him 200 marks 'ad faciendum liberacionem C militibus et C seruientibus qui fuerunt cum eo in Scocia.' There is no other evidence that Saer led the Brabançons, or took a force to Scotland. The date of the payment is 2 February 1211, that is, the force was active before then, probably in 1210. In 1210 Saer was with King John in Ireland, and *Scocia* here is certainly an error for *Hibernia*. *Rot. de Lib.* 240, cf. 203, 208, 223, 227. In a case in the curia regis in the summer of 1212 Saer was essoined in March when going to and returning from Scotland, sent in the king's service; but this was during William's visit to England. *CRR*, vi, 291. Saer witnessed at John's court on 4 and 25 May, and 23 September, but is not found in July or August. *Rot. Chart.*, 186–8. It is possible but unlikely that he led the Brabançons who were to help William. The Melrose chronicle almost ignores Guthred and certainly has nothing on him in 1212 when he was caught and executed.

[92] *Rot. Chart.*, 190.

[93] *Walter of Coventry*, ii, 206.

his forces conspicuously lacked. Historians have generally lined William and Alexander up among John's enemies by then;[94] there is no evidence for this, and much for the contrary view.

But John's fortunes changed. In June 1212 he was at Carlisle, apparently in discussion with Alan of Galloway, who was asked in July to supply 1,000 Galwegians,[95] then at Durham, where he is said to have intended to speak with William. The intention was frustrated by the outbreak of the Welsh revolt.[96] Soon thereafter, according to Roger of Wendover, King William and John's daughter, Joanna, wife of Llewellyn, warned John of the baronial conspiracy which threatened him, and as a result of John's demand for hostages from those he suspected, Eustace de Vescy fled to Scotland. Despite Wendover's unreliability, what he says fits William's relations with John at this time.[97] Six months later, in January 1213, John was again at Norham; to meet him William had faltered from Newbattle east to Haddington, but could go no further. According to Bower he was asked to come or send Alexander on the offer of 'many better things according to their old [or 'original'] triple agreement'. It is difficult to see how this could refer to the 1212 treaty, but a first agreement involving three men, that of 1209 whereby Alexander was to hold William's lands in England of John, fits the context. It explains why William was inclined to agree and to send Alexander, doubtless in the hope that 'better things' would be Northumberland; he had no distrust of John till his advisers worked on him. He was dissuaded, delayed going himself and refused point-blank to allow his son to go on the grounds of youth, inexperience and inability to answer any new proposal of John's.[98] This refusal, when contrasted with the knighting at London in 1212, can only be explained by the fear of Scottish magnates, reported in Bower, that Alexander would be held until de Vescy was surrendered. The point about Alexander's inability had some validity, but there were matters to be discussed, for though William had paid three-quarters of the money agreed in 1209 and been excused the rest, his hostages were still held in England.[99] It may indeed have been John's wish to take de Vescy, but he is more likely to have offered to return hostages for this than to have seized Alexander.

We are left with the impression of a very sick and vacillating William, worried that he will again be bamboozled by this ruthless English king, but,

---

[94] E.g. Painter, *Reign of King John*, 189.

[95] *Rot. Litt. Claus.* i, 131.

[96] *Memorials of St Edmund's Abbey,* ed. T. Arnold, 3 vols, RS XCVI, London, 1890–96, ii, 20–1.

[97] *Wendover*, ii, 61–2; Earl David was forced to hand over Fotheringhay Castle, and was evidently under some suspicion. Stringer, *Earl David*, 49.

[98] 'juxta priscam triplicem confederacionem pociora ei daturum', *Chron. Bower*, iv, 470–3. There is a brief account with less detail in *Chron. Fordun*, i, 279.

[99] In June 1213 John proposed to take seven hostages to France with him; four hostages were transferred to new custody; one had died and one was 'quit'. *Rot. Litt. Claus.* i, 137. It is presumed that all remaining hostages were released in 1215.

even more, fearful that at his death his son will somehow be denied the throne. It is said by Fordun that even on his deathbed in December 1214 he had his prelates and barons recognise Alexander as future king;[100] that might be only Fordun's rhetoric, but it fits so well with the recognition of 1201 and the 1212 treaty that it is also a strong possibility. It is part of a longer pattern which had certainly begun in 1195, whereby William progressed from the opposition of his own magnates over the succession of Otto in 1195 to distrust of them, even paranoia, over the succession of his son. It may have had roots in the opposition of senior men to the adventure of 1173, and in their subsequent lack of interest or opposition when he was tempted to war over Northumberland as in 1200 or to negotiations over it with John, when the full terms of agreements seem to have been concealed as in 1209. William's barons, like John's, were pressed by inflation and by royal demands for aids, and while they apparently paid up, they became steadily more hostile to foreign commitments and to the sticky embrace of King John.

Alexander II succeeded in December 1214 without contention, and without John's help or protection; he may already have been in contact with his brothers-in-law Ros and Vescy, leaders of the northerners, for Article 46 of the Articles of the Barons promised that in the matters of the return of hostages, of his liberties and his right, the king would act to Alexander according to the form in which he acts toward the barons of England unless (and here the wording is identical to that for Llewellyn) in the judgement of the archbishop and others whom he, the archbishop, wishes to have with him, charters which the king (John) has show that it should be otherwise. These terms refer to Article 38, that hostages and charters given as sureties be given up, and to Article 25 promising restoration to anyone disseised of liberties or right without judgement, with decision by the twenty-five barons if there were disagreement; the purpose is to give Alexander the rights of an English baron, but not what William had conceded – his daughters and their marriages.

Magna Carta Clause 59 added the king's sisters in first place: 'faciemus de sororibus suis et obsidibus reddendis et libertatibus suis'. This does not, I think, mean 'concerning the return of his sisters and hostages', but 'concerning his sisters, and the return of hostages, and his liberties', for the sisters were not hostages, and their return was not in question, since their dowries had been paid. Alexander wanted a return on the best part of 15,000 marks. The charters held by John, having been dropped from Llewellyn's clause, were now defined as King William's, but decision about them was given to 'judgement of [Alexander's] peers in our court', not to ecclesiastics. Holt explains this by the recognition of John as lord in the treaties of 1209 and 1212, which would be a secular issue between lord and vassal.[101] But both treaties had been secured by oaths on the souls of both kings, which were certainly matters of ecclesiastical concern,

---

[100] *Chron. Fordun,* iv, 279: 'filio suo ab episcopis comitibus et baronibus in regem futurum recepto'.

[101] Holt, *Magna Carta,* 287–9.

and the shift here was away from those treaties, dowry and hostages, to Alexander's right as a tenant of John and a peer of John's barons, a right to the earldom of Northumbria.

Alexander must have heard of the content of Magna Carta about the end of June 1215, for he despatched an embassy headed by Malveisin to John on 7 July.[102] Whether he promised an oath to the Charter and the Twenty-Five we do not know, but it would seem likely that his messengers were at the fruitless council of Oxford. A baronial judgement (probably in September) awarded the lands of Northumberland, Cumberland and Westmorland to Alexander and he was given seisin of them while at the siege of Norham probably on 22 October 1215, when the barons of Northumberland did him homage as they had been instructed by letters from the Twenty-Five; the latter also ordered the city of Carlisle to surrender to him, perhaps vainly. John was provoked into a fierce response in January 1216, the first royal invasion of Scotland since 1072, the first by an English army since 1097. He took and burned Berwick, Roxburgh, Dunbar and Haddington, but the pressure of other dangers denied him a stay of more than ten days in Scotland, and he withdrew without reaching Edinburgh.[103] The aim of the campaign was to deprive the northerners of Alexander's support, to drive the red fox back into his lair,[104] and John's position in the north did improve somewhat as a result of his activity.

In February Alexander besieged Carlisle unsuccessfully, then seems to have withdrawn again. The arrival of Louis in May prompted him into another attack on the city, which he took in August, crossing the Pennines and then moving swiftly south. On this journey I suggest that he reached the agreement with the barons over certain marriages, clearly of his sisters, which may have promised return of them and the dowry. To his passing through London probably belongs the treaty between him and the barons and the city of London, and a separate letter of the city, both described as being 'against King John', though in what sense is not said. At Canterbury he met Louis and with several northern barons did homage to him at Dover, receiving Louis's confirmation charter of the baronial concession of the northern earldom. The guarantee was an oath by Louis and the rebels that they would make no peace with John without the king of Scots.[105]

Of course with John's death all turned to ashes for Alexander. But the events of 1215–16 are revealing of the aspirations of the Scottish king. De Vescy used a baton to invest Alexander II at Norham with the *Comitatus Northumbrie*, which can be translated as the shire of Northumberland. But Alexander was adjudged lands of three northern shires, and there is no doubt that he sought to

---

[102] *Rot. Litt. Pat.*, 150.

[103] *Hist. ducs de Normandie*, 163–4.

[104] As *Hist. ducs de Normandie* has it. But *Chronica Majora*, ii, 641–2 uses the contrary metaphor: 'we shall hunt the red fox-cub from his lairs'.

[105] *Chron. Melrose*, 62–4; *Hist. ducs de Normandie,* 179; the letters are listed in the Scottish inventories and thence in the Appendix.

become lord of all the barons of these shires and that the rebels there sought to 'introduce the king of Scotland as a buffer between themselves and their old masters'.[106] In what role? The answer surely has to be as lord of the *comitatus*, earldom, not shire, of Northumbria. Holt rightly, in my view, concluded that Alexander sought these lands in the kingdom of England, and not as king of Scots (despite the hesitation introduced in his second edition).[107] If Alexander sought annexation, there was an occasion to achieve it – as a price of support in September 1216 when he met Louis. Instead he did homage and received Louis's charter, evidently because he expected to hold these lands of the new ruler of England, having failed to persuade John to invest him in them. This issue was not resolved till the Treaty of York in 1237.

I have not discussed the lordship of the English Crown over Scotland, and for a very good reason: it was scarcely an issue. Despite the view (for which Gerald of Wales is the only contemporary support[108]) that William did not fully recover the independence of Scotland in 1189 and that he surrendered it in 1209 and 1212, there is no evidence of a liege-homage surviving 1189 and screwed on to a reluctant William twenty years later. On the contrary, John's demand for castles in 1209 shows that he then considered re-establishing the 1174 vassalage ended in 1189, but was persuaded to settle for two lassies and 15,000 marks. The supposed rights of the English crown haunt writing on the period, replacing discussion of the lost texts of the treaties, for two reasons: William called the English king his lord, which of course he was, as Philip Augustus was lord of Henry II and his sons; and Edward I, in accounts which ignored the quittance of 1189, but have since dominated English and Scottish historiography, said that homage was done for Scotland, which it was not. In 1174 there was a charter explicitly acknowledging that lordship and an oath by William's barons to support the English king against the Scottish king if he rejected the former's authority; no such undertaking or oath survived 1189. We do an injustice to both John and William if we seek to explain their tortuous relationship in terms of feudal subjection of Scotland, for thereby we miss its real nature – that the circumspection of Scotland's rulers in accepting the logic of their poorer resources, should make formal subjugation to England unnecessary. The king of Scots learned to be the complaisant friend of his English neighbour, to abjure a role in Anglo-French tensions, to limit his ambitions to the lands north of Tweed and Solway. David I thought to cross those limits from 1136, winning the damnable heritage of the Northumbrian earldom. King William in 1173 chose the painful way to learn the lesson again; but by 1199 he was a reluctant graduate of the school of hard knocks who took a further blow, probably undeserved, in 1209. Alexander II, having crossed the limits in 1215, was fortunate that neither the papacy nor the bankrupt English regency after 1217 was in any position to impose a penalty. He too learned his lesson.

---

[106] Holt, *The Northerners*, 133.
[107] Holt, *The Northerners*, 131–3, xxii n.
[108] *Giraldi Cambrensis Opera*, viii, 156–7.

By 1200, to the English magnates, except for some northerners, with two of whom, Ros and Vescy, William had established a family relationship, Scotland was a land of distant cousins, to whom a redundant spinster might on occasion be married. After 1157, to Henry II and his sons, it was a kingdom to be treated with familiar condescension, its rights recognised so long as it remained isolated from the tensions of the Angevin empire. Should it disappear under the sea, there would be little grief, but it was a kingdom of Christendom, its barons poor relations, but recognisably part of chivalric order; it was not a land for forcible colonisation like savage and immoral Ireland, heretic Toulouse, pagan Spain, or Outremer. Despite the English xenophobia towards Scots which John Gillingham has traced to 1138, Scottish kings were regarded as neighbours, masters in their own house, and generally a heap less troublesome than the descendants of Hugh Capet. This article has sought to show that the tension of Anglo-Scottish relations arose from a demand, not Scottish but by the Scottish king, for Northumbria, and from a reluctance of the English king to address the demand. But crisis occurred only when Philip II of France cranked up the tension by offering alliance to the Scottish king in pursuit of his own agenda: the recovery of Normandy. Whatever King John's failings as 'Softsword' whose word no man might trust, it is difficult to fault his treatment of Scotland for more than procrastination punctuated by impatience.

Looking through the other end of the telescope, we can ask how the magnates of Scotland reacted to the situations in which their king placed himself? For long we assumed that their sense of political identity and therefore rights appeared suddenly after 1286; in the 1960s Barrow first made a strong case for the development of a community by that date. But we have not shown how it had grown during the thirteenth century, nor when it first manifested itself. If it was defined by the existence of an other, the distinct societies, Gaelic and Norse in the west and north, were different from the comity of Anglophones elsewhere in Britain; William and his magnates still struggled to subordinate those societies, that other. But there was a different other, within the Anglophone community, a kingdom with an unjust king responsible for heavy burdens, not only upon his own subjects but also upon the kingdom of Scotland. In this other kingdom the world was truly turned upside down, for as a Scottish poet remarked of 1215:

> A new state of things begun in England, anyone hearing such a thing would call it wonderful to relate, for the body wished to rule the head, and the people sought to rule the king.[109]

The poet gave a wildly distorted account of the rebellion against John, led by knights recruiting reluctant barons – but that distortion tells us how little understanding the Scots now had of the English political community. The documented resentment of Scots at the terms of 1209 and their suspicions in 1213 suggest that a distinct political culture was already in the making in Scotland,

---

[109] *Chron. Melrose*, 60.

perhaps with its origins in the oath demanded by Henry II of William's vassals. If John in 1209 had bullied William into accepting feudal subjection, I doubt that the barons of Scotland would have shown themselves as obediently submissive as had their fathers at York in 1175.

Appendix

Entries from 1199–1216 in the inventories of Scottish records drawn up 1282–92. Not all entries can be dated and some may have been included here which are not of John's reign. The inventories are printed in *Acts of the Parliaments of Scotland*, i, 107–18, and are numbered I, II, VI and VIII. The last has nothing of the period. I have omitted the word 'Item' at the beginning of each entry, and added the Arabic numbering of items.

I. Inventory of 1282

1. Littera regis Johannis quod non possit castrum firmari super portum de Twedmuth.
2. Littera regis Johannis ad recipiendum vii^m et D marc' ad opus regis Anglie pro quodam fine et de residuo remittendo.
3. Littera regis Anglie de die statuto apud Norham.
4. Confederacio inter regem Scocie et barones Anglie olim facta. (II, 2?)
5. Adiudicacio terrarum Northumbrie et Cumbirlandie et Westmerlandie per barones Anglie regi Scocie. (II, 2?)
6. . . . littera convencionalis inter regem Scocie at barones Anglie super quibusdam matrimoniis.
7. Mandatum baronum Anglie facta civitati Carliolensi super reddicione et adiudi[cacione terr]arum Northumbrie Cumbirlandie et Westmerlandie. (II, 4)
8. Mandatum baronum Anglie directum baronibus Northumbrie Cumbirlandie et Westmerlandie per regem Scocie. (II, 5)
9. Littera maioris et burgensium Lundonie. (II, 6)
10. Excusacio nunciorum regis Scocie facta per eosdem super quadam summa pecunie deponenda ad Templum Lundonie.
11. Littera Roberti de Ros et Eustacii de Vescy.
12. Littera Lodouici filii regis Francie de confirmacione carte baronum Anglie. (II, 1?)
13. Alia confederacio inter Scotos et Anglicos. (II, 3?)
14. Solucio iii^m vii^c marcarum et quinquaginta marcarum facta regi Anglie.
15. Littera Ludouici filii regis Francie de Northumbria Cumbirland et Westmerlandia. (II, 1?)
16. Littera de tribus milibus librarum et amplius solutis regi Anglie.

II. Inventory of 1291

1. Carta Lodouici filii regis Francie facta regi Scocie. (I, 12 or 15)
2. Carta baronum Anglie missa regi Scocie contra Johannem regem Anglie. (I, 4 or 5?)
3. Carta baronum Anglie et ciuium Londonie missa regi Scocie contra Johannem regem Anglie. (I, 13?)
4. Carta baronum Anglie missa probis hominibus Carleolensibus contra Johannem regem Anglie de civitate Carleoli reddenda regi Scocie. (I, 7)
5. Item carta baronum Anglie missa tenentibus Northumbrie Westmerlandie Cumbr' contra Johannem regem Anglie. (I, 8)
6. Littera maioris et ciuium Londonie missa regi Scocie contra Johannem regem Anglie. (I, 9)
7. Littera regis Anglie missa regi Scocie et Dauid fratri suo.
8. Carta Johannis regis Anglie missa Willelmo regi Scocie de tractatu maritagii inter regem Francie et filiam Willelmi regis Scocie.
9. Unus baculus unde Eustachius de Vescy seysiuit Regem A[lexandrum] in comitatu Northumbrie cum esset at Norham ad castella obsidenda.

VI. Inventory of 1292

1. In octauo sacculo . . . quedam peticiones facta regibus Anglie per reges Scocie et responsiones ad quasdam.

King John and Wales

Ifor W. Rowlands

While it is true that familiarity is no substitute for political sagacity, it is certain that King John came to the throne with more experience of Wales than any of his predecessors and that, in the course of his reign, he itinerated within it or along its frontiers more frequently than any previous English monarch. Having made due allowance for the greater abundance of surviving royal records and any resulting distortion, it is demonstrable that the period 1199–1216 brought what may be termed Anglo-Welsh relations into sharper focus than before. More correctly perhaps we should speak of the relations between the English state and the congeries of lordships, both native and settler, that so uneasily coexisted within the bounds of *Wallia*. What, in this peripheral region of the Angevin Empire, was the impact of the rule of John?

'King John and Wales' might appear self-defining in terms of that king's dealings with *Wallia* or *terra Wallie* and its inhabitants. Yet it might be pertinent to ask 'which Wales?' Whatever Wales was in 1199 it was not a unitary state as was Scotland nor was it perceived as an indivisible lordship annexed to the English Crown as in the case of Ireland. While its people were readily comprehended as a *gens* or *natio*, neither they nor the country approximated to a single *regnum*, *principatum* or *dominium*. Native Welsh law, it appears, did not admit of a 'high kingship', though it is arguable that Gruffydd ap Llywelyn's position by 1063 was an unarticulated version of such an ascendancy. Wales was in essence made up of parts and was the sum of those parts. In the Chancery enrolments the regional hegemonies are duly identified – Gwynedd (*Nordwallia*), Deheubarth (*Sudwallia*) and Powys (*Powis*).[1] In these records the Welsh princes themselves appear, significantly or not, to be territorially detached as it were and generally their given style is a simple patronymic. In this way at least their lack of title and territorial designation assimilates them to the status of English barons (save the comital ones).[2] This may also reflect the Crown's perception that Welsh lordship was personal before it was territorial.

The above hegemonies and their satellites may be described as 'native Wales' – a convenient modern label corresponding to no contemporary concept

---

[1] *Rot. Chart*, 63 (1199). Grant to Gwenwynwyn of lands in 'tam in Norwallia quam in Sudwall et Powis'.

[2] *Rot. Litt. Pat.*, 39, 40 and 44, where Llywelyn is titled *princeps Norwallie*. These are infrequent designations.

– to distinguish them from those parts of Wales which had not escaped Anglo-Norman conquest and settlement to which the contemporary terms *Marchia* or *Marchie Wallie* were, by John's reign, more routinely applied. Their relative novelty as appellations for the sum of English lordships in Wales is indicated by their continued use to describe particular and localised military commands or commissions in Wales or on its frontier, for example, to *custodes marchiae Walliae*.[3] The 'March' was, one suspects, 'marches' before it became 'the March'. The convenience of the term should not, however, be allowed to conceal the continued existence within those English lordships of sometimes extensive Welsh communities subject more immediately to native dynasties and to Welsh law. The term 'March', though increasingly used in the records in contradistinction to native Wales, described in 1199 a more shifting and fluid reality than what may be called the more mature March of post-1284 which included newly created lordships such as Denbigh but also lordships such as Oswestry and Clun which were withdrawn from shire ground in the course of the thirteenth century. While by 1199 some of the English lordships could trace their histories back to the first or second generation of Anglo-Norman *conquistadores*, others in the so-called 'Middle March' (in Maelienydd and Elfael for instance) were much more recent and less securely held. Indeed Richard I's conciliar government had been very interventionist here. Given this, the historian of the period should be wary of obscuring realities by too loose a usage of the term 'Marcher'. Proximity to the frontier itself is not enough. A true Marcher was defined by a territorial stake and active interest in Wales and, one might add, by close contact (hostile or otherwise) with the native people. John was confronted in Wales, then, by a duality of authority and lordship (Welsh and English) and by two foci of allegiance and obedience (native and settler). Everything was plural and multifaceted while nothing stemmed from a single construction of lordship or dominion. John, like his predecessors, was not even titular 'lord of Wales' for there was no such all-inclusive honour or lordship with which he could be invested or could indeed acquire – short of conquest. There was no *dominium Wallie* corresponding to *dominium Hiberne*. The creation of the March itself ensured that the Welsh people (*natio*) were not commensurate with a single political entity. The English government would first have to wait for the Welsh to invent such a polity in 1267 before they could then annex it in 1284 and reinvent it as the Principality of Wales in 1301.

What were John's *iura* and *negotia* in Wales in 1199? These were primarily the lordships, with their services, jurisdictions and administrations, of Carmarthen (royal from 1105 but the castle had been twice taken and six times attacked by the Welsh thereafter); the county of Pembroke (in royal hands since c.1154 when Richard fitz Gilbert was deprived it it); Glamorgan and Gwynllŵg (both acquired by John by his marriage to Isabella of Gloucester in 1189 and retained after its annulment) and Gower (retained by the Crown after the death of

---

[3] For fuller discussion, see K. Mann, 'The March of Wales: A Question of Terminology', *Welsh History Review* 18, 1996, 1–12.

William, earl of Warwick in 1184).[4] The location, in part accidental, of these royal lordships in the south and west had its geopolitical consequences. The Angevins' interest in Ireland after 1167 and reinforced in 1185 highlighted the strategic importance of the south-west (the Pembroke–Carmarthen axis). This was precisely the region where stability was most imperilled by the segmental conflicts that engulfed the dynasty of Deheubarth from 1197 onwards. John early on profited from this by the acquisition of Cardigan (a base forward of Carmarthen) in 1199, but some time in 1200–1201 he gave Pembroke to William Marshal and in 1203 bestowed Gower (a link between Glamorgan and Carmarthen) upon William de Braose.[5] Not for the last time did the political imperatives of his management of the English baronage override the exigencies of Wales.

John had also of course the homages and fealties of the lords of the March, tenants-in-chief who held their lordships of the Crown and were subject to the normal feudal incidents but not, in general, to aids, scutages and specified military service on the English model. Given the opportunity, a king such as Henry I, for instance, could create a March, as it were, in his own image, for the rights incident upon feudal overlordship and the existence of compact honorial blocs made this possible. Wales was a valuable replenishment to royal sources of patronage. William Marshal was made earl of Pembroke on John's coronation day and William de Braose who likewise played a leading role in smoothing John's path to the throne was another early beneficiary.[6]

Braose, descendant of a family with more than a century of Marcher history and experience, already held the lordships of Brecon, Builth, Radnor and Abergavenny and had annexed Elfael by 1195. His elder son had custody of Monmouth until 1205 and another, Giles, became bishop of Hereford in 1200. William, sheriff of 'Herefordshire in Wales' in 1199 was truly an 'earl of March' *manqué* and his subsequent career almost reads like a sub-text of John's reign. The Marshal, seised *de uxore* of Striguil and Usk in 1189, was only episodically a major force in the March and the same is even truer of Earl Ranulf of Chester.[7] This has not prevented historians from regarding Ranulf as part of John's balancing act in the March as he sought an equilibrium between the three major interests of Chester, Braose and the Marshal (as if a revival of the earlier trinity of Avranches, Montgomery and Fitz Osbern!).[8] Earl Ranulf assuredly had a vulnerable frontier against Gwynedd yet the twelfth-century earls of Chester were, in so far as Wales was concerned, 'dogs that did not bark in the night'. Ranulf may have sought to protect his flank by making overtures to Gwenwynwyn of Powys in 1204 and by building castles at Deganwy and

---

4   To a certain extent, therefore, John inherited a March created by his father.
5   For the grant of Pembroke, see I.W. Rowlands, 'William Marshal, Pembroke Castle and the Historian', *Chateau-Gaillard (Etudes de Castellologie Medievale)* 17, 1996, 154–5.
6   *Ann. Mon.*, i, 24–5.
7   Crouch, *William Marshal*, does not single out the Marshal's involvement in Wales and the March.
8   Warren, *King John*, 197–8.

Holywell in 1210 but his political ambitions and horizons lay elsewhere – in Richmondshire and the Midlands.[9] It is arguable that a more robust stance on his western frontier by Earl Ranulf after 1199, when Mold was lost, may have deterred Llywelyn, but he had significant other priorities. As to the rest of the triumvirate the further promotion of Braose in the Middle March was likely prompted by the menace of Gwenwynwyn while the claim of Marshal upon Pembroke would have been difficult to resist. Other Marchers or frontier lords such as Clifford, Monmouth, Lacy, Mortimer and fitz Alan carried weight, as it were, as leaders of Welsh levies and as an affinity.[10] In turn bullied and seduced by John, the first four became active royal partisans in 1215–16, calculating that by then they had more to fear from the Welsh than from the Crown.

In native Wales John might expect to receive the fealties and homages of its rulers as heir to an as yet ill-defined and only periodically uttered overlordship and a tradition of royal interventionism evident in the Anglo-Norman period and in the reigns of both his father and brother.[11] But there was, as yet, no continuity in all this, and much of it was the product of particular circumstances, the forming of personal bonds of fealty or mutual aid and protection between king and native prince, of homages given to deflect royal anger. Welsh lords regarded homages done to the king as personal rather than territorial. They took royal power into account in their political calculations if they were politic enough and appreciated the value of royal protection. It was an in-built feature of their political landscape by 1199, but not a constant and predictive constraint on their actions. They did not regard themselves, as English barons did, as part of an institutionalised network of fealties. Native rulers acknowledged when needful or opportune a dependence on the Crown which was in practice disregarded. They recognised the dominance of the king but did not conduct themselves as if subject to his domination. For an English king it was a matter of maintaining a benign status quo or intervening, diplomatically and militarily, if royal interests were threatened or the wider imperatives of Angevin politics demanded, and all this without necessarily invoking feudal overlordship. Royal aims could be achieved by means other than war or feudal discipline – by favouring one party in a dynastic conflict, by bribes and pensions and other manifestations of royal benevolence.[12]

In native Wales, John was confronted by a kaleidoscope of competing dynastic hegemonies, some contracting and others expanding, whose cohesion was often distorted by internal segmentation, partible inheritance and relatively primitive realisations of administrative and territorial lordship. Contested border areas, therefore, were often flashpoints of conflict, and could suck in Marchers and

---

[9] Holt, *Magna Carta and Medieval Government*, 132–4.

[10] For a fuller treatment of John and the March – and much else– see Kevin Mann, 'King John, Wales and the March', unpublished University of Wales PhD thesis, 1991.

[11] Warren, *Henry II*, 153–69 gives an excellent analysis of these matters.

[12] For the wider context, see R.R. Davies, *Domination and Conquest: The Experience of Ireland, Scotland and Wales*, Cambridge 1990.

Crown alike. A notable instance in Richard's reign was the Middle March of Maelienydd, Elfael and Gwerthrynion which drew in the rulers of Powys, Deheubarth, Braose and Mortimer and, eventually, royal forces.[13] The waxing and waning of these hegemonies or of the more successful dynasts was one of the few constancies. The instability consequent upon internal segmentation was evident enough in Gwynedd between 1170 and 1200, and it proved mortal to Deheubarth after 1197. Indeed the fragmentation of the latter, which endured up to the Edwardian Conquest, was a major destabilising factor in South Wales throughout John's reign.[14] Until it was partitioned in an agreed settlement in 1216 under the supervision of Llywelyn ap Iorwerth of Gwynedd, the strife between Rhys ap Gruffydd's descendants spilled over to embroil the Crown, the Marcher lords (notably the Marshal) and the rulers of both Powys and Gwynedd. It enabled John in 1199 to obtain possession of Cardigan, and William Marshal in 1204 to capture Cilgerran and in this way reconstruct the wider Clare earldom of Pembroke.[15] It was clearly a matter of concern to the Crown whenever Deheubarth's weakness fuelled the expansionism of Powys and Gwynedd and it could not always play the part of a detached observer but had sometimes to immerse itself as a party to these segmental rivalries.

Elsewhere in native Wales it was the more aggressive posture of the other two leading players that demanded atttention, namely Gwenwynwyn of southern Powys from 1198, and Llywelyn of Gwynedd from 1199.[16] The greater proximity of the former to the English border and the core of the March lands and his assault on Painscastle made him appear the greater immediate threat. This may have averted John's gaze from the danger signals from Gwynedd for Llywelyn had in 1199 captured the castle of Mold (some twelve miles from Chester) and in the following year proceeded to assume sole dominion over the principality. Initially, however, Llywelyn may have been regarded as a counter to Gwenwynwyn. This is why the former was given royal recognition of his position in 1199 as a prelude to negotiations which culminated in a treaty ('pax') with John in 1201.[17]

How effectively did John protect his interests in Wales? Earlier historians were content to write of John's Welsh 'policy'. Thus, in his classic *History of Wales*, published in 1911, J.E. Lloyd said

in dealing with Wales he pursued, on the whole, a settled and consistent policy. His aim was to divide and disintegrate, to checkmate the designs of

---

[13] For the strategic significance of this region, see J. Beverley Smith, 'The Middle March in the Thirteenth Century', *Bulletin of the Board of Celtic Studies* 24, 1970–72, 77–93. It looms large too in the pipe rolls of the reign of Richard I.

[14] The detailed narrative is to be found in J.E. Lloyd, *A History of Wales from the Earliest Times to the Edwardian Conquest*, 3rd edn, London 1939, ii, chapter xvii.

[15] Crouch, *William Marshal*, 78–9 provides the context.

[16] Llywelyn's success has so hypnotised Welsh historians that his Powysian contemporary and rival has suffered, I think, from undue neglect. He should be rescued.

[17] *Rot. Litt. Pat.*, 8–9. This remarkable agreement, negotiated on John's behalf by Hubert Walter and Geoffrey fitz Peter, merits fuller treatment than is accorded it here and I hope to treat it at greater length elsewhere.

the more formidable chiefs by favouring their rivals, so that thus the land might be torn by the strife of opposing and not ill-balanced parties. It was a policy which for many years bade fair to be successful and only failed because the statesmanship of Llywelyn enabled him to take advantage of the serious difficulties in which the king involved himself as his reign drew to a close.[18]

Later Welsh historians have been largely content to refine rather than refute this analysis. Naturally, Lloyd's perspective was different and necessarily Cambrocentric. His discussion of the period treats essentially of the career of Llywelyn the Great (d. 1240), whose mastery of the Welsh political scene after 1215 provided Lloyd with his conceptual structure and mode of interpretation. Limited use was made of the record evidence other than the Chancery rolls, yet it is curious that so little use was made of the 1201 peace between John and Llywelyn enrolled as letters patent.[19] He apparently did not know of the existence of the Franco–Welsh alliance of 1212 and the text of Llywelyn's charter of security in 1211 (demanded of him by John) remained unpublished until 1984.[20] The pipe rolls of the Exchequer would have further illuminated such matters as Welsh royal pensioners, the recruitment of Welsh infantry, military disbursements in Wales in the years immediately prior to 1211. Narrative and the inter-play of personalities mattered more to Lloyd – the niceties of feudal dependence were the concern of a later school of historians. Concern with matters constitutional, with the feudal nexus between native rulers and the English Crown, and with English 'proto-imperialism' has provided a new and fruitful context for analysing the subordination and eventual elimination of native rule and the non- appearance of a unitary Welsh state. Particular attention has been paid to the friction between jurisdictional 'plates' or, in Powicke's succinct phrase, 'the conflict of laws'.[21]

For Rees Davies, in his magisterial contribution to the *Oxford History of Wales*, the reign of John was a 'formative period in Anglo-Welsh relations'.[22] The parameters within which these would in future be played out had found their defining moment in the reign of the last Angevin. 'John had shown that the English monarchy had assembled the theoretical pretext and the military means to convert overlordship of Wales to direct lordship should it wish'. It remained for a conjunction of will and opportunity. Written documents such as the 1201 treaty, the 1208 *conventio* between John and Gwenwynwyn of Powys and Llywelyn's charter of security of 1211 all played their part in the episodic, but

---

[18] J.E. Lloyd, *A History of Wales*, ii, 614.

[19] This is remedied in R.R. Davies, *Conquest, Coexistence and Change: Wales, 1063–1415*, Oxford 1987, 294–5.

[20] J. Beverley Smith, 'Magna Carta and the Charters of the Welsh Princes', *EHR* 94, 1984, 344–62; R.F. Treharne, 'The Franco–Welsh Treaty of Alliance in 1212', *Bulletin of the Board of Celtic Studies* 18, 1958–60, 60–75.

[21] The title of chapter xv in *Henry III and The Lord Edward*, Oxford 1947.

[22] R.R. Davies, *Conflict, Coexistence and Change*, 296.

cumulative, intensification of royal overlordship of native Wales both at the princely and aristocratic level.[23]

These documents illustrate the manner in which, on one level, the Crown increasingly perceived the native Welsh princes as barons of a sensibly English kind; their status was being assimilated to that of English tenants-in-chief. There was the opportunistic intrusion, whenever a relationship was being defined, of the concepts of *fidelitas* and *servitium*. By the terms of the peace of 1201 Llywelyn came 'into the king's service' and then he and (significantly) his great men were to swear fealty; when John returns to England, Llywelyn is to do homage to him 'sicut domino suo ligio'.[24] Earlier, a cluster of charters in favour of individual Welsh lords (Gwenwynwyn of Powys, Maelgwn ap Rhys of Deheubarth among them) issued at Poitiers in 1199 contains, with only slight variations, a formula which holds the recipients liable for homage and service and in words suggestive of liege-homage: 'ita quod nobis fideliter serviet [in this instance Gruffydd ap Cynan of Meirionydd] et nobis fideliter existet contra omnes mortales'.[25] This tenor is starkest in the humiliation of Gwenwynwyn of Powys in October 1208 when he was required to hand over twenty named hostages for his life and limbs after swearing 'quod fideliter serviet eidem domino regi de se et terra sua in perpetuum'.[26] Significantly, Llywelyn in 1201 was permitted to decide whether certain actions that may be taken against him concerning right title to the land he held (he was not to be vexed by possessory actions) should proceed by Welsh law; Gwenwynwyn, on the contrary, 'stabit iuri in curia ipsius regis ad summonicionem suam de omnibus quae erga ipsum proponentur'. Llywelyn was in a position to negotiate, Gwenwynwyn came as a suppliant. In 1211 Llywelyn himself was compelled to accept terms for the remission of the king's 'malevolence and indignation', amongst which the making of John his heir for Gwynedd should he not have his own heir by his wife Joan (the king's daughter) most clearly demonstrated the perils of being enmeshed within the feudal nexus. In a vain attempt to contain Llywelyn, in the following year John granted to the former's dynastic rivals Owain ap Gruffudd and Gruffydd ap Rhodri lands and castles in the Perfeddwlad and they were to hold them of the king and his heirs and, more significantly, to do specified military service for them.[27]

Where the *ius scriptum* is in this fashion, the *iustum bellum* is not far behind: such documents could be used to legitimise punitive campaigns of annexation

---

[23] The terms imposed on Gwenwynwyn are in Rymer's *Foedera*, I i, 101.

[24] Was it this treaty that was referred to in a bull of Honorius III of 1226 when he confirmed to Llywelyn 'libertates tibi a clare memoriae Johanne rege Anglorum de regali liberalite concessas prout in ipsius litteris dicitur plenius contineri sicut eas iuste ac pacifice obtines'? *Littere Wallie, preserved in Liber A in the Public Record Office*, ed. J.G. Edwards, London 1935, 34.

[25] *Rot. Chart.*, 63.

[26] Rymer's *Foedera*, I i, 101. Four of the named witnesses were Marcher lords, namely, William fitz Alan, Robert Corbet, Hugh Pantulf and John L'Estrange.

[27] *Rot. Chart.*, 188. For 1247, see C.W. Lewis, 'The Treaty of Woodstock: its Background and Significance', *Welsh History Review* 2, 1964–65, 37–65.

and disinheritance in the guise of feudal discipline. John's second successful Welsh campaign of 1211 had indeed demonstrated the possibility and potentiality of an English ascendancy in Wales. After 1216, the memory of this fleeting hegemony was to be a powerfully motivating political legacy, attractive to Crown and Marchers alike. For the Welsh, too, the period had been equally formative: the options had been clarified because narrowed. 1211 must have revealed in the starkest terms the choices between vassalage, unity or conquest. The following three-quarters of a century were to show that they could neither accommodate the first nor achieve the second.

The narrative framework for the history of Anglo-Welsh relations between 1199 and 1216 now stands well established and R.R. Davies has refined, conceptually and otherwise, their significance for the history of medieval Wales. My intention here is simply to focus more narrowly on some features of John's dealings with Wales which resonate with the wider context of his personal rule and to assess their impact on relations between Wales and the English state. My brief confines me to Wales, but the wider 'British' context should be borne in mind. The 'Celtic fringe', though by now a term so ingrained as to be beyond eradication, is a historically meaningless construct both as to 'Celtic' and to 'fringe'.[28] Within the wider context of British history as properly understood, there is more to the study of these than their assumed 'Celticity' and certainly more that is central about them than is peripheral. In John's reign, it is the differences between Scotland, Wales and Ireland that are striking – Scotland was a separate kingdom, Ireland was a unitary lordship and Wales was neither. There are obvious parallels – closest perhaps between the lands of incomplete conquest, Wales and Ireland, who both had their Marches and where there were localised areas of royal demesne and lordship. Important, too, were the tenurial links, the cross-channel holdings of such men as William Marshal, William de Braose and the Lacys – great men in Wales and Ireland.

In Wales much of John's interventionism and methods were traditional, drawing on Angevin and Anglo-Norman practice as much the forte of Henry I and Henry II. In part this meant the exploitation of those fissures, dynastic and constitutional, inherent in the socio-political structure of native Wales itself. In other areas, the closest parallels are with his father's reign. Henry II undertook three campaigns in Wales in the first part of his reign (1157, 1163 and 1165) and the last of them, though it proved abortive, was by all accounts a major affair, suggesting to his modern biographer that 'Henry, it seems, intended to settle the Welsh problem once and for all.' After leading back a retreating army, the king ordered the mutilation and hanging of twenty-two Welsh hostages.[29] In

---

[28] The most recent foray is the section on 'John and the British Isles', in Turner, *King John*, London 1994, 135ff. Celticity is so clear a sub-text here that the Welsh (p. 137) are termed 'Gaelic'.

[29] Warren, *Henry II*, 163. The fate of the hostages is in *Brut y Tywysogyon (Peniarth Ms, 20 version)*, ed. T. Jones, Cardiff 1952, 64–5 (henceforth all references to the *Brut* are to this version).

1211 John led two campaigns into Wales against Llywelyn (the first aborted through supply shortages); in the following year a host mustered for a French campaign was redirected to Chester for a new offensive against Llywelyn and his allies who had rejected the settlement imposed upon him. The impressive preparations for this campaign, which included the impressment of just under 8,500 labourers, has been seen in rather similar terms, namely, as John's attempt to find a final solution to the problem of Wales by intending 'to establish a permanent basis for English rule'.[30] When he was thwarted by intelligence of a baronial conspiracy, he vented his anger by the hanging of twenty-eight Welsh hostages; like father, like son.[31]

The matter of hostages has recently been highlighted by Seán Duffy in a study of King John's 1210 expedition to Ireland and, more particularly, his dealings with the two most powerful native rulers Cathal Crobderg, king of Connacht, and Aed Meith O Neill, king of Cenel Eogain in Ulster.[32] Negotiations between them and John foundered on the issue of the hostages demanded by John. When King William of Scotland felt it politic to submit to John in 1209, the latter demanded twelve or more hostages from the sons of the Scottish nobility together with two of William's daughters whose promised marriages did not materialise.[33] When Llywelyn was compelled to submit two years later, he agreed to hand over his son Gruffydd 'tenendum semper et ad faciendum inde voluntatem suam' and released to John 'obsides de terra mea quos et quot et de quibus habere voluerit'.[34] The return of such hostages would figure prominently in the negotiations between the Welsh princes and John in the months leading up to Magna Carta. It is perhaps with regard to Gwenwynwyn's submission on 8 October 1208 that such a 'hostage policy' receives its most elaborate and even ritualised documented form. The twenty hostages are all named save in two instances where they are specified as 'primogenitus . . . de uxore [or 'de sponse'] sua'; twelve are to be handed over within the following eight days during which time Gwenwynwyn's body is at the king's will and he will remain in custody until the remaining eight are delivered.[35] John then had refined his 'hostage policy' in his dealings with the Welsh, Irish and Scots before deploying it as an instrument of political discipline in England.[36] There might have been an ease about hostage-giving (not under compulsion) when done to affirm a relationship or as a voluntary sign of peace or submission; it was surely a different matter when one party insisted in this manner, when the

---

[30] Introduction to the *Pipe Roll 14 John*, xv–xvi.

[31] The chroniclers differ as to the number of hostages put to death but Wendover, Gervase of Canterbury and the 'Barnwell' annalist are agreed on the fact of the executions.

[32] 'King John's Expedition to Ireland, 1210: the Evidence Reconsidered', *Irish Historical Studies* 30, no. 17, 1996, 1–24.

[33] Duncan, *Scotland*, 245–9.

[34] J. Beverley Smith, 'Magna Carta', 361–2.

[35] Rymer's *Foedera,* I i, 101.

[36] On John's hostage-taking in England, see J.C. Holt, 'Feudal Society and the Family in Early Medieval England, III: Patronage and Politics', *TRHS* 4th ser., 1984, 13–14.

giver's plans for the succession and inheritance were taken out of his hands in this way. Hostages given to John might be forgiven for entertaining but low expectations of an honourable confinement. If by the mid-twelfth century, chivalrous convention dictated a different treatment of French or English hostages from 'barbarous' Irish or Welsh ones, it was a convention that John crossed. It is at the very least arguable that John's extravagant demands for, and treatment of, hostages poisoned to some extent his relationships with the native princes.

In the more benign matter of marriage alliances, Henry II's initiatives are replicated in the reign of his youngest son. In 1175 Dafydd ab Owain, temporarily successful in the sibling rivalries of the Gwynedd dynasty, was married to the king's half-sister, Emma, natural daughter of Geoffrey of Anjou, with the Shropshire manor of Ellesmere as her marriage portion. In 1205, as he sought to bind Llywelyn to him, John conveyed to him his natural daughter Joan and the same manor of Ellesmere.[37] Such marriage arrangements could have more sinister outcomes as King William of Scotland might have realised in 1209 and 1212 and as Llywelyn was to realise in 1211 when he undertook to convey Gwynedd itself as an escheat to King John should he not have an heir by his wife Joan.

While this clause was novel and suggests that Llywelyn's position in John's eyes approximated to that of a tenant-in-chief in England, a traditional concern of the Crown is revealed in Llywelyn's reparations, namely, contributions towards military supplies.[38] Unlike Scotland, Wales could not be tapped as a source of silver pennies but it was, under the Angevins, exploited as a recruiting ground for troops.[39] In the short-lived Treaty of Woodstock of 1247, a triumphant Henry III was able to make specified military service an obligation upon the then rulers of Gwynedd.[40] John provided a precedent when, as we have seen, he conveyed lands in the Perfeddwlad in 1212 to Owain ap Dafydd and Gruffudd ap Rhodri.[41] Welsh troops were either recruited directly from the royal lordships in Wales (especially Glamorgan), from the Marcher lordships (especially the Braose lands after 1209), from Welsh friendlies or from native rulers (such as the Lord Rhys in 1173–74 and Llywelyn in 1209) who either thought it politic to volunteer such assistance or were pressurised to do so.[42] Both Henry II and Richard had used paid Welsh levies in their French campaigns; the latter in 1196 collected the surprisingly high total of over 2,100 Welsh foot.[43] John was to continue this practice not only for his campaigns in

---

[37] Dafydd ab Owian died an exile in England, in 1203. *Brut y Tywysogyon*, 82.

[38] J. Beverley Smith, 'Magna Carta', 362: 'dabo eidem domino meo regi pro expensis suis decem ilia vaccarum et quadraginta dextrarios et sexaginta chascurios'.

[39] Warren, *Henry II*, 158: 'Fighting men from the Welsh mountains were, indeed, the Gurkhas of the twelfth century.'

[40] J.G. Edwards, *Littere Wallie*, 7–8.

[41] *Rot. Chart.*, 188: 'ibunt in servicium nostrum cum gentibus de dictis cantredis'.

[42] The Introductions to the pipe rolls of 1154–1216 provide plentiful references to the Crown's recruitment of Welsh footmen.

[43] *C.R. 8 Richard I*, xvii–xviii.

France but also in England itself when, as count of Mortain, he used them during the crisis of 1191.[44] He recruited them likewise in the crisis of 1215, and his overtures to the Welsh rulers of the Middle March in July 1216 may in part have been inspired by similar considerations.[45]

The campaigns to defend Normandy and the other Angevin territories in France and the efforts, ultimately abortive, to recover the duchy and other lands lost from 1204 onwards explain the militarisation that informs so much of John's reign.[46] Wales, in this regard supplied manpower (and in 1211 material) but this overarching preoccupation resonated in other ways, too. John's 'hot war' (1199–1203) for the defence of Normandy and his largely 'cold war' for its recovery (1203–13) had an impact upon the king's dealings outside England itself. W.L. Warren explored some of these interconnections, particularly with regard to John's relations with the great Anglo-Norman lords in the lordship of Ireland.[47] In Wales John's patronage in the years up to 1205/6 of Marshal, Braose and Lacy may well be explained by their commitment to the defence of Normandy in which they had a significant territorial investment and, after 1204 (with the exception of the Marshal), compensation for losses sustained in the duchy.[48] At a later stage, but equally telling was the intrusion into custodies and offices in the March and the royal lordships there after the fall of Braose of those who had displayed conspicuous loyalty and support overseas: men such as Engelard de Cigogné and Gerard de Athies from Touraine and Falkes de Bréauté from Normandy. Wales did not escape the consequences of the fact that John had lost King Richard's war (1199–1204) and could not win his own (1213–14).

Nowhere is this brought into clearer focus than the still somewhat neglected matter of the treaty between Llywelyn and Philip Augustus. This is referred to in a letter from the Welsh ruler to the king of France which its editor assigned to some date in July or early August 1212.[49] A close reading of the letter suggests that Llywelyn assumed the treaty to be already in force and, if so, it is possible that it would have been negotiated in May or June 1212. King John's impressive preparations for his campaign into Wales (diverting all this from a proposed expedition to Poitou) – while surely a response to the Welsh *revanchiste* offensives after his conquests of 1211 – may therefore be explained by some intelligence or foreknowledge on his part of such a pact. John reacted

---

[44] E.g. *Rot. Litt. Claus.*, i, 210 (August, 1214) for Welsh troops summoned for embarkation at Portsmouth; the writ is addressed to Engelard de Cigogné, then keeper of the Braose estates. Payment was also arranged at this time for 300 Welsh brought by Gruffudd ap Rhodri to whom John had granted lands in the Perfeddwlad in 1212 (see n.27 above).

[45] E.g. *Rot. Litt. Claus.*, i, 214 (June 1215) Fawkes de Bréauté to send 400 Welsh to Salisbury by 9 June.

[46] 'There is a strong military colour to his rule throughout': Jolliffe, 'Chamber', 118.

[47] W.L. Warren, 'King John and Ireland', 26–42.

[48] E.g. *Rot. Chart.*, 66 (June 1200): licence to William de Braose to seize lands from his Welsh enemies 'in incrementum baronie sue de Radenorure'.

[49] R.F. Treharne, 'The Franco–Welsh Treaty', 66–70.

in a similar way in 1209 when he 'had every reason to think that he faced the likelihood of a political alliance between the French king and the Scottish king'.[50] He would not be unaware, one imagines, of the decision in the same year of Innocent III to lift the interdict on the lands of Llywelyn, Gwenwynwyn of Powys and their confederates as a way of increasing the pressure on John.[51] The French Crown and the papacy could exploit those tensions and resentments in Wales which John's campaigns in 1211 and the subsequent settlement had created.

The collapse of the royal position in Wales by early 1216 – in large measure a delayed response by the Welsh to that settlement – was as sudden as it was dramatic. In the autumn of 1211 the Crown's position in Wales was, in terms of territorial extent, larger than it ever had been. John's conquest of the Perfeddwlad (Gwynedd between the Conwy and the Dee), his continuing occupation of the Braose lordships, his annexation of Aberystwyth and its environs, and control of the Lacy lands enhanced a presence already secured by the lordships of Cardigan, Carmarthen and Glamorgan. All this betokened a dangerous and menacing novelty for the Welsh. John was a Welsh landlord on a scale not matched until 1277. Those who had been disinherited and dispossessed in 1211 would seek recovery; those who had not might well fear the same fate. The resulting backlash, informed most crucially by the way the other Welsh princes got in line behind Llywelyn (including Gwenwynwyn of Powys whom Llywelyn had dispossessed in 1209), was, as seen, given added potency by the involvement of Philip Augustus and Innocent III. John was not so much the victim of his own success in 1211, rather he was deceived by it. After securing a rather similar ascendancy in 1277, Edward I had to make a huge financial investment in castle-building to underpin it. In 1212 John, in terms of castle-building, invested less and paid a disproportionate political price.[52] By 1276 Edward I had the support not only of Llywelyn ap Gruffydd's brother Dafydd, but also of Gruffydd ap Gwenwynwyn of Powys. John had effectively emasculated Gwenwynwyn of Powys so that when the latter eventually committed himself to the Crown in 1216 he was a broken reed. John would have been better advised to protect the Powysian ruler in 1208 as a means of containing Llywelyn; John's decision to opt for a rapprochement with the northern prince was a close call but, in retrospect, the wrong one.

John's problems in Wales by 1212–13 were not insurmountable and by negotiation and military interventions he was able to contain them until

---

[50] Duncan, *Scotland*, 243–4.

[51] *Brut y Tywysogyon*, 87: 'And he enjoined upon them, *for the remission of their sins*, to direct friendly endeavour and actions against the iniquity of that king' (the italics are mine).

[52] The labour force impressed in 1212 strongly suggests that John had an extensive castle-building programme in mind (n. 30 above) but little had been achieved after the 1211 campaigns, save at Aberystwyth and (by Robert de Vieuxpoint) at Mathrafal in Powys. Deganwy and Holywell were fortified in 1210 by the earl of Chester.

1215.[53] He had lost the Perfeddwlad and control over the Aberystwyth pocket but he was not without Welsh allies; the storm was one he could weather, given time. Time was the one commodity he did not have in 1215; the great gamble of 1214 had not paid off. John's miscalculations in Wales now ensured that as the political storm in England gathered about his head there could be no *cordon sanitaire* around Wales; it could not be insulated from the collapse of royal authority in England. There was in Wales itself no natural constituency for him. In much of Wales John had ensured that when the crunch came more would be against him than with him. In the March and its environs, to be sure, he could rely on the Marshal, and he had managed to attach to him de Lacy, Clifford, Mortimer, L'Estrange and Monmouth but, in addition to William and John fitz Alan, the sons of the disinherited William de Braose – Giles, bishop of Hereford, and his brother Reginald – were to continue their father's feud against the king.

By the spring of 1215 the particular idiom of John's dealings with Wales conspired with baronial disaffection in England to confront him with a trinity so novel that it had no precedent – a powerful group of English barons formed a league against him; all the leading Welsh princes were already leagued against him and now *both* allied with each other.[54] Previous English kings had faced the first of these threats, and occasionally the second, but none had faced all three simultaneously – until John. (We may add, too, that his northern vassals were to do homage to the king of Scots.) A notable outcome of this hybrid coalition was Llywelyn's capture of the castle and borough of Shrewsbury in 1215, 'surrendered without resistance'.[55] The account of this remarkable event in the Welsh chronicle suggests that it coordinated with the baronial entry into London in May of that year. This cannot be confirmed but it is at least conceivable that it was not only (though chiefly) the loss of London that brought John to take negotiations seriously, but also a Welsh presence in a city well within the bounds of his kingdom and one which had never encountered such a fate before. Nothing else is known of this brief Welsh occupation and it is possible that it was restored by Llywelyn after the sealing of Magna Carta which provided, *inter alia*, for the restoration of Welsh hostages and of his (and other) charters of submission.

From 1213 onwards Llywelyn was to establish an ascendancy in Wales not enjoyed by a Welsh ruler since the 1060s and this at the expense both of the Crown and the Marchers. Especially dramatic was his onslaught in December 1215 upon the Marcher castles of the south.[56] William Marshal's much vaunted military reputation took a severe knock as Cardigan and Carmarthen fell – both

---

[53] J.E. Lloyd, *A History of Wales*, ii. 637–643.

[54] *Brut y Tywysogyon*, 89.

[55] *Brut y Tywysogyon*, 90.

[56] *Brut y Tywysogyon*, 91–2. Llywelyn's success in 1215–16 is in part explained by the fact that he took advantage of a clement December to undertake a winter campaign.

were in his charge.[57] Alone of the important ones, his own fortress of Pembroke was not to be assaulted (though Welsh raiding came close enough); perhaps it was by then too formidable an obstacle and, to the astute Llywelyn, a castle too far.[58] By the time of John's death, the March had been severely battered and the Crown's territorial stake in Wales had been reduced to a rump in the south-east. Retreat on this scale eclipsed those losses incurred in Stephen's reign.

There was a stench of failure everywhere and nowhere more noxious perhaps than in Wales and the March. Where the Crown was in retreat, Llywelyn had established a military alliance and political federation that was to become a *de facto* principality. The mastery that John had achieved in 1211, which so impressed the chroniclers, proved illusory and began to unravel within a year.[59] It was a temporary ascendancy imposed by conquest, the threat of further annexations and by bullying. It was not cushioned against any serious challenge or change in its equilibrium. Having decided from 1201 to extend his grace and benevolence to the clearly expansionist Llywelyn and delaying a confrontation until 1210–11, John had given himself less room to manoeuvre and had in the process undermined the power and credibility of Llywelyn's only serious rival, Gwenwynwyn of Powys. When the latter seceded from Llywelyn's federation in 1216, he was of little use to the Crown. When John determined to move against Llywelyn in 1211, he engineered the least advantageous outcome: he had left Llywelyn humbled but not defeated. The resultant Welsh reaction caught him unprepared and when he did decide in 1212 to complete what had been unfinished the year before, he was prevented from doing so. In 1211, it might be said, it was not the case that he had gone too far but rather that he had not gone far enough. Short-termism and the allure of an easy triumph likewise informed his actions elsewhere.

John's hardening stance against Llywelyn in 1210 may in part have resulted from the latter's support for William de Braose whose fall from favour in 1208 and subsequent outlawry provided vivid confirmation, if such were needed, of the vindictive force of John's malevolence. Of more relevance in a Welsh context was the resultant political 'fall-out' which the king may not have foreseen. Braose's removal and his attempts to stir up trouble in his erstwhile lordships (the most extensive in the March) destabilised the whole area. It stirred the ambitions of opportunist Welsh rulers and it engendered, in the later attempts of William's sons to recover their patrimony, a Marcher–Welsh alliance and an early Braose attachment to the rebel faction of 1215. The Braose lands were entrusted to John's alien familiars – Engelard de Cigogné, Gerard de Athies and Falkes de Bréauté. No English baron, and assuredly no Marcher, was to profit from the downfall of one of their number as might have happened

---

[57] The earl's castle of Cilgerran, which had been seized in 1202, was also lost to the Welsh, *Brut y Tywysogyon*, 92.

[58] I.W. Rowlands, 'William Marshal', 154–5 for a discussion of the Marshal's works at Pembroke.

[59] E.g. *Walter of Coventry*, 203.

under Henry I or Henry II. In this instance John's actions in Wales are eloquent of the weft and weave – of the very texture – of his personal rule.

John's successor was left to contend with this self-evident failure in Wales. Yet, as Rees Davies has shown, John's legacy was not wholly a poisonous one. John had demonstrated what a properly prepared military strike (and one beyond the Conway river) could achieve and how an increasing definition of royal overlordship could provide the occasion for such an enterprise. He had also bequeathed to his infant son and his council a divided kingdom in whose affairs the matter of Wales was to loom large. This was the most immediate legacy. All this was presaged in 1215 when Welsh demands appeared in the Articles of the Barons and in Magna Carta itself and more so (if the evidence is to be believed) when Llywelyn, together with Alexander of Scotland, was invited by the barons to elect a new king.[60] The regent of England in 1216 was a man whose chief territorial interests lay in Wales (and in Ireland) and a successor as dominant counsellor, Hubert de Burgh, likewise had Marcher ambitions. A settlement with Llywelyn was an early pressing concern of the minority government and thereafter when Henry III assumed personal rule the matter of Wales became, if not routinely so, at least a not insignificant constituent of the *magna negotia regni*. If Henry II had given John the lordship of Ireland, John in a sense bequeathed to Henry III the overlordship of Wales.

[60] Duncan, *Scotland*, 523 and n.9.

John and the Church of Rome

Christopher Harper-Bill

If the political identity of England, and latterly even of the United Kingdom, has come over the last four centuries to be moulded by a Reformation perceived to have been Protestant, the conflict between King John and Pope Innocent III quickly took its place as an important, if abortive, prelude to the momentous struggle of the sixteenth century. In the accounts of the Tudor historians of England, and consequently in Shakespeare's dramatic rendering, the king is blamed not so much for tyranny, political miscalculation or even the loss of his French provinces, as for his surrender, after a promising start which prefigured Henry VIII's militant stance, to the aggression and the blandishments of the church of Rome. The memory lingers on. On 3 February 1997 Sister Lavinia Byrne, in her 'thought for the day' on BBC Radio 4's *Today* programme, cited Innocent III's interdict on England as one of the residual reasons for British hostility to Europe, a folk-memory of which the details have long been obscured, but nevertheless engraved upon the national consciousness. So certainly the topic still matters, and although very little can be added to the magisterial accounts of C.R. Cheney,[1] who devoted much of a lifetime of distinguished scholarship to the subject, reiteration in this volume may not be entirely superfluous.[2]

The Condition of the Church on the Eve of the Interdict

Two diametrically opposed views might be taken of the state of the English church at the turn of the twelfth and thirteenth centuries. When compared with

---

[1] Cheney, *From Becket to Langton*; *Hubert Walter*; *Innocent III and England*. Also 'King John and the Papal Interdict', 'King John's Reaction to the Interdict on England', 'A Recent View of the General Interdict on England', 'The Alleged Deposition of King John' and 'The Church and Magna Carta', all repr. in *The Papacy and England: 12th–14th Centuries*, London 1982. Cheney, of course, also took the lead in the edition of *Letters of Innocent III*, *SLI* and *C & S* 2.

[2] For other good short accounts, see Painter, *Reign of King John*, 151–202; Warren, *King John*, 154–73, 206–16; Turner, *King John*, 147–74; C.H. Lawrence, ed., *The English Church and the Papacy in the Middle Ages*, London 1965, chapters 3–4; B.M. Bolton, 'Philip Augustus and John: Two Sons in Innocent III's Vineyard', in *The Church and Sovereignty: c. 590–1918: Essays in Honour of Michael Wilks*, ed. D. Wood, *SCH subsidia* 9, 1991, 113–34.

the vision proclaimed by the papal reformers of the late eleventh century, an ideal enthusiastically (if perhaps anachronistically) taken up by Thomas Becket in the 1160s, it was a poor thing, enjoying little of the liberty which Pope Gregory VII had proclaimed to be essential for the fulfilment of the church's mission, and regulated by custom, which the same pope had asserted to be the antithesis of Truth.[3] Most importantly, the Crown retained effective control over the appointment of bishops and abbots. Free election may have been conceded in theory, but might mean something very different in practice. The reality was indeed expressed by the writ allegedly sent by Henry II to the monks of Winchester in 1173: 'I order you to hold a free election; nevertheless, I forbid you to elect anyone save Richard my clerk.'[4] It would be a brave electoral body which would dare to incur the *malevolentia*, the institutionalised ill-will, of an Angevin king; and indeed the secular cathedral chapters, packed with royal clerks, felt no inclination to do so. The men appointed to the episcopal bench after the Compromise of Avranches of 1173 were of the same type as those consecrated before the Becket conflict – royal servants, the younger sons of baronial families in the king's favour, only the occasional holy man who had captured the ruler's imagination.

Vacancies following the deaths of prelates were prolonged, to increase the revenues which were taken into the king's hands. During vacancies, moreover, the Crown might tallage the tenants of a greater church. From Lincoln, for example, in the vacancy following the death of Hugh of Avalon, between November 1200 and July 1202, the Crown took a net profit of £2,649.[5] Bishoprics and the major Benedictine abbeys were burdened by military service to the Crown in return for the tenure of their lands. The church owed the service of 741½ knights, about one-seventh of the total *servitium debitum* of England,[6] paid scutage in lieu of this service, and was also charged those fines levied in addition for the 'privilege' of paying rather than actually sending trained cavalry.

All disputes relating to the real estate of the church, including rights of patronage, were reserved to the royal courts, and bishops often had to appear there as litigants in cases relating to churches, manors and knights' fees. In other ways, too, royal intervention in the administration of the English church, outlined as customary in the Constitutions of Clarendon of 1164, becomes more clearly visible in the early thirteenth century due to the enrolment of Chancery writs and most especially of records of the *curia regis*. Bishops and their officers were bombarded by writs and mandates from the secular government.

---

[3] For convenient accounts of the development of the papal position, see R.W. Southern, *Western Society and the Church in the Middle Ages*, Harmondsworth 1970, chapter 11; C. Morris, *The Papal Monarchy: the Western Church from 1050 to 1250*, Oxford 1989, chapters 4–5, 8–9, 17.

[4] This was reported to the pope by the Young King during his conflict with his father (*RHF* xiv, 645).

[5] M. Howell, *Regalian Right in Medieval England*, London 1962, 223.

[6] H.M. Chew, *The English Ecclesiastical Tenants-in-Chief and Knight Service*, Oxford 1932, 4–6.

The bishop was required, when a case in the royal courts turned on a matter judicable in the ecclesiastical forum, to enquire into a disputed question of legitimate birth or marriage and to report to the king's justices. The diocesan authorities were ordered to sequestrate the ecclesiastical revenues of clerks who had no lay fee or who had failed to appear when cited to the royal court. The ambiguous borderline between royal and ecclesiastical jurisdiction was determined by the Crown. Writs of prohibition, introduced under Henry II, were increasingly used to terminate proceedings in church courts, and ecclesiastical judges were frequently summoned to explain to royal justices why they had heard cases beyond their alleged competence. Benefit of clergy, the immediate cause of the conflict between Becket and Henry II, might have been conceded, but even that privilege was carefully regulated by the royal courts. None of this was seriously challenged by the bishops, some of whom themselves served the king on the judicial bench.

The church in England, and in the king of England's other dominions, was most certainly acknowledged to be part of a universal church, at whose head was the bishop of Rome, the ultimate arbiter in matters of faith and doctrine. The Papacy and its publicists had, since the late eleventh century, built up a formidable armoury of theological justifications for its supremacy within the church, its plenitude of power balanced by its duty of solicitude for all churches. Indeed, it has been suggested that until the rediscovery and absorption in western Europe of Aristotle's concept of the state as a consensual political association, the political theology of the Papacy was incontrovertible.[7] In practice, however, kings since William the Conqueror had clearly demonstrated that papal authority could only be exercised effectively in regions controlled by a strong central authority, and then by the tolerance of the royal power. The remarkable thing, perhaps, was that this formidable measure of royal control over the church in the Angevin dominions was gained 'without recourse to political theory; Henry II produced no theory of royal power. Probably, as has been suggested, he did not even have one'.[8]

Viewed from another perspective, however, the English church around 1200 appears as a remarkably healthy body. The parochial structure was now nearly complete. Since about AD 900 over nine thousand parishes had been created, virtually a church for every centre of population, while great cities such as London, Norwich, Winchester and York had numerous churches serving very small neighbourhoods.[9] The Gregorian reform had emphasised the distinctiveness of the clerical order and its superiority to the laity, but in the vast majority

---

[7] This is one of the main themes running through the work of Walter Ullmann; see, most conveniently, *A History of Political Thought: the Middle Ages*, Harmondsworth 1965, chapter 4, 'The Hierocratic Doctrine in its Maturity'.

[8] J.A. Watt, 'Spiritual and Temporal Powers', in *The Cambridge History of Medieval Political Thought, c. 350–c.1450*, Cambridge 1988, 367–423, at p. 392.

[9] For an overview, see J. Blair, 'Introduction: From Minster to Parish Church', in *idem*, ed., *Minsters and Parish Churches: the Local Church in Transition 950–1200*, Oxford University Committee for Archaeology monograph 17, 1988, 1–20.

of English parishes which provided only a living wage for their rectors, and also those well-endowed parishes where the absentee rector employed a resident vicar or chaplain, the parson was far closer to his flock, physically and in mentality, than had been the itinerant priests of the old Anglo-Saxon minster churches with their extended *parochiae*. Evidence concerning the standard of parochial ministry is rare before the fifteenth century, but it is certain that few of the country clergy had any great education. Historians of the late-medieval English church have, however, recently emphasised that learning might even be a barrier between priest and people; that what was expected was that the priest should be a man who could recite the magical formulae (both in the consecration of the elements of the Mass and in the cursing of caterpillars in the fields), that what was appreciated was discretion in the resolution of conflict through the annual Easter confession, and charity in the bringing of comfort and the sacraments to the sick and dying.[10] Shared experience of subsistence farming might be more valuable than a precise knowledge of the nature of the Trinity or even, despite constant papal and episcopal strictures, celibacy. Advice to the parish priest was, moreover, surely available at the diocesan synod from the bishop's penitentiary and other learned clerks in his service. Between 1208 and 1215 the Englishman Robert of Flamborough was compiling his *Liber Poenitentialis*, which would be an aid to priests of the next generation, but which surely did not emerge from a vacuum.[11]

The credit for the creation of this parochial system must go in part to lords of manors and cooperatives of urban artisans and traders, but also to the English episcopate which sanctioned and increasingly supervised the process. It is possible now to know far more about the activities of the bishops than it was twenty years ago, due to the systematic edition of their *acta* which provide an insight into the routine administration of their dioceses rather than their involvement in the great controversies of the age, highlighted in chronicles and letter-collections long in print.[12] Many of the bishops inherited by John or appointed in the early years of his reign were, indeed, royal clerks who continued in the king's service after their consecration, but none so far investigated can be said to have neglected their pastoral role. When absent from their dioceses they appointed worthy and hard-working deputies. Improvement in Christian observance, most particularly through the concerted attempt to provide an adequate resident priest in every parish, may for them have been a matter of administrative efficiency rather than of charismatic inspiration, but

---

[10] For a convenient survey of work on the late medieval parochial clergy, see C. Harper-Bill, *The Pre-Reformation Church in England, 1400–1530*, rev. edn London 1996, chapter 5.

[11] Robert was a canon of St Victor in Paris. For a brief biography, see J.W. Baldwin, *Masters, Princes and Merchants: the Social Views of Peter the Chanter and his Circle*, 2 vols; Princeton 1970, 1, 32–4 and 2, index *s.n.* Robert of Flamborough. Around 1215, too, Thomas of Chobham produced his *Summa confessorum*; see *ibid.* 1, 34–6.

[12] For the project, see C.N.L. Brooke, 'English Episcopal Acta of the Twelfth and Thirteenth Centuries', in *Medieval Ecclesiastical Studies in Honour of Dorothy M. Owen*, ed. M.F. Franklin and C. Harper-Bill, Woodbridge 1995, 41–56.

the work was done and improvement there certainly was, before rather than as a result of the decrees for reform promulgated by Pope Innocent III at the Fourth Lateran Council of 1215.[13] In the earliest years of the thirteenth century the initiative came from Hubert Walter, reviled by many contemporaries because he combined the archbishopric of Canterbury with the royal chancellorship, clear contrary to Becket's example. His provincial council of 1200 laid down a blueprint for continuing reform of administrative structure and of clerical and lay conduct.[14] Robert Brentano, writing in 1968 of Cheney's study of the archbishop, remarks that '. . . Hubert Walter, that old model of secular prelacy, looked at hard and freshly, can be shown to be "genuinely zealous for the welfare of the church", with even the suggestion of "a deeper conviction".' In a footnote Brentano adds: 'this seems to me a remarkable revelation. Cheney seems to change Hubert Walter as one watches.'[15] Thirty years on, it appears perhaps less remarkable. A study of William de Ste Mère-Eglise emphasises not only his efficient governance of the diocese of London, but also the courage shown by this former royal clerk in confronting the king with the pope's increasingly indignant mandates relating to the Canterbury election dispute.[16] Another former royal servant, Eustace bishop of Ely, stood shoulder to shoulder with him, and his concern for his pastoral responsibilities had been revealed by the series of questions which he addressed to the pope and which elicited the important decretal *Pastoralis officii diligentia*.[17] Of the bishops of John's reign, only his own half-brother, Geoffrey archbishop of York, appears at all scandalous, as he hit out at his king, his suffragan, his cathedral chapter and anyone else whom he perceived to have thwarted his Angevin ambition.[18]

The point may be emphasised by reference to two bishops who, politically, took diametrically opposed stances. Of Giles de Braose, to whom King John 'gave' the see of Hereford in 1200 to cement his relationship with his father William, Painter remarked that 'there is no reason for thinking that he was not merely a wild marcher lord covered with clerical vestments'.[19] Yet the collection of his *acta* shows him to have been as active as his contemporaries in the administration of his notoriously unruly diocese, enforcing the provisions of the rapidly evolving canon law and frequently being commissioned by the pope as

---

[13] For example, the creation of vicarages in an attempt to ensure that there was a resident priest in every parish; see Cheney, *From Becket to Langton*, 131–6; B.R. Kemp, 'Monastic Possession of Parish Churches in the Twelfth Century', *JEH* 31, 1980, 133–60.

[14] The statutes are heavily reliant on those of the Third Lateran Council, but draw too on legislation from Rouen and on recent papal decretals; *C & S* 1 (2), 1,055–74.

[15] R. Brentano, *Two Churches: England and Italy in the Thirteenth Century*, Berkeley and Los Angeles, new edn 1988, 221 and n.106.

[16] R.V. Turner, *Men Raised from the Dust: Administrative Service and Upward Mobility in Angevin England*, Philadelphia 1988, 20–34.

[17] Pd with translation, *SLI* no. 22.

[18] D.L. Douie, *Archbishop Geoffrey Plantaganet and the Chapter of York*, Borthwick Pamphlet 18, York 1960. A full-scale study is promised by Dr M. Lovatt.

[19] Painter, *Reign of King John*, 155.

a judge-delegate.[20] It was only after the king had turned upon his father, and Giles himself had been forced to accompany John as a surety and the Hereford estates had been confiscated, that he escaped into exile, after the bishops of London, Ely and Worcester but with more reason than they to appreciate the justification of Innocent's strictures against the king; and it was only after his mother and brother had been starved to death by John that Giles began, on his return from exile, to create mayhem on the marches in association with Llywelyn ap Iorworth.

Of John de Gray, keeper of the royal seal and advanced to the see of Norwich in 1200, Painter writes: 'he was a man of purely secular interests – a competent captain and efficient civil servant. There was no man in England whom King John trusted so completely and so consistently as he did John de Gray.'[21] After his elevation, he continued in the royal service, and from 1201 to 1208 was among the most regular witnesses of royal writs and charters, as well as presiding on the judicial bench; from 1208 to 1213 he was justiciar of Ireland. Yet his *acta* indicate that his diocese was efficiently administered, even if much of the work was done by his excellent Official, Master Ranulf of Warham, monk of the cathedral priory, who subsequently became bishop of Chichester. Most significantly, by a series of detailed *conventiones* which must have involved long negotiation, Gray brought to an end the conflict between bishop and monks at Norwich which, while less well known, had threatened to become as bitter as those at Canterbury and Coventry.[22] John de Gray, of course, was the king's candidate for Canterbury in 1205, and his candidature then and now has been dismissed as a prime example of royal intimidation. Yet it may be that the monks of Canterbury were unwise not to accept him with unanimous equanimity, for his record suggests not only that he would have been accommodating to them, but that he would have been a primate very much in the tradition of Hubert Walter in the style of his provincial administration.

In the history of the religious orders a plateau had been reached. The Black monks had been criticised from the 1120s for their excessive involvement in the world, and the cathedral priories especially had been the target of episcopal hostility in the 1190s. The Cistercians' evolution from their original ideals of pristine purity had made them the butt of sardonic humour in the milieu of Henry II's court.[23] The great age of monastic foundation had come to an end with the establishment in the last quarter of the twelfth century of an important group of houses of Augustinian canons, many endowed by servants of the Angevin monarchy. By 1200, however, saturation point had been reached. There were, for example, in Norfolk and Suffolk some fifty-two conventual

[20] J. Barrow, ed., *EEA 7: Hereford 1079–1234*, London 1993, nos 243–91.

[21] Painter, *Reign of King John*, 155.

[22] C. Harper-Bill, ed., *EEA 6: Norwich 1070–1214*, London 1990, xxxvii–xxxix, nos 320–431.

[23] Knowles, *Monastic Order*, chapter 17, 'The Hostility of the Bishops to the Black Monks'; chapter 39, 'The Critics of the Monks'.

communities and thirty-eight small dependent houses and cells.[24] All over England religious orders held considerable landed estates, and this was an age of land-hunger. If there were few new monastic foundations, grants to existing communities continued, albeit on a smaller scale. Certainly there were very many more men and women living in communities under a rule in 1216 than in 1100 – the increase may be estimated at approximately 2,700 to 9,700 for males, 440 to 3,000 for nuns.[25] From 1200, too, until the advent of the friars in the 1220s and indeed beyond, numerous hospitals were founded throughout England, where brother and sisters living a quasi-monastic life provided at least spiritual medicine for the sick and needy.[26]

It is extraordinarily difficult to gauge the spiritual climate of England in the early years of John's reign. Certainly there was the odour of sanctity. Gilbert of Sempringham, founder of the only native English religious order, was canonised in 1202, only thirteen years after his death, to be followed the next year by Wulfstan, the eleventh-century bishop of Worcester.[27] When Bishop Hugh of Lincoln died in 1200, his holiness was already recognised,[28] and the cult of the hermit Robert of Knaresborough developed very soon after the latter's death in 1218.[29] There was certainly an appetite for the wondrous. When William, a baker of Perth, was murdered in 1201 at Rochester on his way to Becket's shrine, miracles were immediately reported at the scene of the crime,[30] as they were in Kent and Yorkshire during the preaching tours in 1200–1201 of the charismatic preacher Eustace of Flay, who on his second visit came armed with a letter from Christ, sent down from heaven and found at Jerusalem,

---

[24] *MRH, passim.*

[25] *MRH,* 489–95.

[26] Two important developments in the history of the religious orders in England were signalled in the years before the Interdict. First, as links with Normandy were severed in 1204, albeit as was thought temporarily, there was inaugurated almost immediately a policy of royal exploitation of the English assets of Norman monasteries now in enemy territory; estates were seized and the export of money to mother-houses forbidden. The priors of the dependencies began from late 1204 to pay fines for the custody of their own lands, and soon afterward there are instances of Norman abbots paying for the restoration of English possessions. John's measures provided a model for the policies adopted after 1294 by Edward I and his successors (D. Matthew, *The Norman Monasteries and their English Possessions*, Oxford 1962, 73–81). Secondly, on 17 March 1207 the pope ordered the priors of the Augustinian houses of the province of York to meet annually for a provincial chapter, foreshadowing the universal regulation for Benedictine and Augustinian chapters of the Fourth Lateran Council (*Letters of Innocent III*, no. 743).

[27] D.H. Farmer, *The Oxford Dictionary of Saints*, Oxford 1978, 171–2, 413–14. For Gilbert's canonisation process, see R. Foreville and G. Kerr, eds, *The Book of St Gilbert*, OMT 1987.

[28] *Oxford Dictionary of Saints*, 199–200; D.H. Farmer, *St Hugh of Lincoln*, London 1985; H. Mayr-Harting, ed., *St Hugh of Lincoln*, Oxford 1987.

[29] *Oxford Dictionary of Saints*, 344; B. Golding, 'The Hermit and the Hunter', in *The Cloister and the World: Essays in Medieval History in Honour of Barbara Harvey*, Oxford 1996, 95–117.

[30] *Oxford Dictionary of Saints*, 405–6.

proclaiming the urgent need for repentance and observance of the sabbath.[31] Many Sunday markets were apparently closed down because of his exhortations, but as one chronicler observes, as soon as he left, speeded on his way by less than enthusiastic bishops, the people returned to their former ways. On one matter at least, however, the evangelist and the hierarchy agreed: the need for charity. Eustace urged the well-to-do to have bowls on their tables to collect leftovers for the poor, while the archbishop's insistence on social responsibility is indicated by a mandate, probably of 1203, that the parochial clergy should give alms to the destitute at a time of great hardship.[32]

The overall picture is of a church that was efficiently administered and which provided the essential means of salvation, if not an intellectual interpretation of the Gospels, to the whole population of England. This is not to say that all was well, that there was no need for reform and regeneration. There were certainly scandals, such as the well-documented case of Abbot Roger Norreys of Evesham, a palpably unworthy superior who was able to cling onto office by confusing his personal position with the battle of his community for exemption from the bishop of Worcester, itself an example of the jurisdictional disputes which could distract the church from its mission;[33] or the siege of Faversham church which resulted from the struggle for patronage between king and archbishop on one side and the monks of St Augustine's Canterbury on the other, symptomatic of the desperate concern of all parties to maximise even indirect profits from local churches.[34] Yet such scandals were a minor disfigurement on a healthy body. Despite, or perhaps because of, firm royal control, at least tolerated by bishops, many of whom who had risen through the ranks of the king's administration, the English church was experiencing in the years before the crisis of the Interdict most of the reforming measures advanced as a universal programme at the Fourth Lateran Council, and was providing a ministry satisfactory to the laity, at least to the extent that there were none of those outbreaks of heresy which characterised contemporary Italy, Languedoc and Flanders.

It remains to fit the role of the Papacy into this more optimistic view of the English church. The drama of Innocent III's conflict with King John has inevitably distracted attention from the pope's role as the universal ordinary, the ultimate judge for the reconciliation of disputes within the church, and father in God to all Christian people.[35] Claims to supreme authority have tended to

---

[31] *Howden* iv 123–4, 167–71. See J.L. Cate, 'The English Mission of Eustace of Flay, 1200–1', in *Etudes d'histoire dédiées a la mémoire de Henri Pirenne*, Brussels 1937, 67–89.

[32] *C & S* 1 (2), 1,076–7.

[33] Knowles, *Monastic Order*, 331–45.

[34] The St Augustine's account is conveniently translated in A.H. Davis, ed., *William Thorne's Chronicle of St Augustine's Abbey, Canterbury*, Oxford 1934, 137–62; cf. E. John, 'The Litigation of an Exempt House: St Augustine's, Canterbury, 1182–1237', *BJRL* 39, 1956–7, 390–415.

[35] For a good recent study, see J. Sayers, *Innocent III, Leader of Europe, 1198–1216*, London 1994.

obscure the concern for all churches shown by the pontiff, who styled himself 'servant of the servants of God'. Certainly Innocent sought to increase revenue from the English church in order to finance his costly projects in Sicily and Germany; in 1199 he was the first pope to impose a comprehensive income tax (of one-fortieth of their revenues) on the clergy,[36] and in 1205 he attempted to maximise receipts from Peter's Pence, assessed on the basis of a penny from every English household, of which he believed the receipts to be diverted to the pockets of middlemen.[37] Much, however, was given in return, albeit at a charge for every individual transaction. During the twelfth century, English institutions and English people (and not only churchmen) had increasingly resorted to the court of Rome in search of security and of justice, dispensed by a tribunal staffed by the best legal minds of the age. In 1100 traffic between England at the *curia* had been rare, by 1200 it had become the norm, largely by volition rather than compulsion. The smallest monastery sought papal confirmation of its possessions; disputes over the division of tithes in a single small rural parish were decided, after appeal to Rome, by papal judges-delegate, themselves local ecclesiastics, appointed by the Papacy.[38] All of this was, by the turn of the century, utterly commonplace. There were, of course, major conflicts within the *ecclesia Anglicana*, and it is probably a tribute to Innocent's own skill as a judge that the long-running quarrel between the archbishop and the monks of Christ Church Canterbury over the status of Lambeth, and the disputed election at St Davids, its claim for metropolitan status and for the autonomy of the Welsh church, were finally settled by the papal court in the early years of his pontificate.[39] His concern for evidence is revealed by the more rigorous procedures for the investigation of sanctity and miracles introduced in the processes of St Gilbert and St Wulfstan,[40] and his own weighing of testimony and mastery of legal minutiae is well illustrated by the decretal addressed in 1202 to Hubert Walter concerning the abbot of Thorney, whom the archbishop had deposed,[41] and even better by his response two years earlier to Hubert's enquiry whether the election to Worcester of Mauger should be allowed, because he was illegitimate – that 'beautiful decretal', as it was called by the Worcester chronicler, in which after lengthy exegesis of the law he declared that although the election was invalid because of his bastardy, because of

---

[36] W.E. Lunt, *Financial Relations of the Papacy with England to 1327*, Cambridge, Mass. 1939, 240–2.

[37] *Letters of Innocent III*, no. 673; cf. Vincent, *Peter des Roches*, 75.

[38] J.E. Sayers, *Papal Judges Delegate in the Province of Canterbury, 1198–1254*, Oxford 1971.

[39] For Lambeth, Cheney, *Innocent III*, 208–20; *Hubert Walter*, 148–50; for St Davids, Cheney, *Innocent III*, 134–41; M. Richter. *Giraldus Cambrensis: the Growth of the Welsh Nation*, Aberystwyth 1976, 94–127.

[40] Cheney, *Innocent III*, 513–8; for the wider context, E.W. Kemp, *Canonisation and Authority in the Western Church*, Oxford 1948, chapter 5.

[41] *Letters of Innocent III*, no. 421; *SLI*, no. 15.

Mauger's great merits the monks might postulate him to the pope. The probity of the man was, in the final analysis, of greater consequence than his birth.[42]

Important rulings directed to English recipients contributed to clarification of the rapidly evolving law of marriage – that a man might not marry the god-mother of his child, nor the goddaughter of his parent, and that despite a husband's adultery with his wife's sister, the marriage should remain valid, although ideally there should be henceforth no marital intercourse.[43] Most revealing of all are three letters, in which Innocent responded to the concerns of ' humble petitioners: instructing the abbot of Leicester to make provision for a Jewish convert, the death of whose noble patron had left him destitute;[44] to a neurotic canon of Norton, who feared that because he had taken a new name at his monastic profession God would not recognise prayers offered for him after his death in either name;[45] and concerning a priest whose horse had bolted and killed a baby, and who was tormented by doubt as to whether he was guilty and whether he might celebrate Mass.[46] It is salutary to balance such letters against the grandiose statements of authority addressed to emperors and kings.

Against this record of ready recourse to the *curia* and the 'equity and com-passion' of papal judgements[47] must be set the reputation of the city of Rome, and particularly of lawyers and papal officials, for fiscality and even venality.[48] By the thirteenth century this had become widespread. It is a theme to which Walter Map, writing at Henry II's, court, constantly returned, and it was taken up by Gerald of Wales, despite his obvious admiration for Innocent III himself. It was not, moreover, merely a literary topos; there are allusions to the strategic disbursement of money at the *curia* in the Lambeth, St Davids and Evesham cases, while the pope himself wrote to Archbishop Hubert of the rumours he had heard about the peculation of Master Philip the notary, sent to England in 1200 to superintend the collection of the crusading fortieth.[49] It is impossible to gauge the extent to which this perception of Roman greed and graft dis-inclined the more learned and influential members of the clergy to enter into wholehearted support of the papal position during the Interdict, even if they recognised absolutely the pope's right to suspend the administration of the sacraments.

The Interdict and the threat of excommunication naturally threw a shadow over John's reputation as a Christian king. How would it stand if the

---

[42] *Letters of Innocent III*, no. 189; *SLI*, no. 6.
[43] *Letters of Innocent III*, nos 54. 397, 466.
[44] *Letters of Innocent III*, no. 169.
[45] *Letters of Innocent III*, no. 712; *SLI*, no. 27.
[46] *Letters of Innocent III*, no. 267; *SLI*, no. 7.
[47] C. Duggan, 'Equity and Compassion in Papal Marriage Decretals to England', in *Love and Marriage in the Twelfth Century*, ed. W. van Hoecke and A. Welkenhuysen, *Medievalia Lovaniensia*, series 1, *studia* 8, Louvain 1981, 59–87.
[48] J.A. Yunck, *The Lineage of Lady Meed*, Notre Dame 1963, 61–116; Cheney, *From Becket to Langton*, 67–9.
[49] *Letters of Innocent III*, no. 433; *SLI*, no. 16.

controversy over the Canterbury election had not escalated? It is very difficult to determine anything of his personal sentiments; we certainly do not have the type of evidence which has recently allowed it to be argued, surprisingly but very convincingly, that the much maligned Richard III exhibited deep inner piety.[50] John's devotion to St Wulfstan, canonised in 1202 and alongside whom he was eventually buried, appears initially to have been without any political calculation, although he subsequently used the legend of that saint's staff to justify the royal appointment of bishops.[51] John gave a piece of the skull of St Philip to Reading abbey.[52] There was certainly charitable giving, recorded on the *mise* and pipe rolls; the pipe roll for his fourth year records revenue of about £24,000 and alms, mostly to religious houses and hospitals, of about £1,450, 6% of the total.[53] Much of this charity, however, was institutionalised, initiated by his predecessors and disbursed annually without a thought;[54] so much so that when in 1210 the Cistercian houses refused to give a subsidy to the king and in reprisal he took from them 25,000 marks, the traditional royal alms to the order continued to be paid.

Two unconnected sources shed incidental light on John's parsimony. At the first Easter of his reign, when St Hugh was celebrating Mass at Fontevrault, the king was extremely reluctant to make an offering of the twelve gold coins which one of his servants placed in his hand.[55] And when immediately after his coronation he went to Bury St Edmunds, the monks expected a notable oblation to the royal saint, but at the great ceremony of his formal reception he gave only a silken cloth which he had borrowed from the sacrist and never paid for; at Mass on the day of his departure he left only twelve pence for all the hospitality he had received.[56] Traditional standing charges on the county farm for charity were one thing, the personal giving of alms quite another. That touched the king's own pocket, and seems to have hurt him.

It was the duty of any king to protect and even extend his patronal and financial rights over churches, but there are some slight indications of John's particular ruthlessness. The chronicler of St Augustine's abbey certainly blamed him in person for the ugly scenes at Faversham in 1201, relating how, when he

---

[50] J. Hughes, *The Religious Life of Richard III*, Gloucester 1997.

[51] E. Mason, *St Wulfstan of Worcester, c.1008–1095*, Oxford 1990, 113–14, 281–3; *idem*, 'St Wulfstan's Staff: a Legend and its Uses', *Medium Aevum* 53, 1984, 157–79 (cf. J. Martindale, 'The Sword on the Stone: some Resonances of a Medieval Symbol of Power', *ANS* 15, 1993, 199–241).

[52] B.R. Kemp, ed., *Reading Abbey Cartularies*, 2 vols, Camden 4th ser. 31, 33, 1986–7, 1, no. 230.

[53] C.R. Young, 'King John of England: an Illustration of the Medieval Practice of Charity', *Church History* 24, 1960, 264–74.

[54] The historian of solitary religious in England has suggested a slight shift in policy; whereas Richard I was eager to dispense alms to enclosed anchorites, John preferred more practical hermits, the custodians of bridges and the like; see A.K. Warren, *Anchorites and their Patrons in Medieval England*, Berkeley and Los Angeles 1985, 151–5.

[55] *Life of St Hugh* ii, 142–4.

[56] H.E. Butler, ed., *The Chronicle of Jocelin of Brakelond*, NMT 1949, 116–17.

heard that the monks had occupied the church and parsonage in order to fore-stall royal presentation, John 'as if turned to madness' ordered the entire complex to be set on fire, with the monks still inside, and only when nobody would obey this command ordered the sheriff to expel them.[57] More prosaic, but perhaps more fully credible, are records indicating minor predations uncon-nected with the Interdict. In 1207 the king took money from the monks of Montacute before ordering the bishop of Bath to depose an unsatisfactory prior. The next year the convent had to give John a further sixty marks not to inter-vene to restore him, but rather to help them find a suitable superior.[58] In 1209 the king reached an agreement with Séez abbey in Normandy whereby the abbot might nominate a choice of candidates as prior of Lancaster, in return for payment of 200 marks and two palfreys.[59] Behind the formal language of the rolls it seems likely there lie personal royal interventions to extract the maximum profit from monastic difficulties.

There is some evidence of royal contrition in the face of sanctity. John appar-ently softened after an implied rebuke from Robert of Knaresborough, accord-ing to the Metrical Life, and the rolls indeed show a donation to him.[60] It was allegedly the death of St Hugh of Lincoln, at whose funeral John acted as a pall-bearer, that prompted him to remit his anger against the Cistercians for an earlier failure to contribute adequately to revenues. Not only did he enter into confraternity with the order, but two years later he founded Beaulieu abbey, his one major religious initiative.[61] This Hampshire monastery received a comfort-able, but not lavish, endowment; it is clear that the idea was Archbishop Hubert Walter's, and the investment was little enough for a monarch of John's resources.[62]

The relationship between King John and Pope Innocent III was complicated, before the crisis provoked by the vacancy at Canterbury in 1205, by two factors of international significance: the question of the Empire and the conflict between John and the Capetian king of France. From the time that Innocent threw his weight behind Otto's imperial candidature in 1200 until he tem-porarily detached himself in 1207, the pope cajoled John to pay his nephew the legacy left to him by Richard I and to aid him in other ways,[63] which John could

---

[57] Davis, *Thorne* (as n.34), 141.

[58] S. Wood, *English Monasteries and their Patrons in the Thirteenth Century*, Oxford 1955, 147 and refs there given.

[59] Wood, *English Monasteries and their Patrons*, 58.

[60] Golding, 'The Hermit and the Hunter' (as n.29), 100–101.

[61] *Life of St Hugh* ii, 188, 225, 232.

[62] For its early history, see F. Hockey, *Beaulieu, King John's Abbey*, Beaulieu 1976, chapters 2–4; C. Holdsworth, 'Royal Cistercians: Beaulieu, her Daughters and Rewley', in *Thirteenth Century England 4*, ed. P.R. Coss and S.D. Lloyd, Woodbridge 1992, 139–50.

[63] *Letters of Innocent III*, nos 264–5, 293–5, 354, 465, 640, 689–93, 799A; cf. *Handbook of Church History 4: From the High Middle Ages to the Eve of the Reformation*, trans. A. Biggs, London 1970, 150: 'So long as the contest for the German throne remained undecided, Innocent was indulgent to John despite the king's brutal ecclesiastical policy, especially since John occasionally showed himself submissive in the face of papal threats.'

initially refuse to do because of the contract made with Philip II at Le Goulet in May 1200. From 1202, however, the conflict between the two kings not only offended against the papal vision of peace within a united Christian commonwealth, but also militated against Innocent's most cherished aim, a successful crusading expedition.[64]

Despite conflict between king and pope regarding several individual churches within his dominions, John was initially treated in other matters with consideration. The annulment of his marriage to Isabelle of Gloucester was authorised by two tribunals of bishops, in Normandy and Aquitaine, without any papal intervention, in marked contrast to Innocent's insistence on the validity of Philip II's marriage to his discarded wife, Ingeborg of Denmark.[65] The pope attempted to make peace between the kings, and although the famous decretal *Novit ille* was more important in later canonical theory than in any brake which it might have put upon Philip's victorious advance, once John was on the defensive the pope might be thought, by the Capetians at least, to have been acting in his favour.[66] Yet once it became obvious that Philip had been successful in the demolition of Angevin power in western France, Innocent accepted the *fait accompli*. When asked by the Norman bishops early in 1205 whether they should render fealty to Philip, the pope merely instructed them to do what law and custom demanded. This was, in Cheney's view, 'an abnegation of authority, a ceremonial hand-washing',[67] however realistic and prudent, and it may surely have been a contributory factor in John's rejection for the archbishopric of Canterbury of a papal nominee who had been so long in Paris.

Long before this, there had been sharp conflicts over other major churches, most of them, however, in John's dominions outside England. He was first lambasted by the pope even before he became king, in a letter of 18 September 1198.[68] John Cumin, archbishop of Dublin, a loyal servant of the Angevins who had been at the heart of Henry II's campaign against Becket, had complained that he had been driven into exile by John; the bishop of Leighlin had protested that the prince's justiciar was obstructing his consecration, and other appeals had been made from his Irish lands. In urging John to allow these bishops free exercise of their offices, Innocent, without threatening specific sanctions, gave a warning: he had committed offences against God and ecclesiastical liberty, and should remember the fate of King Ozias; it would be unwise of him to

---

[64] 'The unusual course of events in England, culminating in what was at least an external success on the part of Innocent III, shows the pope in almost every phase of the dramatic succession of events not merely as the tenacious "master of politics", but also at the same time as guided by the religious concerns and motives of his pontificate: freedom of the church, the crusade and peace among nations.' (*Handbook of Church History* 4, 152).

[65] Cheney, *Innocent III*, 99–100.

[66] For the text of *Novit ille*, see B. Tierney, *The Crisis of Church and State, 1050–1300*, Englewood Cliffs 1964, 134–5; cf. Cheney, *Innocent III*, 290.

[67] Cheney, *Innocent III*, 291.

[68] J.A. Watt, *The Church and the Two Nations in Medieval Ireland*, Cambridge 1970, 69 n.1; Cheney, *Innocent III*, 281–2.

convince the pope that he would behave even worse if he became king, for this would preclude assent being given to his promotion – which may imply that the pope expected some say in the eventual succession to Richard.

In March 1202 Innocent had high hopes of John who, as the archbishop of Canterbury reported, had made confession to him of his past misdeeds and had promised to found a Cistercian house and fund knights for the Holy Land.[69] Later that year, however, trouble broke out again in Dublin, apparently over the incursion of the royal forest onto the lands of the see. Archbishop Cumin was again exiled, in the outcome for three years. On 20 February 1203 Innocent directed to the king a long letter of complaint.[70] In a fit of petulance when the pope had not been able to concede to *all* the petitions brought to the curia by his envoys, John had forbidden the reception of any papal legate; he had impeded the pope's delegated jurisdiction in England (presumably by writs of prohibition); he had persecuted the bishops of Limoges and Poitiers (both of whom had probably sided with the Lusignans against John in 1201); he had prolonged the vacancy at Lincoln, harassed the canons of Séez for failing to elect his candidate, and in some unspecified way had persecuted the church of Coutances. His worst offence, however, was with regard to Dublin, where he had driven the aged and infirm archbishop from his see and forced him to beg for the necessities of life; there followed an appeal to the king's conscience and sense of Christian duty. When three months later Innocent learned that John had confiscated the temporalities and ordered the archbishop of Cashel to administer the see, the king was warned that if he did not readmit Cumin, any diocese throughout his dominions where the king might be would be laid under interdict.[71] By December 1204 Innocent ordered that if all else failed, the province of Dublin should be placed under this ban;[72] but a few months later Archbishop Hubert Walter, just before his own death, apparently effected a reconciliation.[73] In the meantime, however, John had become involved in the Armagh election dispute, which lasted from 1202 to 1207.[74] Out of a confused electoral process there emerged an Irish elect, Eugenius, abbot of Bangor, to whom the English colony strongly objected. John appealed to the papal legate that he had not given assent, and when Eugenius went to Rome, ordered the Armagh electors to choose his own man. In the end, however, he was constrained to accept Eugenius, and in 1206 apparently accepted money for the restitution of the temporalities.

Innocent's letter of March 1203 reveals that there had also been complaints about John's conduct in ecclesiastical matters on the continent. In 1200 the bishop of Le Mans had brought unspecified charges against him at the papal

---

[69] *Letters of Innocent III*, no. 398; *SLI*, no. 13.
[70] *Letters of Innocent III*, no 465; *SLI*, no. 17.
[71] *Letters of Innocent III*, nos 476–7.
[72] *Letters of Innocent III*, nos 578–9.
[73] Cheney, *Innocent III*, 304 n.2.
[74] For an account, see Watt, *Church and the Two Nations* (as n.68), Appendix 2, 226–30.

curia, and in November the same year John appealed to Rome against the dean and chapter of Lisieux for conducting an episcopal election without his consent.[75] The main crisis in Normandy came in 1202, the same year that John, contrary to custom, imposed a tallage on the lands of the church in the duchy, as well as in England.[76] John complained strongly to the pope both of the election and the papal confirmation of the archdeacon Sylvester as bishop of Séez.[77] Innocent's reply was the threat of an interdict on Normandy, which in the current political and military situation in the duchy simply could not be ignored. On 9 October 1203 John admitted Sylvester to the see, despite this being 'contrary to the dignity and liberty of ourself and our land' and the assurance that he would renew his appeal to the pope.

It is rather remarkable how seldom John was upbraided by Innocent for his ecclesiastical policy in England. The potential crisis, looming as a result of the Cistercians' refusal to pay the carucage of 1200 and the king's threat of reprisals, was defused by Hubert Walter's mediation and, apparently, the impact upon the king of St Hugh's death.[78] The king was condemned by the pope in 1203 for his persecution of the church of Lincoln by his prolongation of the vacancy until he might ensure the election of a royal candidate.[79] He was rebuked, too, for his harassment of the rector of Chieveley (Berks.) until he resigned.[80] There was very little more within the kingdom. Indeed, in 1205, when the disputed Winchester election was taken to Rome, the royal candidate, Peter des Roches, emerged there as the unanimous choice of the hitherto hostile parties when they were compelled to conduct a new election in the pope's presence, and he returned to England with papal consecration and a plethora of privileges.[81]

News of des Roches's consecration at Rome on 25 September 1205 would have reached England probably after the monks of Canterbury had elected their own subprior, Reginald, as archbishop, and certainly before their second election, made in the king's presence, of John de Gray on 11 December. The success at the curia of his own candidate for Winchester must have convinced John that he would get his own way at Canterbury too, and pushed to the back of his mind the series of disputes in his other dominions where his own will had been contraverted by the pope.

John was probably no more assertive or rapacious in his relationship with the church before 1205, and even before 1208, than his royal predecessors. They had frequently leaned heavily on electoral bodies, and the men who attained episcopal office through his influence or intimidation were no different in type to the appointees of Henry I or Henry II; like them, they often turned out,

---

[75] Cheney, *Innocent III*, 100 and n.14.
[76] Powicke, *Loss of Normandy*, 347.
[77] Cheney, *Innocent III*, 127–8; Turner, *King John*, 152–3.
[78] *Coggeshall*, 101–5.
[79] *Letters of Innocent III*, no. 465; *SLI*, no. 17. In July 1203 the chapter did elect one of their own number, William of Blois.
[80] *Letters of Innocent III*, no. 184; *SLI*, no. 5.
[81] Vincent, *Peter des Roches*, 47–55.

despite their previous careers and manner of promotion, to be surprisingly good bishops. John's prolongation of vacancies was no more scandalous than in the past, and if he increased the yield to the royal coffers by more frequent tallages of ecclesiastical estates during vacancies, this was an aspect of war finance, which bore heavily on the revenues of secular lords as well.[82] On the other hand, John did openly flout the customs of the Norman church, observed in form by both Richard I and by Philip Augustus without any loss of the substance of power; and it is notable that Philip, despite the long shadow cast by his 'divorce' from Ingeborg, and despite the fact that his renunciation of regalian right hardly affected his exploitation of the Norman church, achieved a reputation as a defender of ecclesiastical liberties.[83] It may be that, as so often with John, it was a matter of perception, and that the king's image was tarnished in Innocent's mind by the reports of aggrieved visitors from the Angevin dominions to the papal court.

The Interdict

The quashing of both elections held at Canterbury in late 1205, the new election of Stephen Langton in the pope's presence in autumn 1206 and his consecration by Innocent in June 1207 in the face of the king's implacable resistance, led almost inexorably to the imposition of an interdict on England in March 1208, which, despite continuing negotiation, was to last for over six years, to 2 July 1214.[84] The details of administration and religious observance remain, as Cheney observed in his definitive study in 1948, remarkably obscure.[85] Despite the recent imposition of several interdicts by a pope who was a very skilled lawyer,[86] there was, as yet, no firm canonical definition of what an interdict entailed. The three bishops who published it in England in 1208 were instructed that there were to be no church services in England, save for the baptism of infants and the confession and absolution of the dying.[87] Early in 1209 the pope allowed monastic communities to celebrate Mass once a week behind closed doors and this, it is reported, caused

---

[82] Howell, *Regalian Right* (as n.5), Appendix A, 211–33.

[83] Powicke, *Loss of Normandy*, 405–7; J. Bradbury, *Philip Augustus, King of France, 1180–1223*, London 1998, 195–202; R.V. Turner, 'King John in his Context: a Comparison with his Contemporaries', *Haskins Society Journal* 3, 1991, 190.

[84] Apart from the instances mentioned above, Innocent had previously threatened interdict in 1198 in the hope of coercing Richard into peace with Philip Augustus (*Letters of Innocent III*, nos 43–4); in 1199, to pressurise him to come to terms with his half-brother, Geoffrey, archbishop of York (no. 109); in 1200, to coerce John into paying Queen Berengaria's dowry (no. 217); and in December 1207, to force John to offer redress to Archbishop Geoffrey (no. 775).

[85] Cheney, 'King John and the Papal Interdict', 295. What follows is heavily reliant on this article.

[86] On the kingdom of Leon, 1198–1204; on France in 1199 and in 1200; on Normandy in 1199 and 1203 (Cheney, 'King John and the Papal Interdict', 296).

[87] *Letters of Innocent III*, no. 799; *SLI*, no. 36.

resentment among the parochial clergy and people.[88] Late in 1212 the viaticum for the dying was authorised.[89] No burial was permitted in consecrated ground, and there is evidence from several places of new unconsecrated burial grounds being set aside. Theoretically, lay entry to churches was totally prohibited, although there are indications that curates were allowed to open their churches on patronal festivals. It also seems that confession was encouraged, no doubt because of its essential role, through its concomitants of reconciliation and restitution, in the calming of village feuds. Crosses were set up in churchyards on Good Friday. Miracles are recorded at the tombs of the saintly former bishops of Lincoln, Salisbury and Worcester, and at Worksop priory, which implies that some laity at least were allowed access to these shrines;[90] and the thirst for the wonderful is perhaps revealed by the reported miracles at the grave in the Isle of Wight of Simon of Atherfield, apparently murdered in 1211 with the complicity of his wife.[91] Royal almsgiving to churches continued, even to the Cistercian houses at the time of the king's greatest anger against the white monks in 1210; so, too, presumably, did the gifts of the aristocracy and knightly class to their own favoured houses, although as so few charters were dated, this is difficult to demonstrate. Ecclesiastical building programmes were not disrupted.

The Margam annalist states that all the laity and most of the clergy supported the king at the outset – no doubt influenced by the propaganda campaign mounted within England to demonstrate the justice of his cause.[92] Certainly magnates, both secular and ecclesiastical, and even knights, may have feared for their own ecclesiastical patronage should John capitulate to the pope. Ecclesiastical commentators, from Gerald of Wales to the Cistercian homilist John of Ford, of course lamented the deprivation of the people's means of salvation. It is impossible to estimate the impact that the consequences of the Interdict had upon the hearts and minds of the great mass of the population. Certainly the rhythm of life was totally disrupted, without attendance at the local church and the hearing of Mass, however passively, every Sunday and feast day. The matter is somewhat ambiguous. It was, after all, the Fourth Lateran Council of 1215 which decreed that all adults should take communion at least once a year, at Easter, which presumably means that before this many did not. On the other hand, it has been demonstrated that the Eucharist did mean a great deal to the medieval peasantry, even if they were seldom active participants.[93] It is not clear if sacramentals, such as the blessing of animals and crops, were also

---

88 *Letters of Innocent III*, no. 835.
89 *Coggeshall*, 165.
90 Cheney, 'King John and the Papal Interdict', 316.
91 The story has recently been elucidated by N. Vincent, 'Simon of Atherfield (d. 1211): a Martyr to his Wife', *Analecta Bollandiana* 113, 1995, 349–61.
92 *Ann. Mon.* 1. 28.
93 M. Rubin, 'What did the Eucharist mean to Thirteenth-Century Villagers?', in *Thirteenth-Century England* 4 (as n.62), 47–56.

suspended. Certainly there would have been no point in the blessing of the bells to avert storms by their pealing. Matthew Paris illustrated his account of the Interdict by a drawing of bell-ropes tied up;[94] and how eerily quiet both town and countryside must have been without their ringing – this too must have created a profound impression of the abnormal. Throughout all this enforced ecclesiastical inactivity, tithes continued to be paid; four trustworthy men from each parish were commissioned by the Crown to guard the church barns. There must, surely, have been a feeling that a tenth of produce was being given to the church for nothing, that the contract had been broken, and this may even have made the people more receptive to the radical mediterranean friars when they arrived in England a few years later.

John's response to the Interdict was the imposition of economic sanctions, rather than violent retribution.[95] He ordered the confiscation of the assets of all ecclesiastical corporations and individuals who observed the ban as, in legalistic terms, they were failing to provide the spiritual services to which they were contractually bound by the grant of their endowment. It is a measure of papal authority that there is no evidence of any priest (outside the monasteries when so licensed), not even royal clerks, continuing to celebrate Mass. The direct administration by the Crown of the revenues of all the monasteries, let alone of some nine thousand parish churches, was obviously totally impossible, and it was merely realistic to allow the vast majority of the English clergy to pay a fine to the Crown for the privilege of administering their own estates. Nearly all the monasteries, except Christ Church Canterbury, Battle and Tewkesbury, recovered administration of their revenues at a price, and only lost it again, as was normal, during vacancies; St Albans, for example, paid 600 marks for the farm of its estates, and a further 500 marks for the privilege of being allowed so to do.[96] In the case of parish clergy, additional revenue was raised, and embarrassment caused to the church, by taking into custody clerical wives or mistresses, and then ransoming them. All the clergy of England suffered financially, but there is no indication that they were driven to penury, let alone starvation. The king's quarrel was with the pope, not with the *ecclesia Anglicana*, and his real animosity was reserved for those who deserted his side and went into exile; and apart from the majority of the bishops, who felt it prudent to leave the country between 1209 and 1213 when the king himself was excommunicate, there were very few clerical refugees, dozens rather than hundreds. John certainly profited financially from the Interdict; the calculation of losses and damages in 1213 was 100,000 marks, and the English clergy complained that this was an underestimate.[97] The official assessment works out at approximately £11,000 per annum extracted from the church for six years,

---

[94] Cited by Cheney, 'King John and the Papal Interdict', 314.
[95] 'The imposition of the Interdict served more to confuse than to compel the English clergy.' (Vincent, *Nicholas des Roches*, 79).
[96] Cheney, 'King John and the Papal Interdict', 305.
[97] *Letters of Innocent III*, no. 947; *SLI*, no. 64.

presumably in addition to the income from vacant sees and abbeys, which would have been taken by the Crown in normal circumstances. John's exactions must, however, be set in the context of a conservative estimate of English ecclesiastical income at £80,000 per annum, and no material assets were lost in the long term.[98]

Despite the removal of almost all the diocesan bishops, either by death or by exile, the routine administration of the church did not grind to a halt. In most dioceses there is by this time evidence of an Official, delegated to exercise all the administrative functions of his bishop and assisted by clerks who had been educated and trained in the cathedral schools. Benefices were filled as they fell vacant, even if the new incumbent was unable for the time being to fulfil his most important role. Although there was obviously a hiatus in papal jurisdiction, the activities of judges-delegate being suspended, the church courts continued to sit, and the rolls of the king's court provide evidence for continued royal dealings with them. The mechanisms of ecclesiastical government were still fully in place when the lifting of the Interdict allowed the church once more to resume its essential spiritual functions.

The Aftermath[99]

In autumn 1212 King John, fearing mounting baronial discontent in England and the prospect of Capetian invasion, determined to accept the terms for reconciliation which he had rejected when they were offered by the papal nuncios in summer 1211. One of the latter, the papal subdeacon Pandulph, returned to England in spring 1213, preceded by letters from Innocent reiterating the conditions and threatening deposition should John once more become recalcitrant.[100] On the day that Pandulph landed, 13 May, the king formally accepted the papal terms and two days later surrendered the kingdoms of England and Ireland, which were to be held henceforth by him and his successors as vassals of the apostolic see, in token of which they would pay an annual tribute of one thousand marks (of which 300 were for Ireland).[101] It is not clear whether the initiative for the enfeoffment came from pope or king. The relationship was, of course, that proposed by Pope Gregory VII in 1080 and then indignantly rejected by William the Conqueror.[102] Papal overlordship, however, had hardly been a restraint on the control exercised by the Norman rulers of the kingdom of

---

[98] The yield of one of the three twentieths collected by Pandulph was well over £4,000 (Lunt, *Financial Relations*, 247). The Valuation of Norwich of 1254 sets the annual income of the English church at around £102,000; and this, an increase of more than 25% on the 1217 valuation, was itself low (*ibid.*, 260–1).

[99] A most valuable recent account is provided by N. Vincent in *Peter des Roches* and in his introduction to *Guala's Letters*, on which the following section is heavily reliant.

[100] *Letters of Innocent III*, no. 905; *SLI*, no. 45.

[101] *C & S* 2 (1), 13–19.

[102] *EHD 1042–1189*, 646–7.

Sicily over the church in their territories,[103] nor did the king of Aragon, who also became a vassal of Innocent III, feel his royal dignity to be diminished.[104] In terms of his relationship with the *ecclesia Anglicana*, John's calculation proved to be astute, for he lost little in terms of revenue or patronage; in the wider political context, it proved to be a masterstroke.

Although the king himself was absolved from excommunication in May 1213 by Stephen Langton, shortly after his return to England, the raising of the Interdict was delayed because the archbishop in particular was insistent that this should not happen until full financial reparations had been made. John had originally promised to satisfy in full for their losses all clergy who had suffered confiscation since 1208, especially the exiles. Such restitution was to be made by Easter 1214, but by Christmas 1213 only 27,000 marks had been reimbursed. Early in 1214 the royal embassy at Rome reached a compromise with the pope, that the Interdict should be lifted when the Crown had paid 100,000 marks as security against individual claims.[105] John had by now embarked upon his continental campaign, and certainly some of the money from the tallage imposed to raise this sum was redirected to war finance.[106] The ambassadors at the curia obtained a further concession: the Interdict should end when 40,000 marks had been paid, and the remainder should be discharged in five annual instalments of 12,000 marks.[107] The bishop of Winchester, Peter des Roches, now Justiciar, with other guarantors pledged not only 60,000 marks for the five instalments, but also the 13,000 marks still needed to make up the full initial payment; at the beginning of July 1214 the Interdict was ended by decree of Nicholas of Tusculum, the papal legate, who had apparently been more eager than the archbishop to see a swift end to the matter.[108] In the four months up to November 1214 a further 6,000 marks was paid, bringing the total to 33,000 marks. In that month, an enquiry into compensation was said to be in progress, but the remaining money, two-thirds of the agreed sum which itself was considered by the victims to be a gross underestimate, seems simply to have been forgotten. Richard Marsh, the king's main agent in such matters, was touring monastic houses and coercing the convents into abandoning any claims, and Langton and four other bishops settled resignedly for grants of privileges to their sees. It was perhaps in this context that John, on 21 November, issued a charter granting that in all the greater churches of England, cathedral and conventual, there should henceforth be free election of prelates[109] – a concession which was repugnant to the king, but the terms of which could be obscured or evaded, and which at least did not immediately cost any cash.

---

[103] I.S. Robinson, *The Papacy, 1073–1198: Continuity and Innovation*, Cambridge 1990, 367–97.
[104] Sayers, *Innocent III*, 83–4.
[105] *Letters of Innocent III*, no. 947; *SLI*, no. 64.
[106] Vincent, *Peter des Roches*, 92.
[107] *Letters of Innocent III*, no. 976; *SLI*, no. 70.
[108] *C & S* 2 (1), 36–8.
[109] *Letters of Innocent III*, no. 1,004; *SLI*, no. 76.

This grant of free elections does appear to mark a watershed for English monasteries.[110] Hitherto, in the greater houses of royal foundation, the monks had normally accepted the royal nominee, although there had been a seven-year vacancy at Ramsey from 1206 to 1214 because of the convent's refusal to elect John's candidate, and the potential extent of royal pressure is revealed by the detailed account of the Bury election dispute from 1213–15;[111] here the king never formally retracted his objection to the election of Hugh of Northwold, but after his general concession it was likely that his resistance would be circumvented, as it eventually was by the decision of papal judges-delegate on 10 March 1215. Henceforth, both in houses under royal patronage and others, the patron's rights in this matter were normally confined to the grant of a licence to elect and subsequent formal assent.

The matter was rather different with regard to episcopal elections. Langton, on his return to England, was, perhaps understandably, set against John's predictable desire to have his own candidates promoted to vacant bishoprics. The pope, having at last vindicated his stance over the Canterbury election, adopted a more realistic stance. Writing to Nicholas of Tusculum on 31 October 1213, he informed him that he had instructed the chapters of vacant churches to accept his legatine recommendations and reminded him that the new prelates 'should be men not only distinguished by their lives and learning, but also loyal to the king, profitable to the kingdom and capable of giving counsel and help – the king's assent having been requested'.[112] The legate rapidly struck up a good working relationship with Peter des Roches, the Justiciar, who from February 1214 was authorised to give assent to elections, which were to be supervised by a committee of five, deliberately constructed so as to exclude Langton's influence. Already in January Walter de Gray, the king's Chancellor, had been elected to Worcester; now des Roches in the summer secured the election of William of Cornhill, Exchequer clerk, to Coventry. Simon of Apulia was elected to Exeter in early October 1214 by the persuasion of legate and Justiciar; although an Italian, he had lived in England for a quarter of a century and had been a clerk of Geoffrey, archbishop of York, where he subsequently became dean. Even at Rochester, traditionally in the archbishop's patronage, after negotiations from late June 1214 the candidate to emerge, Benedict of Sawston, if acceptable to Langton because he was a master of Paris, had previously served in the royal Exchequer. The king, it is true, did not always get his way completely. A plan to translate des Roches himself to the archbishopric of York and to secure the election of Richard Marsh to Winchester was thwarted by the hostility of the York electors and papal reluctance, perhaps engendered by the same complaints from Langton and others which led to the recall of the

---

[110] S. Wood, *English Monasteries and their Patrons* (as n.58), 71.

[111] R.M. Thomson, ed., *The Chronicle of the Election of Hugh, Abbot of Bury St Edmunds and later Bishop of Ely*, OMT 1974.

[112] *Letters of Innocent III*, no. 938; *SLI*, no. 62.

legate late in 1214.[113] Innocent, however, in accordance with the king's wishes, prohibited the election to York of Simon Langton,[114] the archbishop's brother, and eventually at the Lateran Council a delegation of canons postulated, and the pope confirmed, Walter de Gray of Worcester. At Durham the election of Richard Poore, dean of Salisbury, in autumn 1213, was nullified before it was formally announced because Innocent was aware of the king's desire for the translation of John de Gray, by whom the pope had presumably been impressed when he was on embassy to the curia. Gray, however, died in October 1214 before consecration, and the see of Durham was kept vacant until after the king's own death, until it was eventually filled in summer 1217 by Richard Marsh, the most notorious of the king's agents during the Interdict.[115] Of all the episcopal appointments, that most obviously the result of papal influence was the election of Pandulph Verracclo, the nuncio, to Norwich in July 1215, but since the reconciliation between pope and king he had shown himself zealous for royal interests, so John did not object to him and in the event, as papal legate from 1218 to 1221, he was to render signal service to the young Henry III.[116] In general, therefore, the king's wishes were not thwarted in the reconstruction of the English episcopate; although it is notable that, in marked contrast to previous practice, very little money appears to have been received by the Crown, immediately after the reconciliation with Rome, from the exploitation of episcopal estates during the vacancies.

John, then, had lost remarkably little of the additional revenues which had accrued to the royal coffers during the Interdict, nor, whatever precise forms were observed in elections, of his effective ecclesiastical patronage. The political advantage, moreover, which stemmed from his submission to the papacy was considerable, both before and after his unexpected death. Into Innocent's letters can be read rather more than simple priestly joy at the repentance of a sinner. The rhetoric of accusation and retribution was transformed rapidly into that of praise and exhortation, fortified by threatened sanctions against the king's enemies at home and across the Channel. When Langton and the exiled bishops had returned to England in the summer of 1213 they had come with papal letters, one giving them authority to reimpose interdict and excommunication and to ensure that no heir of John should be anointed or crowned, should the agreed terms of submission not be observed.[117] On 6 July, however, the new overlord of England and Ireland

---

[113] For complaints against Roches and Nicholas of Tusculum, see *Letters of Innocent III*, nos 967–8.

[114] *Letters of Innocent III*, no. 1,017; *SLI*, no. 81.

[115] *Fasti* ii, *Monastic Cathedrals 1066–1300*, 30–1. The earlier rehabilitation, in January 1214, of Marsh, the most notorious agent of royal exactions during the Interdict, is particularly remarkable (*Letters of Innocent III*, nos 949–51).

[116] For a short account of his career, N. Vincent, 'The Election of Pandulph Verracclo as Bishop of Norwich (1215)', *Historical Research* 68, 1995, 143–63.

[117] *Letters of Innocent III*, no. 910; *SLI*, no. 49. The other letters are *Letters of Innocent III*, nos 907–8 (dated 7 March), 909; *SLI*, nos 47–8.

rejoiced that 'the kingdom is become a royal priesthood and the priesthood a kingdom of priests', assuring John that his title was now more exalted and secure, and ratifying in advance any sentence which might be passed by the legate on rebellious subjects.[118] In late October the pope ordered all prelates and lay magnates of England to be obedient to their king,[119] and also instructed that Langton should hand over to the legate the letters which he had for use in case of John's intransigence, so that they might now be destroyed.[120] In April 1214, when Innocent certainly knew that John had embarked on an expedition to France, he instructed that he was not to be excommunicated except by special mandate of the apostolic see,[121] although a week later he was urging an end to the war through arbitration and that there should be a truce at least until after the forthcoming general council.[122] When the allied campaign collapsed and a truce was indeed agreed, John claimed to the pope that this had been done so that a crusade for the relief of the Holy Land might be launched. This came as manna from heaven to Innocent, and marked the final phase of John's rehabilitation at Rome.[123] On 19 March 1215 a letter to the baronage of England condemned leagues and conspiracies against the king, most especially since such might thwart his 'good intention' of embarking on crusade.[124] On the same day a letter was despatched to Archbishop Langton – the first clear sign of papal displeasure: he was rebuked for failing to mediate between the king and the dissidents, and for reportedly even giving aid and comfort to John's enemies. The pope acidly remarked that the demands made by some of John's vassals since Langton had arrived in England were unprecedented.[125] On 1 April Innocent turned to specifics, ordering that the barons should pay to the king last year's Poitevin scutage, lest John's 'good intention' should be delayed; there was no need, he optimistically exhorted them, to attempt to coerce the king, since he was prepared to offer justice to all petitioners.[126] On 7 July he rebuked those English bishops who showed little enthusiasm for the crusade, as they had clearly shown by the scant help which they had given the king against the disturbers of his realm; indeed, they might be seen as accomplices in a wicked conspiracy against a worthy king who was intent on his holy expedition. They should rather excommunicate the contrariants, or else themselves face suspension

---

[118] *Letters of Innocent III*, no. 925; *SLI*, no. 53.
[119] *Letters of Innocent III*, no. 930; *SLI*, no. 57. Similar letters were simultaneously sent to Ireland and to the king of Scots (*Letters of Innocent III*, nos 931–2).
[120] *Letters of Innocent III*, no. 936; *SLI*, no. 60.
[121] *Letters of Innocent III*, no. 960; *SLI*, no. 66.
[122] *Letters of Innocent III*, no. 963; *SLI*, no. 68.
[123] *Letters of Innocent III*, no. 982; *SLI*, no. 72.
[124] *Letters of Innocent III*, no. 1001; *SLI*, no. 74.
[125] *Letters of Innocent III*, no. 1002; *SLI*, no. 75.
[126] *Letters of Innocent III*, no. 1005; *SLI*, no. 77; at about the same time the pope despatched letter no. 1010 (78) to John: he will be a splendid leader of the crusade, but he is exhorted to haste.

from office.[127] On 24 August Innocent condemned and invalidated Magna Carta, on the grounds both that settlement of any dispute about the conduct of government pertained to the pope as overlord, and that John had been coerced into acquiescence. The Charter and its terms were 'not only demeaning and shameful but also illegal and unjust'; it represented 'a serious danger to the whole crusade, a danger that would be imminent if the concessions thus wrested from a great king who has taken the Cross were not cancelled by our authority'.[128] On 4 November he confirmed the suspension of Archbishop Langton, so optimistically imposed by his authority on the monks of Canterbury and the church in England nine years before,[129] and on 16 December announced the excommunication of thirty-one named rebels, the citizens of London who were the prime movers in this wickedness, and others, as promulgated at the Lateran Council.[130]

Following John's request for a new papal legate in England, Cardinal Guala Bicchieri arrived on 20 May 1216, the day before Prince Louis of France landed to pursue, at the head of the rebel forces, his claim to the throne through his wife, a granddaughter of Henry II.[131] On his journey through France the legate had already condemned the proposed invasion and had succeeded at least in dissuading Philip Augustus from open support for the venture.[132] Guala was given exceptionally wide-ranging legatine powers,[133] and was sent with the twin aims of providing ecclesiastical leadership in the void left by Langton's suspension and of giving papal support on the spot to Innocent's royal vassal, not least so that John might set out sooner on crusade. On 29 May at Winchester, Guala promulgated solemn sentence of excommunication against Louis and his adherents, and this was repeated and extended over the next few months to embrace their allies in Scotland and Wales.[134]

When news of the death of Innocent III reached England, probably towards the end of August 1216, there was hope among John's enemies that there would be a change of papal policy, but there was no time to see if this optimism was justified before the king himself died on 19 October. There is

---

[127] *Letters of Innocent III*, no. 1016; *SLI*, no. 80.

[128] *Letters of Innocent III*, nos 1018–19; *SLI*, nos 182–3.

[129] *Letters of Innocent III*, nos 1026–7; *SLI*, no. 84. The standard account of the archbishop's career is still F.M. Powicke, *Stephen Langton*, Oxford 1928. Although the account of the Interdict presented by H.G. Richardson and G.O. Sayles, *The Governance of Medieval England from the Conquest to Magna Carta*, Edinburgh 1963, has been strongly criticised by Cheney ('A Recent View of the General Interdict on England', as n.1 above), they are perhaps right (p. 342) in their strongly expressed view as to how unsuitable Langton was for the archiepiscopal office. Rather like Anselm a century before, a great scholar failed to appreciate the need for political manoeuvring and for compromise well understood at the Roman *curia*.

[130] *Letters of Innocent III*, no. 1029; *SLI*, no. 85.

[131] For the legation, see *Guala's Letters*, with its extended introduction.

[132] Bradbury, *Philip Augustus*, 318–19.

[133] *Guala's Letters*, xlvi.

[134] *Guala's Letters*, no. 56.

prescience, as well as pathos, in John's deathbed letter to Pope Honorius III, in which he committed his young heir and his realm to the custody of the papacy, asking that the pope should provide for Henry's succession and for the perpetual confusion of the enemies of the king and of the Roman church.[135] Almost as soon as news reached Rome, Honorius on 1 December ordered all those who had rebelled against John to return now to the path of loyalty, since Henry's age itself demonstrated his innocence. Two days later a letter to Guala, who was maintained in post, instructed him to give the maximum aid and protection to John's sons, who were wards of the pope, and to declare invalid all oaths taken to Louis in the matter of his invasion and claim to the throne.[136] Guala applied himself wholeheartedly to his commission, transforming the royalist campaign into a holy war – at the Battle of Lincoln on 20 May 1217 the loyalists wore white crosses over their armour. Guala's insistence on excluding Simon Langton and three other clerks who had orchestrated Louis's propaganda campaign from any general peace settlement aborted the negotiations of June 1217, but the naval victory over the French fleet off Sandwich caused the dauphin to back down even on this point in the treaty negotiated at Kingston and concluded at Lambeth between 12 and 20 September.[137] The terms were moderate for the failed secular invaders and rebels, but all dissident clergy were to be deprived of their benefices. Guala concluded his work in this matter by taking a leading role in negotiations with the Scots and Welsh rulers who had sought to exploit the confused situation in England.[138] Until he returned to Rome in December 1218, recalled at his own request, Guala played a crucial, perhaps an instrumental, role in the stabilisation of England and the restoration of the Angevin monarchy to control of the whole realm; this was 'the greatest of the legate's achievements',[139] and his work was taken up assiduously by his successor Pandulph, who already had much experience of the English political scene.[140]

The efforts of Guala and Pandulph to recreate political stability in England were recognised by near-contemporary observers.[141] The longer-term consequences of the kingdom's greater exposure, because of its vassal status, to those increasing fiscal demands on the western church as a whole imposed in the thirteenth century are more problematic. Henry III, throughout his long reign, 'never forgot what he owed to the papacy and relations between the English court and the Roman Curia remained close and cordial'; 'they were never again

---

[135] *Guala's Letters*, no. 140b.
[136] J. Sayers, *Papal Government and England during the Pontificate of Honorius III (1216–27)*, Cambridge 1984, 166–7; J. Pressuti, ed., *Regesta Honorii Papae III*, 2 vols, Rome 1888–95, nos 131, 142.
[137] *Guala's Letters*, no. 58; cf. no. 59.
[138] *Guala's Letters*, nos 112, 125.
[139] *Guala's Letters*, xlix.
[140] Vincent, 'Election of Pandulph' (as n. 116); Sayers, *Papal Government*, 173–5.
[141] *Guala's Letters*, xlv; D.A. Carpenter, *The Minority of Henry III*, London 1990, 254, citing Matthew Paris.

so close and warm'.[142] Twice the king requested the despatch of a legate. Cardinal Otto Candidus came from 1237 to January 1241, when Henry wanted papal support in extricating himself from the political restraints placed on him in 1234.[143] Cardinal Ottobuono Fieschi arrived in 1265, despatched as the crisis between royalists and Montfordians was coming to a head.[144] Both worked for peace, and Ottobuono in particular was the architect of the Dictum of Kenilworth and of the process of reconciliation after the civil war. Both, too, promulgated legislation for the English church so fundamental that it was constantly cited to the very eve of the break with Rome. Their presence, however, provided a focus for deep resentment against the rising tide of papal taxation of the English clergy, accentuated by the procurations levied for the support of legates, nuncios and resident collectors.

Submission to Rome also led to an influx of Italian incumbents into the most lucrative of English ecclesiastical benefices. Their introduction, it has been emphasised in a recent study, was thought by contemporary observers to be the most salient feature of Guala's legation.[145] He had effective control of presentations pertaining to the king and collated also to benefices confiscated from rebel clergy or in the gift of rebel lords; in over half the recorded cases the beneficiary of his patronage was one of his compatriots. Once given to an Italian, such valuable livings tended to stay in Italian hands for several turns, so that by mid-century about one tenth of the revenues of the *ecclesia Anglicana* was held by the recipients of papal or legatine patronage, most of whom were from the peninsula. Resentment against this led, within a few years, to the anti-Italian movement of 1231–32, when Italian clerks were thrown into the duck ponds of Yorkshire, and ultimately to the mid-fourteenth-century parliamentary legislation against papal provisions.

As for the feudal subjection of the English crown to Rome and the payment of the census, a policy of delay and evasion was already being adopted by the closing years of Henry III's reign, perhaps by the prompting of the Lord Edward, who as king was even more reluctant to pay, and raised ideological objections to the submission of his realm to the papacy.[146] The conflict over clerical taxation between Edward and Pope Boniface VIII, and the subsequent

---

[142] C.H. Lawrence, 'The Thirteenth Century', in *idem*, ed., *The English Church and the Papacy* (as n.2), 131–2. This gratitude did not, however, amount to subservience. In 1244 Henry III, when rebuking the papal nuncio for undermining the abbot of Peterborough's rights of patronage, observed sharply that 'legates only come here when we ask the apostolic see to send them. Those who have come, however important their duties were, have never tried to pervert the apostolic mandate to the detriment of our rights or the rights of our magnates' (cited by F.M. Powicke, *Henry III and the Lord Edward*, Oxford 1947, 354).

[143] *C & S* 2 (1), 237–59; D.M. Williamson, 'Some Aspects of the Legation of Cardinal Otto in England, 1237–41', *EHR* 64, 1949, 147–73.

[144] *C & S* 2 (2), 725–92; and see Powicke, *Henry III and the Lord Edward*, index s.n. Ottobuono Fieschi.

[145] *Guala's Letters*, lxvii–lxxiv.

[146] Lunt, *Financial Relations* (as n. 36), 141–71.

removal of the papacy to Avignon, with all the connotations for Englishmen of French domination of the apostolic see, prompted even greater prevarication, and the last payment of the tribute was made, without reimbursement for years of arrears, in 1333. The relationship was finally repudiated in 1366. The direct consequences of John's submission were, therefore, limited to the reign of his son. By the time of Edward I there had emerged a new, or at least revived, theory of the state, forged by the scholastic commentators on Aristotle, which held that the ruler drew his authority, through the people, from God directly, without the mediation of the pope.[147] In the fourteenth century, Edward II and Richard II might in the end be murdered by their own subjects, but while they lived they did not need to go cap in hand to the pope nor endure the strictures of a Becket or a Langton. Henry II and John, stronger and probably more capable monarchs, lacked this intellectual armour, and John's capitulation is the most obvious manifestation in English history of that extraordinary phenomenon in the history of the western church, the capacity of the papacy between 1070 and 1250 to challenge and undermine royal control of churches which were hitherto tribal and thereafter national. This aberration was not forgotten nor forgiven. In 1533, when God had long become an Englishman,[148] the imperial ambassador Chapuys reported that Henry VIII was determined 'to repair the error of kings Henry II and John, who by deceit, being in difficulties, had made this realm and Ireland tributary'.[149]

To return to the beginning of this essay: since, for the majority of the population, history begins with the Tudors, Sister Lavinia Byrne in her 'thought for the day' was palpably correct. There is a direct line from the anti-alien movement of the early thirteenth century to the Eurosceptics, by way of the Tudor historians. In the early years of Henry III's reign the Poitevins, not long before admired because they came from the cultural centre of the Angevin world, were now regarded as avaricious carpet-baggers, and the Italians as representatives of a voracious bureaucracy whose universal pretensions were a mere cover for graft and peculation. It only needed the Reformation to complete the myth, for the papacy could then be condemned not only as rapacious but as wrong. In the chronicler Ralph Holinshed's condemnation of John primarily for consenting to become a papal vassal after hearing 'the saucie speech of proud Pandulph the pope's lewd legate',[150] can we not see the genesis of a hundred tabloid headlines targeted at the pusillanimity of the British government and the iniquities of Jacques Delors and the European Commission?

---

[147] Ullmann, *A History of Political Thought: the Middle Ages* (as n.7), chapters 6–8.

[148] J.W. McKenna, 'How God became an Englishman', in *Tudor Rule and Revolution: Essays for G.R. Elton*, ed. D.J. Guth and J.W. McKenna, Cambridge 1982, 25–43.

[149] Cited by W.E. Lunt, *Financial Relations of the Papacy with England, 1327–1534*, Cambridge, Mass. 1962, 73.

[150] Cited by M. McKisack, *Medieval History in the Tudor Age*, Oxford 1971, 119.

John and Justice

Ralph V. Turner

Almost thirty years ago, a reworked version of my doctoral thesis on justice in England under King John and during Henry III's minority and early majority was published as *The King and His Courts*.[1] My aim was to compare the administration of justice before and after *Magna Carta*. It strikes me that a useful way of discussing 'John and Justice' here is to re-examine that book, to take note of work done on the topic since I wrote it, and to consider how I should change it, were I to rewrite it. Surely most scholars would welcome the opportunity to rewrite their first book.

Years of teaching surveys of medieval England have widened my knowledge of justice in the centuries before and after John's reign, and that perspective gives his administration of justice greater importance than I had realised. The legal reforms under Henry II and his two sons built upon England's unique situation during the so-called 'feudal transformation', the eleventh century. In both the late Anglo-Saxon and Norman periods, England was the sole principality where public tribunals capable of rendering definite and relatively impartial judgements over freemen survived, and where central political authority exercised sufficient coercive power to enforce judgements of such courts.[2] Angevin judicial reforms, then, marked a strengthened ruler–subject relationship that was threatening the magnates' traditional control over local communities and creating direct ties between the crown and the knightly class. The surest sign of this expansion of the monarch's power is the protection extended to freemen's property by the *curia regis*.[3]

Activity of the Bench and the eyres between 1194 and 1215 marks a high point for royal authority in medieval England, for such moves in the direction of a centralised state proved premature. By Henry III's middle years, the royal government was surrendering local peace-keeping and dispute settlement to an aristocracy determined to dominate the localities. Both David Crouch and David Carpenter locate in the thirteenth century 'a pattern of magnate rule in

---

[1] *The King and His Courts: The Role of King John and Henry III in the Administration of Justice, 1199–1240*, Ithaca NY, 1968.

[2] For a useful historiographical survey, see Patrick Geary, 'Vivre en conflit dans une France sans Etat: typologie des mécanismes de réglement de conflits (1050–1200)', *Annales, économies, sociétés, civilisations* 41, 1986, 1,107–33.

[3] Peter Coss, 'Bastard Feudalism Revised', *Past and Present* 125, 1989, 41–2.

the shires similar to that which was to dominate England in the later middle ages'.[4] This breakdown of royal authority is usually associated with 'bastard feudalism'; in Peter Coss's words, its effect was 'to deflect and pervert the development of the centralized state'.[5] What happened in the later Middle Ages heightens our awareness of King John's achievement in extending royal justice to humble landholders, and of the fragile and fleeting existence of this great expansion of royal jurisdiction.

The inspiration for my early investigation of justice under John, J.E.A. Jolliffe's book *Angevin Kingship*, showed through administrative records the continued power of the king's *vis et voluntas*. J.C. Holt's work, *The Northerners*, documented John's maltreatment of individual barons – often within the letter of the law – which aroused baronial opposition. Doris M. Stenton's British Academy lecture had already begun a new evaluation of King John. She noted 'the continuing close supervision by the King of his judges' work in the courts' and concluded that 'in the matter of judicial administration King John deserves credit rather than blame'.[6]

My thesis had begun as an investigation of the Angevins' theories of kingship and an assessment of the impact of political theory on the work of justice. During the writing, the political theory largely disappeared from the thesis, and it became a study of the courts' practice based on *curia regis* rolls and assize rolls. Only recently did I return to King John's political thought, recovering his own statements on the royal role in justice from charters and writs.[7] John's words show support for an authoritarian monarchy, supported by custom. Like many rulers whose authority is challenged, he found historical precedent for traditional royal prerogatives; and he depicted his opponents, first the papacy and then the rebel barons, as the innovators.

John found support for his authoritarian views in the 'tutorial principle' of kingship set forth by St Augustine.[8] Roman principles of the responsibility of the *princeps* for his subjects' welfare which had survived the collapse of Carolingian government and the 'feudal transformation' preserved this tutorial view of kingship, and the twelfth-century revival of Roman legal doctrines of *necessitas* strengthened it. Such Roman legal principles penetrated to a wider public than previously acknowledged, and it is now clear that clerics among the Angevin kings' justices knew some Roman Law. I attempted to confirm this in

---

[4] D.A. Carpenter, 'King, Magnates, and Society: The Personal Rule of King Henry III, 1234–1258', in *The Reign of Henry III*, London 1996, 76. Also David Crouch, David Carpenter and Peter Coss, 'Debate: Bastard Feudalism Revised', *Past and Present* 131, 1991, 165–203.

[5] Coss, 'Bastard Feudalism Revised', 41–50.

[6] King John and the Courts of Justice', reprinted in *English Justice between the Norman Conquest and the Great Charter 1066–1215*, Philadelphia 1964, 88–114.

[7] 'King John's Concept of Royal Authority', *History of Political Thought* 17, 1996, 157–78.

[8] As in the *Dialogus de Scaccario*, God entrusted the king with 'the general care of his subjects', 28, lib. ii, cap. vii.

my 1990 paper, 'Who Was the Author of *Glanvill*?'[9] Other scholars' work reinforces the likelihood that some justices were competent Romanists, demonstrating that in the last quarter of the twelfth century 'All who aspired to be lawyers in England, canonists and secular lawyers alike' had access to instruction in Roman law.[10] Thanks to S.E. Thorne's redating of *Bracton*, we can now see a 'Bractonian clerical tradition of Roman law learning in the judiciary' stretching from John's time to the 1220s–1230s and beyond.[11]

Closely linked to the Romanist tradition of the monarch's responsibility for his subjects' well-being is his obligation to give justice to his people, hallowed in the coronation oath. Post-Conquest kings had continued Anglo-Saxon traditions of justice, intervening in instances of *defectus justiciae* or *injustum judicium*.[12] Perhaps this responsibility weighed upon John, although that is a more benign explanation for his surveillance of his courts than is usually offered. His goal was to assert the continued primacy of royal justice. John's creation of the court *coram rege*, an alternative to the Bench at Westminster, points to his commitment to justice.[13] This new court arose partly out of John's desire for more smoothly functioning judicial machinery. Although his court *coram rege* differed little from the Bench, it gave his subjects an opportunity to conclude their cases more promptly, as his travels brought him to their vicinity, saving them from the inconvenience of travelling to Westminster during the long intervals between eyres. Like so much in John's reign, however, the evidence can support a less indulgent interpretation. John's establishment of his own tribunal travelling with his household can be seen as a royal attempt to preserve 'familiar' or 'household' government. Certainly less altruistic motives account for his suspension of the Bench at Westminster between 1209 and 1214.

Notions of royal authority derived from theology and Roman law represent only one stream in twelfth- and thirteenth-century debates on kingship. John could also seek justification for his arbitrary acts in the 'feudal' practice of his predecessors. He regarded extra-judicial seizure of his tenants' lands for default of payments or services as normal administrative practice, and references to

---

[9] Who was the Author of *Glanvill*? Reflections on the Education of Henry II's Common Lawyers', in *Judges, Administrators and Common Law*, London 1994, 71–101.

[10] Quotation, Francis de Zulueta and Peter Stein, *The Teaching of Roman Law in England around 1200*, Selden Society, suppl. ser. VIII, London 1990, xxx. See also Richard Helmholz, 'The Early History of the Grand Jury and the Common Law', *University of Chicago Law Review* 50, 1983, 613–27; Joseph Biancalana, 'For Want of Justice', *Columbia Law Review* 88, 1988, 476.

[11] Quotation from Paul Brand, review of Milsom's *Studies in the History of Common Law*, London 1985, *Law and History Review* 6, 1988.

[12] Stephanie L. Mooers [Christelow], 'A Reevaluation of Royal Justice under Henry I of England', *AHR* 93, 1988: Judith A. Green, *The Government of England under Henry I*, Cambridge 1986.

[13] Turner, 'The Origins of Common Pleas and King's Bench', in *Judges, Administrators and Common Law*, 17–33.

disseizins *per voluntatem* or *per preceptum regis* dot the records.[14] The English barons as royal tenants-in-chief underwent arbitrary disseizins from which the common law protected their own tenants. Yet their experiences in honour courts, bolstered by churchmen's theories, convinced them that no one – least of all themselves – ought to be dispossessed of property unless by lawful judgement.[15]

Not only were the barons subject to disseizin at the king's will, but they lacked their tenants' right to have complaints against their lord moved to a higher, supposedly less partial, tribunal, settling disputes by juries. A writ of right could hardly be purchased by magnates whose immediate lord was the king; neither could barons purchase writs of novel disseizin summoning juries to declare that the king had taken property 'unjustly and without judgement'.[16]As Holt states in *Magna Carta*, 'The plain truth was that in 1215 the undertenant had access to a system of justice which was far more predictable than that available to the great man opposed to his equal in the king's court. . . . The magnate in the king's court was altogether less certain and secure [than the undertenant].'[17]

John's baronial opponents called for government *per judicium* and *per consilium*. They tended to mingle these two concepts, for both feudal courts and traditional public courts settled disputes by collective judgements, reached by a process of negotiation. King John could convince himself that he ruled in accord with those principles, since his definition of them had so little connection with that of his barons.[18] While he could accept an obligation to proceed *per judicium*, his definition was not the barons' concept of judgement *per consilium procerum regni sui*, that is, the honorial court's tradition of collective judgement by peers. As Holt points out, the court of twenty-five barons forced upon John by *Magna Carta* fulfilled this baronial desire for 'lawful judgement of peers between barons for baronies before the king as lord'.[19]

For John, judgement by professional royal servants at the Bench or Exchequer and administrative actions such as distraint of land for default of services constituted 'the law of the land'. His *curia regis* often took the form

---

[14] Turner, 'The Royal Courts Treat Disseizin by the King: John and Henry III, 1199–1240', in *Judges, Administrators and Common Law*, 251–68.

[15] E.g. *Leges Henrici Primi*, ed. L.J. Downer, Oxford 1972, 102, 8.1.b; circulating in an early thirteenth-century collection of Old English Laws, F. Liebermann, *Die Gesetze der Angelsachsen*, 3 vols, Halle 1898–1916, i, 544.

[16] *Bracton*, ed. S.E. Thorne, 4 vols, Selden Society, Cambridge Mass 1968–77, iii, 34, fo. 171b; Holt, *Magna Carta*, 128, 132.

[17] *Magna Carta*, 162–64.

[18] E.g. John's 1215 letter ordering seizure of Stephen Langton's temporalities; John cautioned his justiciar to proceed only if 'you have the power by English law to deprive the archbishop of Canterbury of his temporalities by a judgment of our Court'. PRO Anc. Corr., i, 6; ed. and trans. V.H. Galbraith, *Studies in the Public Records*, London 1948, 136–7, 161–2.

[19] E.g. an early thirteenth-century tract *Quot sit officium regis* stating the king's duty to render justice *per consilium procerum regni sui*. Liebermann, *Gesetze*, 1: 636. Holt, *Magna Carta*, p. 331, and Chapters, 52, 55, 61 of the Charter.

not of a great council of magnates, but an informal and ill-defined body of royal intimates, household knights and domestic officials. Most commonly, the barons encountered the *curia regis* as a collection agency for crown debts in the shape of the Barons of the Exchequer, administering the *lex scaccarii*; application of this administrative law could result in imprisonment of crown debtors and impoundment of their estates.[20] Indeed, John specifically identified the *lex scaccarii* with customary law. In a royal letter drafted to justify his harrying of William de Briouze, the king declared that he had proceeded 'secundum consuetudinem regni nostri et per legem scaccarii'.[21] In the barons' view, such administrative steps were arbitrary acts, denying them possessions or privileges, and a result of debt burdens forced upon them to pay for what was already theirs by right.

The plea rolls from John's reign record no hearings before great councils that could be termed 'state trials', similar to William II's trial of William de Saint-Calais or Henry II's prosecution of Thomas Becket. The king did not submit major disputes over succession to baronies to the judgement of peers; for example, the earl of Salisbury's suit against the earl of Hereford for the barony of Trowbridge, seat of the Bohuns, came before the professional justices *coram rege*. John sought to remove only four lawsuits that came before his justices to a council of his barons. All four disputes date from the years before 1205, and they lay between high-ranking figures whom the king did not wish to offend, such as Earl Ranulf of Chester or William Marshal, earl of Pembroke.[22]

Baronial disputes with King John have little in common with routine proceedings in the common-law courts brought by knights or smaller landholders to sort out quarrels over a few acres. Were I to rewrite *The King and His Courts*, the most important change to be made would be to discriminate sharply between these two levels of royal justice. My concentration on the plea rolls caused me to ignore some major disputes between magnates in which the king played a part, yet left little impression on the *curia regis* rolls. Examples are the longstanding rivalry between Roger Bigod, his step-mother and his half-brother over the earldom of Norfolk, or Saer de Quency's claim to the earldom of Leicester. The distinction between the routinely functioning common-law courts and the king's immediate jurisdiction over his tenants-in-chief is clearer in my 1994 biography of King John, as well as in Holt's second edition of his *Magna Carta*.[23]

Feudal custom in England allowed the king to regulate the lives of his tenants-in-chief much more closely than any French lord outside the duchy of

---

[20] E.g. *PR 6 John*, 7, 47, 120. *PR 13 John*, xxx–xxxi, for more examples of imprisonment for debt.

[21] Rymer's *Foedera* I i, 107–8.

[22] *CRR*, i, 392, the earl of Chester versus William de Béthune; iii, 147, the countess of Devon versus William Marshal; *Howden*, iv, 118, William de Stuteville versus William de Mowbray; *CRR*, iii, 131, plea of contempt of the king's command heard in the Bishop of Durham's court.

[23] Turner, *King John*, 202; Holt, *Magna Carta*, chap 5, 'Justice and Jurisdiction'.

Normandy could manage his nobles. Royal control over inheritance to English estates held in-chief of the Crown allowed wide scope for the king's will. John and his predecessors clung to the custom that an heir to a tenement held of the king could not succeed automatically, but took possession only after the king had accepted his homage and agreed upon the amount of relief. Even sons succeeding by right of primogeniture to their fathers' baronies might find themselves forced to offer exorbitant reliefs or fines, or to purchase influential courtiers' aid to win possession of what they considered their rightful heritage. They remained subject to the law of the Exchequer until they had fully paid their relief.[24] Barons with some flaw in the title to their inheritance could never rest easy, for, should they fall from royal favour, they might find rivals reviving long-dormant claims with King John's support. Finances, politics and patronage played as large a role in settlement of such cases as abstract law.

Chances of mortality gave the king ample occasion to intervene in successions to earldoms and baronies. Scott Waugh's study of the descent of 192 baronies between 1200 and 1327 shows only thirty-six baronies passing continuously from father to son. In 22.7% of the successions (144 instances) the holder died childless with the property passing to collateral heirs.[25] This led to uncertainty about the rightful heir or heirs, and such cases were often concluded through bargaining before the Exchequer or before the king, in consultation with his *privata familia regis*. What Holt wrote about the Anglo-Normans remained true under the Angevins, 'The more distant or debatable the claim, the more substantial would be the overlord's '[king's] consent and more likely would he be concerned with the political impact of the settlement.'[26]

Doubts appeared when no son survived, but brothers, nephews – that is, younger sons 'representing' a deceased elder brother – or more distant male kin claimed an inheritance. Disputes between uncles and nephews caused special concern for royal justices, since they recalled the *casus regis*, John's disputed succession to the English throne in preference to his nephew, Arthur of Brittany.[27] Under John, a case that raised this issue was the disputed succession to the Percy honour of Topcliffe, Yorkshire. William de Percy III, one of the claimants, was the ward of William Briwerre, one of King John's *familiares* and sometime royal justice. This case placed John in an awkward position, and he decided on partition, a rare instance of division between male heirs.[28]

---

[24] Holt, *Magna Carta*, 152; and *Northerners, passim.*

[25] Scott L. Waugh, *The Lordship of England: Royal Wardships and Marriages in English Society and Politics 1217–1327*, Princeton NJ 1988, 17–28.

[26] Holt, 'Politics and Property in Medieval England', *Past and Present* 57, 1972, 22.

[27] Holt, 'The *Casus Regis*: The Law and Politics of Succession in the Plantagenet Dominions, 1185–1247', in *Law in Medieval Life and Thought*, ed. Edward B. King and Susan J. Ridyard, *Sewanee Mediaeval Studies* v, Sewanee TN 1990.

[28] Turner, 'The King's Will in Inheritance of Baronies', in *Judges, Administrators and Common Law*, 280–82. Also Holt, *Northerners*, 240, a dispute between Hugh Buissel and his uncle, Geoffrey, and then with Geoffrey's son, c.1189–1205.

During John's reign, ten baronies passed from brother to brother, and the succeeding brothers made proffers ranging from £100 to 10,000 marks, an average fine of 1575 marks.[29] Successive marriages by barons could produce half-brothers to contend for rights of inheritance. Rivalry between Roger Bigod II and his half-brother Hugh for the earldom of Norfolk attracted both Richard the Lionheart and John's attention. The dispute began when Roger's step-mother sought the earldom of Norfolk for Hugh, her son. In 1190, Roger offered the king 1,000 marks for his inheritance and to prevent his half-brother from being awarded any of their father's lands 'nisi per judicium curie domini regis factum per pares suos'.[30] Then in 1195–96, he offered another fine – only 100 marks – not to be disseized of three estates that Hugh Bigod was claiming against him, 'nisi per judicium curie domini regis'; but while Roger was with Richard I in Normandy, the king required him to raise his proffer to 700 marks.[31] The dispute continued, and as late as 1206 Roger was offering King John fines for dismissal of his half-brother's claims.[32]

In the case of female heirs, partition among co-heirs was necessary in sixty-seven of the baronies tracked by Scott Waugh.[33] Rarely would King John ignore entirely one co-heiress's claim, but he might require her to proffer a hefty fine or else content herself with less than an equal portion.[34] Even a single daughter's succession to her inheritance might require a large fine; Beatrice de Wormegay, for example, owed £1,650 for her father's barony.[35]

---

[29] Castle Carey, Somerset: Henry Lovel II offered 300 marks and 7 palfreys for his brother's lands, *PR 9 John*, 60; Clifford, Herefs: Richard de Clifford II offered 300 marks for confirmation of lands formerly held by his brother, *PR 1 John*, 76; Cogges, Oxon: Robert Arsic offered £100, *PR 7 John*, 151; Cottingham and Knaresborough, Yorks: Nicholas de Stuteville offered 10,000 marks for his brother's inheritance, *PR 7 John*, 59; *Rot. Litt. Claus.*, i, 45b; Hedingham, Essex: Robert I de Vere offered 1,000 marks for his brother's earldom, *PR 16 John*, 11; *Rot. Litt. Claus.*, i, 173; North Cadbury, Somerset: James de Newmarket offered 200 marks for his brother's barony, *Rot. de Obl.*, 205; Pleshy, Essex: William de Mandeville was charged £100 for his brother Geoffrey's inheritance, Sanders, *English Baronies*, Oxford 1960, 71; Swanscombe, Kent: Warin de Mountchesney offered 2000 marks for his brother's barony, *Rot. de Obl.*, 514; Tattersall, Lincs: Robert de Tattersall was charged £100 relief for his brother's barony, *PR 3 John*, 23; Whitchurch, Beds: Hugh de Bolbec offered 200 marks for his brother's barony, *Rot. de Obl.*, 314.

[30] *PR 2 Ric. I*, 101; R. Allen Brown, 'Framlingham Castle and Bigod, 1154–1216', 199–200 and n.64, in his *Castles, Conquest and Charters*, Woodbridge 1989.

[31] *Memoranda Roll 1 John*, PRS new ser. 21, London 1943, 86; *Chancellor's Roll 8 Ric. I*, PRS new ser. 45, London 1930, 138. Also in 1196 Earl Roger brought an assize of mort d'ancestor against Countess Gundreda, *Memoranda Roll 10 John*, PRS new ser. 31, London 1955, 83.

[32] *PR 8 John*, 32.

[33] Waugh, *Lordship of England*, 17–21.

[34] 'The King's Will in Inheritance of Baronies', in *Judges, Administrators and Common Law*, 273.

[35] *PR 12 John*, 50. Beatrice was then the widow of Doun Bardolf. Margaret de Chesney, heir to Blythborough, Suff., made fine for £1000 in 1214 that she not be required to remarry, for her inheritance, for release from Jewish debts and for her dower, *PR 16 John*, 175.

As is well known, John exploited the 'feudal incidents' shamelessly, continuing to exercise feudal prerogatives that his earls and barons had difficulty in imposing on their own tenants.[36] The king's need to pass on the acceptability of his tenants-in-chief led to his insistence on a role in selecting the husbands for female heirs, whether or not they were his wards, and for widows of his barons. With less reason, King John also insisted on giving consent to the marriages of minor male heirs. Roger de Cressy, heir to Blythborough, Suffolk, had to offer John 1,200 marks and twelve palfreys for the restoration of lands seized when he married without royal consent.[37] John's interventions in such situations afford striking evidence of his control over the lives of the English aristocracy, and recent studies of wardship and marriage detail how 'truly mercenary' royal lordship had become by John's time.[38] Scott Waugh's study of Angevin wardship policies finds relatively modest fines for wardships under Henry II, but an increase under Richard from an average of 176 marks to 1,158 marks, and to 3,068 marks under John.[39] Widows paid moderate sums to Henry II for consent to marry or freedom from remarrying, but Janet Loengard characterizes Richard I's 1198 'sweep of eligible widows' as 'little less than an act of extortion,' raising 1,689 marks. John continued to pressure widows, their proffers increasing in his reign to a total of 41,490 marks.[40]

Another emendation of *The King and His Courts* which should be made is a treatment of influential royal servants' manipulation of the courts for their own advantage. They could easily operate as 'influence peddlers', as petitioners sought their intervention with the king on their behalf. Churchmen were willing to pay Peter des Roches large fees for his advice on the most advantageous presentation of their cases to the king.[41] Often royal intervention in disputed successions to baronies came *not* at John's initiative, but was inspired by royal officials, for example, lawsuits brought by Geoffrey fitz Peter or William Briwerre. Such ambitious royal agents used their access to the king to secure

---

[36] Nick Barratt, 'The Revenue of King John', *EHR* 111, 1996, 849, 846–7; Tables 4, 5.1. By 1211, John had expanded his revenue from 'feudal' sources to £7000.

[37] *PR 9 John*, 178; *Rot. de Obl.*, 397. Also William fitz Ralph and Baldwin Wac offered 1000 marks for Baldwin's land in England and Normandy, and William promised not to permit Baldwin to marry without the king's counsel, *PR 3 John*, 22; the bishop of Norwich offered 400 marks for custody of Oliver de Aincourt II and for marrying him 'by the king's counsel whereby he should not be disparaged', *Rot. de Obl.*, 173; Thomas de Erdingham offered 5000 marks for custody of the barony of Oswestry and marrying one of his daughters to its heir, *PR 16 John*, xxiv, 121; Stephen Haringot offered 400 marks and 4 palfreys for marrying William de Tresgoz's son to his daughter, *PR 16 John*, 7.

[38] Quotation from Waugh, *Lordship of England*, 158.

[39] Waugh, *Lordship of England*, 157–8.

[40] Janet S. Loengard, 'Of the Gift of her Husband: English Dower and its Consequences in the Year 1200', in *Women of the Medieval World*, ed. Julius Kirshner and Suzanne F. Wemple, Oxford 1985, 234–5. Figures from Waugh, *Lordship of England*, 159–60, Table 4.4.

[41] Nicholas Vincent, *Peter des Roches: an Alien in English Politics 1205–1238*, Cambridge 1996, 72.

custodies of rich heirs, whom they then married off to their offspring, later launching lawsuits to add as much of the inheritance as possible to their own holdings.[42] William Briwerre, for example, became an expert at procuring portions of baronies partitioned among co-heirs as custodies and at bringing lawsuits on behalf of minors in his custody.[43] Not surprisingly, losers in such suits viewed King John as making justice an instrument for favouring his friends and pursuing his enemies. Ambitious men outside the circle of *curiales* might seek to play the same game, proffering large fines for wardships, marriages or other privileges which they expected to produce large enough profits to cover the promised payments at the Exchequer. Among the barons rebelling against John were such frustrated speculators as Peter de Brus, Simon of Kyme and William de Huntingfield.[44]

The bulk of disputes heard before John's professional justices, whether at Westminster or on eyre, did not deal with baronial concerns, but centred on suits brought by knights and smaller freeholders, often against their lords. Angevin legal innovations became popular surprisingly quickly with litigants from a wide social spectrum, who sued for properties of only a few acres. Final concords made before the royal justices, filed as the feet of fines, soon became a routine mechanism for land transfers between freeholders.[45] John encouraged the purchase of writs that brought more pleas into the royal courts; the pipe rolls show increased purchases of the writ *praecipe*, and also expanded numbers of fines from creditors seeking recovery of debts in the royal courts.[46] The Great Charter itself reveals a popular desire for more, not less, royal justice; Chapter 18 called for quarterly visits to the counties by royal judges.

Smallholders' petty pleas held little interest for King John apart from the revenues that they generated, and most proceeded without any direct royal intervention. Yet the monarch exercised close supervisory jurisdiction over the common pleas. The justices were careful to consult him about cases that touched his interest in some way, and he sent them instructions about individual

---

[42] E.g. Thomas Basset's 500-mark fine for custody of the heir to the earldom of Warwick, and for his marriage to Thomas's daughter, *PR 7 John*, 32; Sanders, *English Baronies*, 93. For William Briwerre's marriages of his wards to his daughters, Turner, *Men Raised from the Dust*, Philadelphia 1988, 83. Thomas of Moulton married his two sons to wards, heiresses to Egremont and Papcastle, *ibid.*, 117–18.

[43] Turner 'Exercise of the King's Will in Inheritance of Baronies: The Example of King John and William Briwerre', reprinted in *Judges, Administrators and Common Law*, 269–87; and 'The Mandeville Inheritance, 1189–1236: Its Legal, Political and Social Context', *ibid.*, 289–306.

[44] See M.J. Vine, 'Two Yorkshire Rebels: Peter de Brus and Richard de Percy', *Yorkshire Archaeological Journal* 47, 1975, 69–74; Brian Golding, 'Simon of Kyme, the Making of a Rebel', *Nottingham Medieval Studies* 27, 1983; and my entry, 'Huntingfield, William de,' in the *New Dictionary of National Biography*, forthcoming, who sought advancement through marrying Isolda Biset, assuming her 1000-mark fine for wardship of her son, whom he married to his daughter.

[45] Holt, *Sewanee Studies*, 16; *Magna Carta*, 123–5.

[46] Doris M. Stenton, *PR 10 John*, xxi–xxii.

cases, often in response to a fine or oblation offered by one of the parties. Whether John's intervention was due to his forced residence in England, to his administrative habit of mind, to his mistrustful character, to genuine concern for justice, or to all these factors still leaves historians perplexed.

Because of these two distinct spheres of judicial activity – pleas between the king and his magnates, and common pleas between individual freeholders – King John's barons could complain bitterly about their failure to secure justice, yet the mass of his subjects could remain well satisfied with the justice they were receiving in his common-law courts. In his new edition of *Magna Carta*, Holt states, '[B]y and large, for the ordinary litigant, knight or freeman, it was an effective system, probably more so than anything else available in western Christendom.'[47] Widows, for example, flocked to the royal courts to claim their dower. About 450 claims between 1194 and 1216 can be traced to their conclusion; of these, 382 (85%) ended favourably for the widow. A recent doctoral thesis finds that widows seeking their dower could approach the royal justices 'with qualified optimism' and could expect 'the possibility of a lenient court'.[48]

A recent study of knights in Angevin Yorkshire concludes that royal justice succeeded in limiting, at least to some extent, lawless violence by members of the knightly class.[49] Itinerant justices clearly sought to curtail the local influence of knightly offenders, sometimes moving to Westminster actions in which the latter were accused of homicide or other acts of violence.[50] There, accused knights had to offer large fines, often £100, for settlement.[51] Justices sought to curb violence even when it meant stretching the law beyond its letter. *Glanvill* and *Bracton* both declare that a woman could only launch an appeal for rape or for her husband's death; the itinerant justices, however, consistently entertained appeals by women for the deaths or wounding of other relatives.[52]

Nonetheless, the king did not maintain his common-law courts merely out of a sense of obligation to do justice to his subjects. Justice was a product to be sold at a profit, and in revising my book, the search for profits from justice must receive greater emphasis. Nick Barratt's study of King John's revenues, calculated from the pipe rolls, gives concrete figures.[53] Income from the eyres – not all of it strictly judicial – rose during the first half of John's reign, a result of the 1198–99 general eyre begun under Richard I and two others in 1201–03 and

---

[47] Holt, *Magna Carta*, 125. Also Hugh Thomas, 'It was by no means unknown for minor tenants to win cases over land against the gentry', *Vassals, Heiresses, Crusaders, and Thugs: The Gentry of Angevin Yorkshire 1154–1216*, Philadelphia 1993, 73–85.

[48] Patricia Orr, 'English Women at Law: Actions in the King's Courts of Justice, 1194–1222', unpublished Rice University PhD Dissertation, Houston TX 1989, 94–116.

[49] Thomas, *Vassals, Heiresses, Crusaders*, 73–85.

[50] E.g. *CRR*, i: 49, 379; 7: 19, 340.

[51] For fines offered for settlements that indicate the justices' dim view of the knightly class's violence, see *PR 5 John*, 213; *Rot. de Obl.*, 138.

[52] September D. Barnes, 'Women in the English Criminal Courts 1200–1250', MA Thesis, Florida State University 1994, 46–7.

[53] Barratt, 'Revenues', 849; Tables, 846–7.

1208–09. Eyre revenue of almost £2,000 or nearly 10% of Exchequer cash totals is recorded for 1200; over £3,500 or 17.6% for 1203; and over £3,300 or 11.5% for 1209. Revenues reached 'unprecedented levels of exploitation' after the autumn 1210 circuits;[54] the £5,000 raised by the 'autumnal justices' comprised about 13% of pipe-roll totals for 1211.

One of Barratt's categories of exchequer revenues is 'judicial', fees for writs or fines to speed the course of justice or for some special procedure, in effect, 'sale of justice'. His figures for this class of income generally range between £1,700 and £4,000; he calculates this at 21% of total pipe-roll revenues in John's first two years, but dropping substantially after 1208 to single-digit percentages. Barratt notes that his 'miscellaneous' column also includes 'quasi-judicial profits', such as fines for the king's goodwill; he finds revenue rising dramatically from this category between 1207 and 1211, ranging from £2,250 to £3,400.

Growing emphasis on the fund-raising aspects of the justices' work had potential for conflict of interest. On the one hand, itinerant justices had an obligation to render justice impartially; on the other, they had a duty to increase royal income. The 'autumnal justices' sent on eyre in 1210 while King John was in Ireland were, in Lady Stenton's words, 'charged in the first place with raising money'. Amercements were for unusual offences, with perjury ranking high among them, and the sums imposed appear to have been based more on ability to pay than on the nature of the offence. Lady Stenton contrasted what she called 'a disgraceful operation carried out in a slovenly manner without supervision' with earlier 'ordered judicial eyres sent out by Geoffrey fitz Peter'.[55]

With the exception of the 1210 circuits, John's quest for funds from eyres does not seem to have overwhelmed his desire to do justice. David Carpenter, however, reaches rather pessimistic findings about Henry III's eyres and the need to increase royal revenues. The crown continued to regard the eyres as a major source of revenue; the visitation of 1226–29 brought in over £7,000.[56] Robert C. Stacey has calculated royal income for the early 1240s; he finds Henry III's cash revenues from justice ranging between £2,100 and £6,000 or between 8% and 20% of the total, with nearly all of this produced by general eyres.[57] C.A.F. Meekings estimated that the general eyre of 1246–49 raised about £4,000–5,000 a year or between 16% and 21% of annual royal income.[58] Thus fines and amercements imposed during general eyres reached a peak

[54] *PR 13 John*, xxxv.

[55] *PR 13 John*, xxxiv–xxxv; *PR 12 John*, pp. xv–xvi, xxii.

[56] Carpenter, *The Minority of Henry III*, Berkeley and Los Angeles 1990, 99–100, 382.

[57] Stacey, *Politics, Policy and Finance under Henry III, 1216–1245*, Oxford 1987, 213–14; Tables 6.1, 206; 6.4, 210.

[58] Meekings, *Crown Pleas of the Wiltshire Eyre 1249*, Wilts Archaeol. & Natural Hist. Soc. Records Branch xvi, 1960, 112–13, estimates Henry III's average annual income at £24,000, lower than Stacey's estimate (206) of £28,000 for 1240–45.

under Henry III, not under his father, and popular resentment against the eyre grew in the mid-thirteenth century.[59]

Generally, historians hold a high opinion of the justices' performance throughout John's reign and much of Henry III's.[60] They echo John's contemporaries who voiced few complaints of judicial corruption, unlike the criticisms of Henry II's judges penned by disappointed and disillusioned courtiers.[61] Those moralists had depicted the new administrative class as careerists, 'new men' whose ambition and jockeying for royal patronage threatened good governance.[62] The surge of lawsuits brought by ordinary freemen in John's time is powerful proof of the reputation of his courts and the royal justices. Litigants appear to have been confident that the standard of justice at Westminster was higher than that at the papal *curia* in Rome, where lawsuits could cost thousands of marks.[63]

John's judges accepted hospitality and gifts from litigants, and they responded by offering legal advice and 'expediting' pleas, but this remained within acceptable bounds until the mid-thirteenth century. Medieval attitudes toward gifts to smooth the course of justice differed markedly from twentieth-century standards of judicial conduct. John of Salisbury wrote that spontaneously offered *munera* – offerings – were good; only gifts offered as a price for official action were bad.[64] As royal justices became more professional, however, proceedings followed a routine that respected custom and established procedures; in short, the judges grew to respect 'due process'.[65] Furthermore, loyalty to the king and advancement of his interest entailed giving impartial justice in common pleas, for justice was a profitable commodity; and in order to attract customers, it had to be an untainted product.

Judicial venality, then, does not seem to have reached serious proportions

---

[59] W.M. Ormrod, 'Royal Finances in Thirteenth-Century England', *Thirteenth Century England* v, 1995, ed. Peter Coss and Simon Lloyd, Woodbridge 1996, 147.

[60] E.g. R.F. Treharne, *The Baronial Plan of Reform, 1258–1263*, Manchester 1932, 41, 'This was the golden age of medieval justice, and at no other time did the prestige of the courts stand so high . . .'

[61] E.g. John of Salisbury, Walter Map and Peter of Blois, in Turner, 'The Reputation of Royal Judges under the Angevin Kings', in *Judges, Administrators and Common Law*, 103–5.

[62] Turner, 'Changing Perceptions of the New Administrative Class in Anglo–Norman and Angevin England: The *Curiales* and their Conservative Critics', in *Judges, Administrators and Common Law*, 225–49.

[63] According to the *Hist. Guillaume le Maréchal*, 'Palms must always be greased at the court of Rome; it is not necessary to chant psalms, for the relics of St Rufinus [gold] are as much prized there as those of St Albinus [silver]', 2: 44, lines 11,360–9. See C.R. Cheney, *Pope Innocent III and England*, Stuttgart 1979, 109–10, 188, on the high cost of English suits at Rome.

[64] John T. Noonan, Jr, 'Bribery in John of Salisbury', *Monumenta Iuris Canonici*, ser. C: Subsidia 8, *Proc. Seventh International Congress of Medieval Canon Law*, ed. Peter Linehan, Vatican City 1988, 200.

[65] M.T. Clanchy, 'Magna Carta and the Common Pleas', in *Studies in Medieval History Presented to R.H.C. Davis*, ed. Henry Mayr-Harting and R.I. Moore, London 1985, 228.

until Henry III's middle years or later.[66] It would always be difficult for a small band of justices centred at Westminster to maintain a countrywide system of justice without local interests dominating it in some districts.[67] Carpenter suggests that only under John's successor did the magnates learn to manipulate the machinery of royal justice by methods that became common in the later Middle Ages: retaining judges, maintaining dependants, tampering with juries and intimidating local royal agents.[68] Significant evidence for judicial retainers first dates from the later thirteenth century, once financial accounts of magnates and monastic houses survive to show them regularly granting fees to judges.[69] The earliest evidence for widespread laxness in judicial ethics dates from 1289–98, when three justices of Edward I's court of King's Bench, four Common Pleas justices and four eyre justices were dismissed from office for misconduct and subjected to substantial fines. Brand has concluded that levels of corruption uncovered at these proceedings 'did not differ greatly from what was normal . . .'.[70] King John, of course, maintained tighter control over his judiciary than did his son or grandson; and John's father and brother had capable justiciars to exercise effective supervision. Also they employed *curiales* as sheriffs, barons of the Exchequer and justices.

Under Henry III, the disappearance of the curial sheriff and decay of the general eyre left the shires 'far more open to magnate and gentry control'.[71] While the reputation of the justices at Westminster remained high, increasing reliance on middling local landholders as commissioners of assize or gaol delivery by the 1220s created ripe conditions for corruption in the counties. The king's Lusignan relatives and his other friends at court could defy royal agents in the counties, forcing them to oppress lesser men more harshly in order to raise required revenues. Records of eyre revenues, for example, show more and heavier amercements for absences of lesser-ranking persons summoned to the

---

[66] Henry of Bath, senior justice of King's Bench, dismissed and punished for misconduct in 1251, Paul Brand, 'Edward I and the Judges: The "State Trials" of 1289–93', in *The Making of the Common Law*, London 1992, 152.

[67] Alan Harding, *The Law Courts of Medieval England*, London 1973, 75.

[68] Carpenter, 'Bastard Feudalism: Debate', 178. *Documents of the Baronial Movement of Reform and Rebellion 1258–1267*, ed. R.E. Treharne and I.J. Sanders, Oxford 1973, 160–3, provisions for a 1260 eyre. David Crouch has shown recently, however, how the earl of Warwick dominated Warwickshire in the 1220s through his influence over local justices, coroners and undersheriffs. 'The Local Influence of the Earls of Warwick, 1088–1242: A Study in Decline and Resourcefulness', *Midland History* 21, 1996, 9, 13.

[69] J.R. Maddicott, 'Law and Lordship: Royal Justices as Retainers in Thirteenth- and Fourteenth-Century England', *Past and Present*, Supplement iv, 1978, 4; Peter Coss, 'Bastard Feudalism Revised', 51.

[70] Brand, 'Edward I and the Judges', 110; and Brand, 'Edward I and the Transformation of the English Judiciary', also in *Making of the Common Law*, 148–56.

[71] Carpenter, 'Bastard Feudalism: Debate', 179. Also Carpenter, 'The Decline of the Curial Sheriff in England', *Reign of Henry III*, 151–182; David Crook, 'The Later Eyres', *EHR* 97, 1982.

proceedings.[72] Local office-holders no longer expected promotion to higher posts through sponsorship by the monarch or his household officials, but supplemented their income with the patronage of local lords. Some barons seized this opportunity to build bastions of local power, cementing ties of patronage with local officials, purchasing their support with fees of retainer; or as Carpenter expresses it, '[L]ords rendered the Angevin revolution in government harmless by spinning a bastard feudal web over the system.' Thus the decay of royal justice can be connected with the decline of the *curiales* as county officials.[73]

Strongest evidence for judges' corruption or incorruptibility comes from their biographies. *The King and His Courts* had been written with little awareness of the justiciar or the justices as individuals, without considering the impact of their ambitions, experience and prejudices on the law and the courts. Remedying this eventually resulted in my second book, *The English Judiciary in the Age of Glanvill and Bracton*. In my pursuit of evidence for the king's hand in pleas, I doubtless under-valued the justiciar's day-to-day supervision of the courts. It is clear that Geoffrey fitz Peter presided over the courts with ability during his justiciarship, 1198–1213, although he has always suffered by comparison with Hubert Walter, his predecessor. Geoffrey was not the innovator that Hubert Walter was, yet he played an important part in subjecting the royal courts to the routine of direction by professionals. Perhaps the chief difference between Geoffrey fitz Peter and Hubert Walter lay not in their abilities, but in their opportunities. Hubert, serving the absentee ruler Richard Lionheart, had greater scope for earning distinction than did Geoffrey, serving a ruler resident in England.[74] Geoffrey organised three general eyres and in intervals between eyres held sessions in the counties during summers, when the Bench at Westminster was on vacation. Geoffrey issued a steady stream of instructions to the justices at Westminster, to itinerant justices and to sheriffs about the conduct of cases; and he often joined John's court *coram rege* before 1209.[75]

Composition of John's judiciary owed more to his justiciars than to his personal appointments. Many of his justices were holdovers from Richard's reign named by Hubert Walter; five justices of the Bench were appointees of Geoffrey fitz Peter.[76] Most outstanding was Simon of Pattishall, whose ability John recognised; the king made him senior justice of his court *coram rege*, and he took him to Ireland in 1210 to introduce English law there.[77]

[72] J.R. Maddicott, 'Magna Carta and the Local Community', *Past and Present* 102, 1984, 47–58.

[73] Carpenter, 'Bastard Feudalism: Debate', 189, also 181–3. See Scott L. Waugh, 'Reluctant Knights and Jurors: Respites, Exemptions, and Public Obligations in the Reign of Henry III', *Speculum* 58, 1983, 976–83.

[74] Francis West, *The Justiciarship in England 1066–1232*, Cambridge 1966, 109.

[75] *Men Raised from the Dust*, 48–50.

[76] *Ibid.*, 49–50.

[77] See Turner, 'Simon of Pattishall, Early Common Law Judge from Northamptonshire', in *Judges, Administrators and Common Law*, 213.

One of John's 'aliens', Peter des Roches, bishop of Winchester, succeeded to the justiciarship early in 1214. Peter had begun his career in the Lionheart's Chamber, and he became the leader of a clique of foreign *familiares*, who wielded wide influence in John's household after 1204.[78] Peter des Roches had ample Exchequer experience, but no expertise in the common law. As formal head of the judicial system, he depended upon a veteran corps of justices, chief of whom was Simon of Pattishall. Once King John left for the Continent in 1214, Simon and his fellow judges from the court *coram rege* returned to Westminster, reviving the Bench that had been suspended since 1209. Peter des Roches recruited to his household Master Eustace de Fauconberg, a former justice who had come to the Bench from the household of Godfrey de Lucy, bishop of Winchester, himself a long-time justice and son of a justiciar. Doubtless, Eustace had absorbed legal learning from Bishop Godfrey, a possible author of *Glanvill*.[79] Eustace thus connected des Roches to the long line of legal learning extending back to the original implementers of Henry II's legal reforms.[80] Nonetheless, the bishop of Winchester made little impact upon the law or the practice of the courts. Yet he did try to make justice accessible, clearing accumulated assizes of novel disseizin as he travelled about the shires on the king's business.[81]

No doubt, the aspect of my book that stands in greatest need of revision is the section comparing pre- and post-Magna Carta justice. In the 1960s, all views of Henry III's reign – including the impact of the Charter – were shaped by F.M. Powicke. In recent years, however, a new generation of scholars is revising Powicke's venerable picture of the thirteenth century. My examination of Henry III's early years convinced me that lessons of the Charter had largely been learned and that, generally, the barons no longer had to endure arbitrary acts by the king. Holt stresses major improvements in the justice available to the baronage under Henry III in his revised *Magna Carta*. He finds that the magnates had 'largely achieved' the legal protections that only under-tenants had enjoyed prior to Magna Carta, gaining access to common-law procedures notably through the writ *praecipe in capite*. As Holt phrases it, 'The protection of the law moved up, not down, the social scale.'[82]

Now Carpenter has challenged this view of the consequences of Magna Carta and the standard of justice under Henry III. While recognizing that litigation by royal tenants-in-chief was 'less expensive and less dangerous' after John's death, he concludes that Holt overstates the contrast. Carpenter writes, 'The litigation of great men in the minority of Henry III and thereafter was still contaminated by politics and fragmented by government intervention. . . . The lord

---

[78] Vincent, *Peter des Roches*, 103. See chapter 3, 'The Justiciarship', 89–113.

[79] Turner, 'Who Was the Author of *Glanvill*?', in *Judges, Administrators and Common Law*, 95–9.

[80] *Ibid.*, 101–2.

[81] West, *Justiciarship*, chapter 6, 184–7, 191–202; on assizes of novel disseizin, *PR 16 John*, xxv–xxvi; Vincent, *Peter des Roches*, 101.

[82] Holt, *Magna Carta*, 123.

never achieved the "regular procedure" enjoyed by the undertenant.' Carpenter discounts Holt's finding that the *praecipe in capite* eased the way for baronial litigation. His basic point is that lawsuits involving the magnates could never be routine, that such suits always involved 'considerations of politics and patronage' inevitably leading to royal intervention.[83] Carpenter, despite concluding that litigation involving landholdings of Henry III's magnates remained subject to the monarch's intervention, does acknowledge that much changed after Magna Carta. He finds few instances of arbitrary disseizin by Henry III before Peter des Roches' return to England in 1231; this brought back to court 'the one man most closely associated with the person and practices of King John'.[84]

Nicholas Vincent's new book supplies a much-needed study of this mis-named 'Poitevin' and a narrative of the crisis of 1232–34, precipitated by des Roches and his nephew Peter de Rivallis. The bishop of Winchester after his return in 1231 quickly made himself the king's most influential counsellor, while his nephew Peter de Rivallis accumulated 'an extraordinary concentration of offices . . . virtually unprecedented in the history of England or any other medieval state'.[85] The two, in their zeal for rehabilitation of their fellow aliens, urged on the king a policy of revoking his earlier grants by royal charter in order to restore aliens to their possessions, lost in the 1220s. With Peter des Roches' return to power, Henry III obliged his father's dispossessed aliens by annulling his own charters. This royal action undermined baronial security of tenure, posing 'a threat to the very basis of property-holding throughout the realm'.[86] It was the major cause of the upheavals that resulted in the disgrace of the two Tourangeaux by 1234, a 'lesson in kingship' for Henry, teaching him that Chapter 39 of Magna Carta bound him, and firmly fixing the Charter as England's law of the land.[87] Victims of des Roches and de Rivallis brought a series of suits to recover their land in 1234 and 1235 that were *quo warranto* actions, extraordinary proceedings, sanctioned by the king in order to shift responsibility for the arbitrary disseizins from himself onto his disgraced servants.[88]

As Carpenter acknowledges, enforcement of Chapter 39 of the Great Charter was no longer at issue after the crisis of 1232–36; Henry's writs from the 1240s

---

[83] Carpenter, 'Justice and Jurisdiction under King John and King Henry III', *Reign of Henry III*, 17–43.

[84] Carpenter, 'Justice and Jurisdiction', 39; quotation, Vincent, *Peter des Roches*, 292.

[85] Vincent, *Peter des Roches*, 298–9.

[86] Vincent, 336. E.g. Henry's disseizin of Gilbert Basset's manor of Upavon, Wilts, to return to Peter de Mauley, Carpenter, 'Justice and Jurisdiction', 38.

[87] Carpenter, 'Justice and Jurisdiction', 39; and Turner, 'Royal Courts Treat Disseizin by the King', in *Judges, Administrators and Common Law*, 264–7. F.M. Powicke, *Henry III and the Lord Edward*, Oxford 1947, chapter iv, 'Henry III's Lesson in Kingship', 143, sees the 1232–34 crisis as 'probably more important than the better known and more prolonged assertion of baronial opinion . . . a quarter of a century later'.

[88] Carpenter, 'Justice and Jurisdiction', 24–5.

and 1250s express his desire not to disseize anyone unjustly or without judgement.[89] Afterwards, complaints against Henry III's administration of justice centred on Chapter 40, forbidding sale, denial or delay of justice. A set of grievances against the English king submitted to St Louis in 1264 complained that Henry's judges could be bribed or intimidated into denying lesser men redress at the *curia regis*:

> [A]lthough in the charter it is laid down that to no one shall the king sell, deny, or delay right or justice . . . after the arrival of certain aliens whom the king, scorning his native subjects, drew to his counsels, no justice could be obtained in the lord king's court against these men or against certain courtiers [*curiales*] . . . no matter how gravely they had offended, nor even could writs of common justice, which by custom of the realm should be granted to every petitioner, nor any other remedy at law be obtained.[90]

Evidence from the 1258–59 eyre supports this, for example, a plaintiff's protest that he was unable to prosecute his action of debt 'on account of the favour in which [his debtor] stood with William de Valence, the king's brother'.[91]

Carpenter attributes this denial of justice less to Henry III personally than to powerful barons and foreign courtiers. Henry's weakness prevented him from resisting the pressures of great men who were corrupting the entire judicial system; an 'under-mighty king' was no match for his over-mighty subjects.[92] Despite Carpenter's useful corrective about the extraordinary character of all proceedings involving magnates, the Great Charter stood as the standard by which good government was measured.[93] The justice who pronounced judgement in May 1234 overturning Henry's outlawry of Hubert de Burgh and other enemies of the 'Poitevins' was William of Raleigh, the 'prime mover' behind the treatise called *Bracton* and likely author of the famous *addicio de cartis*, a statement that the earls and barons must restrain the king with the bridle of the law.[94] Raleigh had been the clerk of the royal judge, Martin of Pattishall, who had apprenticed as clerk to Simon of Pattishall, King John's senior justice. Surely Raleigh's intellectual ancestry tells us much about King John's common-law courts.

[89] Carpenter, 'King, Magnates, and Society', *Reign of Henry III*, 43.

[90] *Documents of the Baronial Reform*, 270–3, Doc. 37C, cap. 3: Also 276–7. See Carpenter's comments, 'Justice and Jurisdiction', 35–7; 'King, Magnates, and Society', 80–5.

[91] Maddicott, 'Magna Carta and the Local community', 57, citing PRO JUST. 1/873 m 18d; JUST. 1/1187 m 7.

[92] Coss, 'Bastard Feudalism Revised', 28, quoting K.B. McFarlane.

[93] Maddicott, 'Magna Carta and the Local Community', 30–1.

[94] S.E. Thorne established Raleigh's authorship or sponsorship of *Bracton* 3: xxx, xxxv; for Raleigh's constitutionalism, see Carpenter, 'Justice and Jurisdiction', 39–41. Stacey, *Politics, Policy and Finance*, 104, depicts Raleigh as the 'guiding spirit' behind Henry's financial reforms, 1236–39, making him an even more significant figure.

King John and the Empire

Natalie Fryde

There can be no doubt that we as British scholars when dealing with foreign policy under John live to a certain extent in the shadow of F.M. Powicke's mighty tome *The Loss of Normandy*.[1] Powicke's admirable work, accurate and perceptive as it is, is basically a study of the bilateral relations between England and France at the beginning of the thirteenth century. The remaining European political scene is observed from this axis and John and Philip Augustus are seen in a profile which is almost certainly distorted. In this respect Georges Duby's book, which took the critical battle of Bouvines of 1214 as its focus and attempted to explain its role in European politics as a whole, is in principle a useful alternative point of view.[2] We are extremely lucky in having two excellent, if older, detailed and conscientious (if indigestible) narratives, Cartellieri on Philip Augustus and Kienast on the German princes, to steer us through the complicated and ever-changing foreign relations in this period.[3] Narratives on the detailed scale of these books were only possible because the level of diplomatic contacts between the western European powers increased dramatically in the late twelfth century. The exigencies of dynastic marriage, dynastic rivalry, the increased ability and desire of the papacy to play a role in European politics and the common desire of the Christian kings of Europe to win the Holy Land combined to produce an explosion in the volume of diplomatic correspondence at the turn of the twelfth century. Restricted by space, one is forced to put a rather old-fashioned spotlight on the main characters on a stage where many who will remain unmentioned were also playing important roles. One cannot fail to see under the spotlight the awesome figure of Pope Innocent III, the huge figure of the Welf Otto in Germany, his rival the brilliant and popular Philip of Swabia, in the background the king of Castile with his eye on Gascony. In fact at the very front of the stage stood the powers from the Low Countries

---

[1] 2nd edn, Manchester 1960.

[2] *The Legend of Bouvines*, trans. C. Tihanyi, Berkeley and Los Angeles 1990.

[3] Alexander Cartellieri, *Philip II. August König von Frankreich* vol. 4, 1199–1223, Leipzig 1921–22 and Aalen 1984. Walther Kienast, *Die deutschen Fürsten im Dienste der Westmächte bis zum Tode Philipps des Schoenen von Frankreich*, vol. 1, Utrecht 1924. The best version in English remains that of A.L. Poole, *From Domesday Book to Magna Carta*, Oxford 1951, 455–63 which is also a useful introduction to the part played by the powers in the Low Countries. See also the brief survey by Fritz Trautz, *Die Koenige von England und das Reich*, Heidelberg 1961, 81–101.

exploiting the leading players for their own ends and being exploited by them: charismatic figures like the able Henry of Brabant and Reginald Dammartin count of Boulogne or Adolf of Altena, archbishop of Cologne, play fateful roles until, at the battle of Bouvines, their allegiances eventually decide the fate of Europe and, in England, precipitate Magna Carta.

A volume on medieval foreign policy which has just been published bemoans the lack of an analysis employing methods of political scientists on the basis of 'systems theory' and understanding of the principles of medieval 'decision making'.[4] Foreign policy is, however, a relatively neglected, if up-and-coming, field of medieval studies, and to some extent the raw material of correct facts and basic understanding which would enable us to construct such theories is lacking. All we have to serve as the basis of this article are scattered studies of bilateral relations. Also missing is a convincing study of the theory and practice of the evolution of the standard medieval political structure, the monarchy, and in particular its role in determining the development of the nation state and the foundation of the modern state. All that can be done in this paper, therefore, is to focus on John's relations with the Empire, concentrating in the old-fashioned way on his relationship with Otto of Brunswick.

Although he initially espoused Otto's cause to become king with far less enthusiasm than his brother Richard the Lionheart, John's striking lack of diplomatic contact with Philip of Swabia reflects the fact that, for all his cold-blooded pragmatism in his need to withstand Philip Augustus, his foreign policy towards the Empire was in no way innovative. It remained as Welf-orientated as that of his father, Henry II, while his system of granting fiefs and money fiefs to the princes of north Germany and the Low Countries was taken over from his brother Richard.[5] It is also interesting that Philip Augustus, ruthless as he was, at no time considered an alliance with Otto. In his case, there is evidence that it was less any doubtful tradition of alliance with the Hohenstaufen than a healthy terror of Otto, whose ability and achievements he calculated far more seriously than modern historians until recently have done.

One can detect five stages in John's relations with the Empire: firstly, a period of waiting and distance between his accession and April 1202; secondly, a period of active alliance until John abandoned Normandy at the end of 1203; thirdly, a period between 1203 and 1208, when John remained cautiously helpful toward Otto while being preoccupied with his own affairs; fourthly, the crucial and active stage in the relationship between 1208 and the battle of Bouvines when Otto was temporarily without a serious rival in the Empire and John finally recognized him as an indispensable ally in the struggle against Philip Augustus; and finally, the period after Bouvines, which is not without

---

[4] Dieter Berg, *Deutschland und seine Nachbarn*, 1200–1500. Enzyklopaedie deutscher Geschichte, vol. 40, Munich 1997, 1–4.

[5] A.L. Poole, 'Richard the First's Alliances with the German Princes in 1194', in *Studies in Medieval History presented to Frederick Maurice Powicke*, ed. R.W. Hunt *et al.*, Oxford 1948, 90–99.

interest despite what one might initially think would be the case. The fact that John continued to send substantial sums of money to Otto after their defeat shows that he regarded Bouvines not as the final battle which would change the European balance of power, rather he saw it as a serious but only temporary setback. For John his policy towards the Empire was certainly of secondary importance to his tense and fateful relationship with Philip Augustus of France. This is reflected in Wendover's chronicle where Otto hardly puts in an appearance.[6] Howden also devotes rather less space to Otto than he does to John's father, Henry the Lion. It is significant that John's earliest initiatives in foreign policy were directed not towards the Empire but towards Castile, Portugal and Flanders.[7]

It is difficult to imagine that John's initial reaction to the situation in the Empire was other than ambivalent. After the premature and unexpected death of the Hohenstaufen Emperor Henry VI in 1196, a primarily north German party, fundamentally dissatisfied with Hohenstaufen rule, and led by the archbishop of Cologne, formed a coalition. After offering the German crown to various congenial candidates, including Richard Coeur de Lion himself, the allies opted for the Welf prince, Otto.[8] Otto was crowned emperor on 12 July 1198 in Aachen largely, it has to be said, thanks to his uncle Richard's money.[9]

John will have regarded Otto with scepticism since, as an earlier favourite of King Richard, he had been a potential rival for the English Crown. This threat had been removed firstly by Otto's own preference for the German and Imperial candidature in 1198 and ultimately with Richard's deathbed acknowledgement of John. The threat to John now came from his nephew Arthur of Brittany whose cause had been taken up by Philip Augustus. Otto's position was still shaky and his future uncertain in 1199 when John became king. Quite apart from the probably bitter memory of rivalry for the role of crown prince, it is unlikely that John felt his freedom of movement in any way impaired by sentiment for Otto as a former favourite of Richard and a person who reminded observers physically of his uncle. Otto's insistence that John hand over a substantial inheritance in money and jewels from Richard probably also did nothing to endear the Welf to John.[10]

The foreign policy between John and Otto was, therefore, based upon a very asymmetrical relationship, since, for Otto, John was an indispensable ally. From the point of view of day-to-day survival, without a solid territorial basis in

---

6   *Wendover*, II, 169, 183, 249.

7   Rymer's *Foedera*, I i, 76.

8   Hugo Stehkaemper, 'Der Kölner Erzbischof Adolf von Altena und die deutsche Königswahl (1195–1205)', *Gesellschaft für Rheinische Geschichtskunde* 19, 1973. Another prince approached was Henry of Brabant, a fact which must be borne in mind when considering his subsequent relationship with Otto IV.

9   *Idem*, 'England und die Stadt Köln als Wahlmacher König Ottos IV (1198)', *Mitteilungen aus dem Stadtarchiv Köln* 60, 1971, 213–44.

10 The best discussion of this legacy remains Alexander Cartellieri, *Philip II August*, 1984, 38 and n.1.

Germany to rival the Hohenstaufen in Swabia or the financial means to hire mercenaries, Otto desperately needed English money.[11] It is not surprising, therefore, that Otto in his early correspondence with John reminded him how useful it was to have a friend on the eastern frontier to his deadly enemy France.[12]

Otto soon felt the effects of Richard's death on 6 April 1199. Although in August John initially agreed to repay the debts which Richard had undertaken to finance Otto,[13] as early as October he made an initial truce with Philip Augustus, which was then renewed in January.[14] In the provisions of this truce it was clear that John was prepared to abandon Otto. This readiness to abandon Otto became definitive in the treaty of Le Goulet on 22 May 1200. John agreed neither to help Otto directly or through others, with money or with men.[15] John was not the first Plantagenet to make a temporary peace with Philip Augustus and, in this respect, this was not a complete volte-face in Plantagenet foreign policy.[16] There was no love lost between any of the parties although, according to Howden, Philip Augustus particularly and irrationally detested John.[17] Foreign policy at this time was entirely opportunistic and without loyalty or sentiment. Philip Augustus' statement that people were little more than dish-cloths was in practice shared by all the other parties involved. The nature of the settlement of Le Goulet, however, gave Philip Augustus an enormous psychological advantage over John from the beginning of his reign. The treaty in general probably needs to be examined more closely. Such an undertaking is beyond the scope of this article. Briefly stated, the fundamental question is whether John's position in France was so weak in the face of the threat posed by Philip Augustus and his protégé Arthur that the far-reaching concessions in money (20,000 silver marks) and land in Le Goulet were required.[18] Perhaps Otto who, according to Howden, pressed John to fight on, had summed up the

---

[11] For Otto's finances and money sent from England, Natalie Fryde, 'Deutsch- England-kaufleute in frühhansischer Zeit', *Hansische Geschichtfsblätter* 97, 1979, 1–14. Bernd-Ulrich Hucker, *Kaiser Otto IV*, Monumenta Germaniae Historica. Schriften, 34, Hannover 1990, 25–32.

[12] *Howden*, 96.

[13] Walther Kienast, *Die deutschen Fürsten*, 156 and n.2–4: 23 August 1,000 marks which Hugh Oisel had given Otto. Rymer's *Foedera*, I i, 78: 25 August 1199, order to repay the Speroni and Bagarotti of Piacenza 2,125 marks. Hugh Oisel of Ypres, whom John gave the formal title of 'royal merchant' on 26 August 1199, may also have belonged to the circle of merchants who initially came to John's notice thanks to the need to make transfers to Otto. *Hansisches Urkundenbuch* (HU) I, 975–1300, ed. K. Hoehlbaum, Halle 1876, 51, 27 (26 August 1199).

[14] Kienast, *Die deutschen Fuersten*, 157ff.

[15] 'In conventionibus istis habet rex Anglie conventionem, quod ipse Ottoni nullum faciet auxilium, neque per pecuniam, neque per gentes, nec per alium, nisi per consilium nostrum.' *Howden*, 151.

[16] Cartellieri, *Philipp II. August*, 105ff; Kienast, *Die deutschen Fürsten*, 146–7.

[17] 'Rex Francie, quare sic oderat Johannem regem Angliae, quinunquam illi malum fecerat.' *Howden*, 95.

[18] Powicke, *Loss of Normandy*, 134–8.

situation better.[19] Philip Augustus was financially the weaker party and had been excommunicated for trying to divorce his Danish wife, Ingeborg. From the point of view of John's relationship with the Empire, the treaty is important in that in its insistence that John abandon any help to Otto, it shows that Philip Augustus regarded Otto as a real threat. Earlier generations of German historians had regarded Otto as a mere ripple in the charismatic flow of Hohenstaufen rule in Germany. Philip Augustus' antipathy to Otto, clear in the treaty, was the result of the active role which Otto had played in his uncle Richard's campaigns against Philip Augustus in France.[20] Later, in 1208, he bitterly complained to the pope of Otto's behaviour as count of Poitou when he had burned French territory, including churches, and never paid reparations.[21]

The treaty understandably led to a rupture in relations between John and Otto and no doubt Otto's two brothers, Henry and William, who arriving in England in September 1200 seeking the handover of Richard's legacy, received a chilly reception: they returned home empty-handed.[22] Howden repeats John's excuse: that the handover of the money would have infringed the treaty of Le Goulet. The very ebb in Otto's fortunes, however, brought a new and powerful ally to the Welf side. Pope Innocent III espoused his cause. Otto, who was very good at composing fawning letters, had written to him directly after Richard's death, flatteringly describing him as his 'only hope and support' now that his uncle was dead (a remark which throws interesting light on Otto's minimal expectations of John).

Otto, who intrinsically lacked the Hohenstaufen pretensions and claims in southern Italy and whose territorial base was far away in Saxony and the Rhineland, had considerable attractions as an Imperial candidate in Innocent's eyes. Otto played his game shrewdly and in an undated letter from about this time, reminded Innocent of his father's services to the Holy See against the Hohenstaufen. In March 1201, Innocent formally recognized him as king of Germany. The pope tried to persuade Philip Augustus to abandon his traditional support for the Hohenstaufen in Otto's favour.[23] In the summer of 1201, under pressure from the pope who was demanding a crusade, John and Philip drew together and John visited Paris.

It is quite significant that the improvement in the relationship between Philip Augustus and John was not accompanied by any let-up in the king of France's enmity towards Otto. On the contrary, at the end of 1201 or beginning of 1202 Philip Augustus wrote to the pope that he regarded the imminent coronation of Otto as emperor as a fundamental threat to his realm. It is impossible to escape from the impression that he was more scared of the hegemonial claims of Otto

---

[19] 'Mandavit Johanni regi Angliae avunculo suo, ut ipse modicum temporis sustineret et differet pacem facere cum Philippo rege Francie.' *Howden*, p. 96.

[20] Hucker, *Otto IV*, 12–16.

[21] Cartellieri, *Philipp II. August*, 272–3.

[22] According to Howden the brothers also demanded the handover of the counties of York and Poitou which Richard had granted Otto. *Howden*, 116.

[23] Cartellieri, *Philipp II. August*, 67.

than of the territorial power in France of John. Repeated appeals by Innocent, who was terrified of Hohenstaufen power in Italy, to support Otto were in vain. Innocent's letter of 26 March 1202 to Philip is interesting since he gives his interpretation of relations between John and Otto – Otto would never attack France since John in practice had not helped Otto. On the contrary the Staufer nourished plans to attack France.[24] This confirms my feeling that there was no love lost between John and Otto. The nightmare vision, that the kings of France should swear allegiance to the emperor, had been raised by Henry VI's projected alliance with Richard the Lionheart against Philip in 1195.[25] This episode and the danger on his eastern frontier were always at the back of Philip's mind. In the view of Cartellieri, Philip remained deaf to all the pope's pleas and continued to regard Otto as his most dangerous enemy.[26] The pope, on the other hand, regarded Otto as his salvation from the Staufer in Italy, and on 28 March 1202 demanded that John hand over Richard's inheritance to Otto. Nothing seems to have come of this.[27] Innocent's increasing warmth to Otto was viewed with suspicion by the archbishop of Cologne, Adolf of Altena, who had never liked the Welf candidature for the crown in the first place. Adolf came from a comital family in Westphalia with many branches and with extensive lands lying near the towns of Berg, Altena, Mark and Isenberg. He was the fourth member of his family to hold the see and his nephew Engelbert succeeded him. He feared the Welf because they threatened the lands and title which had fallen to the see of Cologne after the fall and exile of Henry the Lion. In addition his family had profited from the carve-up of the mighty Welf duchy. Otto's grant to his brother, Henry, the count palatine of the cities of Stade and Bremen, and his revival for him of the title of duke of Saxony threatened the archbishop's interests. In 1199 he was in a strong position in Germany because his rival the archbishop of Mainz, who had the traditional right to crown the monarch, was away on Crusade. Otto, however, had sufficient skill not to leave Adolf much room for manoeuvre. He allied himself with the count of Flanders and betrothed himself to the duke of Brabant's daughter. Henry of Brabant, a former friend of Richard the Lionheart, and one of the emperor's most important vassals, was carving out of a relatively modest inheritance a mighty duchy which was to change the balance of power on the north-western border of the Empire.[28] He was in, addition, a military power out of proportion even to the size and strategic value of his duchy, since Brabant was renowned at this time for the quality and quantity of its mercenary troops. Between now and 1215 John, too, was to exert himself to keep Henry of Brabant on his side, no mean undertaking since

---

[24] *Ibid.*, 89.
[25] Kienast, *Die deutschen Fürsten*, 146–7; *idem, Deutschland und Frankreich in der Kaiserzeit* (900–1270) vol. 1, Stuttgart 1974, 244 and n.601; Cartellieri, *Philipp II. August*, 69.
[26] Cartellieri, *Philip II. August*, 69.
[27] *Ibid.*, 103 and n.3.
[28] The house of Brabant was, however, extremely prestigious because of its direct descent from Charlemagne.

Philip Augustus spared no effort to lure the unscrupulous man away from the Welf–Plantagenet alliance.

Otto stationed troops in Cologne as a brake on Adolf and increased the city's rights at the expense of the archbishop by exempting merchants from certain duties and tolls. His influence permeated the cathedral chapter of Cologne where Adolf was never popular and which, in September 1202, made an oath to support the archbishop only as long as he remained loyal to Otto. The oath was underwritten by the city's greatest families. More practically they also repaid Otto's debts to the archbishop. John played his part here too. In return for these services to his ally, he renewed the safe-conduct of the Cologne merchants for trading in England. The citizens were particularly anxious to preserve friendly relations with England at this point because the war between England and France was offering them a better market for their goods, particularly their wine, in England. In 1202 they even went as far as to drive Adolf out of the city. Pope Innocent obliged by providing them with a counter-candidate, Bruno of Sayn, and King John followed this up with additional privileges for their independent stance.

Philip Augustus' clear preparations for an attack on Normandy at Easter 1202 forced John to return to the more traditional policy of active alliance with the Welf.[29] Philip's alliance with Castile in January 1202, whose ruler was claiming Gascony, prompted John's alliance with Navarre on 5 February 1202, which cannot have been regarded by Philip Augustus as harmless.[30] After 24 March and the fruitless meeting near Le Goulet and the demand by Philip that John give up his continental possessions and appear in Paris before his court on 22 April, war was inevitable.[31] Exactly at this time the subsidies to Otto recommence, though a formal and rather vague alliance between the two was not concluded until 8 September 1202, a lateness which suggests reluctance on John's part.[32] In a letter to the pope, Otto stressed that the alliance was not intended to harm France, but we can dismiss this as mere rhetoric.[33] On the same day as the alliance was concluded, John requested a subsidy from the diocese of Canterbury to support Otto whom he described as a particularly faithful son of the church.[34] On 11 April 1203, John was urging the citizens of Cologne to support Otto.[35] An undated letter from this period referred to gifts which John had sent, and Otto made the remarkable offer that he would make a two-year truce with Philip of Swabia in order to attack Philip Augustus from Rheims or Cambrai. There is no evidence that John, who was in severe trouble on all fronts and had grave problems with Innocent III, took much interest in Otto's offer. He was

---

[29] Powicke, *Loss of Normandy*, 147–8.
[30] Rymer's *Foedera*, I i, 86.
[31] Powicke, *Loss of Normandy*, 148.
[32] Trautz, *Könige von England*, 94.
[33] Cartellieri, *Philipp II. August*, 124.
[34] Rymer's *Foedera*, I i, 87.
[35] *Ibid.*, 88.

losing castles everywhere in France and at the end of 1203 left for England leaving the vital castle of Château-Gaillard to fend for itself.[36] One cannot escape the conclusion that a prompter and more active cooperation between the two allies would have been advantageous for both parties. At least in April 1204 John thanked the citizens of Cologne for helping Otto and confirmed their privileges.[37]

Normandy was lost and John used his remaining strength in England to gather troops to recover it. This in turn meant that he could give no assistance to Otto who was in deep trouble in his fight against Philip of Swabia, where four of the most prominent German princes, including his brother and the archbishop of Cologne, had abandoned his cause.[38] At this point John stopped sending Otto money.[39] Significantly, in his initial truce with Philip Augustus after the loss of Normandy on 6 October 1206, John, in the middle of the conflict over the election of Stephen Langton to the see of Canterbury, made no mention of Otto.[40]

In April 1207, Philip of Swabia was able to enter Cologne, and Otto's fortunes had reached their lowest point. The main help Otto obtained from outside was from Denmark.[41] When in April 1207 Otto came in Danish ships to England, he must have been in a very desperate military and political situation, and John gave him 6,000 marks.[42] On 9 December that year messengers of John returned from the Empire bringing from Otto a 'great crown' and other purple insignia of imperial office.[43] This gift needs to be looked at more carefully. There may have been an element of symbolism in it – Otto was giving the symbols of his office into John's hands. In the description of them, the value of the articles is precisely noted, so the more prosaic explanation may be that Otto handed them over as surety for more financial help.

The frequent transfers of money from England to Otto led to an increased use of foreign merchants for this purpose by John although this interesting financial policy had clearly been inaugurated by Richard.[44] These merchants came from

---

[36] Powicke, *Loss of Normandy*, 255–7.
[37] *Hansisches Urkundenbuch* (HU), no. 9, 108 (11 April 1204).
[38] Hucker, *Otto IV*, 78–94.
[39] *Ibid.*, 196.
[40] Rymer's, *Foedera*, I i, 95.
[41] Kienast, *Die deutschen Fürsten*, 173.
[42] The exact sum is the object of dissension in the records, Cartellieri, *Philipp II. August*, 262.
[43] 'Et baltheum de orfrasio cum lapidibus; unum per sotularium et frettas de orfrasio; 1 par cirothecarum et dalmaticam de nigra purpura et pallium regale de purpura cum morsu et brocha auri et pannum sericum ad ferendum supra regem in coronatione sua et magnum sceptrum eiusdem regalis, virgam auream cum columba in summo et 11 censes scilicet ensem Tristrami et alium ensem de eodem regali, cupam auri ponderis 8 marcarum et duarum unciarum et unam crucem auri ponderis trium marcarum et 1 unciarum et dimidium.' Rymer's *Foedera*, I i, 99, *Rot. Litt. Pat.*, 77 (9 December 1207).
[44] See above, p. 338.

Piacenza and Ghent.[45] They were initially in Otto's service and their appearance in England is an important stage in the use of foreign merchants as agents of the English crown. The constant need to supply ambassadors with funds meant that, as in the case of the bishop of London who borrowed 100 pounds sterling in London, the merchants who lent him the money were made quit for the same sum of the Fifteenth customarily imposed on merchants in England.[46] Secondly, there was a substantial group of Germans high in favour at King John's court, some of them like Walerand being given military control over strategic royal castles like Berkhamsted and lucrative jobs as keeper of the stannaries in Cornwall.[47] They had either come in the train of Henry the Lion, or more probably were Otto's men from the time of his service to his uncle Richard the Lionheart. Very likely they were mercenary commanders. It is only in the latter stages of the reign that John began to send English messengers on the same scale to Otto and these are more often relatively formal ambassadors. We are here, however, confronted with the problem that we have insufficient household records to offer a complete picture. At all events, through his own background and the use of these men resident in England, Otto will have been far better informed about the situation in England than John about that in Germany.

The murder on 21 June 1208 of Philip of Swabia changed the face of European international politics.[48] The Empire appears to have been war weary. The general recognition of Otto as king meant an emergency for Philip Augustus and a chance for John. Philip wrote in panic to the pope to prevent Otto being crowned emperor. When the pope declined to comply, Philip took the step, extraordinary for the time, of rudely expelling the papal legates.[49] In March John organized a formidable series of alliances with various princes in the Low Countries.[50] No wonder that in May Philip Augustus claimed in a meeting with a messenger from the pope that he was threatened on two sides from powerful and wild lions who would do all they could to endanger

---

[45] John repaid loans granted by Sprok and Saphir at the beginning of his reign. At its end he was still employing them. *Rot. Litt. Claus.*, i, 180, 183.

[46] *Rot. Litt. Pat.* i, 39 (28 March 1204).

[47] See the prosopographic section of Hucker, *Otto IV*, 376–508 here p. 468. For Walerand ('de Leenburg'= Limburg') *Rot. Litt. Claus.*, i, 53. (4 October 1213) and in the Stannaries, PRO E364/1 (Foreign Account Roll). For Terricus Teutonius and the difficulties of sorting out personalities with common names see Natalie Fryde, 'Ein mittelalterlicher deutscher Großunternehmer. Terricus Teutonicus de Colnia in England 1217–1247', *Vierteljahrschrift für Sozial- und Wirtschaftsgeschichte*, Beihefte 125, Wiesbaden 1997, 22ff. Terricus must have been highly in favour with King John because when he was captured in Germany, presumably by the Hohenstaufen, John paid 'pro redempcione sua' 44 marks. E101/349/3 (11 John).

[48] John was well informed about what was going on by, amongst others, Conrad von Wilre, Otto's seneschal, who, with his men, received a safe-conduct on 24 March 1208 (*Rot. Litt. Pat.*, 89).

[49] Cartellieri, *Philipp II. August*, 281.

[50] Rymer's *Foedera*, I i, 103.

France.[51] Characteristic of John in the conduct of his foreign policy is that when the constellation fell in his favour he was capable of becoming quite energetic and of taking the initiative. He seized his chance and sent the earl of Salisbury to Germany to organize an alliance against Philip Augustus.[52] His intervention in Flanders, where he attempted to win over Flemish knights, is also quite impressive. The pope was to some extent grateful for an alternative to the Hohenstaufen who represented both a theoretical threat to his claim for hegemony in Europe and a practical military threat of encirclement in Italy. Thus, as part of a conscious attempt to play off one candidate against the other, Innocent crowned Otto as emperor on 4 October 1209.[53] Innocent had probably already nervously noticed the strength of the army which accompanied Otto and the vigour with which he brought the rebellious Lombard cities under his control. A dramatic turnabout in relations between the two took place that autumn, for already in November 1209 Otto, who had married one of Philip of Swabia's daughters, completely assumed the Hohenstaufen political legacy and began to conquer Sicily. Relations between the pope and the man whom he regarded as his 'creation' deteriorated after the beginning of 1210. In September Pope Innocent III went so far as to beg Philip Augustus for 200 knights to help him against Otto and to influence the German princes to rise in rebellion against the Welf. Philip cynically refused the knights on the ground that they could not reach the pope safely since land and harbours were in Imperial hands. As to the demand that he try to persuade the German princes to rise, Philip answered that he had already tried this. Philip showed his distrust of Innocent's equally cynical policy fully in that he demanded written assurances that the pope would not change his mind and make peace with Otto, and he maintained that the German princes demanded the same assurances.[54]

Philip's assurance has to be seen against the background of his transformed finances. With the conquest of Normandy he had not only achieved a military victory and psychological advantage over John but also taken over huge potential sources of revenue in the duchy. Real enmity and hatred between Philip Augustus and Otto was once again manifest. When Otto attempted to make peace with the pope at the end of 1210 or beginning of 1211 he demanded revenge against Philip Augustus for his seizure of English territories in Normandy and for the speeches which Philip had made against him. For his part Philip Augustus promised to attack the empire.[55] In the spring of 1212, Otto apparently wept with rage over Philip Augustus in the presence of many witnesses.[56]

[51] Cartellieri, *Philipp II. August*, 270.
[52] See his letter patent to the most important princes of the Empire of 24 March 1209 authorizing Salisbury (*Rot. Litt. Pat.*, 91–2). For other diplomatic moves see Rymer's *Foedera*, I i, 104–8.
[53] Hucker, *Otto IV*, 117. John gave Henry Sudendorf, who brought news of Otto's coronation, the handsome gift of 10 marks, PRO E101/349/1b.
[54] Cartellieri, *Philipp II. August*, 289–90, 294–5.
[55] *Ibid.*, 298.
[56] *Ibid.*, 311.

Otto seems to have organised the change of front of Rainald of Boulogne who in May 1212 publicly made his allegiance to John. There is evidence of them working together well in the spring of 1212. Lots of letters went out in May 1212 and payments were made to Netherlandish knights.[57] John was diplomatically very active at this time and one can almost pity him that events were turning against both him and Otto. Otto received huge sums of money, on one occasion alone 10,000 marks.[58] John was, however, forced to abandon his intervention on the continent because of the dangerous uprising of Llywelyn ap Iorwerth in Wales and had to be content with sending Otto huge sums of money.[59]

His problem was that through his many conquests Philip Augustus was now able to support his own candidate in the Empire with substantial financial help. In September 1212 the teenage Hohenstaufen candidate Frederick II came to Germany. On 18 November 1212 he met with the crown prince, Louis of France, at Vaucouleurs. It is clear that Philip of France had paid huge sums to support Frederick (20,000 marks), symptomatic of his hatred and fear of Otto.[60] How did John react? He kept up his diplomatic pressure. He put Ferrand of Flanders under pressure to win over Henry of Brabant, who had temporarily gone over to the French side. On 5 December 1212 Frederick was elected in Frankfurt.[61] Using Rainald of Boulogne as his middle-man, John won over in the spring Theobold of Bar and William, count of Holland.[62] England was in danger of invasion and Philip's preparations were impressive. On 15 May, John turned the tables when he did homage to Innocent III for his possessions and saved the country.[63] Almost simultaneously France's chances were ruined by

[57] Helped by the fact, as Kienast nicely put it, that it 'rained sterling again', *Die deutschen Fürsten*, 195.

[58] *Rot. Litt. Claus.*, i, 124. To speak of 'feverish' diplomatic activity, as in Trautz, *Die Könige von England*, 97, is an exaggeration.

[59] 'Conrado de Wilre et Lambekino de Colonia et fratri Willelmode Sancto Audemaro et . . . Templario nunciis Imperatoris adopus Imperatoris de dono 10000 marcas' (PRO E101/349/3). William of St Omer was subsequently sent on to Rome and received 10 marks for his expenses. The Templars were more than once responsible for money transfers. *Rot. Litt. Claus.*, i, 124.

[60] Philip Augustus made a potentially extremely threatening treaty with Llywelyn ap Iorwerth, Prince of Wales, see R.F. Treharne, 'The Franco–Welsh Treaty of Alliance in 1212', *Bulletin of the Board of Celtic Studies* 18, 1958–60, 60–75. John was forced to abandon his preparations for war against Philip Augustus because of the danger from Llywelyn and subsequently forced to abandon his expedition to Wales because of a threat on his life (R.R. Davies, *The Age of Conquest: Wales 1063–1415*, 206; Kienast, *Die deutschen Fürsten*, 195).

[61] The most recent account is in W. Stuerner, *Friedrich II. Teil I. Die Königsherrschaft in Sizilien und Deutschland 1194–1220*, Darmstadt 1992.

[62] Trautz, *Die Könige von England*, 96. Using Rainauld who was well acquainted with the complicated political scene in the Low Countries was practical for John, but the king delivered himself to some extent into Rainauld's unscrupulous hands.

[63] The story is well told in F.M. Powicke's *Stephen Langton*, 74–101.

the English navy, which destroyed the French boats in Damme in May 1213, rendering the fleet useless.[64]

One of the first signs that John was once again taking the diplomatic initiative was that on 24 July 1213 he freed the Guildhall of Cologne from its yearly rent and gave the merchants of Cologne a safe-conduct for all his lands.[65] Two days later followed a privilege to the men of Bremen as subjects of Otto.[66] John accompanied his diplomatic turnabout with Innocent with an aggressive seizure of the initiative against France. The tables turned and France was now in danger as John began the campaign in Poitou, for once not without success. At the beginning of 1214 a messenger of Otto was helping to organize the crossing. In March the duke of Brabant was won over and the marriage of Maria of Brabant with Otto, whose year-long delay had angered that critical and dubious ally Henry of Brabant, took place on 19 May 1214. In the same week Ferrand of Flanders' daughter married Waldemar of Denmark, brother of Ingeborg. On 23 March in Aachen, Otto treated with Ferrand of Flanders and Rainauld of Boulogne and discussed with them how they could help John.

Catastrophic as the battle of Bouvines was, John does not seem to have recognized its definitive character. Although his treasury was pretty empty, he promptly sent Otto a huge sum of money (2,000 marks).[67] In the truce after the battle, Philip Augustus and John were still allowed to support their candidates in Germany, against the will of the other, without it being regarded as a declaration of war.[68] This underlines the importance which the Empire had assumed for both parties and John's refusal to recognize that Otto was no longer worth supporting. As it was, the latter two had both lost the initiative. Both had had too many fronts to fight on – Otto, Italy and Germany; John, France, Wales and the Low Countries. Philip Augustus' concerns were more concentrated, and he was more purposeful. We see him, like John, getting furious, but, unlike John, not losing his nerve. Philip Augustus was ready for the next step, a renewed attempt to invade England. Kienast's verdict that John's best service was to die at the right time is the right way to end.[69]

---

[64] Turner, *King John*, 131–2. The attack seems to have taken place on 30 May.

[65] *Hansisches Urkundenbuch* (HU), 41, 43 (24 July 1213).

[66] *Ibid.*, 110, 46 (26 July 1213).

[67] See Kienast, *Die deutschen Fürsten*, 216 and n.2 for money transfers and presents of wine after Bouvines.

[68] 'Fredericus rex Romanorum et Siciliae erit in ista nostra treuga, si voluerit et rex Otho similter erit in treuga regis Anglie si voluerit. Et si alter illorum noluerit essein treuga, nos poterimus juvare Fredericum in imperio et rex ÿ Anglie Othonem in imperio similiter absque meffacere et absque faciendo guerram inter Johannem regem Anglie et nos de terris nostris.' Rymer's *Foedera*, I i, 91.

[69] Kienast, *Die deutschen Fürsten*, 221.

Philip Augustus and King John: Personality and History

Jim Bradbury

This paper attempts to answer a simple question: what did contemporary chroniclers make of these two men as human beings? The sub-question is, did this contemporary view match the picture we get from modern historians? Lawrence Durrell once wrote: 'The whole notion of human personality is a sort of fiction. We think we are *personae*, but we are just a melting mass of electrons, a million personalities.'[1] How much greater then is the problem of determining an historical personality. We form an idea of historical personality, imbibed from a variety of sources. Our views are affected by novels, films, Robin Hood and Ivanhoe. It is not easy to separate legend from history. Even historians tend to fill the gaps, and mould a personality in their minds. To shift this mind-image takes a major effort. A view that has taken centuries to form, may gradually, almost imperceptibly, have moved away from the view of contemporaries. At best we can see at second hand how a person was perceived. We need to assess the mirror as well as the subject reflected: the bias, political hostility, personal connection, religious attitude, liking for the nice classical phrase which suits the occasion, and so on; but easier said than done.

With a few exceptions, historians have damned both of our kings as men. In the case of John this may be because few, if any, chroniclers were sympathetic to the king. With Philip the kinder chroniclers had the fatal flaw, for English historians, of being French, and therefore eulogists, and therefore unreliable. Recent argument by and large has been that record materials tell a different story from the narrative sources and give a truer picture. But if this diverges from the narrative-source picture, then perhaps something has gone wrong.

A Note on the Contemporary Sources

No chronicler is entirely favourable to John as a man, but the most strictly contemporary are often the least hostile. Gerald of Wales is less critical of John than of Henry or Richard. Roger of Howden, was not especially critical of him as a person, though his chronicle ends before John's chief failures. The major exceptions, in this regard, are the French chroniclers together with Roger of Wendover. The latter is frequently dismissed as not being a reliable source. For

---

[1] G. Bowker, *Through the Dark Labyrinth: a Biography of Lawrence Durrell*, London 1996, 326. *The Times*, 9 March 1968, 21.

Warren: 'his chronicle is full of anecdotes of a highly dubious nature'.[2] He is often called a 'later' source, but his *Flores* may have been commenced in 1204, much of his work was from the 1220s, and he died in 1236. He deserves to be treated as a contemporary source, even if a hostile one.[3]

Of the French chroniclers, Rigord, lived to about 1206. He was a monk at St-Denis, who wrote a life of Philip. The major chronicler is William the Breton, who became a chaplain at Philip's court, represented Philip on embassies, and was tutor to Philip's illegitimate son, Philip Charlot. William wrote the *Philippide* in verse, and a continuation of Rigord's Life. He was present at many major events including the siege of Château-Gaillard and the battle of Bouvines.

The Personality of John

Let us examine views on each king in turn: a brief summary of recent opinion matched with contemporary comment. Seven areas have been selected as a framework for discussion. They are an arbitrary choice except that, being areas in which each king has been criticized, they allow some comparison. To summarize, the areas selected are as (1) commander and soldier; (2) Christian ruler; (3) one committing atrocities; (4) lord; (5) husband; (6) family member; and (7) in general.

The modern tendency has been to see John as an able military leader, albeit not entirely successful. Both Lewis Warren and Ralph Turner, in the best recent biographies, agree on this. The latter sees him as a competent planner 'especially at strategy', whose military skill has been underestimated. John's ability is demonstrated by the victory of Mirebeau; the strategy to save Château-Gaillard; the victory at Damme, the strategy against Philip in 1214; by the siege of Rochester, and the post Magna Carta campaign. Turner has written: 'many who tangled with John . . . underrated his capability and found themselves quickly defeated'. Cowardice is a constant criticism, though Turner rebuts his 'reputed lack of courage', arguing that Gervase used the nickname 'Softsword' because John preferred peace to war. Turner, like Warren, considers Wendover unreliable, and says that modern historians do *not* find John a coward. Gillingham has criticized this view, noting John's consistent failure to oppose Philip on the continent, and of the 1215 French invasion of England comments: 'this time it was on the beaches of England that John chose not to fight'.[4]

What did contemporary chroniclers make of John as a warrior? Roger of Howden compared him unfavourably with Richard as a leader; under John, he says, they had no one to lead them in the same way as Richard.[5] William the

---

[2] Warren, *King John*, 11.
[3] A. Gransden, *Historical Writing in England c.550 to c.1307*, London 1974, 359.
[4] Turner, *King John*, 14–15, 120; Gillingham, *Angevin Empire*, 80.
[5] *Howden*, 253: 'quia non habebant cui principaliter tanquam domino regi adhaererent'.

Breton emphasizes his cowardice: he dared not fight at La Roche-au-Moine, and left his men to suffer while safely escaping over the Loire. Sensible military retreat was always a butt for enemy chroniclers, but cowardice is a common charge against John. With Normandy invaded John says, according to the Breton, 'I will stay in a safe place with my dog'. Later he was called 'coeur de poupée' (doll's heart). Gervase of Canterbury adds to the epithet 'Softsword', that John was 'prudent rather than pugnacious'. The Lionheart's comment, from Howden – 'my brother John is not the man to subjugate a country if there is a person able to make the slightest resistance' – is confirmation of the Softsword nickname. The Margam Annals accuse John of not daring to fight against Philip, while the Barnwell Chronicle thought John allowed the conquest of Normandy 'without much slaughter or bloodshed'.[6] This range of opinion suggests that John actually was seen as 'Softsword' in the traditional interpretation of that epithet.

Is John's military ability recognized at all? William the Breton, though unlikely to know the king's thoughts, suggests that John was responsible for the strategy in 1214: planning attack from east and west so that Philip would be 'enveloped from all sides by enemy troops'. The Barnwell Chronicle claims, with a degree of exaggeration, that John was successful in his British wars, in Ireland, Scotland and Wales. Wendover praises John's speed at Mirebeau: 'quicker than is to be believed'. But there is criticism of his lethargy on other occasions. When he received appeals to save Château-Gaillard, John 'was enjoying all the pleasures of life with his queen'. Roger of Howden thought him a poor commander – on Richard's death he comments: 'they had no one under whose guidance they could be led, as they would have under our lord king'.[7] On balance, the contemporary comment is unfavourable. John's good military reputation is largely a modern interpretation. Even if his strategy has defenders for Château-Gaillard and 1214, both efforts failed. He did have some successes at first and second hand, notably the naval attack on Philip's fleet for invasion at Damme, and the taking of Rochester, but they were not sufficient to impress contemporary chroniclers that he was a good warrior king.

The crux of the matter must be the loss of Normandy and of the bulk of the continental empire that his father had constructed. It seems likely that John was little, if at all, lagging behind Philip in wealth and resources. The explanation of the defeat does not reside in economics. It rests between John's faults as a commander and his faults as a man. He could not keep the loyalty of vital lords within his territories; he could not inspire a fight to defend his lands. Even with hired men and with himself in command, little was ever done militarily. At key moments he cut and ran. This was not the tactical and sensible withdrawal and

---

6 *Guillaume le Breton*, 181, 184: l. 192: 'ego cum cane tuta tuebor'; G. Guiart, see Philip Mouskes, *Chronique rimée*, ed. de Reiffenberg, 2 vols, Brussels 1836–38, ii, 379: 'cuer-de-poupée'; *Gervase*, ii, 92–3; *Howden*, iii, 198; *Ann. Mon.*, i, 27; *Walter of Coventry*, ii, 197.

7 *Guillaume le Breton*, ed. Guizot, 256; *Walter of Coventry*, ii, 203; *Wendover*, i, 314: 'citius quam credi fas est'; ii, 8.

retreat which may well be praised in a medieval commander. John retreated, but he rarely returned; he did not hold the line when necessary. Those months when he abandoned Normandy to its fate are the key to the matter. Given his problems in raising troops, no commander worth his salt would so lamely have let his best territories fall without a serious fight of some kind. His personal presence and effort would have been rewarded with at least some support and some genuine resistance. His flight from La Roche-au-Moine supports the contention that John failed to make a fight. Again the retreat was complete and John returned to England leaving what had seemed a promising campaign in ruins. Retreat in order to regroup and fight another day was one thing; retreat without return can have no justification. Its consequence was defeat and loss on a major scale.

We shall not debate John's religious policy, only his attitude to religion. In this respect he has won some friends among modern historians. His resistance to the papacy is sometimes admired, and the wealth accumulated during this resistance praised. If John was less than devout, that can be tolerated in our modern age. According to Warren, John was 'at least conventionally devout', though he did not give much to monasteries which kept chronicles.[8] Brenda Bolton has been more generous than most to the eponymous figurehead of our conference, suggesting that his gifts to religious houses were on a normal level, and show 'respect for the religious life'.[9] He employed two Cistercian abbots as confessors, and made pilgrimages. The only favourable contemporary comment on John's religion that Warren can find was that the chaplains of Chichester said masses to 'his blessed memory'.[10] Again it is modern interpretation, not the view of the chroniclers, which allows a defence for John.

Greed is the main motive suggested for his acts in England during the dispute with Rome. According to the Breton, 'the wretch' in his greed took church wealth, expelled bishops, attacked Cistercians and Cluniacs, forbade music in church and encouraged paganism; England was deprived of the worship of God for seven years. Wendover accuses John of pillaging church wealth: 'inglorious spoil will never end in good'. In submitting to the papacy, John was hypocritical according to the Breton: he 'feigned contrition'. The submission is seen as a good diplomatic move by historians, but few thought it so at the time. Wendover suggests he submitted not from piety, but because 'he dreaded the arrival of the French king'. Only later, in Matthew Paris, does one find John as a sceptical unbeliever, though the biographer of St Hugh says that he did not attend communion as an adult.[11] The contemporary Plantagenet chroniclers,

---

[8] Warren, *King John*, 171–2.
[9] B. Bolton, 'Philip Augustus and John: Two Sons in Innocent III's Vineyard', in *The Church and Sovereignty c.590–1918*, ed. D. Wood, Oxford 1991, 113–34.
[10] Warren, *King John*, 172.
[11] *Guillaume le Breton*, ed. Guizot, 248–9, 260, 266; *Wendover*, ii. 69; *Chronica Majora*, ii, 560–3.

though, are less damning than one might have expected; the worst criticism is certainly from William the Breton.

Historians agree that John possessed a cruel streak, and if they dispute the veracity of some of the atrocities, they do not attempt to wipe the slate clean. Holt, with relative kindness, suggests that later thirteenth-century chroniclers turned John into the prototype of a bad king, and Warren says: 'the monster of depravity portrayed by Wendover and Paris must be dismissed for ever'.[12] Turner sees a 'capacity for cruelty', but believes that 'his brutality differed little from that of fellow rulers'. He finds John guilty of four political murders, but remarks that 'compared to Hitler, Stalin, or Pol Pot, he seems quite tame'.[13] The modern view is to soften the edges of this charge.

But John's actions went beyond what was acceptable in his day. The Breton describes him taking Évreux, pretending to be acting for Philip, and then slaying the garrison and parading their heads on poles.[14] The same chronicler reports the starving to death of forty knights captured at Mirebeau, and accuses John of killing infants and hostages. Wendover has the killing of Geoffrey of Norwich, chained up, pressed in a lead cloak, and left to starve. The chronicler seems to have the wrong Geoffrey, though another of the name did die in prison. But he also has the story of the Braoses with the killing of Matilda and her son; and the vicious execution of Peter of Wakefield, dragged at the horse's tail: 'to many it did not seem that he deserved to be punished by such a cruel death'. The Barnwell Chronicle adds that John executed Peter's son in case he shared his father's views. Wendover relates the influence of Alexander the Mason over John, 'inviting the king to acts of cruelty'. He describes the atrocities of John's armies: hanging men by the hands, by the thumbs, putting salt and vinegar in prisoners' eyes, roasting them on tripods and gridirons.[15] It is currently thought best to take Wendover with a pinch of salt. But if Wendover exaggerates, should we simply dismiss him? In any case, the evidence is against John on this count.

A major accusation has been that John possessed a flaw of character which made it difficult for him to trust his own men, and resulted in failure to win their loyalty. Warren found him 'secretive and suspicious, over-sensitive to the merest flicker of opposition'. Turner agrees on 'his inability to manage his magnates', 'his suspicion of them contributing to their distrust of him'. Gillingham repeats that, 'treacherous himself, he was always on the lookout for treachery in others'.[16] There is no dispute on this point, only some attempts to mitigate, for example on the grounds of unfortunate childhood experience, but, if proven, this remains a damaging criticism.

[12] Holt, *Magna Carta*, 290–1; Warren, *King John*, 291, 257.

[13] Turner, *King John*, 262.

[14] Powicke, *Loss of Normandy*, 152, 192; *Guillaume le Breton*, ii, 115.

[15] *Wendover*, ii, 42–3, 48–9, 62–3, 76–7, 94; Warren, *King John*, 12–13; *Guillaume le Breton*, ed. Guizot, 261.

[16] Warren, *King John*, 191; Turner, *King John*, 20–1, 125; Gillingham, *Richard Coeur de Lion*, 199.

There is ample evidence of John's distrustful behaviour towards William de Braose, William des Roches, and even William the Marshal. But though the poem *Guillaume le Maréchal* mentions John's lack of gratitude, it stresses the Marshal's fidelity rather than his monarch's failings. At John's death the poet is content to say that William was always loyal, whatever the king had done to him. For harsh comment on John's lordship one turns to Wendover, who says the barons absolved from their allegiance were 'much pleased'. John failed at La Roche-au-Moine because his Poitevin vassals refused to fight for him. Wendover claims that the English rebellion resulted from John's personal conduct: 'the king's enemies were as numerous as his nobles'.[17] But most chroniclers describe John's loss of support without commenting in terms of character.

John's sexual conduct has aroused some comment: lusting after young girls and aristocratic women to the detriment of his political security. Historians justify John's choice of Isabella of Angoulême for his second wife on political grounds, for example Turner and Gillingham. Most give John the benefit of the doubt on motive, though it is more difficult to condone his failure to placate the Lusignans – but that is another matter. As to the aristocratic ladies, either one accepts the sources that say such things, or dismisses them out of hand. Certainly John had extra-marital liaisons and illegitimate children. The number we know of is small, and hardly justifies derogatory comment on a medieval king.[18] The accusation against John, however, suggests a possibility of perversion in his approach, and an inclination to tyrannical behaviour.

To French chroniclers taking Isabella from Hugh the Brown was 'against God and her husband' (they were not actually married). Howden says that John 'had a fancy for her', and Wendover that there were 'many nobles whose wives and daughters the king had violated to the indignation of their husbands and fathers'. The Breton suggests William of Salisbury's wife was one of John's fancies, with her husband imprisoned after Bouvines. This, though generally accepted, has recently been presented as unlikely.[19] But even the harshest contemporary comment is of a rake rather than a pervert.

There are other charges against John as regards his family. He joined rebellion against his father; he conspired with Philip against Richard, offering bribes to prolong his brother's captivity. It is believed John had a part in the death of his nephew, Arthur of Brittany. William the Breton and Gerald comment on his disloyalty: William says he killed Henry (by betrayal), betrayed his brother and murdered his nephew. Richard distrusted John, demanding an oath to stay out of England for three years during the crusade. During Richard's absence

---

[17] *Wendover*, ii, 63: 'cum se cognovissent ab ejus fidelitate solutos, gavisi sunt valde'; 'tot fere habere hostes, quot habuit magnates'.

[18] Turner, *King John*, 216.

[19] *Guillaume le Breton*, 155; *Howden*, iv, 199; *Wendover*, ii, 63; Brock W. Holden, 'The Balance of Patronage: King John and the Earl of Salisbury', *Haskins Society Journal*, 14, 1995, opposes the story; D.A. Carpenter, *The Minority of Henry III*, London 1990, 30, accepts it.

Wendover claimed that John 'made arrangements to be crowned in his brother's place'; Howden that he attacked his brother's lands in league with Philip. On the deals with Henry VI, Howden protests: 'behold how they loved him!' Richard pardoned him later, but with contempt for his childish behaviour.[20]

John was accused of murdering Arthur of Brittany. The Breton says that John sought a murderer for the act, but finding none, seized Arthur by the hair and drove a sword into his stomach, piercing his head for good measure. In the Margam Annals, possibly late, but believed to be based on Braose information, John himself kills Arthur, ties the body to a stone, and drops it into the Seine.[21] Most Plantagenet chroniclers are less direct. Even Wendover only says that John's guilt was rumoured in France, but adds that as a result many turned against him. He also has the story of John's treatment of the de Braose family (an account confirmed by Margam and Barnwell): driving William into exile and starving his wife and son to death. In Wendover, Matilda claims John has 'basely murdered his nephew Arthur'; and there is the French claim that John 'forfeited his kingdom by the murder of Arthur'.[22] Most Plantagenet chroniclers hesitate to accuse of murder, but the evidence is weighted in that direction.

The general modern comment on John as a man and a king is to suggest his failings have been exaggerated, but to accept that there were failings. He was a hard-working administrator, an able man, an able general. Warren thought that 'everyone underestimated him'; he 'possessed . . . high administrative ability'; 'the mental abilities of a great king, but the inclinations of a petty tyrant'.[23] Turner agrees that Wendover and Paris were 'most influential in creating John's bad historical reputation' and, like Warren, is not prepared to trust them. He sums up that chroniclers 'exaggerated John's moral flaws and underestimated his skills as a soldier', concluding that he was 'a man with ability and potential for greatness'. He finds the US presidents Johnson and Nixon to have 'personality flaws that seem similar to John's'.[24] Both modern biographers present a tragic figure, a man of great parts brought low by his faults.

From films on Robin Hood or reworkings of Ivanhoe, to historical novels, in the popular imagination, John is cruel, treacherous, a thoroughly nasty piece of work. In recent times the attempt to revise our view has been based on administrative records, but has not been universally accepted. Powicke thought his 'mismanagement' lost the Angevin Empire, and Gillingham that he is 'the most overrated king in English history', who 'appears to be efficient only because the beginning of his reign coincides with the beginning of a much more bureaucratic system of record-keeping'.[25]

[20] *Guillaume le Breton*, ed. Guizot, 362; *Wendover*, ed. Giles, i, 131; *Howden*, iii, 229, 198.
[21] *Guillaume le Breton*, ed. Guizot, 171–4; *Ann. Mon.*, i, 27.
[22] *Wendover*, ed. Giles, i, 206; ii, 48–9, 63; *Ann. Mon.*, 30; *Walter of Coventry*, 201.
[23] Warren, *King John*, 191, 258–9.
[24] Turner, *King John*, 13–19.
[25] Powicke, *Loss of Normandy*, 237; Gillingham, *Richard the Lionheart*, 278.

How was he viewed by his contemporaries? Gerald of Wales gives a physical portrait: short in stature, but good looking for his size, renowned for his virtues! Few others had such praise for his early career: marked by failure in Ireland, and the betrayals of Henry and Richard. Richard of Devizes excuses him as 'a light-minded youth' which, taken with his brother's remarks, suggests immaturity.[26] To the French he lost his life and realm for his 'crimes', the just judgement of church and people; for killing Arthur he was a Nero, a new Judas, a second Herod, comparable to those who crucified Christ.[27]

Plantagenet chroniclers see John as unlucky, as John himself claimed in the wake of Bouvines, according to Wendover: 'everything unlucky has happened to me'.[28] This might be considered as at least an attempt to suggest that John was not entirely responsible for his troubles. Barnwell calls John 'a great prince, but less great in luck'. This is the one source which has a few kind words on his death, albeit with a sting in the tail: 'munificent and liberal abroad, though a plunderer at home, confident more in foreigners than in his own men, so that before the end he was deserted by his own, and in the end was not greatly mourned'.[29] It is about the best that even the Plantagenet sources can say for him.

The Personality of Philip Augustus

French historians on the whole have appreciated the achievements of Philip Augustus. Philip has inspired the collection of papers edited by Bautier, who himself contributed an article on his personality, though it deals with his life and kingship rather than personality.[30] In the volume Raymonde Foreville examines the image of Philip, but concentrates on religious policy rather than on personality. Cartellieri's Philip is a great achiever, but a hazy personality, blurred by too much evidence and too little analysis. The most influential work for our views of the reign in modern times is John W. Baldwin's study of Philip's government. But on personality as on narrative material, he is content to follow Cartellieri.[31] Like Warren for John, Baldwin relies on charter evidence and stresses Philip's administrative ability. Bordonove's recent work on Philip

---

[26] *Giraldi Cambrensis Opera*, viii, 173–5; A.L. Poole, *Domesday Book to Magna Carta* 2nd edn, Oxford 1955, 486, n.2: when the grave was opened in 1797 the body was said to measure 5 feet 5 inches, see V. Green, *An Account of the Discovery of the Body of King John in the Cathedral Church of Worcester, July 17 1797, London 1797*; *Devizes*, 60: 'leuis animi adolescens'.

[27] *Guillaume le Breton*, ed. Guizot, 174.

[28] *Wendover*, ii, 110.

[29] *Walter of Coventry*, ii, 232: 'princeps quidem magnus, sed minus felix'; 'munificus et liberalis in exteros, sed suorum depraedator, plus in alienis quam in suis confidens, unde et a suis ante finem derelictus est, et in fine modicum luctus'.

[30] *La France de Philippe Auguste, le Temps des Mutations*, ed. R.-H. Bautier, Paris 1982; Bautier, 'La Personnalité du Roi', 33–57; R. Foreville, 'L'Image de Philippe Auguste dans les Sources Contemporaines', 115–32.

[31] A. Cartellieri, *Philippe II. August, König von Frankreich*, 4 vols, Leipzig 1899–1922; Baldwin, *Government*.

is relatively slight and more popular in approach. Philip becomes more a person, but less tied to the sources.[32]

English historians do not deny Philip's achievements, but few have thought him likeable or admirable. Hallam comments: 'if in many ways an unattractive figure, his achievements were remarkable'.[33] We have some idea of his appearance. The oldest descriptions of Philip are of a well-built man with a ruddy complexion, who enjoyed wine and good food.[34] He lost his hair on crusade. A host of historians, including Runciman, Riley-Smith and Duby, are convinced that he also lost an eye.[35] There does not seem to be contemporary evidence, beyond the statement that the archbishop of Rheims was 'the vigilant eye of his councils and the right hand of his affairs', which does not suggest blindness, unless it suggests also one-handedness.[36] There is a fictional tale by Boccaccio about a one-eyed king, which despite its slight connection with fact, may be the source. Probably the whole thing is a modern error.[37]

In his warfare Philip has also been seen as cowardly. Oddly, although Gillingham justifies Richard's caution in crusading warfare, he condemns a similar approach by Philip in the west as that of a 'timid' commander. Somehow in most modern works Philip's victory against John is explained without praise for Philip, despite attempts to present John as a good military man. Baldwin even gives credit for the command at Bouvines to Brother Guérin, the minister, rather than to Philip.[38]

The author of the *Itinerarium* considered Philip's reason for returning from crusade was cowardice, not the 'alleged sickness'. In Plantagenet chronicles, when Philip retreats it is cowardice, when he makes peace it is weakness. When the bridge broke at Gisors, he fell in the river 'and had to drink of it'. He even rode an elderly horse. For Wendover, Philip's flight at Verneuil was to the 'eternal disgrace and infamy' of the French; Bouvines an 'unexpected victory'. Bertran de Born thought: 'Richard is a lion, but King Philip looks like a lamb to me.'[39] It might be noted that the lamb later, having got the better of the Plantagenets, turned Bertran out of his estate.

[32] G. Bordonove, *Philippe Auguste, le Conquérant*, Paris 1986.

[33] E.M. Hallam, *Capetian France, 987–1328*, Harlow 1980, 127.

[34] A. Luchaire, 'Philippe Auguste', in E. Lavisse, *Histoire de France depuis les Origines jusqu'à la Révolution*, iii pt. I, Paris 1911, Chronicle of Tours.

[35] S. Runciman, *A History of the Crusades*, iii, Cambridge 1955, 35; J. Riley-Smith, *The Crusades, a Short History*, London 1987, 114; A. Bridge, *Richard the Lionheart*, London 1989, 63; G. Duby, *The Legend of Bouvines*, Cambridge 1990, 20.

[36] Baldwin, *Government*, 32; *Actes de Philippe Auguste*, i, 109.

[37] Boccaccio, *The Decameron*, London 1954, 61: the fifth tale on the first day has the king of France, Philip the One-Eyed, leaving on crusade with the marquess of Monferrato – whose wife he falls in love with. The context suggests Philip II as the most likely king for the basis of the tale.

[38] Gillingham, *Richard Coeur de Lion*, 214; Baldwin, *Government*, 219.

[39] 'Itinerarium', in *Chronicles and Memorials of the Reign of Richard I*, ed. Stubbs, 2 vols, RS xxxviii, London 1864–65, i, 236–7; *Howden*, iv, 56–60, 56: 'et bibit ex ea'; *The Poems of the Troubadour Bertran de Born*, ed. W.D. Paden, Berkeley CA 1986, 426, l. 51: 'el reis Felips agnels me par'.

In the French sources Philip is more of a soldierly type than we are used to expect. To the Breton his 'arm was powerful in the use of weapons'. He acted speedily, coming to Mantes riding fast with dust on his face, or covering a week's march of 140 miles to Vaudreuil in three days. During one siege, William comments: 'nothing made Philip fear', and he acted 'with extraordinary vigour'.[40] On crusade he advanced in person and shot against the enemy, as Richard did later. Why do we hear about the latter but not the former? Perhaps to our surprise, Richard makes the cowardly retreats at places which the Plantagenet chroniclers conveniently forget, while Philip shows courage. At Gisors Philip manages a successful escape, going through the water without harm. He shows 'valour' at Les Andelys, 'wisdom united to courage', and, as is his wont, determination to finish an enterprise once begun. He avoided battle in general, and fought none against the Plantagenets directly but, when forced to fight at Bouvines, did so bravely and effectively, inspiring his men in advance, organizing his forces, employing excellent tactics, losing his horse three times but fighting on, and commanding with distinction. To the Breton he was an 'invincible prince', the victor of the greatest battle of his age.[41] Though Bouvines was fought against Otto IV rather than John, it was a conflict against forces brought together through John's activities and included a force sent directly by him under the command of the earl of Salisbury, as well as many allies encouraged by him including Renaud de Dammartin. Philip's command in the battle deserves praise. His main concern before combat commenced was that he might be outflanked on his left. He therefore attacked in echelon, folding the imperial forces inwards and preventing the danger of outflanking. At every point the imperial army was outmanoeuvred. At a crucial moment, when Otto seemed to be making progress, Philip himself joined the fray with his cavalry in the centre, halting Otto's advance.

Elsewhere I shall suggest that militarily Philip was a match for both Henry II and Richard I.[42] There is little question that he was more than a match for John. He began cautiously, weighing up the new king's abilities. And at first John seemed able to hold on, so that Philip was contented to accept some important territorial concessions and recognize John at Le Goulet. But a close examination of Philip's activities shows that he was never still. In the years before the attack on Normandy, he hovered on the border, testing defences and routes. In 1200, after Le Goulet, and again in 1201, Philip moved about from Senlis, to Vernon, Gisors, Mantes and Pontoise: an ever-present reminder on the Norman border of his power – to the local lords as well as to John. He mopped up the places promised him in 1200 but not always handed to him peacefully,

---

[40] *Guillaume le Breton*, 125, l. 18.; *Guillaume le Breton*, ed. Guizot, 5 (arm), 61 (fear), 67 (vigour), 81 (dust).

[41] Ambroise, *The Crusade of Richard Lionheart*, ed. M.J. Hubert and J.J. La Monte, New York 1976, 203; *L'Estoire de la Guerre Sainte*, ed. G. Paris, Paris 1897; *Guillaume le Breton*, ed. Guizot, 141–2, 202 (determination to finish), 204, 336 (single combat), 374 (invincible prince), 226, ('wisdom united with courage').

[42] J. Bradbury, *Philip Augustus: King of France 1180–1223*, Harlow 1998.

establishing a much firmer hold on the eastern fringe of the duchy. His invasion of Normandy was no last minute improvisation. Philip prepared the way by taking important strongholds along the Seine, and then struck deep into Normandy when ready. In 1202 he moved much further west – to Gournay and as far as Arques. Suddenly from a border threat Philip transformed his attack to one against the heart of the duchy. As it happened this first major effort in 1202 had to be delayed because of John's success at Mirebeau, but it proved only to be a postponement. His successful invasion in 1203 depended on taking vital centres. His first task was to renew the hold on the border strongholds along the line of the Seine. He isolated Les Andelys by taking Conches and then Le Vaudreuil. Montfort-sur-Risle and Beaumont-le-Roger surrendered to him. Radepont was besieged and taken. Le Vaudreuil and Radepont being almost opposite each other gave Philip something close to a stranglehold on Seine traffic and added to the problems of defending Les Andelys. The fall of Château-Gaillard took months of siege, but Philip persisted against various possible distractions until the supposedly invulnerable castle was in his hands. He then isolated and took Rouen with a mix of propaganda and force. There are many reasons that contributed to John's continental losses, but Philip's superior military ability seems clear throughout.

There are parallels with John in Philip's relations with the church. Philip has been seen as lacking sincerity, niggardly in his gifts. Foreville considered him 'not generous', he died 'in a far more pious way than he had lived'. Brenda Bolton has him submissive to the church only for political reasons. She dismisses the favourable view of Philip's religious acts retailed by Rigord and the Breton, and considers him 'reluctant to found new churches or to give alms'.[43] His gifts to newer orders, and such as the lepers, is not often noted. Philip like John earned the censure of Innocent III. Philip crusaded, but briefly, he assisted the Albigensian Crusade, but reluctantly. He persecuted Jews and heretics, which does not please modern historians as much as chroniclers and the papacy.

Walter Map has Henry II generously contributing aid for crusading at Senlis, whereas Philip 'as if suddenly smitten by an arrow, and all his nobles, were struck dumb'. But Wendover praised Philip for his toughness against the pope, and for inflicting 'the punishment of God' on the Cathars. He also quotes Philip's claim: 'I have always been a devoted and faithful ally of our lord the pope', favourably contrasting Philip to John. Gerald of Wales compared the sobriety of the Capetian court with that of the Plantagenets.[44]

There is favourable comment from the French chroniclers. Philip always asked aid from God and gave thanks afterwards, praying before Bouvines, founding a house for the Victorines in commemoration afterwards. To Rigord he was 'always faithful to God'; to the Breton he was 'very pious'. Both describe him barefoot in procession, seeking divine aid against the flooding of

---

[43] Hallam, 198, 135; Bolton, 128–9.
[44] *Map*, ed. Tupper and Ogle, 302; *Wendover*, ii, 89, 178; *Giraldi Cambrensis Opera*, viii, 328.

the Seine. Philip forbade swearing at court, and punished offenders with a fine of twenty sous for the poor of Christ, or a ducking. Philip's attack on heresy was 'holy severity'; his motive for the crusade, anger at the desecration of the Holy Places. Philip's ban on tournaments, telling his son to avoid them, obeyed papal policy, as did his tolerance of freedom in church elections. William reports Philip saying 'I leave it to men of God to deal with matters of divine worship. It is enough for laymen to deal with the affairs of the world.' When the papacy forbade the invasion of England, which it had previously encouraged, Philip was annoyed but obeyed. When his son invaded in defiance of papal wishes, he got no support from Philip, 'not wishing to offend the pope'. Philip's chroniclers have more to say of a positive kind on his attitude to religion than have John's. The criticisms may have something in common, but the praise has not. If Philip lacks devotion, it is in the minds of modern historians rather than in the chronicles.[45]

The scale of any atrocities committed by Philip do not compare to John's. Many have found him cold, even cruel. Hallam sees the favourable comment in Rigord and William as an attempt to 'justify his bad deeds'.[46] There are accusations with regard to military affairs by modern historians, some of which do not comprehend the accepted code of the day. Howden accused Philip of blinding prisoners in the war against Richard, to which Richard retaliated in kind, but French chroniclers have it the other way round.[47] He executed some heretics, encouraged by the Church and praised by chroniclers. Much the same is true of his treatment of the Jews in Paris, which was more in terms of confiscation and expulsion than death or torture. He expelled them, the church approved and his chroniclers enthused, though they were less keen when he allowed the Jews back sixteen years later. There is barely a case to answer on Philip over atrocities.

Philip's treatment of his men allowed grounds for criticism, but nothing like as damning as that of John. Some turned against him, the outstanding example being Renaud de Dammartin. Even Renaud, whose disloyalty and treachery are well chronicled, and who had already reneged on a previous pardon, though kept uncomfortably chained until his death, was not executed. Philip's practice was to pardon rebels, but demand security, ensuring future loyalty by threats of financial penalties. After Bouvines the Breton considered that Philip acted with 'admirable clemency'. William said early in the reign that Philip 'never refused to pardon a repentant enemy'.[48] This was not quite true by the end of the reign, but broadly reflects his policy. Philip was considerate to his own men. On the way to Sicily a number suffered losses at sea, which he compensated. Philip gained the kind of loyalty which John could not command. His officials and

---

[45] *Guillaume le Breton*, i, 23, 359; ii, 395–400; 15, l. 201: ('rex sacratus'); 25, l. 445: ('divini zelo'); *Guillaume le Breton*, ed. Guizot, 223 (men of God).

[46] Hallam, 127.

[47] *Howden*, ed. Giles, 427; *Guillaume le Breton*, ed. Guizot, 137, 353 (pardon), 364 (compassion).

[48] *Guillaume le Breton*, ed. Guizot, 33 ('the clement king'), 154, 183 ('magnanimous'), 292 'admirable clemency'.

entourage gave him unswerving loyalty. He was able to preserve his position through the loyalty of nobility and clergy at times of crisis.

Philip's sex life leaves one puzzled rather than critical, since his motives are unknown. He attempted to separate from his first wife, Isabella of Hainault, while his second marriage, to Ingeborg of Denmark, was probably never consummated. Philip made Agnes de Méran his third wife, a liaison which the papacy condemned. The crisis only ended with the death of Agnes, when Ingeborg was restored, though in name only. The attempted divorce from Isabella may have been a political move to sway the allegiance of Isabella's father. It seems probable that personal motives were involved. They had been betrothed while Isabella was a child, and though all was not well in 1184, they were soon reconciled. The Hainault chronicler, Giselbert of Mons, is the only one to criticize Philip for treating her 'unjustly'.[49] After Isabella's death, Philip underwent a physical revulsion when meeting his second wife, Ingeborg of Denmark, and they never lived as man and wife. He 'married' Agnes de Méran, by whom he had two children. The French clergy allowed the third marriage, until the papacy condemned it. His refusal to restore Ingeborg led to an interdict.

Though the French prelates allowed the third marriage, his chroniclers criticized it. They described his reaction to Ingeborg: turning pale and trembling. Their explanation is her sorcery. Philip had children by Isabella, Agnes and at least one other woman, but possibly his repulsion prevented him from performing with Ingeborg. The sorcery charge may suggest this, since it could be used as an explanation of impotence. The Breton declares that her spells led the king to deprive her of her rights in the marriage bed and of his person. Concerning the relationship with Agnes, Rigord says that for five years Philip opposed the law and the will of God; he implies disagreement with the legitimization of her children; William calls Agnes 'his concubine', and says he failed to 'fulfil the obligations of marriage' with Ingeborg. Howden declares that Philip 'unjustly repudiated his wife', and refers to Agnes as the 'German adulteress'.[50] Ingeborg refused to be divorced and was denied comforts as well as freedom. Philip was reconciled to the papacy only after the death of Agnes, when Ingeborg was restored. Later Philip, though he never lived with her as a husband, dealt reasonably with his 'own very dear wife' in his will.[51]

Philip's family relations created problems. But his father, Louis VII, was inordinately fond of his 'God-given' son. Philip's own son, Louis, did have differences with his father over the invasion of England and the Albigensian Crusade, favouring more aggressive action than his father. It never turned into full-scale hostility, and in his will Philip was generous to his 'own very dear

---

[49] *La Chronique de Giselbert de Mons*, ed. L. Vanderkindere, Brussels 1904, 152.
[50] *Guillaume le Breton*, 195; *Rigord*, 124: 'instigante diabolo . . . maleficiis per sorciarias', 150–1; R. Foreville, 'L'Image', 121; *Howden*, iv, 113, 147–8.
[51] *Guillaume le Breton*, ed. Guizot, continuation, ii, 346. Ingeborg did claim that the marriage had been consummated, which seems unlikely given Philip's feelings towards her, but was part of her case to prevent an annulment.

son'. Howden says that Philip 'persecuted' his mother, and 'drove her out of his dominions', but it was part of declaring his independence from her Champagne relatives, and later they were reconciled. Adela and her brother were regents during the crusade.[52]

Philip is seen as an unattractive man but a successful king. He has been portrayed as mean, treacherous and devious. The accepted picture is of an administratively effective king, but one lacking in humanity. Part of his cold image is the result of propaganda on his behalf, a distancing process: the comparison to Charlemagne – the pious king in the Capetian mould. The chroniclers present some more human faults: he treated his second wife badly, he insisted on continuing the liaison with Agnes. William of Newburgh and Wendover say he was envious of Richard. Philip sometimes showed a violent temper. When one opponent escaped, his face turned scarlet with rage.[53] There is the story of Henry II sitting in the shade during the two-day conference near Gisors, and smugly commenting, 'when I lose this tree, I shall agree to the loss of all this land'. Philip in anger ordered the tree to be cut down. Normally he was more restrained. The Breton comments of his relations with John, he 'prefers to vanquish by patience'. Howden called him 'that sower of discord', which to the Plantagenets he was, though others might call it clever diplomacy.[54] He was decisive. There is a story of him waking in the night with the determination to invade England, at once calling for his immediate counsellors. Another incident has him pacing the palace, looking out over Paris. He noticed the smell and mess, and decided to clean up the city and pave its streets. Philip was respected. The Breton wrote: 'one could not know if the king loved his people more than his people loved the king'. He showed 'paternal affection', he was just, he protected the Church, and he was fair.[55]

Philip and John had much in common. They were born just a year apart. John's mother had been married to Philip's father. Philip's half-sister, Margaret, married John's brother Henry. Philip's sister Alice was betrothed to Richard and a possible wife for John. In his youth John went to Paris. During Richard's captivity they were allies. As kings they were opponents in a conflict which brought success, conquest and glory to Philip, failure and defeat for John. Summit conferences between them were regular. At one they came 'face to face for an hour, no one except themselves being within hearing'. At another, 'no one spoke except those two', after which John went on to Paris as Philip's guest.[56]

Modern minds have lumped them together as unpleasant and unadmirable human beings. In chronicles the difference in how they were seen is more

---

[52] *Guillaume le Breton*, ed. Guizot, 193 (God-given); continuation, 346 (dear son); *Howden*, ed. Giles, 519.

[53] *Guillaume le Breton*, ed. Guizot, 49.

[54] *Guillaume le Breton*, 71, l. 169; *Guillaume le Breton*, ed. Guizot, 157 (patience); *Howden*, ii, 345.

[55] *Guillaume le Breton*, ed. Guizot, 362 ('loved his people'), 360 ('affection for the king'), 362 ('paternal affection').

[56] *Howden*, iii, 141; iv, 94.

notable. Rigord called Philip 'Augustus', explaining the portmanteau soubri-
quet: his character 'always august', born in August, comparable to the Caesars,
the increaser of territory from a pun on *augere*. He thought him wise in giving
advice, good at keeping promises, active in enterprises he undertook, generous
with largesse. He was a 'young lion', 'the light of his people'. The Breton
called him 'magnanimous', his deeds those of 'a great man'. 'Nothing made
Philip fear'. The phrases used by the Breton are too eulogistic for modern taste,
but display genuine admiration. To a later writer he was 'the venerable Philip',
'the king of kings of the world', the 'ardent defender of the treasures of the
catholic faith, the light and glory of the French nation'.[57]

In time a legend of Philip the good king grew, demonstrated in the *exempla*.[58]
These anecdotes, which began to appear in Philip's reign, though many are
later, illustrate moral points. In them Philip is the just king, the defender of
rights, the protector of poor clergy, the enemy of swindling officials and bullying knights. One illustrates his shrewdness (or meanness). A beggar asked for
alms in the name of the king's ancestors. Philip asked the ancestors on which
side? The beggar replied, on the side of Adam. The king gave an obol. The
beggar studied the small coin, and asked if that was all his ancestors were
worth. Philip answered that if he gave an obol for every ancestor in that line, he
would be beggared. Another concerned the king's illness. He desired some of
his favourite wine. The doctor demurred unless he drank water with it. Philip
said at least let me drink some wine first and the water after. The physician
yielded. The king drank the wine, but when offered the water, refused, saying
he was no longer thirsty. Such tales are not necessarily entirely without truth.

So what is our conclusion to this muddle of views medieval and modern?
John's chroniclers were critical of him as a man. Some were more neutral than
others, but none were positive about him as a person. It is said this was because
of his dispute with the church: the chroniclers being ecclesiastics, and therefore
hostile. But Philip also resisted papal demands, suffered an interdict, and never
submitted as completely as John. Philip's chroniclers were also churchmen, and
they disapproved of his relationship with Agnes, *but* they could still find much
to praise in his character. Therein lies the difference. The contrast between
Philip and John as seen at the time seems clear: the accusations against John are
deep and enduring, those against Philip are less severe, and are balanced by
laudatory views. On the whole modern historians have been kinder to John than
he deserves, and less kind to Philip than *he* deserves. Of course my Philip and
John are the genuine article, but as for yours . . .

---

[57] *Rigord*, ed. Guizot, 1, 3, 28 (advice), 81 (lion, light); *Guillaume le Breton*, ed. Guizot, 183
(mag/great man); Nicolas de Bray, in *Oeuvres*, ed. Guizot, 390.
[58] J. Le Goff, 'Philippe Auguste dans les *Exempla*', in Bautier, 135–55.